PULITZER

W. A. Rogers.

PULITZER

A Life in Politics, Print, and Power

JAMES McGRATH MORRIS

HARPER PERENNIAL

NEW YORK • LONDON • TORONTO • SYDNEY • NEW DELHI • AUCKLAND

HARPER ● PERENNIAL

FIRST HARPER PERENNIAL EDITION PUBLISHED 2011.

Designed by Eric Butler

The Library of Congress has catalogued the hardcover edition as follows:
Morris, James McGrath.
   Pulitzer : a life in politics, print, and power / James McGrath Morris.
     p.   cm.
   Summary: "Comprehensive biography of media mogul Joseph Pulitzer"—
Provided by publisher.
   ISBN 978-0-06-079869-7 (hardback)
   1. Pulitzer, Joseph, 1847–1911. 2. Journalists—United States—
Biography. I. Title.
PN4874.P8M67   2010
070'.92—dc22
[B]   2009027501

ISBN 978-0-06-079870-3 (pbk.)

11   12   13   14   15   OV/RRD   10 9 8 7 6 5 4 3 2 1

To Dean M. Sagar

CONTENTS

PART III: 1888–1911

Don't tell stories about me.
Keep them until I am dead.

JOSEPH PULITZER (1847–1911)

AUTHOR'S NOTE

L ike Alfred Nobel, Joseph Pulitzer is better known today for the prize that bears his name than for his contribution to history. This is a shame. In the nineteenth century, when America became an industrial nation and Carnegie provided the steel, Rockefeller the oil, Morgan the money, and Vanderbilt the railroads, Joseph Pulitzer was the midwife to the birth of the modern mass media. What he accomplished was as significant in his time as the creation of television would be in the twentieth century, and it remains deeply relevant in today's information age.

Pulitzer's lasting achievement was to transform American journalism into a medium of mass consumption and immense influence. He accomplished this by being the first media lord to recognize the vast social changes that the industrial revolution triggered, and by harnessing all the converging elements of entertainment, technology, business, and demographics. This accomplishment alone would make him worthy of a biography.

His fascinating life, however, makes him an irresistible subject. Ted Turner-like in his innovative abilities, Teddy Roosevelt-like in his power to transform history, and Howard Hughes-like in the reclusive second half of his life as a blind man tormented by sound, Pulitzer's tale provides all the elements of a life story that is important, timely, and compelling.

This book benefits from several fortunate and remarkable discoveries of items previously unavailable to other biographers.

Nearly a century ago, it was reported in newspapers that Pulitzer's only living brother had written a memoir shortly before committing suicide in 1909. In 2005, I located the manuscript in the custody of his granddaughter in Paris. An extraordinarily talented sculptor of religious figures, the late Muriel Pulitzer had guarded the work all her life after her father failed to get it published as he had hoped. The memoir sheds new light on the Pulitzers' childhood in Hungary, their separate journeys to the United States, their rise as American newspaper publishers, and the prickly relationship between them.

Another important source of material was rescued from a trash bin in St. Louis. More than twenty years ago, the contractor Pat Fogarty spotted some wooden cigar boxes in a Dumpster near a building undergoing renovation. He thought they were too nice to be thrown out, so he took them home. When he opened them he discovered they were filled with documents from the 1800s that had once belonged to Joseph Pulitzer's *St. Louis Post-Dispatch*. He put the boxes in his basement for safekeeping, thinking someday he might be able to sell the items.

In 2008, Pat and Leslie Fogarty generously shared the contents with me. The papers turned out to be historically significant. They included the original receipts for Pulitzer's purchase of the *Dispatch* at auction in 1878, the original merger agreement several days later between the *Dispatch* and the *Post*, hundreds of canceled checks signed by Pulitzer, and a loan agreement revealing who provided Pulitzer with the money to operate his first newspaper.

Two other noteworthy sets of documents surfaced in St. Louis during my research. Eric P. Newman provided a copy of a financial note signed by Pulitzer that was instrumental in piecing together his partial ownership of the *Westliche Post*. The St. Louis Police Department Library gave me access to the 1872 Minutes of the St. Louis Police Commission contained in books that had been found abandoned in a closet.

In Washington, D.C., I pursued at length a large cache of documents relating to President Theodore Roosevelt's attempt to imprison Pulitzer for criminal libel. After years of claims by archivists that there were no such files, a threat of a lawsuit under the Freedom of Information Act from a prominent Washington law firm sped their discovery. The files provide for the first time an inside look at this important episode in abuse of presidential power.

Last, a small file folder at the Lake County Historical Society in Ohio contained a set of intriguing love letters to Kate Pulitzer while she was married to Joseph. They were signed only with an initial. But another set of documents, donated to Syracuse University in 2001, helped me identify her lover.

These were just several of the sources that had not been available to previous researchers and have greatly enhanced the story of Pulitzer's life. At the same time, these findings and others also contradict a number of frequently repeated tales about him. These range from the claim that his mother was Catholic to the myth that he purchased the *New York World* while on his way to a vacation in Europe with his family. Rather than bog down the narrative of this book, I have placed any disagreements with previous accounts in my endnotes.

JAMES McGRATH MORRIS
TESUQUE, NEW MEXICO

PULITZER

HAVANA 1909

O n the afternoon of February 17, 1909, a small boat pushed off from a dock in Havana's harbor, cut through the pearl-green waters hugging the shoreline, and slid into the ultramarine-blue bay. Out ahead of it, one of the most luxurious private yachts in the world lay at anchor.

The length of a football field, the *Liberty* was rivaled in size and extravagance only by J. P. Morgan's *Corsair*, which had set the standard of seagoing opulence for a decade. With two raked masts front and aft of a large smokestack, the white-hulled *Liberty* was like the beautiful schooners that had plied the oceans years earlier. "I have never seen a vessel of more beautiful lines," said one man on board, who had served on a yacht belonging to the second white raja of Sarawak. Inside, the spacious vessel contained a gymnasium, a library, drawing and smoking rooms, an oak-paneled dining room that could easily seat a dozen people, quarters for its forty-five-man crew, and twelve staterooms fitted by a decorator who had designed furnishings for London's Victoria and Albert Museum.

At this hour, on board all was still. The engines were silent, the bulkhead doors remained closed, and the upper deck gangways were roped off. The *Liberty*'s owner, Joseph Pulitzer, had just gone down for his after-lunch nap, and severe consequences would befall anyone who disturbed the repose of America's most powerful newspaper publisher.

Since becoming blind at the apex of his rise to the top, the sixty-one-year-old Pulitzer suffered from insomnia as well as numerous other real and imagined ailments, and was tormented by even the smallest sound.

Every consideration possible was made to eliminate noise on board. Engraved brass plaques in the forward part of the ship warned, "This door shall not be opened until Mr. Pulitzer is awake." At sea, the ship's twin steam engines drove propellers set at different pitches and running at varying speeds in order to minimize vibrations carried through the hull. The *Liberty* was a temple of silence.

It was also Pulitzer's cocoon. The demons that beset him never rested. For two decades, he had roamed the globe. At any moment, he might be found consulting doctors in Germany, taking baths in southern France, resting on the Riviera, walking in a private garden in London, riding on Jekyll Island, hiding in his tower of silence in Maine, or at sea. Since his yacht was launched the year before, water had become his constant habitat. In fact, the *Liberty* carried sufficient coal to cross and re-cross the Atlantic without refueling.

Wherever he went, it was in the company of an all-male retinue of secretaries, readers, pianists, and valets. In every practical sense, they had replaced his wife and children. From morning to night, these men tended to his every whim and kept the world at bay. By long practice, they had mastered handling his correspondence, discerned the most soothing manner by which to read books aloud from his well-stocked traveling library, and found ways to entertain at meals.

However, during his long exile Pulitzer never relaxed his grip on the *World*, his influential New York newspaper that had ushered in the modern era of mass communications. An almost unbroken stream of telegrams, all written in code, flowed from ports and distant destinations to New York, directing every part of the paper's operation. The messages even included such details as the typeface used in an advertisement and the vacation schedule of editors. Managers shipped back reams of financial data, editorial reports, and espionage-style accounts of one another's work. Although he had set foot in his skyscraper headquarters on Park Row only three times, whenever anyone talked about the newspaper it was always "Pulitzer's *World*."

And it was talked about. Since Pulitzer took over the moribund newspaper in 1883 and introduced his brand of journalism to New York, the *World* had grown at meteoric speed, becoming, at one point, the largest circulating newspaper on the globe. Six acres of spruce trees were felled a day to keep up with its demand for paper, and almost every day enough lead was melted into type to set an entire Bible into print.

* * *

Variously credited with having elected presidents, governors, and mayors; sending politicians to jail; and dictating the public agenda, the *World* was a potent instrument of change. As a young man in a hurry, Pulitzer had unabashedly used the paper as a handmaiden of reform, to raise social consciousness and promote a progressive—almost radical—political agenda. The changes he had called for, like the outlandish ideas of taxing inheritances, income, and corporations, had become widely accepted.

"*The World* should be more powerful than the President," Pulitzer once said. "He is fettered by partisanship and politicians and has only a four-year term. The paper goes on year after year and is absolutely free to tell the truth and perform every service that should be performed in the public interest."

Like Pulitzer himself, however, the *World* was aging. Its politics had grown conservative, its novelty had spawned dozens of imitators, and its great achievements lay in the past. Most readers couldn't remember a time before newspapers, thick as magazines, circulated in the millions, sold for as little as a penny, and were filled with dramatically written news, riveting sports coverage, comics, marital advice, recipes, fiction, and even sheet music.

On this day, a reminder of the paper's fabled past stood nearby. Rising from the waters of Havana Bay like a cadaver's finger was the top portion of a mast. It was the only visible remains of the USS *Maine*, which blew up a decade before, killing most of its crew. The disaster, coming at a time of rising tension between Spain and America, became incendiary kindling in the hands of battling newspaper editors in New York.

William Randolph Hearst, a young upstart imitator from California armed with an immense family fortune, had done the unthinkable. In 1898 his paper, the *New York Journal*, was closing in on the *World*'s dominance of Park Row. Fighting down to the last possible reader, each seeking to outdo the other in its eagerness to lead the nation into war, the two journalistic behemoths fueled an outburst of jingoistic fever. And when the war came, they continued their cutthroat competition by marshaling armies of reporters, illustrators, and photographers to cover every detail of its promised glory.

The no-holds-barred attitude of the *World* and *Journal* put the newspapers into a spiraling descent of sensationalism, outright fabrications, and profligate spending. If left unchecked, it threatened to bankrupt both their credibility and their businesses. Like Sherlock Holmes and Professor Moriarty, they fought it out at the edge of a precipice that could mean death to both combatants.

In the end, the two survived this short but intense circulation war. But their rivalry became almost as famous as the Spanish-American War itself. Pulitzer was indissolubly linked with Hearst as a purveyor of vile Yellow Journalism. In fact, some critics suspected that Pulitzer's current plans to endow a journalism school at Columbia University and create a national prize for journalists were thinly veiled attempts to cleanse his legacy before his approaching death.

In addition to forever sullying his name, remembrance of the war pained the publisher for another reason. Pulitzer's most formidable political foe had come home a hero. Worse, Pulitzer had contributed to this enemy's glory. When Theodore Roosevelt led his famous Rough Riders to victory on Cuba's San Juan Hill, he had brought the press along. After unleashing and glorifying the power of the press, Pulitzer watched his nemesis Roosevelt harness it as the most potent tool of political leadership in the modern age.

For a quarter of a century, the Republican Roosevelt and the Democratic Pulitzer had battled for the soul of America's reform movement. It had been an epic clash. On one side was an egotistical, hard-boiled politician, convinced that Pulitzer was an impediment to the resplendent future his own leadership offered the nation. On the other side was a sanctimonious publisher who believed he was saving the republic from a demagogue. "I think God Almighty made it for the benefit of the *World* when he made me blind," Pulitzer had confided to one of his editorial writers a few months before. "Because I don't meet anybody, I am a recluse. Like a Blind Goddess of Justice, I sit aloof and uninfluenced. I have no friends; the *World* is therefore absolutely free."

Now, as twilight descended on his presidency, Roosevelt hoped to take revenge for all the years of abuse. The immigrant son of Hungarian Jews—blind, tempestuous, and neurotic—had become the bête noir of the brawny, bellicose scion of the American aristocracy. Triggering the president's wrath was the temerity of Pulitzer's *World* in raising the possibility that the Panama Canal, Roosevelt's most sacred accomplishment, had been tainted by corruption. Under presidential orders the

Justice Department was madly combing through dusty century-old law books hoping to find some means to punish Pulitzer for his most recent affront. Grand juries were convened in Washington and New York. If Roosevelt had his way, Pulitzer would spend his last years alive locked up in prison.

At last the small boat from the harbor reached the *Liberty*. It pulled alongside and a handwritten copy of a cable from New York was passed up to Pulitzer's loyal valet and confidant, Jabez Dunningham. When he read it, Dunningham rushed to the ship's bridge and gave orders to the captain to put out to sea.

Roosevelt's grand jury in Washington had announced its decision.

Part I

1847–1878

Chapter One

HUNGARY

———————————◆———————————

On a Sabbath in the spring of 1847, Fülöp and Elize Pulitzer anxiously awaited the birth of their fourth child. Their trepidation was well founded. Two of the last three children born to them in their nine years of marriage had died. Infant mortality was then common, but the siege of death surrounding the Pulitzers was not. By sundown, the news was promising. Elize's labor ended safely with the birth of a son. This one would live. Yet before he reached his teenage years, he would lose a parent and all but one of his eight siblings. For the newborn Joseph Pulitzer, death would be the most constant element of family life.

The prospect of mortality attending the birth of Fülöp and Elize's children robbed them of the pleasures they should have enjoyed as the last in a line of successful Jewish merchants in the small farming town of Makó on the fringes of the Habsburg Empire. Nestled in a crook of the tranquil Maros River, the agrarian outpost was a lonely spot in the midst of the Great Alföld, a flat expanse the size of Holland running east and west across the country. Makó was like an island, surrounded in the winter by a sea of furrowed black soil stretching outward as far as the eye could see, and in the spring and summer by an undulating tapestry of green.

By the time of Joseph's birth, the Pulitzers had been in Makó for three generations. Their ancestors were among a migration of Jews from Moravia in the 1700s, drawn by the promise of greater tolerance and a better economic life in the Austro-Hungarian Empire. Like many other Moravians, they fit easily into a Germanic culture. Hungarian landowners, eager for the services of merchants and tradesmen, enlisted the newcomers to market the products of their estates, creating a symbiotic relationship that enriched both the Jews and the nobility. Over the years, the only connection the Pulitzers retained to their Moravian roots was their name. Since Ashkenazi Jews had no tradition of using surnames, the family adopted "Pulitzer" after the village of Pullitz they had left behind, in order to meet the legal requirement for a hereditary family name.

In Makó, the Pulitzers prospered, benefiting from the town's growth into an important provincial market center. Joseph's great-grandfather Baruch Simon Pulitzer, the earliest known ancestor in Makó, sold rawhide and later grain. Unusually for Jews at that time, he owned his own house, and he was one of the leaders of the Hevrah Kadisha, which helped arrange burials in Jewish congregations. His son Mihály, Joseph's grandfather, met with even greater commercial success. He took wool and grain from Makó to market in Pest, the rapidly growing city in the north adjacent to Buda, and returned with an array of consumer goods such as spices, sugar, grapes, cloth, candles, and playing cards. Mihály was soon paying some of the highest taxes among Makó's Jews and even lent money to members of the city council.

When Joseph's father, Fülöp, was old enough, he joined the flourishing family business, eventually establishing his own store. Tall, bearded, with chestnut hair, blue eyes, and a pronounced hooked nose, all traits he would pass on to Joseph, Fülöp cast about for a wife. As the third in line of wealthy tradesmen, Fülöp could have easily found one among his town's women. Instead he broke with tradition and proposed to Elize Berger, whom he had met on his frequent business trips to Pest. A sophisticated city woman, Berger complemented Fülöp's social and financial position in Makó. The tall, dark-haired young Berger was soon "regarded an enviable woman in the society of our little town," according to one of the Pulitzer children.

The couple made their home across the street from Makó's marketplace in a two-story L-shaped house, considerably larger than many in town. A carriage entrance graced the front of the house, and stables extended perpendicularly from the rear. It was in this house that Joseph was born on April 10, 1847.

Following Jewish custom, Joseph received his Brit Milah, or circumcision, eight days later. The Hungarian Jewish community, into which Joseph was welcomed, was no longer that of his forebearers. Support for Orthodox Judaism was waning in Makó and in other towns that fell into the cultural orbit of Pest. In these places, Jews such as the Pulitzers were joining a reformist wing of Judaism known as Neolog. It sought to abandon many of the strictures of Orthodoxy that clashed with the growing desire among Hungarian Jews to assimilate. Neologs, for instance, removed the *mehitza*—the lattice barriers hiding women congregants—though women remained seated apart from the men; and these reformists also brought the bimah (somewhat akin to a Christian altar) from its traditional place in the center of the synagogue to the front. Joseph's Judaic life would be less isolated from Christian life than that of young Jews growing up elsewhere in Europe.

Nonetheless, as Jews the Pulitzers remained decidedly in the minority in Makó. Only 6 percent of the population was Jewish. Catholics, Greek Orthodox, and Calvinists dominated the city. Members of each faith lived in distinct neighborhoods that divided the town like wedges of a pie, each piece anchored by a place of worship. The tall steeples of the Calvinist and Catholic churches soared high above the flat landscape, and the pealing of their bells carried for miles. It took only a glance to know if one had wandered from the Christian neighborhoods. They were well laid out, with large houses erected by prosperous farmers who could afford to live away from their fields. The Jewish neighborhood, on the other hand, had evolved more haphazardly, with crooked streets and dead-end alleys. The synagogues were small and humble. Joseph would not be more than a few years old before he would have learned his place in the social order of the town.

In 1848, the year following Joseph's birth, a political tsunami of revolutionary fervor swept across Europe, disturbing the order of life even in isolated Makó. Its epicenter was Paris, where a mob chased King Louis-Philippe from his throne and established the fragile but democratic Second Republic. From France the revolution spread to Italy, Germany, and all corners of the Austro-Hungarian Empire. Hungarians saw this moment as a chance to establish their own state. A new government led by the nationalist Lajos Kossuth took power in Pest and established a free press, taxed the nobility, and unshackled peasants from centuries-old feudalistic practices. Jews supported the revolution in large numbers. In return, the government granted them legal emancipation. But it was a Pyrrhic victory. By the summer of 1849, what little was left of the rebellion was in retreat. Kossuth himself spent a night in Makó, just a few days before Austrian troops entered the city, and then he fled to the United States.

Despite the revolution's ignoble end, the Pulitzers clung to their ideals. Two of Joseph's uncles had served in the revolution's national guard, and his father's store had supplied the troops. (Wisely, his father also supplied the Austrian occupiers, avoiding retribution.) The uprising cemented the Pulitzers' identification with nationalism. Although they were Jewish in religion, they regarded themselves as Hungarians in nationality and sentiment. Like most Jews, they came to view their social and economic fate as inextricably linked to that of the nation. In his diary, Joseph's younger brother Albert neatly inscribed a poem by Sándor Petöfi, the revolution's poet laureate, who perished in one of its battles. "Rise Magyar, your country calls!" it began. "The time for now or never falls! Are we to live as slaves or free? Choose one! This is our destiny."

The end of the revolution had personal consequences for the Pulitzer children. "The Hungarian language, Hungarian manners, Hungarian traditions, were all under a ban. People would hardly dare to speak Hungarian in the lowest whispers," recalled Albert. "And thus it came that the native babble of my childhood was soon a stranger to me." School life was also altered. The new government-funded Jewish grammar school in Makó that Joseph briefly attended was tinged with secularism and less Orthodox than older schools, diminishing even farther the importance of Judaic traditions.

There was nothing modern, however, about discipline in the Pulitzer household. The children learned early that "the Hungarian child never answers his father back," Albert said. When disciplining his three boys, their father terrified them by recounting the Roman historian Livy's tale of Titus Manlius who decapitated his own son for defending the family's honor in battle because he had not first sought his father's permission. For serious infractions, Fülöp banished the offender to the stables for the night, without dinner. Elize, however, frequently smuggled out food from the kitchen.

In the spring of 1855, Fülöp decided to follow his father's and brother's footsteps and move his family to Pest. Thousands were making a similar trek, leaving Hungary's small towns for the economic opportunity and political freedom of the big city. Officials granted the Pulitzers' application to move, and Fülöp and Elize sold their house to one of the city's judges, closed the store, and set off to the north by wagon.

For eight-year-old Joseph, the city of Pest at the end of the two-day journey was an astonishing sight. A cityscape as imperial and as majestic as that of Paris or Vienna unfolded before him as his family joined the procession of wagons navigating the cobblestone boulevards. Instead of the monochromatic Alföld of his youth, Joseph was surrounded by stone or brick buildings reaching four, five, and sometimes six stories high, many stuccoed in pastels with intricate, curlicue plaster cornices.

Unlike Buda, which had developed around the royal court's massive palace on a hilly perch across the Danube, low-lying Pest was the creation of merchants and artisans. As a result it was maturing into one of the most strikingly beautiful cities in Europe. Large boulevards, lined with majestic examples of Italian architecture, flowed across Pest like paved rivers from each huge square to the next, dividing the city into well-defined neighborhoods.

The Pulitzers' wagon made its way to the Golden Stern Inn, two blocks from Joseph's grandparents' house at the center of the city, where Jews had been permitted to live for eighty years. At first, only a few "tolerated Jews" had been able to rent apartments and maintain shops whose doors had to remain closed and which were barren of signs or window displays. But in subsequent years the laws were liberalized. By the time the Pulitzers arrived, approximately one-fifth of the city's population was Jewish. Not only had Pest become the center of the nation's economy, music, literature, art, and politics; it was now the center of Hungary's Judaism as well.

The move to Pest proved to be an economic boon for the family. Within a year, Fülöp's business made enough money to be considered for incorporation and he was invited to become a member of the Commercial and Industrial Chamber of Pest. Increasingly wealthy, the family moved into a flat closer to the Danube, in the portion of the quarter regarded as the neighborhood of the Jewish bourgeoisie. The buildings there reached deep into the interior of each block and contained inner courtyards ringed with balconies that led to one- and two-bedroom apartments.

Because of the family's elevated social position, the parents sought to educate their children for a city trade. The eldest boy was consigned to a school of economics in Vienna, Joseph was sent to a nearby trade school, and Albert was dispatched to a boarding school. After a while, the family turned to tutors. Joseph mastered German and learned to speak French. He was a difficult pupil, however, and displayed a volcanic temper. According to Albert, Joseph once chased a tutor out the window (one assumes on the ground floor) when the tutor made the mistake of insisting on teaching mathematics rather than entertaining the youth with war stories from history.

If Joseph didn't take well to formal instruction, he succumbed to the pleasures of reading. The Pulitzer flat was filled with books, as the parents used their increased wealth to indulge their literary passion. Elize's favorite novelist was the English writer Edward Bulwer-Lytton, whose works had been translated into German. In particular, she loved his novel *The Pilgrims of the Rhine*. (He later became notorious for having penned the line "It was a dark and stormy night.") Both Joseph and Albert adopted their parents' habit. "As a child I used to devour books which were far beyond my age," recalled Albert, who had the more romantic mind of the two brothers. Among his favorite authors was the Jewish philosopher Moses Mendelssohn, known as the "German Plato." Joseph considered philosophy of little use and instead favored works of history and biography.

For Joseph, Pest was an education equal to books. Whenever he crossed the city's largest market to visit his grandparents, he saw and learned about life from all parts of Europe. It was a Babel of tongues and a panoply of apparel colors, a striking contrast to the drab peasant costume of his birthplace. Here, merchants and buyers from Turkey, Serbia, Bosnia, Austria, and Germany plied their trades on a city square of covered stalls acres larger than anything Joseph would have seen in Makó.

Leaving the market, and nearing his grandparents' home, Joseph entered a tranquil street with neoclassical buildings whose inner courtyards housed gold- and silversmiths, jewelers, and spice, fruit, and textile dealers. There was no mistaking that those who lived in this portion of the Jewish quarter had done well. Grandfather Mihály's success as a merchant earned him the description "the rich Mr. Pulitzer" among his neighbors. "He lived in a house of his own," said Albert, "a rare distinction in large Austrian towns where often twenty to one hundred families occupied flats or apartments in the same 'rent palaces.'"

A short stroll in the other direction from Joseph's home led to the banks of the Danube River, an irresistible draw for any young boy. For upwards of a mile, riverboats from distant European cities tied up to the embankment on the Pest side of the river, where the current was less swift. There they unloaded goods from distant lands. Like the market, the Danube River revealed a tantalizing promise of a world beyond.

Any exploration of the city that Joseph undertook was unfettered by his being Jewish. There were few other major European cities of the era where Jews were freer or more integrated into society. The cosmopolitan pageant of Pest's wealthy paraded by Joseph's home as carriages ferrying nobles, wealthy merchants, priests, and city officials came down the boulevard abutting his street. In the evenings, the city's elite dashed to balls, where the well-to-do displayed their equality with the ruling classes of other nations. And when not at balls, the elegant crowds gathered outside at the theater, opera, and casinos only a few blocks away. At first, only the wealthiest of Jews who had converted to Christianity were able to enter this world. But by the time the Pulitzers came to Pest the imperative to give up one's faith had greatly diminished. In fact, the Jews of Pest had their own thriving social, economic, and cultural institutions.

The wealth, success, and prominence of the burgeoning Jewish quarter was symbolized by the construction of the Neolog Dohány synagogue, about five blocks south of Joseph's neighborhood. Almost a block in area, it rose to become the largest synagogue in the world, seating 3,000 congregants. The sanctuary was divided by arches from the nave, like the apse of a Christian church, and the bimah was located in the front. An organ and two pulpits were installed, both unheard of in synagogues until then. It required religious finesse to get around the Jewish prohibition against playing musical instruments on the Sabbath: a Christian was hired to play the organ. The synagogue was soon called the "Israelite cathedral" and became an architectural display of assimilation.

Like the synagogue's architecture, Joseph's religious instruction in Pest renounced the strict observance of what were deemed antiquated religious laws; also, this instruction was less concerned with the careful study of the Torah. By the time Joseph reached his teenage years, being Jewish remained a part of his life, but no longer the center of it.

Despite having secured a place in the upper echelons of Pest Jewish society, the succession of deaths continued to haunt the Pulitzers. Before leaving Makó, they had lost two of their children. In Pest, five more died. Because they were living in a prosperous urban setting where infant death had become rarer, the loss of these children was harder to bear than before. The deaths in Pest included their eldest son, who succumbed to tuberculosis, ending their plans for him to take over the family business. Death's grip on the family did not end here. On July 16, 1858, Fülöp died. Only forty-seven years old and at the peak of his business success, he also had contracted tuberculosis.

Four years older than Albert, Joseph understood more fully the extent of the calamity. He had been nine when his older brother died, ten when his younger brothers and sister died, eleven when his father died, and thirteen at the death of his last sister. Albert, in contrast, was not yet nine when the last sibling died. Under the best of circumstances, Joseph would have felt guilty for having survived. But in his case, he responded in other ways as well. The deaths led to an obsession with his health that would remain with him until the end of his life. Every ailment, no matter how small, was accompanied by an underlying fear that he was dying. Further, he developed a phobia of funerals. Even when his closest friends died, Joseph would refuse to attend their burials, and, pointedly, he would not attend the funeral of either his mother or his only surviving brother.

As an additional cruelty, his father's death created a financial nightmare. In his will, Fülöp instructed that his estate be divided among his surviving children, with his wife as ward of the shares. But Fülöp's prolonged illness had depleted his savings. By the time the executor sent ten florins to the Jewish hospital and to a poorhouse, about the price of an *eimer* (pail) of wine, there was almost nothing left.

"Thus was my mother," said Albert, "left to provide for her boys and one daughter, alone and unfriended." Since she had no business experience, it was only a matter of time before the enterprise went bankrupt. Within six months their property was seized by authorities for failure to pay taxes. The family limped along. Elize did her best to earn an income and to keep paying for the education of her children. "What efforts she put forth to give us a thorough education," said Albert. "How she deprived herself of all that she held most dear to her comfort and well being!"

Financial relief appeared in the form of a marriage proposal. Max Frey, a merchant from the southeastern Hungarian town of Detta, won

Elize's consent but not that of Joseph or Albert. It's common that a child's longing for a dead father triggers a rejection of a substitute, even a well-intentioned one. In Joseph's case Frey's entrance into the family, or what little was left of the family, increased his sense of loss and solitariness. Years later, writing an intimate, confessional letter, he conveyed the toll from the deaths and the remarriage. He described himself as "a poor orphan who never even enjoyed as much of a luxury as a father."

Frey's romantic interest in Elize may have also threatened Joseph's intense devotion to his mother, the one remaining vestige of childhood. Pulitzer transformed his love for his mother into a more abstract reverence, so that photographs of her took on an iconic quality. Those who became Pulitzer's friends during his young adulthood were continually shown a locket-sized illustration of his mother that he kept with him at all times. The illustration remained so important to Joseph that late in his life, when his eyes were failing, his wife commissioned an enlargement of the portrait so he could see it.

The deaths and the remarriage of their mother severed the ties that bound Joseph and Albert to home and family. Early in 1864, Albert, not yet fourteen, became the first to leave. He moved into his grandfather's house and obtained work as a clerk at a life insurance company. Joseph, on the other hand, had grander plans. He was anxious to leave Hungary entirely.

Walking across the square near his house one day, Joseph encountered a childhood playmate from Makó. Joseph filled his friend in on the death of his father and the financial misfortunes that had befallen his family. He then asked if he would like to go to America.

"Well," replied his friend, "are you going to America?"

"Yes," said Pulitzer. "I must go because my mother cannot support us and here there is no work."

Going to the United States was not an outlandish plan for an ambitious Hungarian youth. Since the end of the revolution of 1848, a Jewish Emigration Society in Pest had popularized the notion, and the massive migration from Europe to the United States had begun. But Pulitzer had no money, so his options were limited. He decided his salvation lay in the path taken by his maternal uncle Wilhelm Berger, with whom he had been close. Berger had joined the Austro-Hungarian army, which was open to Jews. That spring Berger had left Hungary for Mexico to serve under Prince Maximilian, who believed he was destined to become that nation's emperor. It was not military life that Pulitzer sought, but the escape it offered.

Pulitzer had grown tall—six feet one inch—and had a head of thick wavy chestnut hair, like his late father. A Roman nose, supporting thick glasses, and an angular chin protruded from his pale, smooth-skinned, boyish face. Although he was very thin, with long arms, his body had matured into a manly figure. But his poor eyesight barred his entry into to the Austrian army.

Events in the United States presented him with another opportunity. The American Civil War was in its third year, soldiers were dying at a rate of 13,000 a month, and the government had instituted a draft to meet the insatiable demand for more men. To meet the quota imposed on their city, a group of wealthy Bostonians looked eastward for able bodies. They wagered that there were thousands of young men in Europe who would join the American military provided their passage could be paid. The Bostonians commissioned Julian Allen, a member of a new entrepreneurial class of men finding profit in the draft law's loopholes, to sail to Europe and launch a recruiting drive. For the plan's backers, the venture, if successful, could be politically profitable; for Allen, it could be financially profitable.

Allen set up shop in Hamburg, Germany. He printed recruitment circulars and placed advertisements in European newspapers that reached Pest. He promised that those who joined would be paid travel expenses, a bounty of $100 when they reached the United States, and $12 a month while in the service in the military. As each man could fetch $900 or more as a substitute soldier, Allen hoped to make at least $650 on each transaction. The scheme became Pulitzer's escape route.

In early summer of 1864, Pulitzer began making his way to Hamburg, nearly 600 miles northwest. He stopped in Vienna and met up with a cousin and two friends. They all dined at the famous Zum Lothringer inn, known for its selection of Bavarian beers and favored by many Viennese notables. After dinner, Pulitzer and one of his companions sat on a park bench and talked until dawn until he caught a train from the Nordbahnhof for Hamburg.

There Pulitzer located Allen. He was still recruiting men, but by now his methods were attracting unwanted scrutiny. Complaints were made that the men who accepted Allen's offer of free passage were being misled into thinking they were headed for laboring jobs in the United States. Still, if Pulitzer heard of the complaints, he wasn't deterred. Following Allen's instructions, he traveled to the seaport of Antwerp, 285 miles west of Hamburg, from where the next ship of emigrants was scheduled to depart.

For this voyage, Allen chartered the *Garland*, a German 548-ton, square-rigged sailing vessel. On July 18, 1864, Pulitzer and 253 other men walked up the gangway. In comparison with any other ship taking on passengers in Antwerp that day, the *Garland* was an unusual sight. Every passenger was male and of military age. No other ship in the harbor sailing to the New World left without families with children.

Pulitzer was among the last to board. As was customary, he was quizzed by an officer filling out the ship's manifest. Pulitzer said he was a twenty-year-old laborer. His actual age was seventeen; that he lied about this suggests he knew the purpose of the voyage—being underage would have disqualified him for military service. But there were some men who did not know and found out only after the ship cleared the harbor. They probably learned of their fate from a New York recruiter who had sneaked on board in hopes of luring some of the men to his city. The men became riled and protested so vigorously that the captain was compelled to offer to let them off on the coast of England. The group held a meeting and after considering that they were penniless and spoke no English, they decided to go on with the voyage; in the words of the captain, "stand their lot."

And so the *Garland* sailed westward.

Chapter Two

BOOTS AND SADDLES

◆

After nearly six weeks at sea, Pulitzer saw the craggy coastline of northeastern America on the horizon. It had been an uneventful passage until the *Garland* reached the calm waters of Boston harbor on August 29, 1864. There the ship and its unusual cargo were met with a forceful reception.

Boats bearing federal soldiers intercepted the *Garland* as it neared the first of the islands that separated the harbor from Massachusetts Bay. The soldiers ordered the men on board to take their belongings and lower themselves over the side of the ship onto the smaller vessels. Clueless as to what was happening, Pulitzer and the others found themselves being ferried to Deer Island, which Allen and his partners had selected as a secure place to conduct the final bit of their business after having lost their first batch of European mercenaries to bounty hunters. Under the watchful guard of the soldiers, the men were handed military enlistment documents to sign. Those who complied were given food, a chance to rest, and $100 in greenbacks.

Pulitzer knew the $100 payment was a small fraction of the money earned by the organizers of the voyage for each recruit. The New York bounty hunter, traveling incognito with the men, had promised that larger bonuses could be had in his city. Weighing his options, Pulitzer decided he didn't like the economics of Allen's contract and pursued an escape clause. Along with perhaps one or two dozen others, he sneaked away from Deer Island by wading across the narrow and shallow channel of water separating the landmass from the mainland and headed south.

Reaching New York City, Pulitzer joined the hundreds of men milling about the military recruiting tents at City Hall Park, across the street from Park Row, where Horace Greeley and other giants of American newspapers plied their trade. A new recruit could get cash bounties totaling $675, a tempting offer for many, considering that the total annual earnings for a soldier were less than $150 a year. The city had just finished erecting a 216-foot-long narrow wooden recruitment building featuring the latest in technology to ward off bounty brokers. Inside, each recruit was seated on a special armchair against a wall with a movable panel. When the recruit signed the documents and was handed his cash bounty, a switch was depressed releasing a spring that swiveled the chair and the wall leaving the recruit isolated in a back room until his transfer to a training camp.

Despite such efforts, bounty brokers remained busy, and the city's walls and lampposts were plastered with recruiting posters, including some in German that Pulitzer could read. One town eager for recruits was Kingston, New York, whose draft board made the eighty-mile trip down the Hudson River Valley to set up a tent in City Hall Park. The board members had completed a round of the draft a few days earlier, but the district's quota had not been met. Furthermore, many among those who were drafted wanted to take advantage of the law's provision that allowed one to pay another to take one's place. Among those seeking a substitute was twenty-two-year-old Henry Vosburgh, a member of a family of farmers in Coxsackie, in Greene County.

Pulitzer became Vosburgh's salvation. At the Kingston tent, on September 20, 1864, Pulitzer agreed to serve as a soldier in his place for one year in return for approximately $200. To do so, Pulitzer swore two separate times that he was twenty years old, though he was still only seventeen. The district's provost marshal, a commissioner of the board as well as the surgeon of the board, certified that the gangly teenager before them was "free from all bodily defects and mental infirmity . . . sober . . . of lawful age" and signed Pulitzer's papers.

With money in his pocket, Pulitzer entered a New York jewelry store. He had a tiny hole drilled into an 1864 gold dollar, a small coin about a half an inch in diameter. A delicate chain fastened the coin to a gold ring, thereby making a device by which a woman could hold her handkerchief, then a fashion accessory in Hungary. On the reverse side of the coin, the jeweler engraved Elize's maiden initials, "E.B." Pulitzer mailed the resulting creation to his mother, better proof than any letter of his success in the New World.

A few days after enlisting, Pulitzer walked south past City Hall Park to the tip of Manhattan and boarded the steamer *John Romer* with other recruits. It took them rapidly up the East River, past Throgs Neck and into the western end of the Long Island Sound to the skinny, 100-acre Hart Island. The army used this isolated spot to train its recruits, but the ragtag, multilingual collection of misfits now arriving posed a considerable challenge. The brigadier general in charge was reaching the end of his patience. Draft boards were meeting recruitment quotas, he said, "with men whom they can obtain by any means of bargain, deception or fraud, with which to liquidate upon paper their old obligations to the Government, regardless alike as to whether the men so obtained are fit for soldiers." By his count only about half the recruits made decent soldiers. In the coming months, he would discharge forty-five recruits upon their examination at Hart Island, seventeen of them for being underage. Pulitzer, however, escaped his detection.

Pulitzer also avoided joining the less desirable and more deadly infantry. Good timing and his childhood knowledge of horseback riding landed him a place in a cavalry company. "I wanted to ride a horse, to be a horse-soldier," Pulitzer said. "I did not like to walk." He knew that in European armies regiments were often named after famous people, such as royalty. "So I inquired for the names of some of the regiments of horsemen, and was told of one called Lincoln. I knew who he was and so went to that regiment."

The First New York "Lincoln" Cavalry, as it was called, was organized at the beginning of hostilities by Carl Schurz, one of the best-known German "forty-eighters" who had come to the United States following the suppression of the revolutionary movement. By the time Pulitzer joined the First Lincoln regiment, its original luster had worn off. Three long years of chasing Confederates in Virginia, West Virginia, Pennsylvania, and Maryland had taken their toll; and the men, at the end of their tours of duty, were mustering out in large numbers.

On November 12, 1864, Pulitzer joined his regiment at Remount Camp near Harpers Ferry. The reinforcements were a welcome sight throughout the camps. "For a time, their arrival, appearance, equipment, created an excitement," an Ohio soldier wrote in his diary. "Many were the surmises that many of them would be minus some of their fancy equipment before another week."

Pulitzer was assigned to Company L, one of four German-speaking companies under the command of German-speaking officers. The men in his company were brewers, locksmiths, mechanics, painters, tailors, and bakers from Switzerland, Austria, Hungary, Germany, and Prussia and were older than both Pulitzer's real age and his false age, which by now he gave as eighteen when asked. In completing the paperwork upon arrival, he also told his superiors that if something were to happen to him they were to contact his grandfather Mihály Pulitzer; he made no mention of his mother or stepfather.

Although it was a relief to be among German speakers, Pulitzer did not get along well with the men. He may not have been at fault. Veterans who had been fighting for years resented recruits who had joined solely for the bounty. They felt, as one soldier wrote, "those money soldiers are not worth as much as they cost for when you hear firing ahead you may see them hid in the woods."

When Pulitzer joined his regiment, the presidential election had just concluded and the news of Lincoln's reelection was reaching the soldiers. Pulitzer witnessed the jubilant celebration, especially among German-Americans, who overwhelmingly supported Lincoln. The moment was a remarkable contrast to the world Pulitzer had left behind. Here were troops in the midst of war voting and even permitted—though certainly not encouraged—to vote against their commander in chief. It was Pulitzer's first taste of American electoral politics.

A less significant introduction to another American custom followed a few weeks later. On November 28, the men took a pause from their military duties to celebrate Thanksgiving, which Lincoln had recently proclaimed a national holiday. Turkeys and other food sent to battlefields by families, friends, and citizens in New York were distributed around the camps. "With one eye on the lookout for hungry rebels prowling around the camp, we eat our Thanksgiving feast without further molestation, and are thankful," wrote a lieutenant in Pulitzer's regiment.

For the remainder of November and December 1864, Pulitzer rode about the Shenandoah Valley as General Sheridan moved his forces like chess pieces, threatening but rarely engaging the enemy. Typical of Pulitzer's rare encounters with Confederate forces was one on November 22, when his company crossed the Shenandoah River and rode in a double line toward a long hill. A line of Confederate infantrymen rose to the crest from the other side. Shots were exchanged, but no bullets found their mark, and the two forces then went their own ways.

Long rides were the center of Pulitzer's life as a cavalryman. At times, engagements between Union and Confederate forces in the Shenandoah Valley that winter caused serious losses on each side; but Pulitzer spent his time traveling up and down the valley, confronting snowy, sleety weather but hardly any rebels. Nonetheless, it was arduous work. For a tall city lad like Pulitzer, the days spent in the hard wood-and-leather saddle produced chafed legs, cramps, and a sore back. At night, exhausted, he tended his horse and cleaned his weaponry during the little time that remained before bedding down.

Pulitzer's pain and exhaustion were soon replaced by tedium and boredom when, at the end of December, the men set up camp for the winter near Winchester, Virginia. Pulitzer's winter home consisted of a hut made of log walls, three to five feet high, with a canvas roof and a brick or stone fireplace. Now, instead of endless miles of riding, he settled into a routine regulated by a bugle. Its call signaled each day's activities, including endless drill formations at the sound of "Boots and Saddles."

Warfare resumed with the advent of spring but Pulitzer remained far from harm's way. Instead of following his company to the battle lines, he was assigned to a detachment protecting a general who remained encamped far behind the lines of engagement. The only combat Pulitzer saw was on a chessboard at which he and another recruit had, in the words of his opponent, "the pleasure of whiling away many weary hours." In this manner Pulitzer served out the end of the war only seventy-five miles from where he first joined his company.

April 1865 brought elation and sadness to the troops. On April 9, Lee surrendered to Grant at Appomattox, signaling an end to the war. Five days later, President Lincoln was assassinated. "The effect of the news of the death of the President cannot be described," wrote one member of Pulitzer's regiment. "All through the camps there was unwonted silence. . . . It was the saddest day in camp that the soldiers had ever known. It was as if a pall had been let down upon them."

* * *

The war at an end, Pulitzer rejoined his company in Alexandria, Virginia. The victorious Union commanders planned a massive review of the forces in Washington. In the early morning of May 22, 1865, Pulitzer rode with the gathered cavalrymen west across the Long Bridge, a narrow wooden bridge that traversed the Potomac and emptied near Fourteenth Street. They continued on to Bladensburg, a few miles northeast of Washington in Maryland, where they camped for the night and groomed their horses and themselves for the grand review in the morning.

May 23 dawned bright, cool, and breezy. Rain had fallen earlier in the week, subduing the dust—perfect conditions for a parade. Pulitzer woke at four o'clock when reveille was sounded. After downing breakfast, he and the men rode into Washington, halting three blocks east of the Capitol. Like the nation, the Capitol had been greatly transformed during the war years. New wings extending on each side had more than doubled its size and a cast-iron dome weighing 8.9 million pounds, topped by a statue called *Freedom Triumphant in War and Peace*, rose 287 feet 5.5 inches above the soldiers. In his homeland, the imperial government buildings were built for rulers whose power stemmed from their heritage; Pulitzer now stood before an equally impressive edifice that celebrated democracy.

Promptly at nine, the review began. Pulitzer's company fell in behind General Custer, whose men wore a "Custer tie": a red scarf thrown dramatically over the shoulder. The regiment marched in such tight formation, with horses lined from curb to curb, that the only things in Pulitzer's line of vision were the man and horse on each side and ahead of him. Years later, he would recall little "but how sore my knees became riding in close formation and pressed against the others in line."

The procession moved past the north side of the Capitol and down the hill into Pennsylvania Avenue. On the hillside, hundreds of schoolchildren were gathered, the girls wearing colorful ribbons and the boys sashes; they sang "The Battle Cry of Freedom." Ahead of the soldiers, for as far as they could see, men and women lined the avenue leading to the Executive Mansion. The crowds were orderly—liquor sales having been banned for two days—and cheered lustily. In front of the White House, a reviewing stand was festooned with flags and floral arrangements. There the new president, Andrew Johnson; generals Grant and Sherman; and cabinet members sat, rising to their feet as the various division commanders passed. It was not until three in the afternoon that the last battery of artillery rumbled past.

The reviews over, Pulitzer's military career was at an end. The government wanted to quickly disband the hundreds of thousands of armed, uniformed men. While awaiting their turn to muster out, the members of Pulitzer's Lincoln Cavalry were kept on the move. At first they camped in the hills of Annandale, roughly ten miles south of Washington; then they were relocated to a busy encampment closer to the Potomac River. Rumors swept through the camp that they might be deployed south, this time to Mexico, to enforce the Monroe Doctrine against French troops fighting against Maximilian. The news was disconcerting to the soldiers, and particularly troubling for Pulitzer. His uncle Wilhelm Berger was serving under Maximilian. The rumor died, but the troop movements didn't. For several days they moved back and forth from one encampment to another, until at last they were instructed to begin surrendering their gear and horses.

When Pulitzer's turn came, he had the horse but not all of the government-issued equipment. He was missing two saddle straps; one carbine socket, sling, cartridge box, and swivel; one currycomb; one saddle blanket; one bridle; a pair of spurs and straps; and his horse's feed bag. The items were part of the standard gear given to cavalrymen. The carbine socket, for example, was a small leather thimble-like device through which one slipped the barrel of a rifle so that the weapon would be held in place when worn on one's back while riding. The clerk described Pulitzer's loss of equipment as "by his own carelessness." It may have been. But it was very likely that Pulitzer, like other men, had found it profitable to sell his equipment or, in some cases, even use it in a wager. Pulitzer was docked $13.25. On June 5, 1865, he received his honorable discharge after completing about 270 days in uniform, less than three-quarters of his promised term of enrollment. For his service to the Union cause, Pulitzer pocketed $135.35.

With money to spend, the troops celebrated at night, under a full moon, with bonfires, civilian food, and illicit alcohol. The soldiers knew that they were returning to a civilian workforce already suffering considerable unemployment. The men in Pulitzer's company, all with homes overseas, had to decide where to go in the United States. The choice was soon made for them.

On June 26, the regiment marched to the railroad station to begin the trip back to New York. After a journey filled with delays, the troops reached New York two days later. Because of the tardy arrival the reception committee had dismissed a musical band of thirty pieces, as well as a cavalry escort. So the men marched up Broadway unaccompanied and unnoticed except by the odd pedestrian who recognized the regimental colors, battered and torn on the battlefield. At the Eighth Regiment Armory, on Twenty-Third Street, the men were seated at tables, which had been loaded with fruit and flowers the day before, and were served the dinner that had sat waiting for them. After they finished their meal, and the dignitaries concluded their welcoming speeches—not a word of which was understandable to Pulitzer—the men marched back down Broadway to the Battery and rode the *John Romer* out to Hart Island, where they had begun their military service.

Peace had its risks. On July 7, Pulitzer joined legions of unemployed soldiers on the streets of New York. The economy could not accommodate all the veterans looking for work. Although many returned to their farms or prewar jobs as craftsmen or professionals, others, in particular foreign-born recruits, were looking for new situations. With few employable skills and still unable to speak English, Pulitzer had no luck in finding work. His money soon ran out.

Bewildered, alone, and desperate, he turned homeward for help and wrote to his family for money. In the interim he continued to look—in vain—for work, wandering the streets of New York at day, and at night sleeping in doorways and any other place he could find. Frequently his bed was a bench in City Hall Park in front of French's Hotel and the newspaper buildings that lined Park Row. "Every pleasant night until I found employment," Pulitzer said, "I slept upon the bench, and my summons to breakfast was frequently the rap of a policeman's club."

One day, as he sat on his bench, Pulitzer was approached by a man who asked if he wanted a job. What kind of job? asked Pulitzer. Three years' work, replied the stranger. Food and lodging were included. Pulitzer agreed to follow him. They went down a side street to a small, unkempt office whose reception room was crowded with men, most of whom were drunk. The office belonged to a shipping agency recruiting men to ship out on a whaling vessel. Unwilling to enter a maritime purgatory, Pulitzer declined and after some effort escaped the clutches of the recruiter, whom he called a "land shark."

At last, the long-awaited money arrived from Pest. Pulitzer decided to leave New York and try his luck in St. Louis. The city's large German population was like a safe harbor, and its promise of jobs was drawing German-speaking immigrants like a beacon. Passage on an immigrant railcar, with its plain bench seats and communal cooking stoves, could be had for only a few dollars. Pulitzer paid the fare for what he hoped would be a fresh start at finding a place for himself in postwar America.

Once again, he headed west.

Chapter Three

THE PROMISED LAND

———————————◆———————————

When Pulitzer got off from the train at the end of its journey, he found that too much water and too little money kept him from his destination. Though railroad construction had resumed with a vengeance since the end of the war, there was still no bridge spanning the Mississippi River when Pulitzer reached its eastern bank in the fall of 1865. The only way across to St. Louis was to pay the Wiggins Ferry Company, which held a monopoly on the busy cross-river traffic. But Pulitzer had not a cent left. "I was hungry, and I was shivering with cold," he said. "I had no dinner, no overcoat. The lights of St. Louis looked like a promised land to me."

Through the darkness, Pulitzer spotted a ferry pulling into a slip on his side of the river. He edged his way to the gate and, as he neared it, he overheard a pair of deck hands conversing. Surprisingly, they were speaking in German. He called out to them. One walked over and struck up a conversation with him. Finally, Pulitzer asked if there was a way he could get across. The deck hand told him that a fireman had quit and offered to go and find out if the ferry company needed to hire a replacement.

The deck hand returned in the company of the engineer, who asked Pulitzer if he could fire a boiler. "I said I could," Pulitzer recalled. "In my condition I was willing to say anything and do anything." They opened the gate and led Pulitzer to the boiler, which sat exposed on an open deck, gave him a shovel, and told him to start feeding coal to the fire. "I opened the fire box door and a blast of fiery hot air struck me in the face. At the same time a blast of cold driven rain struck me in the back. I was roasting in the front and freezing in the back." Long into the night,

Pulitzer fed coal to the boiler. "I don't remember how many trips back and forth across the river I made that night, but the next day I went ashore and walked the streets of St. Louis."

It was like coming home. The boats along the riverbank were tied up in the same fashion as the barges that clung to the Danube's shore a few blocks from his boyhood home. Walking past the throngs of steamboat hands, stevedores, levee rats, and river men in gaiters, Pulitzer reached Second Street, where signs directed traffic to eateries and inns such as the Brod- und Kuchenbäcker, the Eichenkranz, the Basel, and the Pfälzer Hof. Men and women greeted each other with "*Guten Tag*," and boys hawked newspapers published in German. "One who passed through this street could imagine himself transplanted to Germany," recalled one immigrant.

St. Louis was already one of the most important and most rapidly growing cities of the West. Despite recurring floods, visitations of cholera, and a fire that destroyed much of the downtown, the fourteen-square-mile city had risen to become the eighth most populated city in the United States. The war was over; local leaders predicted a golden age for their river city. But rather than the promise of St. Louis, it was the pollution from the soft Illinois coal burned in homes and businesses that visitors first noticed.

"The smoke," wrote Mark Twain, "used to bank itself in a dense billowy black canopy over the town, and hide the sky from view." Nor did visitors forget their first sip of St. Louis water. Drawn from the Mississippi River, the water served in restaurants and homes was thick and muddy. "My first impression at the table d'hôte was that everyone was drinking coffee in tumblers, and from its rich color I concluded that it must be very good," said one British traveler. "How great was my dismay, therefore, when I touched the glass, and found it icy cold. 'Iced coffee,' I thought; then I sipped a little, and in great disgust set it down. It was simply muddy water!"

Despite its foul air and dirty water, St. Louis was a vibrant place, drawing hundreds of newcomers every week. Its streets teamed with a multitude of nationalities and races. The original French-flavored atmosphere had become a distant memory. Germans were in the ascendant. For Pulitzer, who spoke no English, the city was a utopia.

He found work and accommodations on the south side of downtown in a ward that was two-thirds German. One could wander from one end to the other without hearing any language but German. Not only were the words familiar and comfortable to Pulitzer, but so were the street noises, smells, and tastes. During the day, when the sound of a beer keg being tapped at Tony Niederwiester's Valhalla or George Wolbrecht's Tivoli rang out, work would stop so that the workers could get a fresh glass. Between ten and noon, tavern keepers would offer workers lunches of rye bread, blood or summer sausage, salted dried herring, dill pickles, and gallons of lager beer, a new, lighter style of beer. Lager had grown so popular that commercial brewers had just achieved a national production record of 1 million barrels in a year.

For the first several months after reaching St. Louis, Pulitzer worked at a variety of jobs. He tended mules for a short time at the Benton military barracks, which had served as an encampment for Union troops during the war. "Never in my life did I have a more trying task," said Pulitzer. "The man who has not cared for sixteen mules does not know what work and trouble are." Next, he landed work as a coachman for a well-to-do family. The family members were apparently impressed by their French- and German-speaking driver and referred to Pulitzer as their "educated coachy."

In 1866 Pulitzer labored as a deck hand on a riverboat. During his evening breaks, he would sit behind a stove on board and read one of the city's many German newspapers. The boat's captain spoke to his wife in French, hoping to keep his communications from the ears of his deck hand. Pulitzer let him know he would have to use a language other than French or German if he did not want to be understood. Ironically, that could still include English.

Despite Pulitzer's inability to speak much English, he continued to pick up jobs. He worked as a stevedore unloading bales and barrels from river steamers and as a day laborer in construction. He even tried working as a waiter at Tony Faust's Oyster House on Carlonet Avenue close to his rooms. "The trial period for proprietor, guests, and, last but not least, the novice waiter was very brief," one close friend remembered. "It came to a conclusion at the end of the second meal when a beefsteak, having been rejected in a rather impolite manner, found itself, after an exchange of words that quickly developed into personal affronts, dropped onto the head of the guest rather than onto his plate, thereby bringing an end as abrupt as it was drastic to the serving glory of the presenter."

One time Pulitzer, along with about forty other men, responded to an advertisement promising high-paid jobs on a sugar plantation in Louisiana. The employment agent informed the men they would need to pay $5 each as a fee for transportation down the river. That night they boarded a steamer and headed downstream. At three in the morning, they were rousted and disembarked at a deserted spot some forty miles south of the city. Realizing they had been had, the men marched back to St. Louis together, with murderous intentions. Fortunately for the agent, he was nowhere to be found.

The various jobs allowed Pulitzer to improve his English and get a toehold in St. Louis. As soon as he had set aside a little money, he paid his room and board for weeks ahead. "Thus I was secure," he said. "I did not have to worry and could look about for something better." Late in 1866, Pulitzer did find something better. The *Deutsche Gesellschaft*, the German Immigrant Aid Society in St. Louis, recommended him for an opening as a clerk. Many immigrants owed their first employment to this aid society. It had been created seven years earlier to provide job placement and other assistance to new German-speaking residents and was funded by established members of the German community who had not forgotten their own early struggles.

In Pulitzer's case the German aid society had located an assistant clerk's job at Theo Strauss's lumberyard on Franklin Street, not far from where Pulitzer roomed. Upon meeting Pulitzer, Strauss and his family were impressed. "We found him to be bright and highly educated, speaking German and French without an accent and very good English," said Theo's son Adalbert Strauss. The younger Strauss and Pulitzer were about the same age. "I was drawn to him," said Strauss, "by his uniformly kind manner and great courtesy." When meeting Strauss's mother, Pulitzer would exclaim, *"Ich küss die Hand gnädige Frau,"* a characteristically Viennese expression from courtly etiquette. Visiting Pulitzer in his room, Strauss also learned about his new friend's devotion to his own mother when Pulitzer showed the miniature portrait of his mother he had brought with him from Hungary.

Strauss was also a witness to Pulitzer's strong will. One day, Pulitzer showed up at work late, explaining that he had hardly slept, on account of an aching molar. "When I asked him how he obtained relief," said Strauss, "he informed me that he had heated an eightpenny nail red hot in the flame of a gas burner and inserted it into the cavity."

*   *   *

With the steady pay from his job at the lumberyard, Pulitzer began to explore his new home. He discovered the Mercantile Library, one of the city's gems. A vastly successful civic project, the library was created in 1846 as a stock corporation by a group of merchants who were inspired by the example of New York City's Mercantile Library. Young single men, these merchants reasoned, lived primarily in boardinghouses with no parlors in which to entertain themselves when they were not working. A library could offer lectures, concerts, and classes for "mutual improvement," then considered the path of social and economic elevation, a much better alternative to bars and other less virtuous haunts.

Pulitzer paid the $2 initiation fee and $3 annual dues and signed his name in the members' ledger on July 18, 1866. He was one of 275 clerks who joined the library that year, many enticed by a discounted membership aimed at recruiting them. Housed in a three-story building at Fifth and Locust streets, the library held a large collection of books, carried newspapers from all over the country and abroad, and was open each day of the week from morning until late at night. Pulitzer spent every free moment he had at the Mercantile, often bringing a pair of apples for sustenance so as not to waste a moment leaving the library for a meal. In the elegant library's main room, he had his choice of 27,000 books stored behind glass on shelving extending to the ceiling, with a small catwalk to reach the higher shelves. Sitting at one of the eight-sided desks, above which rested busts of important writers from the past, Pulitzer applied himself to polishing his rudimentary English.

He approached the task with marked diligence and persistence. For instance, to expand his vocabulary he studied synonyms for all the words he was learning—a habit he recalled later as "the wisest weakness I had as a youth in acquiring some deeper knowledge of the English language." The librarian, who lived in a chamber off the reading room, did not entirely approve of Pulitzer's quest to use the library to learn English, because he didn't confine himself solely to books. In fact, Pulitzer badgered members in hopes of persuading, or in some cases provoking, them into conversation. To the librarian Pulitzer seemed "just a noisy and unruly young man who ignored the posted signs commanding silence."

His hours in the library paid off. Not only did he polish his English, but Pulitzer came into contact with lawyers, newspapermen, politicians, and other leading figures. One group of men, in particular, exerted considerable influence on the atmosphere of the library. A few months before Pulitzer joined, a dozen or so men had created the St. Louis Philosophical Society under the leadership of Henry C. Brockmeyer, a Prussian Jew who was said to be a "midwestern Thoreau."

His moniker stemmed from an episode during the previous decade, when he had spent two years in a backwoods Missouri cabin studying the work of the German philosopher Georg Wilhelm Friedrich Hegel with such intensity that he might have succumbed to fever and other sicknesses had he not been found by a schoolteacher who nursed him back to health at civilization's closest outpost, St. Louis. In no time this small clutch of would-be philosophers made its mark on the city's cultural landscape, and Hegel was the rage. At the library, spirited members frequently blocked traffic at the checkout desk while arguing a philosophical point. No young member of the city's German community with intellectual leanings remained free of its influence.

When he wasn't studying, Pulitzer loved to spend time in a popular chess room off the reading room. Since childhood, he had loved chess, and in the Civil War he had sharpened his skill during his monotonous winter encampment. His play attracted attention. "When he played, everyone in the room hovered about his game and watched it closely," recalled one young boy. "The attraction, of course, was his superlative playing."

Among the men who took an interest in the young, studious chess player were Emil Preetorius, one of the owners of the *Westliche Post*; and non-German professionals such as the lawyer William Patrick, who had an office in a building on Market Street, four blocks south of the library. Patrick soon gave Pulitzer some occasional work serving legal papers and running errands.

Pulitzer quit his post at the Strauss lumberyard when he was passed over for the job of head bookkeeper. "The only thing that stood in his way," recalled Adalbert Strauss, "was his handwriting which was almost vertical, very large and heavy and at a distance looking a little like Chinese." After giving up his desk at the lumberyard, Pulitzer became a regular fixture in the Market Street office building, picking up whatever work he could find. "We inferred that he was not making much of a go as his exchequer was concerned and it was a struggle with him," said a teenager who worked in Jones & Sibley's drugstore, on the first floor of the building.

By the spring of 1867, Pulitzer felt confident that his future lay in the United States. On March 6, he entered a St. Louis courtroom as a subject of the emperor of Austria and left as an American citizen. Once again, Pulitzer displayed no aversion to deceiving the government. As he had done when he inflated his age to join the Union military, Pulitzer lied about how long he had been in the United States now that he sought to become a citizen. Naturalization law required, among other things, that an applicant reside in the United States for a period of five years before being eligible for citizenship. Pulitzer had been in the country for less than three years. Eight days later, he returned to court and went before the clerk to complete the necessary paperwork, as well as take an oath, to become a notary public. This time, however, there was no need for any deception; the requirements were few.

Pulitzer continued working at his mix of jobs connected with the law offices on Market Street. At one point he accepted the task of recording land deeds for the Atlantic and Pacific Railroad in a dozen counties to the southwest of St. Louis where the railroad planned to build a line to Springfield, Missouri. Following his railroad work, Pulitzer accepted a position as secretary of the Deutsche Gesellschaft, which had provided him with his job at the lumberyard the previous year. Now it was his turn to locate work for new immigrants. His work at the library paid off. The new post required that he write letters in English.

After a few months at the immigrant society, Pulitzer learned about a job opening at the *Westliche Post*. Many of the highly educated and literate German refugees from the 1848 revolution found work in the bourgeoning German press that served the 5 million to 6 million German immigrants with a cultural fondness for reading newspapers. The *Westliche Post* was owned by two of the city's most eminent Germans: Carl Schurz, the former Civil War general in whose cavalry Pulitzer had served, and Emil Preetorius, with whom Pulitzer had made friends in the Mercantile chess room. Under their management, the paper was one of the most widely circulated German-language publications in the United States.

Prosperous and growing, the *Westliche Post* was casting about for a new reporter. For Pulitzer the timing was fortunate. Not only did Pulitzer know Preetorius, but in recent months the elder man, as president of the German Immigration Aid Society, had observed his diligence. Louis Willich, the paper's city editor, also knew Pulitzer. As secretary of the society, Pulitzer had frequently passed on information and stories from the most recent German immigrants arriving in St. Louis. Willich had been impressed with Pulitzer's news sense. He was offered the job.

"I could not believe it," Pulitzer recalled. "I, the unknown, the luckless, almost a boy of the streets, selected for such a responsibility. It all seemed like a dream."

Preetorius and Willich were not disappointed. It took Pulitzer no time to confirm they had made the right decision in taking a chance on the twenty-year-old. What he lacked in experience he more than made up for with raw, resolute effort. "His time for work seemed to be all the time," said Preetorius. "I never called on him at any hour that he did not immediately respond."

It wasn't long, either, before Pulitzer caught the attention of his new colleagues. On a muggy, hot summer day a pack of reporters gathered behind the city's post office to badger an official for a story. "Suddenly," said one of the men, "there appeared among us the new reporter, of whom we had heard but not yet seen." He was hard to miss. Having rushed from the office, Pulitzer was without his collar and jacket but he did have his pad of paper in one hand and his pencil in the other. Within an instant, he informed the crowd of reporters that he was with the *Westliche Post*, as if this might impress them, and began to ask questions. "For a beginner he was exasperatingly inquisitive," said the reporter who recorded the moment. "He was so industrious, indeed, that he became a positive annoyance to others who felt less inclined to work."

If Pulitzer believed his new job would be glamorous, or at least easier than the numerous jobs he had held so far, the delusion was quickly shattered. The working day never ended. There was only one other reporter on the paper, so the duty of finding and reporting all the local news rested on the two men. Also, Pulitzer was unwilling to put forward anything but his best effort. "We would get one of his stories into type," said the compositor who handset all the type, "and when Pulitzer got the proof read there would hardly be a word left as he wrote it in the first place."

While Pulitzer honed his new craft that summer, his sixteen-year-old brother in Pest was preparing to join him in the United States. Albert's motivation was political, not pecuniary. His family-bred republican ardor, combined with a fanciful imagination, had led him to believe he could divest Europe of its emperors, kings, and other potentates. "Obviously, I said to myself, if I could do so wonderful a thing I should attain the very summit of human glory. But how could I accomplish so difficult, so gigantic, apparently almost so impossible a task?" He devised a plan to cross the Atlantic, rouse the American people, and return with an army to dethrone the sovereigns of Europe.

Reaching the United States was an expensive undertaking. The Civil War was over, so there were no American benefactors willing to pay for the passage. Not surprisingly, Grandfather Mihály called Albert's idea a "ridiculous project" and refused to provide any financial support. "My poor mother, seeing that a refusal would not stop me, as I was too unalterably bent upon the realization of my scheme, cried a good deal, but finally yielded a reluctant consent," Albert said. Elize accompanied her son to Hamburg and purchased him a ticket on the *Allemannia*. Hanging a $20 gold piece around his neck, hidden in a tiny cotton bag under his shirt, she consigned the last of her two living children to America.

Albert was ill prepared for the journey. He failed to bring any necessary items such as toiletries, towels, or bedding, and without a bowl, plate, or pan he had no way to eat the ship's meals. So he remained in his hammock deep in the ship, among the 600 others in steerage. "There I lay stupefied, benumbed, absolutely paralyzed from breathing this polluted, nauseating atmosphere," Albert said. Fortunately, several Italian women took pity on him and made sure he got sustenance. On July 20, 1867, Albert reached New York, but he was soon stranded by youth and inexperience. To ward off the July heat, he impetuously consumed flavored ices. "My $20.00 capital was melting away nearly as fast as the ice-cream which I enjoyed so hugely," he said. "Thus I was fain to obey the call of my elder and only surviving brother, Joseph."

After a separation of three years, the two were reunited in St. Louis. Now, Albert stood as tall as Joseph, at more than six feet, and was very slender, but without his older brother's awkward angularity. That they were brothers was undeniable. They had the same thick curly hair, high forehead, and blue eyes, but Albert's face was more balanced, with a less pronounced nose. He was the handsomer of the pair.

Although the reunion was warm, the practicalities of life rapidly took center stage. Albert needed a job and his own place to live. Joseph's small room was not intended for two. Each day Albert went out and tried to find work, even going from house to house. "My inquiries always resulted either in a negative reply or, what was still more hopeless, in no reply whatsoever," he said. Albert was not alone in his bad luck. The city was filled with job seekers. Joseph showed no sympathy. After all, he had found work when he came to St. Louis two years earlier. Each morning he asked if his brother had obtained a job yet. "This query being repeated daily, irritated, upset me," said Albert. "I became restless, peevish, fretful." One evening the pair got into a heated argument over Albert's inability to secure work. Joseph, as was his habit, vented his anger with an outburst of sarcasm. He flippantly said that if things were to go on as they were, Albert might as well make an end of it by shooting himself.

"Excellent advice," replied Albert grabbing the revolver his brother kept in the room and putting the barrel to his mouth.

"Not here!" yelled Joseph.

No, thought Albert. "It would not do to have a coroner's inquest in this very room. I desisted."

Albert redoubled his efforts but still had no luck. The two brothers continued to share Joseph's cramped room, and life was glum. Again, the issue came to a head.

"If you do not desire me to stay here any longer, just say the word 'go' and I shall go," said Albert.

"Go," replied Joseph, in a tone that sounded to Albert as "though he really did not mean for me to go but was curious to know whether I was plucky enough to carry out my own menace." So, in the dead of the night, Albert left. It was a gesture characteristic of the impulsive nature the two brothers shared, especially in decision making. Albert wandered aimlessly until he came to a park and a bench on which to sleep. "But my slumber did not last long." A policeman woke him and told him he could be arrested for sleeping on a bench. Albert spent the rest of the night dozing on and off, keeping watch for any approaching police officers.

After spending yet another futile day searching for work, Albert returned for the night to his bench. At last, the next day he obtained a position as a door-to-door salesman for *Die Gartenlaube,* an immensely popular illustrated family newspaper featuring articles about culture, art, history, and science, as well as short stories, serialized novels, poetry, and puzzles. With his earnings, he secured a small room in a boardinghouse.

Settled at last, Albert made learning English a priority. Before leaving Hungary he had engaged an inexpensive English tutor, one so inept that Albert remained clueless as to how the language was pronounced. In St. Louis, Albert took his brother's path and turned to the Mercantile Library. "My great delight used to be to haunt its precincts from morn till night," said Albert. "I was able to see all the English and American reviews, and familiarize myself with current English and American literature, even though I could not make much progress learning the pronunciation and idiomatic use of the language."

For Joseph the *Westliche Post* became a gateway to the German community's leading politicians, lawyers, merchants, and writers. They came to the Chestnut Street newspaper building each day to discuss the news of the day or to plot election strategy with Preetorius and Schurz. The likelihood that Schurz would become a U.S. senator made the *Westliche Post* a mandatory stop for anyone of significance traveling through St. Louis. Often the daytime gatherings continued into the night at Preetorius's house, which Pulitzer also frequented. Preetorius's wife, Anna, took a liking to the young reporter and doted on him, especially as he often entertained her infant son. The world into which Pulitzer peeked seemed to be one with limitless possibilities. To be a newspaper editor was to do more than report on the world; it was to shape it.

Pulitzer was comfortable in the cultured and political atmosphere of the paper, and during the evenings at Preetorius's house. He was unschooled, but not uneducated. Like his younger brother, he had been inculcated with a love of literature, music, and the arts; and his strong drive to learn made up for any lack of formal instruction. It was not long before the visitors took an interest in Pulitzer. "That young fellow clinches the future," said Brockmeyer, the principal mover behind the Hegelian St. Louis Philosophical Society. "They think because he trundles about with himself a big cob-nose, a whopper jaw, and bull-frog eyes that he has no sense; but I tell you, he possesses greater dialectical ability than all of them put together—I know it for I have felt it."

Pulitzer attended a few of the study groups spawned by Brockmeyer's Philosophical Society. For many of the participants, it was as though they had found the key to the universe in Hegel. Their study created a kind of secret fraternity of understanding for every field of activity from music and art to history and politics. They saw the Civil War as an inevitable conflict of the Hegelian dialectic, playing out the inherent conflict of Southern rights and the Northern morality. Most significant of all, their belief that their city would emerge as the new center of post-war America helped spark a broader "St. Louis movement" that spread among citizens, giving rise to pamphlets, books, and even legislation calling for relocating the nation's capital to St. Louis. The philosophical society "took the character of a subtle pervasive influence, rather than an organized propaganda," said one member. "Its life pulsed in the small coteries which met usually in parlors or private rooms for the study of some special book or subject."

But for Pulitzer, it was not the society's philosophical insights that changed his life. Rather, the society brought him Thomas Davidson, into whose orbit he would be drawn, first as a pupil, then as something more.

A nomadic philosopher from Scotland, Davidson arrived in St. Louis in the fall of 1867, shortly after alighting in Boston where he had been welcomed by the transcendentalists. The superintendent of the St. Louis school system offered the twenty-seven-year-old Davidson a position teaching Latin and Greek, in hopes of making him part of the coterie of Hegelians. It worked. Shortly after arriving, Davidson was elected an associate of the St. Louis Philosophical Society.

In contrast to the serious Hegelians, the broad-framed itinerant philosopher stood out from the crowd. Davidson's rural Scottish origins, red hair, bright blue eyes, and mellifluent voice with its almost musical cadence gave him a personal charm that caught the attention of many. He was ebullient, and his laugh was infectious. "Davidson's native mood was happy," said one close friend. "He took optimistic views of life and his own share in it. A sort of personal satisfaction radiated on his face." Even when posing formally for a photograph, Davidson looked as though concealing a smile was nearly impossible.

The Scot's charms engendered idolatrous feelings among young men. "His capacity for friendship was seemingly boundless, drawing to him extremes of the most startling sort among men," according to one description published shortly after his death. Women were also attracted to Davidson because he was one of the few teachers who treated them as equal to males. But Davidson was unable to sustain a romantic relationship with a woman. He broke off an eight-year engagement to the only woman he found sexually appealing. "I am cursed with a nature that makes all real marriage impossible. When I am physically attracted to a woman I always despise her," he wrote. "When I love a woman spiritually, I am always repelled from her with fearful force, that is, physically."

If Davidson was attracted sexually to men, he was not about to proclaim it. With almost no exception, men in his time did not reveal their homosexuality. On the other hand, wherever he went, Davidson left a trail of young men with broken hearts. In 1867, for instance, one young Englishman wrote to Davidson, now in the United States, "I will never forget how queer I felt about my heart when once at 'Jacques Lorgues' both seated on the same sofa, you put your arms round my neck and gazing fondly in my face, you pressed me into your loving arms and said: 'Oh! If I were a woman!!' . . . then you rested your head on my bosom. I felt as if you had been yourself my sweet-loving bride."

Five years earlier, another young man had been even more direct about the loss of Davidson's companionship. "You were pure, beautiful, intelligent and good and around you the tendrils of adoration and love—the holiest and tenderest feelings of my heart became hopefully entwined," he wrote. "The thought that *you* might be my wife completely filled the measure of my hopes in this world."

Davidson himself confessed considerable emotional turmoil over his attraction to men. "I am not loose or wicked in my behavior, but I am naturally endowed with fearfully strong passions so much so that I am often driven by them to the verge of committing suicide."

Pulitzer fell under Davidson's spell. Over time, the two came to spend nights together in each other's quarters where, as Pulitzer lay on a bed, Davidson would expound upon the classics, literature, and philosophy. These nights filled an emotional void in Pulitzer, a youth stranded in a foreign land, his father dead and his mother married to another man. Sharing a bed was a rare gesture for Pulitzer. Intimacy—especially physical intimacy—was not easy for him. He was very ill at ease when he was around others and not fully clothed. "From his earliest days he slept alone," a longtime associate would later say, "save when he shared a bed with Professor Davidson, remarking after that this unwonted intimacy showed how much he thought of his learned friend."

As when Davidson abandoned other young men, Pulitzer's deep passionate bond with him came to the surface in pained letters. "If Faust had been such a cold-blooded heartless chap as you are, Goethe and Mephisto would have had a much harder time indeed," a crestfallen Pulitzer wrote when Davidson left for Boston. "But I'll have my revenge even if I have to go all the way to Massachusetts to get it." Pulitzer promised to pardon Davidson if he wrote at least once a week while they were apart.

Davidson ignored this request. Calling him a "villain," Pulitzer again unburdened himself. "What a fool your friend must be to cling to you still," he wrote. "But never fear, it is my mission as it is the mission of great men to reform and perseverance like your wisdom knows no limit. Whether you go to Massachusetts, or still further north as far even the north-pole I shall stick to you—stick to you until grim death.

"Do you know what I have been guilty of? I have *thought!* Terrible isn't it? But worse still—I have thought of *you!* And worse and worse—I never had that familiar Grecian countenance framed in Scottish red in my mind's eye without another face close to it—softer still, prettier still, and fully as intelligent and gentle. I have that strange face before me now." Pulitzer vowed that in two weeks time he would come to Gloucester, and he closed the letter with "Yours forever."

Ten days later, Pulitzer received a reply from Davidson. It was less than he hoped. "Tom!!!" Pulitzer wrote back. "The battles of Salamis, Sadaina or Ledars were nothing compared with the struggle that just closed in my breast." Pulitzer was looking for a signal to join Davidson in the East. There was none. Instead he chose to take a business trip to Denver. Had Davidson been more forthcoming, Pulitzer said, his decision might have been different. "Well, there is hope yet. I'll be back in less than fourteen days and, if upon my return, I find a less mysterious and more detailed epistle I'll go right on to Boston."

In the end, however, Davidson remained in the East and Pulitzer in St. Louis. The philosopher had abandoned Pulitzer, as he had abandoned other young men everywhere he went. But in this case, Davidson left behind a pupil whose unschooled intelligence had been polished into a studied intellect. It had been an emotionally wrenching passage for Pulitzer. Except for the letters he would write to women he later courted, there is no other existing Pulitzer correspondence so wrought with feelings. His friendship with Davidson was the deepest that he would have with anyone else except his wife. For unlike Davidson, Pulitzer would marry and father children.

Chapter Four

POLITICS AND JOURNALISM

———————————◆———————————

Politics and journalism were two sides of the same coin when Pulitzer joined the staff of the *Westliche Post*. Out-of-work politicians became newspaper editors, and successful editors became elected politicians. Most newspapers remained financially tied to political patrons, and often their political origins were reflected in their names, such as the *Missouri Republican* and *Missouri Democrat*.* Even the few new independent newspapers made it an all-consuming task to cover politics. Politics was the lifeblood of journalism. "Every newspaper man, if not a politician, took an interest therein," said Pulitzer's friend Charles Johnson. By coming to work for the city's most widely circulated German newspaper, Pulitzer stepped into the world of Republican politics.

Germans in St. Louis were ardent Republicans, a loyalty that grew from their devotion to abolition. Radical Republicans—those members of the party who favored more punitive Reconstruction measures, the destruction of Confederate sympathies, and protection of freed slaves—were in control of Missouri. They conducted politics as they had the war, with a kind of scorched earth approach. Opposing Radical rule was futile.

The keystone of Republican dominance of Missouri was a punitive constitution adopted at the end of the war. During the early years of Reconstruction, Missouri Radicals went farther than those in any other state in creating a system of registration, tests, and oaths to keep former

---

*Confusingly to modern readers, the *Republican* was the Democratic paper and the *Democrat* was, yes, the Republican paper.

rebels and their sympathizers from the ballot box and civic life. Missourians could not vote, become teachers, lawyers, or even ministers without stating in writing that they had never favored or supported the Confederacy. Thousands were disenfranchised on the basis of a definition of disloyalty so vague as to include men whose distant cousins might have fought on the wrong side of the war.

Republicans feared that they would lose their grip on power without the constitution's loyalty provisions. But though these provisions squelched Democratic opposition, a threat was growing from within the party. The more moderate members wanted to restore suffrage to all white voters and feared that the long-run interest of the party was in danger if the restrictions weren't lifted. Among the Germans, this wing was led by Preetorius and Schurz, who was settling in as copublisher of the paper. In the English-speaking community the movement was led by politicians such as Pulitzer's friend Johnson.

Pulitzer fell in line like a foot soldier. Taking orders from Schurz provided him with an apprenticeship in American immigrant politics. In the three years he had been in St. Louis, Pulitzer had worked hard to develop friendships with men whom he perceived to be on a path to power or success. Now he was with one who had both. Remarkably, Schurz was also among the very first American political figures Pulitzer had learned about when he arrived in the United States. It was Schurz, after all, who had created the First Lincoln Cavalry, in which Pulitzer served.

Schurz placed the *Westliche Post* and himself in the service of the 1868 Republican presidential campaign, using the newspaper to persuade Germans in St. Louis that General Ulysses Grant was their man—and using his oratorical skills to persuade Germans in other states. For Schurz, journalism was one weapon on the political battlefield. His speeches were another. None of this was lost on Pulitzer, who had now spent two years working at the paper. "He was my chief," said Pulitzer. "We often traveled together, yet in all that time I never saw him pass an idle moment, either in the office or on the road, or anywhere else."

Pulitzer not only assumed the Republican faith of his boss but followed Schurz's model. "Pulitzer," said Johnson, "as soon as he was fairly in harness as a reporter, became active in politics." He joined his neighborhood's Republican organization; and by August 1868 he was rewarded for his efforts by being selected as the secretary of the Radical club of the Fifth Ward. Pulitzer's ambition did not go unnoticed. "There never seemed to be any doubt in his mind," said Preetorius, "that he would succeed in something."

In November, with the election won, Missouri Republicans turned their attention to selecting their next U.S. senator. Even though Schurz had barely arrived in the state, he set his sights on winning the seat. Republicans in St. Louis, heavily German, were intent on regaining control of the party from Senator Charles Drake, whom they despised.

The contest gave Pulitzer a front-row seat at a battle of Reconstruction politics. One of his friends, William M. Grosvenor, editor of the *Missouri Democrat*, was among a group of three leaders backing Schurz who also included Gratz Brown (a former U.S. senator) and Preetorius. They considered Schurz an ideal candidate for the Senate. He had no political battle scars from Missouri, and thus few enemies; he was a Republican whose support of the party went back to Lincoln's first presidential campaign; and he had the support of the considerable German population.

A New Englander of uncommon talent, Grosvenor was a big, fleshy man with olive skin and a mane of hair, a bushy beard, and heavy eyebrows that gave him the fierce look of a lion. Although one worked for a German paper and the other for an English paper, Pulitzer and Grosvenor found they shared a reformist agenda. They both wanted to restore the vote to disenfranchised Democrats and compete openly in elections. They thought it was their job as journalists to bring this about.

In early January 1869, Pulitzer accompanied Preetorius and Schurz to Jefferson City, the state capital, as the legislature met and prepared to select Missouri's next senator. Schurz told the Republican caucus what it wanted to hear, that he supported President Grant and the Fifteenth Amendment, giving black citizens the right to vote. But he added that the time had also come to lift voting restrictions on disenfranchised white citizens. The appeal triggered an attack from Drake, the architect of the plan to keep Democrats from the voting booth. Drake could hardly contain his temper, and he became especially provoked when Schurz continually interrupted his speech to take issue with his various accusations. Then Drake made a fatal mistake. He broadened his assault on Schurz to include all German immigrants and questioned their loyalty.

His maneuver gave Schurz the opportunity he sought. He was merciless in his rebuttal. Declaring his pride in being German-born, he reminded the audience that he and other Germans had fought to save the Union and damned Drake for having wavered on the issue of slavery. It worked. The caucus voted for Schurz. "I had one of the greatest triumphs of my life last night," he told Preetorius. "Drake was completely crushed."

Preetorius and Pulitzer rushed their own accounts of the triumph into print. Preetorius's was in the refined classical German most commonly found in the paper. Pulitzer's was sprinkled with rollicking humor, biting sarcasm, and double entendres, including one that alluded to menstruation with regard to Schurz's opponent. He invoked his favorite theme as a reporter: the press illuminates the dark recesses of government to which politicians retreat at decision-making time. "A great step forward was taken with yesterday's open caucus in the Hall of Representatives," Pulitzer wrote. "The battle for the Senate has been lifted from the basement of secret intrigues to the public forum. Initially revealed to the people by the press, now it will be sorted out verbally in front of everyone in the halls of the Capitol." It was sorted out. A few days later the legislature followed the caucus's lead and gave Schurz the job.

Schurz's election altered life at the *Westliche Post*. Soon he had gone to Washington and was overwhelmed with political work. "I have hardly time to read the newspaper, let alone to write for it," Schurz wrote back from the capital. Normally Preetorius would have picked up more of the editorial responsibilities, but he was ill. So the management of the paper fell on the shoulders of its ill-equipped city editor, Louis Willich, a twenty-seven-year-old who had been in St. Louis for less time than Pulitzer and was hardly an expert on the city or its political topology.

The vacuum at the top of the staff became an opportunity at the bottom for Pulitzer. His work soon became the mainstay of the paper. He wandered around St. Louis at all hours, visiting schools and public institutions, attending public meetings and ward meetings, knocking on doors of lawyers and politicians, and opening those doors that didn't yield to a knock. "His thirst for news was unquenchable," recalled a stenographer at the St. Louis Police Commission. The commissioners often met behind closed doors. "Not infrequently on those occasions the door would softly open, and a pale, spectacled face would intrude itself on the privacy of the session, with the inquiry 'any news?' followed by the roughest but good natured cry 'Get out of here!' and a hearty laugh at the persistency of the inquisitor."

Pulitzer even took his door-opening to the state capital. One night a group of Democratic legislators were caucusing, and only reporters from Democratic newspapers had been permitted in the room. Suddenly the doors were thrown open, recalled another reporter, and "through the open casement calmly walked the correspondent of the *Westliche Post*. He stepped to the reporters' table without a word, placed a pad of paper before him, and took his seat without question or objection from the members."

It wasn't long before just about every politician and reporter had caught a glimpse of this peripatetic member of the press. Pulitzer's appearance alone was conversation-worthy and was a source of much merriment among reporters. He wore buff-colored pants too short for his long legs, a coarse hickory shirt without a tie, and a soiled jacket. To complete his singular apparel with the required head covering, he made do with a chip hat of plaited split palm leaves, probably bought for 15 cents and held together with an ordinary piece of grocer's string.

Reporters poked fun at him. "They laughed at his ungainly form, his primitive attire; they made sport of his nose, coupling it with his peculiar cognomen 'pull-it-sir' in a way that was calculated to drive a supersensitive person to distraction," recalled the police stenographer. Some called him "Joey the Jew." The more charitable ones gave him the moniker "Shakespeare" for his resemblance to the bard's profile. But Pull-it-sir ignored the taunting. "He pursued his course heedless of the rebuffs and coarse witticisms and they soon began to recognize his worth," recalled the stenographer. "It was then that he won their confidence and esteem."

For good reason. Although Pulitzer cut a strange figure among the reporters, there was nothing lacking in the stories he churned out for the *Westliche Post*. In addition to writing an endless stream of local news, the bread and butter of the business, Pulitzer wrote pithy, cogent stories on St. Louis politics in an inimitable style that stood out from the more classical, restrained German used by Preetorius and others. "We all soon learned to appreciate and make the most of his extraordinary capacity for news gathering," admitted a reporter for the competing *Republican*. "He was an able reporter—trenchant with the pen," Johnson said, "fearless in attacking wrong or corruption, and at times bitter and acrimonious in his assaults."

As Pulitzer mastered English, though he still spoke it with a heavy accent, he widened his social circle, and Johnson became one of his best friends outside the German community. The thirty-year-old Johnson, nine years Pulitzer's senior, liked reporters, having worked in the printing trade and published a small newspaper as a teenager. After serving a term as city attorney, he had been appointed state attorney for St. Louis in 1866.

Although Johnson admired his young friend's aggressive reporting, others were less enthusiastic. It worried the city councilor Anthony Ittner, another man with whom Pulitzer made friends in the course of covering politics. Like Johnson, Ittner was about a decade older than Pulitzer. He had been in St. Louis since he was seven, had built up his bricklaying trade, and was now running his own brickyard. Ittner believed Pulitzer went too far in the tone of his articles and in his arguments with others, and that he was devoid of fear. "It was not an uncommon thing for him to use language in a heated controversy or dispute that went beyond the limit," Ittner said. "In fact, I cautioned him that he must become more conservative and forbearing for fear that he might someday meet a person like himself and then there would be trouble."

In Pulitzer's eyes, the villain of his new world was the notoriously corrupt county government. St. Louis County was probably no worse a den of political iniquity than most burgeoning urban areas in the years following the Civil War. Here, as in other cities, businessmen, party leaders, politicians, and, in many cases, newspaper publishers developed a web of financially beneficial relationships. Businessmen obtained lucrative contracts, party leaders gained favors for their troops of loyal followers, and politicians won elected office and enhanced their earnings. Newspapers weren't exempt from wrongdoing, either. Publishers who favored those in power were awarded legal advertisements, printing contracts, and sometimes even cash payments.

In the summer of 1869 the county government's excesses were all too visible during the construction of a new insane asylum. It was an irresistible topic for Pulitzer's caustic pen. Five stories tall, with a cupola, the asylum had been built at a cost of $700,000, nearly twice the original estimate. Everything about the project had the odor of corruption. For instance, when the construction firm that had been engaged to drill a well failed to strike water at a reasonable depth, it just continued merrily drilling down. The resulting hole, 3,850 feet deep, still without water, became the second-deepest shaft in the world and an object of local ridicule when Pulitzer dubbed it the "well of fools."

Pulitzer tenaciously reported on each step of the county's handling of the project. One day he discovered that county politicians were going to erase a financial mistake made by some lawyers. During the construction of the asylum, these attorneys had acted as guarantors to a brick supplier. The supplier failed to deliver all the promised materials when he realized that he had bid too low for the job and would lose money. The lawyers, in their capacity as guarantors, were thus required to pay for the undelivered bricks. Pulitzer learned that the lawyers were seeking to have the county pay them for their loss. In a session where only four of the seven county judges were in attendance, the county court agreed.

From the pages of the *Westliche Post,* Pulitzer lashed out at the judges. Using what had become one of his favorite reportorial techniques, he filled his copy with questions for his readers: "Do the citizens want to let this infamous County Court pull the wool over their eyes? Do they want to concede, with quiet acceptance of what transpired and indifferent behavior, that the County Court can do what it wants with public money? Has the Insane Asylum not cost them enough already?" Then Pulitzer changed from questioner to instructor. "We want the citizens to answer these questions for themselves, and we want those answers in the form of energetic action. It is high time that they make their position clear to the County Court and explain to them that they were not elected to squander communal money, still damp with the people's sweat, but rather to guard this with utmost providence!"

Under this withering attack, the full court voted to revoke the payment. It was a triumph for Pulitzer. He magnanimously shared the credit for the victory with Preetorius, Ittner, and several others who had promised to file suit to stop the payment if the court had not reversed itself. Pulitzer warned that the victory was limited to this one issue. There was more to be gained. "The eternal waffling on important issues, the revoltingly frivolous handling of public money, the revocation thereof only hours prior: All of this leads to only one conclusion, that the current county judges are either totally incapable of representing the interest of their constituents and the county, or that something is very rotten here." Pulitzer demanded that the judges resign. It would be a miracle if this happened, he conceded. "How can the current situation best be changed? Hereupon we answer with the words that have appeared at the head of our local column numerous times in the past weeks: Down with the County Court!"

In battling the county court, Pulitzer elevated his own reputation. Even though newspapers carried no bylines, most readers and politicians knew who was the author of the attacks. He had earlier earned the respect of his colleagues in the press for his persistence and perspicacity, and now he was being noticed by people outside the ranks of the fourth estate. "Pulitzer was fighting the most powerful and corrupt ring in St. Louis with money and patronage to back it," the lime merchant Theodore Welge said, "and could have had any amount of money in the shape of gifts or otherwise. He was without funds except for the small salary he drew as a reporter for the *Westliche Post*."

In October 1869, Pulitzer became city editor when Willich left the paper. With control of the *Westliche Post*'s news pages, Pulitzer intensified his assault on the county government. During the fall, he reported on other exorbitant payments to contractors, on the county's insistence on paying men to light the gas streetlights rather than using the new electric ignition systems, and on the shoddy brickwork at the jail.

The county court faced a new and effective enemy.

Despite the interminable hours at the paper and his work with the Republican organization in his ward, Pulitzer still found time to socialize and widen his circle of friends. "When first meeting JP one would find him to be rather distant and serious, bent only on his work," recalled a friend at the police department. "But when one got to know him one found he was genial and social." At the end of the day, Pulitzer could often be found at Fritz Roeslein's bookstore, a popular gathering place for bookish Germans. The books, however, were beyond Pulitzer's reach, with the little he earned. An errand boy who worked at Roeslein's remembered Pulitzer taking an interest in a dinner of homemade sausage and bread the boy's mother had packed. "Mr. J.P. saw me go after it, he asked me what it was, I then offered some and he helped me finish up."

At night, Pulitzer retreated to 307 South Third Street, only a few short blocks from the newspaper. There he rented a small room in a boardinghouse run by an aging widow and her two daughters. It was a gloomy two-story building across the street from a bathhouse that gave the block a stench of sulfur. He was, however, in good company. His friend the poet Udo Brachvogel and an editor from the *Anzeiger des Westens* also took rooms there. The three of them often sat together, talking, late into the night.

Joseph's brother Albert, however, was still a wandering soul. After his stint selling magazines door to door, Albert had taken a tutoring job on a German farm and had taught German in the St. Louis schools. In late spring of 1868, he walked into a wealthy neighborhood south of his brother's home and came across a group of boys sitting on the steps of one of the more handsome houses on the block. Albert asked a passerby whose house it was and learned that it belonged to Thomas Allen, president of the Iron Mountain Railway and a figure of considerable political influence in St. Louis.

"In my desperate lonely position," Albert said, "I cast to the winds all timidity, boldly walked up to the doorstep." He asked if Allen was home. To his amazement he was led into the house. "I stammered out that I knew German and might teach the German language to those bright boys I had seen on the doorstep." Allen said the idea appealed to him but he and his family were leaving to spend the summer in Pittsfield, Massachusetts. "Though I did not have the faintest idea where Pittsfield might be, I, nothing daunted, intimated as well as I could in broken English that I would be delighted to wend my way Pittsfield-ward."

It turned into an idyllic summer. Each day after concluding his tutoring lessons, Albert, armed with an English-German dictionary, worked his way through Charles Dickens's *Pickwick Papers*. When the group returned to St. Louis, he spoke a passable form of English. Back at the Mercantile Library, he had a fortunate encounter with a member of the Hegelians who had become superintendent of the public schools. The man had received an inquiry from a school in Leavenworth, Kansas, that was looking for a German teacher. The $100 monthly salary was a princely sum for an eighteen-year-old. But Albert was not successful at the job and was soon returned to St. Louis. Deciding he was not cut out for teaching, he set his sights on entering his brother's field.

This new plan did not sit well with his older brother. Pointing out that Albert was never without a copy of Dickens or Shakespeare in his hands, Joseph instead suggested that a literary career would be more suitable. "Think, Albert, how proud our mother would be," he said. "You are too much of a dreamer ever to make any money for the family. Leave the commercial grind to me."

Ignoring Joseph's advice, Albert headed to Chicago, where, he heard, the *Illinois Staats-Zeitung* was hiring. Astonishingly, without any newspaper training, he duplicated Joseph's luck at getting a job on the *Westliche Post* and landed a reporter's position at $10 a week. "The *Staats-Zeitung*, however, although printed in German, was an excellent school for me, since four-fifths of its new matter was drawn from English-speaking sources. I had perforce to know English first." The paper shared a building with the *Chicago Evening Post*, whose reporters gave him yet more opportunity to work on his English. "His object," recalled one reporter, "was to master the language so that he could take a writing position on an English paper, and he told me that when he felt sure of himself in this respect he should go to New York and begin there."

In November 1869, advertisements appeared in the *Westliche Post*, and other newspapers, announcing a special election in the Fifth and Sixth districts of the General Assembly to fill seats emptied by resignations. Since one of the elections would take place in the ward where Pulitzer served as a Republican Party officer, he went to work hurriedly organizing the nominating meeting necessary to select a candidate. The Democrats held their gathering first, meeting in Uncle Joe Locke's Hall on the night of December 13, 1869. Pulitzer attended in his capacity as a reporter. It was a boisterous affair and several fights almost broke out before the Democrats settled on a candidate.

The Republicans held their meeting the following evening in Turner's Hall. They had little hope of victory in the election. The ward had been solidly Democratic for the past twenty-five years. Nonetheless Pulitzer urged that Republicans turn out for the meeting. "No one," he wrote in the *Westliche Post*, "should be nominated who does not possess the absolute trust of a majority of the citizenry and can be considered their representative."

Despite bad weather, a sufficient number of Republicans turned out that night to hold the nominating meeting. It quickly became clear, however, that the man they had hoped would run was not interested in the nomination. In the disarray one man moved that the ward secretary, Pulitzer, who was then out of the room, be declared the candidate. This motion was followed by one to close the nominations, and Pulitzer was selected unanimously. The hall reacted with applause, according to Republican press accounts—or with laughter if the Democratic reporters were to be believed. More commotion arose when Pulitzer reentered the hall, unaware of what had just occurred.

The next morning, Pulitzer the reporter gave a third-person account of the reaction of Pulitzer the politician. "In a few, apparently heart-felt words that he spoke to the meeting, he explained that he in no way had sought out this office, that he did not believe himself worthy of the trust that his fellow citizens had placed in him with this nomination, but that if elected, it would be always his highest and only goal to reward this trust." The *Democrat*, doing its best to hold up the Republican Party banner, described Pulitzer as "well-known . . . a gentleman of character, considerable attainment, and decided and energetic" and one "who stands high in the estimation of the Germans in the ward" with "many friends among the Americans." The paper predicted an election victory.

The wishful thinking suddenly became a possibility when the Democrats ran into candidate trouble. Their first choice declined the nomination. The party turned next to Stilson Hutchins, a Democratic friend of Pulitzer who was a newspaper editor, but he too turned it down. So with only four days left before the election, the Democrats settled on a tobacco dealer with no political experience. The stand-in candidate received a rapid political baptism when Pulitzer tarred him in the *Westliche Post*. "Who is this new candidate exactly?" wrote Pulitzer. "Few know, but they say that he is a bankrupt merchant, who had strong Rebel sympathies during the war." A day later Pulitzer charged that the Democrat was ineligible to be a candidate. "He is neither registered in the ward that he wishes to represent in the legislature, nor has he ever voted in that ward." In this attack, Pulitzer was playing with fire. He himself was constitutionally ineligible for the office. The minimum age to serve in the General Assembly was twenty-four. Pulitzer was not yet twenty-three.

With three days remaining before the election, Pulitzer went to the registrar's office to sign a loyalty oath, as required by the Reconstruction constitution. In signing the oath, Pulitzer fulfilled a requirement for election, but he also engaged once again in dishonesty about his age. The same day, the *Westliche Post* published a letter of support for Pulitzer's candidacy signed by a "Soldier and Worker." It defended Pulitzer against what it called the "arrogant nose-turning and diplomatic shoulder-shrugging about the young age of the Radical candidate." His youth, it argued, was no fault of his own and would "dissipate with each passing day." The letter sounded suspiciously like the work of the candidate himself.

Not a day had passed when Pulitzer did not use the pages of the paper to tout his candidacy. In humble prose, sounding rather like Dickens's Uriah Heep, Pulitzer wrote—in the third person—that he would have surrendered the nomination to a more seasoned candidate had one emerged. "It is therefore the unforbearable duty of Mr. Pulitzer to accept this unanimously imposed candidacy and see it through." He contrasted his attributes of watchfulness, tirelessness, and fearlessness with his opponent's supposed Confederate sympathies, rumored bankruptcy, and alleged ineligibility. The Radical ticket is "pure gold compared to the candidates of the Irish Democrats. . . . They say that they would vote for the Devil himself in order to defeat the candidates of the Germans," Pulitzer wrote on election eve. "What do our German friends have to say about that?"

On election day snow and freezing rain poured down. Only a little more than 300 voters, less than one-fourth the usual turnout, managed to make their way to the two polling stations: the German Emigration Society, on the river side of the ward; and R. Eitman's Grocery Store, on the western side. The eastern portion of the ward, more densely German, cast 156 votes for Pulitzer and 66 for the Democrat. The margin for Pulitzer allowed him to overcome the Democrat's anemic victory in the more Irish side of the ward, which the Democratic Party took by a vote of 81 to 53. The final count of 209 to 147 gave Pulitzer the seat in the legislature.

"We doubt that an election has ever taken place in our city under such unfavorable conditions and turned out as relatively satisfying," wrote journalist and legislator-elect Pulitzer in the next day's *Westliche Post*. The Radical victory in the Fifth Ward was important because the ward, though not a "fortress of local Democrats" and "Rebel elements" like the neighboring Sixth Ward, might still be considered a Democratic enclave, Pulitzer said. "Regardless the ward elected a Radical representative yesterday in place of its previous Democratic one. The majority of 62 that elected Mr. Pulitzer may seem small, but not when one takes into account that the total votes for both candidates in both precincts did not top 356."

As if he were giving a victory night speech, Pulitzer continued his postelection analysis by thanking his colleagues. "The local press exhibited, with one single exception, such an honorable and collegial spirit with regard to Mr. Pulitzer's campaign, that it is a true pleasure to give voice to our grateful recognition." The one miscreant was the rival German newspaper *Neue Anzeiger*, which, according to Pulitzer, "deviated spitefully from the generous stance of the entire rest of the press." His sensitivity to the one sour note of public criticism revealed that it had not yet dawned on Pulitzer that he had crossed the Rubicon. In only five years he had grown from a bounty-hunting Hungarian teenager to an American lawmaker.

He was now an elected politician.

Chapter Five

POLITICS AND GUNPOWDER

◆

Shortly after New Year's Day 1870, Pulitzer left St. Louis for the state capital, Jefferson City, and his new life as a legislator. It was a short, bucolic train ride along the meandering Missouri River, whose banks alternated between rich farmland and high overhanging cliffs. For those having political business in the capital, the trip was often gratis, as the Missouri Pacific Railroad gladly offered free passage to those who were in a position to return favors. In fact, it was a common practice for newspapermen, public officials, judges, politicians, and lawmakers to ride "deadhead," as it was called. Pulitzer, who was among the poorest lawmakers that year, opted instead to obtain a travel per diem from the state.

The state capital, though not necessarily a backwater, was not a destination of choice for politicians from St. Louis and Kansas City. Many legislators remained unconvinced that this isolated former river trading post was a suitable spot for their deliberations; and when Pulitzer arrived, they were still introducing resolutions to move the state capital. The annual descent of lawmakers was about the only thing that disturbed the calm of Jefferson City.

Bringing with them a carnival atmosphere, the legislators packed Schmidt's Hotel and caused its bartenders to stock extra supplies. Although Pulitzer would take his meals there, he avoided Schmidt's pricey rooms. Instead, he chose to room with his friend Anthony Ittner, who had also been elected as a state legislator. The pair obtained lodgings in a boardinghouse, nicknamed the "German Diet" because of the preponderance of German legislators who favored the place.

On January 5, 1870, as the legislature opened for business, Pulitzer took his oath of office, swearing, for the second time in a month, to uphold the state's constitution but meanwhile violating its minimum age for service in the legislature. For one born in Europe, state legislatures were a marvel of American democracy beyond compare. Each state had its own semi-sovereign government with a legislature in session, on average, eighty-seven days a year. Almost every law of significance— criminal, social, or economic—was made by state legislatures. It would be another half century before the federal government would begin to assume its modern dominant role in governance.

In Jefferson City, and in fourteen other state capitals that month, lawyers, doctors, farmers, merchants, businessmen, and even newspapermen gathered to make the laws of the land. It was exhilarating, and Pulitzer was eager to join in. On his first day, he offered two resolutions, one dealing with printing the governor's annual message in German, the other a routine measure for printing copies of the House rules for use by members.

Pulitzer's fellow Radical Republicans controlled the legislature and had one of their own in the governor's seat. Having disenfranchised some 60,000 citizens with the loyalty oath, the Radicals were at the apex of their power. But political fissures were growing among the ranks of the party. Republican rule was an unnatural state of affairs in a state with strong and deep Democratic Party roots. As in other border states, Republicans had neither a popular base nor public support.

Suffrage was the dominant and most divisive issue before the lawmakers. The governor urged them to ratify the Fifteenth Amendment, giving black American men the right to vote, and to similarly amend the state constitution. But he startled many in his own party by suggesting it was time to lift voting restrictions on Democrats. Although it was only a vague promise, it gave voice to a central issue facing Republicans. How much longer could they deny taxpaying, law-abiding white voters the franchise?

Pulitzer, like a growing number of Republicans, felt that the party had to respond to constituents' demands if it wanted to take permanent root in the state. Five years after the end of the war, a considerable amount of reconciliation had already taken place in Missouri, and the hatred engendered by the conflict was greatly diminished. The animus toward former rebels seemed particularly hard to justify if former slaves were to be given the vote.

The state's constitution, passed during the first years of Reconstruction, specified that the legislature would be constitutionally free to begin tampering with its onerous voting restrictions in 1871. But many Republicans were unwilling to wait. They feared entering the fall campaign with only a promise to do something about lifting the restrictions later. The growing consensus among the moderates was to submit to voters that fall a constitutional amendment which would enfranchise all adult males.

From the start, Pulitzer was in the moderates' camp. On his first full day, he proposed a roll-call vote to help defeat a measure aimed at stemming a slight expansion of suffrage. There was no question in his mind that the right to vote must be given to all men, regardless of their participation in the war or the color of their skin. His faith in the expansion of suffrage was sustained by his sense of wonder at American politics, his absolute faith in democracy, and his youthful idealism. Unlike the veteran legislators, he had not considered the electoral math should the vote be restored to thousands of Democrats. He "is with us," a Democratic Party leader happily told his mostly disenfranchised colleagues in Pulitzer's Fifth Ward.

On a Sunday evening in late January, Pulitzer boarded a train for Jefferson City after spending the weekend in St. Louis. As the train neared Hermann, a German river town about halfway to the capital, the track, probably weakened by the winter cold, broke in three places. The locomotive remained on the railway, but the express car and the sleeping car in the rear came uncoupled and rolled down the steep embankment leading to the river. The remaining cars, including the one in which Pulitzer rode, left the track but remained upright, although teetering and appearing as if they would follow the others down the hill.

Pulitzer scrambled out with the other uninjured travelers and surveyed the scene. "Picture a large sleeping-car, in which at that moment was occupied by over 50 people (and for the most part undressed and sleeping)," Pulitzer said. "One must imagine this car, imagine it rolling down a 20-foot high railroad embankment with increasing momentum until a mighty tree obstructs its passage, the car's interior smashed into a thousand pieces, and the car rests on the ground, but not in its typical position, but rather vice versa, i.e. on its head, and one will have a rough idea of how the scene of the catastrophe looked."

The immediate danger was fire. Pulitzer explored the overturned wagons and found their stoves, filled with glowing ambers, hanging from what was now the ceiling. As rescuers removed the more seriously injured passengers through the windows, several small fires broke out but were quickly extinguished. Most of the injuries were lacerations and broken bones, but one woman had a broken spine and later died.

The passengers stayed the night at the scene of the accident while the wounded were tended to and the serviceable wagons were put back on the track. With the break of day, what remained of the train made its way to Jefferson City, arriving late Monday morning. The legislators who were on the train along with Pulitzer were all uninjured and joined their colleagues on the floor, where their ordeal soon become the topic of conversation.

The new week marked the opening of the lobbying season. Railroad men, lawyers, county politicians, and businessmen flocked to the capital. These lobbyists were so numerous and so powerful they were called the "third house." One reporter from Kansas City, sitting at his desk on the floor, looked over the men who took the seats in the rear of the chamber. "These are the strange commingling," he wrote, "the Augean stables of legislation—the seething cesspool of legislative faith; men, good, bad, corrupt and designing schemers—dupes, plotters, diminutive Richelieus and Mazarins, and petty Woolseys, all after self."

Pulitzer still regarded corruption in St. Louis County as the paramount issue. His tenure as a city and county reporter had made him a legislator on a mission. In assuming his new post, Pulitzer did not give up his old one as a reporter. In his singular position as both a legislator and a journalist, he used his reporting to advance his political work. In Pulitzer's eyes the lobbyists descending on the capital were an army of darkness. Calling them "courthouse corruption aristocrats," he wrote, "The train that arrived yesterday evening seems to have transported half of St. Louis here. One encounters faces everywhere that usually lurk about the Courthouse and Fourth Street."

Among the arriving men, Pulitzer singled out Edward Augustine, a notorious contractor from St. Louis County. Pulitzer had first encountered Augustine, at least by reputation, during his first summer in St. Louis. The city was preparing for a predicted return of cholera, which had killed nearly one in ten of its residents seventeen years earlier. Most of the city's ponds had been drained as a precaution, but in Pulitzer's neighborhood many residents were concerned about a quarry filled with dirty, stagnant water. It was owned by Augustine and situated on the path Pulitzer took each day to work. City officials were at first unwilling to confront Augustine, who had deep political connections, but a public demonstration changed their minds. In the years since, Augustine had risen to become an important contractor in St. Louis, participating in building the county's scandalously expensive insane asylum. In fact, it was he who held the contract to dig the unproductive well that Pulitzer had named the "well of fools."

Before boarding the train for Jefferson City, Augustine had stopped in at the office of the lime merchant Theodore Welge, who rented kilns from him. Augustine asked if Welge would accompany him to take a glass of beer at Lemps, one of the largest of thirty breweries in St. Louis. Augustine was fuming. As they downed their beers, he deplored Pulitzer's activities. He told his drinking companion that he was heading for Jefferson City "to insult and publicly spit in the face of Mr. Joseph Pulitzer, to force him to stop advocating a bill that takes away from him his valuable contract with the county."

On the morning of January 26, as the courthouse crowd from St. Louis settled in at Schmidt's Hotel, Pulitzer dropped a legislative bombshell. He introduced a bill to abolish the existing St. Louis county court government. In the past, county pols had considered it a nuisance when the *Westliche Post* advocated the abolition of the county court, but now that its representative in Jefferson City was moving to convert editorial policy into public policy, it became a threat.

The city-county relationship had long been contentious. As seven-eighths of the county's population resided in the city, its residents chafed at being under the rule of county politicians. After the Civil War, the struggle between the city and county was acerbated by a new revelation of corruption in the county government. Only two months before the legislature met, it had become public knowledge that six county officers were making $120,000 a year each from fee collections while, in comparison, the mayor of St. Louis was paid only $4,000.

Specifically, Pulitzer's bill would require the county court to draw up new election districts and increase the number of judges elected from within the city. This would effectively put the city in charge of all county business. The new judges would be elected in early April, less than three months away; would be paid $1,000 a year; and would be barred from participating in any county contracts or selling anything to the county. All proceedings of the new county court as well as all its expenses and revenues would be published in the largest-circulation English and German newspapers. This last provision raised criticism that Pulitzer was seeking only to enrich his own paper with government advertising.

Although Pulitzer's bill was offered as a program to "reorganize the County Court of St. Louis County," its true intent—killing the court's power—was clear to all observers. Pulitzer admitted as much. The bill, he said, "does not propose to allow the present court to exercise their functions up to the general election in November next, but will decapitate them beyond a remedy on the first Tuesday of April." His actions were front-page news in St. Louis. An hour after introducing his bill, Pulitzer was accosted by Augustine and a companion. They were furious. "They spoke of the bill in a highly agitated manner and began making highly insulting comments," said Pulitzer, who excused himself and took refuge in a closed-door meeting.

The next morning, Pulitzer resumed his print warfare on the lobbyists by publishing their names. For some, like his friend Johnson, who was then district attorney and had official business in the capital, this was not a problem. But for those who were mounting a stealth campaign to preserve the county court and its privileges, the mere listing of their names was an accusation. Pulitzer's list also suggested guilt by association. For instance, he sandwiched Augustine's name between those of two notorious lobbyists. At the end of his list, Pulitzer displayed his characteristic cheekiness. "I would like to pose the question," he wrote, changing from German to English, "who pays the expenses? But since this could be misinterpreted by some of these gentlemen, who are genteel types, I prefer to leave this be and turn to a more interesting topic"—and here he abruptly ended his sentence, prompting the readers to look down to the title of the next section of his dispatch from the state capital: "Abolition of the County Court."

That evening the St. Louis delegation met in the parlor of Schmidt's Hotel, a large room, about sixty by fifty feet. Around seven, a dozen or so men gathered, and then their ranks swelled as others came in from supper. Several German legislators were talking with Augustine about

Pulitzer's article when the author himself arrived. Pulitzer asked what they were discussing. "You," they replied. Augustine then asked Pulitzer why he had published such charges, especially as he didn't know the facts. Not so, replied Pulitzer, claiming that he knew the "facts" very well.

"Nothing but a pup could make such a statement, not knowing them to be facts," Augustine said. That phrase crossed the line. In the nineteenth-century code of honor, a reference to a "liar" or a "pup" could provoke a duel. In 1817, Senator Thomas Hart Benton of Missouri used the term "puppy" in reference to the attorney Charles Lucas, and the latter died in the ensuing duel. Pulitzer warned Augustine to be more cautious with his language, and Augustine responded by calling him a "damned liar."

Pulitzer moved away and joined several friends. "Pulitzer, why didn't you knock that man down when he called you a damned liar?" asked one of them, who had overheard the exchange. "You must keep up the *esprit du corps*, man."

"Oh, it's all about the County Court," replied Pulitzer, who then left.

Back at the boardinghouse, Pulitzer flung open the door to his room and stormed in, startling Anthony Ittner, who had just returned from some late-afternoon bowling. Making straight for the lounge chair, Pulitzer removed his pistol from his suitcase and pocketed it, hiding his actions from his roommate. Ittner said he was heading back to the bowling lanes to retrieve a coat he had forgotten. "Hold on, Tony," Pulitzer said, "and I'll go with you."

"That damned Augustine insulted me," Pulitzer told Ittner when they reached the street. "I am going back there to call him every bad name there is in the dictionary, I am going to call him a 'son-of-a-bitch.'" Ittner admonished him not to, reminding Pulitzer that he revered his own mother by carrying her likeness in his pocket watch.

"Well, Tony," Pulitzer replied, "I think you are right and I will be governed by your advice, but I assure you I will call him every other bad name I can think of." The two then walked east. At the corner, Ittner took a right turn toward the bowling alley and Pulitzer went left toward the hotel.

Heading down the hill to the hotel, Pulitzer encountered two newspapermen on their way to the telegraph office. Pulitzer told them that if they headed back to the hotel they would get a good item. "Thinking he was alluding to the meeting of the delegation," one of them said, "I told him we would be back in a few minutes."

When Pulitzer reached the parlor of Schmidt's Hotel, Augustine was still there, talking with a county judge and another man. Pulitzer walked directly across the room, and angry words once again passed between the two men. "Mr. Augustine, just one word, and I hope that it will be the last word that I speak to you," Pulitzer said. "I would like to explain to you that I am no longer inclined to associate with you, and I also do not wish that you speak to me again. Should you, however, persist in insulting me, you will, despite your great physical advantage, find that you have come to the wrong man."

"I want to tell you in clear and understandable English that you are a damned liar and a puppy," replied Augustine in a loud booming voice that all could hear.

"You are a God-damned liar," Pulitzer snapped back.

Words ceased. Augustine moved toward Pulitzer. Bulky and strong, with fists twice the size of an ordinary man's, Augustine had the edge in combat with his beanpole, bespectacled opponent. Pulitzer retreated. "Everyone who knows Augustine knows that one would be hard-pressed to find one man in 100,000 who is built like him," Pulitzer said. "As far as his physical strength is considered, he was ten times my better."

When Pulitzer had completed about ten to twelve paces of his retreat, Augustine raised his fist. In his assailant's hands, Pulitzer thought he saw "a heavy, gleaming yellow instrument," that he presumed to be brass knuckles. Pulitzer withdrew his pistol and fired. Incredibly, the veteran cavalryman missed his massive target. As they struggled across the parlor, Pulitzer pulled the trigger again, but the barrel of the gun was deflected downward and the bullet only grazed Augustine in the right calf.

Nevertheless, the wound in his leg enraged Augustine, who, like a speared bull, charged and pinned Pulitzer in the corner of the room. There he flung Pulitzer down. "I mashed his head against the case-board of the room, and tried to get the pistol out of his hand," Augustine said. Two men rushed over to separate them. When one tried to take the pistol away from Pulitzer, he would not loosen his grip. But when the other friend asked, Pulitzer surrendered the weapon.

Having retrieved his coat from the bowling alley, Ittner was strolling slowly back to his room when he heard a small boy running and yelling that a man had shot another at the hotel. "The thought instantly struck me that this was the result of Pulitzer's controversy with Edward Augustine and that it was a pistol he had taken from his valise on entering our room so abruptly a short while ago," Ittner said. He rushed to the hotel, where he found his roommate surrounded by a crowd, nursing his head wound.

As he drew near, Pulitzer looked up at him with a broad grin on his face and said, "Hello, Tony."

"You've been playing the 'Devil,' Joe, haven't you?" Ittner asked.

Ittner, who was also a friend of Augustine's, left Pulitzer's side and went to see the wounded man in his room upstairs. Augustine was surrounded by many friends and was being tended by a doctor, who was also a fellow legislator. "I found him sitting on the edge of his bed with his wounded leg resting on same, complacently smoking a cigar; the wound being in the calf of leg and not at all dangerous," Ittner said. The crowd in the hotel room was agitated. One legislator "went so far as to suggest taking the law in their own hands," he said, "as it seems that the officers of the law in this town are not disposed to protect citizens of the State from deadly assault with intent to kill."

By the time Ittner returned to the parlor, Pulitzer had left and gone back to the boardinghouse. Ittner rushed to their room. When he arrived, a police officer was knocking on the door. The man asked Pulitzer to accompany him to the station. Ittner followed and posted a bail bond for his roommate. In the morning, Pulitzer appeared in city court, where he acted as his own attorney. He was fined for "breach of peace," a violation of the city's ordinances. Though Pulitzer was only a student of law, he knew he could later face more serious criminal charges, not to mention political consequences.

When the House convened, an angry representative from St. Louis waited impatiently for the conclusion of the chaplain's prayer before rising and asking the Speaker to be recognized. "The disgraceful scenes which transpired at one of the principal hotels of this city last night," he said, "demand an impartial investigation into the causes and circumstances attending that lamentable occurrence." To accomplish this, he offered a resolution to create a three-member committee to investigate the shooting and report back to the House with a recommendation of action "to maintain the dignity of the House." As soon as he concluded reading his resolution, the floor of House erupted in yelling as defenders of Pulitzer and supporters of the county court demanded to be recognized.

Another representative from St. Louis protested that an investigation was unnecessary. If members didn't think that existing criminal laws were sufficient for the safety of citizens, they should amend the laws, he said. An inquiry like the one proposed "was beneath the dignity of the House, and ought not be entertained for a moment." But if Pulitzer was guilty, argued another member, it would affect the dignity of the House. "I do not want to sit with a man who would go to his room and get his pistol and put it to my breast for a trivial offense."

Luckily for Pulitzer, a sympathetic representative stemmed the pressure for an inquiry by raising the specter of the precedent such a step would set. "Should members by their actions here do this it would lead to the investigation of every member's behavior that takes place outside of the House," he said. "If it undertook such a course as this, the next thing would be that when a member goes to a wine party and does something that displeases somebody, the House will investigate that. Some member might happen to kiss a pretty girl, must the House investigate that?"

Seizing the moment, Pulitzer's defenders immediately moved to table the resolution. A sufficient number agreed to forestall the creation of the committee and thus killed the plan. The subject of the debate, meanwhile, was nowhere to be seen. Pulitzer was off settling the $11.50 fine for disturbing the peace. The *St. Louis Times* called it the "Cost of Prince Pulitzer's Pugnacity."

The House probe may have been thwarted, but the interest of Pulitzer's colleagues in the press was undiminished. The correspondent for the *Missouri Democrat* called Pulitzer's act an "insane folly" and reported that "the feeling against Pulitzer was intense, and I remarked a universal indignation at the outrage from every German fellow-citizen, both in and out of the Legislature." The *Kansas City Journal* said, "The town has been all afire with a shooting affair" and "the St. Louis Delegation ran around and condemned Pulitzer in strong terms, except for Ittner and [William] Phelan." Accounts of the shooting even appeared in papers in major cities such as Chicago and New York.

The clamor impelled Pulitzer, who was lying low, to use the *Westliche Post* to rebut his opponents, who were hoping this would end his nascent political career. "To the people!" he wrote. "It is with the same reluctance that I felt during the events of the very nearly tragic scene in the state capital, that I now reach for the quill, not to defend the role that I was forced to play in this affair, but only to offer a faithful description of the affair."

He called Augustine "a man of honor," but added that he "had a tendency toward violence, knew that he often carried a revolver, but always carried so-called 'dumb knuckles' on him, which are at least an equally dangerous weapon." Pulitzer then offered an account of the fight that matched that of other witnesses except for his claim that he saw what he believed to be brass knuckles in Augustine's raised hand. Pulitzer offered "the holes that it left in my head" as his proof.

"Thus, the people are presented with the facts of a case that is surely regretted by no one more than myself," Pulitzer concluded. "All I ask is that before a judgment is pronounced in this matter, that the opposing view be examined and considered. I call for each man to imagine himself for a moment thrust into a similar situation, and then ask himself if he will not cast the first stone."*

The Cole County grand jury was not impressed by Pulitzer's public defense. "The grand jury of this town who are a very 'rambunctious' set at the best, are determined to find a bill against Mr. Pulitzer, charging him with assault with intent to kill," reported one newspaper. Indeed, after listening to testimony from Augustine and others, the grand jury returned an indictment against Pulitzer on a charge of felonious assault. He was arrested, and once again Ittner rescued him by pledging a $1,000 bail bond. His friends rallied, and Charles Johnson agreed to represent Pulitzer and immediately won a postponement of the trial.

Pulitzer sheepishly returned to the floor of the House on February 4, a little more than a week after being the object of a potential expulsion vote. He cast a vote and left. But several days later, he was back in speaking form. Instead of addressing his colleagues' many questions about the shooting, Pulitzer chose to introduce a fairly routine bill to strengthen the qualifications necessary to be a director of the St. Louis public schools.

---

*Pulitzer's use of this analogy is interesting, as his religious upbringing did not include the New Testament.

This was not entirely out of character and reflected his growing understanding of the workings of the legislature. Pulitzer knew he had little to gain by mentioning the shooting, since that would give his critics another opportunity to comment on it. He was better prepared for being a lawmaker than other newcomers to the legislature after having spent time covering the previous session as a reporter.

He showed parliamentary savvy unusual for a freshman legislator when a bill came up to erect a statue of General Nathan Lyon, who is credited with preventing St. Louis from falling into Confederate hands. The funding measure, which Pulitzer supported, was going down to defeat, but there was hope that it might win approval when more members were present. As the bill headed for defeat, Pulitzer changed his vote at the last minute. By being among those who voted "no," he retained the right under parliamentary procedure to call for the bill's reconsideration. He immediately exercised the right and persuaded the House to send the bill back to committee, where it could live for another chance at passage.

Pulitzer's choice of an education measure on his first full day back was good politics. Although he himself had hardly ever seen the inside of a classroom, he knew from his contacts with the Hegelian philosophers and his friendship with Davidson that the public schools were highly valued by Germans in St. Louis. Any assault on schools was seen by Germans as an attack on their community. In early March a bill reached the floor that would require the city's school board to give $10 to each pupil attending a private school. If it was enacted, the school system would effectively be bankrupt. In battling the bill, Pulitzer found himself up against his old foes, including the doctor-legislator who had attended Augustine after the shooting. Pulitzer won, warding off what the press called "a death blow aimed at their public school system" and frustrating the county court crowd, who thought they had seen the last of him.

A reinvigorated Pulitzer returned to ferreting out corruption. On March 8, he seized another chance to pursue his efforts. A Democrat from St. Francois rose on the floor to give public voice to a rumor that bribes were being used widely to gain passage of legislation. Though he did not specify the source or purposes of the payments, it was widely understood that he was speaking of railroad interests. The House opted to create a five-member committee with the power to issue subpoenas to investigate these claims.

Pulitzer immediately moved that the committee's charge be expanded to include determining "whether any members of the House had been employed as an attorney in any case that was pending in this body, and, as such, received any compensation whatever." His alteration was accepted. The House voted to establish the committee, and Pulitzer was given one of five seats on it. The assignment was a plum for a freshman seeking publicity, but also a minefield because it would look at the behavior of more senior and more powerful legislators. Two days later, the committee reported its recommendation that a member be expelled from the House for accepting bribes.

The legislative session ground onward, and Pulitzer knew that time was running out for his main objective—throwing out the county court in St. Louis. Since introducing his measure, Pulitzer had expanded on his original efforts to restructure the county government by writing a bill that would provide for the election, rather than the appointment, of the collector, assessor, and engineer in St. Louis County.

On March 10, members of the St. Louis delegation met with Pulitzer in the Senate chambers to consider his proposal languishing in legislative limbo. For two hours, the men argued. Finally, the group put the plan to a vote. Pulitzer's bill survived by a one-vote margin. Next, opponents tried to water down the bill. Again, he survived the attack by one vote. Seeking to broaden support, Pulitzer's supporters persuaded him to amend the proposal slightly by delaying the election for the new county court to the fall. Next they decided to rush the new version of the bill through the Senate and prepare for a fight in the House, where the county's strongest defenders lay in waiting.

The plan almost worked. A week later, Ittner brought the moderated version up for consideration in the House. Together, he and Pulitzer argued strenuously for the bill, claiming that it would eliminate the scandalous fee-based salaries and clean up the corrupt county government, even once again bringing up the court's extravagance on Augustine's "well of fools." But it was to no avail. Though the final tally was 56 to 36 in favor of the bill, the rules required a majority of the entire House, not just those present. Pulitzer's measure fell 23 votes short.

As the first day of spring approached, the session's end neared. The weather hardly seemed springlike. Late winter snow and deep cold gripped Jefferson City, and, to his misfortune, Pulitzer, along with his roommate, fell prey to a gang of coat thieves who swept through the capital, raiding the rooms of legislators careless enough to leave their doors unlocked. Pulitzer and Ittner were thus among three legislators who "made their appearance shivering" on March 12, "one of the coldest and dreariest of the session."

On March 24 the session drew to a close. The train to St. Louis carried back to the city a very different man from the one who had arrived in the state capital that winter. Although none of his bills had become law, and although the county court retained the upper hand, Pulitzer's legislative efforts had turned him into a well-known figure, made him new political allies, and placed him in an emerging Liberal Republican movement poised to take center stage.

Chapter Six

LEFT BEHIND

———————————————◆———————————————

In March 1870, when the lawmakers went back to their farms, law
offices, or places of business, Pulitzer returned to the *Westliche Post*.
But instead of being merely a reporter covering political ward meetings,
he was now a player in Missouri politics. No longer was the *Westliche
Post* identified solely as the paper belonging to Schurz and Preetorius; it
was now also the newspaper where Pulitzer worked.

The shooting of Augustine had given Pulitzer considerable notoriety,
which in his quixotic struggle against the county court was not neces-
sarily a bad thing. But it also created a serious legal problem. After all,
he had shot someone, perhaps with the intent to kill. So far, thanks to
the legal skills of his friend Johnson, the day of reckoning had been
postponed. But at some point, Pulitzer would have to face a trial.

The prospect of mounting a decent legal defense improved. Theodore
Welge, the lime merchant who did business with Augustine, decided to
come forward. Although he considered himself a friend of Augustine's,
Welge admired Pulitzer for his efforts against political corruption. "I
made up my mind, come what will, that I would call on Mr. Pulitzer
and tell him what Augustine told me he was going up to Jefferson City
for," Welge said. So he made his way to Pulitzer's boardinghouse on
Third Street.

At first, the landlady informed Welge that Pulitzer could not be dis-
turbed. "I told her to go back and say to him, that a party wanted to tell
him important news probably greatly affecting his future." A few mo-
ments later, Welge was admitted to Pulitzer's room. "When I told him
about the talk I had with Augustine, he stood up in a white night shirt

looking like a ghost," said Welge. "I told him I was ready at any time to go to Jefferson City to testify without any summons." Pulitzer hugged his surprise visitor and repeatedly thanked him for coming.

The trial was still months away, and so was the fall political season. In the interim, Pulitzer returned to Hungary for the first time since he had left six years earlier. To obtain a U.S. passport, he once again lied about his age, moving his birth back two years to conform to his previous deceptions. With the $410 that he had earned for his service in the legislative session, he booked passage out of New York on the *Allemannia*, the same ship that had brought Albert to the United States, and sailed to Europe on May 24. Pulitzer's return to his native land was a heady experience. The penniless teenager who had left in 1864 came back to his family and friends as a twenty-three-year-old American lawmaker with money in his pocket. He used his status to open new doors—calling, for instance, on the mayor of Buda, Ferenc Házmán, who, after years of work, was nearing his goal of uniting Buda and Pest into one city.

By mid-July, Pulitzer was back in Missouri and deep in electoral politics. On August 25, 1870, he ran the Fifth Ward Republican meeting at Wolbrecht's Tivoli Concert Hall and was selected as one of the delegates for the coming state convention. There was trouble brewing for the Republican governor, Joseph McClurg. At Pulitzer's meeting, the delegates decided not to support McClurg's renomination as governor. In fact, it was a bad night throughout St. Louis for the incumbent governor. When all the ward meetings had concluded their business, McClurg won no support whatsoever. Instead, all of St. Louis's delegates lined up behind the reformist B. Gratz Brown.

A former U.S. senator and Free Soil Democrat who had worked to end his party's pro-slavery position, Brown was winning favor with Republicans who wanted to restore the vote to former rebels. Pulitzer and his friend William Grosvenor, who edited the *Missouri Democrat*, threw their lot in with Brown. Pulitzer's German readers were already on board, but Grosvenor's editorials in favor of Brown emboldened moderate English-speaking Republicans who were growing weary of their party's extremism, which for many appeared to be sustained by hate. In addition, the clamor for reforming the civil service and the tariff was gaining strength among moderate Republicans, who had an economic interest in a growing economy as well as efficient, honest urban governments.

Radicals were quick to perceive the danger posed by these "Liberal

Republicans." They were called heretics, and party operatives warned President Grant that he would have to put down this Missouri rebellion politically, just as he had ended the Southern rebellion militarily.

Five days following the city ward meetings, Pulitzer, Senator Schurz, and Grosvenor went to Jefferson City for the Republican state convention. At the capitol, more than 700 delegates crowded into the House chamber, which was regularly used by other groups when the legislature was not in session, and even for religious services on Sundays. This, however, was no church meeting. Within twenty-four hours the Liberals mounted their attack and turned McClurg's hoped-for political coronation into chaos.

The initial confrontations developed when a resolution came to the floor supporting the suffrage amendments on the fall ballot that would immediately remove all voting disqualifications. Seeking to avoid an immediate, divisive vote, the resolutions were referred to the resolutions committee chaired by Schurz. The committee, by a slim majority, returned to the hall with an endorsement of the proposal.

"Upon this question," proclaimed Schurz, "we cannot yield." The delegates, however, yielded and defeated the motion on a vote of 439 to 342. One of the Liberal delegates, yelling as loudly as he could over the noise of agitated delegates, called for those who had voted for the majority report to withdraw to the Senate chambers. Schurz, Grosvenor, and Pulitzer led the exodus.

Once resettled on the other side of the capitol, the rebellious Republicans made Schurz chairman and proceeded immediately to nominate a ticket, with Gratz Brown at its head, and draft a platform. Written by Grosvenor, it contained the text of the defeated majority resolution and other planks of the Liberal cause. Before adjourning, the renegade assembly appointed Pulitzer secretary to the state executive committee. The rebellion had made a team of the beefy Grosvenor and the ectomorphic Pulitzer.

Meanwhile, in the House chamber, the Radicals renominated McClurg and adjourned. The news of the bolt reached all parts of the country. "The Republican Party of Missouri has split in twain on the question of enfranchising the ex-rebels," reported the *Chicago Tribune*. "The Missouri Radicals are in trouble," proclaimed the *Mountain Democrat* in Placerville, California.

The split between Liberal and Radical Republicans was far more than a debate over who should be able to vote and when. It was the beginning of a fight over the soul of the Republican Party. Liberals believed that the Radicals' opposition to restoring the vote and the corruption surrounding Grant were a betrayal of the party's ideals. For Pulitzer, Grant was Pope Leo X and the corruption scandals were the church indulgences that drove Martin Luther to pin his ninety-five theses on the church door in Wittenberg. It was a matter of political faith, not politics.

With the conventions done, Pulitzer and Grosvenor returned to St. Louis to prepare for the fall electoral battle. Pulitzer threw himself into the fray. He bore all the grunt work of the Liberals' executive committee while continuing his work at the *Westliche Post*. On September 20, he single-handedly ran the Republican First Congressional District meeting in Turner Hall, which was filled almost entirely with Liberal Republicans. He chaired the resolutions committee, read aloud the Liberal Republican platform, obtained approval for it, and shepherded the congressional nomination to his friend Johnson, who was home ill.

As exciting as it was to be at the center of a political rebellion, Pulitzer had his own reelection ahead. On October 18, he was renominated without opposition. But Radical Republicans were intent on punishing Liberal Republicans and mounted behind-the-scenes efforts to enlist new black voters, who were not eager to enfranchise former slave masters. "On the McClurg ticket," wrote Pulitzer, "the Germans are distinguished by—their absence. Of course! McClurg and Co. are depending on Negroes to carry their cause, and obviously do not expect to receive a single German vote."

On their side, the Liberals counted on Democrats, many more of whom could come to the polls in 1870 because the state had eased its strict enforcement of the loyalty oath. Brown was a former Democrat, and the Democrats had no one of their party on the top of the ticket to support. But in other races, such as those for the legislature, the Democrats were fielding candidates. A high turnout among Democrats might elect Pulitzer's gubernatorial candidate but would be bad news for his own reelection.

Grosvenor did his best at the *Missouri Democrat* to push Pulitzer's candidacy. "He makes mistakes at times, and is sometimes misinformed," he told the readers, "but the people appreciate a man who never fears to say what he thinks, and never yields to compromise of principle, and so, while he makes some enemies, he makes more friends." But Grosvenor knew that Pulitzer was in trouble.

On November 3, Liberal Republicans of St. Louis gathered for a torch-light procession and rally in a large public market. Pulitzer, Anthony Ittner, and Preetorius, of the *Westliche Post*, were among the speakers. Later, Pulitzer went to the courthouse and signed another loyalty oath to ensure his legality as a candidate. In doing so, he once again betrayed the oath he took. Constitutionally he still remained too young to serve in the legislature.

All the rhetoric, charges, countercharges, campaigning, and torchlight parades came to an end on November 8, 1870, Election Day. Brown's victory was expected, but for Pulitzer the picture looked gloomy. "In the Fifth district Mr. Pulitzer, the Liberal Republican candidate, has the opposition of the county court and court-house ring against him, on ac-count of his opposition to their schemes in the last legislature," reported the morning's edition of the *Missouri Republican*. "Mr. Bell is confident of being elected by a two hundred majority."

In the morning, the extent of Brown's victory astonished everyone. He carried the state by a huge margin. Liberal Republicans were ec-static. The election of their man as governor and the 88 percent vote they garnered for the amendments were a rebuke to Radicalism and, in particular, to the Grant administration. It was "the most remarkable political revolution of the age," said the New York *Journal of Commerce*. "Let men look to Missouri if they would learn how the political revolu-tion of the future is to be brought about."

In Pulitzer's ward, for instance, Brown swamped McClurg by a three-to-one margin. But in Pulitzer's camp, the mood was somber. The high turnout among Democrats that propelled Brown to victory spelled trou-ble. Pulitzer's Democratic opponent won 991 votes to Pulitzer's 673. The vote was a complete reversal of Pulitzer's victory the prior year. Writing in the *Westliche Post* the following day, Pulitzer blamed his loss on 250 Negroes and 60 Frenchmen: "In general, the Negroes and the white McClurgites voted according to the maxim, better to see Democrats elected than the Liberals."

The electoral truth of the matter was simple. Pulitzer had won in 1869 because the unusual political configurations had favored him. The continued legal suppression of Democratic voters, the party's ineptitude in selecting a candidate, and the traditional low voter turnout for a special election hampered by bad weather had produced Pulitzer's winning margin. A year later, with Democrats returning to the polls in large numbers, Pulitzer as a Republican—even a Liberal Republican—was doomed.

Pulitzer's friend Joseph Keppler, the cartoonist, rendered a graphic interpretation of the loss. In a cartoon captioned "Too heavy a load," Keppler drew Pulitzer and two other losing politicians on a wooden platform supported by Brown, Schurz, and Grosvenor. Brown is bending down, unable to bear the weight, and Pulitzer is falling off. The revolution in which Pulitzer had played an important role had been won, but it had left him behind.

Out of office but not out of work, Pulitzer returned to Jefferson City in the second week of January 1871 to cover Gratz Brown's inauguration for the *Westliche Post*. Instead of taking a seat as a lawmaker, he watched as a reporter when Brown was escorted to the Speaker's dais in the house chamber. "We have arrived at the close of a revolution," Brown told the hundreds who crowded the hall. "The lingering animosities of Civil War have been supplanted by an accepted reconciliation on all sides."

Not quite. Schurz and Grosvenor were complaining that Democrats were gaining the upper hand and that the governor, a onetime Democrat, was being excessively friendly to his former party. As far as they could see, too many jobs in the state government were going to Democrats.

Pulitzer did not share his partners' intense hostility toward Democrats. While it was certainly true that he had lost his reelection bid to a Democrat, Pulitzer recognized that the seat he had briefly held traditionally belonged to Democrats. As a newcomer to politics, he was relatively free of the war-related party animosity, unlike Grosvenor and Schurz, who were twelve and eighteen years his senior, respectively. Democrats were among his closest friends. For instance, both Charles Johnson, who was defending him in court, and Stilson Hutchins, a newspaperman, were supporting the Liberal Republican movement. To Pulitzer, it made little sense to think of Democrats as the enemy.

Any concern about looming political fratricide was soon forgotten because Brown, Schurz, and Grosvenor all had a common enemy— Grant. Besides, a more serious blow to Liberal Republicans' harmony now came from the owners of the *Missouri Democrat*. For mysterious and suspicious reasons, they had fallen back into the ranks of Grant Republicans and fired Grosvenor. "Much as I had been warned that they would go back and throw me overboard as a journalist," Grosvenor wrote to Schurz, "I did not believe they would dare to do either, or be mean enough to do the latter."

In 1870, the loss of the *Missouri Democrat* would have been fatal to the cause. But in 1871, editors such as Horace White at the *Chicago Tribune*, Samuel Bowles at the *Springfield Republican*, Murat Halstead at the *Cincinnati Commercial*, and Henry Watterson at the *Louisville Courier-Journal* were spreading the gospel.

The growing movement thrilled Pulitzer, but he had a more mundane concern. The previous year, he had boosted his income considerably with his service in the state legislature. The election opened a fountainhead of patronage posts and Pulitzer sought one in the legislature. State Senator Louis Benecke, a Democrat who had worked with Pulitzer in the fall campaign, hired Pulitzer as a clerk for the committee on banks and corporations, which he chaired. For a second year in a row, Pulitzer spent the winter months in the capital.

When the legislative session ended in March 1871, Pulitzer returned full-time to St. Louis and his work at the *Westliche Post*. The presidential election was still more than a year away, yet the excitement generated by Missouri's Republican rebellion infected Pulitzer's friends, most of whom were working for the cause. Optimism ran high. "And why may not the campaign of 1870 in Missouri, be reenacted in the nation?" asked Brown.

Since being fired from the *Missouri Democrat*, Grosvenor was spending all his time directing the affairs of the ad hoc Liberal Republican organization. Schurz, though still holding out hope of taking back the party from Grant stalwarts, was increasingly identified in the national press as the movement's leader. And Preetorius was overseeing a barrage of editorials intended to rally Germans to the cause. Working at the *Westliche Post* put Pulitzer at the center of this growing political movement, though in the shadows of its better-known leaders.

But that too was changing. A few months later, when the magazine *Every Saturday* commissioned the artist Alfred Waudran to produce a full page of engravings featuring the faces of about four dozen "of the foremost St. Louisans," he included, along with his depictions of Schurz, Hutchins, and Grosvenor, one of Pulitzer. A profile view accenting Pulitzer's protruding chin and nose, the drawing shows a clean-shaven Pulitzer sporting small wire-rim glasses.

As the summer and fall of 1871 passed, Pulitzer divided his days between working for the *Westliche Post* and promoting the Liberal Republican cause with Grosvenor. The Radicals, eager to extinguish the Liberal Republican committee, set a trap. They invited all Republican leaders to an October meeting in St. Louis in order to issue a joint call for a state convention in January.

Members of the State Republican Committee voted to accept the call, but Pulitzer and Grosvenor worked to organize a "no" vote by the Liberals. Accusations immediately flew that the two were violating party rules by using proxies wrongly. "Under the ill-famed leadership of Joe Pulitzer and Bill Grosvenor, Liberals bolted from that resolution, and filled up its deficit by proxies of very dubious authority," reported the *Missouri Staats-Zeitung*.

Pulitzer's patron, State Senator Benecke, offered advice on countering the charge. "I desire to inform you," Benecke wrote to Pulitzer on October 26, "that the various lies reported in the *Missouri Democrat* in reference to yourself and the action of the Committee should be 'nailed' which could easily be done by publishing the whole proceedings of our Committee." Pulitzer, as well as Grosvenor, left the complaints unanswered. It was becoming increasingly clear that the Liberal Republicans now had the upper hand.

If Pulitzer wanted to serve the cause in the presidential battle of 1872, he would need another, more substantial, patronage job. But to earn a gubernatorial political appointment he would have to overcome a major hurdle. Still hanging over him was an indictment in Cole County for felonious assault, stemming from his having grazed Augustine's leg with a bullet. The lobbyist had recovered from his wounds, but the political damage to Pulitzer lingered.

Charles Johnson came to Pulitzer's rescue. Since the shooting, he had acted as Pulitzer's pro bono counsel. So far, each time a court date neared, Johnson had obtained a delay, often so close to the appointed time that Augustine and other witnesses had already made the trek to Jefferson City in anticipation of their day in court. By fall of 1871, delay was no longer an option. On November 20, Pulitzer stood before a Cole

County judge. By his side stood Johnson, who as circuit attorney for St. Louis prosecuted criminals in his city for the state. Also appearing for Pulitzer was Britton A. Hill, a 300-pound St. Louis attorney with a reputation for coarseness and bluntness. One suspects that the prosecutor of bucolic Cole County didn't stand a chance against these big-city heavy hitters and might have been glad to be rid of the case.

The charge was rapidly settled with a modest fine. In all, aside from the embarrassment, the Augustine affair cost Pulitzer approximately $400 in court costs, travel, and other expenses. It was money that he did not have. Johnson borrowed it from Pulitzer's friends. When Pulitzer became wealthy years later, he wrote to Johnson and settled his debts with the lenders who had come to his aid.

Freed from this legal encumbrance, Pulitzer was now eligible for a patronage post if Governor Brown was willing to grant one. There was good reason to believe he was. Brown was increasingly convinced that he could be the Liberal Republican candidate for president in 1872, and Pulitzer had been a good foot soldier since 1870. Again, Johnson took on Pulitzer's cause.

A seat on the St. Louis Police Commission was about to open up as the result of a resignation. It required very few hours of work and paid $1,000 a year, at a time when the average skilled worker earned less than $600 a year working six days a week. On January 12, 1872, Johnson met with the governor and was assured that he would appoint Pulitzer to serve out the unexpired term. Returning to St. Louis, Johnson told Pulitzer the news. But when, several days later, the nomination was sent to the state senate, Pulitzer developed cold feet. Johnson went to see him and was surprised by his reaction. "He is one of the most unreasonable men I ever knew withal," Johnson wrote in his diary. "He is really foolish."

All day, Pulitzer remained obstinate. After meeting with Johnson one last time, he left the distinct impression that he would not take the job. Apparently Pulitzer feared that he would be trading one job for another, that by accepting Brown's nomination he would lose his job with the paper. If so, his fear was not without merit. Earlier that week, when Johnson stopped in at the *Westliche Post*, Preetorius had suggested that Pulitzer might have to leave the paper if he became a police commissioner. In the end, Pulitzer's reluctance disappeared as quickly as it had developed. He accepted the nomination and kept his job at the paper.

The conservative *Anzeiger des Westens* railed against the appointment: the job of police commissioner required tact, dignity, and other qualities of a virtuous character, "and you will not find any of them in Pulitzer. He is undoubtedly a clever political runner. Maybe the governor fancies that in the next nomination for President the new Police Commissioner will be of good service. All of this is possible; but as Police Commissioner, Mr. Pulitzer will remain a caricature—a most ridiculous farce." The Irish newspaper *The Western Celt* also damned the selection: "A more infamous prostitution of the gubernatorial power it would be difficult to imagine."

The grumbling by the press mattered little. The nomination moved to a vote. During the debate it was asked if Pulitzer was not the member of the House who "did a little shooting up here two years ago?" It was confirmed that he was, indeed, the man, but the senate was in a forgiving mood and approved the nomination.

Chapter Seven

POLITICS AND REBELLION

In late January 1872, Pulitzer and Grosvenor headed to Jefferson City to light the spark of a national political rebellion. The Liberal Republican state executive committee was convening to issue a national call to disaffected Republicans to gather and select a ticket to run against President Grant. "The time is ripe for an uprising of the people, in kind not unlike that which swept this state in 1870," Grosvenor said.

As these reform-minded activists traveled by train to Jefferson City for an act of popular sovereignty, the capital's station was a scene of celebration that morning for a symbol of the undemocratic Old World. A huge crowd stood in the damp cold to await Russia's Grand Duke Alexis, who was coming in his $3,500-a-day private train, to lunch with Governor Brown at the new executive mansion. The completion of the mansion was also going to be celebrated with a ball, preparation for which had required many ladies to sleep upright lest they ruin their new coiffures.

As Liberal Republican activists descended amid this hallabaloo, they grabbed the last remaining hotel rooms, to the immense pleasure of the innkeepers. "There is a big crowd here—make no mistake about that," reported Joseph McCullagh. "That is to say, the hotels are what the landlords will call very comfortably, and what the guests will consider very uncomfortably, full."

McCullagh was among the throngs in Jefferson City on assignment to cover the meeting for the *Missouri Democrat*. He had recently rejoined the paper, where he had worked as a young reporter before the war. Since his modest start, McCullagh had served as a Civil War correspondent and then won national fame as a Washington correspondent who published a series of interviews with the embattled president, Andrew Johnson. McCullagh made a memorable impression on most who met him. Born in Dublin, Ireland, the short, thick, and pugnacious reporter was known to all simply as "Mack." According to the novelist Theodore Dreiser, "He was so short, so sturdy, so napoleonic, so ursine rather than leonine, that he pleased and yet frightened me."

On his first night in Jefferson City, McCullagh noticed that Senator Schurz had remained in Washington and left his less-known lieutenants Pulitzer and Grosvenor in charge. "If I had to select from the large crowds that throng the halls and doorways the most prominent managers of the Liberal movement," McCullagh wrote, "I should, at a guess, point to Joe and Bill, as they are familiarly called by each other and by all their acquaintances." From Schurz's perspective this was a worrisome state of affairs. If the convention were a henhouse, Grosvenor would be the farmhand in charge, Brown a fox, and Pulitzer an unreliable watchdog.

That night Pulitzer and Grosvenor conferred with Brown, who left the festivities at the mansion to come to Schmidt's Hotel. The prospects were good. About 130 had showed for the meeting. An equally promising sign was the diversity of the delegates. "In fact, while Liberal Republicans of all classes were more fully represented than ever before," Grosvenor observed. "It was remarked with pleasure and surprise by German Liberals, that, for the first time, they were outnumbered by American Liberals."

The following day, a few minutes before noon, Grosvenor and Pulitzer were caught in the sea of delegates and spectators jamming the floor of the House chambers.

"Joe," Grosvenor yelled.

"All right, Bill," replied Pulitzer from deep in the crowd on the floor as he made his way over to Grosvenor.

"Let's organize the damned thing," Grosvenor said when Pulitzer reached him.

"All right, Bill. You get into the chair and call them to order," Pulitzer instructed.

Grosvenor ascended the dais and welcomed the "vanguard in the army of reform," eliciting a wave of enthusiastic applause. "The time has come, gentlemen," he said. "We are here because we can be nowhere else. The Republican party still clings to abuses which no true Republican can excuse." Charles Johnson followed Grosvenor, and stirred the crowd even further with a harangue about the Grant administration. "The word 'carpet-baggers' figured around hundreds of times in his speech," McCullagh, a defender of Grant, said.

The like-minded delegates took no time to issue the call for a convention to be held in Cincinnati on May 1 and ratify the draft of a platform calling for universal suffrage and amnesty, civil service and tariff reform, and control of big business. "The times demand an uprising of honest citizens to sweep from power the men who prostitute the name of an honored party for selfish interests," proclaimed the document that was finally adopted.

Their work complete, the delegates called on Governor Brown to address the convention. He promised that if Missouri led the fight against executive despotism and corruption, others would rally to the cause. It was a bit much for McCullagh, who simply couldn't resist pointing out Brown's hypocrisy to his readers. The governor, he said, had failed to give one single "instance in which Grant had made such an unfit appointment as that which has recently disgraced his own administration. I mean, of course, Pulitzer as Police Commissioner, which stands out single and alone, and challenges comparison with history or tradition."

Grosvenor and Pulitzer were keenly aware that the fortunes of the Missouri declaration depended on successfully conveying to the nation's press an impression of a political groundswell. To that end, they enlisted William Hyde, the managing editor and part owner of the *Missouri Republican*. He persuaded the Associated Press to transmit his sympathetic coverage of the meeting. The plan succeeded to a great extent, and countless newspapers described the meeting as a political prairie fire. The success of the propaganda left the anti-movement *New York Times* fuming: "The *Missouri Democrat*, through its well-known correspondent 'Mack,' instantly exposed the fraud, but the exaggeration had got twenty-four hours start in the head-lines of thousands of newspapers all over the land, and the truth never overtook it." The "truth," according to the *New York Times*, "was that the Convention was contemptible in numbers and more than contemptible in the political standing of its members."

In the short span of a few days, both the good and the bad press coming from the convention closely identified Pulitzer with the movement. "Among the by-no-means unimportant factors in the great multiple of Liberalism, was and is the brilliant Pulitzer, Senator Schurz's whimsical lieutenant on the *Westliche Post,* of St. Louis," noted one newspaper. The Jefferson City convention was a triumph for the political partnership between Pulitzer and Grosvenor, one that even McCullagh was forced to concede. "Writing now a day after the whole matter has gone into history," he said, "I cannot see a better title for it than the Bill-and-Joe Convention. What there was of it that didn't belong to Bill was purely Joe-ical, and vice versa."

When he got back to St. Louis, Pulitzer took his seat on the four-member police commission. One of the other members was William Patrick, the lawyer who had given Pulitzer some work during his first years in St. Louis. Providing police protection was a serious affair. The city was the fourth-largest in the United States and quite spread out. The geographic area patrolled was larger than that of any American city except for Philadelphia. As a result, St. Louis maintained a good-sized police department with a force of 432, including detectives, sergeants, and captains, and a large budget.

The police commission was charged with overseeing its operation, approving all expenses, reviewing citizens' complaints, and enforcing discipline. The last of these was a not infrequent occupation of the board. For instance, in the summer of 1872, a patrolman, Patrick Conway, was found intoxicated in a house of prostitution. That he was a police officer was evident, because he was in uniform. Drunk, he had nevertheless remained true at least to one of the police department requirements: that one remain in uniform at all times.

For the first few months, Pulitzer diligently attended the biweekly meetings of the commission. He was asked to look into the police force's effectiveness at coping with gambling—a rising problem in the city. But the duties of police commissioner were not high in his mind. Rather, politics took first place. Grosvenor put Pulitzer on the road and he spent most of February and March in the East, drumming up support for the national convention.

As the Cincinnati convention neared, Pulitzer continued promoting the governor's presidential candidacy. "Brown has . . . given Joseph an office to reward his service for an anti-patronage candidate, and the rewarded one is faithful," the *Missouri Democrat* snidely reported. But Pulitzer's partners were acting coy about whom they supported, particularly Schurz, who still harbored resentment at Brown's postelection behavior.

There were four viable candidates for the Liberal Republican nomination aside from Brown: Charles Francis Adams, a former congressman and diplomat who was the son of President John Quincy Adams; Supreme Court Justice David Davis, appointed by Lincoln and known for having written the opinion in a landmark civil liberties case; Senator Lyman Trumbull of Illinois, who alternately was a Democrat and a Republican but while a Republican broke with his party and voted against the conviction of President Johnson during the impeachment; and Horace Greeley, the aging, famous editor of the *New York Tribune*. This last candidate had the virtue of unquestioned integrity, especially in contrast to Grant, but he was seen as somewhat of a screwball who supported temperance and women's rights and dabbled in a decidedly un-American European import, socialism.

On an April evening, Pulitzer and Stilson Hutchins went to Johnson's house to work on plans to secure the nomination for Brown. When Hutchins went home, Johnson and Pulitzer moved to Brown's house, where they worked until two in the morning. "He is very confident of getting the nomination at Cincinnati," Johnson wrote of Brown that night in his diary. "He fears Adams of Massachusetts. Schurz is playing shy. Nobody knows how he stands."

Pulitzer and Grosvenor left town by train on April 24 to arrive in advance of most delegates. Reporters from around the country were heading the same way. On the leg from Chicago, Pulitzer sat with William A. Croffut, the managing editor of the *Chicago Tribune*. "This tall, rawboned youth was twenty-four years old," Croffut recalled, "had a nose like Julius Caesar, had already acquired a picturesque history."

Reaching Cincinnati in the early morning of April 25, Pulitzer and Grosvenor immediately repaired to the St. James Hotel, where they set up their political headquarters. "They kept their camp fires burning from dawn until after midnight," said one Chicago reporter. The St. James was the center of press attention. In particular, reporters sought out the Missourians, who had one of the largest state delegations and were considered the progenitors of the rebellion. "Considering themselves the parents of the Liberal movement," noted the Chicago reporter, "the delegation labored under the delusion that their points could be easily carried."

The press was intensely interested in the convention. Only once before had Cincinnati been the host of a national political convention: in 1856, contentious Democrats had taken seventeen ballots to nominate James Buchanan for president. There was similar potential for drama at the Liberal Republicans' convention, as no candidate had enough votes to win the nomination.

Not only did the convention put Pulitzer at the center of an exciting political battle, but he also met journalists from around the country. In particular, he was drawn to a local press figure, John A. Cockerill, the managing editor of the *Cincinnati Enquirer*. The two had a lot in common. Both were over six feet tall—six inches taller than the average American—and they were only two years apart in age. Most important, their passion for politics, reform, and journalism created an instant bond between them, which years later would bring them together in a legendary journalistic partnership.

The convention was a striking example of the confluence of independent journalism and politics. Like a fly on the wall, Pulitzer witnessed a few of the nation's most powerful publishers try to impose their will on the convention. They met secretly in a room adjacent to Schurz's that Pulitzer frequented. There were five men: Schurz; Henry Watterson, of the *Louisville Courier-Journal*; Samuel Bowles, of the *Springfield Republican*; Murat Halstead, of the *Cincinnati Commercial*; *and* Horace White, of the *Chicago Tribune*. Though they numbered five, they named themselves the Quadrilateral, after four northern Italian fortresses that had been prominent in the Milanese insurgency of 1848. As they saw it, the task before them was not solely to report the news of the convention but to shape it.

The group agreed that the convention should choose either Adams or Trumbull. "The first serious business that engaged us was the killing of the boom for Judge David Davis," said Watterson. "The power of the press must be invoked. It was our chief if not our only weapon."

Sitting at the same table, the editors wrote editorials for their respective papers, saying that there was no support among the delegates for Davis, despite the arrival of 700 of his supporters in Cincinnati, and that he was allied with Democrats to steal the convention away from the movement. After the editorials had been wired to the newspapers, they were reprinted in the *Cincinnati Commercial,* impressing on the arriving delegates the futility of supporting Davis. The editors failed, however, to shroud their machinations. It wasn't long before the *New York Times* traced the "demoralization" of Davis's followers to "a newspaper caucus of independent journalists late at night, in which it was determined to kill off Davis instantly by an editorial blast in four quarters of the country."

On May 1, the convention got down to business. Delegates and spectators, on foot and in carriages, streamed from hotels toward the wood-framed Exposition Hall. They were a motley group. "A livelier and more variegated omnium-gatherum was never assembled," said Watterson. "They were long-haired and spectacled doctrinaires from New England, spliced by short-haired and stumpy emissaries from New York. . . . The full contingent of Washington correspondents was there, of course, with sharpened eyes and pens to make the most of what they had already begun to christen a conclave of cranks."

The *Sängerhalle,* as it was known to the large German population of the city, was ready. The three stages, typically used by musical choruses, were decorated with flags and emblems; and a larger single stage was set at the center with 300 to 400 chairs for the conventiongoers to watch each state's delegation parade in. A last-minute crisis was averted when someone discovered that the ladies' gallery—the only place in the hall where the fair sex would be permitted—had been inadvertently closed but was able to get it opened in time.

At noon, Grosvenor called the convention to order. To Pulitzer and Grosvenor, who had run the Jefferson City enclave that created this gathering, the sight was an impressive achievement. Seven hundred delegates from every state in the union except Delaware sat expectantly in rows on the floor below, surrounded by stands filled with 6,000 or 7,000 spectators, many of whom had come long distances. At that time, political conventions made for good theater. "This convention originated in a single state and has now embraced representatives of the Republican Party from every state of the union," Grosvenor said, to thunderous applause. As their first order of business, the delegates accepted the nomination of officers, including Pulitzer, who was rewarded for his work by being selected as one of the secretaries.

Opening business concluded, the delegates began to clamor for

Schurz to speak. He declined, despite noisy cries of "Now! Now!"—but he said there would be time later. It was an intoxicating moment for Pulitzer, standing on the floor sporting a new mustache and a little tuft of a beard on his chin. Grosvenor, his political partner, held the convention's gavel, and the man for whom the audience clamored was his mentor. The Bill and Joe Show had launched a national movement.

The next day the main order of business was the long-awaited speech by Schurz. He began with a litany of criticisms of the Grant administration, ranging from its alleged disrespect for law to its tyrannical tendencies. But Schurz knew that a music hall filled with idealistic Republicans would not be enough to prevail in the fall. "I earnestly deprecate the cry we have heard so frequently, 'Anybody to beat Grant,'" said Schurz. "We don't want a mere change of persons in the administration of government. We want the overthrow of a pernicious system."

Schurz's speech concluded, the delegates went to work on adopting a platform. Most of the planks were polished versions of the well-known Liberal calls for reform. With the exception of a tortured compromise on the tariff plank, the platform looked pretty much like the one adopted in Jefferson City four months ago when Grosvenor and Pulitzer ran the show. In fact, one newspaper called the convention's final platform "a literal transcript from the platform of Bill and Joe."

The delegates went back to their hotels for a night's rest before the anticipated long struggle to select the man who would lead the party into the fall elections. The coming battle caused the first split between Pulitzer and his mentor. Schurz had grown increasingly hostile toward Brown since the 1870 election and now favored Adams for the nomination. Pulitzer remained loyal to Brown. He was not planning to desert his political patron even if his mentor did.

During the day, one of Brown's delegates had wired the governor to say that Schurz and Grosvenor were working to deny him the nomination. Brown immediately boarded a train for Cincinnati—a dramatic action in an era when candidates were expected to stay away from a nominating convention. In the company of Senator Francis Blair, Brown reached the city late that evening and went directly to the St. James Hotel. Running up and down corridors and knocking on doors, Grosvenor yelled, "Get up! Get up! Blair and Brown are here from St. Louis!"

When the bleary-eyed delegates came down to the lobby, Grosvenor told them that Brown had come to Cincinnati to withdraw from the race and throw his support to Greeley. The startled delegates—especially those who supported Adams or Trumbull—stayed up into the morning hours reworking their strategies for the coming day of balloting. Members of the Quadrilateral also milled about, but they were mostly powerless because time was too short to write editorials, wire them, and publish them back home.

At long last, the moment arrived to select the convention's candidate. Nominating speeches were not permitted, and the first roll call got under way. Brown, who was seated with the Missouri delegation, sent a note up to Schurz asking to be permitted to address the convention. Remarkably, Schurz consented.

On the floor Pulitzer watched his candidate ascend the steps of the platform. With the light from a window far above beaming down on him, Brown thanked the delegates for voting for him. Even though the first tally had not yet been announced, most delegates kept their own count and knew he had close to 100 votes. Then Brown made public what those who had been up most of the night anticipated. He would no longer be a candidate. Instead he asked that his delegates support Greeley. Applause and hisses filled the hall, the former coming from the ladies' gallery because Greeley supported women's rights.

Brown returned to his seat, and the results from the first round of balloting were announced. Adams led with 205 votes, Greeley had 147, and the other five candidates divided the remainder. The math was ominous for Adams and Trumbull. If Brown's votes went to Greeley, the New York publisher would equal or outdistance Adams.

Watterson, who had been absent during the morning, arrived in the hall and found Pulitzer, who filled him in on what had just occurred. He struggled to explain why Schurz had stuck to his pledge of neutrality when he assumed the convention chair. Like many delegates, Pulitzer was convinced that Schurz had the power to direct the convention. "A word from him at that crisis would have completely routed Blair and squelched Brown," Pulitzer told Watterson. "It was simply not in him to speak it."

The contest narrowed to Adams and Greeley. On the second ballot, to the relief of Adams's supporters, Brown's endorsement of Greeley was not as strong as they had feared. Their man still had the lead, though only slightly. As the balloting continued, Adams inched toward the nomination. On the fifth ballot, delegate-rich Illinois decided to throw its lot in with Adams. As the sixth ballot began, everyone assumed it would be the last. But Illinois made a tactical mistake. It decided to pass. Instead Indiana, which had swung to Greeley, announced its change of heart, setting off chaos in the hall. It looked as if Greeley might win, after all. The chair could hardly restore order.

When Illinois finally reported its vote, Adams was back in the lead, but the tide had turned in Greeley's favor, washing away any chance Adams had of winning. In many conventions, a candidate whose fortune rises quickly becomes unstoppable. States changed their votes, and the convention surged in Greeley's favor. He became the nominee. Pulitzer's man, Brown, was immediately rewarded with the vice presidential nomination, and then it was over.

Despite all of Schurz's work in bringing the rebellion to this point, the delegates he inspired had selected an aging editor with no electoral experience and a running mate whom Schurz regarded as his opponent. For Pulitzer, his first national convention taught him that outcomes were hard to control and even hard to predict. Schurz and Pulitzer retreated to the house of Judge John Stallo, who was an Ohioan and a Hegelian and, like Schurz, had raised a regiment of Germans during the Civil War. There the men drank and ate until evening. The convention had turned into a wake. "Reformers hoist by their own petard," said Watterson.

This was a disconcerting moment for Pulitzer. Schurz was distraught by the convention's outcome. Brown, to whom Pulitzer owed his patronage post, was elated by his selection for the national ticket. But in winning his prize, Brown had wrecked Schurz's plans for the convention. This left Pulitzer at a crossroads. He couldn't oppose Brown, but to actively support him would be a blow against the man who had given him his start in politics.

Back in St. Louis, Pulitzer made his choice. He, along with Grosvenor, joined the Greeley-Brown campaign while Schurz retreated to Washington to nurse his political wounds. Schurz said he didn't care if his reputation was hurt by his silence; such damage paled in comparison with "the disappointment caused by the loss of so great an opportunity as we had."

Much of the German community was dismayed by the selection of Greeley, but Pulitzer gave his support unhesitatingly. He took on the job of secretary of the Liberal state executive committee in addition to continuing his work as city editor of the *Westliche Post*. Conveniently, the committee's offices shared the same Chestnut Street building that housed the paper.

Greeley's favorable attitude toward temperance was both an economic and a cultural affront to Germans. Pulitzer urged Whitelaw Reid at the *New York Tribune* to persuade his boss to make some sort of personal statement distinguishing his personal views on alcohol from those he held as a candidate. Though Reid was ten years older than Pulitzer, and more experienced, the two journalists found they had much in common serving as assistants to famous politicians and were soon carrying on a backstairs correspondence about their bosses.

Of concern to Reid was a meeting in New York at which leading Liberal Republicans, including Schurz, plotted to dump the convention's choice. "I knew of the danger of that conference in New York but have no fears," Pulitzer wrote. "I really think that the conference will result in strengthening Mr. Greeley though the very opposite was its original object. Our element will have the majority in it and our views will prevail."

A sense of optimism prevailed in the St. Louis Liberal Republican office. Perhaps matters were not as bleak at they seemed. On June 14, Grosvenor and Pulitzer convened a meeting of the executive committee and told the press that a "larger number of Liberal Republicans in Missouri now support the ticket nominated by the Cincinnati National Convention than supported the Liberal State Ticket in 1870."

But Pulitzer's work for the Greeley campaign was a nonstop effort at damage control. Not only was the candidate prone to gaffes; Pulitzer's colleagues in the press were unimpressed by having one of their own as a candidate. Riding a train to New York in midsummer, Pulitzer read in the Philadelphia papers that only one German newspaper supported Greeley, the inconsequential Davenport, Iowa, *Demokrat*. The *Westliche Post*, the article added, was also maintaining "an ominous silence." Pulitzer was incensed. It was bad enough for the item to appear in the Philadelphia Republican press; an appearance in other newspapers around the country would damage the ticket. "Each reprint," Pulitzer said, is "the theft of a falsehood."

Upon reaching New York, Pulitzer immediately published an irate correction in the *New York Tribune*, Greeley's paper. "Instead of 'but a single German Republican daily still clinging to Greeley,'" he wrote, "every single German Republican daily (except one) that supported the principles of the Liberal movement previous to the Cincinnati Convention, now supports Horace Greeley."

As for the "ominous silence of the *Westliche Post*," he continued, "I simply say that the paper was never more earnest and outspoken in the good cause than now. I do not hesitate to predict that when the vote shall have been counted in November it will appear even to the blindest or wildest Grant criers that Mr. Greeley has received a much larger proportion of the German vote than has ever before been united upon any Presidential candidate."

In New York, Pulitzer was cheered by some good news. The Democrats, meeting in Baltimore, decided to support the Liberal Republican ticket and, for first time in party history, chose not to nominate a candidate of their own. But Pulitzer's growing skill at electoral math left little doubt that even the Democrats' support would not change the uphill nature of the election. Greeley, one of the most eccentric men ever nominated for president, was not inspiring voters. It did not take much in the way of political tea leaf reading to sense that the election was shaping up as a disaster for Liberal Republicans.

After New York, Pulitzer returned briefly to St. Louis. The campaign had ended Pulitzer's diligent attendance to his duties with the St. Louis police commission. He missed all the meetings in July and almost every meeting until December. If Pulitzer worried about his attendance, his qualms did not restrain him from collecting his salary. He did make a stab, of sorts, at resigning. He confirmed to a reporter in St. Louis that he had sent a letter of resignation to Governor Brown.

"Has he accepted the resignation?" asked the reporter.

"I don't know," replied Pulitzer, smiling.

"As far as you know, has he accepted the resignation?"

"I don't know—no; the governor wrote me that he wasn't prepared . . ." said Pulitzer without finishing the thought.

"Then he hasn't accepted it yet?"

"No."

Police commission work felt inconsequential to Pulitzer. He was giving his entire effort to sustaining the *Westliche Post* and supporting the Greeley campaign. Working every day from eight in the morning

to midnight, he seamlessly switched from editor to campaigner, some-
times making no distinction between the roles.

As fall approached, Pulitzer began traveling for the ticket. In an era
when speeches were considered beneath the candidates' dignity, others
made passionate campaign speeches on their behalf. In September Pu-
litzer was on the stump almost full-time. By one count, he delivered
sixty speeches to German audiences in Indiana and Ohio. His campaign
trail crossed the path of Simon Wolf, a prominent Jewish lawyer from
Washington, D.C., who was campaigning for Grant's reelection. Wolf sat
in a hotel reading the newspaper after completing a campaign speech in
the same town where Pulitzer was speaking on behalf of Greeley. Two
men came into the hotel, sat down near Wolf, and ordered drinks. "Did
you ever hear such German as that man Pulitzer got off? Nobody could
understand him," said one man to the other.

"Naturally," said Wolf. "Pulitzer had spoken over their heads and they
were disgusted with his culture. When I met Pulitzer that same evening,
I told him, and we had a laugh at his expense."

The campaign produced a surprising dividend for Pulitzer. "Some of the
proprietors of the *Westliche Post*," he said, "became nervous, wanted to
retire, thought the paper was ruined by the Greeley campaign." They ap-
proached him to see if he would like to buy into the paper. Pulitzer was
the most valuable member of their staff and had toiled for them for five
years. Before newspapers became big businesses, journalists dreamed of
owning at least part of a newspaper. There was no money to be made in
writing for a paper, only in owning one.

The potential changes in the ownership of the *Westliche Post* were
soon a subject of gossip among St. Louis Republicans. The rumors
reached the *Missouri Democrat*, whose editors dispatched a reporter to
follow up on them. "Schurz was said to be disgusted with the course of
the paper, and Plate, the senior member of the firm, anxious to buy the
other proprietors out," reported the *Democrat*.

"What's the news?" asked Pulitzer when the reporter climbed the last
flights of stairs leading into the *Westliche Post* editorial rooms.

"I don't know; I hear there is trouble in the *Post* office."

"How?" replied Pulitzer, smiling at the visitor from a desk stacked
high with paper.

"Well, there are rumors on the street that there is trouble in the office between Mr. Plate and Mr. Schurz and Preetorius; that he wants to buy them out, or have them buy him out."

"Whoever heard of such a damned thing?" said Pulitzer, laughing and leaning back in his chair.

"Then it's not true?"

"No. It's a lie, it's a damned lie. Why, it's so absurd."

At best, Pulitzer was being disingenuous. As in his previous dealings with reporters, Pulitzer was willing to misinform if it was to his advantage. He was not ready to make public that twenty-four hours earlier he had signed a note payable to Preetorius. It provided Pulitzer with $4,500 in credit at an interest rate of 8 percent, 2 percent lower than the rate common at the time for such loans. Pulitzer was in the process of signing other, similar notes. With these funds he bought a stake in the paper on, in his words, "very liberal terms."

"They thought I was necessary to the paper," he said. "They probably would have done the same thing to any other man who worked sixteen hours a day, as I did through that campaign."

Within a week, he was an owner. By late September 1872, Pulitzer was referring to the *Westliche Post* as "our newspaper" in a letter to Schurz. Thus seven years after reading his first copy of the *Westliche Post* in hopes of finding employment in St. Louis, Pulitzer was an American newspaper publisher.

While Pulitzer's stock rose, Greeley's and Brown's sank. The prospect of victory was becoming increasingly dim. "Everything depends on the result of the October elections," Pulitzer wrote to Schurz in Washington in late September, referring to the states that held a first round of voting a month before others. "Here in St. Louis and Missouri it is looking miserable. The area crazies are ruining much, and it seems advisable to me that you temporarily make no arrangements for speeches but rather return as soon as possible."

Pulitzer's forecast and Schurz's nightmare turned out to be true. On Election Day, Greeley and Brown carried only six states: Georgia, Kentucky, Maryland, Tennessee, Texas, and Missouri. The ticket could manage only a slim victory in the state where the movement began. Democrats carried the day in other states' races. Even St. Louis, city and county, returned to the Democratic fold.

For two years Pulitzer had dutifully served the Liberal Republican cause, renouncing the Republican Party, where he had begun his political life. His break had been a principled one over fundamental political differences. Pulitzer believed in the Liberal Republican Party's precepts and had tied his political fortunes to the party's success. Greeley's ignominious defeat not only killed the party, but politically stranded Pulitzer as a man without a party in the partisan world of nineteenth-century America.

Chapter Eight

POLITICS AND PRINCIPLE

◆

The crushing defeat of the Liberal Republican movement imperiled Pulitzer's tenuous hold on his patronage post. His one-year term on the St. Louis police commission was set to expire in February, leaving his reappointment in the hands of the newly elected governor, the first Democrat in Missouri's executive mansion since before the Civil War. Although Governor Silas Woodson knew that he partially owed his election to Liberal Republicans, he had little interest in retaining any Republicans—Liberal or other—in state offices.

Pulitzer mounted a campaign to remain on the commission. Keeping the job would allow him to retain a small foothold in politics and continue earning easy money. Governor Woodson hadn't even been sworn in before Pulitzer's loyalists took action. His friend James Broadhead, an unwavering Democrat who had been both a Unionist and a defender of slavery, was among the first to tell Woodson that Pulitzer had high standing in St. Louis, had done a good job, and represented the important German interests in the city. Others joined in. Newspaper editors, such as those at the *St. Louis Dispatch* and *St. Louis Times*, and city officeholders, including the city council president and city registrar, also wrote in support of Pulitzer.

Pulitzer turned for help to Hutchins and Johnson, who now had considerable political influence. For them, the election of 1872 had been munificent. Hutchins won a seat in the House and Johnson was elected as Woodson's lieutenant governor. With friends like these, Pulitzer's case for reappointment looked strong. The governor, however, didn't show his hand. Pulitzer may have had allies in high places, but he still had strong enemies, particularly among politicians in St. Louis County who had not forgotten his efforts to depose them and deny them the pecuniary rewards of their work.

Word leaked from the governor's office that Woodson was preparing to send his selections to the state senate on Monday afternoon, January 20, 1873. Hutchins feared that Pulitzer's name would not appear on the list and pleaded on behalf of his man. "If undecided to make the appointment requested by Lt. Governor Johnson and myself," Hutchins wrote Woodson, "do me the favor to hold it in abeyance until I can see you."

Monday came and went without any appointments coming down from the governor's office. A silence worthy of the Vatican descended. For several weeks Pulitzer's supporters continued their campaign, framing the issue around complex ethnic politics. "The Germans of this city ought to be represented on the Police Board not for nativistical reasons but so as to make sure that not only Irish Policemen are sent into German districts," wrote one man. But this approach was undercut by the reluctance of the city's best-known representative of German interests to join the bandwagon. The *Westliche Post* remained mum.

Preetorius was opposed to a second term for Pulitzer. In a private letter to Grosvenor, he explained his reasoning. "It was that, not in spite, but rather in consequences of my good wishes for Mr. Pulitzer, I could not recommend his reappointment," he wrote. His opposition stemmed from Pulitzer's confessions to him during his first year on the commission in which he "earnestly declared by himself, as wholly at variance with his qualifications as well as his own taste and liking."

On March 4, a month after Pulitzer's term legally expired, the governor finally broke his silence. Pulitzer, he announced, would be replaced with a former Confederate and loyal Democrat. Woodson's selection left the police commission devoid of any Germans. It took only a few hours for the news to reach St. Louis. Pulitzer was infuriated. He put pencil to paper and angrily scrawled out a letter to Senator Benecke, his old ally in the state senate.

Woodson's appointments were so unthinkable that Pulitzer said he couldn't find anyone who believed the report. Hurriedly he continued, impetuously scratching out unsatisfactory words as he wrote, "Nobody held it possible that the highest officer of our state evinced such a lack of all feelings of justice and propriety because it was supposed Mr. Woodson knew what everybody else knew, namely that since the existence of the Police Commission the German element always had one and for the greatest part of the time even *two* representatives in said Commission.

"If Mr. Woodson should insist upon these appointments and put himself on the record as an 'ignoramus' and 'knownothing,'" concluded Pulitzer, "then we hope that at least the Senate will prove that it knows its duty. We have a right to expect from the Senate the prompt rejection of such ridiculous appointments." The senate did not share Pulitzer's sentiments, and the nominees were promptly approved. With this loss, it seemed as if Pulitzer's political career was at an end. He had been voted out of his House seat; the promising Liberal Republican movement had ingloriously died; and now, even with one of his best friends serving as lieutenant governor, he could not win reappointment to the police board. Pulitzer the politician was out in the cold.

Pulitzer's career in journalism was also imperiled. Schurz's and Preetorius's ardor for their young protégé had cooled. The editorial office had grown too small for all three men. Preetorius's opposition to Pulitzer's reappointment to the police commission strained their relationship. Schurz, who was now a pariah in his party and knew that his reelection to the U.S. Senate was doomed, resented having to share the last bit of the public stage he held. To readers, the *Westliche Post* had become almost as closely identified with Pulitzer as with the mostly absent Schurz. Schurz and Preetorius offered to buy Pulitzer out. The price they proposed was commensurate with their desire to be free of him. On March 19, 1873, the men concluded a deal. After paying off his notes to Preetorius and others, Pulitzer walked away from the *Westliche Post* with about $30,000, three to six times his original investment.

Pulitzer immediately sought out Theodore Welge, who had assisted him in his defense after he shot Augustine. He was at a loss as to what to do with his vast sum of money. "This money he wanted me to deposit for him, which I declined to do," Welge said. Instead, he introduced Pulitzer to an entrepreneur who had created a shipping empire of riverboats operating out of St. Louis. The man persuaded Pulitzer to entrust the money to the nineteen-year-old State Savings Institution, which paid 3 percent interest.

Freed from the necessity of work for a while, Pulitzer left Missouri's journalism and politics behind and headed for Europe. That he would return to St. Louis, however, was certain. Before leaving, he paid a year's rent on a room adjoining Johnson's law offices. He had the room carpeted and purchased a writing desk for it.

On his way to Europe, Pulitzer visited his brother, who now lived in New York. Albert had become captivated by journalism. His choice of vocation did little to lessen the competition between the brothers. After landing a job on the *Illinois Staats-Zeitung* in 1869, Albert had become fluent in English by obsessively studying Dickens and Shakespeare and engaging anyone he could in conversation. Later, he set his sights on New York and on breaking out of German-language journalism. "Chicago has treated your dear Baruch very well indeed," he wrote to their mother, using the Jewish name meaning "blessed," "but he is going to try his fortune once more in New York. Don't be alarmed. *It is destiny.*"

Albert arrived in New York in 1871 with no prospect of work. He rented a dark room on Bleecker Street for $1 a week and sustained himself with apples that cost a penny apiece. He began his quest for a job by knocking on doors along Park Row, home to the nation's leading newspapers. James Gordon Bennett's *New York Herald*, Greeley's *New York Tribune*, and Charles Dana's *New York Sun*, along with less-known papers such as the *New York Times* and the *World*, all plied their trade within earshot of one another. It was America's Fleet Street.

Only twenty years old and with only brief experience at a German paper in Chicago, Albert audaciously applied to the *Sun*, the most successful newspaper in the nation. Established by Benjamin Henry Day in 1833, the *Sun* had launched a new style of journalism in antebellum America. Instead of reporting on international and national events of limited interest to the masses, it focused on city news, violence being its favorite topic, and presented this news in a highly readable, though sometimes flippant, style. In comparison with the stodgy journals favored by city's elite, the *Sun* was a blast of fresh air. It was compact, always four pages long, and, as the nation's first penny newspaper, it was cheap.

At the time Albert approached the *Sun*'s six-story building at Nassau and Frankfort streets, the paper was at the height of its fame and selling more than 100,000 copies a day. It had been bought three years earlier by Dana, who had been Greeley's managing editor at the *Tribune* and was considered a genius among editors. Building on the paper's original mission, Dana inspired and enforced a regime of tight, coherent, bright, lively writing intended to provide "a daily photograph of the whole world's doings in the most luminous and lively manner," as he put it in his first editorial. The paper was a pastiche or quilt of urban tales. It was an irresistible feast of information that won wide attention in an era of generally dull journalism.

Under Dana's regime, the paper prospered even more, and its circulation rose to new, unheard-of heights. Whereas Joseph could only dream of working for Dana, Albert was not intimidated. He walked up the flight of stairs to the *Sun*'s newsroom and spoke to the night editor. The editor asked Albert how long he had worked for a city newspaper.

"Only a short time, sir," Albert replied.

"That's rather vague," the editor said, adding, "You have a slight accent."

"I shall not have the accent long, sir. And I write better than I speak."

The editor decided to give Albert a test assignment, a rather difficult one intended to discourage the youth. Albert "made a Parisian bow and disappeared," said the editor. But to his surprise, Albert returned with the story and won himself a trial period on the staff of what many considered the best-written paper in town. In fact, soon after Albert landed this job, a letter appeared in the *Sun* from one reader in St. Louis. "I read *The Sun* regularly," Joseph Pulitzer wrote. "In my opinion it is the most piquant, entertaining, and, without exception, the best newspaper in the world."

Albert rose rapidly in the ranks of city reporters. His big break came when he was assigned to cover the Halstead murder in Newark, the city's first murder in four years. General O. S. "Pet" Halstead had been shot dead in the rooms of Mary S. Wilson, described by the *New York Times* as "a woman of the worst character." Apparently George "Charcoal" Botts, a charcoal peddler who paid for her lodgings and company, did not take kindly to the presence of Halstead in Wilson's bedroom. Albert wrote colorful accounts of the courtroom scenes and even obtained an interview with the condemned man a few days before his execution. "It was a kind of reporting that was new in those days, especially in Newark, and made a decided hit in this city," a writer for the *Newark Advertiser* recalled.

In February 1873, Albert moved to the *New York Herald*. Started by

James Gordon Bennett in 1835, the *Herald* was in a different class from the *Sun*. It had pioneered the use of many modern reporting methods, such as telegraphing news and dispatching an army of correspondents to the far-flung reaches of the globe. Its in-depth reporting on finances, politics, and society, mixed with a healthy dose of crime and scandal, gave the *Herald* a huge circulation. Its large circulation was accompanied by heft. Unlike the *Sun*, the *Herald* was taken seriously.

The fit was a good one for the tall, rosy-cheeked, twenty-one-year-old Albert, although his writing style was considerably different from that of his colleagues. "Everybody on the *Herald* admitted that Albert Pulitzer's style was rather florid," said an editor. "He was saturated with Dumas, Balzac, and other French writers and could 'pile on agony' in a court scene to an extent to which not another man about the place would have ventured."

After the brotherly reunion, Joseph sailed for Europe. It was the second time he had gone abroad since arriving in the United States in 1864. In Paris, he met up with Henry Watterson, one of the Quadrilateral editors who had worked behind the scenes of the Liberal Republican convention. The two spent a day wandering through Montmartre, a popular drinking and entertainment *quartier*. They arrived at a theater (a "hole-in-the-wall" said Watterson) where *Les Brigands* was playing. The three-act opera by Henri Meilhac and Ludovic Halévy, set to music by Jacques Offenbach, provided a theatrical revenge for the French, who had lost the Franco-Prussian war two years earlier. Parisians erupted in wild applause when the heroine, Joan the Maid, sent the beer-guzzling Teuton chieftain sprawling onto the sawdust-covered floor.

As Pulitzer and Watterson walked away from the entertainment, Pulitzer said, "We are brigands, differing according to individual character, to race and pursuit. If I were writing that play, I should represent the villain as a tyrannous city editor, meanly executing the orders of a niggardly proprietor."

"And the heroine?" asked Watterson.

"She should be a beautiful and rich young lady who buys the newspaper and marries the cub—rescuing genius from poverty and persecution," Pulitzer replied.

In the fall, Pulitzer drifted back to St. Louis. On November 13, 1873, his friends there put on a grand celebration to mark his return. The event, held at the Southern Hotel, was so elaborate that it included a printed menu "in Commemoration of his Evacuation of Europe and Re-Invasion of St. Louis" featuring a cartoon showing a towering, skinny Pulitzer holding a top hat and looking over a crowd that included recognizable caricatures of Grosvenor, Hutchins, Johnson, and other friends.

With plates filled with salmon, lobster, venison (with jelly sauce), croquettes of chicken à l'anglaise, beef, turkey, duck, and quail, the group toasted Pulitzer with Ike Cook's Imperial Champagne, bottled locally by the American Wine Company. Johnson led off the tributes and was followed by Hutchins and Grosvenor. Though he may have been without a defined place in the St. Louis establishment, this night Pulitzer was surrounded by the many successful friends he had made since he was a cub reporter on the *Westliche Post* six years earlier. Tellingly, neither Schurz nor Preetorius attended.

Pulitzer resumed his on-again, off-again study of law in the building where he had rented a room before his trip. He spent his time studying Johnson's law books and books lent to him by another lawyer friend, William Patrick, with whom he had served on the police board. The erstwhile philosopher Brockmeyer and another attorney took turns tutoring Pulitzer. "He was charmed with the excitement and horrors of the courtroom and determined to quit journalism and become a lawyer," recalled one friend. Johnson, however, was unconvinced of the value of Pulitzer's legal studies. "To tell the truth," he said, "I never thought him cut out for a lawyer. He was too easily agitated, too restless, of too nervous a temperament."

Pulitzer had not been long at the law books before he spotted a journalistic business opportunity. Although he had been enjoying a genteel life of travel, secure with a healthy bank balance, millions of others in 1873 faced a far different fate. On September 18, the collapse of the banking firm Jay Cooke and Company, which acted as the chief financing agent for the nation's railroads, started a severe national depression. Among the victims of the economic downturn was the *Staats-Zeitung*, a small German-language newspaper in St. Louis.

The paper was put on the auction block on January 6, 1874. No newspaper had changed hands in the city since 1872, and considering the economic conditions it was unlikely that there would be many, if any, bidders for this one. But Pulitzer saw value where others didn't. He won the auction, paying a modest sum, and announced that it was his intention to start a German evening paper. This was a smoke screen.

The *Staats-Zeitung* had too few subscribers to make it viable as a newspaper. But what the corporation owned caught Pulitzer's attention. Aside from presses and typefaces, the *Staats-Zeitung* was a member of the Associated Press (AP). The AP had been created as a news cooperative in 1849 by leading New York newspapers to share the high costs of news dispatches rapidly distributed by the recently invented telegraph. Because it restricted its news items to its members, a membership in AP was a valuable asset. Those that were not members were excluded from a vast source of national and international news.

Membership in AP gave a newspaper a tremendous competitive advantage, and midwestern publishers had quickly grasped the importance of this cooperative monopoly. In St. Louis, all the major German and English newspapers were members of the Western Associated Press except the *St. Louis Globe,* which had been started by Pulitzer's friends William McKee and Daniel Houser after they lost their share of ownership in the *Missouri Democrat* in a contentious court case. Their *St. Louis Globe* was hamstrung without membership in AP. But when they tried to buy a membership, the surviving owner of the *Democrat* vetoed their application.

Neither McKee nor Houser had thought to bid for the *Staats-Zeitung*. The mistake cost them. With the German newspaper's corporate papers in his hands, Pulitzer went to them with a proposal. If they bought the entire corporation, they would gain membership in AP. Pulitzer would then buy back the presses, type, and office equipment that they didn't need. The following morning, the *St. Louis Globe* was carrying AP stories. Its masthead explained how: McKee and Houser had purchased the *Staats-Zeitung* corporation and its AP membership. Then they had changed the language of the German paper to English and its name to the *St. Louis Globe*.

The owner of the *Democrat* was enraged by the legal chicanery. He called for an immediate meeting of the St. Louis board of the Western Associated Press. Gathering in the library of the *Missouri Republican*, the owners of the eight major newspapers listened as Houser and McKee explained the transaction and examined the documents showing their purchase of the *Staats-Zeitung* corporation and its assets.

Hutchins then offered a resolution recognizing the legitimacy of Pulitzer's sale. It prevailed.

The legal maneuvering over and the last of the insults lobbed, Pulitzer disposed of the *Staats-Zeitung* presses, typefaces, and office furniture. These were bought by a group of investors who made a short-lived attempt to publish a German newspaper. In his forty-eight-hour tenure as a newspaper publisher Pulitzer netted between $11,000 and $20,000. For the second time in a year, he had parlayed a newspaper investment into a considerable cash return. He now had between $30,000 and $40,000 in capital. This time, instead of looking for a safe place to stash his earnings, Pulitzer was ready to gamble.

In the spring of 1874, James B. Eads, one of the nation's best-known engineers, was putting the final touches on his massive stone-and-steel bridge across the Mississippi. When completed, it would be the longest arch bridge in the world and would connect St. Louis to eastern train traffic for the first time—to the horror of the Wiggins family, whose ferry had brought Pulitzer across the river nine years earlier.

Eads was now looking south to an even riskier engineering challenge. He had proposed to the federal government to deepen the key channel that led from the Mississippi River into the Gulf of Mexico. If he succeeded, the government would pay him between $1 million and $2 million. But under the terms, if Eads failed the entire cost of the attempt would rest with him.

Pulitzer confessed that he knew little about "jetties" but had great faith in Eads, whom he had known for five years. He took $20,000 of his capital and invested it in Eads's scheme, knowing, as Eads warned, that the "payments by the government depended wholly upon our securing deep water, and that if the jetties failed to secure the specified depths you would lose your investment."

After turning the money over to Eads, Pulitzer returned to his study of law and took on the air of a gentleman of leisure. He purchased a horse and every morning rode in the company of friends; he also took rooms on the elegant street where Schurz lived. Charles Balmer, a composer of some note who had conducted the music at President Lincoln's funeral in Springfield, Illinois, also lived on this street. He had five unmarried daughters, whom Pulitzer called the "five nightingales." The

Balmer house held a musical salon that Pulitzer, often in the company of the poet Eugene Field, would attend.

"The front door would open and in one of them would stride, like it or not orating from some Shakespeare play," recalled Lillian Balmer, one of the five nightingales. A feast of potato herring salad, sauerbraten, beer, and wine would be set out, and soon the room would be full of music and singing, with the father on the piano and one of the daughters on the violin. Pulitzer was intrigued by Bertha Balmer, who was the more stately and intellectual of the daughters and had a fine soprano voice. But even though they were frequently left alone, nothing came of his advances.

Financial freedom also permitted Pulitzer to indulge his passion for music, "the denial of which from mere poverty and the necessity of earning my livelihood was for many years the greatest of my regrets," Pulitzer said. For those with money, St. Louis offered concerts, operas, theater, and social galas. At a charity ball, the French artist Edward Jump captured Pulitzer dancing. Taller than all the other tailcoat-clad men, Pulitzer is dapper, with a new mustache and goatee, wearing pince-nez, and dancing with an unidentified woman only as tall as his shoulders. Pulitzer even joined a theater production at the Germania Club. He took the part of Mephistopheles, with a St. Louis belle, widely noted for her beauty, playing Faust's love Gretchen.

Finally feeling prepared, Pulitzer stood successfully for the bar in late June. With the coming of fall, Pulitzer's interest, as always, turned to the oncoming elections. By 1874, Liberal Republicans had begun a slow drift back into the ranks of the Republican Party after their ignominious defeat in 1872. For Democrats, such as Johnson, there was no shame in returning to the fold of the party, because the Liberal Republican movement had helped restore its health. But for Pulitzer, Schurz, Preetorius, and Grosvenor, no one was welcoming them back.

The treatment the bolters received from the Republican Party had been harsh. The Grant administration and party leaders did everything they could to drive the rebels out like an infestation. "Here at home," wrote an out-of-state reporter from St. Louis, "the Liberals have received no better treatment. They have been constantly insulted, vilified and persecuted by the Republican leaders during the past four years and will never be forgiven."

A decision by the Missouri Grange to enter politics created an opportunity for Liberals to forestall their day of reckoning. Originally a social and educational organization for farmers, the National Grange jumped into electoral politics to fight exorbitant railroad freight rates. In July 1874, the Missouri Grange issued a call for a convention to meet in Jefferson City to create a People's Party that would be above partisan bickering. Newspapers, particularly Republican ones, applauded the idea, believing it might reunite the party under a new umbrella and provide the strength to beat the Democrats.

The idea was quickly embraced by party leaders, who announced that there would be no Republican convention that year. Schurz and Grosvenor jumped at the prospect of repeating their success of 1870 and restarting the reform movement under a new banner. Pulitzer followed along. After all, Schurz was his former mentor and Grosvenor his political partner, the other half of the "political firm of Bill and Joe."

On September 2, 1874, the new party met in Jefferson City to select its candidates. For governor, the party members settled on William Gentry, a prosperous, affable farmer who had no political experience and was entirely clueless regarding the major reform issues. The choice was an echo of the Cincinnati convention of 1872. The ebullient gathering, clamoring for reform, selected a candidate who pleased few of the ardent reformers. Schurz and Grosvenor supported the convention's choice. Pulitzer couldn't. He renounced the selection and abandoned the movement. In an interview in the *St. Louis Globe*, Pulitzer proclaimed his conversion. He repudiated his mentor and ended the political partnership on which he had risen to the top of a national movement. "The firm of Bill and Joe did not last long," said the *Globe*, "but it was a grand firm while it lasted."

Pulitzer charged that the newspaper's interview with him was fraudulent yet he did not dispute its contents. The next day he explained his conversion in a long article in the *Missouri Republican*. Pulitzer said he did not question the honesty of "Farmer Gentry"; nor did he impugn his friends' participation in the convention. But neither Gentry's honesty nor the good intentions of his fellow reformists could "reconcile me to so palpable a result of politics without principle."

The concept of politics *with* principle might seem oxymoronic, given the nature of politics at the time, but Pulitzer was sincere. Unlike those who had risen through ward politics in the chaos of competing parties, interests, and causes, Pulitzer had entered politics with an inordinate amount of idealism. As a young newcomer he had been exhilarated by Schurz's rebellion against corruption. Whereas his compatriots now sought the spoils of electoral victory, Pulitzer sought principle; where they saw compromise, he saw a betrayal of promise.

For Pulitzer, the convention created not a party of reform, but rather a Trojan horse carrying Grant's Republicans into power. "To men of thought and principle, both platform and ticket are deaf and dumb," Pulitzer said. "Selecting candidates upon the whole very much inferior to those of the Democracy, the convention remained still further behind by failing to protest against the real causes of the prostrate condition of the country—the corruption, the lawlessness, the usurpation and profligacy of the national administration."

Drawn into civic life for idealistic reasons, Pulitzer believed that such compromises were like lying down with the devil. His belief in democracy was a civic religion, and reform was its holiest tenet. For Schurz and Grosvenor, the good fight had been waged and lost, as often happened in politics. Rejoining the party ranks was coming home for these two, who had spent all their political lives as Republicans. "I am a Liberal Republican, and nothing else," said Grosvenor in 1873. "Because that is true, I am a Republican whenever the old issues are brought up, and the choice is between the Republican and the Democratic parties. 'Do the duty that lies nearest thee,' says Goethe."

But Pulitzer had none of those allegiances and was unwilling to beg forgiveness from leaders whom he perceived as having defiled democracy's temple. He was now a Democrat.

The Missouri Democratic Party embraced its new member. In October, Pulitzer was dispatched on a statewide canvass for the Democratic ticket, beginning in Sedalia, a new but rapidly growing town on the Missouri Pacific rail line in the western part of the state. The town's paper, stalwartly Democratic, hailed his conversion and promoted him as a new star in the party. "Wherever Mr. Pulitzer speaks," it reported, "the people crowd to hear him, and those who hear him become convinced of the truth he so eloquently utters."

In his speech, which lasted close to an hour, Pulitzer explained his conversion. "The war with bullets was over. But it left us a legacy, a war with ballots," Pulitzer began. "The enemies of the country are no longer in the South. They are in Washington." In this struggle, Pulitzer said, he was volunteering to fight "as the same humble private as which in the last war I stood on the side of the Union," thereby answering the obligatory question of whose side one had favored, still a hurdle for many aspiring Democratic politicians.

The enemy in this new conflict is "the great army of office-holders, carpet-baggers, monopolists, protectionists and all those selfish people interested naturally in alliance with the 'powers that be,'" Pulitzer told the crowd at Sedalia. Across the nation they are easy to identify because they run under the Republican banner, but not so in Missouri, where reform has had the upper hand and the Republicans have gone into hiding, he said. "And so in this State alone do we enjoy the spectacle of seeing the Grant party turn with band and baggage, postmaster, gaugers, assessors, disfranchisers, colored brothers and all, into 'people,' and hear how lustily they cry for reform! Reform!"

Like the James boys, highway robbers who wore masks, the People's Party was the Republican Party in disguise, Pulitzer said. To prove his point, he exhaustively compared the new party's platform with that of previous Republican Party platforms. "They say it is a party of reform, and we see as the most officious reformers, the most notorious postmasters, Federal office holders and corrupt demagogues in the state." Pulitzer lumped both Schurz and Grosvenor, mentioning them by name, in with the forces of Grant and corruption, though he studiously avoided accusing either one directly of wrongdoing.

As at a revival, Pulitzer washed himself of the sin of having been a Republican. "I confess that coming fresh from the army not much more than a boy, for a very short time, I have myself belonged to the party of proscription." But his sin, he insisted, was not as great as that of the party, because when he served in the legislature he had campaigned for elimination of the disenfranchisement provisions. Opponents claimed that this action would drive out Union men and re-enslave the Negroes or, worse, massacre them. "Well, these rebels have now voted for four years, and show me the first Union man who has been disturbed, show me one Negro who has been molested on account of his Union sentiments! The only Negro who has been molested that I know of in the whole state was a fellow in St. Louis County who ravished a poor girl. And he was only lynched. Not by rebels, however, but by honest Germans and strong Union men."

Not an eyebrow would have been raised at Pulitzer's approbation of a lynching. Between 50 and 100 lynchings took place each year, and almost always the victims were blacks charged with some alleged sexual crime for which there was little or no evidence. Only a few Americans, such as Ida B. Wells, spoke out against the horror. The government's effort to stop this domestic terrorism consisted solely of President Grant's Civil Rights Act of 1871, which strengthened the federal government's hand against the Ku Klux Klan. Pulitzer's animosity to Grant, fueled by his experiences with Schurz, Grosvenor, and Brown, blinded him to the virtues of that law.

Like many whites, Pulitzer was indifferent to the plight of black Americans. There was little in his own experience to relate to their oppression. As a Jew in Hungary, he had experienced hardly any discrimination. He had joined the Civil War late, had remained cocooned in a platoon of non-English-speaking recruits, and was not exposed to the abolitionists' antebellum propaganda or to their triumphant rhetoric at the conclusion of the war. The worst injustice he had endured as a civilian was being the butt of anti-Semitic humor, but it had not thwarted his efforts at landing a job, finding housing, or making friends.

After Sedalia, it was on to Versailles, Warrensburg, and Knob Noster. A Republican newspaper reporter was on hand to chronicle Pulitzer's visit to the small town of Knob Noster. Casting Pulitzer as a pretentious Bourbon Democrat aghast at the provincialism of rural Missouri, the reporter spun a humorous, sarcastic tale. Like his cartoonist brethren, the reporter highlighted Pulitzer's nose from the start, describing Pulitzer's arrival at the train station and his discovery that the town had no hotels. "The look of surprise and indignation that overspread his nasal protuberance was fearful to contemplate," wrote the reporter.

The highlighting of Pulitzer's nose—three times in the article—was more than a humorous jab to score partisan points. Like the caricatures by Pulitzer's friend Keppler, these depictions were a minimally disguised way to let readers know that the subject was Jewish. Just as readers of *Tom Sawyer* knew when Jim said, "She tole me to go an' git dis water," that the speaker was black, newspaper readers knew that a person with a "nasal protuberance" was a Hebrew.

The nose became a common symbol because many of the traditional markers that societies favored to distinguish Jews had fallen into disuse by the late nineteenth century. For instance, the notion that Jews could be distinguished by their "swarthy skin" had gone by the wayside when it had become widely accepted that color—with the obvious exception of "coloreds"—could be modified over time by migration and other factors. Instead, an emerging generation of social scientists obsessed with racial classification turned to the "Jew nose." They studied the "nostrility" of the Jew and connected the characteristics of the "Jewish, or Hawknose" with their view of Jews as shrewd and capable of turning an insight into profit. They determined that the "Jew nose" became even more evident in the children of mixed marriages. Thus even a Jew who gave up his or her cultural accouterments retained a marker still visible a generation later.

From Knob Noster, Pulitzer turned back toward St. Louis. One of the last stops of the speech-a-day statewide tour was in Boonville. The visit offered a wonderful window into the era's partisan press. The *Boonville Advertiser*, the Democratic paper, referred to Pulitzer as "the eloquent German orator" and told readers he had "delivered an able and logical speech [and] was listened to with marked attention." The Republican *Boonville Weekly Eagle* saw things differently: "The general impression was that he had more nose than eloquence. The fact was at once palpable, but we did not like to *seize it*," said the paper, adding italics for its readers insufficiently witty to pick up on the editor's humor.

Pulitzer's speeches were coherent, well organized, carefully composed, and weighty. It had been only a decade since his arrival in the United States as a teenager unable to speak more than a word or two of English. Now twenty-seven years old and a U.S. citizen, Pulitzer was using his newly acquired tongue with enough skill to earn praise from his supporters and to draw derision from his detractors. He still had an accent, but he was no longer simply a German orator.

A few weeks after the tour, Pulitzer's gubernatorial candidate was swept into office. Had Pulitzer stood for office as a Democrat, he might have also returned to the state legislature. As it was, the election offered him a chance to relaunch his political career. By a very narrow margin (283 votes out of 222,315), voters called for a constitutional convention. Pulitzer threw his hat into the ring and joined the campaign for the sixty-eight delegate seats. On January 26, 1875, his friends James Broadhead the lawyer and Henry Brockmeyer the philosopher were among those selected by the voters. And, to Pulitzer's joy, the voters had picked him as well. His old paper, the *Westliche Post,* angry at his conversion to the Democracy, greeted his election with derision. It said Pulitzer was as ill-suited to draft a constitution as a hedgehog was to shave one's face.

Chapter Nine

FOUNDING FATHER

◆

On the evening of February 21, 1875, Pulitzer and Joseph McCullagh, of the *St. Louis Globe*, caught up with A. C. Hesing, the publisher of *Illinois Staats-Zeitung* in a hall of the elegant Southern Hotel of St. Louis, where Pulitzer now lodged. The publisher, a Republican leader of such power in Chicago that he was called "Boss Hesing," was the most sought-after man that night, according to McCullagh. "As he stood, sat or walked in the corridors of the Southern, last night, there was no minute when he was not either talking or listening to some party or other, anxious to look at him, stand by his side and hear him talk."

McCullagh wanted to interview Hesing for an article. Pulitzer had a more pressing personal need. Although they were members of opposing parties, Pulitzer wanted Hesing's take on the changing political landscape. It had been only a few months since Pulitzer had converted to the Democratic Party, and he was still seeking confirmation that he had made the right decision. He got it from Hesing.

"Everything is getting more and more Democratic day by day," Hesing said.

What will happen to those Republicans who supported Greeley and Brown in 1872? McCullagh asked.

"Probably fuse with the true Democratic Party," Hesing said. "I know they will in my state, and in many others. There's no doubt but that they are thoroughly and eternally disgusted with the present Radical Administration."

"And Carl Schurz?"

"Well, I tell you what I think," said Hesing, who was not only a fellow Republican but a German like Schurz. "I don't think so very much of Schurz either as a journalist or politician."

Hesing's words were comforting. Pulitzer had been wise to throw his lot in with Democrats and had also made a timely end to his allegiance with his mentor Schurz. For their part, Democrats were thrilled to have Pulitzer. He had toiled in their successful effort to retain the governor's mansion, and they worked to make him feel welcome.

With his political fortunes on the rise, Pulitzer's fiscal affairs also took a turn upward. James Eads's scheme for dredging the Mississippi delta, in which Pulitzer had invested $20,000, was a triumph. The payoff gave Pulitzer enough money to live for a number of years. He could concentrate on politics without any concern for finding work. Pulitzer expressed his gratitude to Eads by joining dozens of other prominent St. Louisans in the parlor (No. 5) of the Southern Hotel to plan a banquet in Eads's honor. The first to speak was Pulitzer himself. "Twenty years from now," he said, "we will have Eads Places, Eads Avenues, and, I hope, Eads monuments."

Leaving the committee of citizens to do its work, Pulitzer headed east a few days later on the first of what would be half a dozen trips to New York that year. He had in mind breaking into journalism in New York. But, unlike his brother Albert, he didn't want to work for someone else's paper; he wanted to use his capital to acquire his own. He set his eyes on the *Belletristisches Journal*, a German weekly run by Rudolph Lexow, but the two men could not come to terms.

On this trip, as well as on subsequent visits to New York in the 1870s, Pulitzer favored the Fifth Avenue Hotel between West Twenty-Third and West Twenty-Fourth streets. Completed in 1858, the six-story, marble-fronted hotel was the first to have a "vertical railroad"—or what would later be called an elevator. It became very popular after the Civil War for its luxurious rooms, each with fireplaces and private bathrooms. Deep-pile carpets with the sultry smells of anthracite and coffee in its immense public rooms, the hotel was favored for party conferences by Republicans, including Liberal Republicans when their stock was rising.

By the 1870s, however, newer hotels eclipsed the Fifth Avenue. "The hotel, for all its sober state, was no longer fashionable," lamented

Edith Wharton in her novella *New Year's Day*. "No one, in my memory, had ever known anyone who went there; it was frequented by 'politicians' and 'Westerners,' two classes of citizens whom my mother's intonation always seemed to deprive of their vote by ranking them with illiterates and criminals."

At the Fifth Avenue Hotel one day in March, Pulitzer came across a newspaper from St. Louis. Eager to catch up on news from his city, he dived into the issue. Suddenly he spotted his name, in connection with a prominent trial. Several years before, in 1872, a group of businessmen in St. Louis had invested money to rejuvenate the aging Varieties Theater. Pulitzer's friend Hutchins had sunk a considerable sum into the project. It soon failed, but during the ensuing fiscal and legal chaos, Hutchins expanded his investment by buying out other members' shares, at a steep discount. His plan was to force a bankruptcy sale of the theater and its fixtures and then make a claim to the proceeds as a creditor. But other creditors and investors had outmaneuvered Hutchins. As a last resort, he sued.

Pulitzer had not been involved in any part of the business and was not accused of any wrongdoing. Yet he was swept up into the scandal because of his friendship with Hutchins. The defendants wanted to put Pulitzer on the stand because they believed he would contradict Hutchins's claims and corroborate testimony helpful to them.

Two of the city's most notorious and colorful attorneys, Frank J. Bowman and Britton A. Hill, who had helped Pulitzer's defense in the shooting case four years earlier, represented the defense. The legal duo made a most unlikely pairing. Bowman was a tiny man, said to weigh only 125 pounds. He looked even more minuscule next to the 300-pound Hill. But what he lacked in size, Bowman, nicknamed the "Machiavelli of the St. Louis Bar," made up for in bulldog-like tenacity. He was widely feared by attorneys and businessmen because he had little patience for legal ethics and took his legal battles outside the court, on more than one occasion, by challenging his opponent to a duel.

The legal machinations of the case were so complicated that only the most sophisticated lawyers could understand the particulars. But that didn't matter. With so many prominent St. Louisans ensnared, the trial had become the city's most popular soap opera in the spring of 1875.

The press suggested that Pulitzer was absent—hiding, in fact—in order to help his friend Hutchins.

* * *

After setting down the newspaper at his New York hotel, Pulitzer telegraphed the judge in the case. "Never heard anything of the case until just now, and stand ready to take the next train and leave for home and testify," Pulitzer wired. "Please telegraph immediately whether there will be time enough." No reply came, but Pulitzer decided to return anyway. He boarded a train bound for St. Louis the next night, reaching the city on March 20, 1875.

An enterprising reporter for the *Missouri Republican* got word that Pulitzer was back in town and sought him out. He first asked for Pulitzer at the Southern Hotel. "No, sah, not in," said the clerk. Next he tried the *Westliche Post*. A young reporter assured him not only that was Pulitzer not there but that he rarely set foot in the building. Deterred, the reporter retreated to his office. A few minutes before midnight, a messenger delivered a letter from Pulitzer. It was addressed to the "Press of St. Louis."

"Just returning from New York," wrote Pulitzer, "I am both amused and amazed by the animadversions on the part of the generous and unbiased press of St. Louis to connect my purely accidental absence from the city with a pending suit of a scandalous nature." The *Missouri Republican*, which was used to Pulitzer's lack of honesty with the press, published his comments but added that they "must be taken as 'sarkasm'" and deemed unbelievable "the calm and lofty manner in which he remarks that the opera-house suit was too infinitesimal in proportions to have been heard of by him."

The paper was correct. In both his telegram to the judge and his letter to the press, Pulitzer was playing fast and loose with the facts. He had been in St. Louis on March 9, and as an avid newspaper reader, he knew that Hutchins's widely publicized trial was opening on March 8.

When the trial convened for its final day on March 23, visitors to the courthouse might have thought they had taken a wrong turn and entered the city's playhouse. That was certainly the image on the mind of the reporter from the *Missouri Republican*. "A good play of any kind is sure to draw, and Mr. Bowman has put on the stage the best play of the season," he wrote. "The plot of the piece is intricate, the positions startling, and the players all stars. It is no wonder therefore that the play has drawn full houses for over two weeks."

The seats in the courtroom were all filled an hour before the curtain was to rise on the last act, and still spectators streamed in. Former mayors, legislators, businessmen, and even judges from other courts had come to watch. Pulitzer knew most of the audience. Among others, there were James Broadhead and Lewis Gottschalk, fellow delegates to the coming constitutional convention; and Colonel Alonzo Slayback, a prominent Democratic attorney with whom Pulitzer had worked in the campaign the previous year.

A few minutes before ten o'clock, Bowman made his appearance, and at ten sharp the judge entered. Pulitzer immediately pressed to the front of the courtroom and announced his presence. He said he had learned through the papers that he had been subpoenaed and was prepared to give his testimony.

"Not subpoenaed, Mr. Pulitzer," replied the judge. "Subpoenas were issued for you, but returned 'not found.'"

"It has been intimated that I went away to avoid being summoned," Pulitzer continued, undeterred. "Now, your honor, I am perfectly willing to tell anything I know about the matter."

The judge was unmoved. He told Pulitzer the time for testimony had passed and the case was closed. "You are a member of the bar, and, of course, understand that no further testimony can be introduced after the case is closed."

Pulitzer, however, would not desist. "May it please the court," he said, "I have seen in the papers, flings and innuendoes, and insinuations calculated to throw discredit upon me, and I would like the opportunity to make a statement in my own defense."

"You are not upon trial," interrupted the judge.

"All I ask is simple justice, and this is a court of justice."

"Not for everybody," quipped the judge, causing laughter and Pulitzer's retreat. Bowman then rose and began his two-hour summation. That afternoon the jury rewarded the loquacious attorney and returned a verdict in favor of the defense. Bowman had triumphed and Hutchins was out of his money.

Hard feelings put aside, many of the same men who had battled in the courtroom gathered the following night for the planned celebration of James Eads at the Southern Hotel. Dining on Solid Rock Oysters, Mock Turtle Soup, Boiled California Salmon with Anchovy Sauce, mutton, beef, turkey, chicken, venison, and sweetbreads, and washing them down with Château Margaux and Krug champagne, the men praised the past and future achievements of their city's famous bridge builder, and Pulitzer celebrated his financial windfall from his association with Eads.

In early May 1875, Pulitzer was riding the train to Jefferson City. As he had done five years earlier, he was traveling to the capital as an elected official. This time he was on his way to join sixty-seven other delegates to the constitutional convention in the chambers of the Missouri house of representatives at the capitol. The lobby was filled with spectators eager to see the men who had the task of coming up with a new constitution. The delegates were a fairly homogeneous group; all male, as women did not yet have the right to vote; wealthy, since only a few could afford to spend several weeks away from work; and mostly lawyers. Politically, they represented a backlash against Radical rule. Democrats had complete control of the proceedings. In fact, the convention was almost a Confederate reunion, with more than half of the delegates having served in the Confederacy or having been sympathetic to the cause.

At age twenty-eight, Pulitzer was by far the youngest of the delegates—in fact, about twenty years younger than the average. He certainly stood out. He was the only one to have his photograph taken with a hat on, cocked ever so slightly to his right. It was a slouch hat, a style introduced to the United States by the revolutionary leader Lajos Kossuth when he fled Hungary. Along with this hat Pulitzer wore a pince-nez, a mustache, a narrow pointed goatee trimmed in a style known as a Napoleon III, and a royale (a tuft of hair under the lower lip)—if he was seeking to be noticed, he succeeded.

Pulitzer had done his research, and he exuded confidence. His tenure as a reporter and a lawmaker had provided him with considerable parliamentary skills, which he was not reluctant to wield. But his sharp tongue, which had aroused Augustine's anger in 1870, was also soon heard. This time he took aim at Lewis Gottschalk, a fellow delegate from St. Louis. As the convention got under way, Gottschalk asked that the secretary of state be directed to report to the convention on rumors appearing in the press about supplementary election returns, which, if counted, would reverse the election results calling for the convention. "I believe," Pulitzer said, "it will be self-evident that the resolution is an insult to the intelligence of this Convention, which is offered by my very learned and honored colleague; and it is certainly an insult to his own intelligence."

The war of words rapidly escalated. Gottschalk wanted the new constitution to include an acknowledgment that the state of Missouri and its people were part of the American nation. By themselves the words were innocuous, but coming a decade after the end of the Civil War, they were an attack on the delegates' loyalty to the Union, and they struck a nerve with Pulitzer.

"Well, Mr. Chairman, I stand here as an American representative, and as an American," said Pulitzer as he took the floor. "You might as well ask a child to state in writing that he or she is the off-spring of the parent," he continued. "I ask further, Mr. Chairman, I ask the Convention upon what ground, upon what logic other than that of fear, than that of catering to an extravagant and extreme partisan spirit which for a selfish and cowardly purpose . . ."

"Mr. Chairman," interrupted Gottschalk. "I call the gentleman to order."

"I expected it," said Pulitzer, to the laughter of the delegates.

"I undertake to say that this language is unparliamentary," said Gottschalk, at which point the chairman joined in. "Mr. Pulitzer will come to order," he said.

"Well, the truth is never unparliamentary," rejoined Pulitzer, again eliciting a wave of laughter.

"The Gentleman will confine himself to the proposition before the Committee," ordered the chairman, trying to bring an end to the dispute, which was threatening to disrupt the work of the delegates. Pulitzer prevailed and the amendment died. Despite the impression of acrimony between Gottschalk and his impertinent young sparring partner, the two men remained good friends.

As the summer heat settled down on Jefferson City, the delegates worked day in and day out on crafting a new, acceptable constitution. They began their day at eight in the morning and sat until six-thirty in the evening. After a break for dinner, they met in committees, often until ten or eleven at night. "Really it is the hardest working body I ever saw," one of Pulitzer's friends wrote home.

Pulitzer's style as a delegate was unchanged from when he had been a legislator. He was uninterested in the structure and form of the proposed state government. Instead he stuck to his far more parochial aim of freeing St. Louis, the city, from county rule and from state interference. The rural delegates resented St. Louis's insistence on unique consideration in the constitution. But Pulitzer and his old friend Brockmeyer argued that the city deserved preferential treatment because it held a quarter of the state's population and provided half of the state's revenue. A special committee was created to consider St. Louis's demands.

Behind closed doors, the committee struggled to produce a consensus that could win the delegates' support. Pulitzer was excluded from its work. Instead, he resorted to being a gadfly on the floor, never letting the issue rest. For instance, when other delegates worried about setting an unusual and difficult precedent by caving in to the city's demands, Pulitzer applied his rhetorical weapon of choice—sarcasm. Precedent, he said, is "the feeble expression of a feeble mind, lacking the inherent ability to express original views that is compelled to seek refuge in a still feebler vestige of ancient, decayed precedents."

In the end the committee produced a compromise that would allow St. Louis to separate from county jurisdiction, permanently delineate its city limits, and create its own autonomous governing institutions. The following year, the "great divorce" was mediated by the city and county governments. The city, as Pulitzer and other reformers had hoped, gained independence. St. Louis became the first American city to enact a home rule charter, and the achievement was widely hailed as the nation began to look for innovative ways to govern its burgeoning metropolises. But Pulitzer and other advocates did not foresee that their well-intentioned remedy would eventually cripple St. Louis. Barred from annexing land and facing severe constitutional restrictions on raising taxes, the city would, over time, become impoverished, deserted by its wealthier citizens, and transformed into a destitute urban core surrounded by a wealthy county.

As the convention neared its end, a short-lived debate arose on freedom of the press. A delegate wanted to expand the legal safeguards for newspapers against libel suits. He modeled his amendment on an existing clause in Pennsylvania's recently adopted constitution. Under its provisions, both public and private individuals would have to convince a jury that the offending article had been maliciously or negligently published.

Pulitzer was only one of three delegates to speak about the proposal. Years before he would become a publisher besieged with libel suits, he delivered his earliest public view on freedom of the press. Pulitzer said that he, like the author of the amendment, had worked in newspapers. "I, sir, stand with a guilty conscience ready to admit that the law under which I contributed some little activity perhaps in that branch of the profession should in my opinion be rather strengthened than weakened. I am sorry to say it, ready to confess that perhaps I have been myself guilty of slandering and libeling persons, not maliciously, certainly not."

Under the proposed plan, he said, it would be impossible to convict any proprietor of a newspaper, because proprietors so rarely have anything to do with the content of newspapers. Rather, a newspaper is assembled by editors and reporters. "In other words those who own newspapers scarcely ever make them." For evidence he pointed to the newspapers of St. Louis. "The leading papers in that city today are run and conducted by persons who do not own them and . . . the persons who do own them are scarcely fit to write the smallest and most unimportant part of the paper."

The law, Pulitzer claimed, needed no alteration, and newspapers required no additional constitutional protections. "The power of the press, Mr. President, is sufficiently large," Pulitzer said. "They have prospered and grown powerful under the very laws which the gentleman from Boone now charges with being dangerous and working great injustice."

Then, in a singular moment, Pulitzer turned to confession. He told his fellow delegates that he had been part of three or four libel suits while at the *Westliche Post*. "I do not know of a single instance where injustice was done to the press and I could mention several instances to the contrary. Perhaps, if I have at this moment impressed any of my friends who have no occasion to become familiar with the practical workings of the newspaper fraternity, I shall consider it in the nature of an atonement for many acts heretofore committed for which I am sorry." Years later, when his enemies sought to rein in Pulitzer's power as a newspaper publisher, no one thought to consult the convention transcript.

In July the convention ended, its work complete. Pulitzer returned to a St. Louis that seemed increasingly empty. He was unwelcome at the *Westliche Post* and in the homes of Schurz and Preetorius. Equally discouraging, many of his best friends were moving east to Washington and New York. Pulitzer was once again at a crossroads. Professionally, it was a stretch for him to consider himself a lawyer, as he had no established practice. Nor could he call himself a journalist, as he had no permanent affiliation to any newspaper. His small political revival as a member of the constitutional convention was at an end and there were no other such opportunities on the horizon. Financially, he had a comfortable place in his adopted country, but he remained socially adrift and professionally rudderless.

In the fall of 1875, Pulitzer retreated to a quiet life in St. Louis. He handled a few minor legal chores and took on some occasional newspaper work for Hutchins at the *St. Louis Times*. After years that had promised success in journalism and politics, Pulitzer entered a barren stretch, compounding his aimlessness. He was twenty-eight years old. He had no definite profession, and not even a home other than a room at the Southern Hotel.

A sense of failure hung over him. Even his characteristic combativeness was subdued. He declined, for instance, to enter a squabble involving Schurz, instead writing to his friend Hermann Raster, editor of the *Illinois Staats-Zeitung* in Chicago, "I naturally would *prefer* not to be pulled into the controversy, since I do not have a newspaper at my disposal."

The only good news on the horizon was that Pulitzer and his Liberal Republican friends had been the cause of the newest scandal facing the Grant administration. It was sweet revenge. The public was learning that during the Missouri Republican insurgency, Grant had dispatched his supervisor general of internal revenue to St. Louis to fight the rebellion. To fund his counterinsurgency efforts, the supervisor and others recruited distillers, storekeepers, and revenue agents and others into a conspiracy to sell more whiskey than was reported, thereby defrauding the government of thousands of dollars of taxes. The money of the "Whiskey Ring" then was redirected to newspapers that favored their cause and also served to create financial incentives for those newspapers that still remained on the fence.

In May, when Pulitzer had been in Jefferson City working on the new constitution, federal agents apprehended the swindlers. The five ringleaders included William McKee, formerly of the *Democrat* but now the proprietor of the *St. Louis Globe*. Suddenly, it became clear to Pulitzer and others why McKee had fired Grosvenor during the 1872 election and returned to the ranks of Grant's supporters.

In December a grand jury in St. Louis indicted General Orville E. Babcock, Grant's private secretary, on a charge of conspiracy to defraud the U.S. Treasury. Babcock's trial was set for February 7, 1876, and wags in the local press promised that the event would be as important as the trial of Aaron Burr or the impeachment of President Johnson. Reporters came from all parts of the nation. Among them was Albert Pulitzer.

No longer a teenage waif camping in Joseph's room at the boarding-house, Albert returned to St. Louis for the trial as a tall, slender, dapper, twenty-five-year-old correspondent for the *New York Herald*. His softly spoken English betrayed only the slightest accent. His ascendency to the *New York Herald* had completed Albert's professional metamorpho-sis and also brought a dramatic change in his personal life.

During his first year at the paper he was sent to the Grand Central Hotel, then the largest hotel in the country, to follow up on a story of an Englishwoman who, even in the company of a chaperone, had been de-frauded of all her money upon arriving in New York. Albert located the victim and discovered that she was young, attractive, and unattached. His interview for the paper turned into a courtship and on June 15, 1873, Fanny Barnard and Albert Pulitzer were married.

At the *Herald,* Albert won a reputation for his interviews. "Cool, genial, winning, indefatigable, incapable of being rebuffed, he was the champion interviewer of his paper," said one noted British journalist and politician. "No one could hold a candle to him." He was certainly persistent in pur-suit of his quarries. Once he obtained an interview with the embattled Mayor Oakey Hall, caught up in the Tweed scandal, by shouting ques-tions through the keyhole of a bathroom where the mayor was hiding.

Joseph joined Albert at Babcock's trial. Hutchins had assigned Joseph to cover the event for his *St. Louis Times,* a minor paper in compari-son with Albert's. A small journalistic triumph, though, helped Joseph overcome the discomfort of being overshadowed by his younger brother. About a week before the trial got under way, the attorney general sent a letter to prosecutors prohibiting any plea bargaining. The letter ostensi-bly reflected the "no deal" policy that the president had proclaimed in an effort to seem supportive of a vigorous criminal investigation. However, the real effect of the letter, as any lawyer knew, would be to scare off witnesses and curtail a prosecutor's best means of persuading guilty par-ties to testify against higher-ups.

When he received his letter, U.S. District Attorney David P. Dyer in St. Louis immediately understood what its publication could do to his case. He sealed it up in another envelope and put it away. "I did not think it prudent at the time to publish the letter or let any one have it; there was no man in my office, not even my assistants, that saw it," Dyer said.

A few days later, Joseph came to the U.S. attorney's office and handed Dyer a clipping from the *Illinois Staats-Zeitung*. Laughing, Pulitzer said, "I wish you would read this slip." Dyer took the sheet from Pulitzer, gazed at it for a moment, and replied that, as he could not read German, the only word he recognized was the name of the attorney general.

"Now," Pulitzer said, "I want to read you the translation I have made of that letter and I want to know whether you have such a letter in your possession." Pulitzer then read his English translation. Dyer confirmed that, indeed, he had a letter that sounded very much like the one Pulitzer had just read.

"Won't you permit me to examine your letter and compare it with my translation, to see whether the translation is correct?" asked Pulitzer.

"No," Dyer said, "you cannot see any official letter in my office."

"I will publish the letter anyhow tomorrow morning, whether you give it to me or not, and if not correct, you will have to take it to be correct."

"You can publish what you please from other papers, but you cannot get my letters."

Pulitzer returned to the *St. Louis Times* office. The next morning the paper published the letter. A furious Dyer, in the company of James Broadhead, who after serving in the convention with Pulitzer was now working as an assistant U.S. attorney, arrived at the office. They went immediately to see Hutchins and Pulitzer. Dyer told Hutchins he had made a mistake in publishing the letter if he really wanted to help convict the ring's members. Its publication was crippling the prosecution. His remarks were greeted by laughter by Hutchins and Pulitzer, but as a small concession, the *Times* ran an item the next day stating that Dyer was not the source of the leaked letter.

In April, Pulitzer's restlessness prevailed. Even with the 1876 nominating season approaching, Pulitzer left for New York and took a ship bound for Europe. He went first to Paris, armed with a letter of introduction from former senator John Henderson of Missouri to Elihu Washburne, the American minister to France. Henderson detailed the political service of "my young friend" and asked that he be extended official courtesies. Washburne complied and even offered to supply Pulitzer with theater or opera tickets. Pulitzer, however, cut short his stay in Paris without availing himself of Washburne's cultural amenities.

In Germany, Pulitzer took in a political meeting. Unlike the boisterous affairs he had become used to in the United States, the German gathering was orderly and businesslike. Its conclusion was also a shock for an American. "Suddenly a hitherto silent and quiet man arose upon the platform and walked up to the chairman," Pulitzer said. The chairman then interrupted the speaker and the unknown man replaced him at the podium. He revealed that he was an officer of the law and declared that the meeting was over because the speaker had violated the law by criticizing the cabinet. "The chairman muttered some words of protest," Pulitzer said, there "were some indignant expressions in the audience, but the interrupted speaker spoke no more, and in a very few moments the meeting was actually dissolved."

As much as Europe captivated Pulitzer, the calendar inexorably drew him back to the United States. It was an election year—a presidential one. Ever since witnessing Lincoln's reelection while in the Union army, Pulitzer regarded elections as the high holy days of democracy. They couldn't be missed.

Chapter Ten

FRAUD AND HIS
FRAUDULENCY

◆

The presidential campaign was under way by the time Pulitzer
boarded the Cunard steamship *Bothnia* in Liverpool on July 15,
1876. Disembarking in New York eleven days later, he repaired to the
Fifth Avenue Hotel, where, in possession of New York newspapers, he
caught up on the political news, having survived for three months on the
incomplete and dated dispatches that reached Europe.

By his absence, Pulitzer had passed up a chance to attend the Demo-
cratic national convention, which had concluded the previous month in
St. Louis. His friends and political partners hadn't missed it. Hutchins
and Slayback were delegates from Missouri, and Watterson was a del-
egate from Kentucky. In fact, Watterson had brought the hall to its feet
when he urged delegates—descendants of Jackson, as he called them—
"to wrest the government . . . from the clutches of rings and robbers."
The Democrats were convinced they had, at long last, picked a winner
in selecting as their candidate Governor Samuel J. Tilden of New York,
who prosecuted Boss Tweed. If corruption was the issue, no better white
knight could be found.

Pulitzer was elated with the choice and immediately put himself at
the service of the party. While his friends were asked to work solely in
their own political backyards, Pulitzer was invited to engage the enemy
on the important battleground of Ohio and Indiana. Because they held
their state government elections in October, the two states were con-
sidered bellwethers, exercising extraordinary influence on November's

federal elections. Pulitzer's status as a former Republican, widely known among German voters, made him useful in reaching voters in the two states, each of which had a large German population.

In early September, Pulitzer made a jubilant return to Indianapolis, where he had campaigned in vain for Greeley four years earlier. This time he was convinced that he was traveling on behalf of a winning ticket. The Republican convention's nomination of Rutherford Hayes, whose main attribute was his inoffensiveness, only increased Democratic optimism. "The hosts of reform are marching to victory all over the state, and the days of Grantism and Mortonism are doomed," prophesied the Democratic *Indianapolis Sentinel*. The euphoric sense of an approaching Democratic triumph infected thousands of party stalwarts. On Saturday night, September 2, they marched to the Grand Hotel to escort Pulitzer to the hall where he was to give his address. The main thoroughfare teemed with Democrats bearing torches. "As far as the eye could reach out Delaware Street, the lights were seen until they blended in one almost on the horizon," reported the *Sentinel*.

When Pulitzer and his entourage reached the hall, only a few seats remained empty. As the rambunctious audience quieted, Pulitzer began by describing the suppression of the political meeting in Germany he had witnessed a few months earlier. "Such is liberty in Europe!" exclaimed Pulitzer, "I, too, though but a stranger there, felt the outrage; but greater than my indignation at that moment was my pride in knowing that I, too, was an American, a free man in whose country no peaceable meeting could be dispersed at the bidding of the police."

However, he continued, his pride in his American freedoms had been damaged by the actions of Republicans. In the decade since he had become an American, he had seen a president impeached in an act of "reckless partisanship"; the South given up to "public plunder like so much conquered booty"; a reconstruction act turn masters into "political slaves" and slaves into "masters"; the election of a president who had never "read the Constitution," with a "servile Senate at his feet"; a "self-confessed thief" in the cabinet; and political appointees consorting with "notorious thieves." At the heart of his complaint was that the Republican Party—the party founded on a belief in equality—"gave up principles for power," said Pulitzer. "I saw laws and Constitution trampled upon, and crime and corruption flourish."

For more than an hour, Pulitzer's attacks on his former political party enthralled his decidedly partisan audience. Although he was still called a "German orator" and his command of English had been long in coming, he now displayed the erudition inspired by Davidson and acquired at the Mercantile Library. The speech was well organized, with broad themes supported by clever use of examples, possessed an effective cadence, built on alliterative lines, and marshaled such linguistic force that it both inspired converts and won grudging respect from the opposition. The *Indianapolis Sentinel* reproduced his speech in full, and it was quoted in newspapers as far away as Texas.

Fresh from his triumph in Indianapolis, Pulitzer dashed around the state, speaking at a dozen smaller venues. He took time to stop in Cincinnati and visit with John Cockerill, whom he had met at the Liberal Republican Convention. As in 1872, Pulitzer and Cockerill were on the same side politically, but now only one of them commanded a newspaper. It wasn't Pulitzer. Cockerill had risen to become managing editor of the *Cincinnati Enquirer*, a Democratic paper, and was using every part of his seven-column editorial page to boost Tilden's candidacy, accusing the Republicans of illicit use of money and power.

In mid-September, Pulitzer dropped off the campaign trail for two days of rest in St. Louis. From his room at the Southern Hotel, he sent an exultant letter to the famous journalist George Alfred Townsend, another veteran of Greeley's campaign. "My success was probably as astonishing to myself as it was to others. If you looked at the Western papers you probably saw how undeservedly well I was treated." The false humility of the letter was betrayed by his real objective in writing. Pulitzer wanted Townsend to publish a sketch about his life. To that end, he enclosed an entry about him from a new book. "You certainly have sufficient data now," Pulitzer wrote. "If possible try to get it into the Philadelphia *Times*." Campaigning for Tilden served the party's cause, but it also benefited Pulitzer's cause. "Whether Tilden or Hayes be elected," Pulitzer said, "I shall strive to bring some reputation out of this campaign."

The next day Pulitzer returned to the railroad and a grueling campaign schedule that took him to Chicago, Milwaukee, Detroit, Boston, and New York. On the road, he continued to hammer away at Hayes, and at Levi Morton, financial chairman of the Republican National Committee. But he added a new target. With growing regularity, Pulitzer took aim at Carl Schurz, who had come in from the cold and was now supporting the Republican ticket. "If the great Schurz tells the truth, the great Morton is a liar," Pulitzer said in one speech, highlighting the inconsistencies of the two men and drawing cheers. "If the great Morton tells the truth, the great Schurz is a liar," he continued, to increasing cheers. And then, bringing down the house, he concluded, "If they both speak the truth they must both be liars!"

To the delight of the press, Pulitzer challenged Schurz to debate him. Schurz's spokesman gave a dismissive response wrapped in courteous language. "In arranging for a joint discussion between gentlemen," said the spokesman, "certainly some regard should be had to their character, services, and reputation. Having this in view, of course the proposition is declined." Pulitzer's friend Hutchins couldn't resist joining the fray with a jab or two of his own in the *St. Louis Times*. "Of course, Mr. Schurz will not consent to a discussion of the issues of the campaign with Mr. Pulitzer, because he would be the last man to acknowledge the intellectual equality of his former lieutenant and associate."

Although Schurz remained above the fray, his paper did not let the attack pass unchallenged. The *Westliche Post* published a long, scathing article on its former star reporter, editor, and part owner. "The advantage and gain, should such a debate have taken place, would all be on the side of Pulitzer," said the paper, taking Pulitzer's favorite tack: sarcasm. "The contest would have been like one between a louse and an elephant—the former could climb upon the latter, but the elephant would crush the louse with his left toe." Even the *New York Times*, which had excoriated Schurz during the Liberal Republican revolt, now took his side. Pulitzer "belongs to the large class of unappreciated fools who mistake themselves for great men. Who is there to mourn for Pulitzer? No one."

Pulitzer sought to portray his feud with Schurz as political, not personal. But his actions wounded their friendship, and Pulitzer confessed as much in late September. "I followed myself in the course of this counterfeit reformer with enthusiasm and admiration only possible to the warm impulses of youth that blind cold judgment," he said. "But however much I should have preferred in ordinary times to remain silent at the grave of departed friendship, the present crisis in our history must dwarf all personal considerations."

* * *

The drudgery of stump speeches, the tedium of railway travel, and battered friendships faded as October brought encouraging news. Democrats won the state elections in both Indiana and Ohio. The result was the very outcome that Tilden's opponent, Hayes, feared. It seemed as if a victory for Tilden was now only a matter of time. With a favorable political wind at his back, Pulitzer appeared at the biggest venue yet—Detroit's opera house—on October 18. He was introduced to the capacity audience as the man Schurz wouldn't face. "And," said the speaker introducing him, "Mr. Pulitzer, I promise you, will first analyze Mr. Schurz and then pulverize him."

As in his other speeches, Pulitzer tore into Schurz. But this time he also offered his most direct explanation yet of his political migration during the past decade. "I am glad to say I am no partisan," he said. "I cordially cooperated with the Republican Party so long as it pursued the right path, and as cordially oppose it now, convinced that it is a mass of corruption. I do battle willingly for Tilden and Reform and will as freely oppose misrule by the Democratic Party."

At the end of October, Pulitzer reached New York City. By this time he had given more than seventy speeches, but he remained willing to deliver a few more in Brooklyn, in Queens, and across the river in Hoboken, New Jersey. New York Democrats rewarded him with an honor, including him among the guests at a reception at the Manhattan Club for the party's presidential candidate. About 300 politicians attended, including members of the Democratic National Committee; August Belmont, the banker and American minister; and Oakey Hall, the former mayor, whom Albert had famously trapped in a bathroom for an interview.

Pulitzer's role in the campaign came to an end the following evening with a speech at Cooper Union, the great hall where, in 1860, a relatively unknown Abraham Lincoln had given a famous address that set him on the path to the White House. To cheers and the accompaniment of a band, Pulitzer once again took up Schurz as his theme. "I came here to answer Carl Schurz," he said. "And in speaking of him you will pardon me for saying that I do so more in a spirit of sorrow than of anger. I have no ill feeling against him.

"In earlier days I followed the leadership of that man, but I am free to say that if I ever did think he was a great light which any patriotic citizen could follow, I think now that he is but a great Will 'o the wisp," he continued, to the laughter of the mostly German crowd. Then, casting doubt on his claim that he had no ill feeling toward Schurz, Pulitzer continued his attack, like a dog unwilling to loosen its grip on a bone. He highlighted all of Schurz's inconsistencies, changes of heart, and electoral vacillations. "He is perfectly consistent in advocating the election of every popular candidate whose nomination he had previously denounced and damned, and also damning and denouncing the nomination of every popular candidate whose election he afterward supported and favored."

Bringing his assault on Schurz to a close, Pulitzer then made his pitch to elect a Democrat for the first time since before the Civil War. "I stand here to say the war is over, and it is time that it should be," Pulitzer said. Ringing out one applause line after another, he told the audience that the Union had not been saved for robbers, thieves, and carpetbaggers. "The Southern people belong to us and we belong to them. Their interests are our interests; their rights should be our rights; their wrongs should be our wrongs. Their prosperity is our prosperity; their poverty is our poverty," he said, to waves of applause and cheers. "We are one people, one country, and one government; and whoever endeavors to make the union of all the people impossible, is a traitor to his country."

The *New York Sun* gave front-page coverage to Pulitzer's address at Cooper Union. As an unabashed admirer of the *Sun* and of its editor, Pulitzer went to call on Charles Dana. The *Sun* was on the same block of Park Row as the *New York Tribune*'s new building, which rose ten stories and towered over everything else in New York except the spire of Trinity Church. As newspapers sought new ways to find readers, the circulation wars of Park Row expanded into architecture. Dana had abstained from this new battle. The structure that housed his enterprise, which had once served as headquarters to Tammany Hall, was aging and run-down. To reach Dana's office, Pulitzer ascended a narrow iron spiral staircase and passed through a cavernous loft filled with reporters and editors dashing about, shouting, in an atmosphere of controlled bedlam.

The famous editor's office was a quiet refuge. From its door, its occupant and his long, white flowing beard and gleaming, bespectacled eyes gave him almost a look of Santa Claus. (Years later, after Dana's time, the *Sun* published the famous editorial "Yes, Virginia, There Is a Santa Claus.") But Dana's personality was hardly charitable. Not only were his editorials direct, pointed, often caustic, and at times abusive; he also ran a very efficient, no-nonsense, parsimonious business.

Although he was much Dana's junior, Pulitzer had a lot in common with him politically. The Grant administration had caused them both to abandon the Republican camp. But, unlike Schurz, Dana was willing to support a Democrat. Tilden had been a favorite of Dana's since his fight against the Tweed Ring, and the *Sun* had contributed heavily to his election as governor of New York. Now Dana hoped his paper would help put his man in the White House.

After a while, Dana brought Pulitzer out of his office and introduced him to his editor and heir apparent, Edward P. Mitchell. The paper was in a frenzy over the election, but the topic foremost on Pulitzer's mind was his own desire to get a perch in New York journalism. He had tried and failed to buy the *New York Belletristisches Journal.* Only months before, while walking with a friend in Washington, he had confessed that he still couldn't shake off his ambition to run a New York paper. Now he shared his idea with Mitchell and Dana.

Pulitzer told the men he wanted to launch a German edition of the *Sun* to compete with the *New York Staats-Zeitung,* a prominent German paper. The plan he put forward was that the *Sun* would own and publish the new paper but that he would edit it, translate for it, and add his own material. Dana, however, was uninterested, and Pulitzer left, no closer to breaking into Park Row.

On election night, the nation's telegraph lines transmitted the results to New York, where the parties had their headquarters. As predicted, Hayes carried most of New England, but his margins were weaker than those of Grant four years earlier. Tilden carried New York and New Jersey, both states that Grant had won. In the Midwest, Tilden won Indiana, Missouri, and a solid swatch of states to the south. It looked as though the electoral count, though close, would be in the Democrats' favor for the first time since before the Civil War. The popular vote was unquestionably for the Democrat: Tilden had 51 percent of it, and Hayes 48 percent.

But as the night went on, Oregon and three states in the South refused to fall into the Democratic column. The southern states were

South Carolina, Florida, and Louisiana—coincidentally, the last re-maining Confederate states in which Grant still kept federal troops. As officials squabbled over the results, the electoral votes from the four dis-puted states were not tallied. In the morning, Tilden had 184 electoral votes, one short of the majority needed to win. Hayes had 165.

The nation's partisan press roared to life, each newspaper declaring its man the winner and refusing to concede. Pulitzer quickly joined the fray. Writing in the *St. Louis Times,* he bravely proclaimed that the "hopes of Republicans about the result of the election are as groundless as the fears of the Democrats. Mr. Tilden is elected." Whether he was putting on a brave face, believing that this was tactically smart, or was unable to concede that his side might have lost, Pulitzer continued to claim Tilden had won.

"I do not share the grave apprehensions of nearly all my Democratic friends," he said a week later. In every scenario that he could dream up, such as the election's being thrown into the House or the Senate's certifying the contested states, the result would still give the presidency to the Democrats. "For these reasons I don't think there's much ground for serious alarm about the final results," he said. If it were to come out differently, Grant and the Republicans "would be the rebels fighting against their country."

In New York, Dana refused to doubt that the election was anything but a victory for Tilden. But it became clear that the outcome would be resolved by Congress. For the second time in a decade, Dana hired Pulitzer to write for the paper. He asked him to go to Washington and cover the disputed election. It was a choice assignment. When Pulitzer arrived in Washington in late December, the unresolved election had stirred the city into a frenzy. Armed conflict did not seem out of the question, especially after President Grant stationed additional soldiers near the city. "It is not impossible that such a condition of affairs might have led to bloodshed," wrote one politically savvy observer.

As a member of the Washington press corps, Pulitzer watched the com-ings and goings at the Capitol, interviewed members of the Senate, and kept an ear open to the conversations of the city's politicos. His first dis-patches to the *Sun* appeared just after Christmas. They were a marvel of optimism. "There will be no war," he began. "The woman that hesitates is lost. The Republican confederates hesitated. They will lose."

By this point, both the House and the Senate had appointed special committees to devise a means of resolving the election. Pulitzer believed that the outcome rested in the hands of nine Republican senators. "My answer, based upon close observation, direct information, and personal conversation with the members of the Senate, is that these nine will be found on the right side when they are really needed," Pulitzer reported.

Dana permitted Pulitzer a byline, a rare privilege in that era; and, considering that the *Sun* was only a four-page paper, the space devoted to his dispatches gave Pulitzer considerable prominence. For the first two weeks of January 1877, Pulitzer continued to predict a victory for Tilden. Pulitzer's reasoning was not without foundation. By the end of January, the House and Senate had passed, with strong Democratic support, a bill creating the Electoral Commission, whose job it would be to resolve the election, presumably in Tilden's favor.

Pulitzer did not limit his advocacy of Tilden to the pages of the *Sun*. On January 8, 1877, he joined his friend Watterson at a mass meeting at Ford's Theater under the auspices of the Tilden-Hendricks Reform Club. Though the flyers had promised that prominent members of Congress would attend, the two most recognizable speakers turned out to be Watterson and Pulitzer. Watterson offered a fiery denunciation of the Republicans' efforts to thwart Tilden's election. He declared that 100,000 unarmed citizens would descend on the capital on February 14. The announcement startled many Democrats, who had heard of no plans for any demonstration. Pulitzer followed Watterson's lead and delivered a harangue that even a sympathetic newspaper called "incendiary and revolutionary." Pulitzer said he was "ready to bare his breast to the bullets of the tyrant, and rush headlong upon his glittering steel."

Pulitzer's intemperate speech troubled Dana. Pulitzer's dispatches disappeared from the pages of the *Sun* for the remainder of the month. It was not until February 10 that Pulitzer resumed his articles. By then, it was becoming clear Tilden's cause was lost. The Electoral Commission was going to side with the Republicans because a tactical mistake had resulted in giving the deciding vote on the fifteen-member panel to a Republican. "When the work of the returning boards of South Carolina, Louisiana, and Florida was finally completed," Pulitzer wrote, "and these states given to Mr. Hayes, wresting the fruits of success from the party to whom they have seemed to belong, by a bare majority of one, the chagrin of the Democratic Party was deep seated and bitter to the last degree."

On March 2, the wrangling came to an end. Congress awarded the presidency to Hayes. Democrats accepted the result because a tacit deal had been made whereby their acquiescence would be rewarded with a withdrawal of federal troops from the South. In fact, after assuming office, Hayes removed the remaining federal forces from southern state capitals, and Reconstruction came to an effective end. The Democrats lost the White House, but for southern Democrats, their second rebellion against the national government—this one nonviolent—was a success. Dana could not accept the defeat. For the next four years, his paper referred to Hayes as the "Fraudulent President."

Disgusted, Pulitzer left Washington for St. Louis. A week after the inauguration, he admitted the fight was over. "We may have lost much as American citizens, but we have lost little as partisans," he wrote. "It is only four years. We have not been defeated, but defrauded."

The loss stung. Pulitzer understood that politics, though exhilarating, could include defeats, but each path he took came to the same conclusion. As a Republican, he had lost his office. As an insurgent reformer, he had joined a movement that went nowhere. And, now after crossing a political Rubicon by changing his affiliation to a party whose victory seemed inevitable, the result was unchanged. It was not hard to conclude that politics, like journalism, seemed to be a dead end.

In St. Louis Pulitzer took up residence again at the Southern Hotel. This time he took two rooms on the fifth floor. When the six-story Ohio sandstone hotel opened in 1865, to great fanfare, the local press had invoked the image of the Egyptian pyramids. The Southern Hotel was still among the nation's largest, occupying most of a block and capable of accommodating 700 guests.

On April 10, Pulitzer celebrated his thirtieth birthday at a friend's house with Hutchins and others. At midnight, he returned to the Southern, walked through the office past the night clerk, and rode the elevator to his rooms, where he promptly went to bed. A little over an hour later, muffled noises awoke him. He thought he heard the word "fire" but concluded that the voices were coming from the street and that the fire was elsewhere, so he turned over to go back to sleep again. "Suddenly I heard women's shrieks, seemingly in the hotel," Pulitzer said. He jumped from his bed, lit the gas lamp, and looked at his watch. It was one-thirty in the morning.

In his nightshirt, Pulitzer dashed into the hall. It was filled with smoke. He took the stairs down to the fourth floor, where he found two frantic women. "I tried to pacify them and took them to the parlor floor," he said. "The ladies were *en negligée* and I took them to a room of a lady on that floor who gave them apparel." Then, foolishly, Pulitzer ran back upstairs to his own room. There he donned his pants, which contained his wallet, and put on a vest. When he exited his room, the smoke had become so dense that the gaslights no longer illuminated the halls. Yet Pulitzer turned back one more time, to retrieve his eyeglasses, thinking they might help. As he at last descended the stairs, he saw that almost every floor was engulfed in flames.

The fire engines arrived at the hotel a few minutes after Pulitzer reached the street. Red flames burst from first- and second-story windows, and smoke poured from every opening in the building. Guests continued to spill onto the street, but it became obvious to rescuers that many remained inside. "First one window and another in rapid succession were violently raised, heads of men, women, and children were seen everywhere, and a wild cry for help filled the air," said a reporter who arrived on the scene.

As the firemen raised ladders into position, they urged the trapped guests to remain calm. But it soon became apparent that the ladders could not reach above the fourth floor. Panicked guests began climbing down on knotted sheets. One man slid from the sixth floor on tied sheets, only to realize when he got to the end of his makeshift rope that he was still 120 feet above the ground. With flames leaping about him, he jumped. "He was immediately picked up and carried into an adjoining saloon, and lived long enough to say that his name was J. F. Stevens, when he expired," the reporter said. "Two other faces soon appeared at the window from which he had jumped, but the flame and smoke closed them from view almost instantly, and left no doubt of the awful fate that befell them."

By dawn nothing remained of the hotel. Firemen hosed down the embers as the search for bodies began. In all, twenty-one people died in the fire. On April 16, a coroner's inquest was begun. A jury was sworn in over the body of Kate Nolan, one of the servants who had perished in the fire; her body had been kept in the morgue for this purpose.

Pulitzer was the first witness called. He recounted how he had been awakened, had helped the two women, had returned to his room, and then had fled the hotel. One of the jurors asked Pulitzer if he was certain about the time when he awoke. Pulitzer said he didn't know how close his watch was to "telegraph" time, but he felt confident it was between half-past one and quarter to two when he made his escape. "I will say that no alarm was given in the house, so far as I heard," he told the jurors. "I think the shrieks of the women were very fortunate, for had it not been for that, fully one hundred persons would have perished. I know I would have been one, for I am a very sound sleeper."

On April 27, the jury concluded that the fire had originated in the basement of the hotel, possibly in the wine cellar, and that it had spread quickly to the upper floors through the elevator shaft. The building was deemed to have been safe, but the hotel management was faulted for doing an inadequate job of fire prevention.

When the coroner's jury issued its report, Pulitzer was back in New York, again staying at the Fifth Avenue Hotel. He and Albert had received word that their mother was ill and might be dying. They decided that only Albert would go to Hungary. Joseph had no work obligations, but his phobia of funerals overwhelmed his filial devotion. In order to make the trip, Albert persuaded the New York Herald to send him to cover the war between Russia and Turkey, which had just erupted. Before leaving he compiled in a small notebook a list of items to buy in Europe. These included lingerie, gloves, a fan, and a brooch for his wife and alpaca for his son's nurse. For Joseph, he promised to buy a frock coat and an overcoat. On April 26, Albert left New York on the Hammonia, bound for Hamburg.

A month later, Albert reached Detta, the Hungarian city where their mother had moved after remarrying. The day he arrived, Elize died. Upon receiving the news, Albert's wife wrote a consoling letter from their house on Washington Square, where she had remained with their newborn son, Walter. "Oh, why can I not fly to you, my poor, bereaved darling, and mingle my heart-felt tears with thine," Fannie Pulitzer wrote. "I wish you had gone sooner. I suppose the thread of life was so fragile within her that whenever you had gone the shock would have killed her."

Their mother's death left Joseph and Albert the only living members of the large, original family. For Joseph, Elize had been the single most important element of his youth in Hungary. When he reached the United States in 1864, he had sent her the gold coin handkerchief ring, bought with his first earnings. In St. Louis, he had shown his miniature portrait of her to all his new friends. At least twice in the intervening years, he had made the arduous trip home to Hungary to see her. In the best of circumstances, the loss of one's only surviving parent inspires self-reflection. For Joseph—now thirty, and with no specific profession or even a home—such introspection was demoralizing.

Whenever Pulitzer was in turmoil, he would become restless and pick up and go elsewhere, as if he were searching for a geographical solution to his woes. Now he left New York and traveled to Saratoga and then to Springfield, Massachusetts. There he visited Samuel Bowles, another newspaper editor with whom he had been friends during the Liberal Republican crusade. Although Bowles edited the modest *Springfield Republican*, started by his father in 1824, he was one of a few editors outside New York who were nationally famous, such as Halstead in Cincinnati and Watterson in Louisville.

Pulitzer found the aging editor living in a beautiful ivy-covered cottage surrounded by acres of flowers, shrubbery, fountains, and walks amid maple, oak, and magnolia trees. They spent several hours together, talking politics. To his dismay, Pulitzer discovered that Bowles supported the Hayes administration. "He may be wearied by his long fight against both parties; he may be softened by growing years and the growing sweetness of home," said Pulitzer. Because of Bowles's stature, Pulitzer's visit had the flavor of a pilgrimage. He shared the experience in a reverential account published in the *New York Sun*.

The 800-word article, filled with praise for Bowles's journalism, revealed Pulitzer's own literary growth. It was not that Pulitzer had become a polished writer. In fact, many of his allusions seemed forced, his sentences wordy even for an era of breath-challenging sentences, and his choice of vocabulary highly self-conscious. But the piece was the work of a well-read thirty-year-old immigrant comfortable in his new tongue.

He began by introducing his readers to Bowles's hometown. "Trees remarkable for size and beauty; streets picturesquely winding over promontories; every house a garden; the silver stream of the shallow Connecticut obsequiously washing the feet of precipitous bluffs; steeped in the softest green; streets well made and rarely tidy; school houses and churches numerous and of good architecture; Swiss cottages for dwellings; wherever you look, green and air and room—this is the town of Springfield, Mass."

With a flourish, typical of the slow-paced style of the set pieces of the era, Pulitzer laboriously—as if confessing—revealed that the purpose of his journey was to see Samuel Bowles. "I am glad it is out," he wrote. "With all regard for delicacy, one might as well see 'Hamlet' without the part of the Prince of Denmark as write about Springfield with Sam Bowles omitted."

In August, Charles Johnson came east to spend time with Pulitzer, but when he reached the Fifth Avenue Hotel he found that Pulitzer had gone to take the baths at White Sulphur Springs, West Virginia. Johnson wrote and persuaded Pulitzer to meet him at Long Branch, New Jersey, a coastal resort that had become glamorous when President Grant chose to summer there. Other friends, including Alfred Townsend, joined them. They spent their days bathing in the ocean and riding horseback. "In the evening," Johnson said, "we discussed almost everything."

Pulitzer sprained his ankle and was confined to his room. Albert, who had returned from Europe, came down to stay with him. A few days later, the group left Long Branch for New York, where they took in shows, including one in an old railroad depot that had been converted by P. T. Barnum into a hippodrome named Gilmore's Garden in honor of Patrick S. Gilmore, a bandmaster whose best-known composition was "When Johnny Comes Marching Home." (Two years later, the hippodrome was renamed Madison Square Garden.) Pulitzer and Hutchins tried to talk Johnson into accompanying them to the White Mountains in New Hampshire, but he declined.

In early October, Pulitzer returned to St. Louis. He saw a performance of *Hamlet* by Edwin Booth, the nineteenth century's most famous American Shakespearean actor (and brother of the assassin). Just as Hamlet is concerned with his famous question of being, Pulitzer still had no answer for the one that confronted him. At the end of 1877 he was no closer than four years prior, when he had left the *Westliche Post*, to finding a place for himself in his adopted land. Politics had let him down. After experiencing New York, St. Louis confined him. And, aside from a brief attraction to a neighbor's daughter and to one of Schurz's daughters, Pulitzer had thus far remained free of love. By the end of the month, he was on the move again, this time back to Washington.

Chapter Eleven

NANNIE AND KATE

◆

As 1877 ended and 1878 began, Pulitzer was caught between two places, two professions, and two women. The confluence of all three problems pressed the thirty-year-old Pulitzer for decisions. "I am almost tired of this life—aimless, homeless, loveless," he wrote.

St. Louis grew less attractive and Pulitzer spent more time in Washington, which he had come to know while covering the 1876 election debacle for the *New York Sun*. His friend Hutchins had also moved to the capital and was starting a new Democratic newspaper. On December 6, 1877, the first issue of Hutchins's *Washington Post* hit the streets. Four pages long, it looked a lot like the *St. Louis Times*. Although it had no graphics, the *Post* was a lively contrast to the dull papers of Washington. "The newspapers of that city were dreary mockeries of the profession," said the poet and journalist Eugene Field, who used to accompany Pulitzer to musical soirees with the "five nightingales" in St. Louis and had come to work at the *Post*.

Field was not the only one on the *Post* staff that Pulitzer knew. John Cockerill, whom Pulitzer befriended at the convention of 1872, had signed on as Hutchins's managing editor. Under Cockerill's rule, the *Post* packed in more news per square inch than any other paper in town, wrapping it around punchy editorials. The paper was an immediate hit. "It was the marvel of Washington journalism," Field said. "The newspaper world of the continent, who had no idea any good could come out of Nazareth, gaped in astonishment when this bright, saucy, vigorous bantling pranced blithely into the ring."

Journalism, however, was not on Pulitzer's mind. He had come to

Washington not as a reporter but as a lawyer for an election dispute. In Missouri's Third Congressional district, the Democrat, Richard Graham Frost, had been designated the winner, with one vote more than his Republican opponent, Lyne Metcalfe. But Metcalfe persuaded the courts to award him the seat, successfully claiming that Frost's supporters had changed a "7" to a "9" in one of the poll books to supply the winning margin. Now Frost's only remaining recourse was an appeal to the House Committee on Elections. To pursue this, Frost hired Pulitzer, whom he knew as a colleague in the St. Louis bar.

The Committee on Elections began its work in late January. Pulitzer asked the members to order that ballot boxes, roll books, election returns, and other documents be brought from Missouri to Washington. They turned him down and told him that the place for any recounting should be Missouri. The decision was a signal that he faced an uphill fight. He would have only one chance to make his client's case. The committee set February 20 as the last day it would hear any remaining arguments for why Metcalfe should not be seated.

While awaiting judgment day, Pulitzer turned to the *Washington Post*. Already, the paper had given front-page coverage to the dispute and was pushing Pulitzer's argument that the race could not be decided without a recount conducted in Washington. Now Pulitzer gained access to the paper's editorial page. The resulting article was vintage Pulitzer.

If the Committee on Elections should deny Frost the seat in the House, the *Post* editorial began, it would simultaneously decide that he was "a perjurer in several divers and sundry particulars." A decision favoring Metcalfe would mean that Frost had lied under oath. "We do not know how the Committee will act, but we do know that there is not even a political antagonist in the Third Missouri District who would dare to question R. Graham Frost's statement under oath. In fact, those who know him prefer the simple word of R. Graham Frost to the oath of many, if not most, men. Nor do we, in the least, doubt that Mr. Frost was swindled out of his seat by a series of extraordinary frauds."

The editorial had little influence on the members of Congress. On the appointed day the committee listened patiently as Pulitzer read from several affidavits and begged for additional time to build his case. The following day, it unanimously turned down Pulitzer's motions for more time. The seat was Metcalfe's.

* * *

Despite this loss, Washington suited Pulitzer. In the time he had spent there since the fall of 1876, he had developed a busy social life. In the first month of 1878, he was among the guests at a glamorous reception given by the Spanish legation at Wormley's Hotel in honor of their king's wedding. A week later, he was dancing to Jacques Offenbach's music at the Willard Hotel. Pulitzer also helped support the Penny Lunch Room, which opened in January to feed the many citizens who had become destitute as a result of four years of steady wage cuts caused by the economic panic of 1873. He joined a committee to raise money for this lunchroom, participated in a fund-raising ball at the Riggs House, and even ate lunch at the facility to draw attention to its work.

Pulitzer did not lack for friends in the capital. Anthony Ittner, who had been his roommate in Jefferson City, had been elected to the House. Hutchins hosted a popular salon in his parlors that attracted a colorful cast of characters, such as Senator Lucius Quintus Cincinnatus Lamar, who drafted the Mississippi Ordinance of Secession and served in the Confederate diplomatic corps in Russia and other places; Representative James Proctor Knott, whose humor was known to laugh a bill off the floor; and Representative Samuel Sullivan "Sunset" Cox, a former foot soldier with Pulitzer in the 1872 Liberal Republican campaign. The men ate and drank late into the night while the colorful Freemason Albert Pike held the floor with folktales or black singers from a nearby church performed.

On January 12, 1878, Pulitzer attended the wedding of Udo Brach-vogel (who had been his housemate in St. Louis) at the First Trinity Lutheran Church, known as the German church of Washington. In his company was a twenty-five-year-old woman, tall and slim with large dark eyes set in a pale face framed with coils of dark brown hair. "One of the belles of Washington," proclaimed the *Post*. "One of the reigning belles of that city," if an out-of-town newspaper was to be believed.

Her name was Kate Davis, and she was the youngest daughter of a family with both a Confederate and a social pedigree. Representative John B. Clark of Missouri, an old Confederate himself, had introduced her and Pulitzer to each other. Davis's father, William Worthington Davis, came from a Virginian family distantly related to Jefferson Davis, the president of the late Confederacy. Her mother, Catherine Worthington Davis, was a distant cousin of her father's from Baltimore, Maryland. Financially, however, the family was on a decline. William and his three brothers worked a small family farm in Tenleytown, within the city limits, with three servants who were former slaves. But to make ends meet, two of the brothers also held jobs outside the farm, and William served as a justice of the peace.

Though attractive, Davis was passing the age by which most women of her time were married. Her older sister, Clara, was about to turn thirty and no closer to the altar. For his part, Pulitzer's charm, mesmerizing blue eyes, and simmering intensity made up for his awkward, gangly appearance. His intelligence, wit, evident ambition, and appearance of financial means worked to his advantage.

But to Davis's parents, a match between their daughter and Pulitzer was a mixed blessing. Pulitzer had no dependable career. He did have means, having carefully husbanded the money he made from his newspaper deals, his investment with Eads, and land he owned along the south side of the newly created Forest Park in St. Louis. On the other hand, his bloodline was not likely to impress the southern landed gentry. His remaining accent betrayed his eastern European origins, and for churchgoing Episcopalians like the Davises, the issue of his religion was a concern.

Trying to hide his Jewish heritage would have been futile. Although he had stayed clear of synagogues and Jewish life in the United States, he was always immediately identified as a Jew by his friends and publicly in the press. And any illusion that he was something other would have been shattered on the wedding night, as at that time virtually only Jewish males were circumcised. Pulitzer promulgated a tale that his mother had not been Jewish but rather was Catholic. Because Judaism is a maternal religion, this claim explained his Jewish appearance but freed him from its detrimental status, particularly for a family such as the Davises.

Davis was not the only woman in Pulitzer's life that spring. Nannie Tunstall, a beguiling, intense, literary twenty-four-year-old Virginian who was visiting Washington, swept him off his feet. They met while moving in similar Washington social circles. In fact, Tunstall was a friend of Brachvogel's bride and went to the wedding that Pulitzer attended in the company of Davis.

Born in a small town in Virginia, Tunstall was the daughter of a wealthy attorney who had been a state legislator and a railroad executive. The last of six children, all born on a plantation that had been in the family since the 1790s and was farmed by slaves, Tunstall was, like Pulitzer, a child of loss. Four of her siblings and her father had died when she was young, and she had been raised by her mother.

William Corcoran, one of the city's wealthiest men, was a friend of Tunstall's mother, and he invited Nannie to stay with him in Washington. Widowed since he was young, he liked to have company with him at all times. "No one," noted the *Washington Post*, "was more delighted with the society of intelligent and agreeable women than Mr. Corcoran." Tunstall accepted his invitation and soon became a fixture in what she called his "enchanted castle of indolence."

Tunstall certainly filled the bill. Men were drawn to her. "She excites admiration from all," said Corcoran's arts curator, who was among those smitten by Tunstall. She had melancholy eyes, set in a soft, roundish face; a slightly Roman nose; and thick, long, wavy hair. The sculptor Moses Ezekiel was so taken with her that he used her profile for a bas-relief, a bronze copy of which Corcoran purchased.

Tunstall was well-educated, though, like Pulitzer, she had spent little time in school. She read widely and was sufficiently fluent in German to translate poetry; she could also quote French aphorisms in her correspondence, and write poetry and fiction, eventually publishing a novel. She displayed a dramatic excitement over life, literature, and art that seemed daring among the more demure members of Washington's high society. "I have lived fast—emotionally, I have burned the candle at both ends," she confessed late in life.

In February, while he was courting Davis, Pulitzer also pursued Tunstall. "Of course, I have thought of you and would like to see you," he wrote to her when she was visiting relatives in Baltimore. "Of course, you want me to come over to Baltimore. Of course, you are consumed by that tender passion which I return with such powerful profundity and earnestness."

Tunstall demurely left his notes unanswered. An anxious Pulitzer wrote again. "What day, pray? Whenever I receive the signal, Baltimore shall be invaded." Like a nervous suitor, he felt compelled to say more. "Here I *should* stop. But I cannot," he continued. "Brevity may be the soul of wit and it cannot be the wit of sympathetic souls. So I must go on and at least fill this sheet. And say—what? Well, I scarcely know

myself. That I have thought of you much? I see the shake of your clas-
sic head? That I have, in cold blood, determined to admire you? I see
another shake of incredulity that I hope there will be a due appreciation
of that admiration by your ladyship? I hope you now change your gentle
shake from the skeptical to the assenting."

As if at the edge of a precipice, Pulitzer showed tentativeness, almost
like second thoughts, referring to previous loves. "Is it well that we
should fan the embers of congeniality into lurid flames of attachment?"
he asked in one letter. "I really do not like the glare, fear the fire. I
have been burned and too often before both actually and metaphorically
speaking, both internally and externally." Another closed with similar
reluctance. "What! This is going a little too fast, is it not?"

In May, Tunstall put an end to Pulitzer's pursuit. Pulitzer called her
letter cruel. "It has not only unnerved my soul but blasted my hopes," he
wrote. "Your terrible revelation has put an awful chasm between us.

"Is there no hope? Will you not mend? Will you not begin to appreci-
ate the rare qualities of the humble subscriber—in admiring you? Cold
beauty, thy lines are colder yet. The season is rapidly advancing, all nature
laughs and blooms, the very air has sentiment, and poetry grains are free
and sail. In your letters alone there is no spring, in your words alone still
lingers cold winter. How is this for a man who is *not* in love?" Pulitzer's
ardor suffocated Tunstall, who planned to travel unescorted in Europe—
a shocking idea in her era. He was hardly the match for such a soul.

On a spring day, Samuel Bowles, the son of the late publisher of
the *Springfield Republican*, paused for lunch while visiting Washington.
As he looked around the restaurant, he saw Pulitzer lunching with the
prominent suffragist Isabella Beecher Hooker. She was in the capital in
hopes of advancing the passage of a constitutional amendment. Sitting
at a table near the door of the restaurant, Pulitzer and Hooker attracted
attention. "The two," said Bowles, "were engaged in animated conversa-
tion, no doubt discussing the merits of the Sixteenth Amendment, and
the intellectual sparks were pretty surely flying, for they do not agree."

Indeed, Pulitzer was not a supporter of women's suffrage. When he
first confronted the issue as a state legislator in 1870, he seemed some-
what sympathetic. The lawmakers were considering putting a women's
suffrage amendment on a statewide ballot. Before the measure failed,
Pulitzer urged that women of all races over twenty-one years old be
permitted to cast ballots that would be tallied separately and would not

affect the outcome of the vote. But four years later, at the constitutional convention, Pulitzer lined up with opponents of women's suffrage. In fact, he was quite dismissive, suggesting that those who supported it did so only "out of sheer gallantry and courtesy." He even opposed permitting widows and unmarried women over twenty-one who paid school taxes to vote in school elections.

Tunstall's Dear John letter left Pulitzer with only one option, which he pursued with vigor. "If you knew," Pulitzer wrote to Kate Davis, "how much I thought of you these last days and how the thought of you creeps in and connects with every contemplation and plan about the present and future, you would believe it.

"I cannot help saying that I am not worthy of such love, I am too cold and selfish, I know," he continued describing himself truthfully in words that might eventually haunt Davis. By his own admission, Pulitzer was driven by speculative impulses. Until now, his life had unfolded as an undirected but singular pursuit of his own goals, with no care for others. "Still I am not without honor, and that alone would compel me to strive to become worthy of you, worthy of your faith and love, worthy of a better and finer future.

"There now," he wrote, "you have my first love letter."

Pulitzer longed not just for stability, professionally and otherwise, but also for affection and companionship. The deaths in his family led him to think of himself as an orphan, and his competitive relationship with Albert, his only surviving sibling, kept the two apart. Pulitzer frankly described his life to Davis in melancholy terms, a life void of purpose, love, and a home. "I am impatient to turn over a new leaf and start a new life—one of which home must be the foundation, affection, ambition and occupation the corner stones, and you, my dear, my inseparable companion."

They planned a June wedding in Washington. As the date neared, Pulitzer gave Davis many reasons to reconsider. He vacillated on their plans for a honeymoon in Europe. One moment he wanted to rearrange the departure date so as to travel with his actor friend John McCullough, who was appearing at the National Theater. Next, when Pulitzer heard of a newspaper for sale, he broached the idea that they shouldn't go overseas after all.

"You can now see yourself what an utterly inconsistent, uncertain and inconsistent chap I am," he wrote to Davis. He said he could not make up his mind even as to where they would settle. "Funny situation, isn't it? As if to give you a foretaste of the future, you are met by difficulties even before you start on that lifelong journey which philosophers call so perilous; whatever may be thought of your indiscretion, my child, your pluck is really splendid."

A week before the wedding Pulitzer dashed off to New York, again in pursuit of a newspaper. "Prospects look quite favorable for a consummation of a bargain," he wrote, without identifying the prospect—probably the *New York Mail*, which was teetering on the edge of bankruptcy. He admitted that he knew his fiancée was upset by his absence on the eve of their wedding. "It is an important opportunity, perhaps a fortune, and you ought not to expect me to neglect it.

"I must have business to occupy my mind and heart," Pulitzer continued, "you do the latter. Occupation will do the former," in an accurate forecast of the years that lay ahead. "Make all arrangements, complete every preparation upon the assumption that I will be with you on Monday for that important ceremony, thereafter to stay with you forever."

The ceremony actually didn't take place until Wednesday, June 19, 1878. At eight o'clock in the evening, Pulitzer and Davis stood at an altar before a congregation of 100 in the Church of the Epiphany, on G Street in Washington, the church to which the Davis family had belonged almost since its inception in 1842. Theirs was a parish of the powerful and wealthy. In the 1870s, the capital's elite had a choice of four Episcopal churches. The Church of the Epiphany and St. John's were the only two in the mostly residential portions of downtown surrounding the White House. But while the latter served as a house of worship for presidents, the former was larger, more elegant, and more desirable.

Prior to the Civil War, the congregants of the Church of the Epiphany had strong sympathies toward the South. Among their ranks was Kate Davis's distant cousin Jefferson Davis. Those members of the lost cause who had returned to Washington since the war also came back to the church. Sitting on the bride's side of the aisle were Senator Lamar of Mississippi, who knew Pulitzer from Hutchins's salon; Senator John Brown Gordon of Georgia, a lieutenant general in the Confederate army; and Representative John Ezekiel Ellis of Louisiana, a Confederate veteran who had been a prisoner of war.

There were former Confederates on the groom's side also: two Missouri Democrats now in Congress. They were joined by other politicians with whom Pulitzer had become friends in a decade of electoral work. In all, one-third of Missouri's congressional delegation was in attendance, along with friends such as Hutchins and the bridge builder James Eads.

The newlyweds, whose union the politicians, publishers, judges, and notables had come to celebrate, were a study in contrast. The bride was refined, delicate, and graceful. "A more gentle or lovely bride was never led to the altar than she," wrote Hutchins for the front page of the *Washington Post* the next morning. Her betrothed towered over her with angular awkwardness. When they knelt before the altar, Pulitzer was gripped with anxiety about his shoes. His feet were larger than normal, and the soles of his shoes had been chalked with his room number by the hotel staff, who polished them overnight. "I thought with dismay that the people in the back of me would think that I wore No. 17 shoes."

The Reverend John H. Chew pronounced the couple man and wife, and the Hungarian Jew entered the ranks of one of Washington's most established Episcopal congregations. A union with Davis, unlike one with Tunstall, offered considerable benefits. Her family, her pedigree, and her religion completed Pulitzer's metamorphosis. Success, power, and wealth in the United States had only one place of worship, the Episcopal church. Appropriately, the three-paneled stained-glass window above the altar depicted Epiphany, the moment when Jews and Gentiles came together before Christ.

In the fourteen years since his arrival on the shores of the United States, Pulitzer had been a carriage driver, waiter, steamador, journalist, politician, and lawyer. He had shed most traces of his immigrant origins. He had money and a beautiful bride. Still, for all that, Pulitzer remained rudderless. As he walked down the aisle with Kate, he saw the pews filled with his closest friends, each with a successful career, the one thing he still lacked.

Part II

1878–1888

Chapter Twelve

A PAPER OF HIS OWN

In the early morning of July 6, 1878, a carriage ferrying Joseph and Kate Pulitzer made its way across Manhattan and joined a procession of others heading for Pier 52, between West Twelfth and West Fourteenth streets, where the *Britannic* awaited the last of its Liverpool-bound passengers. The newlyweds were among a select group of 175 persons who paid between $160 and $200 in gold for first-class cabins on the White Star Line steamship. The fare was four times what the 1,500 men, women, and children jammed below in steerage paid. The Pulitzers were given staterooms in the middle of the ship, insulated from engine noise and less susceptible to the motion of the waves. By ten o'clock that morning, the *Britannic* set sail and soon cleared Sandy Hook, reaching open water and refreshing ocean breezes.

Ostensibly, Kate and Joseph were off on a two-month honeymoon. But Kate soon learned, or may already have deduced from Joseph's frenetic business pursuits on the eve of their wedding, that her husband's attention would never be hers alone, even on a honeymoon. His mind constantly churned with political and business schemes. As soon as they reached England, Joseph dived into the newspapers, making careful note of everything he read, and buttonholed all he met to ask endless questions.

Having spent all his adult life in the United States, Pulitzer now looked at European life from an American perspective. Landing in England, he was struck by the rigidity of class. The British, he concluded, deluded themselves into thinking that their democracy and court system were open and fair. "A people with such inequalities, such artificial and unnatural arrangements and laws, are like a woman who uses French heels, tight lacing, and paints," Pulitzer wrote. "While they look well, they are like the red decayed apple. As the continuous tight lacing will ruin the woman's lungs and vital organs, and retard the free pulsation of the blood, so will the artificial and unjust arrangements of government eventually ruin the body politic."

When Joseph and Kate reached Germany, he was outraged by the destruction of political freedom caused by Chancellor Otto von Bismarck's drive to suppress an emerging socialist movement. "There was not a single day," Pulitzer wrote, "in which I did not hear, either through the press, or conversation, of cases so arbitrary and unjust, so cruel and despotic, that they would be appalling to any American." What he witnessed fueled his nascent fear of leaders who traded on the passions and prejudices of the masses. "People without liberty have despots. People with too much liberty have demagogues. Both agree in abusing liberty," wrote Pulitzer. "The despot thinks there is too much of it. The demagogue thinks there is not enough. The despot rules from fear of demagogues; the demagogue from fear of despots." This fear of demagoguery remained with Pulitzer all his life. Years later, it would cause him to be one of the only progressive-minded leaders to be on the outs when William Jennings Bryan and Teddy Roosevelt took hold of the American imagination.

To Kate's relief, politics did not consume the entire honeymoon. In Paris the Pulitzers toured the dazzling Exposition Universelle. The exhibits came from all across the globe and included such American technological marvels as Alexander Graham Bell's telephone and Thomas Edison's phonograph. Also on display was the completed head of Frédéric-Auguste Bartholdi's Statue of Liberty. Several years earlier, the French sculptor had begun designing and casting the 150-foot statue, to be presented to the United States on its centenary in 1876. The plan called for French citizens to pay for the statue and for American citizens to pay for the pedestal and foundation. The French were meeting their end of the deal, but the Americans were not.

In Paris, Kate visited the city's fabled couturiers and Joseph indulged her expensive tastes. She also experienced, perhaps for the first time, Joseph's quick anger. As a joke she told him she had purchased a cookstove. He believed her and erupted in anger at her presumed foolishness. But his temper was also short-lived. Kate left Paris pregnant.

*   *   *

The two-month honeymoon came to a close on September 4, when the Pulitzers returned to New York on board the *Russia*, a modest, aging ship of the Cunard Line. The passage presented one of those singular moments in history when two figures whose names will become closely linked pass by each other unknowingly. In New York, among the passengers preparing to board the ship for its return to Europe was fifteen-year-old William Randolph Hearst, accompanied by his mother.

The Pulitzers' European sojourn became a little more costly when customs officials peered into Kate's two trunks. Her Paris dresses caught their attention. One appeared not to have been worn. In the past, clothing bought overseas that had "actual use" was exempt from import duties. But stricter instructions now required that agents assess duty on almost any garment bought overseas unless the passenger was actually wearing it when disembarking. The agents were just about to let Kate's dress pass when one of them spotted a Treasury inspector looking their way. They stopped the Pulitzers and told Joseph he would have to pay a duty on the dress. He protested, and a superior was summoned who, in turn, called an appraiser over to join the debate. After an hour of listening to Pulitzer's pleas, the officials who had gathered around the trunks remained unmoved. Unless he paid the $60 duty in gold coins, they said, his luggage would be confiscated. Pulitzer paid.

Because Pulitzer hated President Hayes, he viewed the episode as a personal affront and an example of the administration's corruption. He dispatched a tempestuous letter to Charles Dana's *New York Sun*, which had already reported the incident (though misidentifying Pulitzer as a former lieutenant governor). "Immediately next to me were two parties, each with probably five times the number of trunks and boxes," Pulitzer wrote. "Not one of those was opened at all—everything was passed smoothly and quickly. Why? Perhaps because at least one of the parties slipped a piece of paper into the hand of his inspector, which probably partook the character of legal tender."

At the *Sun*, Pulitzer met with Dana. The aging editor still held Pulitzer in high regard and agreed to publish his reflections on politics in England, France, and Germany. The resulting six pieces, which ran in the *Sun*'s September and October editions, not only contained astute observations but also displayed the thinking of a writer who had now developed a mature political philosophy. In comparison with the rush-

to-judgment style of Pulitzer's articles in the *Westliche Post,* or even his
recent dispatches for the *Sun* during the Hayes-Tilden electoral dispute,
the articles—essays, really—were dispassionate analyses.

After dissecting German, French, and British society and politics,
Pulitzer reserved his last essay for an ode to his adopted land. He
constructed an imaginary conversation between an American and a
European in which the latter pointed out the many imperfections of
democracy in the United States. Was not the selection of Hayes as presi-
dent a violation of the nation's constitutional practices? the European
asked. True, replied the American, but Hayes, unlike a European mon-
arch, will hold office for only four years. Not one to give up easily, the
European continued his faultfinding and pointed to American women
who sought to marry noblemen. Surely, he said, this proves that Ameri-
cans look to Europe as a model. No, replied the American, it shows only
the mercenary qualities of our women.

The most singular moment in Pulitzer's imaginary dialogue occurred
when the European challenged the premise of universal male suffrage,
one of Pulitzer's most sacred beliefs since his entry into politics. Citing
Alexis de Tocqueville, Pulitzer conceded that the extension of voting
rights did indeed have a tendency to elevate mediocrity, perhaps a lesson
taught by the sting of the elections of 1872 and 1876. But it was a fallacy
to conclude that universal suffrage was the linchpin of democracy, said
Pulitzer's alter ego in the article. "The great advantages of our system
certainly do not consist in giving every man a vote but in giving every
man a better chance for life than other governments allow."

Although long-winded, a bit showy, and at times wandering off the
track, the articles were the equal of any in this genre published in New
York newspapers. Dana even granted Pulitzer a byline, reinforcing his
success in English-language journalism. In fact, the articles marked
Pulitzer's complete transformation into an American. Never once men-
tioning his foreign birth, Pulitzer had opened his series of articles pro-
claiming, "The more I see of Europe, the more American I become."
He confessed his love for the opera houses, museums, castles, and new
palaces of Europe. But he also wrote, "However great the treasures of
art, I prefer the treasures of liberty." Expressing a sentiment similar
to that which brought his brother Albert to the United States, Joseph
added, "I like still more our plain land without the glare of royalty or
nobility."

* * *

The articles in the *New York Sun*, though glamorous, brought Pulitzer no closer to finding suitable employment, a more pressing problem now that he was married. But while languishing in New York, Pulitzer heard that the *Dispatch*, a struggling evening paper in St. Louis, was going to be auctioned off at a bankruptcy sale. He knew the paper well. Stilson Hutchins and Charles Johnson had taken turns owning the *Dispatch*, but neither had made a go of it. Pulitzer telegraphed Johnson as well as John Marmaduke, a former Confederate general who edited an agricultural magazine and had discovered a new lost cause as an agitator against the increasing power of railroads. Pulitzer told them that he and his bride were leaving for St. Louis and that they were to meet him at the Lindell Hotel.

The St. Louis at the end of the train ride was greatly changed from the one that had greeted Pulitzer thirteen years earlier. It was now a thriving industrial and commercial city whose air was so thick with smoke that only a dome or two could be seen through the haze from the train as it crossed the Eads Bridge. When Johnson and Marmaduke met Pulitzer at the hotel, he revealed his plans. He told them he had returned to take a shot at buying the *Dispatch*. The men were enthusiastic—especially Johnson, who had long pressed Pulitzer to abandon his off-and-on legal career. "I zealously urged him to embark on the newspaper business," said Johnson.

Encouraged, Pulitzer next went to see Daniel Houser, the part owner of the *St. Louis Globe-Democrat*, to whom he had sold the AP membership four years earlier. For several evenings Houser and Pulitzer worked on the financial numbers. Houser guessed that Pulitzer might win the auction with a bid of $1,500 to $1,700. Pulitzer had $5,000 in savings, so at that price the paper would be within his reach. Operating the paper, however, was an unresolved question. If Pulitzer could not eliminate its daily deficit, his cash would last only seventeen weeks.

In the early morning of December 9, 1878, the day of the auction, Pulitzer strolled from the Lindell Hotel to the nearby courthouse—a Greek Revival building with a cast-iron dome modeled after St. Peter's Basilica in Rome. By the time he reached the courthouse, a small crowd was already milling around the east side; its members were doing their best to stay warm in the frigid air—this December was one of the coldest months since the city had begun keeping records. Pulitzer knew just about everyone among the thirty or so men, and they, him. "The tall, graceful figure and pale Mephistophelean face of Mr. Joseph Pulitzer, with its expression of keen irony, was the object of marked attention," wrote a reporter.

There were actually two newspapers on the auction block that day. An eight-year-old failed newspaper, the *St. Louis Journal*, was expected to sell for less than the value of its presses, type, and furniture. The *Dispatch*, however, had greater potential. It had been founded as the *St. Louis Union* in 1862 by the late U.S. senator Frank P. Blair, to counter the *Missouri Democrat's* support of John Frémont, who was running against President Lincoln. Two years later, Johnson and a group of investors had bought the failing *St. Louis Union* and converted it to an evening publication called the *Dispatch*. During the following years, the *Dispatch* continued to change hands as different publishers took turns failing to make it financially viable. By 1878, its most recent set of owners could find no one else on whom to unload it, and the sheriff ordered a bankruptcy sale.

Despite its miserable track record, the *Dispatch* still appealed to newspapermen. Among those who came to watch the auction were Houser; the former governor Gratz Brown, now working as an attorney representing the party who held a $15,000 mortgage on the *Dispatch*; John and George Knapp, owners of the *Missouri Republican*, and their editor William Hyde; and John A. Dillon of the *Evening Post*. The assembled newspapermen, lawyers, bankers, and judges tried to guess what the *Dispatch* might fetch. Some thought it might sell for as much as $40,000. The auctioneer suggested that the AP membership alone would be worth at least $20,000, an estimate inspired by Pulitzer's well-rememberd profit in buying and selling the *Staats-Zeitung* in 1874. This time, however, there was no paper in town so badly in need of the AP. The more reasonable men who were present had only modest expectations for the sale, and some had none. Asked what he would pay the paper, William Hyde replied, "I would not give a damn for it."

Within a few minutes of Pulitzer's arrival at the courthouse, the auctioneer climbed onto a chair. "I propose to sell for cash two newspapers—two *live* papers," he said, drawing laughter. Reviewing the lamentable histories of the two papers, he said that they had sometimes made money, but at other times they had not. Again, the audience guffawed. Those who held unpaid financial notes did not share in the merriment. Brown grabbed the auctioneer's chair and warned potential buyers that anyone who purchased one of the two newspapers would be liable for the $15,000 mortgage.

It took only a moment to dispense with the *Journal*. It fetched $600. "Gentlemen," the auctioneer said, "I now propose to sell you the *Evening Dispatch*, a paper that will live when all the other evening papers are dead." After more laughter, the bidding began. Simon J. Arnold, who worked for the city collector, Meyer Rosenblatt, went first, offering $1,000. Rosenblatt was an important figure in the city's Republican politics, and it was presumed that Arnold was doing his bidding. He wasn't. He was Pulitzer's Trojan horse. Pulitzer knew if he were to openly join the bidding, others would assume that he had seen in the paper something of value that had escaped their attention, and the price would soar. Arnold's opening move was countered with a bid for $1,500. The gathered men were baffled. The other bidder, standing behind the crowd in a hallway, was a complete stranger. A reporter asked his name. "I'll tell you after a while," he replied.

Arnold raised his bid to $2,000. The mysterious man topped it with a bid for $2,100. Pulitzer remained silent. His well-made plan seemed to be unraveling. At $3,000, Arnold gave up and walked away. The unidentified man had topped Pulitzer's man by $100. The auctioneer declared the auction over. Pulitzer's game was up. He would not be the new owner of the *Dispatch*. But a commotion arose when the anonymous figure did not come to the front to claim his prize. In fact, he had vanished. Arnold rushed back and announced that he would still be willing to pay $2,500. His offer was accepted, and Arnold and the auctioneer retired to offices across the street to complete the transaction. The identity of the other bidder never emerged.

During the confusion at the end of the auction, Pulitzer slipped away unnoticed. But a reporter caught up with him as he stepped into the elevator at his hotel and pressed him for an interview. "I would grant your rather sudden request with the greatest of pleasure," Pulitzer said, "if it were not for the unfortunate fact that I have been engaged all day, and now am going to see my wife for the first time since breakfast this morning, and I know you wouldn't detain even a humble individual like myself from the bosom of his family for so long a period. Even if the imperious necessities of metropolitan journalism . . ."

"But, Mr. Pulitzer, only a question," broke in the reporter. "You have bought the *Dispatch*, I understand, and I would like you . . ."

Now it was Pulitzer's turn to interrupt. "My dear fellow, without presuming to criticize your intelligence or acumen, which I would hardly dare to question, are you not assuming too much? *I* own the *Dispatch—I?*"

The cat-and-mouse game continued as Pulitzer feigned ignorance, pretended to be unacquainted with Arnold, and conceded only that it was "possible" though not "probable" that he had bought the *Dispatch*. The reporter gave up. "No one better understands the use of language for the purpose for which Talleyrand said it was given—to conceal one's thoughts—than Mr. Pulitzer," wrote the frustrated reporter. "He parries the question like a skillful fencer, and it is as hard to pin him to a point as it is an eel."

The following day, all the newspapers reported that Pulitzer was the new owner, but he had yet to confirm his purchase publicly. "The all-absorbing question this morning in newspaper circles was, had Mr. Joseph Pulitzer really bought the *Evening Dispatch*?" asked Dillon at the *Evening Post*. Gossip had it that Pulitzer intended to merge the *Dispatch* with another paper. "There are so many rumors afloat about evening journalism in St. Louis that we should not be surprised, as the result of all of them, to hear the newsboys crying out 'the *Dispatch-Journal-Post-Star*,'" wrote Mack at the *St. Louis Globe-Democrat*. The rumor of a merger worried Dillon. A combination of the *Dispatch* and *Star* could destroy his *Evening Post*. He wanted to know Pulitzer's plans without disclosing his own fears. He sent one of his reporters off to find Pulitzer and see what could be learned.

Locating Pulitzer was not easy. At the *Dispatch*'s office, the reporter found two or three employees sitting around, idly passing the time with the paper's attorney. Pulitzer was expected, they said. By nine-thirty he had not arrived. Impatient, the reporter left. He spotted his quarry on the street, across from the offices of the *Westliche Post*. That was, however, the extent of his good luck. Pulitzer was still uncooperative. "I do not know that I am the owner of the *Dispatch*," he said. "I do not know that I have authorized anybody to say that I bought it or that I intend to buy it."

Frustrated, the reporter walked to the city collector's office, where Arnold, who had placed the winning bid, was employed. He spoke with Rosenblatt, Arnold's boss.

"Did you buy the paper for Mr. Pulitzer?"

"The *Dispatch* was purchased for Mr. Joseph Pulitzer," replied Rosen-blatt.

"This, of course," the reporter said, "looked like a positive thing, but why on earth was Mr. Pulitzer playing the sphinx?"

The answer was not hard to fathom. His dodges were designed to fan public interest. He had been similarly dishonest with the St. Louis press corps when the sale of the *Westliche Post* was rumored, and he had also done this when he bought the *Staats-Zeitung*. In this present instance, his evasions served to increase the mystery surrounding his actions. The more he could get the St. Louis press to talk about the sale of the paper, the more papers he would sell.

Finally, at noon, Pulitzer walked into the *Dispatch*'s office in the company of the lawyer William Patrick, who had once used Pulitzer as an errand boy. The auctioneer, who had been cooling his heels in the office, rose from his seat. "Mr. Pulitzer comes to take formal possession of the *Evening Dispatch*, and will henceforth be considered its propri-etor," he announced. "I only take possession temporarily and subject to future possibilities," said Pulitzer, quickly retiring to an editorial room upstairs. The two reporters on duty, though bewildered by Pulitzer's cryptic remark, went to work rushing out an edition of the *Dispatch* with what little they could gather in the way of news after having spent the day in idleness.

Pulitzer's antics gained him a second day of front-page coverage in the morning papers. At the *Globe-Democrat,* McCullagh greeted Pulit-zer's return to journalism in St. Louis with a warmhearted editorial. As a statesman, Pulitzer had not been very successful, he said. "What he failed to accomplish with an eloquent tongue, he may yet achieve with a brilliant pen. If the world was made no better by Mr. Pulitzer as an orator, it will, we trust, be made wiser by Mr. Pulitzer as an editor."

Buying the *St. Louis Dispatch* was easy compared with the next hurdle Pulitzer faced. His cash would last only a few weeks; and unlike the *Staats-Zeitung,* the *Dispatch* had no salable assets with which he could turn a quick profit. Rather, Pulitzer's only option was to find new read-ers and do it quickly.

St. Louisans already had two other English-language afternoon newspapers: the *Evening Star* and the *Evening Post*. Unlike the morning newspapers, neither of these was well established. The *Star* had started publishing only a few days earlier, but it had strong financial backing. It counted prominently among its investors Thomas Allen, a railroad magnate and aspiring politician, whose children Albert had tutored one summer. He was sinking money in it, in the hope of having a paper to support his planned bid for the U.S. Senate.

The *Evening Post*, which had been launched eleven months earlier, had the lion's share of readers. Its publisher, Dillon, who looked like a patrician and wore a handlebar mustache, was about Pulitzer's age, was also an experienced journalist, and had similar political leanings. Otherwise the two men were very different. Dillon had been born into one of the leading families of St. Louis. His father was an Irish immigrant merchant who made a considerable sum in real estate. In 1861, the younger Dillon went to Harvard, rather than to war, and returned home an urbane and well-read gentleman. He won the hand of a daughter of one of the French families who founded St. Louis, and the couple spent a two-year honeymoon in Rome—the same years when Pulitzer was struggling to get a foothold in St. Louis.

Their honeymoon ended when Dillon's father died. The engineer James Eads had been appointed executor of the estate, and Dillon discovered that much of his inheritance was tied up in Eads's chancy bridge project. To protect his investment, he became secretary-treasurer of the Illinois–St. Louis Bridge Company. Five years later, when the family's financial affairs were secure, Dillon sought an escape from the dull work. McCullagh offered him a job on the *Globe-Democrat*. Under the guidance of the venerable editor, Dillon developed into an editorial writer of some distinction. His thoughtful writing was graceful and refined. He was soon a well-known figure in St. Louis journalism. In 1878, Dillon decided the time had come to establish his own newspaper. His wife, Blanche, supplied the necessary funds.

Dillon's *Evening Post* was an odd amalgam of his own refined, lofty writing style and McCullagh's muscular journalism. Its coverage of society news appealed to the city's elite but did not lure the potentially large audience for an afternoon paper. This was of some comfort to Pulitzer as he took the helm of the dead-in-the-water *Dispatch*. On one flank he faced a new, untested afternoon paper, the *Star*; and on the other the more established paper, the *Post*, stalled in its search for readers. There was bound to be an opportunity for the *Dispatch*.

*   *   *

Although the flagging fortunes of the three evening papers discouraged others from venturing into the business, Pulitzer was undeterred. He was convinced that evening papers had a great future. He was right. The advent of the telegraph and faster printing presses made it possible to publish an afternoon newspaper with news as fresh as that day, making morning papers look as if they were publishing yesterday's news, which, in fact, they were. Urbanites, particularly workers and professionals heading home, had a voracious appetite for news and were primed to buy an evening paper. Gaslight, and then electric light, also made the newspaper an important evening pastime. In a few years, evening newspapers would outnumber morning ones.

Pulitzer openly professed his faith in the evening press within days of buying the *Dispatch*. "Whether it be a collision in the Sea of Marmosa, a battle in the Peiwar Pass, a revolution in the Sultan's palace, or a row in the British Cabinet, the evening paper is invariably the first to give the news," Pulitzer told his readers. "Moreover, it reaches the subscriber when he has time to read a paper. In a city, as least, there are about three times as many people who have leisure for an evening paper as there are for a morning paper. It is merely a question whether the evening paper can occupy the field, and we propose to occupy it."

Pulitzer's timing was perfect. Not only were evening papers on the rise, but production and newsprint costs were decreasing. Publishers could offer readers more for their money or drop the price. Either strategy provided a stable financial footing, permitting newspapers to wean themselves from subsidies, direct or indirect, from political parties. With this prosperity, an increasing number of newspapers began to call themselves "independent." The more independent a newspaper became, the more it drew readers seeking objective news, entertainment, and advertising to guide their growing purchases. In other words, becoming an independent newspaper was as much an economic as a political decision. "Business prosperity," noted the *Chicago Tribune*, "has increased with all papers in the proportion that they have maintained their independence and their freedom."

Pulitzer gambled he could ride these trends to journalistic and financial success. His business acumen drove him. Although he was at times an innovator in journalism, this was not his strength. Rather, he possessed remarkable foresight and had an uncanny ability to recognize value where others didn't. He was willing to take risks based on his insights when others remained timid.

But none of Pulitzer's ambitious plans would bear fruit on the minuscule subscription rolls of the *Dispatch*. So, like a bridge player, Pulitzer relied on his strong suit. He owned an AP membership, whereas Dillon's *Post* made do with a weaker alternative, the National Associated Press. Dillon could survive without an authentic AP membership, but he feared doing battle with the well-equipped Pulitzer, and he still worried that the *Dispatch* might combine forces with the *Star*.

Pulitzer's ploy worked. Within twenty-four hours, Dillon agreed to merge his paper with Pulitzer's. A merger made good sense. Pulitzer and Dillon shared essentially the same reformist political views. For Dillon, the merger would prevent a potentially disastrous circulation fight. For Pulitzer, it would bring readers and, most important, time.

The two men decided that their respective enterprises were worth $15,000 each. They created a new corporation that issued 300 shares, valued at $100 each. Blanche Dillon, who had funded the *Post*, retained 149 shares; Pulitzer had 149; and two shares were assigned to William Patrick, Pulitzer's attorney, who drew up the papers. Dillon took the posts of president and managing editor, and Pulitzer became vice president and political editor. But the agreement made it clear that Pulitzer renounced no editorial power by accepting the post of second in command. At the last minute, a clause was added to the final text, specifying that he "should write upon any subject political or otherwise without reservation."

Dillon agreed to give Pulitzer free rein because financially he was bringing the most to the table. Although his *Dispatch* had fewer readers and was encumbered by a $15,000 lien from an unpaid mortgage, Pulitzer agreed to fund an expansion of the combined newspapers. Under the terms of the deal, he promised to lend up to $10,000 at 5 percent interest. No mention was made of where Pulitzer, who was down to his last reserves, would obtain such a sum.

The next day, Pulitzer abandoned the *Dispatch*'s headquarters and its staff. Only one employee was invited to come with Pulitzer, and he refused. Wearing a soft hat and a blue chinchilla overcoat, Pulitzer moved what little was worth keeping to the offices of the *Evening Post* on Pine Street, just blocks from where he had lived when he was a reporter for the *Westliche Post*. The following day, the new *Post and Dispatch* appeared.

The new paper was physically unchanged by the merger. It remained four pages long, except on Saturdays, when it promised that it might be as long as ten pages. The details of the merger were to be kept secret but were described as "decreed by immutable destiny" in an editorial that bore all the marks of Pulitzer's hand. The editorial promised that the combination of an almost dead newspaper with another less than a year old would create a publication that would be "one of the best established among the newspapers of the country."

Pulitzer's dominance of the combined papers was in evidence all across the editorial page. He declared the paper's political independence. "The *Post and Dispatch* will serve no party but the people; will be no organ of 'Republicanism,' but the organ of truth; will follow no caucuses but its own convictions; will not support the 'Administration,' but criticize it; will oppose all frauds and shams wherever and whatever they are; will advocate principles and ideas rather than prejudices and partisanship."

The declaration was disingenuous. The merger agreement specified that the *Post and Dispatch* "would be independent with a Democratic leaning." A careful reading of Pulitzer's announcement made the preference clear. The Democrats remained the chosen tribe. But the declaration was the first pronouncement of what would become a tenet of Pulitzerian journalism. In his hands, independent journalism was a political tool. By building journalistic credibility with readers, a newspaper could build independent political power. For Pulitzer, journalism was another route to power.

Anyone who knew Pulitzer knew that power was something he did not readily share. McCullagh, at the *Globe-Democrat*, foresaw trouble for his protégé. To succeed, Dillon would have to tone down "the crude products of Pulitzer's fiery and untamed brain," said McCullagh. This was such a tall order that should he succeed, McCullagh added, Dillon could retire to harness zebras in the wild.

Chapter Thirteen

SUCCESS

◆

B efore the *Post and Dispatch* was a month old, Pulitzer announced that larger quarters and faster presses were needed to meet the surging demand for it. This was sheer chutzpah. St. Louisans weren't exactly rushing into the streets to buy the paper. True, circulation neared 4,000. But Dillon and Pulitzer had merged their subscription lists. The actual number of *new* subscribers was low—hardly a groundswell straining the capacity of the *Globe-Democrat*'s presses, which printed the *Post and Dispatch*. In fact, Pulitzer's plan seemed economically suicidal.

In the following weeks, money slipped rapidly from Dillon and Pulitzer's hands. They leased a building at 111 North Fifth Street that had once been the home of the *Evening Dispatch*. Crews moved in to make needed repairs and alterations. Pulitzer and Dillon ordered one of Richard M. Hoe & Company's newest and speediest four-cylinder presses, capable of printing the paper's entire press run in less than an hour. To old hands in the St. Louis press corps, the expense was unjustified. So far, except for Pulitzer's friends in politics and journalism, few people were paying any attention to the *Post and Dispatch*. Although it led the *Star*, the other afternoon paper, its circulation was one-tenth that of the leading morning newspapers. The essential problem remained. New readers were needed. And for that to happen, the paper had to be noticed.

Years before, when he worked at the *Westliche Post*, Pulitzer had gained attention with his crusading reporting, exposing corruption in the county government and exhorting readers to action. Now, with an entire newspaper at his disposal, he went at it again, but this time he selected a larger target. He took aim at the oligarchs who controlled the city's economic life. "The trouble in St. Louis is not with either our masses or merchants or middle classes," Pulitzer wrote, "but those whose wealth would seem to make it their own interest to lead in every measure of enterprise, but who do not lead, nor even sometimes follow."

He was on to something. Like many other cities of the era, St. Louis had long been under the control of a wealthy, privileged elite. This was not really a matter of corruption and graft, although those, too, certainly existed. Rather, a cabal, comprising many of the descendants of early settlers, ruthlessly safeguarded its own economic interests. City laws ensured that only a select group obtained lucrative business monopolies or provided such public services as streetcar lines and gaslights. By the middle of the 1870s, a growing number of merchants, professionals, and small businessmen chafed under the economic restrictions and monopolistic behavior of this elite. A newspaper that espoused their cause would find a ready audience.

In January 1879 the St. Louis Gas-Light Company quietly sought to regain its financial stranglehold on its customers. For years, this monopoly had forced St. Louisans to pay the highest rates in the nation for heat and light, making a staggering 73 percent profit. But this profitable arrangement was shattered when a court sided with a plan to cancel the gas company's exclusive franchise. Under the pretense of offering a compromise plan, the company promised to pay all the city's legal fees from the lengthy court fight if the city council restored the monopoly. If not for Pulitzer, the plan might have worked.

Like an editorial Paul Revere, Pulitzer sounded the alarm. "This is no compromise," he roared from the pages of his paper. "Hands Off! No surrender to the monopoly." The proposal, he said, reminded him of an old tale about a white man and an Indian dividing a buzzard and a turkey. "Whichever way the proposition is turned, it is the same—the city gets the buzzard, the Gas Company all the turkey." This first volley was followed by another the next day. "The most objectionable feature of this business is that its only possibility of success depends upon bribery," Pulitzer said. "Yes, we write it deliberately, bribery." Lawyers who had previously sold the city's residents into monopolistic bondage were willing to do it again, he continued. "This is an open and unblushing bid to bribe the lawyers of the city by the payment of large fees."

Every day for the next two weeks, Pulitzer shoehorned into the paper articles that detailed the monopolistic practices of the gas company and featured poignant interviews with victimized customers. The flurry of articles, as well as the continuous stream of editorials—appearing, as they usually did, under the banner headline No COMPROMISE! No COMPROMISE! No COMPROMISE!—caught the city's attention. None of the other English-speaking newspapers joined the campaign, and certainly not *The Republican*, whose editor, William Hyde, was a mouthpiece for the oligarchs.

As the campaign ground on, the paper began to sound like a one-note composition. Pulitzer needed another campaign that would goad the oligarchs and attract readers. His staff obliged him by obtaining copies of the tax returns of the city's richest residents. Kept in the assessor's office, the returns were public documents, but they cast an embarrassing hue when published in a newspaper for all to see. Under the headline TAX DODGING: WHOLESALE PERJURY AS A FINE ART, Pulitzer published the financial declarations—especially the dishonest ones—of the city's wealthiest men. The declarations were damning. For example, despite being reputed to be the city's wealthiest resident, one man reported having no money in the bank or on hand and listed the value of his personal property at less than $3,000. No one escaped exposure. Judges, lawyers, politicians, and even members of the St. Louis press, such as Hyde, McCullagh, and Preetorius, found their incomplete tax returns in the paper.

When citizens file incomplete returns, Pulitzer told readers, "they commit—to use the mildest term possible—a falsehood, both ridiculous and monstrous. And a much stronger term could be used without the danger of libel suits." To prove its point, the *Post and Dispatch* reprinted the text of the taxpayers' oath each day, with the headline WHAT TAX-DODGERS SWEAR AND SWALLOW. Pulitzer, who had lied in official oaths himself, told his readers that his paper's reporting revealed "that honor and honesty, law and oath even, are palpably violated by some of our 'eminently respectable' and 'most prominent' citizens."

The gas campaign yielded a victory. The city rejected the plan in late February. The tax exposé, however, failed. A grand jury was convened but decided that there was nothing to probe, because the state law was so full of loopholes.

* * *

Pulitzer concluded that reporting alone wouldn't build circulation no matter how great the story, unless one trumpeted it. To that end, he sent his reporters out to interview citizens about the tax abuses and then published reports on what they thought. This ploy paid a double dividend. It permitted the newspaper to publicize its own gallant work— THE POST AND DISPATCH MEETS WITH GENERAL APPROVAL, read one headline—and it ensured that even people who didn't read the paper learned of its contents. Pulitzer was convinced that news reporting could be combined with promotion, and he pushed his staff to do both. A typical headline would invariably include a subhead such as "Another Exposure by the *Post and Dispatch*." By March, his efforts had secured 540 new readers, an outstanding growth rate that, if maintained, promised profits by the end of the year.

Treating every aspect of city life as unexplored territory, Pulitzer commissioned articles on who lived in the alleys and byways. "Tramps, Darkeys, Goats and Garbage" were what the reporter found. Pulitzer sent his staff to learn who owned the houses that were used as brothels: well-heeled citizens, it turned out. And he had the courage to shatter the myth, steadfastly believed by its citizens, that St. Louis was on its way to becoming the nation's next great city. Instead Pulitzer revealed that it was being outstripped in population and economic growth by its rival, Chicago.

There was hardly anything Pulitzer would not try; he even picked fights with his competitors. He never missed a chance to criticize, embarrass, or simply poke fun at other newspapers, especially Hyde's *Republican*, with which he competed for Democratic readers. Once, he laid a trap for the *Star*. The *Post and Dispatch* published a fake article, said to be a cable dispatch from Lahore, Pakistan, reporting a massacre of an English garrison at the hands of rebellious Afghan war prisoners. The *Star* copied this and published the story prominently in its second edition, with the credit "special cable to the *Star*." The next day, the *Post and Dispatch* revealed on its front page how it had fooled the *Star*.

Pulitzer's goal was to publish every day at least one article so intriguing, so unusual, so provocative that it would cause people to talk about it at the dinner table. Sensationalism was the most common way newspapers tried to attract attention. But for readers in St. Louis that was old hat.

Even the staid *Republican*, for example, regularly ran stories likely to ruin breakfast for anyone with a sensitive stomach. On December 9, 1878, the day Pulitzer was buying the *Dispatch*, the *Republican* put on page one a report of a child's beheading by a train in Nevada. The head had rolled down a bank and had come to rest on the stump of its neck, facing the trainload of passengers. When it was lifted, the eyes opened and the mouth twitched. The mother soon reached the scene and collected her son's head, severed arm, and body, placed them in her apron, and led a procession back to her home.

The *Post and Dispatch* ran its share of these stories. Readers learned about heinous killings by a man in Kentucky in A CRIME UNPARAL-LELED IN WILD AND REVENGEFUL BRUTALITY and got the details of how the rope broke in an executioner's attempt to hang another murderer in THE HORRIBLE CRIME FOR WHICH THE BLACK RASCAL DIED.

Pulitzer had a more ambitious and less imitative scheme for building circulation. He wanted to make news from his own news coverage. A perfect opportunity presented itself in February. Two members of the police commission, on which Pulitzer had once served, were said to have ties to city gambling operations. The state senate dispatched a committee to look quietly into the matter. On Monday morning, February 17, the committee members gathered in one of the parlors of the Laclede Hotel, dismissed everyone else from the room except their secretary, and stationed two policemen at the door. Witnesses were admitted one at a time and were sworn not to reveal anything about the conduct of the hearing. Certain that they had outfoxed the press, the senators began their work.

Pulitzer was not easily put off when he wanted a story. He conferred with his city editor, and they decided to approach a doctor whose offices in the hotel included a waiting room that had a sealed door connecting with the parlor in which the senators were to meet. By holding an ear to the door, a reporter might be able to hear the proceedings. The doctor consented to the plan. When the secret hearings began, a reporter for the *Post and Dispatch* who was familiar with the senators' voices was stationed at the door, while the remainder of the press wandered through the hotel's hallways, clueless about the proceedings. All day Pulitzer's reporter listened, using his hands to cup his ear against the door. Unable to take notes in this awkward, cramped position, he memorized important portions and later dictated them to the city editor.

On Tuesday, the committee resumed its secret work. As its day's work drew to an end, the early edition of the *Post and Dispatch* appeared on the street. "The Veil Is Rent and the Doors of the Star Chamber Fall from Their Fastening," cried the newsboys, reading from the article headlined: A POST AND DISPATCH REPORTER DEFIES LOCKS AND BARS, BRICKS AND MORTAR. When one of the newsboys entered the lobby of the Laclede Hotel, a witness at the hearing grabbed a copy of the paper and incredulously read the first few lines. In seconds, the boy was cleaned out of his supply of papers. A note was sent up to the committee. One of the senators came from the closed chamber, got a copy of the newspaper, and retreated back into the room. Reading the account, the senator soon learned—as the paper proudly reported later—"that the cat was really out of the bag, that the dog was really dead, and that the jig was really up."

The incensed senators summoned Pulitzer's city editor, but he refused to divulge how the paper had obtained its scoop. A policeman was dispatched to examine the doctor's office adjoining the hearing room. Completing his investigation, he told the committee that the door between the rooms, although blocked to traffic, was not necessarily closed to sound. Next, a man was stationed behind the door with sheets of paper to see if one could record what was being said from the other room. When he returned with notes, the senators glumly learned that indeed it was possible and actually quite easy.

For days, the *Post and Dispatch* crowed about its scoop. It reprinted commentary from other papers, published articles about how its coverage had stunned the senators, and made sure no one forgot. "The piece of work," Pulitzer said, "was complete on—so complete, so surprising, so overwhelming, that it commanded recognition and acknowledgment."

After weeks of delay, workers finally completed the renovations to the paper's new offices on North Fifth Street. A good-size crowd was on hand the afternoon of March 10, 1879, when Pulitzer, Dillon, and their staff moved in. For a paper with a modest, though growing, circulation, the plant was impressive. The first floor contained the counting room for the business side of the paper. An open stairway led to the newsroom on the second floor, where Pulitzer had a curtained alcove overlooking the street. The new press, and a boiler to produce the steam to run it, was in a two-story wing off the back, with the composing room on the floor above. Soon after two-thirty that afternoon, the press was started. Slowly, it began printing and folding an eight-page edition of 20,000 copies, carrying the name the paper would use from then on, the *Post-Dispatch*. Pulitzer boasted that this was the largest run of an evening paper in St. Louis's history. Printing the edition, however, turned into an embarrassing challenge. After only a few minutes at full speed, the roar of the press was silenced as the paper tore and jammed the rollers. It was nightfall before copies reached subscribers.

Despite the paper's progress toward financial stability, Pulitzer did not relax or let up. He practically lived in the North Fifth Street office, staying late into the night working by the light of a single gas jet. "I would pass by on my way home between eleven and twelve o'clock and he was always there," recalled one nocturnal St. Louisan. No matter how late he worked, Pulitzer always arrived at the office in the early morning to examine the paper's vital signs. He demanded precise information. Exactly how many copies were printed the day before? Sold? Returned? How were street sales of the paper? How many lines of advertising had run in the last issue? During the last week? Since the beginning of the year? How much money was spent on the staff? For paper? For telegraphs? How much money was taken in? His thirst for details was insatiable.

In these first days of running the *Post-Dispatch*, feeling the sharp anxiety of potential failure, Pulitzer learned to ask questions that provided him with the most realistic take on the financial health of his paper. He measured the number of column inches of classified advertisements, scrutinized sales figures to see if a particular news scoop increased street sales, and analyzed every aspect of the competition. He honed his questioning down to a precise mix of queries yielding a statistical portrait that revealed in a single glance where things stood. Until the end of his life, and no matter how far he wandered from the office or how much he delegated to others, he would never give up this habit. He feigned to be interested only in politics and in writing editorials, but the truth was that Pulitzer knew any power he could accumulate from an Olympian perch could not be kept by Olympian detachment. His success, after all, rested on the pennies readers spent for his paper.

After concluding his business duties, which usually took an hour, Pulitzer would turn to the editorial work. He worked side by side with the reporters and editors, "just as if he was one of them," recalled a reporter. "If he wrote something he particularly fancied, he would read it aloud for the benefit of his staff. If a new reporter wrote a good story, Pulitzer, in his intensely enthusiastic way, would compliment the young fellow." Pulitzer didn't consider it beneath his position to contribute news copy. One day, on his way to work, he witnessed a runaway carriage. Upon reaching the paper, he burst into the newsroom with the enthusiasm of a cub reporter and filed his own account of the accident.

Pulitzer thrived on the hubbub of the newsroom. He simultaneously wrote, edited, and conferred with his staff. "He seemed equally at ease when writing and talking at the same time," said the reporter. Interruptions were continuous. Pulitzer would get started on an editorial, and then the politicos would begin to arrive. He greeted each one with "My dear fellow," followed by an inquiry as to the person's well-being, recalled a reporter. "He would continue to dash off editorials and pungent paragraphs while discussing politics with his visitors. He seemed to be as much immersed in politics as he was in building up his newspaper." To Pulitzer, of course, these were one and the same thing.

After lunch at eateries such as Faust's, where he had once made an inglorious attempt at being a waiter, Pulitzer would return to the office to review the final page proofs, often bringing them to the composition room to explain his changes. At three o'clock, when the first edition of the paper came off the press, Pulitzer would leave his desk and go to the counting room. There he would join other men in distributing bundles of the paper to the boys who would walk the delivery routes or hawk the paper on the street.

The street urchins were critical to a paper's success. They could also be its Achilles' heel. Several times during his early months of managing the paper, Pulitzer clashed with them. In May, for instance, the newsboys went on strike, demanding a 50 percent share of the paper's selling price. The arrangement had been that they purchased copies of the paper at three cents and sold the copies for five cents. "It is hard to fight women, but still harder to argue with boys, especially newsboys," wrote Pulitzer. "However kindly we are disposed toward the little brigades who sell our paper, it is an absurdity which we are fully determined and able to stop—no matter how long the strike may last."

He won.

On April 21, 1879, the St. Louis contractor Edward Augustine returned to his house at dinnertime looking haggard. In the nine years since

Pulitzer had shot him at the hotel in Jefferson City, Augustine had fallen from political power, and without county government contracts, his business ventures had failed. When he entered his house, Augustine found his family at the dinner table. His wife asked him to join them. He refused and instead asked her to come into the front parlor. She demurred—understandably. Only a few days earlier, Augustine had brought home a rifle after telling friends it was for the purpose of murdering his family. He turned and went into the parlor alone. "Then, I'll finish it," he said. A few minutes later, a shot rang out.

Pulitzer resisted the temptation to use his new position to even the score with his old antagonist. In fact, the *Post-Dispatch*'s coverage of Augustine's suicide was muted in comparison with that of the other newspapers, though it included the required graphic description of Augustine's brain "scattered all about the room." Pulitzer may have possessed a volcanic temper and held grudges for long periods, but he could be magnanimous.

Pulitzer didn't have time to worry about old history. The paper needed constant tending. Although it was becoming profitable, the financial foundation of the enterprise was a house of cards. As a precaution, Pulitzer took $300 from his reserve funds and put them in a trunk at home to make sure he could cover the coming expenses of the birth of his first child.

Neither Dillon nor Pulitzer had the capital necessary to continue the paper's growth. The promise of profits would not pay for the new presses or the paper's rising expenses. Pulitzer turned to Louis Gottschalk, a prominent lawyer and Democrat in St. Louis whom he had known since Gratz Brown's election as governor in 1870. In 1875, Pulitzer and Gottschalk had both served as delegates from St. Louis to the state's constitutional convention. Gottschalk, like a number of other Democrats, believed the *Post-Dispatch* under Pulitzer's editorship could benefit the party. He agreed to lend $13,000 so that Pulitzer, in turn, could lend money to the *Post-Dispatch* as promised in the merger agreement.

In addition to the infusion of capital, Pulitzer had a lucky break with the $15,000 mortgage taken out by the *Dispatch*'s former owners and thought to have been conveyed when Pulitzer bought the paper at auction. In fact, Pulitzer had been making interest payments on the mortgage. He had also taken the unusual step of making weekly payments to the Associated Press in the name of the mortgage holder. He worried that the *Post-Dispatch* could lose access to AP because the original embossed membership certificate had been used as collateral and was still in the hands of the mortgage holder.

Lawyers who researched the mortgage discovered that the debt had been contracted personally by one of the former owners, and they reported to Pulitzer that it "was a debt never incurred by him and for which he is not in any respect responsible." As far as he was concerned, the debt was off the books, but he still fretted about the missing official AP membership document.

With his new Hoe presses, Pulitzer was able to increase the space in the *Post-Dispatch* for both news and advertising. To persuade a hesitant readership that an afternoon paper could also carry classifieds, like the established morning papers, Pulitzer gave out classifieds free of charge for several months. The idea was to increase circulation as well as to boost advertising revenue. Pulitzer recognized that many people read the advertisements the way others read the articles. "It is our object to make the advertising columns of the *Post-Dispatch* not less varied and interesting than the news columns," he wrote.

Indeed, the news columns were filled with the kind of stories Pulitzer craved, the kind that made people talk. The *Post-Dispatch* continued its relentless assault on the municipal monopolies, exposed questionable banking practices, detailed shady insurance schemes, and revealed anything else that victimized the middle class. It was scathing in its treatment of the city's upper-class families, many of whom were Pulitzer's neighbors. Editorials dripping with sarcasm poked fun at upper-class rituals and social events. These customs also served as topics for some of the paper's best stories.

Nothing was too private for the circulation-hungry Pulitzer. There was a rumor that Dolly Liggett, the daughter of one of the city's wealthiest tobacco merchants, had defied her parents and married a livery stable's bookkeeper. The family refused the entreaties of two *Post-Dispatch* reporters seeking confirmation. Pulitzer sent off a third reporter, Florence D. White, whose unusual first name had given him the nickname "Flory." White was, at age sixteen, the youngest member of Pulitzer's staff. His passion for journalism had lured him away from Christian Brothers College, an opulent high school whose graduates often pursued more education. Pulitzer saw in White a drive that mirrored his own, and he rewarded his young reporter with increasing trust. His instinct did not let him down. White persuaded the Liggetts' maid to admit him. He returned with an exclusive interview with the mother, a mix of outburst and tears.

Watching with dismay as the *Post-Dispatch*'s circulation rose each week, the owners of the *Star* decided to throw in the towel. It was now their turn on the auction block. On May 14, 1879, the usual crowd gathered on the courthouse steps. Pulitzer joined in the bidding, which started at only $100 but rapidly devolved into a three-way match. When the bids reached the $700 range, Pulitzer dropped out, and one of the remaining two men prevailed with a bid of $790. As when he had bought the *Dispatch* at auction, Pulitzer had fooled the crowd. The man who placed the winning bid was working for him. The afternoon field now belonged solely to the *Post-Dispatch*.

"We have passed the point," Pulitzer wrote, "where the *Post-Dispatch* was an experiment."

Joseph settled the pregnant Kate into a house at 2920 Washington Avenue. It was of brick and had three stories, a mansard roof, a bay window in the front, and stables in the rear. The neighborhood was one of gracious dwellings, crisscrossed by private streets. By choosing this spot, Joseph placed Kate in an enclave of the city's aristocrats, who were objects of his paper's continual attacks. That mattered little to Joseph, for whom confrontation was almost a pleasure. But for Kate it was the beginning of what would be many uncomfortable experiences of being ostracized because of her husband's public conduct.

On June 11, 1879, Kate gave birth to their first son. They named him Ralph. With a child at home and with the paper becoming more successful, Pulitzer carved out more time for his family. He spent Sundays with Kate and baby. All summer he came home early enough to sit on the front stoop with Kate and visit with neighbors, at least those who did not hold the conduct of his paper against him. Those who did referred to the couple as "beauty and the beast."

Usually Kate, with Ralph in her arms, fetched her husband from work by carriage. Joseph would greet her and Ralph with joyous enthusiasm, as if they had been separated by a long journey. "In such an atmosphere, those were happy days for everyone," one of Joseph's reporters recalled. Indeed, even his old friend Johnson noted Joseph's happiness in his diary. Joseph had resumed horseback riding, often taking rides in Forest Park with a friend. On evenings when he did not return to the paper for late work, Joseph gathered friends for cards in his home.

As the summer of 1879 drew to a close, Joseph had found all the things that he had been lacking when he confessed to Kate, on the eve of their wedding a year earlier, his need for a new life. He was now married to an enviably attractive woman, he was the father of a son, and he was no longer fretting about an impending return to poverty. The only thing that was not yet fully in his domain was the paper, which he still had to share with a partner.

In the fall, it became increasingly clear to Dillon and Pulitzer that their partnership would not work. McCullagh, who predicted that the partnership would not last, attributed the breakup to "incompatibility of temper, superinduced, perhaps, by an excess of talent." The truth of the matter was that one did not work with Pulitzer. For him, surely. Against him, often. But not with him. Carl Schurz and Preetorius had learned this in 1872. Now, it was Dillon's turn.

Dillon agreed to sell Pulitzer his half of the enterprise. It had been only a year since Pulitzer had sat late into the night with his friend Houser, counting how many months of operating expenses his few thousand dollars in savings would buy him. Now he could meet Dillon's asking price solely from his share of the paper's first-year profits. On November 29, 1879, the *Post-Dispatch* announced Dillon's departure. Pulitzer was the paper's sole proprietor.

Joseph reorganized the paper's corporate structure. He made Kate vice president, putting one share in her name, and filled the rest of the board with loyal friends such as William Patrick. Next, with his hands unfettered, Pulitzer made wholesale changes to the editorial staff. He didn't want another partner, but he needed someone who could act as one. Within days of Dillon's departure, Pulitzer sent a wire to John Cockerill, whom he had first met at the Liberal Republican convention, offering him the post of managing editor.

That night, Cockerill found the telegram waiting for him when he picked up his room key at Barnum's Hotel in Baltimore. Since his successful run with Hutchins at the *Washington Post*, he had moved on to become editor of the *Baltimore Gazette*. Hutchins still sang his praises. "The really notable newspaper men in the United States can be numbered upon the fingers of one's hands, and Mr. Cockerill's name would be called before the second hand was reached," he wrote. Pulitzer's offer was irresistible. The two men had similar political views, and their enthusiasm for the new journalism of the era was so great that they were like apostles of a faith.

The challenge that came with the job was daunting. Although Cockerill knew of Pulitzer's early successes, the *Post-Dispatch* was still more a promise than an accomplishment. It was nowhere close to challenging the behemoth of St. Louis edited by Cockerill's early boss and friend McCullagh. The city belonged to the *Globe Democrat*. Only the *Boston Herald*, the *New York Herald*, and the *Philadelphia Ledger* had higher circulations. But Cockerill had confidence in Pulitzer. He took the job.

Chapter Fourteen

DARK LANTERN

◆

In January 1880, St. Louisans were astonished to read that the *Post-Dispatch* would soon be on the auction block. Advertisements in the *St. Louis Times* proclaimed that the rival newspaper, its machinery, type, press, furniture, and all components of business would be sold to the highest bidder at the east front of the courthouse. The advertisements were the devious work of *Times* publisher B. M. Chambers, an avowed enemy of Pulitzer who was frequently ill treated in the *Post-Dispatch*.

Chambers was convinced he had found a means to put Pulitzer out of business or, at the least, make his life miserable. Before Pulitzer had bought the *Dispatch*, its former owners kept the paper alive using a loan from the ill-famed attorney Frank Bowman. In return for this last-ditch loan, the owners surrendered to Bowman the original, embossed certificate of the *Dispatch*'s membership in the Associated Press. Chambers had since acquired the note and certificate. With the AP document in his hands, Chambers demanded that Pulitzer pay off the loan to get it back. But Pulitzer's lawyers had rightly concluded that he was not liable for the loan, so Pulitzer refused.

Chambers put his plan for an auction into action. Pulitzer was not worried about the stunt. It would be impossible to sell the paper without a legal determination that it was liable for the old loan. "Is THIS MAN INSANE?" Pulitzer asked in a headline in the *Post-Dispatch*. But the *Post-Dispatch*'s AP membership certificate was another matter, one far more serious. If Chambers somehow caused Pulitzer to lose access to the AP, it might ruin the paper.

Pulitzer sought help from AP president Murat Halstead, whom he had known since the Liberal Republican days, and other members of the news service. But Pulitzer knew that in the high-stakes game of a news monopoly, business interests could trump friendship. So, as insurance, he filed suit to compel the association to issue him a new certificate to replace the one Chambers held and proposed to sell at the auction.

After a week's delay, which gave Pulitzer a chance to continue his frantic work behind the scenes, a crowd assembled at the courthouse believing the sale would finally take place. Several properties were auctioned, but to the audience's disappointment Chambers, the star of the event, never showed up. Instead, he sent his attorney to announce that the sale had been postponed indefinitely. He knew what the crowd was about to learn. He had been beaten.

Rather than a funeral for the *Post-Dispatch*, the moment was a triumph for Pulitzer. He mounted the steps in front of the crowd. With the flourish of a stump speaker, Pulitzer declared that Chambers's allegations were false and that his access to AP dispatches was secure. "Look at this," he cried out and held aloft, for all to see, a new certificate of membership in the AP.

His exuberance stemmed from more than this one victory. For the first time since he had bought the *Dispatch*, Pulitzer felt free. Circulation was increasing at such a rate that it would almost triple by the end of the year. His books showed that if the trend held steady the paper would earn $88,000 that year. "It owes nothing beyond a few accounts which will be adjusted on presentation," wrote Pulitzer, keeping his loan from the wealthy Democrat a secret. "It has no unhappy stockholders, no unpleasant litigation, and its circulation and its patronage show each month a gratifying increase. And that's how the *Post-Dispatch* plunges into the New Year." With Cockerill in place as his trusted lieutenant and the staffing changes complete, Pulitzer no longer needed to give the enterprise his undivided attention.

At home, his growing income allowed him to provide Kate with three servants to run the house and care for the baby. Kate also had an easier entry into St. Louis society. She and Joseph attended the exclusive Home Circle ball at the Lindell Hotel. Described as "a very brilliant brunette," she wore a costume of pale blue and delicate pink satin, with ribbon bows. "The lady's ornaments," noted the press, "were diamonds."

Unencumbered by financial and managerial demands, Pulitzer turned his attention to his most important passion. Since his return to

St. Louis, the silence regarding his political plans had been like waiting for the other shoe to drop. All his friends, as well as his detractors, knew that Pulitzer still wanted to hold office. His success as a newspaper publisher had strengthened his chances and his resolve. The day following his speech at the courthouse, word leaked out that he would run for the U.S. House of Representatives from the second congressional district of St. Louis.

Pulitzer made plans to devote time to his own election, and to the entire Democratic ticket. But they almost all unraveled while he was out of town on his first political trip a couple of weeks later. At quarter past midnight on January 23, 1880, a *Post-Dispatch* employee smelled smoke. He ran into the deserted street yelling "Fire!" A nearby watchman tried to ring an alarm, but his key was so plugged with dirt he couldn't open the box. Luckily, a police officer spotted flames bursting through the windows of the paper's back building and set off an alarm, summoning two corps of firemen.

By one o'clock in the morning, when the business manager arrived on the scene, the facility was a wreck: half burned, half soaked in water. Later, the foreman of the pressroom was found standing disconsolately in the midst of the steaming wreckage. The new Hoe press had been warped by the heat, and the stockpile of paper was rendered useless by the water. Telegrams were dispatched to Pulitzer, who was staying at his favorite New York hotel, the Fifth Avenue. Early estimates put the loss at more than $6,000, probably closer to $8,000. But although he had risked his savings in the enterprise and had operated for many months with little or no cash, Pulitzer had not risked going uninsured. Seven paid-up insurance policies covered his losses.

Awakened with the news of the fire, McCullagh sent word that the paper could be printed at the *Globe-Democrat*, as it had been before the *Post-Dispatch* obtained its own presses. In the morning Cockerill wrote an editorial headlined OUR BLACK FRIDAY, predicting that the paper would take two weeks to get back on its feet. The paper, concluded Cockerill, "is a thoroughly established institution and is able to survive the ordinary vicissitudes of life."

In New York, the fire put Pulitzer in a foul mood. A reporter for the *New York Tribune* approached him about the election prospects for Democrats. A Republican will be in the White House for another four years, Pulitzer curtly replied (leading Hutchins at the *Post* to quip that "Pulitzer should always be interviewed just after dinner and a cursory examination of rent-rolls").

Reports from Cockerill calmed Joseph and he left New York to meet Kate in Washington. There, he and Kate returned to the Church of the Epiphany, this time to baptize Ralph. Kate's unmarried older sister Clara Davis and Joseph's friend U.S. Representative John Bullock Clark Jr. served as witnesses. The priest did not ask Joseph for a profession of faith; only the godparents were required to give that. Yet standing by the baptismal font and agreeing to have his child raised as an Episcopalian, Joseph sealed his departure from Judaism.

By early February, with his family in St. Louis, the paper back in its office, and circulation holding steady, Pulitzer once again turned eagerly to the oncoming election. Despite his dour pronouncement to the *Tribune*'s reporter, all signs pointed to a Democratic victory. In 1878, the party had taken back both houses of Congress for the first time since 1858. The Democrats' political fortunes were such that the presidency, which they had not won since 1856, should at last be theirs.

With a heightened sense of power as one of the new breed of independent newspaper publishers, Pulitzer intended to both direct the Missouri Democratic Party and help the national party find a suitable standard-bearer. He and his friend Henry Watterson, of the *Louisville Courier-Journal*, were determined to anoint a man who could win.

Pulitzer's vision of himself as the party's leader in Missouri did not sit well with William Hyde, editor of the *Missouri Republican*. That paper, managed from an elegant five-story building with Renaissance-style ornamentation, had long been the acknowledged party sheet. Over time, however, its support of the city's oligarchs had left many Democrats out in the cold, especially those in the middle class. They were gravitating to the *Post-Dispatch*, creating a political and economic competition between Pulitzer and Hyde.

Despite the enmity between the two men, both Hyde and Pulitzer sat on a committee assigned to lure the 1880 Democratic national convention back to St. Louis, where it had been held four years earlier. Pulitzer conveniently missed the committee's trip to the Washington meeting where it lost out to Cincinnati. Upon returning to St. Louis, Hyde discovered that Pulitzer had published a telegram suggesting that the committee failed because its members spent their time drinking in Washington's bars. If Hyde's anger was not sufficiently stoked by this, a cheeky poem continuing the paper's abuse of him appeared in the five o'clock edition of the March 1 *Post-Dispatch*.

At six that evening, with—as one reporter described it—anger coursing though his veins "like a mountain-fed stream in the early spring," Hyde left a friend's office and headed down Olive Street to his newspaper. Meanwhile, Pulitzer exited Maranesi's candy store, where he had bought a supply of caramel, and was strolling to Willie Gray's bookstore for a copy of *Harper's Weekly*. At the corner of Olive and Fourth streets, the editors came face-to-face.

"Now damn you, I've got you at last," said Hyde. He swung his fist at Pulitzer, but managed only a glancing blow to the right eye, knocking Pulitzer's glasses off. Blinded, Pulitzer returned the punch with equal ineffectiveness. He then grabbed Hyde by his tie and shirt and wrestled him to the ground. The two scuffled until bystanders pulled them apart in the nick of time. Pulitzer had managed to reach under his heavy overcoat and had withdrawn a pistol from his hip pocket. Before he could get a shot off, one of the men knocked the gun away. A decade after the shooting in Jefferson City, Pulitzer was still taking aim at St. Louis's pols.

Pulitzer was shaken. He couldn't see without his spectacles. In the darkness and cold, he let himself be led to a nearby cigar store. As he stepped away, he yelled in Hyde's direction, "You cow! Anybody could do that." Hyde imperiously dusted himself off, and with an escort of two men retreated to a doorway next to Ettling's barbershop, where he received the congratulations of friends.

The election of 1880 lacked any major issues. The economy had recovered from the doldrums of the 1870s, Reconstruction was a dead issue, and the clamor for civil service reform had faded. The partisans of the time were glad to concoct disputes, but the supposed issues were little more than proxies for regional and factional differences. When it came to the ballot, the nation was still divided by the Mason-Dixon Line.

Early in the race for the Democratic nomination, Tilden was the leading contender. Pulitzer was adamantly against Tilden because he was still angry about the New Yorker's acquiescence in the 1877 bargain that gave the presidency to Hayes. As early as February 1879, Pulitzer argued against the rising tide for Tilden. "It seems absurd that Mr. Tilden should ask a vindication in the shape of the Presidency, when his own inexcusable conduct alone made the success of the electoral crime possible." Pulitzer flirted briefly with other potential candidates, but soon lost interest in them.

With only a month remaining before the selection process began, Pulitzer was still without a man. He feared that if he couldn't find a strong candidate, the party would go back to Tilden. Pulitzer decided to try luring another former New York governor, Horatio Seymour, who had run against Grant in 1868, out of retirement.

If Pulitzer could talk Seymour into running, he would not only save the party but score a journalistic coup. On April 24, 1880, Pulitzer traveled to Utica, New York. He rode a carriage across the Mohawk River and up the Deerfield hills to the Seymour home, a small house framed by tall hemlocks and a century-old black cherry tree in front, perched so high in the hills that it had a twenty-mile view of the valley below. Seymour greeted Pulitzer at the door. Although Seymour would turn seventy years old the following month, Pulitzer thought he hardly looked sixty. He stood tall and erect, his hair had little gray, and his hazel eyes remained clear. His only infirmity was a slight loss of hearing.

They entered the house, which was filled with colonial and revolutionary era antiques. As they sat, Pulitzer displayed rare diffidence and held off raising the question of who should be the Democratic Party's nominee. Instead the two conversed about politics, the "Negro problem" (as it was then called), and the coming election. Finally the all-important topic came up as the two prepared to part. At the door to the house, Seymour said the party had a wide choice of excellent candidates and listed several of the leading ones. "I am too old," said Seymour. "You had better leave me to die gracefully by myself. That is an act few men understand, and perhaps I had best begin to try it now."

"But Governor," Pulitzer replied, "if the people think you are the strongest candidate for your state as well as the country, and if their delegates at Cincinnati fix upon you as the man of all others to lead them in this campaign against centralization and imperialism, I have always said that you were too good a patriot and too good a Democrat to decline the leadership. Have I said wrong?"

Seymour stood at the doorway for a while looking at his guest and made motions as if he were going to say something. Instead, he grasped

Pulitzer's hand and shook it. Pulitzer told him he was satisfied with this silent reply. Seymour laughed. "You had better lay me on the shelf and get a younger man." Despite this final pronouncement Pulitzer rode away "with exultation in my heart," believing that Seymour might still be a candidate.

The harsh light of reality struck Pulitzer upon his return to Missouri. Seymour had been sincere in declining the honor Pulitzer had proffered. There was no realistic way that the aging Seymour could undertake a national campaign. Without a candidate, Pulitzer could only try to deny Tilden the nomination. This goal took on a personal element because the leader of Tilden's crowd in Missouri was none other than William Hyde.

Missouri Democrats gathered in late May for their state convention in Moberly, a railroad town in the middle of the state. Both Hyde and Pulitzer were delegates. When Pulitzer's turn came to address the convention, Hyde's supporters packed the galleries and tried to shout him down. But no matter what Hyde's men tried, Tilden's day had come and gone. There was nothing Hyde could do. The convention selected twenty-one of its thirty national delegates from the ranks of anti-Tilden men. Pulitzer returned to St. Louis triumphant. "A cloud of gloom rests over the Tilden cause," noted the *Washington Post* in reporting the results at Moberly. Hyde avoided complete defeat by securing a spot as a delegate at-large. Pulitzer was selected as one of two delegates from the Second Congressional District, which he hoped to represent after the election.

At the end of June, Pulitzer traveled to Cincinnati for the Democratic national convention. Years earlier, he had come as a dewy-eyed organizer of the insurgent Liberal Republican movement. Then he had been a twenty-five-year-old dissatisfied Republican newspaper editor. Now he was one of the most talked-about newspaper publishers, and comfortable in his new political home among the Democrats.

The convention, which opened on June 22, 1880, looked almost as wild as the renegade gathering of 1872. Nineteen hopefuls sought the presidential nomination. Pulitzer gained a seat on the resolutions committee, chaired by Watterson. Together they crafted a platform of fifteen planks that included opposition to centralization and to protective tariffs, support for the gold standard, and an end to Chinese immigration.

The platform also stated the election of 1876 had been fraudulently stolen and that Tilden should be thanked for his selfless service to the party.

With the preliminaries out of the way, the convention turned to its main business on the morning of June 24. Though stifling heat made the convention hall almost unbearable for the delegates, they began to sift through the many candidates. Tilden gracefully bowed out, and on the first ballot the new leading candidate, General Winfield Hancock, took 23 percent of the vote. It looked as though it could be a long day. But when the second ballot began, delegates abandoned their first choices and formed a bandwagon for Hancock.

Pulitzer faced a quandary. He had promised to speak on behalf of the candidacy of William English, a former Indiana congressman who was now a dark horse. The changing developments on the floor made this impossible, however. "I saw before Missouri was called that the nomination would sweep through the convention like wildfire," Pulitzer later told English. "I did not think it wise to interrupt the room, and sacrificed my own inclination and pleasure rather than do what seemed needless."

Pulitzer's judgment was sound. His own state, which had split its votes among five men on the first ballot, now gave Hancock all but two of those votes. The counting of the ballots would be only a formality. "The mob howled and shrieked, so that for some time no business could be done," said a reporter on the floor. "But while the disorder prevailed there were hurried consultations among the delegates and unmistakable signs of a stampede." It would be for General Hancock.

With that decision made, the convention chair asked for a recess until later in the day. But Pulitzer instead moved that the convention immediately select the "next vice president," with an assurance that caused some laughter. At this moment, Pulitzer's friend English was more fortunate. His status as a former congressman from the important battleground state of Indiana made him an easy choice for the convention, and he was given the second spot on the ticket.

The Republicans, meeting in Chicago, had a harder time making their selection. It took them thirty-six ballots before they settled on U.S. Representative James Garfield, from Ohio, and on the New Yorker Chester Arthur as his running mate.

The Democrats' choice of Hancock meant that Pulitzer had to do some rapid editorial backpedaling. On the eve of the convention, he had warned that selecting a general as a candidate would be a "stupendous mistake" because putting a military man in the White House would be inherently dangerous to liberty. Now he did an about-face. Of all the soldier-politicians, he assured his readers, Hancock was the one most devoted to civilian rule, habeas corpus, and strict interpretation of the Constitution.

On his return to St. Louis, Pulitzer spoke to a large, enthusiastic Democratic rally at the courthouse. Most men would have been physically exhausted by the travel and the long hours of the convention, but Pulitzer displayed dazzling energy, sustained by the adrenaline surge elections gave him. He had not been home for even a day before he wrote to a political operative in Indiana, "Is there anything I can do in your state on the stump? I shall be glad to serve as in 76, of course, at my expense."

Back at his desk, Pulitzer found that his paper had recovered from the fire and had prevailed in a dozen libel suits, including one brought by the famous Italian soprano Carlotta Patti—the *Post-Dispatch* had insinuated that she was very well, perhaps too well, acquainted with liquor. But now a different danger arose. On the streets in late July, newsboys were hawking a new paper, the *Evening Chronicle*. It sold for two cents—three cents less than the *Post-Dispatch*—and the street urchins were excited because they received the paper free of charge and could pocket the entire revenue.

The publisher challenging Pulitzer's dominance of the afternoon field was Edward W. Scripps. Pulitzer was not the only one who had discovered a way to succeed in the new era of independent journalism. Scripps, who had been an Illinois farmboy, launched his first newspaper at age twenty-four in Cleveland. His formula was to produce an inexpensive, tightly edited, but sprightly written paper aimed at the growing working classes of the nation's new industrial centers. His editorial policy matched the goals of the audience he sought. His papers were fierce advocates for labor unions and collective bargaining.

The *Evening Chronicle*'s fresh tone and low price attracted readers, and its pricing policy stirred up the newsboys to demand that Pulitzer sell them three, instead of two, copies of his paper for five cents. When he refused, the boys once again staged a strike of sorts. Some of them stood outside the *Post-Dispatch* offices and taunted others who tried to deliver papers. Pulitzer was unfazed. Unembarrassed to be waging an industrial war against children, Pulitzer knew that, as in his previous skirmish with the boys, he could withstand their assaults. He defended himself to his readers, pointing out he made only as much on each newspaper sold as the newsboys did, "and we furnish the white paper, ink, presswork, type-setting, and just enough brains to keep the thing going."

Pulitzer was comforted also by the *Post-Dispatch*'s continued growth. The paper had already surpassed the circulation of Hyde's *Republican* by 25 percent. Only McCullagh's morning *Globe-Democrat* outsold the *Post-Dispatch*, and Pulitzer anticipated that he would overtake it within months. With the growth in circulation came continued prosperity. Pulitzer's cashier predicted that the paper should net more than $85,000 by the end of 1880.

On August 8, Charles Johnson stopped in at Pulitzer's house and found Pulitzer huddled with Irish ward bosses, discussing his plan to run for Congress. Johnson, who had earlier tried to persuade Pulitzer not to pursue a career in law or politics, told him the project was an act of folly. But Pulitzer wasn't in a mood to listen. His hunger for political office was so overpowering that he ignored both his old friend and his own ethics.

To get the nomination, Pulitzer was willing to dance with the devil. In this case his name was Ed Butler, also known as "de boss of St. Louis" or more unassumingly as "the village blacksmith." Butler, who had been born in Ireland in 1838, ran a smithing business in the Fifth Ward, which Pulitzer had represented in the state legislature. Early on, Butler found it profitable to get involved in city politics. After helping one mayoral candidate in 1872, he earned the contract to shoe the city government's horses and, later, the horses that pulled the city's trolleys. By 1880, Butler's power extended over the entire city. His powerful organization was known to its detractors as the "Dark Lantern."

Butler had a simple system. For the payment of a fee to the Dark Lantern, a candidate would receive the Democratic nomination. Although this was the kind of corrupt practice the *Post-Dispatch* denounced, Pulitzer himself paid between $6,000 and $10,000. It was worth it. Being nominated was tantamount to winning the election, as the Second District was overwhelmingly Democratic.

Believing that his nomination was secure and that he would be in

Congress when the Democrats regained the White House, Pulitzer refocused his energy on the national campaign. As he had in 1872 and 1876, he turned to Indiana. It was widely believed that its 15 electoral votes, perhaps with New York state's 30, would decide the election. Indiana was also one of the states that had additional political importance, because it held its elections for state office in October, helping build momentum for the winning party in the national vote a month later. "We all regard Indiana as *the* battle ground," Pulitzer wrote to the vice presidential candidate, English.

Pulitzer crafted a speech to give in Indianapolis, where Schurz had delivered a long and widely noted address for the Republicans. In a sense, this would be a reprise of the 1876 election, when Pulitzer indirectly debated his former mentor. But in the four years that had passed since then, Pulitzer had become a newspaper publisher whose fame was equal to, if not greater than, Schurz's. The Democratic press now described Pulitzer as the editor of "one of the most influential papers"; Republicans called him "notorious." In either case, he was no longer simply the "German orator."

Pulitzer was pleased with this transformation. He told organizers in Indianapolis that he would make his speech in English. If they insisted, he could deliver a second address in German. "There is no difference to me whatever between the two languages," he said. "I prefer to deliver the principal speech in English solely because I know that will make it more effective—even among Germans."

On the evening of August 14, Pulitzer stood before a large crowd in the Indianapolis Wigwam, an auditorium often used for political functions. For almost an hour, he accused the Republicans of demagoguery and centralization. In an unusually personal moment, Pulitzer said he was better equipped than native-born men to recognize the danger, describing how he came to the United States "friendless, homeless, tongueless, guideless" and how he renounced his allegiance to an emperor to become a citizen. "I joyfully complied with that condition," he said. "I have kept faith; I am only keeping faith now."

Launching his most direct attack yet as a politician, publisher, or orator, Pulitzer challenged America's upper class and the elected officials who did its bidding. In a succession of sentences that left both speaker and audience breathless, Pulitzer said, "Show me a land where one person controls 8,000 miles of railroad, mostly built by government subsidies; where another has forty-seven million of government bonds registered in his name, and where still another can appear at a White House reception with diamonds on her body worth over a million dollars; show me a land where the money power, the organized capital, privileges and monopolies of the country, the railroads, telegraphs, banks, protected manufacturers, etc. are favored and fostered by the government . . . and you have shown me imperialism. It is the issue of the hour and the duty of the Democracy is to meet it, battle it, overthrow it, and restore and re-establish the sane principle of true, popular, self-government."

Pulitzer did not frame the election in terms of commonplace issues such as tariffs or civil service reform. Rather, he argued that the growing prosperity of the nation endangered its political freedoms. The wealthy, who benefited most from industrialization, were seeking to protect their interests by controlling the government. "Let us have prosperity, but never at the expense of liberty, never at the expense of real self-government, and let us never have a government in Washington owing its retention to the power of the millionaires rather than the will of the millions."

In September, Pulitzer set aside his work for the national ticket in order to tend to his own race for Congress. Anyone else might have been simply content to enjoy success as a publisher. But Pulitzer was not yet ready to give up his pursuit of elective office. His ambition had taken root when, at a formative age, he had watched Carl Schurz win office, respect, success, and adulation through journalism. For one who had Pulitzer's ego and need for control, politics was a siren—even more so when, after he had been rejected by voters, it offered redemption in the form of a comeback.

As the primary neared, the acrimony between Pulitzer and Hyde increased. Still stinging from his defeat in Moberly, Hyde was not going to let Pulitzer seize his mantle without a fight. He and his paper's publisher, Charles Knapp, set to work to derail Pulitzer's nomination. They persuaded Thomas Allen, president of Iron Mountain Railroad, to give up his aspirations for the Senate and run for the House seat. Even though he had once charitably given Pulitzer's brother a job, Allen despised the *Post-Dispatch* and the older Pulitzer. There was no doubt how Pulitzer felt about him. When Allen ran for the Senate in 1879, Pulitzer had fired off an editorial barrage, attacking him as a tool of capital, and insisting that if he was elected the railroads would rule the state. "No one outside of the lunatic asylum," Pulitzer wrote, "believes that Tom Allen's name would be even mentioned if, instead of having riches and railroads, he were poor and penniless."

With Allen's entry into the race, the other candidates withdrew, leaving the field to the newspaper publisher and railroad magnate. "His candidacy simply represents the spite, the hatred, the jealousy and business rivalry of the Knapp cabal," wrote Pulitzer in an editorial "There never was a better time to put a quietus on the dictatorial gang of political pirates who infest the *Republican* office."

Calling Pulitzer a demagogue who prostituted his paper by turning it into a mudslinging machine, Hyde said that the *Post-Dispatch* would not thwart Allen's candidacy. "If anybody is to be hurt by the dirt-throwing, which the *Post-Dispatch* began as soon as Mr. Allen consented to run for Congress, it is Pulitzer. His mud will all fall back on himself, and it will stick there."

Hyde enlisted the wealthiest and most influential residents of each ward to serve as delegates, election judges, and clerks in the primary. Together they brought economic pressure to bear on Butler and his Dark Lantern organization by threatening Butler's control of the street-car shoeing business. The plan worked. The night before the primary, Butler's men were ordered to change their votes to Allen.

The *Republican* greeted Election Day with confidence. The campaign had taken such a turn that it was almost like a chapter from *Alice in Wonderland*. Everything was now upside down. Allen, the railroad magnate representing St. Louis's oligarchy, was running as the candidate of reform. Pulitzer, the real enemy of entrenched interests, was tainted by his brief fling with corrupt machine politics. The paper urged voters "to bury Pulitzer out of sight at the Democratic primary election today." That's what they did. Pulitzer received only 721 votes to Allen's 4,274. In Butler's ward, Pulitzer did not receive a single vote. "The machine, as I expected, sold Pulitzer out," Johnson wrote that night in his diary.

When Pulitzer lost his seat in the legislature in 1870, it had been at the hands of the opposing political party. Now his own party rejected him. Despite his ego and his mounting sense of importance, Pulitzer accepted this shellacking. Johnson was impressed. "Pulitzer takes his defeat more philosophically than I should," he said. The day following the election, Pulitzer told his readers, "The past is past. We have nothing to take back. We look and think forward, not backward." The nomination had been settled with the selection of Allen. "The next question is, Shall he be elected? We say, emphatically, Yes!"

Pulitzer wasted no time before returning to the stump for the national ticket, leaving behind a pregnant Kate, nearing her due date. Only a few days after his departure, on October 3, 1880, she gave birth to their second child, Lucille Irma. Father would not meet his new baby for several weeks because in Pulitzer's world little if anything was more important than an election. In this case, he had an executive committee meeting in New York and was to give speeches along the way in Ohio. He arrived at the national Democratic headquarters full of enthusiasm. "I have not the slightest doubt of carrying Indiana," he told a reporter. "Why should I?"

But, the reporter persisted, "the story is here that the Republicans are preparing to send a great deal of money into Indiana."

"I see that this story is circulated," said Pulitzer. "With the shadow of the Presidential contest projected over the State battle, I do not believe money will change enough votes to affect the results in any appreciable manner."

Following the party leaders' meeting, Pulitzer took to the road again. He first went to Boston and then quickly headed back to Indiana and Ohio, predicting victory to all he met. "If Ohio were to elect tomorrow it would go Democratic," Pulitzer told one reporter. But the election would turn on Indiana, he predicted. "It is agreed on all sides that as Indiana goes this year, so goes the Union."

Pulitzer had one major speech scheduled before the Buckeyes and Hoosiers voted. On October 7, he was the main event at a large Democratic, and very German, rally at Memorial Park in Cleveland, Ohio. Pulitzer dug right into his class-based attack on the Republicans. He asked the Germans in the audience if they had not left their native land to escape a government controlled by one class. The ruling class would turn the United States into the same system they had escaped unless their participation in the election turned the tide. Allied against them, he warned, were an army of patronage and a coalition of corporations, banks, and railroads. "The Blaines, Conklings, Shermans and others traveling on special trains, unlike common people; hundreds of thousands, if not millions of dollars raised by Wall Street and capitalists in Boston, New England, and Philadelphia. Raised for what? To corrupt the elections and prevent a change."

Despite the size and enthusiasm of the crowd, Pulitzer sensed that the tide in these two crucial state elections was not in the Democrats' favor. He was right. Several days later, the Republicans scored an easy victory in Ohio and squeaked by in Indiana. The prospects for the White House looked dim once again. Nonetheless Pulitzer continued his campaign, making speeches in the crucial state of New York. Speaking in Chickering Hall on Fifth Avenue, he clung tenaciously to his populist themes. "The country is in danger, not from below, but from above; not from segregation, but from centralization and imperialism—from organized corporations, organized privileges, and from the army of 100,000 office holders."

Pulitzer the journalist dropped any pretense of confidence. He telegraphed a signed article back to the *Post-Dispatch* with a gloomy estimation of Hancock's chances in the election. In fact, Pulitzer went as far as to forecast a victory for Garfield, earning the wrath of other partisan papers. Such a prediction was the political equivalent of violating baseball's prohibition against using the term "no-hitter" before the last batter is out.

When Election Day came, it looked for a brief time as if Pulitzer would be proved wrong. The popular vote turned out to be a virtual tie: each major candidate had 48.3 percent of the vote, with the remainder going to third-party candidates. But the electoral votes gave Garfield the election. With Indiana and Ohio voting Republican, New York turned out to be the key state. A shift of a few thousand votes in the Empire State—5,517, to be precise—would have made Hancock president. The lesson was not lost on Pulitzer, who studied election maps with a mania. If the Democrats were to end their drought, those votes would need to be found in New York.

His dream of owning a New York paper took on new urgency.

Chapter Fifteen

ST. LOUIS GROWS SMALL

◆

O n many nights in early 1881, Pulitzer lay awake in his bed listening to the bells of the St. Louis Pilgrim Congregational Church peal out the passing hours. The third- or fourth-largest set of bells in the United States, they could be easily heard across the city. Pulitzer liked the ringing because it let him know how much time remained until dawn. The long, taxing days and the never-ending demands at the paper had taken a toll. Even though success was near, Pulitzer found it harder to sleep. But his insomnia did not stem from business worries. It was as if he could not shut down.

Neither the *Post-Dispatch* nor Pulitzer had financial woes. The paper's net income was growing every month, and Pulitzer himself brought home more than $4,000 a month—more than what many of his elite neighbors earned. The only business challenge facing Pulitzer that spring was a modest one. The local typographical union wanted the *Post-Dispatch* to recognize it as the bargaining agent for the paper's compositors and printers, as the *Globe-Democrat* had done. Intellectually, Pulitzer was sympathetic to the aims of the labor movement. But this was different from writing an editorial dictating the behavior of others. Pulitzer would not abide anything that challenged his rule within the paper.

A few printers sought to meet with Pulitzer and threatened to stop work if their demands were not met. Pulitzer was absent, so no meeting occurred. Nor would the meeting occur upon his return, because these printers were summarily fired by his managers. The *Post-Dispatch*, Pulitzer declared, "declines to be told who it shall and shall not employ.

It refuses to be instructed as to how to measure its type, feed its press and to be limited to the number of apprentices it shall take into office training." He conceded that workers had the right to organize "but the right to manage the internal affairs of this office, employ and discharge and to direct when and how labor shall be performed, is one that the proprietor reserves to himself." Simply put, Pulitzer was a democrat in politics, but a paternalistic despot in the office.

Pulitzer, however, did not treat his workers badly. In fact, the 1881 campaign by the typographical union came to an end because an overwhelming majority of Pulitzer's compositors had signed a statement proclaiming their happiness with their working conditions and their loyalty to their boss. Pulitzer paid better than other publishers, granted vacation time, frequently rewarded good work with bonuses, and remained intensely loyal to those who served him. He even gave his employees wedding and birthday gifts. At Christmas, he made it a tradition to send turkeys to his staff, and newsboys were invited to yuletide dinners where the tables groaned under the weight of food.

Pulitzer claimed that his benevolence was self-serving. "Without good men you cannot get good work, and without good work no paper can prosper largely," he said. Yet he was deeply charitable. Once he became wealthy, he rarely declined any financial appeal, and he was particularly receptive to appeals from people he had met on his way up. For the remainder of his life, he quietly made arrangements to send monthly checks to widows of men who had toiled for him. He remembered how his mother had faced poverty when her husband died.

That Pulitzer was absent when the printers came to see him was not surprising. As during the 1880 campaign, he used his increasing freedom from managerial responsibilities to spend time in the East. No matter how successful he was in St. Louis, New York remained the center of American journalism and politics. Pulitzer wanted in.

With its theaters, concert halls, museums, banks, corporations, and millionaires, New York was the capital of everything important in the United States. Swampy, uncivilized Washington, D.C., may have been the seat of government, but New York remained the capital of politics. In journalism, Park Row was the dream destination of every reporter and editor. In the few short blocks, more newspapers were clustered than in any other spot of the world. Their offices were so substantial, their circulation was so large, and their news gathering was so extensive that the rest of nation's papers seemed like small-town sheets.

But in the last few years, New York's Park Row had changed greatly. Many of the giants who created its best-known newspapers had died. Gone were the *New York Tribune*'s Horace Greeley, the *New York Herald*'s James Gordon Bennett, Sr., and the *New York Times*'s Henry J. Raymond. The new leaders were men such as Charles Dana at the *New York Sun* and Edwin Lawrence Godkin at the *New York Evening Post*. This group, however, seemed only to be caretakers. A new order of journalism—lively, independent, and crusading—was growing in other cities. It was like theatrical plays previewing out of town, working out their kinks while awaiting their chance on Broadway.

Pulitzer talked Daniel Houser into accompanying him to New York to look for a newspaper to buy. Houser, who co-owned the *Globe-Democrat*, had helped Pulitzer plan his purchase of the *Dispatch* four years earlier. They took rooms at the Fifth Avenue Hotel on June 19, 1881.

After scouting around Park Row, they failed to discover any major newspaper for sale. There was one paper, a daily called *Truth*, which might be bought. It had started in 1879, had been an instant hit, and had quickly attained a circulation of more than 100,000 with its irreverent, light tone, bordering on the vulgar. Recently, it had run into financial difficulties, and Pulitzer made a halfhearted bid of $50,000 for it, but he was turned down. Thinking maybe he would do better to launch his own newspaper, Pulitzer asked Houser to go in with him. "I told him I was tied up with the *Globe-Democrat* and that the only field in New York would be for a Democratic paper, that I could not print a Republican paper in St. Louis and a Democratic paper in New York," Houser recalled. "I advised him not to start a new paper but buy one with a location—an office, a name, a franchise."

Almost as if he did not want to return to St. Louis, Pulitzer found excuses to stay in the East through the summer of 1881. He dashed up to Albany to report for the *Post-Dispatch* on Roscoe Conkling's fruitless bid to win back the Senate seat he had resigned over a patronage dispute with President James Garfield. The political drama culminated on July 2 when Charles Guiteau, an obscure follower of Conkling's stalwart faction who was also a disappointed office seeker himself, pumped two bullets into the president. Doctors spent the summer battling to save Garfield's life.

In September, the president was moved to Elberon, part of the coastal town of Long Branch, New Jersey, where fresh sea air might speed his recovery. Pulitzer joined the pack of reporters at the West End Hotel covering the president's convalescence. It didn't take long for him to become skeptical about the doctors' optimistic bulletins. Probably, most of the reporters were also doubtful about the official pronouncements. But lacking the freedom of writing for a paper they owned, most of them dutifully transmitted to their editors the morsels of upbeat news provided to them by the president's staff. GREATLY IMPROVED reported the *Chicago Tribune*, and the *Washington Post* predicted, THE PRESIDENT SURELY ON THE ROAD TO RECOVERY.

When his turn came at the telegraph office, Pulitzer handed the operator a far gloomier assessment. "There are not many in the inner circle who do not well know that the bulletins are reliable only in this, that they exaggerate and embellish to the uttermost every favorable and utterly ignore every unfavorable sign of the case," he wired to the *Post-Dispatch*. The operator, one of eight brought in by Western Union to handle the volume of traffic, was impressed by what he transmitted. "Mr. Pulitzer always filed what we termed 'good stuff,'" he recalled. "From the first line of his first story, Mr. Pulitzer predicted the death of Garfield and pilloried several of the attending physicians for their false bulletins on the President's condition."

At the beginning of Garfield's second week in Long Branch, ominous reports about his health began circulating. Most reporters, however, continued to report otherwise. They stuck to the story that the president was improving and that any news to the contrary was a product of the sensational press. A few nervous reporters covered their tracks by mentioning the rumors. Pulitzer, on the other hand, pressed on with his baleful version of Garfield's condition. "As I said last week, the President is growing worse," he wrote. "He is wasting away. It is only a question of time. All of his troubles, all his weakness come from the blood. It is poisoned." The doctors, he said, were lying. Pulitzer was convinced that septicemia, which before antibiotics invariably resulted in death, had set in.

On September 15, the president's medical team conceded that Garfield had pyemia, or septicemia. Incredibly, reporters for the *Washington*

Post, the *New York Times*, and other papers downplayed this news. Pulitzer marched to the telegraph office with a blunt dispatch. "Unless his blood can be cured he cannot be saved. I said this over a week ago and I repeat it," Pulitzer wrote. "The physicians and bulletins and reporters have lied for days and weeks and months in denying this fact."

The tide of bad news now overwhelmed the Pollyannas of the press. The *New York Times* had the most backpedaling to do. It claimed that newspapermen were astonished by the new disclosures. The *Post-Dispatch* bragged that the new official bulletins proved its reporting—done by its owner—had been true all along. "Even Dr. Bliss has at last been forced to confess the lamentable truth," Pulitzer said. "He now admits everything he so positively denied every day and almost every hour of the last week."

On Monday morning, September 19, Pulitzer filed his final dispatch. "All hope is dead. The President is dying." That night, with his wife and daughter at his side, Garfield ceased to breathe. In New York, a messenger boy brought the news to Vice President Chester Alan Arthur as church bells began to toll. Pulitzer returned to the city and denounced Garfield's doctors. "If they had been blind-folded they could hardly have shown much less sense."

The day after the president's death, the *Post-Dispatch* defended itself against the censorious complaints it had received during Pulitzer's coverage of Garfield's decline. "We have been charged with 'sensationalism' and with a desire to prematurely dispose of the sufferer," Cockerill wrote. "We were not blinded by the bulletins of the physicians who felt it a part of their duty to keep up the spirit of the country in the face of plain facts. We went behind the bulletins. . . . Our predictions, we are sorry to say, have nearly all been verified."

The success of Pulitzer's *Post-Dispatch* ceased being a novelty. By any measure, the newspaper and its publisher had become as important in St. Louis as the established morning papers—*The Republican* and the *Globe-Democrat*—and the men at their helms. During Pulitzer's reporting from Long Branch, his paper's circulation rose to 28,475 copies, more than three times the average circulation it had at the beginning of the year.

To accommodate his growing staff and new presses, Pulitzer built a four-story building. He installed Richard Hoe's latest press, which could cut and fold the paper at a high rate of speed and included the first counting devices. Since getting his first order from the upstart publisher in 1878, Hoe and his headquarters staff in New York had become very familiar with the Pulitzer name.

Pulitzer trumpeted the link between the newspaper's financial independence and its political independence. "From the very commencement the cardinal principle of the paper and the chief ambition of its owner and conductor has been to achieve and maintain an absolute independence, financially, politically, personally and morally," Pulitzer wrote, celebrating the installation of the latest Hoe press. "We have absolutely no master, and no friend but the great public."

Indeed, the *Post-Dispatch*'s crusading zeal found a loyal middle-class readership. Success, however, came with costs. The paper's campaigns of civic reform left the city's landscape strewn with bruised and injured parties; its drive to clean up the city's illicit pastimes of gambling and prostitution shut down popular forms of entertainment; its continual attacks on the oligarchy embittered the powerful; and the moral haughtiness of its editorials ensured that many, including its supporters, would relish a humbling misstep.

As a consequence, Pulitzer and his family faced growing social ostracism. St. Louis may have projected cosmopolitan airs to visitors, but those who lived there learned quickly that it had the pettiness of a small town. "It is encrusted," said Pulitzer's friend Stilson Hutchins, "with prejudices, which are steadily strengthened by such contemptible creatures as the Knapps—who prat high morality in the columns of their newspapers—traduce and slander everybody whom they can't use or who does not belong to their set."

The hostility grew to the point where Pulitzer was assaulted on the street. In late March, as he was leaving Ecker's restaurant, where he had lunched, a burly man armed with a small whip tried to strike him. Pulitzer seized his assailant by the throat and threw him against a store window, breaking it. The man, who left no clue as to the cause of his anger, ran off, escaping through a nearby saloon.

For Kate, her husband's notoriety was painful. Despite her pedigree, she found herself increasingly snubbed by the social elite whose company she coveted. The Pulitzers moved from their house on Washington Avenue, but there was little they could do to decrease their sense of isolation. Compounding Kate's unhappiness was the uncertain health of the children. Both Ralph and Lucille were delicate. Ralph, in particular, was small and weak for his age and suffered from asthma and other ailments. As 1882 began, Kate was pregnant again. She remained alone a great deal of time, especially as Joseph increasingly spent time away from St. Louis.

In March, on one of half a dozen long trips to the East that year, Pulitzer joined up with Hutchins in Washington to interview Garfield's assassin in the jail where he awaited execution. Charles Guiteau had used as a legal defense the technically correct claim that the president had died not from the bullets but rather from the incompetence of the doctors who, as Pulitzer had reported, had misdiagnosed and mistreated their patient. Despite their shared low regard for Garfield's doctors, Pulitzer was filled with an intense hatred of Guiteau. When he reached the cell, his enmity grew. The prisoner jumped up and greeted Pulitzer in perhaps the most wounding manner possible. "Why, how do you do, Mr. Schurz," said Guiteau. "I know your brother very well—have spoken from the same platform with him. How much you look like him."

Pulitzer turned to Hutchins with a look of disgust and they both shook their heads. "I did not care, however, to lose time by explanations as to his mistake of my identity," said Pulitzer, who decided to let the insulting misidentification go unchallenged. "My business was to study." Perhaps, but Guiteau's business was to make money. He earned about $50 a day selling photographs and autographs to visitors. Before the interview progressed, the required business was transacted, and Pulitzer and Hutchins soon owned their own Guiteau memorabilia.

"He handles his greenbacks," Pulitzer said, "like a bank teller and talks about the different points and features of his different photographs precisely as if he were standing behind the counter selling ribbons or lace." Pulitzer found Guiteau unrepentant. Nor did Guiteau show any signs of lunacy. In fact, Pulitzer thought the man, whose actions had changed the leadership of the nation and the fortunes of thousands of ambitious men, seemed no different from a typical businessman or clerk. "He could have been taken precisely as he stood and transferred behind the counter of some dry-goods store as a perfectly fit figure."

By the end of the visit, Pulitzer was even more repelled by the assassin than he had been at its beginning, almost as if Guiteau's apparent normality made the crime more heinous. As the two newspapermen rode away from the jail, Hutchins noticed that his companion "was constantly engaged in washing his hands with invisible soap in imperceptible water."

Perhaps inspired by his brother's success with the *Post-Dispatch*, Albert Pulitzer was bitten by a similar ambition. He had been working as a $45-a-week reporter on Bennett's *New York Herald* that spring when he shared his plan with a friend who worked at the *New York Times*. Pausing in front of the Equitable Building on Broadway, Albert told his companion that he intended to raise $20,000 to launch a paper in the already crowded New York market. His fellow reporter questioned the wisdom of embarking on such a risky enterprise with so little money. Albert laughed. "If I once get started, I shall not stop," he said. "I can then get more capital."

Albert wanted to create a newspaper that would stand in contrast to the spiritless gray sheets of the time. The idea had come to him while he rode on streetcars and ferryboats. He noticed that newspaper readers gravitated to articles written in a lighter vein. "How would it do, I often asked myself when I thus watched newspaper readers, as they read their different papers, to create a new kind of paper, bright instead of dull, light instead of heavy, gay instead of wearisome?"

During his years at the *Herald*, Albert had become convinced that newspapers were ignoring half of their potential readership. "It is, after all, women who enrich newspaper proprietors, it is the shops who cater to them who make the great newspaper fortunes in this country by the advertising which they pour out like a shower of gold into the columns of the papers." He recalled how, when he sold subscriptions to a German newspaper door-to-door in St. Louis, women remained loyal to a publication that won their affection. Albert's ideal newspaper would be full of material interesting to women.

Albert asked his now wealthy brother for money. Even though Joseph had earlier been so eager to get a foothold into New York newspaperdom that he had been prepared to buy a gossipy rag, he said he wouldn't invest a cent in Albert's scheme. "He kindly proposed that I should come out to St. Louis for a year, go to work on the *Post-Dispatch* and thus learn at least the rudiments of the business side of journalism." The idea of his younger brother seeking to succeed in New York before him raised Joseph's hackles.

Undeterred by either the pessimism of his friends of the parsimony of his brother, Albert began a search for capital. Failing to find anyone in New York willing to invest, in the summer of 1882 Albert sailed for London, where his wit and charm had won over many people in high social circles during his previous reporting trips for the *Herald*. Unlike Joseph, Albert was a bon vivant. "His delightful anecdotes and reminiscences of celebrities he had met at home and abroad, his gift for seizing upon the distinctive qualities of a personality and turning them to the best account, together with his sharp and pungent wit and sparkling repartee," recalled one smitten marquise, "rendered him an exceptionally entertaining companion."

In August, Albert returned triumphantly to New York with $25,000 in capital. He put together a bare-bones staff of editors and reporters and rented space on the sixth floor of the *New York Tribune*'s building on Spruce Street, overlooking the *Sun* and French's Hotel. The *Tribune* agreed to print his newspaper on one of its unused presses, but only after Albert had promised that none of his staff would enter the composing room, where valuable AP dispatches might be purloined.

New York would soon have its first Pulitzer newspaper.

In the fall of 1882, continued concern about Ralph's asthma led the Pulitzers to spend time away from St. Louis. Now with a third child—Katherine Ethel, who had been born on June 30—the family took up residence for the winter in Aiken, South Carolina, which was becoming a popular health resort. Even though this was an election year, Pulitzer left the management of the *Post-Dispatch* in Cockerill's hands. When it came to political coverage, readers were unlikely to notice the difference. Cockerill, if such a thing was possible, became even more excited by elections than his boss—perhaps, as it would turn out, too animated.

The most important contest in St. Louis was an election to fill the congressional seat that had become vacant when Thomas Allen, Pulitzer's former opponent, died in office. The party bosses, specifically the Knapps and Hyde at the *Republican*, favored James Broadhead, an old friend and political ally of Pulitzer's. But under Cockerill's direction, the *Post-Dispatch* vigorously opposed Broadhead on the grounds that he was in the pocket of the gas monopoly and acted as Jay Gould's man in St. Louis. Broadhead's participation in the court cases involving the gas monopoly might have been excused as a mistake, but his affiliation with Gould tainted him indelibly.

If the railroad was the corporate evil of the era, the railroad and industrial magnate Jay Gould was its personification. Easily one of the most hated men of the era, he served as a ready target for the editorial pen of the reformist-minded Pulitzer. Two years earlier, for instance, Pulitzer heard a rumor in New York that Gould had purchased the Democratic *New York World*. "The Democratic party, despite its great vitality, cannot afford to have its press contaminated by such a vampire," wrote Pulitzer on his return to St. Louis. The rumor was true. Gould had unintentionally acquired the paper when he purchased the assets of another corporation.

Gould became Pulitzer's particular devil. Pulitzer began a campaign to warn Missourians of the financier's Mephistophelian intentions. From New York, in March 1882, Pulitzer filed an article claiming that Gould intended to make Missouri "his 'pocket borough,' controlling the Missouri legislature, running all the railroads, steamships, iron mills, and everything else he can gobble up, including one or two of the newspapers." The *Post-Dispatch* took to calling Gould "Missouri's boss."

Broadhead aroused the enmity of the *Post-Dispatch* for two reasons. Not only was he the hand-chosen candidate of Pulitzer's archenemies in St. Louis, but he was also Gould's representative. Still, when Broadhead won the party's nomination, most people assumed the *Post-Dispatch* would support him, as it had done when Allen beat Pulitzer two years earlier. But Cockerill relished a fight. He did not back down. On the contrary, he went after Broadhead with a vengeance, laying out an array of charges of corruption. When the candidate remained silent, Cockerill wrote, "Perhaps the charges are unanswerable."

The attacks greatly upset Broadhead's law partner Alonzo W. Slayback, not a man one would want to anger. Slayback had been a friend of Cockerill's boss since they met during Pulitzer's first political campaign as a Democrat. Slayback had tolerated the *Post-Dispatch*'s excited political pronouncements, and in return Pulitzer had kept Slayback out of the paper's crosshairs. For example, about a year earlier an opponent of Slayback's had published a card* in the *Post-Dispatch* accusing the lawyer of

---

*In the nineteenth century, the term "card" referred to a brief personal note published in a newspaper, similar to a modern letter to the editor. Cards containing strong language were sometimes a preliminary to a duel.

being a coward; at great expense, Pulitzer had the card removed in the middle of a press run.

Now, with Pulitzer out of town and Cockerill in charge, Slayback began to berate the paper to anyone who would listen. One night at the end of September, Slayback went on a verbal rampage against Cockerill and the paper in the reception room of the Elks club, of which Cockerill was the president. Slayback accused Cockerill of being a blackmailer, a term then considered provocation for a duel. Cockerill gently persuaded Slayback to retire to the library, where the two held an extended conversation. When it was concluded, they headed off to drink in the bar, apparently having put their differences aside.

But a dozen days later, Slayback resumed sniping at Cockerill and referred to the paper as a "blackmailing sheet." The renewed attack prompted Cockerill to dig out and print the old insulting card, whose publication Pulitzer had prevented. Only an hour after the edition hit the street, the *Post-Dispatch*'s city editor looked up from his desk to see Slayback charging through the newsroom toward Cockerill's office in the company of William Clopton, another lawyer.

In his office, Cockerill was meeting with the business manager and the composing room foreman. His pistol lay on the desk, where he had placed it in anticipation of putting it into his coat when he left for home in a few minutes. Slayback threw open the door and stepped in, leaving Clopton in the hall. Then, as the men watched, Slayback took out a revolver.

"Well, I'm here, sir," Slayback said. Then, spotting Cockerill's weapon on the desk, he asked, "Is that for me?"

"No, it's for me to use only to defend myself," replied Cockerill.

"You are prepared to draw, then draw," Slayback said.

By this time Clopton had managed to gain entrance to the room and found that the confrontation had developed into a physical struggle between the men. Cockerill pulled the trigger of his gun as Clopton rushed to disarm him. The single shot met its target, traversing both of Slayback's lungs. He slumped to the floor with blood frothing at his mouth. In a moment, Slayback was dead.

When word spread through town that Cockerill had killed Slayback, a mob of detractors of the *Post-Dispatch* gathered in front of its building. The crowd grew angry and might have stormed the building had the police not held the people back. Meanwhile, Cockerill stole away to the

Lindell Hotel. Pulitzer's old friend Charles Johnson, who had defended Pulitzer when he shot Augustine, was summoned. In Johnson's company, Cockerill surrendered to the police that night.

News of the shooting was reported across the country. Reporters found Pulitzer in New York. He strongly defended Cockerill, calling him "one of the quietest persons you ever knew." Even though he admitted he did not know that his editor packed a pistol, Pulitzer said Cockerill must have done so solely for self-defense. He immediately caught a train back to St. Louis.

Upon arriving in St. Louis, Pulitzer went directly to Cockerill's cell and assured his editor that he would stand by him. In the paper's office, Pulitzer scrawled a short editorial, in his large, loopy handwriting, asking readers to withhold judgment until the police and the courts had completed their work. It was doubtful that any official report would please both sides. The only witnesses to the shooting each had a motive to lie. Nor was the prosecutor likely to be considered objective, since the *Post-Dispatch* had supported his election.

Slayback's friend Clopton told the police the victim had been unarmed. The *Post-Dispatch* employees in the room stood by their claim that he had been armed. The gun found on Slayback seemed to corroborate Cockerill's claim of self-defense, but some people believed the gun had been planted. In fact, years later a *Post-Dispatch* employee confessed that he had planted it, to help Cockerill's plea of self-defense. But whether St. Louisans believed the killing was self-defense or murder depended less on evidence and more on their attitude toward the paper. Few sat on the fence, and those who were vindictive were vocal. "If this closes the career of that scandalous sheet it will be a life well spent," one woman wrote to her son.

On October 18, Pulitzer and McCullagh, the *Globe-Democrat* editor who had once been Cockerill's boss, persuaded a judge to release Cockerill on $10,000 bail. A grand jury was convened to determine if Cockerill would be indicted for murder. Pulitzer knew that more than Cockerill's fate hung in the balance. His enemies, particularly those at the *Missouri Republican*, struck at him and the *Post-Dispatch*, claiming that Slayback's death was a direct result of his sensational journalism. For once, it seemed, Hyde had the upper hand. The *Post-Dispatch*'s average daily circulation fell by 2,015, and several national publications joined the chorus of critics. *Harper's Weekly*, for instance, said the killing was "a direct result of personal journalism."

Pulitzer brushed off the *Republican*'s daily attacks and offered a spirited defense of Cockerill in the *Post-Dispatch*. He accepted responsibility for the content of the paper leading up to the shooting and wrote that Cockerill's conduct—in print, not with the gun—had been justified by Slayback's provocation.

But, watching the circulation plummet, Pulitzer knew he had to disassociate the paper from Cockerill. He turned to John Dillon for help. In the three years since they had parted company, Dillon had spent some time writing for the *Globe-Democrat*, had gone to work in Mexico, and had recently returned to St. Louis to take a job with the weekly *Spectator*. Pulitzer now asked him to take over Cockerill's job. Dillon immediately accepted the offer, and within days his restrained, refined prose calmed the editorial page. Any mention of Broadhead's candidacy disappeared from the page.

As part of this restoration, Pulitzer invited his actor friend John McCullough to put on a benefit performance of *Julius Caesar* at the Mercantile Library for the Slayback family. Boxes for the show were auctioned off. Kate bought one for $1,000, although most sold for less than $100. Notably absent were Pulitzer's critics at the *Republican*, who had so ferociously attacked him. In their anger, none of Pulitzer's enemies recognized that the victim had been a friend of his also. Years later, long after Pulitzer was no longer in St. Louis, he provided a job on the paper for Slayback's daughter.

In the end, the grand jury declined to indict Cokerill, convinced that Slayback had provoked the shooting by entering the office with a weapon. Pulitzer and the *Post-Dispatch* had survived the crisis but St. Louis had become even less hospitable to him and his family. Once again, Pulitzer left for New York.

In the early morning hours of November 16, 1882, a few days after Joseph reached New York City, Albert and his newly assembled staff left their offices to get the first copies of *The Morning Journal* as it came off the *New York Tribune*'s presses. The men all returned to their desks to study their first effort and, as all journalists do, mark typos.

One of the men suggested "something wet" to mark the occasion, and Albert sent the office boy out to procure some bottles. Upon his return, the editors and reporters quaffed beer and toasted the paper's birth. Albert, however, chose Apollinaris water instead. There was no food, not even "beef an," the famous ten-cent plate of corned beef and beans from nearby Hitchcock's. "So," noted one of the editors, "the *Journal* was baptized with Apollinaris and beer."

A few hours later, New Yorkers sampled *The Morning Journal*. Readers who couldn't find the time to wade through the daily papers, oversize canvases of dull unbroken type, found the *Journal* a relief. For only a penny—a third or a fourth of the cost of other papers—readers could have their fill of short news items written in a light, breezy style. Women in particular were offered, at last, a newspaper that clearly had their interests in mind. The paper had detailed reports of weddings and balls, romantic news such as the first loves of famous men, and lots of gossipy notices. Albert, one Park Row veteran recalled, "was the first New York editor to realize the fact that shop-girls and poor clerks are interested in the daily lives of the millionaire class. He turned to their 'doings' and paved the way for the new journalism that followed." The paper was soon nicknamed the "chambermaid's delight." From the very first appearance of the *Journal*, Albert found readers. It was the talk of the town.

From his Manhattan hotel room Joseph enviously witnessed his brother's success.

Chapter Sixteen

THE GREAT THEATER

O n April 7, 1883, Jay Gould took his family and friends by private railcar to Philadelphia for the launching of his new yacht, *Atalanta,* named after the huntress of Greek mythology. Built at a cost of $140,000, the yacht was a floating palace with gold-edged curtains, oriental rugs, and a built-in piano. But as Gould participated in the festivities of the day, he was beset with worries. The country was in the midst of a business downturn, his nerves were frayed, and the constant public attacks on him had begun to hit home. For the first time, he was considering retirement. At the very least, it was time to lighten his load.

He decided to rid himself of the burdensome *New York World.* It was a Democratic paper and he was a Republican. But perhaps an even greater sin in the eyes of a railroad and industrial baron was that it had never made a dime since he acquired it four years earlier. "I never cared anything about the *World,"* Gould said. The *World* had an anemic circulation of 15,000 and was losing money every week.

In January, Gould had come close to disposing of the paper to John McLean, the publisher of the *Cincinnati Enquirer,* but McLean had been unwilling to meet the $385,000 price. There was only one man trolling for a New York paper for whom price did not seem to be a consideration. "As Joseph has more stamps than the rest of us, I might say the only one with stamps," said McLean when his bid failed, "I suspect he will get it ultimately."

On the day Gould watched his new yacht slip into the water, Pulitzer was riding a train to New York. The Pulitzer family had just concluded the stay of several months in the South, undertaken out of concern for Ralph's asthma. Joseph and Kate had given up on St. Louis and were looking for a place to buy or rent in New York City. The *Post-Dispatch* practically ran itself. But to be sure that it remained on track, Pulitzer received daily preprinted one-page reports that showed him at a glance all the essential information, such as circulation, advertising, expenses, and the times when the presses started and ended their runs. He was forever asking the men who managed the business side of his operations to be brief in responding to his ceaseless queries. In his words, he wanted the information in "a nutshell."

On the way north, Joseph dropped Kate and the children off in Washington for a stay with her family. He pushed on to New York. If the intelligence he had learned from his friend William H. Smith, director of the Associated Press, was sound and if he played his hand deftly, the *World* could be his. The press was reporting that Gould would leave any day for the West in the company of tycoon Russell Sage. Pulitzer would have to work fast.

He obtained a meeting with Gould at his Western Union office, a few blocks from Park Row. As the two sat facing each other, it was clear there wasn't much to negotiate. For Gould, who had once stacked $53 million in stock certificates on his desk and who lived in a forty-room Gothic mansion, selling the *World* was a Lilliputian deal. True, owning the paper had become an irritation, and Pulitzer was a willing purchaser. But Gould could have easily closed the *World* without making a dent in his petty cash. He wasn't going to grant any favors to a man who made a sport of pillorying him. From a negotiating perspective, Gould's uninterest trumped Pulitzer's desire.

This purchase, unlike that of the *Staats-Zeitung* or the *Dispatch*, was no fire sale. The negotiations dragged on for a couple of weeks over two issues. Gould wanted to retain a small ownership share for his son and wanted the current editor to keep his job. In the end, Gould conceded on both points and Pulitzer met his price of $346,000. The sum, according to Gould, represented the amount he had paid for the paper and the losses incurred during his four years of ownership.

Pulitzer did not have that much cash. If he sold the *Post-Dispatch*, he would be trading a moneymaker for, in his own words, a "mummified corpse of the once bright and lively New York *World*." His craving for the *World* was so intense that he would take a loan from Gould, a man whom he deemed "one of the most sinister figures that have ever flitted bat-like across the vision of the American people."

On April 28, Pulitzer drew up the sales contract in his own hand, with the advice and counsel of the former U.S. senator Roscoe Conkling, whom Pulitzer had befriended since Conkling had fallen out of favor with the Republican Party and opened a law practice. To take possession of the *World*, Pulitzer would give Gould a down payment of $34,600, and Gould would finance the remainder at a 5 percent interest rate. Under the terms of the loan, Pulitzer would pay $79,200 in 1884; $121,100 in 1885; and $121,100 in 1886, as well as the interest on the outstanding balance, which could amount to $33,730. In addition, Pulitzer promised to rent for a decade the Park Row building housing the *World*, for $13,560 a year. Signing the contract put Pulitzer nearly $500,000 in debt. Less than five years after spending his last few thousand dollars to buy the bankrupt *Dispatch*, he was betting he could repeat his success on a far grander scale.

The stakes were high. The *Post-Dispatch*, which had recovered from its slump after Slayback's murder, looked as though it would generate profits of $120,000 to $150,000 in 1883. But the *World* was losing thousands of dollars each month. If New York didn't take to his so-called western journalism, Pulitzer would be ruined.

He confessed his anxiety to Kate, who had installed herself and the children in the Fifth Avenue Hotel. Five years with Joseph had convinced her that it was no use trying to restrain his ambition. He was, as he had promised in his wedding-eve letters, driven by an insatiable need to be occupied, to have meaningful work, to keep moving. On the other hand, Kate had witnessed his talent. She had, after all, accompanied him to St. Louis to spend their last dime on a bankrupt paper. She believed in him and urged him on, even if it meant risking everything they had.

Word of the pending sale began to leak out. It was hard to keep it a secret, with Cockerill shuttling between New York and St. Louis and the *Post-Dispatch* business manager joining Pulitzer in New York. On May 6, the rival *Globe-Democrat* confirmed that Pulitzer had concluded the deal.

On May 9, the day before Gould transferred the *World* to him, Pulitzer proposed to his brother that they consolidate their papers into a new one, to be called the *World-Journal*. Albert's seven-month-old *Journal* had three times the circulation of the *World* and was acquiring thousands of new subscribers each month. If Albert agreed to the merger, Joseph promised him a profit of no less than $100,000 a year.

"That is a good deal of money," Albert said. "I shall be perfectly satisfied if I can even make a fifth of that out of the *Journal*."

"You needn't come to the office at all, if you like you can stay at home in bed all day long," continued Joseph, who could never brook an equal in the office.

In hoping to combine the papers, Joseph was following the game plan he had used in St. Louis when he had merged his new paper there with Dillon's *Post*. But this situation was different: Albert was making money on his own, lots of it, and his paper was not threatened by Joseph. He declined the invitation.

"Don't be so cock-sure of your success," Joseph snapped. "It is the men you have got and who get the paper out every night for you that are making it what it is. When they are gone what will you do?"

That night, Albert confronted this question. He discovered that his managing editor, E. C. Hancock, had resigned, his lead columnist had vanished, and his editorial writer had called in sick. "I did not lose a moment, jumped into a car as I was determined to get at the truth, rode to his house, obtained admission after some difficulty and soon learned that my surmise was true—my whole staff, my three most valuable men whom I had trained with such pains since the first issue of the *Morning Journal*, had gone over in the dead of night to a rival newspaper! This blow was intended to kill me."

Of course, the rival paper was the *World*. In a city teeming with editorial talent, Joseph had chosen to raid his brother's shop. He was seeking more than editors. Driven by jealousy, he wanted to put his kid brother in his place.

At the Fifth Avenue Hotel, a reporter caught up with Pulitzer, eager to learn his plans for the *World*. "I intend to make it a thorough American newspaper—to un-Anglicize it, so to speak," Pulitzer said. He promised that no immediate personnel changes were in the works. "I have no intention to bring any new men to the city for the purpose of placing them on the editorial staff of the paper," he said. Once again Pulitzer was resorting to his old habit of lying when talking to a reporter. He preferred to keep it quiet that Cockerill, with a reputation as an editor who shot complaining readers, was on his way to New York to run the *World*. "In the news sense and in other ways," Pulitzer promised, "I shall, of course, in time make considerable changes in the paper."

In the company of his newly purloined editor from Albert's paper, Pulitzer went to inspect his new property on the evening of May 10. The paper was housed in a fire-damaged building at the lower end of Park Row. The fabled block housed a dozen or more daily papers. This was the newspapers' golden age, and Park Row was the richest vein. But in New York, unlike St. Louis, Pulitzer faced competition from sophisticated, well-funded, worldly publications. Aside from Albert's *Morning Journal*, there were the immensely profitable *New York Herald*, run by James Gordon Bennett Jr.; Charles Dana's *Sun*, still attracting more than 100,000 readers each day with its compact four-page format; the late Horace Greeley's *New York Tribune*, now ruled by Whitelaw Reid, a conservative Republican sheet serving the prosperous. If there was a turtle among these hares, it was the sober *New York Times*, slowly winning a loyal following.

Pulitzer and Hancock entered the *World* newsroom just as the staff was putting the finishing touches on the next day's edition. Although Pulitzer's arrival had been preceded by a memo telling the employees that the new owner wished to retain them in their positions at their current salaries, the nearly 100 reporters, editors, compositors, and printers were anxious to catch a glimpse of this thirty-six-year-old outsider who held their future in his hands. The departure of the existing senior management, fleeing like ship rats, forecast great changes.

Escorting Pulitzer around the newsroom, Hancock urged him to write some sort of pronouncement for the next day's edition. Taking a pen, Pulitzer hurriedly began. While a newspaper must be independent, he wrote for his first editorial in the paper, "it must not be indifferent or neutral on any question involving public interest." Then, collating phrases from his stump speeches and from five years of editorial struggles against entrenched interests in St. Louis, Pulitzer pledged that the *World* would fight against monopolies, organized privilege, corrupt officials, and other threats to democracy. "Its rock of faith must be true Democracy," he wrote. "Not the Democracy of a political machine. Not the Democracy which seeks to win the spoils of office from a political rival, but the Democracy which guards with jealous care the rights of all alike, and perpetuates the free institutions it first established.

"Performance is better than promises. Exuberant assurances are cheap," Pulitzer continued, adding a signed announcement of the change of ownership that he had drafted to accompany his editorial. Simply watch the paper and see for yourself, he said. "There is room in this great and growing city for a journal that is not only cheap but bright, not only bright but large, not only large but truly Democratic—dedicated to the cause of the people rather than that of purse-potentates—devoted more to the news of the New than the Old World—that will expose all fraud and sham, fight all public evils and abuses—that will serve and battle for the people with earnest sincerity." Done, Pulitzer handed the sheets to an eighteen-year-old compositor, who would later become one of his editors, and his words were rapidly set into type in time for the press run.

Before leaving for the night, Pulitzer made one alteration to the look of the paper that hinted at his ambitions. He dropped "New York" from the name and restored the nameplate that had been used when the *World* began in 1860. At its center, framed by the words "The World," was a printing press with rays of light emanating from it like the sun flanked by the two hemispheres of the globe.

While Joseph made plans for his newspaper, Albert made repairs to his. He had managed to locate a new editor. In fact, the replacement turned out to be an improvement, and the stolen Hancock lasted only a few days under Joseph. Still fuming over the raid, Albert ran into Joseph at Madison Square Garden.

"I congratulate you on your new recruits," Albert said. "Perhaps you would now like to offer me a stated sum annually for the sole purpose of looking up and supplying your paper with bright writers?"

Joseph dismissed the sarcastic remark with a wave. "I'll admit that you have a wonderful nose for ferreting out talent," he said. "I have read your paper today and it is really not half bad."

There may have been enough room for two Pulitzer papers in New York, but not enough for two Pulitzers. Although Albert was willing to share the stage, Joseph wasn't. Stung by the malevolent actions of his only living sibling, Albert took an angry swipe at Joseph's handiwork. He told the *Herald* that the success of the *Journal* showed that for a newspaper to find readers "it is not necessary to make it slanderous, vituperative, or nasty."

A few weeks after their encounter, Joseph made an attempt to be civil. He stopped in at Albert's office for fifteen minutes. "He made a closer study of us and took in more during that time than another less observing man would have done in a whole day," Albert wrote, describing the visit to a friend. "After Joe left someone asked, 'I wonder what he dropped in for?' My officious office-boy quickly replied, 'I guess he dropped in to see if there was anyone else he could coax away!'"

After the visit, the two brothers would forever remain estranged. The only two remaining members of Fülöp and Elize Pulitzer's children left in the world found they could not get along.

For those who had watched Pulitzer climb from being a lawyer's errand boy to being a newspaper publisher, his purchase of the *World* held great promise. "You have entered upon the stage of a great theater and stand as if it were before the footlights in presence of the nation," one of his oldest friends from St. Louis wrote. Another compared him to a previous newspaper giant: "The present situation is not unlike that which the elder Bennett found when he moved to attack the established dailies. You are in a magnificent field and you ought to move all of America."

But unless Pulitzer could spark a spectacular increase in circulation he would not ascend a pinnacle of political power. Instead, he would be crushed under an avalanche of debt. Every tactic, device, scheme, plan, and method that he employed in St. Louis would have to work in New York, and he also needed to think up new ones. But before introducing his ideas, he decided to create the appearance of change.

Taking from his bag a trick he had used in St. Louis, Pulitzer sent reporters out to interview leading Democrats about the "new *World,*" even though it still looked like the old one. Flattered by the attention and the promise of free publicity, the party figures immediately studied the paper. Typical was the response of one party official. "I guess we are going to have a real Democratic paper at last," he said. "The paper in its new dress is an immense improvement and the short distinct paragraphs, instead of running everything together, make the paper very readable."

Then—also as he had done in St. Louis—Pulitzer took to reprinting all the press comments on the *World*'s change in ownership. He sought to project a sense of dramatic change. "He took every occasion to blow his horn and tell the public what a good newspaper he was making," remarked the owner of a stationery and newspaper store on the West Side. "This was unusual in New York and by many people it was considered very bad taste on his part to be continually boasting and bragging about the merits of his publication." However distasteful it might have seemed to some, it worked. Within the first few days, circulation had a modest increase. New Yorkers were curious about the *World*.

What they found when they picked up a copy was not all that different from before. Except for Pulitzer's tinkering with the masthead, the layout of the paper remained unchanged. He filled in the empty spaces on each side of the top of the front page with a circle or square containing promotional copy such as "Only 8-Page Newspaper in the United States Sold for 2 Cents." (This little innovation, which he may have stolen from Albert, became known in the business as "ears" and eventually was adopted by most papers.) The front page was divided into six or seven narrow columns, just as in other newspapers. The headlines remained small because convention bound them to the limits of the column width.

But if the new *World* looked like the old, life inside its building certainly didn't. James B. Townsend, a reporter who had been absent at a funeral in Vermont when Pulitzer took over, was startled by what he found upon his return. "It seemed as if a cyclone had entered the building, completely disarranged everything, and had passed away leaving confusion." Avoiding collisions with messenger boys exiting with urgent deliveries, Townsend made his way to the city room and found his colleagues running around excitedly. He asked the general manager what was the cause of all the commotion.

"You will know soon enough, young man," the manager replied. "The new boss will see you in five minutes." He then glanced up at Townsend and added. "After us the deluge—prepare to meet your fate."

Indeed, Townsend was soon summoned to Pulitzer's office. As he entered, Townsend made his first examination of his new boss, and Pulitzer of him. Dressed in a frock coat and gray trousers, Pulitzer stared back through his glasses. "So, this is Mr. T," he said. "Well, Sir, you've heard that I am the new chief of this newspaper. I have already introduced new methods—new ways I proposed to galvanize this force: are you willing to aid me?"

Almost as if the breath had been sucked from him by Pulitzer's vigor, Townsend stammered that he would like to remain on the staff. "Good, I like you," replied Pulitzer. "Get to work."

During the following days, editors and reporters arriving in the early morning found Pulitzer already in his office, often toiling in his shirt-sleeves. When the door was open and he was dictating an editorial, recalled one man, "his speech was so interlarded with sulphurous and searing phrases that the whole staff shuddered. He was the first man I ever heard who split a word to insert an oath. He did it often. His favorite was 'indegoddampendent.'"

As the staff settled in for the day's work, they couldn't escape Pulitzer. One moment he would be in the city room arguing with a reporter about some aspect of a story. No detail was too small. In one case, he was overheard discussing the estimated number of cattle that an editor had expected to arrive in New York from the West the previous day. He loved debating with his staff, usually provoking the arguments himself. "It is by argument," he told Townsend, "that I measure a man, his short-comings, his possession or lack of logic, and, above all, whether he has the courage of his convictions, for no man can long work for me with satisfaction to himself or myself unless he has this courage."

Finished with the city room, Pulitzer would bark out orders in the composing room or dash into the counting room to get a report on revenues. It wasn't long before the old-timers couldn't take it anymore, and new faces, often younger, appeared in the editorial quarters. The men in the composing and printing rooms were content with their new manager, though Pulitzer had one dustup with them. On May 24, he and Cockerill returned from the dedication of the Brooklyn Bridge brimming with ideas about how to cover the momentous occasion, only to discover that forty-three of the fifty-one men had walked off the job in a wage dispute. It took Pulitzer only three hours to capitulate and agree to recognize the men's union. "The whole difficulty has been amicably settled, and the men have returned happy," Pulitzer said as he headed out with the union president and others for a glass of beer at a neighboring bar.

There was a sense that Pulitzer was pushing the *World* forward. "We in the office felt from the first that this remarkable personality, which has so impressed us upon its arrival inside the building, would soon make its impress felt on the great cosmopolitan public of New York," Townsend said, "and in time the country."

* * *

Pulitzer launched his journalistic revolution modestly. The dramatic changes for which he would eventually become known were still years away. At this point, he sought solely to condition his editorial staff to his principles of how a paper should be written and edited. This effort, however modest it may seem, is how the *World* began on its path to becoming the most widely read newspaper in American history. In an era when the printed word ruled supreme and 1,028 newspapers competed for readers, content was the means of competition. The medium was not the message; the message was. This was where Pulitzer started.

The paper abandoned its old, dull headlines. In place of BENCH SHOW OF DOGS: PRIZES AWARDED ON THE SECOND DAY OF THE MEETING IN MADISON SQUARE GARDEN on May 10 came SCREAMING FOR MERCY: HOW THE CRAVEN CORNETTI MOUNTED THE SCAFFOLD on May 12. Two weeks later the *World*'s readers were greeted with BAPTIZED IN BLOOD, on top of a story, complete with a diagram, on how eleven people were crushed to death in a human stampede when panic broke out in a large crowd enjoying a Sunday stroll on the newly opened Brooklyn Bridge. In a city where half a dozen newspapers offered dull, similar fare to readers each morning, Pulitzer's dramatic headlines made the *World* stand out like a racehorse among draft horses.

If the headline was the lure, the copy was the hook. Pulitzer could write all the catchy headlines he wanted, but it was up to the reporters to win over readers. He pushed his staff to give him simplicity and color. He admonished them to write in a buoyant, colloquial style comprising simple nouns, bright verbs, and short, punchy sentences. If there was a "Pulitzer formula," it was a story written so simply that anyone could read it and so colorfully that no one would forget it. The question "Did you see that in the *World*?" Pulitzer instructed his staff, "should be asked every day and something should be designed to cause this."

Pulitzer had an uncanny ability to recognize news in what others ignored. He sent out his reporters to mine the urban dramas that other papers confined to their back pages. They returned with stories that could leave no reader unmoved. Typical, for instance, was the *World*'s front-page tale, which ran soon after Pulitzer took over, of the destitute and widowed Margaret Graham. She had been seen by dockworkers as she walked on the edge of a pier in the East River with an infant in her arms and a two-year-old girl clutching her skirt. "All at once the famished mother clasped the feeble little girl round her waist and, tottering to the brink of the wharf, hurled both her starving young into the river as it whirled by. She stood for a moment on the edge of the stream. The children were too weak and spent to struggle or to cry. Their little helpless heads dotted the brown tide for an instant, then they sank out of sight. The men who looked on stood spellbound." Graham followed her children into the river but was saved by the onlookers and was taken to jail to face murder charges.

For Pulitzer a news story was always a *story*. He pushed his writers to think like Dickens, who wove fiction from the sad tales of urban Victorian London, to create compelling entertainment from the drama of the modern city. To the upper classes, it was sensationalism. To the lower and working classes, it was their life. When they looked at the *World*, they found stories about their world.

In the Lower East Side's notorious bars, known as black and tans, or at dinner in their cramped tenements, men and women did not discuss society news, cultural events, or happenings in the investment houses. Rather, the talk was about the baby who fell to his death from a rooftop, the brutal beating that police officers dispensed to an unfortunate waif, or the rising cost of streetcar fares to the upper reaches of Fifth Avenue and the mansions needing servants. The clear, simple prose of the *World* drew in these readers, many of whom were immigrants struggling to master their first words of English. Writing about the events that mattered in their lives in a way they could understand, Pulitzer's *World* gave these New Yorkers a sense of belonging and a sense of value. In one stroke, he simultaneously elevated the common man and took his spare change to fuel the *World*'s profits.

The moneyed class learned to pick up the *World* with trepidation. Each day brought a fresh assault on privilege and another revelation of the squalor and oppression under which the new members of the laboring class toiled. Pulitzer found readers where other newspaper publishers saw a threat. Immigrants were pouring into New York at a rate never before seen. By the end of the decade, 80 percent of the city's population was either foreign-born or of foreign parentage. Only the *World* seemed to consider the stories of this human tide as deserving news coverage. The other papers wrote about it; the *World* wrote for it.

The *World*'s stories were animated not just by the facts the reporters dug up but by the voices of the city they recorded. Pulitzer drove his staff to aggressively seek out interviews, a relatively new technique in journalism pioneered by his brother, among others. Leading figures of the day were used to a considerable wall of privacy and were affronted by what Pulitzer proudly called "the insolence and impertinence of the reporters for the *World*."

Not only did he have the temerity to dispatch his men to pester politicians, manufacturers, bankers, society figures and others for answers to endless questions, but he instructed them to return with specific personal details that would illustrate the resulting articles. Pulitzer was obsessed with details. A tall man was six feet two inches tall. A beautiful woman had auburn hair, hazel eyes, and demure lips that occasionally turned upward in a coy smile. Vagueness was a sin.

As was inaccuracy. A disciple of the independent press movement, Pulitzer was convinced that accuracy built circulation, credibility, and editorial power. Words could paint brides as blushing, murderers as heinous, politicians as venal, but the facts had to be right. "When you go to New York, ask any of the men in the dome to show you my instructions to them, my letters written from day to day, my cables," Pulitzer told an associate late in life. "You will see that accuracy, accuracy, accuracy, is the first and the most urgent, the most constant demand I have made on them."

Pulitzer practically lived at his cramped headquarters on Park Row. Kate and the children hardly ever saw him. His day began with editorial conferences—an editor who came unprepared never repeated the mistake—and ended under the harsh white gaslight as he read and reread proofs for the next morning's edition. When not writing or editing, Pulitzer studied all the New York papers as well as more than a dozen British, German, and French ones. He demanded a great deal from his staff but even more from himself. When he had been in St. Louis, if the paper was dull he would steal home feeling sick. If it met his standard, he would be elated. As spring turned into summer in New York, Pulitzer was feeling elated.

In his first weeks at the *World*, the paper's circulation soared by 35 percent. "Increasing in circulation? You can just bet it is," said a newsstand operator on the corner of Cortland and Greenwich streets. "I used to sell fourteen *World*s a day. I now sell thirty-four. If that ain't an increase I don't know what is."

*   *   *

The Pulitzers moved from their hotel rooms into a house they rented at 17 Gramercy Park, an elegant neighborhood surrounding a private park on the East Side, off Park Avenue. The aging Samuel Tilden, for whom Pulitzer had toiled in the disputed presidential election of 1876, lived at number 15. Once again there was talk of Tilden's running for president, but Pulitzer would have nothing to do with it. "He belongs to the past and represents an idea," Pulitzer said a few weeks after moving in next door to his famous neighbor. "Now, ideas are stronger than men, but you can't elect an idea."

Even though work consumed most of Pulitzer's waking hours, he found time for socializing, particularly with political New Yorkers. One evening, shortly after taking over the *World*, he reminisced about the campaign of 1876 with the wealthy Democrat William C. Whitney at a dinner of Democrats. Despite their shared political convictions, Pulitzer stood out as an odd duck among the well-heeled dinner guests. "Sharp-faced with bushy hair and scraggy whiskers, an ill-fitting dress suit too large for him, antagonizing people at dinner," Whitney wrote, describing Pulitzer to his wife, who was away. Another night, Pulitzer joined Watterson at Delmonico's for a dinner promoting the Louisville Exposition. By June, Pulitzer was a member of the Manhattan Club, an almost exclusively Democratic society.

Pulitzer even found time and, more remarkably, had enough interest, to take a lunchtime river cruise in Jay Gould's new yacht, along with the *Sun*'s editor Dana and William Dorsheimer, a Democrat starting his term in Congress. That Pulitzer sought the company of these two guests was understandable. He had known both for almost a decade and shared their political beliefs. But his willingness to enjoy Gould's yacht, food, drink, and company betrayed a dichotomy in Pulitzer that widened as he accumulated wealth. He wanted to be accepted by the elite while making a living trashing them in his paper.

Pulitzer may have taunted the wealthy, attacked their political power, and criticized their sense of entitlement, but he planned to be among them. A few weeks after his lunch with Gould, the *World* printed a list of New York's millionaires. "We find the names of only three or four newspaper publishers in the magnificent array," Pulitzer wrote. "By this time next year, as things are going, the list will be beautified with the names of at least a half-dozen journalists. We could name them now, but modesty forbids."

In August, Pulitzer dashed out to Ohio in support of a Democrat, Judge Hoadly, who was a candidate for governor. The campaign had already deteriorated into a raucous, dirty, knockdown fight after a convention that one newspaper reporter said was more akin to a bullfight than a political meeting. Sitting in the smoking car from Urbana to Columbus, Pulitzer struck up a conversation with a reporter for McLean's *Cincinnati Enquirer*, which strongly opposed Hoadly.

"This is a perfect hell you've been raising," Pulitzer said.

"Just a trifle that I couldn't well help," replied the reporter.

Pulitzer was unconvinced and said he thought the *Enquirer's* publisher was seeking revenge against Hoadly, who was involved with a competing paper.

"Well, that's only natural," the reporter said. "You don't publish a newspaper as a matter of sentiment; you publish it to make money."

"Now, I do publish a newspaper as a matter of sentiment—two of them," replied Pulitzer. "My paper in New York City is straight-out Democratic, because in that city I am possessed of the backing of strong Democratic sentiment. My paper in St. Louis is independent, because in that city I have a strong independent sentiment."

The two then shared a number of confidences about the campaign, including Hoadly's belief that his election to governor would make him a leading contender for president the following year. "Bah," said Pulitzer, "the Democratic party will not go to Ohio to find its next candidate, and if it should, nobody need fear that it would select Hoadly."

When the train reached its destination, Pulitzer was met by one of the state's leading Democrats. Pulitzer told him of the conversation on the train. The politician assured Pulitzer that the reporter could be trusted to keep it to himself. None of them, however, took account of the fact that the man in the seat behind them worked for the *New York Times*, which eagerly published a transcript, giving Pulitzer a taste of public embarrassment of the kind he usually dished out.

By the end of August 1883, with the *World's* circulation twice what it had been before he bought the paper, Pulitzer felt sufficiently comfortable to leave New York for almost a month. Henry Villard, one of the nation's most prominent railroad men, had just completed the first northern transcontinental railroad. To do so, he had overstretched his financial resources, and he was deep in debt. Desperate to drum up business for his new line, Villard contrived a huge international celebration. He invited government officials, politicians, foreign dignitaries, and editors from leading newspapers on a cross-country train ride to witness the driving of the last spike. The antirailroad, antimonopolist, and anticorporate Pulitzer accepted the invitation.

On August 28, Villard's private trains began leaving New York. The engines pulled Wagner sleeping cars, beautifully appointed with curtains, leather seats, carpeting, and china spittoons, and configured like long drawing rooms with tables. By the time the two trains reached Chicago, the excursion party had grown to four trains with more than 300 guests including the former president Ulysses Grant. The caravan made stops for parades and banquets. In Bismarck, the delegation laid the cornerstone of the state capitol and listened to a speech by Sitting Bull, who had been released from captivity for the event. On September 8, the trains joined up with ones coming from the West in the valley of Little Blackfoot Creek, about sixty miles from Helena, Montana.

Pulitzer was surprised to find that Villard had built a pavilion, a bandstand, and promenades in this abandoned stretch. Finding a seat, Pulitzer watched as the men rapidly laid the last 1,000 feet of track. The man who had driven in the first spike on the opening of the road came forward to nail the last as the sun began to set behind the mountains. Villard spent $300,000 for the affair but he couldn't have bought better press coverage. Newspapers across the country and in Europe played up the event—that was, all except the *World*, which churlishly said the event was "a comparatively unimportant incident in railroad history."

During Pulitzer's absence from New York, his detractors took the opportunity to spread a rumor that the *World* was still owned by Gould, even though Pulitzer had run a front-page two-column interview with Gould to publicize the change of ownership. The rumor had sufficient credibility, supported by Pulitzer's willingness to float around New York waters with Gould in the latter's yacht, that Cockerill was forced to issue a public statement. Neither Gould nor his son, said Cockerill, "nor any other human being connected with any monopoly or corporation own directly or indirectly one dollar's worth of interest in the *World* or have any more to do with its management than the Emperor of China."

Despite his best efforts the rumors persisted. The *Brooklyn Eagle*, for instance, remarked, Pulitzer "claims that Mr. Gould has nothing to do with the paper, but the claim is simply the rankest sort of nonsense, Mr. Gould still owns the paper."

The rumors were only a nuisance. When he returned from the West, Pulitzer was greeted by proof positive of his success. His competitors had flinched and were cutting their price. The *Tribune* went from four to three cents, the *Times* from four to two, and the *Herald* from three to two. Gloating, Pulitzer proclaimed, "Another victory for the *World*."

As the *World*'s circulation rose each week, Pulitzer sought to use his newfound political leverage to help bring Democrats back to power. From the start he made no pretenses about his plans. "I want to talk to a nation, not to a select committee," he said. Within days of buying the paper, Pulitzer had made his political aims clear and so specific that they formed a ten-point list consisting of only thirty-five words. The first five goals were to tax luxuries, inheritances, large incomes, monopolies, and corporations. The remaining goals were to eliminate protective tariffs, reform the civil service, and punish corrupt government officials and those who bought votes, as well as employers who coerced their employees during elections.

When he returned from his western junket, Pulitzer worked to unite New York's Democrats. In 1880, the party had failed to win the White House when it lost the state by a few thousand votes. Then, Pulitzer had been a bystander. Now that he was in a position of influence in the state, he was determined that 1884 would be different. On September 24, he joined Dana at a rally of Democrats at Cooper Union. With a display of fireworks and a brass band, the Democrats pledged themselves to unity in hopes of ending their quarter-century exile from the White House. Dana, age sixty-four, who was the dean of New York editors, did not object to sharing a stage with his young rival. In May, he had been one of the few publishers in New York to comment favorably on the sale of the *World*, reminding readers that Pulitzer had once been his protégé.

Weeks later, as the Democrats began their usual intra-party bickering, Pulitzer met with the leaders. It seemed to him as if all Democrats in New York were intent on losing the election: he was astonished by the fractious debate on the eve of the voting. One of the veteran party members asked Pulitzer if he knew anything about New York politics.

Pulitzer conceded that his experience was limited to Missouri and other midwestern states but added sarcastically that the longer he lived in New York the less able he was to divine the objectives of the city's politicians.

Pulitzer had shed none of his animus toward the Republican Party, which he was convinced was completely under the thumb of robber barons, monopolies, and corporate interests. "These people seem to have an idea that they are superior people—a sort of upper ruling class, and have a right through the power of their money to rule in this country as the upper classes rule in Europe," he said. "But the millions are more powerful than the millionaires."

In November, Pulitzer was so confident of his paper's success that he taunted his rivals by publishing notarized statements of its circulation. The *World*'s average circulation was now 45,000 copies a day. In six months, he had tripled the circulation and forced his rivals to cut their prices. If he continued at this rate, the previously moribund *World* would be the equal of any newspaper on Park Row within the next six months. If not stopped, it would eclipse them all.

At Albert's *Morning Journal,* there was also cause to celebrate. The circulation of his paper had hit 80,000. One year earlier, most New Yorkers had never heard the name Pulitzer. Now the two most talked-about newspapers belonged to the brothers. For Albert, every upward tick in circulation meant more money. For Joseph, it brought money and political power.

Chapter Seventeen

KINGMAKER

Despite his triumphant seven months at the helm of the *World,* Pulitzer approached the end of 1883 on a depressing note. Kate became sick. The family immediately left New York for warm weather and rest in Cuba. With his health phobias, Joseph was not going to take any chances. But his worst fears materialized, though not with Kate. She recovered. Rather, a few months later, it was his daughter, Katherine Ethel, who fell ill with pneumonia. Katherine died at six in the morning on Friday, May 9, 1884, the eve of Pulitzer's one-year anniversary with the *World.*

In composing the death notice, her parents calculated her age. She was two years, eight months, and ten days old. For Joseph, who had lost all but one of his siblings, the death was what he expected of childhood. Kate, on the other hand, was unprepared. She had never experienced the grief of watching a child in the family die. On Sunday, friends gathered at the Pulitzers' Gramercy Park residence for a quiet funeral service.

Characteristically, Pulitzer made immediate plans to travel, reserving a cabin on a ship to Europe. But he soon rejected any foreign destination. It was an election year, the most promising for Democrats in a generation. Instead, Pulitzer booked rooms at the Curtis Hotel in Lenox, Massachusetts, a small New England town a few hours north of New York that had recently been discovered by the city's wealthy seeking relief from the summer heat. By the time he installed Ralph, now five years old, Lucille, three, and their maid in Lenox, Kate was pregnant with their fourth child.

Along with the summer's heat came the political conventions. The

Republicans selected as their nominee James Blaine, a former House Speaker, U.S. senator from Maine, and secretary of state. It was a poor choice because Blaine had an odor of corruption dating back to suspicious relationships with several major railroads in the 1870s. Many Republicans, particularly the reform-minded ones, were uncomfortable with their party's choice.

As the convention broke up, a reporter for the *World* caught up with one of the disgruntled delegates. At age twenty-five, delegate Theodore Roosevelt was a rising political figure in New York. "I am going cattle-ranching in Dakota for the remainder of the summer and part of the fall," he snapped. The reporter persisted: would he support Blaine? "That question I decline to answer. It is a subject that I do not care to talk about." But, after some reflection at his ranch, a calmer Roosevelt announced that, yes, he would vote for Blaine.

A Republican who portrayed himself as a reformer but was supporting Blaine was too tempting a target for Pulitzer to ignore. When Roosevelt first attracted notice as a municipal reformer in the legislature, Pulitzer had been favorably impressed, even though the man was a Republican. But he concluded that Roosevelt had gone soft in his pursuit of corruption in return for advancement in his party's ranks. "It is not surprising that young Mr. Roosevelt should prefer to offend honesty rather than to displease the machine. He is of the finical dancing-master school of reform, whose disciples are the most useful tools of the political managers," wrote Pulitzer. "We denounced young Mr. Roosevelt as a reform fraud and a Jack-in-the-box politician who disappears whenever his boss applies a gentle pressure to his aspiring head," he said. "In short, we have discovered that young Mr. Roosevelt is a humbug who only masquerades as a reformer while in reality is one of the most subservient of machine politicians."

Roosevelt was a victim of Pulitzer's stubborn, unbending insistence on principle over compromise or expediency. This was an easy stance for the nation's newest and most prominent newspaper publisher to take. His measure of accomplishment was a blistering editorial that excited partisans and attracted readers. But for an ambitious politician like Roosevelt, success demanded results, and these required both political compromise and electoral success.

Had Pulitzer understood the necessity of compromise, he might have forged an alliance with Roosevelt that would have accelerated the political change they both sought. Instead, the editorial shot across Roosevelt's bow became the first of many. None of Pulitzer's attacks would be ignored by Roosevelt, who never forgave or forgot an affront. The two men were so pigheaded that they failed to see their common interest.

Although Blaine had the crucial support of young Theodore Roosevelt in New York, he lacked that of Roscoe Conkling, who still commanded a considerable following. But the former U.S. senator was working as Pulitzer's attorney, fighting the many libel suits brought against the audacious *World*; also he was in no mood to forgive Blaine for their decades-long feud in Congress. "I have given up criminal law," Conkling said when asked if he would endorse Blaine. Instead, he worked secretly with Pulitzer to undermine Blaine by writing a series of critical columns for the *World*, under the pen name "Stalwart."

Pulitzer could hardly restrain his optimism about his party's prospects. He told his readers that Blaine was "the embodiment of corruption in legislation, demagogism in politics and cupidity in affairs." In 1884, unlike 1880, Pulitzer had no trouble backing a candidate. Two years earlier he had cast his lot with Grover Cleveland, the rotund governor of New York, who had a well-deserved reputation for integrity. Then, however, Pulitzer was speaking only to a modest midwestern audience from his editorial pulpit at the *Post-Dispatch*. Now he had the *World* and stood in the center of the most important electoral field of battle. "New York," he said, "again becomes the battleground for the presidency." In 1880, Republicans had staved off defeat in the presidential election by only 5,517 votes in New York. Pulitzer now commanded at least that many votes, if not more.

With each passing day the *World*'s circulation rose. One morning, an observer took an informal census of newspaper preferences on the Fourth Avenue streetcar. Three passengers were reading the *Herald*, four the *Sun,* and five the *World*. Only the *Times* and Albert's *Journal* had more readers. Veterans of the business were astonished by the *World*'s growth. "It cannot be expected to go on forever gaining at the gait which it has been following during the past few months," claimed the trade publication *The Journalist*. But it did.

By midsummer 1884, the *World* was selling 60,000 copies on weekdays and 100,000 on Sundays, closing in on all the leading newspapers. Advertising was booming also. "A year ago the *World* could hardly get advertising at any price," reported *The Journalist*. "It now charges from twenty-five to thirty-five cents a line, and has as much advertising as it can conveniently handle on Sunday."

Nothing his competitors tried seemed to slow his paper's growth. The *Herald* even resorted to taking out full-page advertisements in the *World*. When it cut its price to that of the *World*, the *Herald* compounded its woes by also trimming the commission it paid to wholesalers. One wholesaler decided to order 3,000 copies of the *World* instead of the *Herald* for his customers. "There was no complaint, and the *World* gained 3,000 copies, and the *Herald* lost them," recalled the president of the news dealers association. "I daresay the *World* kept many of them."

In July, sitting with the press in Chicago's Exposition Building, Pulitzer watched the Democrats pick their candidate. Pulitzer did all he could to sway the convention to Cleveland. "When a blathering ward politician objects to Cleveland because he is 'more of a Reformer than a Democrat' he furnishes the best argument in favor of Cleveland's nomination and election," Pulitzer wrote in a long stream of editorials. After a bruising fight, Cleveland won the nomination. If Pulitzer's editorials were little noticed by the delegates, the efforts convinced Cleveland that in the coming election he had an ally upon whom he could depend.

Most of the New York City press—the *Herald*, *Post*, and *Times*—joined in supporting Cleveland. But not Charles Dana at the *Sun*. A couple of years earlier, Cleveland had offended Dana by not granting a patronage job to a friend. Despite having worked hard for Democratic unity with Pulitzer, Dana broke ranks and supported a third-party candidate in hopes of denying Cleveland a victory in the crucial New York returns. Once again, as with Schurz years earlier, Pulitzer found himself at political odds with a man whom he had greatly admired and who had once been his mentor.

On July 29, Pulitzer joined other leading Democrats in Albany to officially convey the nomination to Cleveland and to mark the formal opening of the campaign. Pulitzer was the lone newspaper publisher among the judges, elected officials, and party leaders who rode to the governor's mansion in a parade of twenty-five carriages led by the Albany city band. The deputation made its presentation, and the governor mingled with its members until the doors were opened to the dining room, where a feast had been set out. Later, full of food and optimism, the party broke up to tend to the work ahead. In the drizzling rain and dark, the delegation paraded back into the city along a route lit by torches and fireworks, to large crowds of Democrats awaiting them in the music hall and opera house. Among the few chosen by the party to speak that night was Pulitzer.

Rather than boost Cleveland's candidacy, Pulitzer decided to sink Blaine's. If he could defeat Blaine in New York, the election would be won. As when he tore into Grant in 1872, Hayes in 1876, and Garfield in 1880, Pulitzer filled the pages of the *World* with hyperbolic attacks on Blaine. Readers learned that Blaine favored prohibition, belonged to the Know-Nothing movement that opposed Irish Catholic immigration, and took money from railroads; that his marriage was on the rocks; and that he was depressed. The charges were, at best, based on Blaine's earliest days in politics or in many cases were nothing more than a recycling of well-worn unflattering tales.

Cleveland also carried some unseemly baggage. He was a bachelor, and during the campaign it was revealed that he had fathered an illegitimate child. Cleveland decided to deal with the matter by issuing a simple directive to party officials desperate for instructions on what to say. "Tell the truth," he said. Pulitzer was less circumspect. Calling the accusation slander spread by the Republicans, he publicly blackmailed Blaine by threatening to release salacious information about him.

Pulitzer was only warming up. His stump-speaking style, seasoned by years of campaigning, filled the editorial pages of the *World*. "Is such an offense unpardonable?" Pulitzer asked. "If Grover Cleveland had a whole family of illegitimate children . . . he would be more worthy of the office than Blaine, the beggar at the feet of railroad jobbers, the prostitute in the Speaker's chair, the lawmaking broker in land grabs, the representative and agent of the corruptionists, monopolists, and enemies of the Republic."

A candidate who was the devil's companion and a challenger with clay feet made for great copy. The growing interest in the election increased readership for all newspapers, and particularly for the *World*. The *World*'s office was like a campaign headquarters. Electing Cleveland and boosting circulation were completely intertwined, the latter increasing the chance of the former. Pulitzer and Cockerill were open to any ideas that would push the *World* forward. One fell into their lap.

The artist Walt McDougall of Newark had been peddling comic

sketches, with some success, to *Puck, Harper's Weekly*, and other magazines. In June, he came into the city to see a baseball game. On his way he stopped by *Puck*'s office, where he learned that the editors had turned down his cartoon of Blaine. He didn't want to trudge off to the game carrying a large rolled-up drawing, so he impetuously decided to see if he could sell it to Dana. Cartoons were, at best, a novelty in daily newspapers. It was difficult to reproduce illustrations on the high-speed presses required by newspapers, because the engraving plates regularly became clogged with ink. The presses would then have to be stopped to clean the plates, wasting precious time in a business where every lost minute could diminish circulation.

As McDougall walked toward the *Sun*, he came to the *World* and decided to try his luck there first. When he entered the dim front office he lost his courage and hurriedly handed the cardboard tube to the elevator boy. "Give that to the editor and tell him he can have it if he wants it," said McDougall, who then beat a retreat and headed off to the baseball game.

The next day brought a telegram from Pulitzer asking McDougall to come quickly to the *World*. On his way, McDougall spotted a copy of the *World* at a newsstand. His cartoon ran across five columns of the front page of the paper. After McDougall was ushered into Pulitzer's office, the publisher immediately took him to Cockerill's office across the hall. The editor was as excited as Pulitzer about McDougall's drawing; its style averted the ink-clogging problem, and the sample had survived an entire press run. "We have found the fellow who can make pictures for newspapers!" Pulitzer excitedly told Cockerill. McDougall was hired, given a studio, and paid $50 a week, more than twice the salary of most reporters.

Pulitzer had wanted illustrations in the *World* since he bought the paper. On newsstands and in the arms of newsboys, the gray, unbroken front pages of the city's newspapers were indistinguishable from each other. Both he and Albert, at the *Morning Journal*, found every excuse possible to add illustrations to make their papers stand out. Within his first two weeks with the *World*, Joseph had begun printing drawings of criminals to aid in their apprehension and, of course, to bring credit to the *World*. Just before McDougall dropped off his drawing at the *World*, the newspaper had been celebrating the capture of a fugitive stockbroker by Canadian authorities who recognized him from the sketch that had appeared in the *World*. "This is a decided triumph for our artist," Pulitzer crowed. "Some of our jealous contemporaries have affected great contempt for our efforts in the line of cut-work. The Montreal incident attests to the value of our illustrations, and demonstrates that while we are educating the masses with our pictures we are at the same time lending a helping hand to Justice."

Not all the reading public was ready for illustrations. Complaints were numerous when the *World* included drawings in an article on ladies of Brooklyn. "The *World* made an error of no small magnitude when it published its series of Brooklyn Belles in last Sunday's issue," commented *The Journalist*. "Brooklyn is not used to these wild western methods of journalism." The fuss pleased Pulitzer. None of the ladies who had been portrayed complained, and circulation in Brooklyn soared. "A great many people in the world require to be educated through the eyes, as it were," Pulitzer said, mindful that many of the readers he pursued were struggling to learn English.

Pulitzer enlisted McDougall's talent in going after Blaine. Now a barrage of cartoons accompanied the reams of unflattering news copy and acidic editorials that the *World* published about Blaine. Between August and November's Election Day, McDougall's cartoons appeared twice a week on the front page. All but one of them attacked Blaine or Ben Butler, the third-party candidate supported by Dana. Readers in New York had seen nothing like this before. It was as if a rabid dog had gotten loose at a society dog show.

Pulitzer had no interest in muzzling the sharp bite of the *World*. "It should make enemies constantly, the more the better, for only by making enemies can it expose roguery and serve the public," he said. "The most valuable and most successful paper will generally be that which has the most enemies." The style also continued to win over readers. By the end of September, the *World*'s daily circulation passed the 100,000 mark. "This," Pulitzer exclaimed, "we hold to be our *first* 100,000."

The maliciousness of the *World* perplexed some of Pulitzer's friends. "I have always believed, and do believe, that you are a generous-hearted man," wrote AP's William Henry Smith, complaining that the paper was mercilessly pursuing one official who had already lost his job. "This is not like the Joseph Pulitzer I once knew; and if he is to be forever lost, I shall never cease to regret the share I had in bringing him into this wicked New York World."

Pulitzer beat on, pushing his staff like a coxswain who was never satisfied with his shell's lead.

Pulitzer interrupted his frenetic editorial and campaign work on the afternoon of September 3 to take a leisurely cruise on the Hudson. The idea of owning a yacht was beginning to appeal to him, and he had begun looking into buying one. But, as with everything else this year, this cruise was a political rather than a pleasure trip. Samuel Tilden had sent his vessel, the *Viking,* to the Twenty-Third Street pier to bring a delegation of Democrats upstream to his riverfront mansion in Yonkers. The journey was a well-timed public reminder of Republican dastardliness. The men were delivering an official resolution from the Democratic convention thanking Tilden for his service in the disputed 1876 election. Pulitzer was the only member of the press on board. Sitting at the lunch table near his friend William Whitney, he offered to make himself useful by distributing copies of the prepared remarks to newspapermen when they disembarked.

As the campaign approached its final month, New York Democrats enlisted Pulitzer to speak at a rally aimed at winning the German vote. The resplendent Academy of Music, on Irving Place between Fourteenth and Fifteenth streets, was decorated with German and American flags. A dozen bands as well as fireworks and explosives greeted the huge crowd that entered the hall on the night of September 29. Inside, the publisher of the New York *Staats-Zeitung,* well-known German leaders, and Pulitzer gathered on the stage between two imposing portraits of Cleveland and his running mate, Thomas Hendricks.

When his turn came to speak, Pulitzer continued the evening's portrayal of Blaine as the representative of a bankrupt and corrupt party that had overstayed its turn in power. "He stands for the unholy alliance between prohibition and corruption," Pulitzer said, "while Cleveland is the representative of honesty and honor in politics, and with clean hands will bring us back to purity in official life, which Mr. Blaine could not possibly do."

As he spoke, some of the organizers spied Carl Schurz sitting in one of the boxes. One of them approached Pulitzer and whispered into his ear that the eminent German-American politician was present. Eight years earlier, on a similar New York stage, Pulitzer had attacked and lampooned Schurz. Now that they were once again on the same side,

Pulitzer put aside his prepared remarks. "I have a brilliant finale with which I intended to close my remarks, but what can I say that would be more brilliant than to introduce the man whom you must and will hear—Carl Schurz?"

The crowd roared. A decade of bad blood between the two men came to an end as Pulitzer and Schurz stood before the cheering people. Their old friend from the 1872 rebellion, Murat Halstead, said a photographer could have earned a fortune capturing the moment. "It was a spectacle to see Pulitzer and Schurz meet at last as reformers on the Democratic platform," Halstead said, "and pouring forth their libations of eloquence for Cleveland, each telling of his goodness, and rising to the sublime height of telling us that beloved Europe itself, should be very much exercised about Blaine."

The fall campaign held yet another surprise for Pulitzer. In early October, Tammany Hall nominated him for the Ninth District's congressional seat without even consulting him. It took some coaxing to persuade him to accept the nomination. The district leaders finally succeeded after making a pilgrimage to Pulitzer's office and flattering him by saying that his candidacy would help the ticket. Tammany's designation was bound to be ratified by a later convention and, as the district was overwhelmingly Democratic, it was tantamount to giving Pulitzer a seat in Congress. What he had sought and had been denied in St. Louis was brought to him on a platter in New York.

The nomination was met by cheers at the *Journal*. Despite how Joseph had treated his younger brother, Albert applauded the news. With his special inside knowledge, Albert recounted Joseph's work in Missouri politics and said he would "make a faithful and devoted representative of the people." An editor at *The Journalist* couldn't resist adding, "This is very nice and brotherly, but I very much doubt that Mr. J. Pulitzer would have done as much for Mr. A. Pulitzer under the same circumstances." The editor was right. Joseph viewed his brother's newspaper no differently from any other competitor. When the *Morning Journal* broke the news of Lillie Langtry's pending divorce, Joseph waited until the story was printed in the *Chicago Tribune* so as to be able to use it in the *World* without crediting the *Journal*.

On October 16, Pulitzer was among half a dozen men selected to greet Cleveland at Grand Central Terminal. Then, with a crowd of almost

1,000 in tow, the party made its way to the Fifth Avenue Hotel, where the governor met with selected well-wishers. Once their hands were shaken and their concerns and advice listened to, Cleveland retired to a private lunch with Pulitzer, William Whitney, and a dozen leading Democrats. As always in the campaign, Pulitzer was the only newspaper publisher among the politicians and fund-raisers. Money was becoming an issue. The campaign's coffers were emptying fast, and it looked to Whitney for help. He contributed $20,000 and pressed others to do the same. Pulitzer, however, remained a small player when it came to political money, contributing only $1,000. His real value lay in his work at the *World*.

Pulitzer soon proved his worth. Blaine, exhausted from a speaking tour—something candidates rarely undertook at that time—arrived in New York hoping to hold the state in the closing days of the campaign. On October 29, he committed two mistakes. In Pulitzer's hands, they became politically fatal.

Blaine began his day with a speech before a group of Protestant clergymen at the Fifth Avenue Hotel. The pastor who introduced Blaine called the Democrats the party of "Rum, Romanism, and Rebellion." Too tired or too distracted to notice the dangers posed by this comment, which could turn Irish voters against him, Blaine said nothing. The Democrats, who had a stenographer following Blaine, rushed a copy of the remark to newspapers. Meanwhile, Blaine moved on to a fund-raising dinner at Delmonico's, where he was toasted by nearly 200 of the richest and most powerful men in America.

Pulitzer was the only editor who understood the significance of Blaine's two gaffes. The other pro-Cleveland papers in New York ran their campaign stories on the inside pages. The *Tribune*, which favored Blaine, reported only on the dinner, calling it a triumph. That night, Pulitzer sought out Walt McDougall and Valerian Gribayedoff, the *World*'s other staff artist. He said he needed a large cartoon by morning.

The two retreated to the studio and sketched an unusually wide cartoon. Across it were caricatures of nineteen of the most notorious and hated financial lords who had attended the dinner, seated as in a depiction of the Last Supper. Blaine sat beatifically at the center, with Jay Gould at this right and William H. Vanderbilt at his left. On the table before the men were dishes of food with such labels as "Gould Pie," "Monopoly Soup," and "Lobby Pudding." As a final touch, the artists added an impoverished, bedraggled couple, with a child, approaching the feast in hopes of a handout.

Pulitzer broke open the design of the front page, eliminating the traditional seven columns to accommodate the damning art. Nothing like this had appeared in a New York publication since Thomas Nast dethroned Boss Tweed. Pulitzer topped the dramatic cartoon with the headline THE ROYAL FEAST OF BELSHAZZAR BLAINE AND THE MONEY KINGS.

Pulitzer was not done yet. The *World* revealed every aspect of the dinner, even though the organizers had done their best to bar the press. From the *Timbales à la Reine* and *Soufflés aux Marrons* upon which the men feasted to the thousands of dollars pledged to buy votes, no detail was left out. Even more damning, the main story began with a one-paragraph account of men who had been thrown out of work at a mill in Blaine's home state and were now applying for assistance or emigrating to Canada. Other stories highlighted Blaine's silence at the slur against the Irish and his friendship with Jay Gould, and led the way to the editorial page, where Pulitzer let loose. "Read the list of Blaine's banqueters who are to fill his pockets with money to corrupt the ballot box," he wrote; railroad kings, greedy monopolists, lobbyists, all of them. They had grown rich on public money and special privilege. "Shall Jay Gould rule this country? Shall he own the President?"

The "Royal Feast of Belshazzar" was reprinted by the thousands. Democrats gleefully replaced their election propaganda with copies of the *World*. Republicans gnashed their teeth. In a reversal of politics as usual, Pulitzer's words became more important than those of the Democratic candidate in the closing days of the campaign. It was almost as if the *World* were on the ballot. Only once before, in 1876, had a newspaper played such a prominent role in a presidential election, and in that case its publisher, Horace Greeley, had been a candidate. Here Pulitzer was using the power of the new independent press, whose reporting had far more credibility than that of the old partisan journals, to mobilize voters. "There has been," Pulitzer wrote, "a revolution in journalism in New York."

November 4, 1884, Election Day, brought a deluge of voters in New York City and rain upstate, cheering Democrats who believed the inclement weather would dampen Republican turnout in rural areas. The day, however, ended with no clear decision. The electoral votes were evenly divided between Blaine and Cleveland—except in New York, which held the balance. Whoever won the state would win the White House.

Pulitzer ordered press runs of nearly 250,000 copies, 45,000 more than the *Sun* and 40,000 more than the *Herald*. No matter who won the battle for the White House, Pulitzer had won the newspaper war.

The *World* began reporting a Democratic triumph with its first edition at two o'clock in the morning, but the race was still too close to call. Nor could victory be firmly declared the following day as the voting tabulations continued. "Watch the count," Pulitzer warned his readers. "Guard carefully against any frauds on the part of the Republican inspectors and supervisors."

In the evening, tens of thousands of people crowded into Park Row. The newspapers affixed bulletin boards to the front of their buildings and displayed the latest election bulletins. Fights broke out between rival groups, but mostly the crowds sang songs and parodies and yelled insults. All sorts of rumors began circulating. On hearing one that Jay Gould was tampering with the votes, a crowd surged up Fifth Avenue chanting, "We'll hang Jay Gould to a sour apple tree." Fortunately for the financier, the police hid him in a hotel under guard.

Finally, at week's end, the results became clear. By a margin of 1,149 votes, out of 1,167,169 votes cast, New York fell to the Democrats, and the White House was theirs. A mere 575 voters had thrown the Republicans out of power. By a far more comfortable two-to-one margin, Pulitzer had defeated his Republican congressional opponent without lifting a finger for himself.

Pulitzer basked in the glow of the election results. His chosen candidate was on the way to the White House. He himself had been redeemed from the ignominious election defeats he had suffered in St. Louis. But most important, Pulitzer's gamble on the *World* had paid off. It was now the largest-circulating newspaper in the nation and widely credited with Cleveland's election. "I should say, the election of Cleveland the first time was the most important achievement of the *World*," Pulitzer wrote years later. "Blaine, Conkling and other politicians with whom I was personally acquainted all said the *World* elected Cleveland."

Pulitzer capped off his success with one final act before the year ended. He sat down and made out a check for $252,039 to Jay Gould. The amount represented the balance and interest remaining on the loan to purchase the *World*. Pulitzer paid off the loan two years before it was due. The *World* now belonged entirely to him.

Chapter Eighteen

RAISING LIBERTY

P iled on Pulitzer's desk each day was proof of his success beyond New York. Letters poured in from all parts of the country, filled with ideas on how to boost circulation in places such as Vermont and Nebraska and hopes that he would launch a newspaper in Washington or Chicago. Priests submitted sermons for republication, and ambitious writers begged Pulitzer to open the columns of his newspaper to articles on New Guinea, archaeology, and, in one case, a "light readable history of the Fenian movement [an Irish independence movement] for the last twenty years." One pair of new parents told him they were christening their child "Joseph Pulitzer Conner," and a steamboat builder asked permission to name his newest and fastest craft after Pulitzer.

It was all too much. Pulitzer could not keep up with the deluge of mail and run the *World* at the same time, not to mention overseeing the *Post-Dispatch* in St. Louis. He flirted briefly with the idea of selling the St. Louis paper but decided its income was worth the headaches. Pulitzer knew he needed lieutenants. Finding the right ones was the problem. There was no lack of applicants. "It is approaching somewhat of a craze now in the newspaper circles of the metropolis to get on the *World*," reported *The Journalist*. But Pulitzer had a string of bad luck. He hired one business manager away from the *Herald*, but the manager proceeded to discount advertising sold to big retailers, against Pulitzer's wishes. The next hire turned out to have pocketed some of the advertising revenue at his previous job. Frustrated, Pulitzer telegraphed to James Scott, publisher of the *Chicago Herald*, for help. "I have always found it easier to get good writers than good reliable men for the business office," Scott wrote back. "The business end of the *World* is an immense responsibility and no man of ordinary newspaper experience would be the equal to its management."

The news management of the paper was safely in Cockerill's hands. But he was an exception—Pulitzer had such immense trust in Cockerill that he considered him his equal. For other positions of importance, even if Pulitzer managed to find a suitable man, he was ill suited to delegating work. He never really surrendered the responsibility, and he spent enormous amounts of time instructing, informing, and interfering with the person assigned to handle the work.

His election to Congress and the public's perception that Cleveland owed the presidency to Pulitzer compounded his misery by bringing an onslaught of demands for patronage jobs. Friends and strangers plied him with requests to become postmaster in Colorado, territorial governor of New Mexico, consul to Hawaii, or American minister to Berlin. The parade of supplicants thwarted the civil service commissioner's attempts to meet with Pulitzer on legitimate government business. "I called at your office yesterday," wrote the frustrated official, "but there was such a queue of persons at the desk that I could not wait my turn to send up my card without which formality access to you was denied me." The new Congress would not convene until the end of the year, but already Pulitzer regretted accepting the nomination. After years of wanting to be an elected politician, he found that the appeal of office was fading.

In early February 1885 Pulitzer traveled to Washington to see what awaited him when he assumed office. The Missouri delegation welcomed him and took him to the floor of the House of Representatives, where a debate droned on. After sitting for about an hour, Pulitzer went up to Representative James Burnes of Missouri and asked, "Have I got to stay in this place two years?"

Politics seemed even less attractive when Pulitzer returned to New York. Cleveland was staying on the tenth floor of the Victoria Hotel. Job seekers, well-wishers, party officials, and cranks swarmed into the hotel. The police kept them in line while Cleveland's secretary screened calling cards. Pulitzer arrived at the hotel around noon. He scampered up a private staircase to the tenth floor and gave his card to the secretary, who disappeared into the presidential chambers. When he returned, he said that Pulitzer would have to wait a minute. "I am not accustomed to waiting," Pulitzer snapped, and then bounded down the staircase before the secretary could recover from the angry outburst. Later that evening, Pulitzer was persuaded to return to the hotel to meet Cleveland, and his bruised feelings were further assuaged when he was invited to dine with the president-elect and a small group a couple of nights later.

Pulitzer expected a revolution from Cleveland. In the *World*, he argued that the president should accept no gifts, tolerate no nepotism, tax luxuries, and impose a tariff to protect labor. More important, Pulitzer wanted a political quail hunt. Cleveland needed to flush out all the Republicans in appointed offices, gain access to their supposedly secret records, and expose the skullduggery of past years. Democrats should be the ones to staff the government, Pulitzer said. "A President who is nominated and elected by a party also owes something to that party."

Cleveland didn't share Pulitzer's fervor, and was uninterested in satisfying the party's hunger for patronage jobs after twenty-four years of exile. Even worse, the president ignored Pulitzer's choices. In particular, Pulitzer wanted his friend Charles Gibson of St. Louis appointed to the minister's post in Berlin and met with Cleveland to urge this selection. Gibson himself came to Washington, armed with an endorsement from the *Post-Dispatch* and a privately printed pamphlet. It was all for naught. In late March, Cleveland appointed someone else to the Berlin post.

Pulitzer the reformer turned into a rejected spoils seeker. Cleveland had hardly finished taking the oath of office when it became clear that a fight was brewing between the two men.

Frustrated with President Cleveland, Pulitzer turned his attention to a struggling effort to erect a prominent symbol of American immigration in New York. The French sculptor Frédéric-Auguste Bartholdi's statue of *Liberty Enlightening the World* was collecting dust in crates in France because Americans had not yet raised the money necessary to build its pedestal on Bedloe Island in the middle of New York's harbor.

Seven years earlier, in 1878, Pulitzer had been among those who had seen the head of the statue at the Paris Exposition. Since moving to New York in 1883, he had provided editorial support to the undertaking. His own experience of immigration and his devotion to American liberty made the project immensely appealing to Pulitzer. In fact, within two weeks of taking over the *World*, he had replaced the printing press at the center of the two globes on the masthead with a figure of Liberty, her hand holding the torch aloft.

All that remained to complete the project was to build an 89-foot granite pedestal to support the 151-foot, 225-ton sculpture. But the American fund-raising efforts had been anemic, especially in comparison with the French effort, which had raised more than $750,000. After years of solicitation, the American committee remained $100,000 short of the $250,000 needed for the work. Congress refused to help, other cities complained about New York's being chosen for the statue, and most newspaper editors considered the project too costly. It seemed destined for failure.

But Pulitzer was not going to give up on Lady Liberty. Even in the midst of the tumultuous 1884 election, he had taken time to support the work of the American committee. "Unless the statue goes to the bottom of the ocean," wrote Pulitzer, "it is safe to predict that it will eventually stand upon an American pedestal, and then be referred to for a very long time with more sentiment than we can now dream of."

The scattered editorials in the World had little effect. By spring of 1885, as the French prepared to ship the statue, only the concrete base had been poured. Pulitzer was indignant. "What a burning disgrace it will be to the United States," he wrote, "if the statue of the goddess is brought to our shores on a French government vessel and is met by the intelligence that our people, with all their wealth, have not enough public spirit, liberality and pride to provide a fitting pedestal on which it can be placed!" But his chastisement, published on a Saturday, stirred no one. The other newspapers, especially the Herald, continued to treat the project with puzzlement and disdain.

The following Monday, however, few could any longer feign ignorance of the Statue of Liberty's plight: Pulitzer made it the front-page story in his paper, now selling 150,000 or more copies a day. Under the banner headline WHAT SHALL BE DONE WITH THE GREAT BARTHOLDI STATUE? the World put America's failure to raise the needed funds on display, complete with illustrations of the stalled pedestal construction.

"There is but one thing that can be done," Pulitzer railed from his editorial page. "We must raise the money!" He backed his call with a specific plan. "The World is the people paper, and it now appeals to the people to come forward and raise this money," he wrote. "Let us not wait for the millionaires to give this money. It is not a gift from the millionaires of France to the millionaires of America, but a gift of the whole population of France to the whole people of America."

He called on readers to send money to the paper and promised he would deliver it to the project. "Give something, however little," Pulitzer asked. In return, he pledged that every donor's name would be published in the *World*. For as little as a penny, the poorest New Yorker could have his name in print in the same newspaper whose columns were populated with the names of the Vanderbilts, Whitneys, Rhinelanders, Roosevelts, and Astors.

It was an audacious move. Pulitzer was, after all, asking people to send cash and checks to a corporation just like those which ran the railroads or operated the steel mills. It was only Pulitzer's word that stood as a guarantee that every dime of the money would be accounted for and would be used for the statue. If no one responded, Pulitzer would look like a fool.

By the next morning, contributions began to pour in. "I am a poor man," wrote one reader, "but I will give something and I'll try to get everybody else to give something." Another wrote, "We have read what you say about the Bartholdi statue this morning and send you at once a small collection ($3.31) taken up in our office and expect to send you more very shortly."

Rather than start a fund-raising campaign, Pulitzer could have expediently used his own checkbook to make up the deficit. Instead, he chose to finish the project as it had been intended, by turning to the public for support. In one stroke, Pulitzer set into motion a mammoth public effort and demonstrated the growing power and civic role of the independent press. In the past, only churches and governments had been able to marshal such financial support. Now the fourth estate held an equal power to excite and direct mass public support.

The public service also turned out to be good for business. The *World*'s circulation soared. By June, it would boast that its Sunday edition was the largest in size and in circulation of any newspaper published in the United States. It was consuming 834 miles of newsprint per edition. "No newspaper on the habitable globe consumed so much paper as the *World* yesterday."

The long hours of work and the sleepless nights finally prompted Pulitzer to seek rest. On May 9, he and Kate left New York on the *Etruria*, bound for Europe. Ralph, Lucille, and the baby—Joseph Jr., born on March 21, 1885—were sent off to New Hampshire with nannies and a doctor under the watch of William H. Davis, Kate's younger brother, whom Joseph Sr. had recently hired as a much-needed personal assistant.

While Kate shopped in London and Paris, Joseph talked shop with newspaper publishers who were curious about this American sensation. Not one to be outmatched, Joseph also did his fair share of consuming, with visits to wine merchants and art galleries. He engaged the help of a Parisian art dealer to search for paintings while he and Kate went off to Aix-les-Bains. "I don't think I told you that Vanderbilt has a Pahnaroli in his fine collection and although I do not know it, it will not be a *better* one than yours," the dealer wrote, deftly mentioning the other art collector.

The Pulitzers took baths at Aix-les-Bains and at Bad Kissingen, in Germany, but they had little effect on Joseph. Instead of finding rest in his isolation and distance from New York, Pulitzer continued to meddle in every part of the *World*'s operation. He paid to have his editors come to Europe to meet with him, he read and criticized each issue of the paper sent to him by mail, and he kept telegraph operators busy transmitting instructions back to New York.

Usually Pulitzer's transatlantic chatter consisted of complaints, but he also found cause to praise the work of his staff. By July, readers had sent $75,000 to the *World* for the Statue of Liberty. On August 11, the paper exceeded its goal of $100,000. In less than four months, more than 120,000 readers had responded to the *World*'s campaign. "From every single condition in life—save only the very richest of the rich and their tainted fortunes—did contributions flow," Pulitzer said. "From the honorable rich as well as the poorest of poor—from all parties, all sections, all ages, all sexes, all classes—from the cabinet member and the Union League member—from the poor news boys who sent their pennies, until the unprecedented number of 120,000 widely different contributors had joined in a common spirit for a common cause."

The European sojourn was a failure. Joseph returned home no better rested than when he had left. (Kate, however, was pregnant with their fifth child in seven years of marriage.) Insomnia still gripped him, and he was in a state of nervous exhaustion. His editors suffered. He found fault in everything they did and escalated his demands for time-consuming reports on all aspects of the operation. Men were assigned to tediously count the want-ad lineage in competing papers in order to calculate the *World*'s share of the market. To keep Pulitzer happy the results had to be broken down into categories and boiled down to their essence. "Put the thing in the nutshell," he would say over and over again. "He was the damnedest best man in the world to have in a newspaper office for one hour in the morning," said Cockerill. "For the remainder of the day he was a damned nuisance."

At home it was no better. His family lived in fear. Joseph exploded over even the smallest things and Kate took the brunt of his attacks. "He said that he was uncomfortable, that I did not understand the proper relations between husband and wife," she wrote in her diary that fall. The particulars of his indictment were that she failed in what he called "the duties of a wife" and neglected to make him comfortable at home. "There was not a servant in this house who had worked harder than I had," Kate snapped back at him, losing her temper. "I had made a slave of myself," she continued, telling him that "he was entirely spoilt, that with his disposition he must have something to criticize." Her uncharacteristic outburst caused Joseph to order her from the room, telling her that he would never forgive her. "When will these scenes end or when will I be at rest?" Kate asked that night in her diary.

One friend understood the depth of Joseph's troubles. Writing from St. Louis, his former partner John Dillon spoke lovingly of his admiration for Pulitzer but included a warning. "Overwork in business or in routine work will break a man down but in your case the injury is greater because you have been overworking those powers and faculty which in the main is the type of higher or divine creative power," Dillon wrote. "Not one man in ten thousand has it at all.

"You have overstretched it," he continued. "You have called on it to do more than it should have done, you have put it under the services of your will, you have made it work when it should have rested, you have compelled it to furnish ideas—and you have overworked it." Dillon urged Pulitzer to leave work for six months of rest. In the end, Dillon said, his friend faced a decision. "If you wish you can do the work of a lifetime and break down; or you can do the work of a century in a lifetime, and live while you do it, which is much better." It was the frankest Dillon had ever been with Pulitzer and he asked that the letter be burned.

*   *   *

On the morning of December 3, 1885, a New York City judge was startled to see the names of the mayor and the city's most prominent newspaper publisher in a bundle of documents handed to him. Before him was "William R. Grace, plaintiff, v. Joseph Pulitzer, defendant," prepared by one of the best law firms in the city. The lawsuit alleged that the *World*'s editorial page had damaged Mayor Grace's good name by wrongly linking him to a financial scandal surrounding the demise of the investment firm Grant & Ward and the wreck of the Marine Bank. The collapse had wiped out most of former president Grant's fortune, sent a few men to prison, and set off a minor financial panic. The city lost $1 million in deposits it had in the firm, and the *World* had laid the blame on the mayor.

Grace sought $50,000 in damages. Seeing that the documents were in order, the judge dispatched a deputy sheriff to arrest Pulitzer, as was then the custom in lawsuits. The deputy reached the *World* building and after some delay was admitted into Pulitzer's office. He explained the charges and said bail would be set at $5,000.

"Do you want the money?" asked Pulitzer

"I prefer two bondsmen," replied the deputy.

"All right, but it would be much more convenient to pay the money," Pulitzer said wearily, well used to this legal dance. Since taking over the *World*, Pulitzer's lawyer Roscoe Conkling had been called on to litigate twenty-one libel cases, more than one a month. He was able to successfully defend the paper on ten of them and, with his legal skills, put the eleven others into judicial limbo. Conkling would eventually manage to make Grace's lawsuit disappear as well. But the battle cost tens of thousands of dollars in legal fees and incalculable frayed nerves. Pulitzer, recalled one staff member, "was so obsessed by the fear of libel suits that he nightly read almost every paragraph in the paper." A few days later Pulitzer escaped New York and its legal harassments, though not the crush of work. The Congress elected in 1884 was finally convening, and he headed to Washington.

Pulitzer and the House of Representatives were a bad match from the start. In New York he had power and could make his own decisions. Here he was one of 325 men and nothing happened without collaboration. Even worse, as a freshman he was on the bottom rung. He drew a lot that gave him an unwanted seat in the back of the House chamber, and his assignments to the civil service and commerce committees had so little seniority that they were of little value. He would be a committee chair, he quipped, if six Democrats on one committee and seven on the other didn't show up.

Pulitzer had no time for endless committee meetings, long floor debates, and late-night political socializing. As it was, his pace was already frenetic. He would hold a morning editorial meeting on Park Row, attend a Democratic caucus meeting in the evening in Washington, then breakfast with a Congressional leader the next morning before returning north for dinner with, say, the New York socialite Ward McAllister.

To maintain this schedule was arduous. The tunnel under the Hudson River was still not complete, so Pulitzer had to take a ferry from Fourteenth or Twenty-Third Street to the New Jersey shore and then board a train south. Making this travel even more distasteful to Pulitzer was that he had no interest in the work of a congressman. Once, when he was supposed to be preparing a committee report, Pulitzer was instead attending an art auction in New York. "Day was turned into night and night into day," observed a reporter. "He flew from Washington to New York and from New York to Washington like a cock pigeon with a mate and nest in both places."

Pulitzer found Washington politics clubby and its politicians unappreciative of his brand of journalism. One morning, he and his personal secretary were met at the Washington train station by the *World*'s Washington correspondent. To Pulitzer's great pleasure, the reporter had discovered that the attorney general and several members of the House held stock in the Pan-Electric Telegraph Company, which stood to benefit from some forthcoming legal rulings. "The talk was all about the investigation, which was creating something of a sensation," recalled Pulitzer's personal secretary. The *World* trumpeted the charges, and Pulitzer used his new position as a member of the House to call for an investigation.

Many of Pulitzer's colleagues, who had deep and long-standing political alliances, were unhappy about his attacks on a member of the administration. Unlike his readers, they were not limited to writing angry letters to the editor. A fellow Democrat, Representative Eustace Gibson of West Virginia, rose on the floor and accused the publisher of cowardice. Pulitzer, he said, "did not see fit in his official capacity to attack these gentlemen in an open, honest, and manly way, which a Representative should have done, but undertook to retreat behind the irresponsible columns of his newspapers for the purpose of creating a scandal for what motives I am not here to state."

Another member rose quickly to point out that Pulitzer was not present to defend himself. "I cannot help that. He ought to be here," Gibson said.

When a committee was finally convened in March 1886 to examine the charges, Pulitzer was almost as much a target of the investigation as the accused. The committee members suspected that the *World* had published the allegations in order to profit from manipulating the stock prices of Pan-Electric. Who had made the decision to publish the story, they asked.

"I, and I alone, solely am responsible and no one else is," Pulitzer said. "No human being has tried to influence me in any manner whatever." He explained that he had held the story in one of the pigeonholes of his desk. "I had waited three months in the hopes that a certain gentleman—particularly one gentleman—might rid himself of the possession of Pan-Electric stock."

The gentleman in question was Grover Cleveland's attorney general, Augustus Garland. Several months earlier, Garland had secretly offered to dispose of his stock by turning it over to the *World*. Pulitzer declined the offer, wiring to his Washington correspondent, "Garland's offer to transfer the stock to the *World* is against my inflexible rule never to touch any speculative stock whatever. I must adhere to that principle but if he positively wants to transfer the ~~unclean~~ thing to you not as a representative of the *World* but as a trustee for the sole purpose of getting rid of the embarrassment and publicly disposing of the stock for some charity that might be considered." Nothing came of the idea.

The committee members continued with their questioning, but as they couldn't obtain any useful information from Pulitzer, he was dismissed to catch his train back to New York. Even excluding the experience of being grilled by his colleagues, Pulitzer found Capitol Hill a disappointment and reneged on his responsibilities. He was absent most of the time, never gave a speech on the floor, introduced just two bills, and completed his overdue committee work only after being reprimanded.

When Pulitzer was nominated for Congress two years earlier, he and

Conkling had made ambitious political plans during leisurely carriage rides through Central Park. Only his St. Louisan friend Gibson had pointedly asked him, "How can one man attend to two great newspapers and act a great part on the national stage?" Pulitzer had learned the answer the hard way. On April 10, his thirty-ninth birthday, he sat at his desk and pulled out a sheet of stationery. "Unwilling to hold the honors of a seat in Congress without fully observing all the expectations attached to it," he wrote in a letter to his constituents, "I hereby return to you the trust which you so generously confided to me."

The World's Washington correspondent promised to clean out Pulitzer's desk in the Capitol. "I'm glad you have resigned your seat in Congress," he wrote. "I am sure you have a much better position as editor of the World than any official in Washington."

Pulitzer's congressional career lasted a mere four months, unless one counts the eleven months he spent waiting for the opening of Congress. He donated his salary to help endow a bed in a New York hospital for use by a newspaperman; he donated his stationery allowance to an industrial school for newsboys; and, after much work, he found a recipient for the several quarts of wheat given to members of Congress by the Department of Agriculture to distribute to their constituents. The only thing he had not thought through was the consequences of his resignation. The vacancy he created could not be filled until the next election. In his hurry to dump the job, he left his district with no vote in the House and no procurer of patronage, and young military academy candidates without a sponsor. His departure was as ill-considered as his candidacy had been in the first place.

In late June 1886, when Kate neared her due date, Joseph made plans to travel. As when Lucille and Katherine were about to be born, Joseph did not let Kate's pregnancy restrict his movements, though childbirth carried a considerable risk of mortality until it took place in hospitals, later in the century. Rather, Joseph remained single-mindedly focused on his own health, which continued to bedevil him. He became convinced, for reasons unknown, that the water in the house they rented at 616 Fifth Avenue was unhealthy, even though the house was in one of the toniest sections of Manhattan. Pulitzer hired plumbers to cut off the water to several of the bathrooms.

Since Kate could not travel, Pulitzer enlisted his old friend Thomas

Davidson of St. Louis as a companion. In the midst of the election of the previous year, Pulitzer had paused for a reunion with Davidson. It was the first time in a decade the two had seen each other. In the intervening years, Davidson had wandered through Europe, living for a while as a hermit, and had founded a utopian fellowship that included George Bernard Shaw among its members. Pulitzer insisted that Davidson stay at the house and devised a dinner to which he invited Conkling and other well-known politicians in hopes of impressing his old teacher. It didn't work. After the dinner, the skeptical philosopher wrote to a friend that he found the dinner guests lacking in character. But he was charmed by Kate, whom he had not met before, and found her to be entirely devoted to Joseph.

Davidson and Pulitzer traveled through Europe for a month. Pulitzer kept the European telegraph operators busy and, as usual, was no more rested when he returned than when he had departed. At home, he met his new daughter, who was born on June 19, 1886, and was named Edith. Once again, Joseph did not want to remain in New York during the heat of the summer, so he left with the family for Lenox. But even in the relaxing Berkshires, with daily horse rides, the demands of his newspapers pressed on him. He refused to let his managers manage or his editors edit. Despite the continued success of the papers, he found fault in all they did.

Pulitzer was most frustrated with the quality of the *World's* editorial page. In his conception, this was the most important component of a newspaper. For him, reporting the news served primarily to build a readership that would turn to the editorial page for his own sage counsel on affairs of state and politics. So far, none of the editors he had hired could write an editorial to his liking. He hoped William H. Merrill, who worked at the *Boston Herald*, would solve his problem. At first Merrill agreed to come to the *World,* which he considered "the greatest opportunity now offered in the press of America," but then he got cold feet. Pulitzer left Lenox and went to Boston to persuade Merrill in person. After some hesitation, Merrill was finally won over. The incredible $7,500 salary sufficiently assuaged his fears of working for a publisher with a demanding reputation.

Next Pulitzer dashed out to St. Louis to look over plans for a new *Post-Dispatch* building. It was the first time he had been back since he left the city in 1883. Then he returned to New York in time to celebrate the dedication of the Statue of Liberty. Pulitzer did not want anyone to forget who had made the completion of the statue possible. In front of the *World* offices, he built a triumphal arch sixty feet tall spanning Park Row and festooned with French and American flags. On October 28, a great parade passed under the arch and the *World*'s employees and their families, as well as its advertisers, boarded two steamers. The two ships, led by another with Pulitzer and his family on board, joined a flotilla that made its way to Bedloe's Island. There, President Cleveland and a huge retinue of dignitaries—few of whom had contributed to the pedestal—marked the moment with a long succession of speeches.

Not being among the speakers, Pulitzer reserved his thoughts for the *World*'s editorial page. In his inimitable style, decorated with Old World flourishes, he wrote, "The statue represents, upon a standpoint at last firmly held, the results of centuries of struggle against oppression, ignorance, bigotry and might unsupported by right. It breathes a sense of relief that so much has been won."

Among those who did speak at the ceremonies was Chauncey Depew. He and Pulitzer had recently become friends, and theirs was the first of several friendships Pulitzer made among New York's elite that could challenge his ability to run a newspaper championing the common man. Not only was Depew a Republican; he was president of the New York Central, the rail line controlled by Vanderbilt and the *World*'s most frequent target in its war against monopolies. But Depew had more savvy than most of the *World*'s targets. He recognized that the new medium Pulitzer commanded was, at its core, a business. He and Pulitzer were both captains of industry. The difference was just that Pulitzer made his money tearing apart the other.

As one of the figures in the famous "Belshazzar" cartoon that had irreparably damaged Blaine's presidential campaign, Depew had felt the *World*'s sting. But he believed more was to be gained by being friends with Pulitzer than by being his enemy. A year earlier, Depew had disarmed Pulitzer with a dinner toast in which he recounted their first meeting. Depew said that Pulitzer warned him that the paper would include him in its attacks on New York Central, monopolies, and Vanderbilt. But, Depew said, Pulitzer then added, "'When Mr. Vanderbilt finds that you are attacked, he is a gentleman and broad-minded enough to compensate you and will grant to you both significant promotion and a large increase in salary.'

"Well, gentlemen," Depew told the dinner crowd, "I have only to say that Mr. Pulitzer's experiment has been eminently successful. He has made his newspaper a recognized power and a notable organ of public opinion; its fortunes are made and so are his, and in regard to myself, all he predicted has come true, both in promotion and in enlargement of income."

With the Statue of Liberty now part of New York's landscape, as he had promised, Pulitzer turned his attention to the mayoral election. Although he apparently had three choices—the Democrats' Abram Hewitt, the United Labor Party's Henry George, and the Republicans' Theodore Roosevelt—in fact he had only two. He still considered the twenty-eight-year-old Roosevelt a traitor to the cause of reform. The *World* would have to choose between Hewitt and George.

Hewitt was a competent, honest, experienced politician; George was only famous as the author of *Progress and Poverty*, a wildly popular book that advocated the abolition of most taxes, the abolition of monopolies, and the creation of numerous social programs. If it were up to Pulitzer's working-class readers, the endorsement would have gone to George. But the *World* did not belong to them. Davidson pleaded with Pulitzer to support George. "He will be treated fairly," Pulitzer replied, saying he would meet George. "But I can't promise anything until all the candidates are known. Then I shall do whatever I think is best for the *City*."

In the end, Hewitt won the *World*'s editorial support, but in this election, unlike that of 1884, Pulitzer consented to restrain the news side from attacking Hewitt's opponents. Though the *World* criticized George in its editorials, it gave him a fair break. "You are doing excellently well by George, better than if you openly supported him," wrote Davidson. "His candidacy will, in any case, do much good in making people think and forcing the parties to put forward reputable candidates."

On Election Day, Pulitzer's candidate carried the day. Roosevelt came in a distant third. It was a stinging defeat. "I do not disguise from myself that this is the end of my political career," he told a close friend. Although Pulitzer was not to blame for the loss, he had again etched his name on Roosevelt's enemies list.

The double triumphs of 1886—the statue stood in the harbor, and Roosevelt had fallen in defeat—did not diminish the pressures on Pulitzer. The management of the *World* continued to consume his time and sap his energy. He had hired a personal secretary to cope with the flow of mail, but that put hardly a dent in the problem. "Hundreds of letters come into this office every day that I never see," Pulitzer told one correspondent who complained of not getting a reply.

Most vexing was Pulitzer's spreading fame as a financial success. Masy le Doll, a widow in Martinsburg, West Virginia, read that Pulitzer "was up to his neck in money, had so much he did not know what to do with it." She hoped for some to buy a bucket of coal, some flour, and maybe a turkey for Christmas. The New Yorker Walter Hammond appealed for a donation from Pulitzer because the organized charities denied him relief, believing him to be promiscuous. During a medical exam it was determined that one of Hammond's testicles was larger than the other, and the charity workers took this as proof that he had been sexually active. Hammond denied the charge, giving his word to Pulitzer that he had had sex only with his wife, who had burned to death in a fire six years earlier, and had been celibate since. Such was welfare in 1886.

Work and tension continued to wear Pulitzer down. He began to turn down social invitations, preferring to steal what rest he could at home in the evenings. When he did get out, it was now more often to visit an out-of-town friend such as the newspaper publisher George Childs of Philadelphia, who had a country house. Sitting by a blazing wood fire, Childs (who was older than Pulitzer) often counseled Pulitzer to ease up on his workload. In fact, Childs took it upon himself to deliver the same message to Pulitzer's wife. He wrote anxiously to Kate that Joseph was endangering his health. "He must be careful and remember that he has a wife and children who have a claim on him," Childs wrote. "He must try to learn to take things more rationally, he is under too great a pressure, and is doing more than anyone can do and retain his health. We all think too much of him to let him go on without a word of caution."

When Kate shared Childs's message with Joseph, he was in no mood to listen.

Chapter Nineteen

A BLIND CROESUS

---◆---

Joe Howard, one of the *World*'s leading reporters, was preparing to depart for Montreal on the evening of February 9, 1887, to cover the city's famous winter carnival. The idea had been Pulitzer's, and it was a plum assignment. Howard would spend several days visiting a monolithic illuminated ice palace and attending the carnival's many festivities. As he talked over his plans with editors in the newsroom, Pulitzer came out from his office and walked over to him.

"What have you been doing today, Joe?" asked Pulitzer.

"Nothing. I'm preparing, you know, to go to Montreal," replied Howard.

Upon hearing this, Pulitzer remembered he had also given permission and $100 to Walt McDougall to go to Montreal. Pulitzer had no interest in having—in his words—"two high-priced men off on one job."

"I don't want you to go," Pulitzer brusquely told Howard.

"But," said Howard, "I've bought my tickets and engaged berths for the people who are going with me. One must do that early. There are crowds going to Canada right now."

Pulitzer's face reddened. He raised his right hand and, waving his index finger close to Howard's face, said, "I tell you I don't want you to go."

"Don't you point that at me," Howard snapped back, hurling an insult, later reported as one that described Pulitzer as "a sordid, grasping, covetous Israelite."

Howard's revilement kindled Pulitzer's notorious temper. The publisher, who at six feet two inches towered over the squat reporter, struck Howard on the neck with his fist, sending him to the floor. As Howard fumbled for his eyeglasses, knocked off by the blow, Pulitzer told him he was fired. Rising from the floor, Howard tried to return the assault. But Cockerill and others restrained him and escorted him from the office.

"Joe got so abusive that I got at him and knocked him down, and then discharged him on the spot," Pulitzer admitted to reporters from rival newspapers who chased him down later that day. But, he added, "I wouldn't for the world hurt Joe, so don't say anything about it, please." Naturally, however, the fisticuffs made the front pages of the city's papers, except for the restrained *New York Times*. The *New York Herald*, where Howard had once worked, wrote the incident up like a prizefight, complete with diagrams and sporting-style commentary.

Howard was not the only talent Pulitzer had plucked from Bennett's staff at the *Herald*. While Bennett was in Paris, Pulitzer had persuaded the *Herald*'s managing editor, Ballard Smith, to move over to the *World*. When Bennett returned, he was so angry that he abolished the job, though others ended up doing the work under a different title.

Bennett's wrath was understandable. In the competitive atmosphere of Park Row, staffing remained a constant worry. Reporters were not hard to come by and most jumped at the chance to work for the *World*. But editors were another matter. "It is the man," Pulitzer said, "who decides what is to go into the paper and what is to be left out, and in what shape it is to go in, who has more to do with making the newspaper than the man who simply writes for it." The problem of finding the right editors was even more vexing for Pulitzer than for most publishers because the success of the *World* rested on an approach to news for which most editors were not trained. Pulitzer was betting that Ballard Smith would take to it.

Smith was a Kentuckian who had once worked for Pulitzer's friend Henry Watterson at the *Louisville Courier-Journal*. After coming to New York, Smith served briefly as an editor on the old *World* before going to the *Herald*. Debonair, with an aura of erudition from his education at Dartmouth, he married the only daughter of a wealthy merchant and gained an entrée rare for a journalist into the city's close-knit social life—from which the Pulitzers were excluded.

Although Smith cut an unusual figure in the crass, tumultuous world of a newspaper's city room, Pulitzer recognized in him news instincts similar to his own. Smith was daring, a master of headlines, and, most important, willing to be trained. "I have tried faithfully to reflect exactly your views," Smith wrote to Pulitzer not long after joining the paper. "I confess they often conflicted much with what I thought I knew well before."

Smith, however, did not hit it off with Cockerill, who felt threatened. Like two feral dogs, they circled each other. This was not displeasing to Pulitzer. He had no interest in building a team. Rather, he preferred having managers who competed with one another and for his approbation. Without making himself superfluous, he was taking the first steps toward assembling a structure of management that could run the paper without him.

With Cockerill overseeing the entire operation, Smith enforcing Pulitzer's approach to news gathering, and Merrill writing editorials, Pulitzer was freed from the day-to-day operation of the paper. The change was a necessity. He had become irascible and moody, and his health woes grew more and more apparent to those around him. "Won't you have enough confidence to let us run the place?" asked George Turner, a Bostonian, whom Pulitzer had hired as a business manager. "I am writing this to beg you to cease worrying about the paper and, if a sea voyage is possible, to take a long one where it will be impossible to get reports or issue directions."

Pulitzer booked tickets to Liverpool for April 16.

While Pulitzer waited to depart for Europe, the needs of the paper weighed heavily on him. The libel suits continued to swarm like gnats, despite Pulitzer's interminable precautions, including reading almost every word that went into the paper. The *World Almanac* also required his attention. He had revived the encyclopedic work, which was originally published by the old *World* but had died. Pulitzer saw both promotional and moneymaking opportunities in resurrecting it. He also loved reference works. When he got into arguments—not an infrequent occurrence—he would rush to his collection of such books to find ammunition. But like all his ideas, this one created more work for which he could not find time, and he had been disappointed by the first new editions. "That it has not received the measure of my own concept," he told an editor, "is perhaps because I had not time enough at my disposal to do all I had planned."

In the meantime, Pulitzer had to tend to the opening of a printing plant in Brooklyn, because the *World*'s main presses couldn't keep up with demand. The paper now circulated more than a quarter of a million copies each day. To celebrate this achievement, Pulitzer sent commemorative coins set in plush-lined leather cases to advertisers and leading political figures. Slightly larger than a silver dollar, the coins were 100 percent silver, 17 percent more than the amount of silver the government used in its coins. On one side was a relief of the Statue of Liberty; the other side boasted that the *World*'s circulation was the largest ever attained by an American newspaper.

The paper's average daily circulation was now three times what it had been three years earlier, when Pulitzer had already been considered a stunning success. The new high-water mark astonished newspapermen because 1887 was not an election year, when partisan fever stoked the circulation of newspapers. The *World*'s numerical claims were also credible even in an era when circulation figures were often unsubstantiated bragging. Pulitzer dared anyone to prove him wrong. He offered to open his books to public inspection and promised to donate $10,000 to the press club if someone found he had misstated the figures. "It is a common query in the literary clubs and among the journalistic fraternity," said one commentator. "What in the *World* will Pulitzer do next?"

Even if Pulitzer ceased his constant self-promotion, the success of the *World* was now so widely known that it was spawning imitators in other cities. His formula worked, even for a young dropout from Harvard.

In the spring of 1887, after years of entreaties, twenty-four-year-old William Randolph Hearst persuaded his father to turn over control of the family's money-losing *San Francisco Examiner* to him. He had found Harvard boring in comparison with life's possibilities for someone with money who was eager to prove himself. Commuting to work in a fifty-foot speedboat, the tall, slender, handsome Hearst set about transforming the *Examiner* into a West Coast version of the *World*.

For years Hearst had read, studied, and cut out articles from the *World*. He told his father that he would make the family's newspaper like the "*New York World* which is undoubtedly the best paper of the class to which the *Examiner* belongs—that class which appeals to the people and which depends for its success upon enterprise, energy and a certain startling originality."

"To accomplish this," he continued, "we must have—as the *World* has—active, intelligent, and energetic young men."

Hearst needed first to break his paper's association with its past incarnation, as Pulitzer had done when he took over the *World*. Almost as if he were Pulitzer in New York in 1883, Hearst resorted to every trick from Pulitzer's playbook. He sent his reporters out to scour the poorest neighborhoods in San Francisco for tales that would make readers weep, to look in police stations and courts for crime stories that thrilled, and to search through public records to uncover corruption. The front page not only displayed the reporters' work with headlines bold as neon lights but also trumpeted the paper's successes as if the *Examiner* itself were running for office. Imitation has its rewards. The *Examiner's* circulation began a steady climb.

Hearst's approach to management also mirrored Pulitzer's. He left no part of the operation alone, and his indefatigable presence drove his staff to work even harder. He spent almost every waking hour working on the paper. "I don't suppose I will live more than two or three weeks if this strain keeps up," Hearst wrote his mother, voicing woes similar to those of Pulitzer, though he was almost twenty years Pulitzer's junior.

Although he greatly admired the *World* and imitated it, Hearst disdained its owner. He felt he had more in common with Pulitzer's adversary Bennett, who like Hearst was heir to a family fortune and who had been given his *New York Herald* without spending a cent. "It is an honest and brave paper one can respect," Hearst said. "It is the kind of paper I should like the *Examiner* to be, while the *World* is, because of the Jew that owns it, a nasty, unscrupulous damned sheet that I despise but which is too powerful to insult." But as a copycat, his spite was like that of a man who enjoyed the company of a mistress, which Hearst did, and felt sullied by the experience the morning after.

Despite the imitation there was a vast difference between the men. Pulitzer had started with nothing, and his newspapers were sustained and expanded by their financial success. Hearst, on the other hand, was backed by an endless reserve of family money. For any competitor, this made Hearst dangerous. He was soon boasting of the *Examiner's* success in full-page advertisements calling it "The Monarch of dailies. The largest, brightest and best newspaper on the Pacific Coast."

But conquering the Atlantic coast would have to wait for another day.

* * *

In late March 1887 the kind of criminal case Pulitzer loved to feature in the *World* opened in a New York City courtroom. Assistant District Attorney De Lancey Nicoll, whom Pulitzer admired, was prosecuting several aldermen on charges of corruption. One of the boodlers was defended by Ira Shafer, a colorful lawyer who made for good copy. The *World* illustrated its front-page coverage of the trial with comic drawings of Shafer, and the reporter had fun referring to Shafer's shoes as toboggans and to his mouth as a cave of winds. All this got to be too much for the lawyer. "That dirty, filthy sheet yesterday reviled and insulted me by the publication of a lot of vile caricatures," Shafer informed the jury, whose members were quite surprised, as they had not been permitted to read any newspapers. "A friend said to me this morning: 'Shafer, why don't you shoot that Hungarian Jew? Why don't you horsewhip him?'"

Despite the judge's attempts to rein him in, Shafer continued. "Gentlemen, wait. The day will come when I will meet that Jew face to face, and when I do meet him let him beware," he told the jury, which included three Jewish members. When court adjourned, Shafer went on a similar rampage before reporters in the courthouse hall. "The first time I shall meet Mr. Pulitzer after this trial is over," he said, "I shall kill him."

Lawyers who knew Shafer doubted that his threat was serious, and rather attributed it to his quick-to-anger disposition. The fiery-tempered Pulitzer figured as much. He continued to ride the elevated train to work unescorted, and he dismissed any talk of danger. "If I could have been killed by threats I should have been buried long ago," he said. "If I could be influenced by the hostility of rascals I should have conducted a very different newspaper from the *World* and I should have adopted a different policy when I entered journalism years ago—which was to expose fraud and crime and pursue rascals."

Pulitzer was soon out of Shafer's reach anyway. Leaving Smith, Cockerill, and Merrill to run the shop, he departed with Kate on the most extensive trip they had taken since he bought the paper four years earlier. There had been scarlet fever in their house and they were eager to leave. The children were left in the care of Kate's brother, who greatly pleased seven-year-old Lucille with the purchase of a pony. Pulitzer's friend Childs came up from Philadelphia to see them off. "I have been very anxious about you all," Childs told him. "What with the illness at home and the immense pressure of your great business you had too much to bear."

After a stopover in Scotland, the Pulitzers reached London, where Joseph was immediately confined to his hotel room by doctors worried that his cold was creating congestion in his lungs. Finally, in early May, the Pulitzers began their European trip in earnest—in Paris, a favorite of Kate's. There they dined with J. P. Morgan's partner Joseph Drexel, were feted by the American ambassador Robert McLane, attended balls, and purchased art and jewels.

The Pulitzers took up quarters at the Hotel Bristol. Joseph's brother Albert was only a few blocks away in Le Grand Hotel, but they remained estranged. The success of Albert's *Morning Journal*, though now eclipsed by the *World*, provided him with financial freedom. His fortune made, he spent less and less time in New York and instead resided regally for long stretches in Paris and London. His marriage to Fanny was at an end. In fact, he had been romantically linked with the four-times-married Miriam Leslie, a publishing widow who was a descendant of Huguenots and sometimes went by the title Baroness de Bazus.

An enterprising American reporter could not resist playing the two brothers against each other by seeking their opinions of French news-papers. "I think it is simply disgraceful the kind of thing which they produce here," said Joseph. "They are newspapers in name, but newspa-pers with the news left out. They print neither home news nor foreign news, in fact they print nothing but stories and essays." *Au contraire*, said Albert. "People in France have not got that terrible thirst for 'news' which consumes us at home; they are not at all in a hurry to know about accidents and crimes before it is necessary, and even then they don't want a great mass of sickening details. In many ways their tastes are more elevated than ours."

Joseph and Kate went south for a rest in Aix-les-Bains and then recrossed the Channel to be among the dignitaries and royalty from around the globe who gathered in Westminster Abbey for Queen Vic-toria's celebration of her silver jubilee. Afterward they watched the royal procession from the *World*'s London offices. While they were in London, Pulitzer flirted with the idea of buying a newspaper. Before his arrival, the *World*'s correspondent there had inquired which newspaper could be had and made into a British version of the New York sensation.

It was a tempting proposition. Pulitzer loved London and its museums, theaters, and politics. Kate and his friends who fretted about his health were in a panic.

Nothing came of the idea and Pulitzer resumed his statesmanlike role. The financier Junius Morgan invited the Pulitzers to his country house; "I am but a plain farmer living on my farm," he wrote. Liberal members of Parliament feted Pulitzer in London, and he made a pilgrimage to visit their party leader, William Gladstone, at Dollis Hill Estate. Thrown out of office after his third term, as a consequence of advocating home rule for Ireland, Gladstone was living in political exile about a forty-five-minute carriage ride from Charing Cross. Pulitzer arrived with a delegation of American politicians to present him with an ornamental silver urn, a tribute paid for by contributions from thousands of readers of the *World* for Gladstone's failed efforts on behalf of Ireland.

Gladstone, dressed in a light gray frock coat with a loosely tied blue-and-white polka-dot scarf, greeted the Americans and led them to the wooden box in which the gift had been shipped. Keys were procured and Gladstone lifted the three-foot silver urn from its container. On its top was mounted a small bust of him, and the trophy-like object was engraved with a bas-relief of Homer and Demosthenes and embossed with a rose, thistle, and shamrock.

"Well, let us get the business formality of this out of the way so that everyone can come and look at it," Gladstone said. Then he leaned against the box and turned to Pulitzer, who addressed the crowd. "Mr. Gladstone," he began, "10,689 people of the first city of America ask the first citizen of England to accept this gift." As if he were giving an American stump speech, Pulitzer droned on with praises for Gladstone, with his usual references to liberty, freedom, political equality, and democracy.

While the ceremony continued, an American con man took advantage of the moment. He hid behind a tree and emerged to stand behind Gladstone and Pulitzer when all the dignitaries gathered for a photograph. Later he would imply to others that he was an intimate friend of the Prince of Wales, who he claimed had once taken his picture. When the mark expressed doubts, the American operator would say he thought he might even have the picture with him and would produce a photo, trimmed to show him standing with Gladstone and Pulitzer.

Unaware of the shady operator, Pulitzer relished the moment. He sent instructions to the *World* to play up the ceremony. Smith gave it two columns on the front page. British newspapers were less thrilled and questioned the delegation's claim of speaking for the American people. "In point of fact," said the *Evening Standard*, "they had no more right to such a position than the three tailors of Tooley Street, who addressed the Emperor of Russia, had to represent the people of Great Britain." The last word, however, belonged to Gladstone's daughter Mary. That night she penned a few short lines in her diary about the ceremony. "Sat. A garden party the American presentation to [father], an object of surprising hideousness."

By August the Pulitzers were back in New York. They stayed only briefly, though long enough for Pulitzer to consider yet another proposal to buy a paper. He had given up on acquiring a London newspaper, but he listened attentively to a pitch from William Henry Smith, the AP's director, to acquire the *Chicago Times*. After all, Smith had been one of the men who had guided him to buy the *World*. But reason again prevailed, and Pulitzer declined the opportunity.

Abandoning business and the heat, the Pulitzers spent the remainder of the summer in Lenox, where they rented one of the town's many mansions, referred to by the wealthy as "cottages." Despite the fresh country air, their daughter Lucille fell gravely ill. Three years after losing one daughter, Joseph and Kate faced the horrible possibility again. Joseph was convinced that the plumbing was the culprit, as he had been at their Fifth Avenue house. This time, he may not have been wrong. After Lucille recovered, two doctors discovered that the pipes leading to the cesspool were not properly installed and permitted gases to work their way into the bathroom Lucille had used.

The Pulitzers returned to New York, in time for Joseph to witness, from the officiating yacht, the final race of the 1887 defense of America's Cup. The race had become immensely popular. In fact, during the prior year's race, the *World* had mounted movable miniature yachts on a track across the first floor of its building. As dispatches arrived by telegram every ten minutes, the yachts were drawn across the painted scene by hidden strings. The display attracted crowds so immense that all traffic was blocked from Park Row from morning until night.

Pulitzer finally ended his family's migration from rented house to rented house. He purchased a mansion at 10 East Fifty-Fifth Street, just off Fifth Avenue, from the banker Charles Barney, brother-in-law of Pulitzer's friend Whitney. The house was almost new and had been designed by McKim, Mead, and White, architects to the rich and famous such as the Astors, the Vanderbilts, and other plutocrats who were madly building châteaus on Fifth Avenue. The targets of the *World*'s editorial venom would now be Pulitzer's neighbors.

It was, indeed, quite a neighborhood. A few blocks to the south, William Henry Vanderbilt had bought an entire block and built enormous brownstone houses for his family and two married daughters. His sons soon built their own mansions nearby. Henry Villard, who had taken Pulitzer across the country four years earlier to witness the completion of his cross-country railroad, erected an even more enormous palace comprising six linked brownstones with a courtyard in the center. Also designed by McKim, Mead, and White, the palazzo-like structure consumed a ton of coal a day for heating.

Only in comparison with his neighbors' houses did Pulitzer's $200,000 manor seem modest. Broad stairs led up from the street to a carved stone entrance that opened into a large hall with a winding staircase. Four stories tall, constructed of stone and brick, the house had large, high-ceilinged rooms for entertainment on the first floor, including a magnificent oak-paneled dining room; bedrooms on the second and third floors; and servants' quarters on the fourth floor. In the rear was an attached conservatory.

While negotiating for the house, Pulitzer asked his lawyers to persuade the mortgage holders to let him own it outright. Money was no longer an issue. In addition to the political power and the prominence the *World* gave him, the paper was making Pulitzer very rich. His annual income alone now dwarfed the entire fortune he had gambled on acquiring the *World* four years earlier.

He invested in stocks, paid $185,000 in cash for additional buildings for the paper, and indulged in any luxury he fancied. He toyed with the idea of acquiring a $75,000 yacht, purchased paintings from Parisian and New York art dealers, and ordered 2,000 bottles of French claret from a wine merchant for $25,000. Pulitzer's taste in cigars and wine grew with his income. He stocked his house with Havana cigars and his wine cellar with Château d'Yquem and Château le Crock, among other vintages. His willingness to spend encouraged Tiffany's to put him on a list that offered buyers an early peek at its new line of jewels; and Goupil's Picture Gallery brought paintings to his house for his consideration.

Pulitzer developed a preference for working at home. He had a telephone with a direct line to the office installed so that he could summon editors and business managers for meetings. He rarely left for the office before noon. Reaching the *World*, he would make his way through each department before settling in at his editorial offices. By six, he would be on his way home. On nights when there was a performance at the Metropolitan Opera House, Joseph and Kate could be found in their box, one of the best in the house. Going to the opera, particularly to hear German works, ranked as Joseph's favorite pastime. He rarely missed a performance, and he would whistle operatic airs after hearing them but once. The evening invariably closed with a protracted telephone consultation with the night editors at the paper.

Money bought the Pulitzers more than acquisitions and leisure pursuits. It gave them access to New York's elite society. By day, Joseph may have sparred with the city's rich, but by night he dined with them. New York society began to see a lot of the Pulitzers. Sometimes they were accompanied by the socially well-connected editor Ballard Smith and his wife. The Pulitzers even received an invitation to the prestigious Patriarch Ball in December 1885. This dance was organized by Ward McAllister, a social arbiter who was famous for his list of New York's 400 most elite families. He had also initiated the Patriarchs, a group of heads of prominent families who made a vain attempt to create a social designation that could not be bought. They saw themselves as the last stand of manners and breeding.

The ball was held at Delmonico's on Fifth Avenue. The ballroom was splendidly decorated with flowers and greenery from Charles Klunder, whose plants decked the tables of society. Hidden by banks of flowers, electric lights, still considered a novelty, illuminated the room. The Pulitzers arrived at eleven that evening. Mrs. Astor, the queen of New York society, presided over the soiree, and J. Pierpont Morgan was installed as a Patriarch. Punctually at midnight, two Patriarchs led the couples in the german (a cotillion) before the group retired downstairs for terrapin, canvasback duck, and pâté de foie gras.

The Pulitzers' rising status gave Kate a chance to charm the Fifth

Avenue crowd with her graciousness. She served as a social tour guide when her distant cousin Winnie Davis—the youngest daughter of Jefferson Davis, known as the "daughter of the Confederacy"—came to New York. Dressed in a satin gown trimmed with ostrich feathers and crystal pendants, Kate caught the eye of one society columnist. "Her manner is cordial and fascinating," the journalist wrote. "She has large black eyes fringed with long lashes, a brilliant color, perfect teeth, lovely white sloping shoulders, a head well poised and coils of dark brown hair."

When the Hungarian painter Mihály Munkácsy came to New York the winter before, Pulitzer had given one dinner party in the artist's honor at Delmonico's and a second at home. The guests at both included financial luminaries such as sugar trust attorney John E. Parsons, the businessman Cyrus W. Field, and assorted wealthy politicians and statesmen such as Chauncey Depew, William Evarts, and Levi P. Morton—the same three who were among the figures in the cartoon "Belshazzar's Feast" that Pulitzer published during Blaine's campaign.

In particular, Joseph enjoyed the company of August Belmont and Leonard Jerome, who dined with the Pulitzers on both evenings. Belmont and Jerome were doyens of the city's new rich, and they loved to compete ostentatiously with each other. After the ladies at one of Jerome's dinner parties found gold bracelets in their napkins, Belmont folded platinum bracelets in the napkins at his dinner party. Friendship with such men was seemingly incongruous for the publisher of the nation's leading democratic sheet, which daily proselytized for the virtues of egalitarianism. But Pulitzer did not object to wealth. In fact, he coveted it. However, the kind of wealth mattered. Inherited fortunes were a social evil for Pulitzer; but earned wealth was not, even if it was tinged by illicit gains or exploitive profits.

"J.P. always cherished in his heart a sincere if unacknowledged veneration for rank and family," said the cartoonist McDougall, who spent many long hours with Pulitzer. "This was probably atavistic, coming as he did from a land where rank meant all that is desirable but, to a peasant, unattainable. He showed this feeling by an exaggerated contempt for persons of wealth and standing, yet the truth is that he was moved by quite different feelings, a strong hunger for wealth, luxury, power, predominating over all other emotions."

Pulitzer did not simply socialize with those he pilloried in the pages of the *World*; he also became their financial partner. He joined William

Rockefeller, William Vanderbilt, J. P. Morgan, and others in creating a club on Jekyll Island* off the Georgia coast as a private preserve where the nation's richest and most powerful men could hunt, fish, ride, and socialize in complete privacy.

Despite distaste for his brand of journalism in many quarters of polite society, the gatekeepers could no more close the doors to Pulitzer than they could to other nouveaux riches. The time had passed when Wall Street speculators, industrial titans, and even Democratic politicians could be excluded. In New York—unlike Boston, where the Brahmins had deep roots—money was in the ascendant. But though his wealth gained him a passport to the domain of New York's plutocracy, it did not gain him genuine acceptance. In the eyes of many he remained, as he was born, a Jew.

Up until now, most of the anti-Semitism Pulitzer had faced from gentiles in New York had been coated with a veneer of politeness. German Jews, among whom Pulitzer would have been placed, incurred only mild ostracism. Pulitzer's friend Belmont, a Jew who had converted and changed his name from Schönberg, traveled in all but the most exclusive of New York's circles. But when a tidal wave of Russian Jews flooded New York, the accepting spirit among the elite faded. The Grand Union Hotel in Saratoga Springs barred the Jewish banker Joseph Seligman; the Union Club closed its doors to Jews (even though many were among its founders); and Anna Morton began to insist that her husband, Levi, be referred to as L. P. Morton. A dormant anti-Semitism among New Yorkers awoke.

"To decide a bet between two parties will you kindly answer the following," one reader wrote to the *World*. "Was the Editor of the New York *World* born in the country and is he of Jewish extraction." Pulitzer declined to answer the letter. Despite his Episcopalian wife, his baptized children, and his family's membership in St. Thomas Church on Fifth Avenue, Pulitzer could not shed his Jewish identity in the eyes of others any more than he could deny his foreign birth. In the public mind there was little doubt about Pulitzer's ethnicity.

"In all the multiplicity of Nature's freaks, running from Albino Negroes to seven-legged calves, there is one curiosity that will always cause

---

*The spelling in Pulitzer's time was "Jekyl." The second "l" was added in 1929.

the observer to turn and stare. This freak is a red-headed Jew," began a profile of Pulitzer in the trade publication *The Journalist*. It described "Jewseph Pulitzer" as "combing his hair with talons," "rubbing the sores around his eyes," and remaining in the shadows "in order to escape turning rancid in the hot sun."

The author of this barbarous piece was Leander Richardson, an aspiring actor with a beard and a wavy chevron mustache untrimmed at the ends so as to extend wider than his face. Richardson had worked as a gossip columnist for the *World* under Pulitzer until he was fired for undisclosed reasons in May 1884. He and a partner launched *The Journalist*, and Richardson used his new post on the widely read trade magazine to seek revenge on Pulitzer.

"Any man can make money by publishing a newspaper which will defile its columns with dirty advertisements as those of Jewseph Pulitzer's *World* are defiled," wrote Richardson, referring to personal notices that some people believed were illicit coded messages for rendezvous with prostitutes. "A directory of assignation houses and worse, the recognized organ of prostitutes, pimps and janders," claimed Anthony Comstock, of the New York Society for the Suppression of Vice. When the fuss over the advertisements faded, Richardson didn't relax his attacks. "There was never a greater pretender in American journalism," he said, "than this same Jewseph Pulitzer."

Pulitzer banned *The Journalist* from the office, but the anti-Semitic broadsides against him were not limited to Richardson's personal vendetta in the trade press. In "New Jerusalem," as the *Los Angeles Times* referred to New York City, others among Pulitzer's competitors adopted Richardson's methods. Their anger toward the upstart who was winning the circulation war found expression in attacks on Pulitzer for his Jewish origins. Even a man who had once been his mentor joined in.

The rivalry between Charles Dana and Pulitzer, harsh and vitriolic as it had been during the 1884 election, became bitterly personal in 1887. Since Pulitzer had come to New York, the *Sun's* circulation had shrunk at almost the same rate that the *World's* had soared. In October, Pulitzer launched the *Evening World* to compete with the *Evening Sun*, which Dana had begun publishing in the spring. In his typical fashion, Pulitzer stole one of Dana's editors, Solomon S. Carvalho, to run the new paper. Carvalho, who had a goatee and was always impeccably dressed, had made a reputation as a reporter with a flair for covering murders and suicides when he had first joined the *Sun* nine years earlier. He instantly made the one-cent *Evening World* into an audacious purveyor of titillating and sensational news. Within a few weeks it surpassed the *Evening Sun*'s circulation.

The economic insult to Dana was compounded by a political dispute between him and Pulitzer. In the election for district attorney, Pulitzer was backing De Lancey Nicoll, who had prosecuted the corrupt alderman in the trial that produced the death threat against Pulitzer. Tammany Hall, however, would have nothing to do with a man seemingly hell-bent on putting corrupt politicians in jail. So Nicoll deserted the Democratic Party and won the Republican nomination. In the offing was the kind of political fight Pulitzer relished. By not abandoning Nicoll, he could prove his paper's independence. On the other hand, Dana, who had backed Nicoll, withheld his support now that Nicoll was running as a Republican. Pulitzer, in bellicose prose, demanded an explanation from Dana. He got one.

"We have withdrawn from our support of Mr. Nicoll because we distrust the *World* and its motives," wrote Dana, "and because more than suspicions exist to indicate what these motives are." The *Sun* then rehashed the tale of Cockerill's shooting of Slayback and claimed that Cockerill had avoided a murder charge because the district attorney in St. Louis had been in Pulitzer's pocket.

By bringing up this embarrassment, Dana initiated a verbal brawl between the two publishers that rapidly descended into the gutter. Pulitzer called the *Sun*'s editor "Charles Ananias Dana" and Dana retorted with "Boss Judas Pulitzer" and "Dunghill Cock." As Nicoll campaigned, probably bewildered by the conduct of the two publishers, the editorial volleys worsened. Pulitzer called Dana a "mendacious blackguard" and Dana said Pulitzer was a "renegade Jew who has denied his breed" and "exudes the venom of a snake and wields the bludgeon of a bully.

"The Jews of New York have no reason to be ashamed of Judas Pulitzer if he has denied his race and religion," said Dana. "The insuperable obstacle in the way of his social progress is not the fact that he is a Jew, but in certain offensive personal qualities." So that no reader was left uncertain, Dana listed them. "His face is repulsive, not because the physiography is Hebraic, but because it is Pulitzeresque. . . . Cunning, malice, falsehood, treachery, dishonesty, greed, and venal self-abasement have stamped their unmistakable traits."

Dana's words hit their mark, tormenting Pulitzer. "The stings of that human wasp, Dana of the *Sun*, drove him frantic," the cartoonist McDougall recalled. Depressed and feeling harassed, Pulitzer would sometimes come to McDougall's office and lie on an old sofa. In the room was a desk that had been used by Manton Marable when he was editor of the *World*; it contained bundles of old letters hidden in a cavity. "I used to amuse J.P. by reading some of them to him, and he would in return tell me his troubles and narrate his adventures. I early gathered that he hadn't the courage of Cockerill, but as a writer he was as rashly bold as a rhinoceros. He once told me that the fact that Cockerill had killed Slayback had the effect of kindling his sincere admiration and respect at one time and filling him with a chilled repulsion at another."

The voters soon had their say. Dana and Pulitzer acted as if their names had been on the ballot. Both of them had also spoken at rallies on behalf of their candidates. Nicoll lost, by a large margin. "And now, Pulitzer, a word with you!" wrote a triumphant Dana. Like a judge reading from a defendant's criminal record before imposing a sentence, Dana listed scandal, blackmail, and murder among Pulitzer deeds prior to coming to New York. "We wish, Pulitzer, that you had never come."

An unpleasant future awaited, Dana promised. "Perhaps your lot will be like that of the mythical unfortunate of the same race you belong to and deny, that weird creation of medieval legend, a creation, by the way, far more prepossessing than you are—we mean, The Wandering Jew!

"Move on, Pulitzer," said Dana, "move on!"

A few days after this bitter defeat at the polls, Pulitzer went to the office to look over the next morning's editorials. Unlike Dana, he had little to gloat about. In addition to the painful brawl with Dana, the election results had subjected him to personal ridicule. After taking credit for electing a president, a governor, and a mayor, he had failed to get his man elected to the minor post of district attorney.

Pulitzer had reached the limits of his physical and psychological endurance. "It was a period of terrible strain for me," he said years later. His friend Childs in Philadelphia was worried. "I told a leading newspaper man today," Childs wrote to Pulitzer, "that if your health holds out, you were bound to make the best success of the age, and you can do it, I mean that you can hold it." But despite his persistent insomnia and disregarding pleas from his friends and family, Pulitzer insisted on going to the office. Reading every line of copy before it was published remained a mania with him, even though Merrill and others were among the best editorialists one could hire.

"When I picked up the sheets," said Pulitzer, "I was astonished to find that I could hardly see the writing, let alone read it." It was if a dark curtain had been pulled entirely across his right eye and partially across the left. Having long suffered from bad eyesight, frequently aggravated by reading late into the night under harsh gaslight, Pulitzer decided that this was simply a temporary affliction. He left the building without saying a word about it. The next morning, his vision still not improved, Pulitzer stopped in to consult a doctor on his way to work.

In 1887, optometrists, a term then only a year old, had the use of an ophthalmoscope, which permitted a clear view of the retina and the vitreous body separating it from the lens. When the doctor peered into Pulitzer's eyes it was clear in an instant what had gone wrong. The retina in the right eye had become detached, and the left retina was in danger of detaching. The prognosis was grim. "In a great majority of cases the natural course of the disease is slowly but surely progressive, leading finally to total blindness," wrote one expert at the time. The chief remedies at the time were the application of artificial leeches, a tool that drew blood or other fluids from the patient; mercury drops; or extended bed rest. Pulitzer was ordered home to remain in a darkened room for six weeks.

Pulitzer's doctors were summoned. His primary physician, James W. McLane, was worried that the vision failure was only one manifestation of Pulitzer's health problems, which he listed as insomnia, asthmatic lungs, and almost continuous indigestion. It was as if Pulitzer was having a breakdown.

"I am absolutely and totally unable to read or write, or have any use of my sight," Pulitzer said plaintively, dictating a letter. "I am in the hands of the oculist, who has put me to bed, stripped me of all occupation, and enforces a course of treatment which he says, with care on my part, may give me back my sight in about six weeks. If I am not careful, he also says, I am quite apt to lose my sight altogether."

For six weeks, Cockerill, Merrill, and Smith ran the *World*, coming occasionally to the dark confines of Pulitzer's room for advice. The children were kept at bay, and when Kate's father died, she attended the funeral in Washington alone. Almost as if he were engaged in mortal combat, Dana did not even have the good manners to lessen his attacks. Instead, he continuously reprinted the editorial about the "Jew who does want to be a Jew" under the headline, MOVE ON, PULITZER!—REPUDIATED BY HIS RACE.

At the end of the bed rest, Pulitzer's sight was no better. McLane prescribed a new course of treatment: Pulitzer was to cease all work and go to California for a six-month rest. On January 14, 1888, Joseph, Kate, and Ralph, along with a personal staff, boarded a private railcar in Jersey City. Lucille, Joseph Jr., and Edith were left in the care of nannies.

Congressman Walter Phelps came to see them off. Pulitzer was pessimistic about the plan and prophesied that the climate of California and the fresh air would do him no good. While he was becoming a Croesus, he told Phelps, he would eventually be a blind one.

"That," said Pulitzer, "was the beginning of the end."

Part III

1888–1911

Chapter Twenty

SAMSON AGONISTES

◆

On a moonlit evening in late February 1888, Pulitzer stood on the veranda of San Diego's legendary Hotel del Coronado. Puffing on a cigar, he gazed out at the beach. In the pale soft light, he could discern the contours of the beach and the crashing waves tipped with white foam. "That is beautiful," Pulitzer said to a young reporter who had accompanied him out into the night air.

"I am not blind by any means," he continued, as they went inside. "I can see well enough to enjoy the beauties of the country. Your harbor is wonderfully beautiful, as we saw it in the moonlight this evening."

The rest of the world, however, was fading from his sight. Under the harsh electric lights of the hotel's interior, he could scarcely make out the headlines on display at the newsstand, announcing that St. Louis would be the site of the next Democratic convention. "I am half blind, and have lost the use of one eye," he conceded. "The other eye is of partial use, but I have not read a newspaper for three months."

Pulitzer's doctors in New York had prescribed repose in California. It was like being sent into exile. When the Pulitzers had boarded the train in New York, Kate was handed a note from a onetime *World* editor and Democratic stalwart. "May I beg you to read the next page of this note to Samson Agonistes," it said. "My God, what a calamity for the party that you are ill now."

The journey drained Joseph, even though they crossed the country in the comfort of a private railcar, the nineteenth-century counterpart of the corporate jet. Contributing to his exhaustion was a detour they took to Beauvoir, a crumbling mansion not far from New Orleans in

Biloxi, Mississippi. There Kate's distant cousins Jefferson and Varina Davis, the former president and first lady of the Confederacy, lived in quiet solitude.

The Pulitzers had come to know the Davises during the past eight years and had grown attached to their twenty-two-year-old daughter, whom they asked to be a godmother to one of their children. Winnie, called the "daughter of the Confederacy," was almost as symbolic of the lost cause as were her parents. During the visit to Beauvoir, the Pulitzers tried to talk Winnie into accompanying them on their trip. "A private car offers the two-fold temptation of comfort and economy in seeing a new and interesting country," Jefferson Davis wrote to a family member. "She says, no."

The Pulitzers pushed on, stopping in Texas, where Joseph told reporters that the Confederacy's former leader, though aging, had a mind as clear as that of a thirty-year-old. A few days later, the party reached Los Angeles, where their arrival was front-page news. Joseph declined an interview, saying he had been fatigued by the journey. The group soon repaired to the Raymond Hotel in Pasadena, a popular winter residence for wealthy easterners.

For the next several weeks, Pulitzer and his entourage wandered from one coastal resort to another. In Santa Barbara, the doctors he consulted had only discouraging words and suggested that he consider a sea voyage to the Sandwich Islands (later known as Hawaii), Japan, and China. It was hardly advice he wanted or was willing to follow. He was anxious about not being in charge of the *World* back in New York. Though he trusted Cockerill, circulation had fallen for the first time since Pulitzer bought the paper. Even worse, Pulitzer could play no part in orchestrating the paper's coverage of a terrible snowstorm hammering New York: food and medicine were in short supply, trains stood still, and few telegrams got through.

During the blizzard, Pulitzer's lawyer and crony Roscoe Conkling developed an ear infection after walking from his office on Wall Street to his club at Madison Square. Though it was persistent and nagging, Conkling regarded the infection as only a nuisance. "Would gladly face greater storms to make your eyes strong enough to be squandered reading newspapers," he wired back after receiving Pulitzer's worried inquiries. But the infection created a dangerous abscess that pressed on Conkling's brain. For weeks he lay close to death, finally succumbing on April 17, 1888. All Pulitzer could do was send flowers and a telegram of condolence, and order the *World* to give Conkling a statesmanlike send-off.

Balmy California seemed like a purgatory to him.

Pulitzer nixed the idea of a Pacific voyage. By May he and his family were on a train heading back east. They stopped in St. Louis for two days so that Joseph could confer with his editors at the *Post-Dispatch* and again consider offers to buy his paper. He had been back to St. Louis only twice in the ten years since he had left. The place no longer had any hold on him. This would be his last visit ever. He decided, however, to hold on to the *Post-Dispatch*.

The family reached New York as the *World* celebrated its fifth anniversary under Pulitzer's regime. On the front page, editors reprinted his original statement of principles, published in the first issue; they also listed the newspaper's achievements in its war on monopolists and conspirators, in its efforts to protect immigrants, and in its work on behalf of the poor. "The keystone of *The World*'s arch of triumph is public service," they said. Daily circulation now hovered around 300,000 copies.

Home again, Pulitzer confronted an unchanged prognosis by his doctors. They still insisted on prescribing rest. Stubbornly, he tried to read the *World* and further strained his eyes. At best, all he could now see out his good left eye was a confusion of black spots and occasional flashes of light. His primary physician, Dr. McLane, persuaded him to sail for Europe, where they could together consult renowned medical authorities. On June 9, they boarded the *Etruria*, bound for England. Kate and the children, joined by Winnie Davis, stayed behind and headed north to a rented house in Maine's increasingly fashionable Mount Desert Island.

Once across the ocean, Pulitzer shuttled from one examining room to another in London and Paris. After a summer spent consulting the world's most celebrated physicians, Pulitzer learned nothing he had not already heard from the less famous specialists in New York. He was entirely blind in one eye, and the other was threatened with the same fate. There was no cure, procedure, or therapy. Rest might extend what vision he had left. He ceased to ride horses and take walks. Confined to dim rooms, he grew weaker.

The doctors forbade travel. The order couldn't have come at a worse time. It was September of an election year. For Pulitzer, being confined to Europe was like being a captain watching his ship set sail without him. The presidential contest was in full swing, but for Pulitzer there were no editorial meetings, no strategy sessions with party operatives, no election maps to study, no supplicants seeking the *World*'s editorial benediction. Unnatural silence surrounded him.

In the election, President Cleveland's plan to cut import tariffs became the central issue. He believed that the tariff was an indirect subsidy to businesses, and that it raised prices and hurt labor and farmers. In turn, the Republicans, who nominated Benjamin Harrison, claimed that the high tariff protected American industry and workers from foreign competition.

Still smarting from the president's ungracious attitude toward the *World* and its owner following his election to the White House, Pulitzer cared little if Cleveland went down in defeat. The paper acted as if the only elections of significance that year were those for New York State's governor and New York City's mayor. The *World*'s silence on the presidential race was a frigid rejection of Cleveland, whom it had championed as a political messiah four years earlier. "Temperamentally, no two men could have been farther apart than the President and his foremost supporter," observed one insider at the *World*. "That sturdy statesman was steady and persistent; Mr. Pulitzer fiery and insistent."

Resigned to his exile, Pulitzer telegraphed Kate and asked her to come to Europe with the children. He left London, engaged rooms at the Hotel Bristol in Paris, then traveled to Le Havre on the northwest coast of France to await her ship. For Joseph, this was a rare gesture that reflected his anguish. Kate and the children arrived on September 16, 1888. Kate was now visibly pregnant with their sixth child, conceived during their wanderings in California. Reunited as a family, they settled into a rented house near Paris's graceful Parc Monceau for the fall and winter.

Constance Helen Pulitzer was born on December 13, 1888, and her birth was recorded by the U.S. consul in Paris, who had been appointed by Cleveland. Although Pulitzer could sign the birth certificate, he was incapable of reading or other writing. To cope with his increasing infirmity, he hired thirty-year-old Claude Ponsonby, an Englishman who had some noble relatives. Ponsonby would be the first in a long succession of young men who would handle Pulitzer's correspondence, read aloud to him, play the piano, and provide companionship as the world darkened around him.

Infirm but not incapacitated, Pulitzer sought to remain in command of his journalism empire. The *World* alone now had more than 600 editors, reporters, compositors, pressmen, salesmen, and business managers on its payroll. As his absence from New York became prolonged, he appointed three men to run the paper: Cockerill would manage editorial matters, George Turner would manage the business side, and Kate's brother William Davis would act as Pulitzer's personal representative when the triumvirate met. To communicate with their absent boss, Turner devised a simple cipher scheme so that telegrams could be coded to save words and keep others from understanding them.

Of his newspapers, the *St. Louis Post-Dispatch* held the least interest for Pulitzer. It ran itself, produced a handsome income, and gave him no headaches. His heart was in New York, specifically with the affairs of the morning *World,* referred to as "Senior" in the coded messages of the heavy transatlantic cable traffic. Pulitzer regarded "Junior," the *Evening World,* with a mix of disdain and acceptance. With its base, coarse style, it thrived in the hurly-burly domain of sidewalk sales, where a good headline could sell its entire run of 100,000 copies. Pulitzer knew there was a large and growing appetite for afternoon newspapers, with their fresh news, punchy headlines, and scandalous tales. After all, he had started out as a publisher of an evening paper. Still, although it churned out profits, the *Evening World* was not a maker of presidents. If this were only a matter of money, Pulitzer could have disposed of the whole lot and spent the remainder of his life a wealthy man. Instead, he wanted to keep the reins of the *World* in his hands because it gave him what he coveted most—power.

Aside from creating his triumvirate, Pulitzer embarked on a scheme of retaining control over the hiring of editors and managers. No matter how sick or how far away he might be, he would be the one to fill the key posts. Editors and managers who performed well would be rewarded by bonuses, conveyed by telegraphed instructions to the cashier. Those who didn't would face a Pulitzerian wrath in telegraphic form. Sometimes the telegram or letter would even be read aloud to the recipient by one of the members of the triumvirate. An editor knew he worked for Pulitzer, not for the *World.* Misdirecting his loyalty could mean the end of his employment.

For years, Pulitzer had sought to lure Julius Chambers, whom he had known since 1872, away from the *New York Herald*. That winter Chambers was chafing under the idiosyncratic rule of his publisher, James Bennett—who, coincidently, was running the *Herald* from Paris, giving Pulitzer hope that he might do the same. One day Chambers joined Cockerill for lunch in the famous Room 1 of New York's Astor House. Comparing their experiences in working for absent publishers, Cockerill quickly fathomed Chambers's unhappiness and handed him a telegram he had received from Pulitzer. "See Chambers again," it read, "renew offer of $250 per week and three year contract." Chambers took the job.

By similar means, Pulitzer gained a new editorial writer, hiring George Eggleston from the *New York Commercial Advertiser*. The new hires quickly learned that Pulitzer intended to manage them as if he were in the office rather than simply the source of telegrams piled thick on their desks. "Never fear of troubling me with any suggestion concerning either the welfare of the paper or your own," Pulitzer told Chambers. "Nothing, looking to the elevation and improvement of the paper, is too small to mention."

Although Pulitzer's editors and staff could run the *World* satisfactorily in his absence, they could hardly find room to do their work in the cramped Park Row building he continued to rent from Jay Gould. The *World* needed a new building. Pulitzer owned a lot on Park Row, but it was too small for an edifice like the one he had in mind. He wanted a symbol of his power and success, something that would loom physically over the other Park Row newspapers as his paper had towered over them in circulation.

While Pulitzer was in California the previous year, French's Hotel, which sat on a Park Row block at the entrance of the Brooklyn Bridge, had been put up for sale. Twenty-three years earlier, as an unemployed Civil War veteran, Pulitzer had been thrown out of the hotel's lobby because its guests objected to seeing tattered former soldiers milling about. Since then the hotel had fallen into financial trouble. Pulitzer seized the opportunity and with a $100,000 deposit agreed to pay $630,000 in cash for the site. The former derelict in the lobby now owned the place.

The architect George Brown Post, a student of Richard Morris Hunt, heard about Pulitzer's purchase and wrote to a friend at the *World* asking to be recommended to his boss. Post had just completed a design for a new Park Row building for the *New York Times.* "It would be an interesting problem to construct two buildings in sight of each other for rival papers, and to make the buildings as different as the politics of the papers," he wrote to his friend. Pulitzer decided to hold a design competition. Post entered and won.

From Paris, Pulitzer laid down his conditions. The building had to rise a full fourteen stories, making it the tallest on the globe. The cost could not exceed $950,000, and it had to be completed by October 1, 1890. If he succeeded, Post would receive a $50,000 commission and a $10,000 bonus. If he failed, he would repay $20,000 of the commission. Finally, all design elements had to be approved by Pulitzer before any contracts for the work were awarded. And, added Pulitzer, the final building had to be "at least as good at the *Times* building which is now in the process of construction."

Over the winter Post worked on the design. As the months passed, Pulitzer grew increasingly frustrated. It had been his intention to hire an architect as one hires a portraitist, for his artistry, his vision, and his interpretation. That is not what he got from Post. In March, the architect came to Paris to go over the plans with Pulitzer. The meeting was not a great success. "*In confidence of the strictest nature,* I am bound to say that I am not encouraged to greater faith in our architect by this visit," Pulitzer wrote to Turner, his business manager in New York. "He may be a great architect in carrying out other people's ideas, but he certainly is not, in this case, carrying out many of his own."

Money, of course, was also a point of contention between the two. Post was unable to remain within the budget. He persuaded Pulitzer to spend another $60,000, raising the maximum allowed above $1 million. "I will not allow another cent," Pulitzer immediately informed Turner in New York. But since Pulitzer continued to insist that he be shown final drawings before any work was started at the site, the mandatory transatlantic consultations were bound to imperil the construction schedule and drive up the costs.

Post returned to New York, and the two continued their struggle by mail.

Pulitzer still considered his exile from New York a temporary affair. "I am glad to say that I am better in point of health, able to walk again," he wrote to Turner, his business manager. "I don't know what's the matter with me generally except that my physical machinery is decidedly out of order and in need of repairs; but it is more a question of annoyance than serious danger I suppose—Anyway, the doctors tell me (and, I have enough of them the Lord knows!) that the big vital parts of the machinery are all right except the eyes, and that I really think is improving though awfully slowly."

After Post's visit, Pulitzer headed south to the Riviera and, feeling stronger, embarked on a planned trip to New York in late April with Ponsonby, leaving Kate and the children in Paris. Arriving in New York, he reviewed Post's plans, and the two were soon at loggerheads again. Although it was true that cheaper materials might not meet the requirements for a "first class" building, Post complained that Pulitzer's refusal to approve less expensive choices made it impossible to cut costs. When Post, in frustration, began to demand arbitration, Pulitzer backed down. The *World*'s need for more space was desperate, and Pulitzer was finally willing to compromise.

Pulitzer took time to see his politically-minded friends. Cleveland had lost the election, though he had won the popular vote. President Benjamin Harrison had been in office for a couple of months, and Pulitzer, whose lukewarm support for Cleveland was partially responsible for this state of affairs, suffered graciously by accepting a dinner invitation from his good Republican friend the railroad lawyer Chauncey Depew. At Depew's mansion on Fifty-Fourth Street, Pulitzer sat for a meal with a group of enemies and friends including Theodore Roosevelt, angling for a post in the new administration; the *Tribune*'s editor Whitelaw Reid, who had just been appointed ambassador to France; Pulitzer's own rival Charles Dana; the U.S. senator William Evarts, who had led the fundraising efforts for the Statue of Liberty; and Ward McAllister.

An editor from a rival newspaper ran into Pulitzer during his stay in New York and was surprised at how well he looked. "Physically, he seems to be in perfect health, and the only thing that mars his condition at all is the loss of one eye. I never saw him in better spirits, and his remaining eye seems to be strong, clear and exceedingly alert," he said.

On May 15, 1889, Pulitzer and Ponsonby departed from New York on the *Eider* for Bremen, Germany. Rather than rejoin Kate in Paris, Pulitzer went to Wiesbaden, also in Germany. This city had been attracting the sick and infirm since its thermal baths were first mentioned by Pliny the Elder. In the late nineteenth century it had become one of the leading destinations for those with ample means, including the Russian novelist Fyodor Dostoyevsky and Pulitzer's favorite composer, Richard Wagner.

Pulitzer did his resolute best to ignore work. In a complete break with his usual practice, he instructed that no newspapers be sent to him. "I want to experiment being without them for a fortnight," he wrote. He diligently undertook a regimen of drinking and bathing in the famous mineral and thermal waters in the mornings and taking long carriage rides in the afternoons. He stayed in the elegant Hotel DuRose and dined there in the open air near the city's main imperial building, listening to snatches of music drifting into the night air from the concerts indoors.

After several days Pulitzer asked Ponsonby to send word to Kate in Paris that he was feeling better. His spirits were on the rise and he was hopeful that Wiesbaden's curative powers were having an effect. "But remember again," Pulitzer dictated to his assistant, "all my statements of improvement are *comparative*."

Pulitzer's better mood restrained his trigger-finger temper when he submitted to a well-known doctor's care. "I have to wait sometimes in the hot anteroom with ten other people before I am received for my massage, which never takes more than one or two minutes and never gives me an opportunity to have a real talk, to which he seems opposed," Pulitzer told Kate.

"Well," he added, "he is the first majesty who has made me bow down and dance attendance in the anteroom." The dictation concluded, Pulitzer took the letter from Ponsonby. Then in his own hand, he addressed it "My Dearest" and signed it "sincere love, ever your devoted husband, JP in haste." There would be only a few remaining letters to which he could sign his name. But Pulitzer was optimistic. "My spirit," Joseph told Kate, "is beginning to improve and is again hopeful." Joseph and Kate spent the summer of 1889 together in St. Moritz, the Swiss alpine resort whose 300 days of sunshine each year made it a favorite among the wealthy.

In a decade, Pulitzer had gone from hiding his last savings of $300 in a trunk to earning more than that amount every hour. With money, the Pulitzers had slipped easily into the society of wealthy American expatriates in Europe. They moved about, from Paris to London to St.

Moritz, with an entourage of personal servants and nannies. Kate attended weddings with royalty and wore diamonds said to have once belonged to Marie Antoinette. "And Mrs. Pulitzer has the right to wear them," said one newspaper. "Thirty years ago her husband was shoveling coal and driving drays, but his indomitable energy and active brain have placed him where he can afford to buy out half a dozen royal families."

Pulitzer also increased his philanthropy. In May, he anonymously established a scholarship to send twelve New York City high school students, particularly immigrant children, to college. "My special object is to help the poor—the rich can help themselves," he told the city's school superintendent. But Pulitzer did not want the money to simply increase the earning power of its recipients. "College education is not needed for that," he said. "There are nobler purposes in life, and my hope is not that these scholarships will make better butchers, bakers, brokers, and bank cashiers, but that they will help to make teachers, scholars, physicians, authors, journalists, judges, lawyers, and statesmen." On the other hand, his friend Chauncey Depew predicted that the recipients would end up still being paupers.

In the fall, the Pulitzers returned to Paris, where Joe and Edith, who had spent the summer in the care of Kate's mother and sister in New London, Connecticut, arrived for a short visit. The children found their father preoccupied with the new building for the *World*. Work had been under way for four months, and in October the cornerstone was scheduled to be laid in an elaborate ceremony. Pulitzer had already spent $630,000 for the land and was now paying out another $1 million for the construction. Not a dime was borrowed.

Nothing about the project escaped his attention. He examined sketches and descriptions of the sculptures being made for the exterior and lists of all interior furnishings. With his poor eyesight he could discern only the larger drawings, but details were described verbally by Ponsonby. "I want to be sure that no *false* economy or niggardliness will mar the building inside," he wrote to Kate's brother William Davis, who increasingly acted as his emissary. Pulitzer wanted to know if anyone had seen the inside of the new *Times* building. "You remember the Post contract requires it to be at least as good as that of the *Times*."

On October 10, 1889, onlookers jammed the north end of Park Row as crews prepared to lay the cornerstone of the new Pulitzer building. A platform for the ceremony stood at one corner of the construction site. The intersection in front was covered by a large canopy, under which invited dignitaries gathered, including many admiring colleagues such as George Childes of the *Philadelphia Ledger* and Charles Taylor of the *Boston Globe*. Noticeably absent was the publisher himself. Pulitzer remained at the baths in Wiesbaden.

The first to emerge from the canopy was Thomas Edison, whose electric dynamo, capable of lighting 8,500 incandescent bulbs, was being installed thirty-five feet under the sidewalk. Next, Governor David Hill made his way through the crowd, pausing to shake the hands of workers, some of whom he called by name. Soon the platform was filled with well-known politicians, businessmen, religious leaders, and publishers.

After a blessing from the Missouri Episcopalian bishop, John Cockerill rose. "I am authorized to pledge a faithful adherence to the principles which have won public confidence for this journal," he began, listing many of Pulitzer's principles. "This shall be indeed a temple where the right shall always secure an advocate: where liberty abides, and where justice may find all seasons summer."

Chauncey Depew took the stage next, followed by Governor Hill and the aging Samuel Tilden, for whom Pulitzer had campaigned in 1876. They all heaped praise on the *World* and on Pulitzer's accomplishments. With the speeches at an end, Cockerill returned to the podium. He told the audience he had a cable from Pulitzer. The crowd quieted and Cockerill began to read from it. "God grant that this structure be the enduring home of a newspaper forever unsatisfied with merely printing news, forever fighting forms of wrong, forever independent—forever advancing in enlightenment and progress, forever wedded to truly democratic ideas, forever aspiring to be a moral force, forever rising to a higher plan of perfection as a public institution."

For several minutes Cockerill's voice carried the words of the absent Pulitzer over the construction site and the audience. When done, the crowd exploded into applause and redoubled its clapping when Cockerill announced that the text had been transcribed onto a parchment and would be placed in the cornerstone.

Then the crowd's attention turned to a set of stairs leading up to a platform along a brick wall. In place of Pulitzer, four-year-old Joe, dressed in a sailor suit, began to scale the stairs. His legs were almost too short to reach the steps, but holding his uncle William Davis's hand, he made his way to the top. Once there, he grasped a silver trowel and, using both hands, smoothed the bed of cement that workers had spread on the wall. He backed away, and the cornerstone was moved into place. Little Joe came forward again, tapped the stone twice with his trowel, and declared, "It is well done."

Inside the cornerstone was a copper box made especially for the event. In it, along with the parchment containing Pulitzer's remarks, the men had placed photographs, copies of newspapers, a directory of the *World's* employees, and a recording made on Edison's newest invention, the wax-cylinder voice recorder. It held the voices of three of the *World's* newspapermen discussing the news events of the year, such as the Johnstown flood and the successes of New York City's baseball club.

Many of the nation's newspapers put news of the cornerstone-laying ceremony on their front pages. The *New York Times* did not—it gave a short write-up on page two—but it was one of the few papers that noticed Pulitzer's architectural revenge. "The room of Mr. Charles A. Dana in the *Sun* building overlooks the foundations of the Pulitzer building," said the *Times*. "This will not be the case, however, in a few months. Then, like a certain other eminent gentleman, he, too, will sit in the shade."

Back again in Paris in November, at the house near Parc Monceau, Pulitzer may have regretted his decision to leave Wiesbaden. The house was in turmoil. Ralph and Lucille were being packed off to St. Moritz with tutors and nannies. Little Joseph, back from his trip to New York, Edith, and Constance were noisily playing. The Confederacy's daughter, Winnie Davis, had just arrived, and her ill health added to the convalescent atmosphere. Like Pulitzer, she suffered from vision problems and other hard-to-diagnose ailments. Doctors hoped a six months' stay on the Riviera and in German health resorts would help her. Further complicating matters was Winnie's secret engagement, after a five-year romance, to a Yankee, the disclosure of which was bound to set off a political storm.

Every day the sad group would sit down punctually for lunch at one o'clock and for dinner at seven-thirty. On some days, the *World's* new editorial writer George Eggleston, whom Joseph had brought over to Paris on an all-expenses-paid trip, would join them. Kate did her best to function under the circumstances. She took Winnie and ten-year-old

Ralph to the Paris Opera. "You should have seen the grandeur of that little fellow in his miniature beaver and dress suit!" Winnie wrote to her father. "He opened the box with an air, and altogether behaved like the fine little gentleman he is." But a few hours after she wrote the letter, her father died. Unable to withstand a sea voyage, Winnie remained with the Pulitzers.

It looked increasingly likely that Paris might become a long-term home for the family. Already, the two other publishers of major American newspapers were living there. Whitelaw Reid had arrived to begin his service as ambassador, and James Bennett was established in his home on the Champs-Élysées. Kate began looking for a suitable house but had little luck. "She has climbed up stairs, gone poking around stables to no purpose, however, as just as she thinks she has a house tight and fast away, it goes again," Winnie said.

Joseph decided to get as far away as possible from the bedlam by planning a trip around the globe. Before losing his vision, he had never remained still. The thought of traveling now, however, made him aware of his growing infirmity and his dependence on others. He needed help to travel by train, stay in hotels, and simply get about. A ship, however, offered him a completely self-contained world on the move.

He sent detailed and complicated instructions to Davis in New York about which steamers would most effectively carry mail to him on his journey through India, China, and Japan. He also made it clear what he wanted to receive. "You may judge from this simple rule. As many pleasant and agreeable reports as possible. No *unnecessary* questions for my decisions. Nothing disagreeable or annoying unless of *REAL IMPORTANCE*."

He complained that the "regency" he left in charge of the paper had failed and explained that "you three gentlemen have ample power and discretion to settle any of the ordinary questions that may arise during my absence, and I do not want to have my trip spoilt by ordinary bothers, nor to pay a dollar or two per word for such things."

In her role as Florence Nightingale, Kate took Joseph and Winnie to Naples. They were soon joined by Winnie's American suitor, who arrived in the hope of convincing her that, with her father dead, the time had come to make their engagement public. Ponsonby and others busied themselves with the final arrangements for Joseph's world tour.

The planned journey would be a slow-paced imitation of another global circumnavigation under way at the time. The *World*'s intrepid reporter Nellie Bly had left New York the month before, in an attempt to better the achievement of Jules Verne's fictional Phileas Fogg of *Around the World in Eighty Days*. Her undertaking, which would soon succeed, was generating immense publicity for the paper.

In early December, Pulitzer and Ponsonby, along with servants, boarded the *Peninsular*. In a short time, it crossed the Mediterranean, called at Port Said, then descended the Suez Canal and entered the Red Sea. The protected waters were immensely peaceful. In the hot climate, the men ate their meals often in the company of the financier Charles Fearing under punkahs, swaying ceiling fans of palm fronds or cloth pulled back and forth by a servant.

Just before Christmas, the ship came into the Gulf of Aden. Under a bright electric light, Pulitzer undertook to write a letter to Kate in his own hand. "Fearing and Ponsonby have written to you all about me," he said in the letter, which he wrote hurriedly so it could be posted from the port of Aden. "As it suits their fancy to think I am much better or at least to say so be it so. I am certainly no worse than when I came on ship."

"He is certainly better," said Ponsonby in an accompanying letter, "but he is inclined to take a despondent view of his health and pitches to Charles and myself when we try to cheer him up by making light of his complaints and that he has already improved."

Crossing the Arabian Sea, the ship encountered even more intense heat. It was New Year's Day, and Pulitzer was miserable. He couldn't sleep or shake off the cough he had when he boarded the ship, and he was bothered by what he called his rheumatism. After several more sleepless nights he decided to give up the idea of traveling across India by land and remained aboard the ship, bound for Calcutta. "Of course Fearing is terribly broken up but I am sure that the long RR journey and miserably noisy hotels throughout India would not have been good for me," he dictated in a letter to Kate. "It was the dream of my boyhood to see India and now when I am actually here, I must give up my dream no matter how great the temptation."

His misery was intense. "The year closed, with the one before, represent more suffering than all the rest of my life brought me—ten times as much—I honestly think fifty times as much. And the year which opens with this day—I cannot finish the sentence." Alone, at sea, he poured out his fear that he would never again regain his health. "Travel will not cure me—no more than Metzger [his German doctor]. I am miserable, I cannot trust myself to write more whatever I feel, however, you are still the only being in this world who fills my heart and mind and hope and receives my love and tenderness and affections."

Under the new plan, the men would remain on the ship until Calcutta. There they would change to a series of other vessels that would eventually bring them to Hong Kong, Singapore, Shanghai, and Japan, and then across the Pacific to San Francisco. But it was not to be. Shortly after mailing his despondent letter to Kate, Pulitzer stood on the deck of the ship with Ponsonby. The bright Indian sun beat down on the two men as they looked out over the water. "How dark it is getting," remarked Pulitzer.

His remaining functioning retina had become detached. The darkness had set in.

Chapter Twenty-One

DARKNESS

---◆---

Although he had plenty of newspaper experience, fifty-nine-year-old George W. Hosmer had never gotten an assignment quite like the one he drew in the summer of 1890. A doctor who never practiced medicine and an attorney who never practiced law, Hosmer had put in almost thirty years with Bennett's *New York Herald* before joining the *World*. None of this, however, prepared him for the task he faced. He was to accompany Kate Pulitzer to Europe and return with her nearly blind, bedridden husband.

That spring, the stacks of telegrams from Pulitzer that usually greeted editors at their desks ceased. For months the paper had drifted along, cautiously guided by Cockerill, Davis, and Turner. The few telegrams that did come provided little or no direction. "Silence gives consent and when you do not hear from me assume that I am satisfied," Pulitzer wrote.

Earlier in the year, when the retina in Pulitzer's remaining good eye detached while he was on board a ship bound for India, he and Ponsonby had returned to Europe, where doctors recommended more time in dark rooms. The two men drifted to Paris and eventually to St. Moritz. Pulitzer was entirely in Ponsonby's care, since Kate was no longer in Europe. She and the children had left for the United States shortly after the men had embarked on the ill-fated cruise. She did not rush back across the Atlantic. Kate had learned that the consequences of showing up uninvited could be severe.

But over the succeeding weeks discouraging reports reached Kate. Ponsonby telegraphed that Joseph had contracted acute bronchitis, a dangerous problem in the era before antibiotics, and was growing weak.

Kate decided to launch a rescue mission, and departed with Hosmer in late July. By the time the two reached Joseph, he had been moved to a sanatorium in the Swiss city of Lucerne. They found him so weak that he was spending entire days on the sofa. "He was very ill—in a state so feeble that he could scarcely get around on foot," Hosmer said. "Physical collapse had assumed the form of nervous prostration."

For two weeks, Hosmer and Kate tended him until he was well enough to travel. They went to Paris; after a few more weeks the group moved to a vacation house in Trouville, a summer resort in Normandy. "In the pleasant atmosphere of the seaside," Hosmer said, "a place which was very quiet—for the gay world was already gone—he recovered from bronchitis and to some degree from his great physical debility." Joseph regained sufficient strength to listen again to Ponsonby reading telegrams from New York. His new building neared completion, the fall elections loomed, and the Democrats seemed poised for a rebound.

On October 2, 1890, Kate, Hosmer, and Ponsonby escorted the recovering Joseph onto the *Teutonic* in Queenstown, England, and headed home. Wearing goggle-like dark-blue glasses, Joseph walked on American soil for the first time in eighteen months.

Joseph settled into the familiar surroundings of the Fifty-Fifth Street house, which grew more luxurious with each passing month. The architect Stanford White was busily spending thousands of Pulitzer's dollars employing painters and wall paperers. Silk was hung on the walls in Kate's room, and a wine cellar was being planned. Joseph also acquainted himself with the unfamiliar. He had not spent any time with his daughter Constance since she was a few months old. Kate resumed her place in New York society, attending the opera and putting on dinners such as one for Varina Davis, who was in New York revising her late husband's memoirs.

Soon Pulitzer's days were filled with meetings, with a steady stream of executives and editors making their way uptown. The men's appraisal of the coming congressional elections offered encouraging news. The electorate's faith in President Harrison had been shaken by another economic panic. Support for his Republican Party was also damaged by the profligate spending of the aptly nicknamed "billion-dollar Congress," and by the passage of the McKinley Tariff Act, which increased the cost of goods but kept workers' wages stagnant.

In such circumstances the *World* would have normally opened a floodgate of editorial abuse of Republicans and praise for Democrats. But for the first time, Pulitzer sought to restrain his paper's partisan ardor. Its ferocity was not weakened, but the frequency of its attacks was diminished. "Remember *every day in the year* that though politicians read the editorial page they are probably only 5 percent of our readers," Pulitzer told his main editorial writer. "A larger portion of the remaining 95 percent not being interested in politics at all."

After seven years of unequaled journalistic success and immense financial reward, the political fires burned less strongly in Pulitzer. Like its master, the *World* was also no longer a startling new phenomenon overturning the rule of establishment newspapers and shaking up the political order. Rather, it was now the undisputed monarch of Park Row, and its reign was made even clearer when the scaffolding was peeled away and New Yorkers had their first complete view of Pulitzer's new building. Like the newspaper itself, the scale, audacity, and ornamentation of George Post's creation were impossible to ignore. A monument to Pulitzer's brand of journalism, the edifice transformed the landscape of Park Row.

Towering 345 feet above the sidewalk, the building had two miles of wrought-iron columns, sixteen miles of steel beams, enough iron and steel to lay twenty-nine miles of railway, and sufficient bricks to build 250 ordinary houses. It stood on a foundation thirty feet below street level, supported by twelve-foot brick footings. The cavernous basement held Hoe's newest and fastest presses, which when running at full tilt made their rhythmic beat felt throughout the building.

The gigantic high-speed presses were not mere workhorses. They were one of the technological marvels of the age, capable of churning out enough newspapers in a few hours to supply every New Yorker with a copy, and inspiring awe among the hundreds of visitors who came to watch each day. For members of the fourth estate the smell of ink was intoxicating. Few thrills compared with hearing the sound of the bell announcing the first turns of a press and the ensuing locomotive-like thumping cadence building to a deafening roar as the procession of cut, folded, and gathered pages poured forth with increasing speed. In the minds of reporters, the power of the press was both a figurative and a literal idea.

To enter the Pulitzer Building, one walked through a churchlike three-story vault made of Corsehill stone from Scotland, above which stood a quartet of bronze female torchbearers, representing art, literature, science, and invention. Fast-moving elevators ferried passengers up and down fifteen stories. The first ten floors, coupled vertically with tall, Palladian windows, and banded horizontally by a stone ledge, contained offices leased to insurance salesmen, stockbrokers, and lawyers. The remaining floors, stacked above this hive of commerce, were distinguished by concave corners and four sculptured black copper figures representing the four races—Caucasian, Indian, Mongolian, Negro—and standing as if supporting a large pediment.

The *World* itself began here, on the twelfth floor. A room with a ceiling eighteen feet high housed 210 compositors, who set the morning and evening editions entirely by hand. It was the largest operation of its kind anywhere and required thirty-two tons of lead. The men stood at forty long, raised tables with bins with lead type. Moving with lightning speed, the compositors pulled and dropped each letter of each word into composing sticks that were locked into a form the size of a newspaper page. On a raised platform at the center of the hall, thirty proofreaders worked reviewing printed samples of the composed stories and advertisements.

Above it all, positioned like a throne room, Pulitzer's editorial command post occupied a tower. The largest office, facing east on the second floor of the domed structure, was reserved for Pulitzer. With frescoed ceilings, walls wainscoted with leather, and three floor-to-ceiling windows, the room looked out over the city, the Statue of Liberty in the harbor, and the Watchung Mountains in New Jersey—a privileged view lost on an almost blind publisher. Next door to Pulitzer's office three interconnected offices housed his staff of editorial writers.

Capped with an 850,000-pound gilded dome, the four-story editorial enclave perched on top of the Pulitzer Building reached higher into the sky than even the Statue of Liberty's raised torch. When the sun struck the dome, it reflected a shimmering light that could be seen forty miles out at sea. The first sight of the New World for immigrants entering New York was not a building of commerce, banking, or industry. Rather, it was a temple of America's new mass media.

Kate and Hosmer persuaded Dr. S. Weir Mitchell, the nation's leading neurologist, to see Joseph. Mitchell's medical reputation stemmed from his work with soldiers in the Civil War who suffered injuries to their nerves. His book *Injuries of Nerves and Their Consequence*, based on his experiences, was the most widely used reference for physicians in the United States and Europe. He had also pioneered research examining the relationship between eyestrain and headaches. He seemed the perfect physician for Joseph.

Unfortunately, Mitchell turned out to be yet another in a long series of disappointments. The "Weir Mitchell treatment" consisting of prolonged bed rest with optimum feeding and massages had been prescribed for Pulitzer so often that he was let down when the inventor himself prescribed it. On the other hand, hearing this advice from Mitchell was like reaching the end of a long road. If Mitchell could offer no other solution, there was no recourse.

As he struggled with his near-blindness, Pulitzer entered a kind of netherworld. He did not fit into the sighted world, but neither was he blind—at least not yet. Although he clung to a hope that he could regain his vision, there was little doubt of his fate. To become blind during his era was like being sentenced to a dark internal exile. There were no blind politicians, business leaders, or generals. Helen Keller was still only eight years old. It was assumed that the loss of vision meant the end of a productive life. In fact, newspapers were filled with stories of men who could not face the prospect: "DEATH PREFERRED TO TOTAL BLINDNESS"; "PREFERRING DEATH TO BLINDNESS"; "SHOOTS HIMSELF WHEN EYES FAIL." The Talmud, which Pulitzer had studied as a child, offered a somber interpretation: the blind were thought of as the living dead; and when encountering a blind person, believers were to offer the same benediction as was customary upon the death of a close relative.

On October 16, 1890, a startling announcement greeted readers of the *World*. "Yielding to the advice of his physicians, Mr. Joseph Pulitzer has withdrawn entirely from the editorship of the *World*." Control of the newspaper would be turned over to an executive board comprised of editors who had long been in his service.

News of Pulitzer's abdication spread rapidly. From Bangor, Maine, to Chillicothe, Missouri, and Galveston, Texas, small-town editors who aspired to be the Pulitzers of their communities marked the moment. But it was a neighboring newspaper on Park Row that gave Pulitzer his most gratifying acknowledgment. As if a champion boxer had withdrawn from the ring, the competing *New York Herald* found words of praise. "We droop our colors to him," said Bennett's editorial. "We have not always agreed with the spirit which had made his ideas a journalistic success, and we cannot refrain from regretting that he did not encourage us in the new departure which he made, instead of merely astonishing us, frightening us, and, we may add—now that it is past—perhaps a little bit disgusting us."

"But," Bennett concluded, "*le Roi est mort, vive the Roi!* The *New York World* is dead, long live the *World!*"

Barely two months later, on December 10, the tallest building on earth was ready for its grand opening. Its owner, however, was not. Pulitzer could not bring himself to attend a public event at which he would be led around like the invalid he was getting to be. It would be too humiliating. Instead, he and Kate, along with Hosmer and Ponsonby, reboarded the *Teutonic*, which sailed out of sight of the gold-domed Pulitzer Building only hours before thousands congregated for the ceremonies.

On Park Row, the power and prestige of the *World* were on display. Nine governors and three governors-elect, as well as countless mayors, congressmen, judges, editors, and publishers vied for a chance to have their words mark the occasion. The huge crowd pressed up against the entrance of the building. The sea of visitors inside was so thick that movement from room to room or floor to floor was almost impossible. Even the dignitaries could not get a ride in the E.T. Ellithorpe Improved Air-Cushion with Self-Closing Elevator Door lift.

The final price tag of the building topped $2 million, and not a cent had been borrowed. A PEOPLE'S PALACE WITHOUT A CENT OF DEBT OR MORTGAGE, proclaimed the *World,* which printed a copy of a certificate from the county recorder showing Pulitzer's unencumbered ownership. As a tribute to their publisher, the employees of the *World* commissioned and paid for a twenty-one-inch bas-relief of the building, made of silver melted from the coins of customers who bought copies of the paper.

After reaching England on December 16, Pulitzer and his party made their way to Paris, where they remained until arrangements to charter a British yacht with crew for a Mediterranean cruise were concluded. In early January 1891, the group went south to Menton and boarded the 200-foot, two-year-old steamship *Semiramis*. At the last minute, Kate decided that she could not endure a long sea voyage and begged off.

For almost four months, Pulitzer and his companions lazily circled the Mediterranean. He adhered rigidly to Dr. Mitchell's instructions and avoided all irritation, even remaining out of touch with his editors. "All those days on the yacht, conversation was an abundant resource to lighten the steps of time," said Hosmer. So were books. Ponsonby and Hosmer took turns reading aloud from George Eliot's *The Mill on the Floss* and William Thackeray's *Vanity Fair*, as well as works by the Victorian novelist Hall Caine.

When the men left the yacht at Nice and returned to Paris, Pulitzer felt better but still suffered from anxiety and insomnia. Consulting with Dr. Mitchell, who was in Rome, Pulitzer complained that being separated from his staff and work was creating as much anxiety in him as any work-related woes had done in the past. The doctor was unconvinced and refused to alter his prescription of isolation and rest.

Pulitzer defied Mitchell. He began to catch up on the conduct of the paper in his absence. He was horrified by what he found. Cockerill had taken a twelve-week vacation. He and Turner were acting like owners, and worse, they had let the paper's circulation fall by 16 percent. Pulitzer fired off cables giving Turner, his loyal business manager, a pink slip and punishing Cockerill by ordering his return to St. Louis, an impossible mission considering the fatal episode that had driven him from that city. Turner immediately landed a job as editor of a rival paper. Cockerill went to his watering hole at the Astor House and in three hours rounded up enough investors to start his own newspaper.

Pulitzer's cure for the *World* was worse than the disease. Now his paper was devoid of leadership. He had no option but to return to New York.

Leaving Kate in Paris, Joseph, Ponsonby, and Hosmer rushed to England and booked passage on the *Majestic*. J. P. Morgan was also on board. Despite their membership in the exclusive Jekyll Island club, as a frequent target of the *World*'s acerbic editorials Morgan avoided socializing with Pulitzer. Arriving in New York ahead of schedule on the morning of June 10, the group went straight to Park Row, startling editors and reporters who had not expected Pulitzer this soon. The shock of Pulitzer's presence in the building accentuated the seriousness of the situation. His first visit to the building constructed to the glory of the paper was a rescue mission.

Ballard Smith, the paper's highest-ranking editor now that Cockerill was gone, had not yet come in for the day. Luckily, Davis, Pulitzer's brother-in-law and the only remaining member of the triumvirate that had ruled the paper, was on hand—as was John Dillon, Pulitzer's former partner in St. Louis, who had been running the *Post-Dispatch*. He had rushed to New York after receiving a telegraphed plea from Pulitzer. While Hosmer tended to his boss's luggage, the men conferred, summoning other editors and managers.

Pulitzer's solution to the disarray at the top was to have Smith, who had come into the office at last, officially assume most of Cockerill's duties as editor in chief. Dillon would take over for Turner. For new blood, Pulitzer turned to George B. M. Harvey. Though only twenty-seven years old, Harvey had distinguished himself as a reporter for the *World* and then as editor of the New Jersey and Connecticut editions. Pulitzer made Harvey the managing editor, with a salary higher than he had ever earned, and promised Harvey that he would report only to him and would be exempt from most night work.

With the new structure established, Pulitzer left the *World* and took some time to look over his newest purchase, a $100,000 yacht that had once belonged to the duke of Sutherland. The vessel, rechristened *Romola*, after one of Pulitzer's favorite novels by George Eliot, was ready for his inspection at a Hudson River pier. The test cruise and dinner on board were a disaster.

A heat wave blanketed New York City (the thermometer reached 97 degrees at Hudnut's Pharmacy downtown) and the inside of the yacht was like an oven. Frustrated, Pulitzer ordered the captain to sail to Europe without him. Instead, he secured rooms for the return voyage of the *Majestic* and, along with Hosmer and Ponsonby, said good-bye to New York after only seven days.

A few weeks after Pulitzer's departure, William Randolph Hearst arrived in New York. In the four years since he had taken over his father's bankrupt daily, the *San Francisco Examiner*, Hearst had made a success of it, using all the techniques he had learned by carefully studying Pulitzer. But, just as his role model had felt running the *Post-Dispatch* in St. Louis, Hearst wanted a New York newspaper. "Between you and me," he wrote to his mother during one of many stays in the east, "I am getting so I do hate San Francisco."

Because of his father's death earlier in the year, Hearst anticipated having the capital to pursue his dream. To his shock, however, he discovered that he had inherited none of his father's vast fortune. Instead, it went entirely to his mother. If he wanted to buy another paper, he would need to persuade his mother to write the check. It would have to be a large one. In the seven years since Pulitzer had bought the *World,* buying a New York newspaper had grown costly.

When Hearst reached New York in July, he sought out Cockerill, Pulitzer's former editor. Cockerill offered Hearst a chance to buy into his new *Morning Advertiser,* which sold for a penny on the streets. But Hearst didn't want to acquire a one-cent paper like Cockerill's, or even Albert Pulitzer's *Morning Journal,* which had continued to prosper in the shadow of the *World.* "I think there is another way to get into New York perhaps even better than through Mr. Cockerill," Hearst wrote his mother, with whom he was now campaigning to buy a newspaper.

"I dined with Ballard Smith the other night and we talked newspapers till we were black in the face," he explained. Smith—Pulitzer's managing editor—told Hearst that he believed his boss was going to give him a share of ownership in the *World.* It was an unrealistic expectation. Although Pulitzer paid high salaries, gave huge bonuses, and lavished presents on his editors, he had yet to relinquish any portion of ownership in either newspaper. Nonetheless, Smith's story raised Hearst's hopes. Maybe, given Pulitzer's ill health, the *World* itself could be bought.

Pulitzer's emergency trip to New York had exacted a toll. The heat and his fretting over the paper's management had been toxic for everything that ailed him. "There was a partial loss of even the little eyesight that he possessed," noted an anxious Hosmer. Kate met the returning party in England and they retreated to Paris together. Suffering from what doctors decided was asthma and still unable to sleep through the night, Joseph was packed off to Wiesbaden for another cure. Kate, once again, remained in Paris, attending social events and displaying, as at the British embassy ball, her famous necklace of seven rows of closely set diamonds.

Ponsonby and Hosmer stayed in Wiesbaden with their boss while he underwent a monotonous regimen of baths, massages, walks, and carriage rides. "Many of these days were lightened by literature—reading was the main resource to exclude the devil of worry," Hosmer said. In the company of Trollope and Scott, the three men whiled away the summer.

In the fall, when Pulitzer finally returned to New York, no unpleasant surprises awaited him. During this exile, he had kept up with the affairs of the *World*. The paper was healthy, and the council had proved itself capable of replacing Cockerill and Turner—at least temporarily. When Pulitzer gathered his editors, the 1892 presidential election was on his mind. Governor David Hill of New York, elected and reelected in great part thanks to the *World*, was being touted as a candidate. But he was overshadowed by Grover Cleveland, who had decided to try to regain the White House and was currying favor with Pulitzer. The former president knew firsthand, having experienced Pulitzer's rejection in 1888, that it was better to run for office with the *World* on your side.

Pulitzer feared that the Democrats were growing weak in their resolve to support the gold standard, under which paper money could be redeemed for gold. Along with the Republicans, they had long held that giving paper money real value helped keep the economy stable. But in the House elections of 1890, the Democrats had watched members of the Populist Party win nine Congressional seats at their expense on a "free silver" platform, essentially proposing that the U.S. mint produce an unlimited amount of silver coins.

At first glance, monetary policy would seem to be an arcane subject unlikely to stir up the political cauldron. But monetary policy was widely and contentiously debated because the nation's economic life was regularly punctuated by severe depressions. Many citizens believed that the federal government controlled the value of money and that bad times were largely due to poor exercise of this power. A growing number of Americans became persuaded that the government ought to decrease the value of money to combat a deflation that was wreaking havoc in farm states. Falling prices struck farmers with a one-two punch by simultaneously reducing their income and driving up the costs of their mortgages.

The debate over free silver and the gold standard grew to be more than an economic argument. The banner of free silver united the nation's disaffected citizens, farmers, and some elements of labor. They saw silver as the salvation for all the ills they faced and considered the gold standard to be an exploitive tool of banks. It was a prairie fire that soon alarmed the eastern establishment.

Pulitzer shared most goals of the populists and progressives, but he could not bring himself to advocate abandoning the gold standard. Earlier in his life, he had run the *Post-Dispatch* on a shoestring, and as the owner of the *World* had been in debt to one of the most notorious barons of the Gilded Age; but now he was among the fifty richest Americans. In the last couple of years, the annual profit from the *World* alone had exceeded $1 million. To oversee his money, Pulitzer had engaged Dumont Clarke, a fifty-year-old investment manager who descended from a line of six bank presidents. Unlike the ever-changing guard at the paper, Clarke won Pulitzer's lasting trust by protecting his growing wealth with railroad stocks, one of the few investment options available then aside from bonds. If industrialists and financiers considered the gold standard as the bulwark protecting their fortunes, Pulitzer now had a fortune of his own to safeguard.

Unlike many of the elite, however, Pulitzer was not merely defending wealth. His dread of free silver was entwined with his long-held fear of demagoguery. Even before he was operating his first newspaper or writing his first editorials, Pulitzer had worried that democracy was a breeding ground for ambitious politicians willing to tap popular desires and prejudices to gain power. This was the lesson of Germany under Chancellor Otto van Bismarck—a lesson that Pulitzer had shared in a series of articles on European politics he wrote for Dana's *Sun* a decade before. Nothing in the ensuing years, including his time in elected office, had diminished this fear. "I am a radical myself, progressive, liberal to the core," he told one of his editorial writers years later. "But I do not want to be thrown over by a lot of demagogues, nincompoops, and shallow shouters."

As 1891 closed, Pulitzer's near-blindness, compounded by insomnia, asthma, indigestion, and various vague bodily aches, increased his sense that his working life was at an end. "It seemed as if he might be compelled, as he feared, to give up altogether," noted Hosmer. "He wanted to devote a few months to putting things in good shape out of regard to those that were to follow."

Again, Dr. S. Weir Mitchell was brought in. Since Pulitzer had disobeyed most of his instructions, Mitchell was not in a charitable mood. "I want to say to you for the hundredth time what I think in regard to your present condition," Mitchell told Pulitzer. "I want to say that your present course must inevitably result in the total destruction of what remains of your eyesight; also that it is quite impossible for you to carry on your paper under present condition without total sacrifice of your general health." Mitchell even enlisted Pulitzer's friend George Childs, the Philadelphia publisher. "He agrees with me," Mitchell said, "in thinking that the course in which you are engaged is one of physical and moral disaster."

Pulitzer selected a middle course. He would monitor the *World*, but at a distance. He spent Christmas with his family in New York, and then he, Kate, the children, and their bevy of maids, governesses, as well as valets, headed south to Jekyll Island, stopping in Washington to stay with Kate's mother. While they were in the capital, Joseph continued to mull over his choice for president. Governor Hill had been elected to the Senate, and Pulitzer was still torn between supporting his protégé or resuming his off-and-on alliance with Cleveland.

One of the men in the *World*'s Washington bureau acted as a go-between. Pulitzer offered Hill the *World*'s support if Hill would appoint him American minister to France, a post that Pulitzer's friend the newspaper publisher Whitelaw Reid was soon to vacate. Pulitzer had watched Reid up close during his own extended stays in Paris, and this seemed like the ideal arrangement for his plan of running the *World* by long distance.

Hill declined the deal. Unbeknownst to Pulitzer, Hill had already decided to throw in his lot with Dana's *Sun*. He knew he would have to choose one paper over the other, and he felt the *Sun* was closer to his wing of the party. By default, Cleveland was once again in the *World*'s good graces.

In February, the Pulitzers reached Brunswick, Georgia, their last stop before taking a steamer across a narrow strait to the Jekyll Island club. The townspeople of Brunswick were still not used to the parade of millionaires descending from private railcars in their hamlet to reach this new private island enclave. But the city did have a new hotel, where the Pulitzers stayed while awaiting transit to the island and to which they sometimes returned for dinner. When Kate made her appearance one evening, several weeks later, she caught everyone's attention. "Mrs. Pulitzer is a very handsome brunette, medium height and beautifully formed," wrote a smitten observer. "On her hand she wore two large magnificent diamond rings, while her neck was adorned with a lovely pearl necklace. Her beauty and jewels were the cause of much favorable comment among the guests."

It was Pulitzer's first visit to Jekyll since he had invested in the retreat six years earlier. Unwanted livestock had been chased from the island and replaced with game for hunting. Roads for carriage rides had been built, bridle paths cleared, and docks built. An elegant clubhouse stood ready to receive members. "From a distance," wrote one reporter, "it looks like some English castle with its square-shaped windows and its lofty tower." For Pulitzer it was an ideal refuge. He spent his days in repose, taking walks, being read to, dictating memos to his staff of editorial writers, and adjusting to his sightless life.

By June 1892, Pulitzer had alighted in Paris. Like that of a migratory bird, his path was developing regularity. But while he enjoyed his luxurious Parisian summer, workers at the Homestead Mill in western Pennsylvania were locked in battle with Henry Clay Frick, who managed Andrew Carnegie's steelworks. Frick decided to cease recognizing the union, give up bargaining, and lock the workers out of the plant. The men blocked access to the mills, with the help of the nearly 12,000 residents of Homestead. Frick vowed to reopen the plant with nonunion workers.

To get his way, Frick sent for 300 guards from the Pinkerton company, a famous detective agency that had become a source of mercenaries to fight organized labor. The standoff grew into an electrifying news story. At the *World*, Ballard Smith dispatched his best men to Pennsylvania to report on what the paper called "the iron king's war." At length, the *World* exposed how despite the increasing profitability of the mills, protected by the McKinley Tariff Act, falling wages had driven workers into destitution.

Merrill used the editorial page to support the strikers and linked their suffering to the McKinley Act. "The only beneficiary of the tariff is the capitalist, Carnegie, who lives in a baronial castle in Scotland, his native land." After six years of writing editorials for Pulitzer, Merrill undoubtedly felt that his words would have been those of his absent boss. So did Walt McDougall, who lampooned Carnegie in his cartoons.

Their assumption made sense. Since coming to New York, Pulitzer had expanded his advocacy of labor from the modest support he had offered in St. Louis, where he catered to a more middle-class professional readership. Under Pulitzer, the *World* had exposed sweatshops and supported efforts to limit working hours, protect women and children from abuse in the workplace, and increase the number of schools for laborers' children. In one pro-labor campaign, Pulitzer had come to verbal blows with his antagonist Theodore Roosevelt, who was then a state legislator. Roosevelt had described a bill reducing the working hours for car drivers as communistic. "If it be Communism, nice, dainty, cultured Mr. Roosevelt to say to these favored corporations, 'Twelve hours shall be a legal day's work,'" Pulitzer wrote, "pray what is when the corporations say to their employees, 'You shall slave for sixteen hours a day or starve.'"

In St. Louis, his own workers remained mostly nonunion, but Pulitzer recognized the unions in his New York shop and supported workers in several major strikes, even raising money from his readers for a strike fund. He had also rallied to the side of striking workers at the Missouri Pacific Railroad. "This is the case in a nutshell," he wrote. "Dividends paid on watered stock which was done to add to the hoards of millionaires who are sailing in their floating palaces among the soft breezes of the Antilles. Wages cut down to a miserable pittance of $1 to $1.18 a day, out of which the workman on the Western roads, if a married man, must feed and clothe a family."

It was no wonder that Merrill felt comfortable bringing the *World* to the side of the striking Homestead workers as the conflict continued to escalate. The Pinkerton guards arrived by boat, and they and the strikers engaged in a pitched battle that resulted in deaths on both sides. But the strikers prevailed, and they paraded the captured guards through town like prisoners of war. Frick called on the governor, who sent in 8,000 state militiamen, placed the town under martial law, and reclaimed the mill for the company. The message to labor was clear. When and if workers gained the upper hand, American industry could call upon the power of the state. Merrill was outraged, calling the use of the troops "obnoxious" and "inexcusable."

Pulitzer—who now traveled in floating palaces himself, vacationed with the barons of capitalism at Jekyll Island, and lived like royalty in Paris—learned about the battle of Homestead from French newspapers. He immediately told Ponsonby to cable to New York and obtain a full report on the conduct of the *World*. When he learned that the paper had sided with the workers, he was furious. He cabled Merrill, rebuking him and accusing him of sensationalism and of having disregarded law and order. "There is but one thing for the locked-out men to do. They must submit to the law," Pulitzer said. "They must not resist the authority of the State. They must not make war upon the community."

The Pulitzer who had built up the *Post-Dispatch* and the *World* as voices for the disinherited was gone. The bitter darkness into which he had fallen and the cocoon of wealth that surrounded him had destroyed Pulitzer's empathy. When it came to supporting reform and political and social change, property was now the trump card in Pulitzer's deck.

Angry about his paper's conduct, complaining about all his ailments, and dispirited, Pulitzer found no solace in Paris. He returned to Wiesbaden to see Dr. Hermann Pagenstecher, one of the many doctors with whom he had consulted when the decline in his vision began. Pagenstecher ran the largest eye hospital in Germany and treated famous patients from all over the world. He examined Pulitzer in his private clinic, a large white house with purple-blossomed creepers clinging to its columns and running along its windowsills. Peering into Pulitzer's eyes, he dictated his observations to his assistant, who dutifully recorded them. The doctor offered encouraging words to his patient even though he knew that the prognosis was bleak.

Pagenstecher was more honest with Kate. "As regards to Mr. Pulitzer," he wrote to her, "I should not advise to tell him the real character of the disease of the left eye because it would take away every hope from him and would have a great and unfavorable impression on his total nervous system."

Pulitzer rejoined his family in Baden-Baden, another town known for its baths, located in the western foothills of the Black Forest. The reunion was grim. The daughter of an old friend who joined them wrote to her parents that Joseph was "so melancholy of late that they did not know what to do."

With the coming of fall, Pulitzer returned to Paris. Dissatisfied with the conduct of the *World,* he set off, by telegram, yet another round of editorial and management changes back in New York. Ballard Smith figured he had been given his walking papers when he learned of a farewell dinner at Delmonico's. "Grateful memories for loyal services," wired Pulitzer, "sorry for parting and confident hopes for happy career."

As Pulitzer, from a distance, played musical chairs with his editors, the *World* lumbered on. It survived the managerial gyrations because it held an unchallenged position in New York. That luxury, however, would not last any more than calm waters on the ocean that Pulitzer continually crossed.

Chapter Twenty-Two

CAGED EAGLE

◆

I t took the tenth-anniversary celebration of his ownership of the *World* to bring Pulitzer back to New York from Europe in May 1893, after an absence of more than a year. This was a sea change from the man who years before—when attacking the rich was his stock in trade—had asked his readers, "Why do Millionaires go to Europe to spend so much money? What has Europe to offer that America has not?"

The *Majestic*, one of White Star's luxurious steamships, took Pulitzer across the Atlantic in a stateroom that had been specially altered for him so as to diminish sounds from the hallways and decks. Sailing on his yacht, *Romola*, was out of the question. He had put it up for sale after spending one sleepless night aboard it, off the coast of Italy.

Another publisher in exile, the *New York Herald*'s James Gordon Bennett, was also on board. Bennett admired Pulitzer but also he begrudged him the *World*'s success, which had reduced the *Herald*'s circulation to below 100,000. Almost as if Bennett didn't want his employees to be reminded of Pulitzer's dominance of Park Row, he was on his way to New York to supervise the building of new headquarters far uptown, on a triangular block at Thirty-Fifth Street, where Broadway and Sixth Avenue intersected.

The building made no attempt to rival Pulitzer's stab at the sky. Rather, it was only two stories high. But in keeping with Bennett's European tastes, it was an opulent design conceived by Stanford White to look like a Veronese palazzo. Unlike Pulitzer, Bennett had leased the land on which he was building. "I could not sleep nights if I thought another owned the ground upon which my building stood," Pulitzer told

Bennett in Paris. "I shall not be here to worry about it," the fifty-two-year-old Bennett replied.

The publishers disembarked in New York early in the morning of May 10 and went their separate ways. Awaiting Pulitzer was a 100-page tenth-anniversary edition of the *World* that had been published on Sunday and had sold 400,000 copies. That evening, Pulitzer took twenty of his top editors and managers to dinner at Delmonico's. Bradford Merrill, his editorialist, was seated to his right and Solomon Carvalho, who managed the money, to his left. His old partner John Dillon and his young managing editor George Harvey raised a continual series of toasts late into the night.

Despite the good cheer, Harvey was having second thoughts about working for Pulitzer. A promise from Pulitzer that he would be relieved of night work had not been kept. Harvey had slept most nights at the Pulitzer Building, in the bedroom off the city room. He had little choice. He worked for a boss who insisted that he spend six hours a day reading the papers and two hours a day reading books, while at the same time overseeing the work of the largest newspaper staff on earth.

Pulitzer, for his part, had lost interest in Harvey. He had marked another member of his staff for personal grooming. That spring, David Graham Phillips, a six-foot-three Hoosier-born graduate of Princeton University who turned the heads of the women in the stenographers' pool, had joined the *World* after three years with Dana's *Sun*. He was as ambitious in character as he was striking in physique. Upon arriving in New York, in search of a reporting job, he had written to his father, "Here I am in this great city, and no man, woman or child cares whether I am dead or alive, but I will make them care before I am done with them."

Phillips received an invitation to dine at Pulitzer's house—a considerable honor since the publisher was in New York for only seventy-two hours, and many of the *World*'s staffers wanted time with him. After the meal, the two men retired to the drawing room to discuss politics, poetry, and philosophy. The sartorially splendid Phillips lived up to his advance billing as a charming conversationalist. Pulitzer invited him on the spot to return to Europe with him and become the *World*'s correspondent in London.

Within forty-eight hours, Phillips had packed, put his affairs in order, and caught up with Hosmer, Ponsonby, and Pulitzer on a ship bound for England. His presence greatly enlivened Pulitzer's traveling party. While

Ponsonby and Hosmer tended to the publisher's many needs, Phillips provided the kind of lively intellectual conversation that Pulitzer cherished. More important, Pulitzer saw in Phillips a potential journalistic heir apparent. It seemed unlikely to him that his asthmatic eldest son would ever be able to take over the reins of the paper. Convinced that any one of his maladies could end his own life, Pulitzer worried that the *World* would die with him.

Pulitzer was so completely taken with Phillips that, in a moment of weakness, he consented to give his young traveling companion something he had thus far denied to all his correspondents at the *World*. He would permit Phillips to publish the London dispatches with a byline.

By June, Pulitzer was already back again. He now had two U.S. homes that provided privacy away from New York. He was eager to spend time at his newest one, a beautiful estate that he had leased. It was named Chatwold, and it overlooked the ocean in Bar Harbor, Maine. Despite the distance from New York, this small community was drawing the likes of the Vanderbilts, eclipsing Lenox, Massachusetts, and rivaling Newport, Rhode Island, as a summer haven for the wealthy.

Geographically nearer to the *World* and closer to its day-to-day operations than he had been in more than a year, Pulitzer couldn't resist meddling with its management. Whereas he left the *Post-Dispatch* entirely to itself, he could not keep his hands off the *World*. Actually, at this moment, the paper needed help. Its affairs were in disarray and two of its top managers weren't speaking to each other, communicating only by memo. Pulitzer slashed the salary and powers of one of the two; but, unsurprisingly, that did little to restore harmony.

The problem was larger than an office squabble. Since Pulitzer had sent Cockerill packing, he had never found an editor who was Cockerill's equal. George Harvey worked himself into exhaustion and pneumonia trying to be the next Cockerill, to no avail. The only person who ever met Pulitzer's expectations was Pulitzer himself.

He believed the solution to his troubles was a brash editor working for a competitor in St. Louis. Pulitzer knew that Colonel Charles H. Jones, who had replaced William Hyde at the *Missouri Republican,* had boosted the paper's circulation with an aggressive style of journalism not seen in St. Louis since Pulitzer had left a decade ago. Aside from his undesirable sympathy for the populist free-silver movement, Jones seemed to possess the determination and drive Pulitzer wanted at the helm of the *World*. He sent Jones an invitation to Chatwold, and the editor came and stayed for a week.

No one on the staff in New York knew anything about Pulitzer's intentions until one day in July when Jones walked into the Pulitzer Building and presented himself to Carvalho and Don Carlos Seitz, a rising business manager. The well-dressed man with oversize sideburns and a portentous manner handed them a blue envelope of the kind that usually held Pulitzer's correspondence. When Carvalho and Seitz opened it, they were incredulous. Jones was to have complete dominion over the paper.

"The astonishment of the shop was not at the colonel," Seitz said, "but at the wide scope seemingly given a man with no knowledge of the field, and Mr. Pulitzer's disregard of those who had done much to hold the paper together successfully." Carvalho, in particular, was bewildered. Until this moment he had considered himself Pulitzer's top lieutenant. He learned, as Cockerill and Turner had before him, that while Pulitzer's personal loyalty ran deep, it counted for little in his business affairs.

"It was soon manifest that the new man would not do," Seitz said. The disempowered Carvalho wanted to leave but did not want to go to a lesser paper than the *World*, which still had no equal in New York. Harvey, who had recovered from his pneumonia, went to Bar Harbor and submitted his resignation. Pulitzer was puzzled. He could not understand why anyone would want to leave the *World*. "It seems to me strange, indeed, considering all that I have tried to do, that you should not be on the paper; and most strange that you should have no feelings of regret at the termination of relations, which to me at least, were extremely sympathetic and interesting," he wrote to Harvey.

Amid the managerial confusion under the dome in New York, Pulitzer's promise that Phillips's articles would carry a byline had not been kept. The London correspondent was annoyed that his hard work, including a major scoop in which he had beaten British newspapers, was unnoticed. Without a byline, he complained to Pulitzer, a correspondent's work is lost in the pages of varied and confusing foreign items. "He may have had an excellent reputation as a newspaper man before he left New York but he is soon forgotten."

Pulitzer was unconvinced. He sent Phillips a polite note suggesting that his work might not yet be up to a standard that merited a byline. "The management of the *Sun* and the *Herald* have formed a rather more favorable opinion," Phillips snapped back. "And you will permit me the hope that perhaps you would have shared that better opinion had you had the time to spare to read it." Phillips then grabbed another sheet of paper, wrote out his resignation, and posted it to Jones in New York.

Phillips consented to remain in London until his replacement arrived. Ballard Smith, who thought he was no longer working for the *World* and was idly vacationing, suddenly received orders from Pulitzer to head for London as the *World*'s new correspondent. "Well, I suppose it's the same old story," said Smith to Phillips upon disembarking.

"What story?" asked Phillips

"Bad faith and broken promises."

But when he returned to the United States, Phillips accepted Pulitzer's offer to stay on the *World*. This proved a wise decision on his part. In New York, he won his long-sought byline and gained considerable attention for his work, as well as praise from Pulitzer. He also gathered material for a novel that he was writing at night. The *World,* and especially Pulitzer, provided an abundance of raw material.

Leaving the paper under Jones's shaky rule, Pulitzer returned to Europe. His travels had become a permanent feature of his life. He could easily afford the best accommodations. He was now listed as the twenty-fourth-richest American alive. But hotels, even the best, no longer sufficed. His sensitivity to noise had grown so severe that his wrath would descend on any staffer who made the mistake of taking lodging on a cobblestone street. "The entourage came at times to be skeptical about Mr. Pulitzer's sensitiveness to noise but rarely dared to experiment," Seitz said. "This desire for silence became almost a mania."

Because blind people depend more on their other senses, they tend to listen with greater discrimination. But, contrary to common belief, they do not necessarily develop more acute hearing to compensate for their infirmity, with the possible exception of those who go blind at a very young age. The source of Pulitzer's acousticophobia, and his later sensitivity to odors, was a symptom of a much larger problem. He was so beset with anxiety that it was taking a physical toll.

Pulitzer suffered from what later experts would call hyperesthesia, which in his case, was brought on by generalized anxiety disorder, a psychological condition in which a person is haunted by long-lasting anxieties that are not focused on any particular thing. This was a genuine distress for Pulitzer, not hypochondriacal. No one knows the cause. Some people believe it relates to naturally occurring chemicals in the brain; others think it may stem from life situations; and yet others subscribe to a theory that an event in combination with certain natural and environmental conditions may trigger the disorder. In Pulitzer's case it was likely that the trauma of becoming blind brought on the extreme anxieties and accompanying phobias. In fact, his symptoms manifested themselves only after he began to lose his vision. His condition, in any case, complicated the search for suitable accommodations when he was traveling. "Three or four rooms will never do," Pulitzer said. "I must have all the rooms above me or below me vacant, and as I usually have three to four gentlemen with me, a house with a dozen rooms would be more desirable." He needed a full-time advance man.

"It is all very well to think about paying a salary to a man who will find a quiet hotel or rooms," one Pulitzer man wrote to another, "but no-one who is not intimately acquainted personally with Mr. Pulitzer's wants could not possibly set out on such an expedition with the slightest hope of success." In the end, the man best suited for the job was close by. John Dillon's personal assistant turned out to be perfect. About thirty, and educated at Phillips Exeter and Harvard, George H. Ledlie possessed all the skills, social training, and taste to be the scent hound for the wandering Pulitzer party. He began what would be a decades-long search for the Holy Grail—a place where his boss could find rest and repose.

As if his own health weren't enough of a distraction, Pulitzer also fretted about that of his children. In particular, Ralph remained a constant worry. Ever since he was a baby, his asthma had been a source of concern. Like father, like son—Ralph also developed other woes. Pulitzer sent the boy off to Birmingham General Hospital in England for a complete examination. The British doctors reported that Ralph, who was then fourteen, had a weak lung and was prone to tuberculosis. They prescribed rest at high altitude, and Ralph was promptly sent off to St. Moritz.

The older Pulitzer children, accustomed to long stretches of separation, began corresponding with each other, creating a family among themselves in the absence of their parents. Ralph, alone in St. Moritz, wrote to Lucille, who was a year younger. He described one of the rare joys in his solitary life in the Swiss Alps. He had been allowed to begin studying Greek and abandon his pursuit of Latin, which he hated. "I never imagined a language capable of such filthy, beastly rules and contradictions," he told Lucille. "If it is really a dead language, it must be baking freely in purgatory for its sins in the way of murder of youths."

All winter Joseph drifted around Europe. He visited Ralph in St. Moritz and told Kate that he had found the boy much improved. "The outdoor and sporting life of St. Moritz had done that." But he kept from Kate that he was sending Hosmer all the way to Colorado to look for another place for Ralph. Joseph's mood was turning sour again. It corresponded "with the dark cloudy raining dismal weather outside," he wrote to Kate from Pfäfers-Bad in Ragatz.

In New York, the *World* continued to suffer under Jones's incompetent rule. Not only were long-serving editors chafing under him, but he was sacrilegiously seeking to use the paper to support free silver, in contradiction to Pulitzer's well-established opposition. Distracted by his own problems, Pulitzer did nothing. Only when his friend Chauncey Depew was ill-treated in the paper did he interfere. "I have knocked the perpetrators down with a little cable club," Pulitzer wrote to Depew, "and hope there will be no further lunacies in this line."

But there were to be others.

Jones's ineptitude at the *World* had consequences beyond the bruised feelings of some staffers. He had begun ruining the editorial page, Pulitzer's prized domain, with incoherent and, worse, populist screeds on the financial panic of 1893. Pulitzer's mistake in selecting Jones grew into a public embarrassment noted as far away as Atlanta. "The *World* was published before Mr. Pulitzer lifted Jones out of the hole into which the *St. Louis Republic* dropped him," said the *Atlanta Constitution*. "It was not only published, but had an editorial page—and a much better one than Jones has been able to give it. . . . Soon there will be nothing left of the *World*'s editorial page but an effulgent circulation statement and Jones's whiskers."

With the problem of Jones weighing heavily on his mind, Pulitzer returned to New York at the beginning of the summer in 1894 in the company of Arthur Brisbane, the son of a wealthy, noted reformer, socialist, and advocate of communal living. The younger Brisbane had turned to newspaper work when he was eighteen, landing a job on Dana's *Sun*. In 1890, at the age of twenty-six, he came to work at the *World*. Erudite and accomplished—he had already been a London correspondent—Brisbane possessed maturity and sophistication beyond his years. As he had done with other men of promise, Pulitzer sought to personally groom Brisbane and had brought him to Europe for the past winter.

Unlike the coterie of pliant secretaries who surrounded Pulitzer, Brisbane stood up to him and even teased him. Staying with Pulitzer in Paris, Brisbane had persuaded him to remove the mattresses that blocked the bedroom window, to take longer drives, to resume horseback riding, and to alter some of his eating habits. The two rode horses, read, and played chess and—sometimes for money—cards. Pulitzer had little interest in gambling, but he enjoyed cards and the accompanying conversation. Because of his almost complete lack of sight, the men played with specially designed cards twice the size of those in an ordinary deck. One time, this gave Brisbane an opportunity to get a leg up on his boss. Pulitzer required that many lamps be placed behind him so that he could make out the cards, and Brisbane found that he could see through the cards in Pulitzer's hand. He then pretended that he had discerned the strength of Pulitzer's hand through the tone of his voice, completely confounding him.

Upon arriving in New York, Brisbane returned to the paper, and Pulitzer immediately repaired to Chatwold, which he had recently purchased after renting it for two years. Kate and the children arrived soon afterward. The family remained in Bar Harbor until early fall. It was an election year, so a continuous stream of editors came to confer with Pulitzer, and politicians arrived in hopes of having his blessings conferred upon them.

Senator David Hill of New York, who had been nominated to run for governor again, wanted the *World*'s backing despite having allied himself with Dana's *Sun* in the presidential contest two years earlier. He summoned George McClellan, who was the son of the controversial General Brinton McClellan and who would later become mayor of New York. "George, I want you to take the first train to Bar Harbor," said Hill. "When you get there, see Pulitzer and tell him that if he will agree to support me, I will agree to remove Brockway as soon as I am inaugurated." The prize Hill was offering, Zebulon Reed Brockway, managed the state reformatory in Elmira and was the target of an investigation by the *World* for alleged abuse of the inmates.

The following morning McClellan presented himself at Chatwold. He told Ponsonby he had come with a message from Senator Hill. A few minutes elapsed and Pulitzer entered the room, leaning on Ponsonby's arm. Though McClellan had once worked at the *World*, this was the first time he had ever seen Pulitzer. "In appearance he was very like the newspaper caricatures of him," he thought.

Pulitzer asked Ponsonby to get some cigars and cursed him when he returned with the wrong ones—a treatment which Ponsonby had become used to. At last, McClellan was given a chance to deliver Hill's message as instructed. Even if he lost the election, McClellan continued, Hill would make sure the new governor would carry out his pledge to fire Brockway.

"I am surprised that Hill should make me such a proposition," said Pulitzer. "He knows that I am not for sale, nor is the *World* for sale." McClellan protested that Hill had nothing like that in mind. Rather, it was only suggested as a "friendly little arrangement." Pulitzer admitted he was eager to be rid of Brockway and conceded that he had always liked Hill. "You can tell him that I never make a political bargain. At the same time, if he agrees that Brockway shall go, I agree to support the Democratic ticket," said Pulitzer, adding with a grin, "Understand this is not a bargain, just a friendly little arrangement."

Auspiciously, that summer, a horse named Pulitzer was paying off handsomely at racetracks in New York. But in the 1894 political races, the publisher Pulitzer was not as fortunate. Another financial downturn spurring foreclosures, the embarrassment of begging New York bankers for loans to maintain the government's gold reserves, and the growing free-silver movement sapped the Democrats' strength. In November, the Democratic Party went down to defeat nationally as well as in New York, despite the *World*'s efforts. Brockway kept his job.

As the weather turned cold in Maine, the Pulitzers decamped and moved into a mansion on Bellevue Avenue in Newport, Rhode Island, for a month, before returning to New York City.

The election over, Pulitzer finally turned to the problem of Jones at the paper. It would not be easy to fix. Normally, Pulitzer moved his editors around like pieces on a chessboard and considered them as expendable as pawns. But in his desperate quest for managerial peace, he had foolishly given Jones an ironclad contract specifying both his remuneration and his powers. The cure had proved worse than the ailment.

On his return, Pulitzer met with Jones at the house on Fifty-Fifth Street. Jones may have been ill-suited to run the *World*, but he was no fool. He knew he had the upper hand. He told Pulitzer he would quit the paper on two conditions: he must be given absolute control of the *Post-Dispatch*, and must be allowed to purchase a majority stake in it. Seeing no other way to be rid of Jones in New York, Pulitzer agreed and ordered that a contract be drawn up and sent to Jekyll Island, where he was heading. Fourteen servants worked feverishly to ready a two-story stone "cottage" on Jekyll Island. In an act of kindness, Kate consented to accompany him despite her dislike of the island's isolation, heat, and sand flies. By New Year's Day 1895, the couple, several of their children, and a carload of guns, fishing rods, and traps reached the island.

Jones's contract followed Pulitzer to Jekyll Island. The first draft was absurd. Under its terms, Pulitzer would pay for Jones's shares of the *Post-Dispatch*. Pulitzer was desperate but not mad. For several weeks, the contract traveled back and forth between Jekyll Island and New York until it was finally agreed that Jones would be president, editor, and manager and could own as much stock as he could afford. With a signed contract in his pocket, Jones headed to St. Louis, and Pulitzer, as well as the *World*'s staff, thought he was rid of a nightmare.

For Pulitzer, Jekyll Island's main attraction was complete privacy. When a reporter from Atlanta asked at the clubhouse if he could see Pulitzer, the manager replied, "That is impossible. Mr. Pulitzer has left instructions that no one save the members of his newspaper family is to be allowed near him." Just as the reporter prepared to beat a retreat, Pulitzer entered the room on the arm of one of his secretaries, heading out for a walk. "Oh yes, I am always glad to see newspaper men," Pulitzer said. "That brotherhood which is formed between those who have had to run an item down is as strong as any formed in any other calling."

The three men went out to the steps of the clubhouse, where Pulitzer submitted to a short interview, enjoying a chance to express his frustration with President Cleveland. "Men of all political views voted for him, believing that above all issues would stand the one great and overpowering fact of good government," said Pulitzer. "He has disappointed their expectations and failed in every hope."

Good government, Pulitzer predicted, would be the decisive issue in the 1896 election. "The great issue before the people at all times is not silver, or gold, or the tariff, though they are all important relatively." He was wrong. As he talked with the reporter, William Jennings Bryan, an unknown U.S. representative leaving office and barely old enough to run for president, was beginning a national speaking tour on behalf of free silver. In sixteen months, Bryan would remake the American political landscape.

Even when he was at his best, Joseph made their marriage an ordeal for Kate. If he was not consumed by work, he was haunted by sickness, real and imagined. As his worries about work and his fears for his health mounted, so did his notorious temper and impatience. From a practical point of view, the connubial disharmony had been resolved by an almost continuous separation since the onset of his blindness. Joseph wandered the globe in the company of secretaries, doctors, and valets, while Kate led a busy social life in Paris, London, and New York.

One of the few witnesses to their turbulent domestic life was Felix Webber, a Briton who had a short, unhappy tenure as Pulitzer's secretary. He found Pulitzer an insufferable boss. "He is such an ill-mannered surly brute and keeps throwing in one's teeth that he is paying one for all one does for him—and he is evidently quite determined to get his money's worth out of one," Webber wrote to his sister after taking the post. Bitter and angry, he became the only secretary willing to break the code of silence adhered to by the other men who served as personal aides to Pulitzer.

In December 1894, the Pulitzers' eldest daughter, Lucille, who was then fourteen, required a small, modest operation on her throat. Unfortunately, the wound did not heal properly, and more work had to be done. Kate was distraught and remained by Lucille's side throughout the ordeal. Although he was in New York, Joseph did not even consent to visit Lucille while she was recuperating in her room. One night at dinner, Kate asked why he was shunning his daughter. Did he not pity her?

"Pity Lucille!" Joseph shouted back, according to Webber, who recorded the moment. "No! I'm the one to pity—has no one any pity for me! Does no one realize what I suffer! My own house turned into a hospital! Doctors coming at all hours! You rushing upstairs in the middle of meals, without a word of conversation for me—no one pities me, and you ask me to pity Lucille!"

Kate could not bring herself to speak. She was well used to silences, especially at the beginning of the month, when she and Joseph fought over money. This time, however, she gave Webber orders that Joseph not be allowed upstairs. Contrite the following day, Joseph visited Lucille and sent Webber out to buy flowers for his daughter.

When Joseph had left for Jekyll Island a few weeks later, the household breathed a sigh of relief. "Especially Mrs. P. who got up out of bed as soon as he was gone and received lying in a chaise longue in her boudoir in a vieux rose peignoir and a chinchilla fur rug also lined with vieux rose over her legs and plenty of white frou frou all about her," Webber said. "She was sighing over a a portrait of J.P. which has just come from Paris painted by [Léon] Bonnat two years ago."

"I suppose I ought to hang it in my boudoir, *but I won't*," she told Webber. "Don't you think that a large photograph is enough for me to have in my boudoir?"

Kate had certainly tried her best to tolerate Joseph's outbursts, to tend to his health, and to be with him when he permitted it, aside from the one time when she declined the Mediterranean cruise. But it was a Sisyphean task to please him. Only the year before, Kate, preoccupied with managing the house and children, had let a stretch of time go by without writing to her absent Joseph. "For two weeks you did not write me one word even inquiring whether I was dead or alive," Joseph wrote to her. "Do you think that was right? You know you have the power to keep me awake, that I chafe and worry and brood over the conduct of yours.

"Again," he continued, "after all it is supposed to be the first business of a wife to be interested in the comfort and condition of her husband who is absolutely without family and as helpless as I am." Then, resurrecting his old complaint, he told Kate she never did what he asked. "You like to emphasize the word 'order,' my order, or your order, when you refer to my wishes or when I refer to them, especially a wish that is habitually trampled upon and disregarded. I wish you would not do that because it reminds me how utterly ignored my wishes are."

By March, Kate had enough of Jekyll Island—and Joseph—and returned to New York. She may also have had an ulterior motive for leaving. She was having an affair. Pulitzer's new man, Arthur Brisbane, offered Kate the adoration she could not get from her husband, who was embroiled in his battles with real and doubtful demons of ill health. Only just in her forties, Kate remained an immensely attractive, outgoing, and gregarious woman. She loved parties, culture, and life, while her husband was becoming a recluse.

Her separation from Joseph made it easier for Kate to take a lover, but discretion remained a necessity. "I do not discuss my actual work, much as I should like to, in these letters, because such discussion would give too clear a key to the authorship of these writings should one of them go wrong," Brisbane wrote to Kate in 1895, in a letter that he signed only with the initial "H." Brisbane's ardor was unmistakable. When they planned a rendezvous between Boston and Bar Harbor, he wrote, "That will be one of the most eagerly anticipated journeys I have ever made."

"I could go on writing you for hours, for you are in my mind, and I like even the imitation of talking to you," he wrote in another letter. "The longer you are away from me, the more I want to see you, and the more real and necessary you seem.

"What a shame it is that we have not the power of telegraphing ourselves from place to place. We shall have that power sometime. If we had it now, I should send myself by wire instead of sending this letter by mail, *et alors, tu sais ce qui t'arriverait.*"

In April or early May, Kate discovered that she was pregnant. But whose child was it? It had been seven years since her last pregnancy and the birth of her sixth child since marrying Joseph. It seemed possible that Joseph was the father now, as Kate might have been on Jekyll Island at the time of conception. However, considering Joseph's condition and mood, it was unlikely.

Brisbane allegedly told David Graham Phillips that the child was his. In his clandestine correspondence with Kate, he expressed worries about her health. "Had you taken care of yourself, you would be in good condition now," he wrote. "You are not good to yourself. I wish you would care as much about your own health and future as you do about mine. It would be a good thing for you and for me.

"Do be a good sensible girl and take care of yourself. Some of these days we shall have some fun. Keep your health for that."

Joseph never doubted that the child was his.

* * *

In May, Pulitzer went for a brief stay in a luxurious manor at Kensington, near London's Hyde Park. But peacocks summering in the adjacent park made such a racket with their nighttime mating screeches that Pulitzer was soon on his way back to the United States. It was as if everything conspired to wreck his life just as he reached his zenith. On board the *Teutonic*, Pulitzer wrote to Thomas Davidson, with whom he had fallen out of touch since 1887. "I did suffer more during those eight years by loss of sight, sleep, health and activity than in all my previous existence."

That summer the remodeled Chatwold stood ready to receive Pulitzer and his guests. More than 100 men had worked through the winter rebuilding the country mansion to Pulitzer's specifications. The most difficult task had been an excavation down through fifty feet of rock to sea level, where a steam-heated underground room had been carved out for a plunge bath. Aboveground, the house had been extensively rebuilt, with the addition of a granite tower specially constructed to prevent sound from entering. Inside it, according to one reporter, "the great chief can hide away from the sordid cares of the world and be at peace with his soul—or at war with it—and no one will be the wiser."

The "tower of silence," as his secretaries called it, also revealed that Pulitzer's retreat from the paper was no longer a search for a cure but rather a permanent condition. "So Mr. Pulitzer," noted one of his men, "dictated the destinies of his manifold interests at long distances in intervals between seizures when his infirmities utterly incapacitated him—a giant intelligence eternally condemned to the darkest of dungeons, a caged eagle furiously belaboring the bars."

Pulitzer's talons, however, remained sharp, especially with regard to Theodore Roosevelt. The politician had recently become New York City's police commissioner and was cleaning up its notoriously corrupt police force. This cheered New Yorkers until he also decided to enforce blue laws that forbade saloons—but not private clubs—to serve alcohol on the Sabbath. Roosevelt agreed that the law was pigheaded and led to corruption, but said that he had no choice except to enforce it. Pulitzer, who had long opposed any form of temperance, directed Bradford Merrill to bring up the *World*'s editorial guns.

Roosevelt's claim that his enforcement might actually inspire a lifting of the ban was disingenuous, said the *World*. "You know that those who have such power are in no way annoyed by your nagging and exasperating activity in preventing the hard-working laborer from getting a pitcher of beer for his Sunday dinner," the editorial continued, addressing Roosevelt directly, as the *World* always did when he was the subject of Pulitzer's condemnation. "Does it commend 'reform' to have the innocent annoyed in its name while crime runs riot and criminals go free?"

Reading the editorial, Roosevelt told his friend Senator Henry Cabot Lodge that the *World* was among the New York papers "shrieking with rage." He told another friend that the *World* and *Herald* "are doing everything in their power to make me swerve from my course; but they will fail signally; I shall not flinch one handbreadth." But being despised by drinkers and the New York press had no ill effect on Roosevelt's national popularity. In fact, it increased. One paper asked, "Will he succeed Col. Strong as Mayor; or Levi P. Morton as Governor; or Grover Cleveland as President?"

Indeed, Roosevelt's ambitions far exceeded cleaning up a city's police department. He was certain that his combativeness and manliness were appealing. He was convinced that the entire nation, not just Manhattan, lacked virility. "There is an unhappy tendency among certain of our cultivated people to lose the great manly virtues, the power to strive and fight and conquer, not only in a time of peace, but on the field of battle," he told one audience. He thought the time had come for the United States to flex its military muscle outside its borders, and he saw an opportunity in a crisis brewing in Venezuela.

Roosevelt, who had never seen a battlefield, wanted war. Pulitzer, who had, wanted nothing of it.

For years Venezuela had been bickering with Great Britain about its border with British Guiana. After the discovery of gold, the quarrel intensified. The United States took Venezuela's side, broke off diplomatic relations with England in late 1895, and demanded arbitration. The British, who ruled the seas, considered this an insult and refused.

The rebuff drew an angry message from the president to Congress. Invoking the Monroe Doctrine, Cleveland promised that if England dared to take any land the United States deemed as belonging to Venezuela, the United States would "resist by every means in its power." Congress rushed to the president's side, and the saber rattling put the little-noticed dispute on the front pages. WAR ON EVERY LIP was the

Chicago Tribune's headline. WAR CLOUDS proclaimed the *Atlanta Constitution*. The editorial pages clamored for a fight. "Any American citizen who hesitates to uphold the President of the United States is either an alien or a traitor," said the *Sun*.

Pulitzer refused to let the *World* join in. He thought Cleveland had gone too far. Put the headline A GRAVE BLUNDER on the lead editorial, Pulitzer told one of his writers over the telephone from his rented house in Lakewood, New Jersey. Weighing each word carefully, he composed a four-paragraph assault on the president's logic. Great Britain's actions in Venezuela posed no danger to the United States, he said. "It is a grave blunder to put this government in its attitude of threatening war unless we mean it and are prepared for it and can hopefully appeal to the sympathizers of the civilized world in making it."

Pulitzer had long feared militarism. Seventeen years earlier, he had seen firsthand how Bismarck used the threat of French territorial claims to maintain a large standing army and impose oppressive taxes to pay for it. The ruler's actions created a warlike state, though without battle, much as Thomas Hobbes famously described it in *Leviathan*. "This they call peace!" the young Pulitzer had written. "Next to war itself I cannot imagine anything more terrible to a great nation than such a peace."

Pulitzer now expanded his efforts to douse the war fever. Over his signature, his staff sent telegrams to leading statesmen, clergymen, politicians, editors, leaders of Parliament, and the royal family in Great Britain, urging them to publicly express their opposition to war. Within days, the *World* published replies from the prince of Wales, Gladstone (out of office again), the bishop of London, the archbishop of Westminster, and dozens of other leaders. Each telegram professed England's peaceful intentions and strove to lower the transatlantic rhetoric. "They earnestly trust and cannot but believe the present crisis will be arranged in a manner satisfactory to both countries," read the message from the British throne. "No feelings here but peaceful and brotherly," wired the bishop of Liverpool. "God Speed you in your patriotic endeavor," added the bishop of Chester.

The *World*'s issue for Christmas Day 1895 reproduced the telegrams from the prince of Wales and one from the duke of York under the headline PEACE AND GOOD WILL. Soon, said another of Pulitzer's editorials, the holly and mistletoe would be gone, as would the voices of children singing carols. "But we shall retain our hopes. The white doves, unseen, will be fluttering somewhere."

In England, the telegrams sent by the prince and the duke generated considerable support and were on the front page of most newspapers, reported an excited Ballard Smith. The reaction in the United States was quite different. Roosevelt, who had already written a letter of congratulation to Cleveland for his belligerent threats, told Lodge that Americans were weakening in their resolve for war. "Personally, I rather hope the fight will come soon. The clamor of the peace faction has convinced me that this country needs a war." He was furious at Pulitzer and Edwin Godkin at the *New York Post*, who had joined in urging restraint. "As for the editors of the *Evening Post* and *World*," Roosevelt said, "it would give me great pleasure to have them put in prison the minute hostilities began."

Pulitzer's intervention could not have come at a worse moment for the Cleveland administration. Its gold reserves had fallen to critically low levels again. Since the panic of 1893, the government had dealt with close calls by borrowing and buying gold in Europe. Now that Cleveland faced a new borrowing crisis, Pulitzer's peace campaign had made matters worse by eliciting a proclamation from the Rothschild banking family that Europeans should not buy American bonds.

With the free silver forces gaining strength, the economy still in the doldrums, and Pulitzer causing trouble, Cleveland met secretly with J. P. Morgan. A year earlier, when two U.S. public bond offerings had failed, Morgan had persuaded the president to permit his private syndicate to handle a bond sale like the one the president again had in mind. The first one had saved the government from defaulting on its obligations, but Morgan's alleged profits had further fueled the free-silver movement. Pulitzer had bitterly denounced the deal. He wanted to protect the gold standard, but not at the cost of enriching Morgan. He was also convinced that Morgan's plan could give the "silverites" the White House in 1896. He was dead set on preventing another such deal.

Under such headlines as SMASH THE RING, the *World* claimed that the administration was once again entering into a secret compact with financiers. As Pulitzer had done in the ongoing crisis over Venezuela, he ordered his staff to use the telegraph wires. More than 10,000 telegrams were sent to banks and investment houses asking if they would support a public bond offering, and more than half replied, setting a one-day record for Western Union. Pulitzer then called several of his editors to Lakewood. They took the last New Jersey–bound train out of the city.

"When I got there night had already fallen, and as I was without even so much as a handbag, I anticipated a night of makeshift at the hotel," said George Eggleston, one of the summoned editors.

"Come in quickly. We must talk rapidly and to the point. You think you're to stay here all night, but you're mistaken," Pulitzer told the men as they entered his house. "I've ordered a special train to take you back. It will start at eight o'clock and run through in eighty minutes. Meanwhile, we have much to arrange, so we must get to work.

"What we demand is that these bonds shall be sold to the public at something like their actual value and not to a Wall Street syndicate for many millions less," he said. "You are to write a double-leaded article to occupy the whole editorial page tomorrow morning. You are not to print a line of editorial on any other subject."

Eggleston was to assail the idea of using Morgan as a middleman and argue that the government should sell the bonds directly to the people. "Then," Pulitzer added, "as a guarantee of the sincerity of our convictions you are to say that the *World* offers in advance to take one million dollars of the new bonds at the highest market price, if they are offered to the public in open markets."

Pulitzer dismissed his men. The following morning, the *World* reported that hundreds of banks and bankers had replied to its telegraphed inquiries with pledges to buy the bonds. "To you, Mr. Cleveland, the *World* appeals," read Eggleston's editorial. It pleaded with the president to turn Morgan down and to turn instead to the people. "If you make your appeal to the people they will quickly respond. So sure are we of this that the *World* now offers to head the list with a subscription of one million dollars on its own account."

Pulitzer won. Both Morgan and Cleveland realized that another private sale was now out of the question. On January 6, 1896, the administration announced a public sale of bonds. Cleveland, facing the end of his second term, had grown tired of Pulitzer's outbursts. His secretary of state dug up an old federal statute that made it a crime punishable by imprisonment to communicate with foreign leaders to influence American policy. Roosevelt's friend Senator Lodge brought the matter up in the Senate. He asked his colleagues if they did not think that Pulitzer's telegrams to the prince of Wales and others did not constitute an offense under the law. A Republican senator rose to say he thought they did. "If the President and the Attorney General do their duty," said the senator, "Mr. Pulitzer, if he ever sets foot upon the soil of America as I understand he occasionally does, ought to be prosecuted according to law."

Pulitzer mounted his own defense. The *World* urged that the government use the "aged, obsolete, moldy, moth-eaten, dust-covered" law to prosecute the paper. "It is really time to make an example of the presumptuous editors who dare to interfere to break the force and repair the damage of an imitation jingo policy with its disturbing threat of war."

Tempers cooled. The dispute between England and Venezuela moved to the back pages as the two nations agreed to arbitration. The public bond sale proceeded and was a success. Pulitzer's banker Dumont Clarke placed a bid for $1 million of bonds, as the *World* had promised. When the bid was received at the auction, the secretary of the treasury moved uncomfortably in his seat, and a shadow fell over Morgan's face, reported the *World,* which devoted an entire page to the opening of the bids. "The name of the *World* was not a pleasant sound and it was a bitter thing to be reminded of the past."

A few days later, Clarke reported that the purchase of the bonds would bring a profit of $50,000. After having attacked Morgan for making money from bond transactions, Pulitzer panicked at this potentially embarrassing gain. The *World*'s managers and editors were all called together for a meeting. After two hours of debate, the paper's business manager asked, "Why not keep it?" Pulitzer accepted the advice.

Roosevelt, who had gotten neither war nor a criminal prosecution of Pulitzer, sought his own revenge for the paper's ill-treatment of his police commissionership. He found a vehicle when the *World* compiled a catalog of crimes under his watch, implying that time spent on the saloon issue had left citizens less protected. Roosevelt persuaded the *New York Times*, which was losing $2,500 a week and facing bankruptcy, to publish the city's official report showing the *World*'s list to be a gross exaggeration.

Roosevelt, in this small triumph, summed up a decision that all of Pulitzer's political enemies had to make. "It is always a question how far it is necessary to go in answering a man who is a convicted liar," Roosevelt said. "For the same reason it is a little difficult to decide whether it is necessary to take notice of any statement whatever appearing in Mr. Pulitzer's paper, the *New York World*."

Pulitzer, tucked away in his cottage at Jekyll once again, chose to ignore Roosevelt. A new and more dangerous opponent than a carping politician faced him. A young upstart newspaper publisher was preparing to do to him what Pulitzer had done to the giants of Park Row in 1883.

(*Above*) Migrating Jewish families found economic opportunity in Makó, the Hungarian farming village where Joseph Pulitzer was born in 1847. Landowners, eager for the services of merchants and tradesmen, enlisted the newcomers to market the products of their estates. Members of the Paskesz family, whose business may be seen on the right-hand side of this nineteenth-century photo, later migrated to the United States and opened a Kosher confectionery in Brooklyn.

(*Right*) Pulitzer was devoted to his mother, Elize, seen here with his sister Anna, who died not long after the photograph was taken. In fact, all but one of his eight siblings died before Pulitzer reached his teenage years.

Mother of
Joseph & Albert

(*Left*) Joseph Pulitzer's four-year-younger brother, Albert, was a consummate reader, idealistic and ambitious. In 1867, with a twenty-dollar coin tucked under his shirt in a tiny cotton bag hung around his neck, Albert sailed for the United States and joined his brother in St. Louis.

(*Below*) This rare moment of brotherly togetherness was probably captured by a New York photographer in the spring of 1873. Joseph (*left*) visited Albert on his way to Europe after selling his shares in the *Westliche Post*. Albert had just started working at the *New York Herald*.

(*Above*) German immigrant and American politician Carl Schurz was a role model for Pulitzer in St. Louis.

(*Left*) Pulitzer followed Schurz into the Liberal Republican movement. When the rebellion was defeated, Schurz returned to the Republican Party, but Pulitzer became a Democrat.

(*Left*) With his success as a reporter and the additional income he earned as a state legislator, Pulitzer had improved his dress by 1869, when this photograph was taken.

(*Below*) During his term as a state legislator, Pulitzer's notorious temper got the best of him and he tried to shoot a lobbyist. The scene was captured by well-known cartoonist Joseph Keppler.

(*Above*) By the mid-1870s, Pulitzer had added facial hair to his look. In 1878, he courted two women while living in Washington, D.C.: Kate Davis (*above right*) and Nannie Tunstall (*right*). In the end, Tunstall spurned Pulitzer's affections, and he married Davis. The drawing of Tunstall was done by sculptor Moses J. Ezekiel.

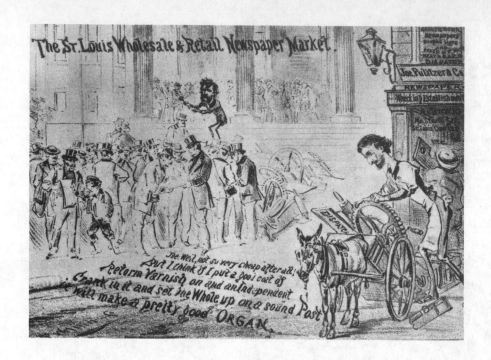

(*Above*) In December 1878, Pulitzer purchased the St. Louis *Dispatch* at a bankruptcy sale on the steps of the courthouse. In this cartoon Pulitzer (*right*) is seen packing up his new paper a few days later to merge it with the St. Louis *Post*, a move alluded to in the comment "set the whole up on a sound Post," at the center of the drawing. The cartoon appeared in the German-language *Die Laterne*.

(*Left*) Within a year of creating the *Post-Dispatch*, Pulitzer persuaded John Cockerill to come to St. Louis to take charge of the news operation of the paper. The two men met at the 1872 Liberal Republican convention. In the years since, Cockerill had worked as an editor at several newspapers, including the newly launched *Washington Post*. With their innovative style and aggressive reporting, Pulitzer and Cockerill changed the face of journalism.

When Pulitzer purchased the *New York World* from Jay Gould in 1883, he also agreed to lease for a decade Gould's Park Row building that housed the paper. But within six years, Pulitzer had made such a success of the *World* that he built the tallest building on the globe (*above*), without incurring a cent of debt. The thirteen-story building, topped with a gilded dome that reflected light forty miles out to sea, became an important symbol of Pulitzer's financial success and how he changed the landscape of journalism. The first sight of the New World for immigrants entering New York's harbor was not a building of commerce, banking, or industry. Rather, it was a temple of America's new mass media.

(*Right*) Don Carlos Seitz was Pulitzer's longest-serving business manager. He was one of the few working for Pulitzer who found a way to survive under his management style. Thirteen years after Pulitzer's death, Seitz became his first biographer.

(*Left*) Arthur Brisbane, one of Joseph Pulitzer's most brilliant news editors, was Kate Pulitzer's lover for several years. In 1897, after Kate called off the relationship, he left the *World* to work for Hearst, where he remained for thirty-nine years and became the nation's highest-paid editor and one of its best-read columnists.

Joseph Pulitzer hoped that David Graham Phillips (*right*) might be trained to lead the *World* after his death. Unfortunately, Phillips had literary aspirations and left the paper to write novels and muckraking articles for leading magazines. Pulitzer was wounded when he discovered that the corrupt publisher portrayed in Phillips's first novel was based, in great part, on himself.

Two publishers and two politicians challenged Pulitzer's power. Charles Dana *(right, top)*, who twice hired Pulitzer to write for his *New York Sun*, grew bitter when the *World* stole his circulation, and he wrote a series of anti-Semitic editorials attacking Pulitzer. William Randolph Hearst *(right, center)* bought the paper that Albert Pulitzer had started and engaged in a crippling circulation war with Joseph Pulitzer's *World* that almost bankrupted both newspapers. Theodore Roosevelt *(right, bottom)* feuded with Pulitzer for almost a quarter of century and sought to use the power of the presidency to put Pulitzer in prison. William Jennings Bryan *(below left)* turned bitter when Pulitzer refused to support his early presidential bids and told the publisher "that the trouble with him is that he has too much money."

(*Above*) When the Pulitzer building was torn down in 1955, the cornerstone was recovered. It contained copies of the *World* and other newspapers, a wax-cylinder voice recording, and photographs of Pulitzer and his family, several of which are reproduced here for the first time since they were encased in the building.

(*Left*) One of the last photographs taken of Joseph Pulitzer before he began to lose his vision. His increasing blindness and tormenting mental and health problems would test Kate Pulitzer's patience and love.

Ralph *(above left)*, the oldest, poses with a rifle at age ten. Joe and his sister Edith *(above right)* wear clothes often favored by wealthy parents. Constance *(below left)* was the only child of the Pulitzers born outside the country; she was born in Paris. Lucille *(below right)*, Joseph Pulitzer's favorite, died of typhoid in 1897, eight years after this photograph was taken. Kate Pulitzer had two other children—Katherine, born in 1882, who died at age two, and Herbert, who would be born in 1895, six years after these photographs were taken.

(*Left*) After becoming almost completely blind, Joseph Pulitzer avoided public appearances and became a recluse. It often fell to his oldest son Ralph to fill in for his ailing father or to accompany him on the rare times he was in New York. Usually Pulitzer (*lower left*) wore goggles to protect his eyes from light and to hide the deterioration visible to others. He increasingly became obsessed with his health and traveled to visit Europe's best doctors and spas accompanied by a large retinue of personal aides.

(*Right*) Joseph Pulitzer's brother Albert sold his New York *Journal* in 1895 for nearly $1 million and spent the remainder of his life mostly in Europe. He committed suicide in 1909, only a few years after this photograph was taken. Although Joseph was only a short train ride away, he chose not to come to the funeral. Albert is buried in the Jewish section of Vienna's Zentralfriedhof cemetery.

(*Below*) In 1911, Pulitzer spent part of his last spring alive in Southern France. This photograph of Pulitzer walking in Monte Carlo with his daughter Edith and his aide Harold Pollard was taken less than seven months from his death. He complained extensively about his health and began that June to take Veronal, a new sedative with dangerous side effects that were not yet known; its use may have lead to Pulitzer's death in October.

Pulitzer used his wealth to build expensive houses in hopes of finding within their walls an escape from business pressures and a shelter from noise. With the decline of his vision, Pulitzer became tormented by sounds of all sorts. For his New York mansion on East Seventy-third Street *(right)*, he hired a Harvard acoustical expert to help create a bedroom insulated from all outside sound. At his palatial estate, Chatwold, on Mt. Desert Island, Maine *(below)*, Pulitzer constructed a special wing of stone that aides nicknamed the "Tower of Silence." Pulitzer was never satisfied by the measures taken to guard him from noise.

(*Above*) Ultimately, Pulitzer came closest to finding a refuge on his yacht, *The Liberty*. The length of a football field, it contained a gymnasium, a library, drawing and smoking rooms, an oak-paneled dining room, quarters for its forty-five-man crew, and twelve elegant staterooms. The ship carried sufficient coal to cross and recross the Atlantic Ocean without refueling. Pulitzer also favored wintering in his house on Jekyll Island (*below*), a private island off the coast of Georgia where the Gilded Age's wealthiest industrialists and financiers vacationed.

Mr. Pulizer's Residence Jekyl 1906

When he died, Pulitzer used his wealth to create two institutions that have ensured his name would live on. A century later, his Pulitzer Prizes for journalism, the literary arts, and music are announced each spring at the Columbia University Graduate School of Journalism, which he endowed. Many felt the creation of the school and the prizes were late-in-life attempts to improve his legacy after years of reckless so-called "Yellow Journalism." For his part, Pulitzer said his goal was to help professionalize his trade. His last will and testament offered his personal motivation, words that remain engraved in the front hall of his school.

SCHOOL·OF·JOURNALISM
ERECTED·AND·ENDOWED·BY
JOSEPH·PULITZER
IN·MEMORY·OF·HIS·DAUGHTER
LUCILLE
MDCCCCXII

Chapter Twenty-Three

TROUBLE FROM THE WEST

◆

In February 1895 an office boy at the *Morning Journal* spotted a corpulent man, probably nearing 300 pounds, trying to unlock the door to Albert Pulitzer's office.

"Hey, there!" said the boy, "You can't go in there. That's a private room."

"I want to get in there, right away," replied the man, smiling.

The boy rushed to the newsroom to tell the city editor that someone was trying to get into the publisher's office. As he tried to give his report, the desk bell from Pulitzer's office began to ring. The boy ran back to see who was ringing it and found the mysterious intruder in the office seated behind the desk. Only then did he realize that it was Albert Pulitzer, who had not been at the paper in a year or two.

"I fooled you, didn't I," said Pulitzer.

"I-I-I, er, beg your pardon, sir, but I didn't know you," replied the boy.

"Oh, that's all right, you are not the only one. I passed the Sunday editor as I was coming through the hall and he actually gave me a stony, British stare."

Albert's immense weight gain made him hard to recognize, but in any case his mere presence in the office was a shock. In the years since the *Morning Journal* had become established, Albert had become an absentee publisher like his brother Joseph at the *World*. He had no health concerns to drive him from New York. Rather, he was more like James Bennett of the *New York Herald*. He simply preferred life in the elegant social circles of London, Paris, and other European capitals. The *Morning Journal*'s purpose had been to make money and it had done that.

At the beginning, Albert had brought the same dedication to running the *Morning Journal* that Joseph had lavished on the *World*. Every morning between three and four o'clock, a messenger brought a copy of the *Morning Journal*, other papers, reports on daily circulation, and the daily ledger. If the man was late, he would find the publisher pacing impatiently on the sidewalk. During breakfast, Pulitzer scrutinized his paper. "When he finished with it," recalled his son, "the thing would look like a pyrotechnical display, for he used both blue and red pencils without stint, and frequently the comments were punctuated with several exclamation points." With remarks such as "Awful!! Don't let this occur again" or "Too Evening-*Post*ish!" plastered over the pages, the paper was sent back to the editors for their review.

From its origin as a scandal sheet, the *Morning Journal* had grown into an immensely successful one-cent paper. It took no interest in politics. "I think one politician in the family is enough," said Albert. "My brother Joseph is welcome to that part of fame which time may allot to the name Pulitzer. Two *World*s would be more than New York could hold."

The *Journal*'s circulation hovered between 175,000 and 200,000. Its success rested on a daily array of human interest stories, spiced with risqué items, humor, and, above all, a slavish devotion to society news. "If the Vanderbilts and Astors were absent from its columns," a rewrite man said, "proprietor Albert, in Vienna or Paris, would want to know the reasons why." Although the profit paled in comparison with that of Joseph's *World*, the $100,000 a year Albert drew supported his leisurely life in Europe. Having divorced Fannie in 1882, after nine years of marriage, he left her to raise their son Walter on her own with a small stipend.

But his years in European capitals, with their more refined journals, had lessened Albert's appetite for prurient news. Upon his return in 1895 he informed his staff that the *Morning Journal* would now become "the least sensational paper published" and would move into the arena of the two-cent papers such as the *World*. He shared the news with his readers in a front-page editorial. "As it once brought New York the gospel of brightness, so the *Journal* will now strive to set an example of a higher, better tone in the treatment of news," he said. "To please, to amuse, to instruct in a fascinating way, to brighten the home circle, and never to offend with an objectionable word, will be our unceasing endeavor."

The readers weren't impressed, and circulation dropped precipitously. Fortunately, John McLean, the successful publisher of the *Cincinnati*

Enquirer, rescued Albert from the consequences of his folly. McLean paid close to $1 million for the *Morning Journal* and its companion German edition, the *Morgen Journal.* He was convinced that he could make money in New York as he had done in Cincinnati. It didn't happen. Rather, the *Morning Journal* continued its decline. McLean dropped the price to a penny again, but to no avail. By the fall of 1895, he had to sell. He found a willing customer in William Randolph Hearst.

After making a success of the *San Francisco Examiner,* Hearst had hungered for a newspaper in New York. His mother, who now held the family fortune, consented to back him. In September 1895, Hearst took the dying *Journal* off of McLean's hands for $150,000, less than 20 percent of what McLean had paid for it the year before.

At long last Hearst had a toehold in New York, and he had gotten it for far less than his model, Joseph Pulitzer, had paid. But in the twelve years since Pulitzer arrived on Park Row, the fabled block had vastly changed. The city had eight other morning newspapers including the dominant *World*; the venerable *Herald, Sun,* and *Tribune*; and the struggling *New York Times.* The once gossipy, now declining sheet that Hearst bought held little promise of competing. "He may come but he can't get a reputable newspaperman in New York to work on his paper," said one editor.

Hearst imported his best talent from San Francisco and, with his checkbook, persuaded several well-known journalists such as Julius Chambers and Julian Ralph to join his staff. He even lured Richard Harding Davis into covering the Harvard-Yale football game for a then unheard-of fee: $500. In November the first issue of the new, redesigned *New York Journal* was out. Advertisements for the paper appeared everywhere in the city and hired bands played on street corners.

The *Journal* displayed many of the same traits that had made the *World* a success. The front page bristled with large bold headlines atop engrossing urban tales. Most striking were the spectacular illustrations of criminals and beautiful girls. Except for the frequency of females in the illustrations—a Hearst touch—the challenger was simply improving on Pulitzer's recipe by using splashier headlines, larger drawings, and more dramatic and compelling copy.

The new kid on the block made the *World* look middle-aged and stodgy. In fact, in Pulitzer's absence, his paper had grown fat on its success, and stale. But no one had dared challenge its supremacy until now. Most threatening to the *World* was that Hearst had the luxury of being able to sacrifice revenue for circulation. He could afford to put out the most expensive newspaper in town and sell it as the cheapest for as long as he wished. Readers didn't care if Hearst was making money. What appealed to them was a newspaper that offered twice the excitement for half the price.

Pulitzer's men at the *World* remained unconcerned. "The new venture at once began to grow, not at the expense of the high-priced but of the low-cost papers," said Don Seitz, who was now one of Pulitzer's top men. Their cockiness did not last long. From the *San Francisco Examiner*'s New York office, on the eleventh floor of the Pulitzer Building, Hearst secretly negotiated with the editor of the Sunday *World*, whose circulation of nearly 500,000 copies made it the most profitable part of the paper. By January 1896, Hearst had persuaded not only the Sunday editor but the entire Sunday staff to join the *Journal*.

Pulitzer found out about this theft when he alighted on Jekyll Island. He telegraphed Solomon Carvalho to get the staff back at any cost. Then, ordering his aides to pack, Pulitzer left the island for New York. When the club tender carrying him reached the mainland, the party ran into James Creelman, a noted *World* reporter, who was waiting for a launch to take him to a promised meeting with the publisher. The weary Creelman had no choice but to reboard the train that had brought him south and have his meeting in Pulitzer's private coach.

After two years as one of the *World*'s most widely traveled and colorful foreign correspondents, Creelman wanted out. He told his boss that he cared little about the *World* but a lot for their friendship. Pulitzer accepted the news with unusual calmness, considering the personnel problems awaiting him in New York. But he recognized traits in Creelman, similar to his own, that made it hard to work in a subordinate position.

While the party traveled northward, Carvalho, in New York, managed to lure the Sunday staff back. But this reprieve lasted only twenty-four hours. Hearst's checkbook was too appealing. "The most extraordinary dollar-matching contest in the history of American journalism had begun," said Seitz, whose own pay would begin a long ascent in return for his loyalty to Pulitzer.

Pulitzer's first action on reaching New York was to terminate the

Examiner's lease in his building. He put Arthur Brisbane in charge of the Sunday edition and convened a war council at his residence in Lakewood. The news was grim. The *Journal*, in less than three months, had come within 35,000 of the *World's* daily circulation. Something had to be done. The business manager, John Norris, who had worked for a penny newspaper, recommended that Pulitzer cut the price of the two-cent morning *World* in half; the *Evening World* already sold for a penny. Carvalho agreed. Only Seitz held out.

Pulitzer couldn't decide. A dozen years earlier he had been the one to force other publishers to cut their prices. Not being able to call the shots was a new and uncomfortable position for him. As Pulitzer prepared to head back to Jekyll Island, he had still not made up his mind, so Carvalho and Norris boarded the train with him. By the time they reached Philadelphia, Pulitzer told them his decision. He would cut the price. The pair left the train and returned to New York.

"The news of the *World's* reduction came like a thunder clap to the great newspaper offices in Park Row," reported the *Chicago Tribune*. An editorial in the *World* announced the change.

"The reason for this reduction is a secret that we are ready to share with all the people. We prefer power to profits."

"The immediate effect was electric, but not as its owner had anticipated," Seitz said. Circulation did go up, by 88,000, but only the smaller competing papers suffered circulation losses. The *Journal* continued to gain. By stooping to compete with Hearst, Pulitzer had brought more attention to the *Journal* and had actually encouraged his rival. "The *World* in reducing to one cent must have recognized the fact that the *Journal* has come to stay," Adolph Ochs, a publisher in Chattanooga, Tennessee, with hopes of someday joining the Park Row fraternity, told Pulitzer.

Both newspapers gained in circulation, but lost money with every copy. "Mr. Hearst felt that he had his antagonist staggering and began a furious assault," said Seitz. "He spent money as it had never been spent before on newspapers in any field." Pulitzer had the resources to match Hearst, but he no longer had the daring of a young man, especially one with inherited wealth.

Hearst's entry into New York gave editors and reporters who could no longer tolerate Pulitzer's eccentric management style a practical exit, even a lucrative one. To Carvalho, who had acted as the publisher of the *World* in all but name, the option looked attractive. He felt as if he were at the end of a yo-yo jerked by Pulitzer's constant changing of orders and reshuffling of authority. In late March 1896, he telephoned Pulitzer on Jekyll Island, a daring act in and of itself, and said that unless his powers were restored by the end of the day—five o'clock in the afternoon, to be precise—he would quit. At five-thirty, Carvalho called Seitz into his office and said he was done, after nine years of managing the *World*. A few days later, he was on the *Journal*'s payroll, where he would remain as Hearst's right-hand man for thirty years. Pulitzer's detractors watched the desertions with glee. The anti-Semitic gossip sheet *Town Topics* asked, "How is Mr. Pulitzer going to get un-leavened bread when the young Egyptian from San Francisco is getting all the dough?"

With his newspaper's supremacy threatened and managerial trouble afoot, Pulitzer found Jekyll Island insufferable. To make matters worse, a government-contracted dredge entered the waters near his cottage, its steam engine clanging as it hoisted buckets of muck to the surface. Pulitzer sent his secretary out to pay the foreman $100 a day to hold off on the work until his stay on the island was over.

On Jekyll Island, word reached Pulitzer that John Cockerill, the editor who served him loyally during his rise at the *Post-Dispatch* and followed him to the *World*, had died in Cairo, Egypt. Since the two had parted company in 1891, Cockerill had run his own newspaper and then become a foreign correspondent for the *New York Herald*. He was on assignment for the *Herald* in Egypt when he succumbed to a brain hemorrhage while in a hotel barber's chair. The *World* made only modest note of his passing. Pulitzer was heading north and could have attended the funeral service when Cockerill's body reached New York in May, but he chose not to. Instead he left it to Chauncey Depew, who had presided with Cockerill at the laying of the cornerstone for the Pulitzer Building, to represent the missing half of the partnership that had transformed New York journalism. A few days later, Cockerill's will was probated. "I name as my executor Joseph Pulitzer," Cockerill had written, "who has been a faithful and sincere friend to me, and to whom I am indebted for much that I enjoy."

Pulitzer found tranquillity at Moray Lodge, the princely manor in Kensington, England. The peacocks were done with their mating and the place was quiet. "No discordant echoes of the city's ceaseless human hum disturb the restful quiet of the place," noted one caller who found Pulitzer in the elegant study, which was lined with the landlord's books. He was in better health than he had been in several years. His worries in New York rested in an untended pile of telegrams and letters strewn over a desk. London was like a tonic.

Its pleasures were made all the greater when, in June 1896, a delegation of British peace societies came to pay homage to Pulitzer and the *World* for helping defuse the Venezuelan crisis. They brought a proclamation, engrossed on vellum, deeming the effort a "beneficent exemplification of the marvelous facilities of modern journalism in the dark days of last December." A decade after Pulitzer had brought an American tribute to Gladstone, his own statesmanship was the subject of British praise.

"I'm deeply touched," Pulitzer told the gathered religious, social, and political leaders, "but am unfortunately an invalid and under a doctor's orders and I ask permission that my response be read by a young American friend—my son."

It thus fell to sixteen-year-old Ralph to read his father's long speech on the value of international arbitration. Pulitzer earnestly believed that war could almost always be avoided. He hated the saber rattling endemic in American political culture and had little taste for the bellicose rhetoric exemplified by men like Theodore Roosevelt. "Civilization is no more possible without peace than permanent peace is possible without arbitration," Ralph said, as he made his way through the thousands of words.

Yet an American war loomed as Ralph read his father's speech. In Cuba, an independence movement had gained such strength that the Spanish government dispatched 150,000 troops to put it down. The Cubans who resisted were being turned into heroes by the *World*, the *Journal*, and other newspapers.

Before returning to the United States, Pulitzer detoured to Wiesbaden, Germany, for a short stay at the Hotel Kaiserhof, adjacent to the Augusta Victoria baths. There, between Turkish baths and mud and hot sand treatments, Pulitzer gave more thought to his problems back in New York. "We must recognize the extraordinary competition, no doubt, but we must also recognize extraordinary foolishness, not imitate it," he wrote to Norris. Publishing a penny newspaper constrained the size of the paper but not its quality. "I regard it as more important to have the *best* paper than the biggest in size."

Unable to let his staff do their jobs without his constant interference, Pulitzer sent a stream of telegrams through the underwater Atlantic cable bearing instructions on topics ranging from the rate for help-wanted classifieds to changing the grade of paper used in certain editions. He instructed Brisbane to make the Sunday edition of interest to intelligent readers ("Make real popular magazine not a magazine of horrors"); reviewed the *World*'s printing capacity ("Shall we order six new color presses in order that we may meet the *Journal*?"); and pushed him to compete with the *Journal* for out-of-town readers ("if you are sure of your grounds and more particularly of the ground the *Journal* occupies").

By midsummer, Pulitzer was at Chatwold, readying himself for the fall's political battles. The Democrats were preparing for their convention in Chicago and the Republicans for theirs in St. Louis. Pulitzer faced a daunting political problem. Choosing whom to support in a national election remained both a political and an economic decision. Readers still regarded their selection of a newspaper as a political act. The wrong presidential choice could seriously damage the *World*, especially with Hearst's *Journal* nipping at its heels. When Pulitzer had made his bid for supremacy in New York in 1884, he had triumphed over Dana in great part because the *Sun* had abandoned the Democratic Party. The choice he made in the 1896 election posed similar risks for Pulitzer.

The strength of the silver movement caught the old guard of the Democratic Party, including Pulitzer, by surprise. "There is not the remotest shadow of a chance that free silver can ever become a reality in the United States," Pulitzer told a reporter in June. But when William Jennings Bryan spoke to the convention he lit a political prairie fire. Bellowing to the cheering delegates whose excitement rose with each phrase of inspired rhetoric, Bryan proclaimed the movement's answer to the defenders of the gold standard. "You shall not press down upon the brow of labor this crown of thorns, you shall not crucify mankind upon a cross of gold." Then, he stepped back, held his arms out and stood Christ-like before the hall. "The floor of the convention seemed to heave up," reported the *World*. "Everybody seemed to go mad at once."

Pulitzer summoned the *World*'s editorial writer George Eggleston to Bar Harbor. He had correctly predicted Bryan's nomination, unlike the other men covering the convention for the *World*. While Pulitzer and

Eggleston conferred, an emissary from Bryan's campaign arrived. Since only one Democrat had been elected to the White House in forty years, and then with the support of the *World*, such a political pilgrimage was mandatory.

Pulitzer instructed Eggleston to meet the representative. The man informed Eggleston that Bryan would win by a large majority with or without the support of the *World*. "For the sake of the press, and especially of so great a newspaper as the *World*, therefore, Mr. Bryan asked Mr. Pulitzer's attention to this danger to prestige." Nothing that could have been said was more likely to have a worse effect on Pulitzer.

When Eggleston delivered the message, Pulitzer laughed. As the two men sat on the small porch, Pulitzer asked him to jot down figures. The publisher rapidly named the states and the number of electoral votes that would go to Bryan. "I don't often predict—never unless I know," he said. His calculations predicted defeat. "Let that be our answer to Mr. Bryan's audacious message." Pulitzer's electoral math was uncannily correct. "Mr. Pulitzer correctly named every state that would give its electoral vote to each candidate, and the returns of the election—four months later—varies from his prediction by only two electoral votes out of four hundred and forty-seven."

But, in a larger sense, Pulitzer had misread the political tea leaves, for the first time in his life. He failed to grasp that free silver was not a public policy debate but a cry for help from the very people for whom he had built his paper.

Eggleston and Pulitzer crafted an unusually long editorial as the campaign season opened. The *World*, it said, sympathized with any candidate who stood against Wall Street's domination and for the creation of an income tax. But before the paper could throw its support to Bryan, it raised twenty ponderous objections to the more extreme elements in the party's platform—primarily those dealing with free silver. These policies, Pulitzer claimed, could destroy the economy. If Bryan disowned these planks, then he could win over the undecided voters.

"You can, if you will, decide a majority of them to vote their party's ticket," the editorial promised, "as they would very much prefer to do if they can be satisfied that it will be right and safe to do so. Will you not try to convince them?" But it was really Pulitzer who needed convincing. He strongly opposed McKinley's candidacy but could not bring himself to support Bryan. In hopes of resolving this quandary, he lured Creelman back to the paper to take on a special assignment. Creelman was to follow Bryan's campaign tour. But he was to write for two audiences: the *World's* readers and its publisher. Each day he sent long reports to Bar Harbor, where they were read to Pulitzer, who immediately dictated questions that were wired back. At the end of the campaign, although it had been Creelman who logged thousands of miles as Pulitzer's political eyes and ears, it was the boss who complained of exhaustion.

For his part, Hearst had no reservations in supporting Bryan. He published a free weekly campaign edition and covered the nominee's every move, speech, and utterance. His support was so unquestionable that the candidate himself sent a telegram on election eve to Hearst, thanking him for it.

Bryan went down to defeat but the *Journal* did not. Hearst had beaten Pulitzer at his own game. On the basis of his battle with the *Sun* in 1884, Pulitzer had anticipated that Bryan's defeat would be a crippling blow to the *Journal*, which had been the only major Park Row newspaper to support the insurgent Democrat in the decidedly anti-silver New York. But Pulitzer was wrong. Hearst's alliance with the Bryan campaign gave the *Journal* exactly what it needed. Its vigorous support for a champion of the underdog established the *Journal* as the city's brash newspaper for the masses and an entertaining jester of established politics while the *World* equivocated. In thirteen years, Pulitzer's *World* had gone from being the bad boy of Park Row to being a stodgy defender of the political establishment.

As he had done after other setbacks, Pulitzer reacted to this one by leaving New York. Taking his old friend and editor John Dillon with him, he sailed for the Riviera, leaving his family to celebrate Christmas without him. His first stop, Monte Carlo, proved to be a nightmare. The bells of ships in the harbor rang incessantly. Two decades earlier, he had defended a church in St. Louis that rang its bells at night. Now such tolling tormented him. Scrambling, his assistants located a more suitable refuge at Hotel Cap Martin on a peninsula to the east, bathed in sea air perfumed by tangerines, lemons, and orange groves.

The beauty of the setting did little to lighten Pulitzer's mood. "I have never seen him so steadily and persistently gloomy or in so deep a gloom," Alfred Butes, an English secretary who had joined Pulitzer's retinue, wrote to Kate back in New York. "His health is worse than at any time in years," Butes said. Pulitzer moped behind closed shutters, bored, and fretting about the children. "He needs more gaiety around him. And, unfortunately, that must always be accompanied by noise. Dear! Oh Dear! It's a big problem. And we haven't solved it yet."

Efforts to relieve Pulitzer's ills continued, though with a touch of the comic. Dr. Ernst Schweninger, famous for helping the hefty German chancellor Bismarck lose weight, was brought to the hotel for two days of treatments. To Pulitzer, the bearded, beady-eyed doctor looked like a wild anarchist and also seemed to act like one. "He says Mr. P. can be practically cured," Butes told Kate. "Probably could, I think, if he could survive the remedies which seem too almost drastic. I hear he laid Mr. P. down on the floor and knelt on his stomach! This is the latest, most scientific way of forcing a man to take a deep breath—and it is humorous too!"

Pulitzer gave up claret and cigars, but these New Year's resolutions were soon broken. "I am, in fact, kept busy from morning to night with massages and exercises," he reported to Kate. "But I have been so miserable yet in spite of, or perhaps, on account of this, I am more miserable in some respects (physical) than I have been in years." As soon as the Atlantic weather reports became encouraging, the party headed back to New York.

After years of wandering the globe, Pulitzer had become expendable. In fact, his original newspaper, the *Post-Dispatch,* functioned smoothly and successfully in the hands of seasoned editors and managers, with only the occasional counsel from its owner. But ceding control of his beloved *World* to others would be an admission of surrender to his blindness and infirmities. The *World* was his public identity. When other newspapers or politicians cited it, they always referred to it as "Pulitzer's *World.*" He could not give that up. It had been what he had worked to achieve, and the paper remained his greatest love.

Instead, Pulitzer continued to delegate broad, but overlapping, powers to an executive council of his top three or four men. No one man had dominion over the paper or even his own portion of the operation. A single telegram sent by Pulitzer from some distant city could reduce anyone's power in an instant. Every move his men made was second-guessed. The only certainty was that each man knew that the others were watching and reporting his every move to Pulitzer in an endless series of diaries read aloud by his secretaries. This gave the council an atmosphere of intrigue reminiscent of the Roman senate.

Compounding the council's woes was Pulitzer's constant vacillating over how much power to cede to his managers. One moment he would tell them to act on their own; the next minute he would micromanage even the smallest decision. For instance, Pulitzer became annoyed when he learned that one of his lieutenants had a sign saying "Editorial Manager" on his door. He sent detailed instruction to Seitz to inform the painting department that no such sign should be made without his explicit approval and to arrange for the offending sign to be removed. "But," he added quickly, "really do it early in the morning so that nobody will notice it."

As the day neared in January 1897 for Pulitzer's ship from Europe to reach New York, the *World*'s staff was put to work preparing written reports that could be read to him by those secretaries whose voices he preferred. Butes bluntly instructed Seitz on the boss's preferences. "He asks for this as conversation—especially conversations with you—has a headachy tendency and really does not furnish him with the same large number of facts which you can produce on paper." (Pulitzer also refused to eat with Seitz, because Seitz crunched his toast, smacked his lips, and talked with food in the mouth.)

Pulitzer stayed in New York only long enough to receive his many reports. He discovered that his lieutenants, especially Brisbane, whom he had put in charge of the Sunday flagship edition and all news coverage, had boosted the *World*'s circulation by descending into a sensationalist word-to-word combat with the *Journal*. Hearst had not only succeeded in gaining circulation but had also lured the *World* down into what many people in the city regarded as gutter journalism. The *World* had always had a sensationalistic streak, and the libel lawsuits to prove it. But in its desperate competition with Hearst the paper's baser tendencies were unrestrained.

What had been called "new journalism" was soon disparagingly renamed "Yellow," after Richard F. Outcault's comic strip. His "Hogan's Alley," published in the *World,* was one of the first Sunday color comics. It featured the immensely popular tenement adventures of the "Yellow Kid," an odd-looking child in a long yellow nightshirt. Hearst coveted it, as he did all the *World*'s other successes; and he lured Outcault away from Pulitzer. Since the *World* retained the rights to it, "Hogan's Alley" continued to appear, and both papers published Sunday comics featuring a yellow kid. These gave rise to the term "Yellow Journalism" to describe the antics of the *World* and the *Journal*.

Clubs and libraries around the city began to have doubts about permitting these newspapers in their reading rooms. The General Society of Mechanics and Tradesmen ordered that the *World* and *Journal* be removed from its reading rooms. "There can be no doubt that these two papers exercise a most demoralizing influence upon adults, and that they tend to corrupt the minds of the coming generation," a trustee of the society told a reporter from the *New York Times*, which gleefully printed his remarks. The Young Men's Christian Association Library in Brooklyn had avoided the *Journal*; now it dumped the *World*. "The paper brought into our rooms a very undesirable class of readers," said the librarian.

Pulitzer knew nothing of the boycott. "It has been carefully kept from his knowledge by his family and secretaries," recalled an employee at the *World*, "and upon his arrival in the golden dome he made many discoveries which should have revealed to him the weakness of his system of espionage and divided responsibilities, but it made him only more strenuous in keeping tabs on each one of his aides and stricter in requiring daily accounts of everything published in his paper."

Pulitzer now realized to his horror that Hearst's *Journal* threatened not only his financial success but the *World's* reputation and political power, which he valued above all. He directed his editors to focus their energy less on competing with the *Journal* and more on improving the character of the *World*. Recovering the respect and confidence of the public, he told them, would destroy "the notion that we are in the same class with the *Journal*, in recklessness and unreliability." He also instructed Seitz to dig deeper into Hearst's operation. "Please find somebody in *Journal* office with whom you can connect to discover who furnished their ideas, who is dissatisfied and obtainable or available even in the second class of executive ranks. We are getting shorter and shorter and need recruiting."

In a state of depression and panic, Pulitzer fled to Jekyll Island. His private Pullman train beat the one bearing J. P. Morgan to Brunswick, Georgia, by fifteen minutes. The Jekyll Club's management, sensitive to the animosity between the two tycoons, sent separate steamships to ferry them from Brunswick to the island. On Jekyll Island, Pulitzer inspected his newest purchase, a magnificent three-story wood-shingled cottage with rounded corners and large second-story porch.

After a month's rest, Pulitzer went to Washington, where he rented a mansion—Kate called it a mausoleum—from the widow of a Civil War general, who had preserved and kept on display all of her late husband's swords, uniforms, and other relics. Joseph sent for Seitz and began to hold court for Democrats, now once again as far removed from power as they had been before Cleveland's election in 1884.

Among those who came to see Pulitzer was the Democratic Party's standard-bearer. Despite his defeat, Bryan remained the most important figure in the party. Pulitzer had given orders to his staff to treat him kindly. But together in the same room, the two argued vigorously. When Bryan prepared to leave, Pulitzer asked to run his hands over Bryan's face. Bryan took Pulitzer's hands, with their long delicate fingers, into his and passed them over his jaw. "You see, Mr. Pulitzer, I am a fighter," said Bryan. In turn, Pulitzer took Bryan's hands and ran them over his bearded jaw and chin. "You see I am one, too," he said.

When Pulitzer reached Bar Harbor in early summer, he received good news. His long fight against Jones was over. In the two years since he had given Jones dominion over the *Post-Dispatch* in order to get him out of New York, the paper had became an embarrassing thorn in Pulitzer's side. Here he was waging an editorial war in the *World* against the Bryan tide and Jones had turned the *Post-Dispatch* into a proponent of free silver. As a result, Pulitzer looked like an opportunist who supported free silver where it was strong and opposed it where it was weak.

Almost as soon as Jones had arrived in St. Louis, Pulitzer had launched an internecine corporate war to rectify his blunder of giving Jones control of the *Post-Dispatch*. It spilled over into the courts and went all the way to the Missouri supreme court, which ruled that Jones's contract was ironclad. Pulitzer won a small victory, though, by paying for the lawsuit with profits Jones had generated at the *Post-Dispatch*.

Jones grew tired of his struggles with the obstinate publisher and sought terms of surrender. In June, Pulitzer agreed to pay Jones $100,000 to resign and return the stock he held. The agreement stipu-lated that no announcement of the change would be made. The paper, Pulitzer instructed, would make Jones's departure known only by its return to Pulitzer's editorial positions. "Don't want a word of national politics except against tariff, trusts, monopoly, plutocracy, corruption . . . not one word about Chicago platform and free silver this year."

With the Jones episode at an end and no elections of importance in sight, Pulitzer turned to his own personal wants. Even though he already owned a palace in Maine, with its "tower of silence"; a house on Fifty-Fifth Street in New York; and a hideaway on Jekyll Island, Pulitzer suddenly had a hankering to acquire William Rockefeller's Rockwood Hall, on the Hudson River. Rockefeller's public complaint about the taxes on this estate gave the impression he might sell it. Pulitzer sent Dillon and Seitz, who were well used to running personal errands for their boss, to investigate—under strict instructions of secrecy, especially about whom they represented. The men telegraphed Pulitzer a full report on the house, furniture, riding trails, and cost of maintaining the grounds, and even on whether trains could be heard from inside the house. In the end, though, the secret mission was a waste of time. As a phone call might have determined, Rockefeller had no interest in selling Rockwood.

Investing in the Rockefeller mansion would have been fiscal folly that wiser heads would have counseled Pulitzer to abandon anyway. Aside from Dumont Clarke, who managed his personal fortune, Pulitzer trusted J. Angus Shaw, who watched over the finances of the *World*. The news from Shaw was terrifying. The nearly $1 million income that Pulitzer had drawn from the *World* each year had fallen to less than $350,000. Pulitzer ordered budget cuts and payroll reductions. But he knew that he could not economize his way out of the financial free fall the *World* had taken since Hearst's arrival in New York. Unless he, or his editors, came up with a solution, Pulitzer's fate would be like that of Dana and the *Sun* in 1884. The *World* would recede into history as an interesting episode in American journalism.

No one was exempt from the reductions—not even Kate, who did not take kindly to the idea. Several years before, she and Joseph had worked out an agreement that she was to receive $6,000 a month to run the household and to cover her personal expenses and those of the children. But Kate continued to accumulate debts in Europe and New York. She told Butes the bills had to be paid. "I count, as I always do, upon you," she wrote, "to make things as little disagreeable as possible.

"Money is such a contemptible thing to so constantly fight about," Kate told Butes, whom she had come to treat as a confidant. "I do not ask it for myself for I can do without money, the things I should love to do—the charities, the enumerable helpful things I could do for the openly poor and for the poor too proud and too well born to make their wants known. This is one of my crosses."

In August 1897, Kate and Joseph were with their children at Chatwold in Maine. It was a rare moment of togetherness for the family, which had spread itself across two continents. Though Joseph and Kate often bickered about money, Kate had reconciled herself to her marriage. She had terminated her amorous relationship with Brisbane the previous year. "Separate you from me, if you think you must for your own peace of mind," Brisbane wrote upon receiving Kate's Dear John letter. "I am what I am, and I think you have seen and known the best of me.

"You know that I admire you, and you know my other feelings. I do not write freely about such things, even on an anonymous machine," Brisbane typed. Yet, he offered a frank assessment of their differences. "I know first of all that no living man could ever satisfy you—and no dead one for that matter," he wrote. "As regards my feeling—change in my regard for you, etc.—you are entirely wrong. When you have urged me to make promises as to what I would or would not do, I have always told you that I could not make promises, and I think I have been more frank and truthful than many men would be—if they felt the anxiety I feel to have your good opinion."

In the fall of 1897, Brisbane and Joseph broke up also. Brisbane yearned to write a column, with a byline, in the *Evening World*, over which Pulitzer had given him dominion. However, Pulitzer was unbending in his prohibition of signed editorial columns. Brisbane went ahead with his plan anyway. An angry Pulitzer suspended him. It was hardly a punishing move, now that the *Journal*'s doors were open to any disgruntled editor from the *World*.

Hearst offered to put Brisbane in charge of the *Evening Journal* and to give him a high enough salary to repay the $8,000 in advances he had taken from Pulitzer, with the promise of a bonus for a circulation increase. Brisbane would remain with Hearst for thirty-nine years and would become the nation's highest-paid editor and one of its best-read columnists.

The social season at Bar Harbor was in full swing. "August follows in the wake of July with an array of brilliant events that must almost turn the summer girl's head," said one giddy society columnist. The Pulitzers joined in by giving Lucille a lavish coming-out party. Joseph, who continually complained about Kate's extravagances, agreed to spend $10,000 on the event. Chatwold "was transformed into a fairyland," according to one newspaper in Maine. More than 120 guests attended, most leaving with party favors—canaries in cages.

Lucille made a classic debutante. She had Kate's abundant brown hair, sought-after porcelain skin, and her father's deep-set eyes, which conveyed an air of melancholy. "She was a most beautiful young girl, spiritual of face and distinguished in manner and with talents seldom equaled by a society girl of the Bar Harbor colony," said one observer. Of all his children, Lucille was the one who had not disappointed Joseph. She was most like him and the most willing to follow his social proscriptions and educational prescriptions. In comparison with her sisters, she took little interest in society and instead applied herself to her studies, learning to speak half a dozen languages, play musical instruments, and draw.

Not long after the lavish soiree, Lucille developed a fever and complained of other ailments. Doctors diagnosed typhoid fever, which she had probably contracted from contaminated food or water. Cables summoned more doctors, including many of the physicians who had attended Pulitzer in New York and Europe. Nurses were assigned to Lucille's care twenty-four hours a day. Using steam and electricity, the house was heated and moistened like a tropical greenhouse. Despite everyone's best efforts, the disease took its brutal course.

In October there was some improvement in the girl's health. "Thank God," Pulitzer wrote to his friend Tom Davidson, "Lucille is better and we are again hopeful of her convalescence." Merrill told Brisbane the good news. "I am sure you know that I am very glad of that," Brisbane wrote to Kate, "very glad for Lucille's own sake and very glad to think that you are free from worry." It was a false hope. The patient's condition worsened again, and by December there was little optimism in the house. "Poor Lucille is still very ill and I need not tell you that I have been worried almost to death," Pulitzer wrote to Davidson. "I have a frightful headache and am sick at heart and all broken up by Lucille's grave condition."

As the winter holidays neared, Lucille rallied. She had made sure that each family member had a present. The Pulitzers spent Christmas

Day together in her bedroom, joined by some of the household help to whom she was attached. Joseph, feeling more confident about Lucille's condition, made plans to move on to Jekyll Island after New Year's and sent his horse and a dozen servants ahead. Lucille's improvement, however, was a final, cruel deception. With both parents, and her brothers and sisters, by her side, Lucille died six days later, at four o'clock on New Year's Eve.

It was left to Butes to inform the *World*. "Grieved to tell you poor Lucille just died," he telegraphed Norris. "Chief much broken. Send him no business."

Chapter Twenty-Four

YELLOW

———————————————◆———————————————

In the early morning of January 2, 1898, a private train lumbered from the railyard in Bangor, Maine, and headed south to pick up the Pulitzers at the Mount Desert ferry. The family had already held Lucille's funeral service at Chatwold, and all that remained now was to accompany her body home to New York. Two days later, on a cold morning, they gathered before a plot at Woodlawn Cemetery in the Bronx that had been purchased fourteen years earlier for Lucille's baby sister Katherine. Reverend William Stephen Rainsford, the rector of the tony St. George's Church, read from the Book of Common Prayer as fine snow swirled in the breezes and thousands celebrated the early opening of the skating season in the adjacent Van Cortlandt Park.

This was the second time the Pulitzers had buried a child. For Joseph, the ritual was a sorrowful return to his own childhood, when he saw all but one of his eight siblings go to the grave. Now, he was staggered by the loss of Lucille. For years afterward, Pulitzer looked for ways to commemorate her life. At first, he settled on establishing a perpetual Lucille Pulitzer Scholarship at Barnard College. In the end, he quietly dedicated one of his two most famous legacies to her. Only the inscription in the floor of the marble foyer of the Columbia University Journalism College reveals that the famous school was built in the "memory of my daughter Lucille."

In death as in sickness, Lucille had brought Joseph, Kate, and the children together in a single place at a single time.

The moment didn't last long. Joseph left immediately for Jekyll Island with two of the children. Kate returned to the house on Fifty-Fifth

Street and to the care of her physician. She remained indoors for a month until her doctor convinced her that a trip would be beneficial. She enlisted her much-favored cousin Winnie Davis, who, never having married her Yankee beau, had come to spend increasing time in Kate's company. Together, with Ralph, on leave from Harvard, they departed for a sightseeing journey in Egypt.

Meanwhile, Joseph remained in deep seclusion on Jekyll Island, with his faithful Dr. Hosmer, Butes, and a few aides for company. In a tender moment, he sent Kate an unusually warm message that included no reproaches. "Darling," she wrote back, "your telegram gave me great pleasure as any word of tenderness from you always does." Knowing that her communication would be read aloud, she continued, "Dr. Hosmer must hide his blushes now—I slept with it under my pillow. I think I forget I am an old married woman with five great children."

The warmth between the two dissipated as Joseph's mood once again turned dark and frantic. He wanted Ralph to be working at the paper in New York rather than traipsing through Egypt with Kate. He became obsessed with this idea and didn't trust his secretaries to forward his orders. "He took the cable to the office himself as he evidently suspected Butes might not send it," Hosmer wrote to Kate. "The sudden change followed an attack of indigestion after two hours of work in his usual overwhelming style."

Five hundred miles due south from Jekyll Island, on the moonless night of February 15, 1898, Lieutenant John Hood took a seat on the port side of the battleship *Maine*, anchored in Havana Bay. As chief watch officer, Hood had the duty of keeping vigil. His charge, the largest ship in the harbor, was the white-hulled *Maine*.* President McKinley had directed it to Havana two weeks earlier in a high-wire act of diplomatic and symbolic gestures aimed at placating the growing ranks of American supporters of Cuban independence while at the same time averting war with Spain.

Hood hoisted his feet onto the rail and looked across the harbor at the lights of the city twinkling on the calm water's surface. In a flash, his reverie was shattered by an explosion coming from the front of the vessel. The massive ship lurched upward and was engulfed in flames.

---

*It was then customary for the U.S. Navy to paint its ships white during peacetime.

The harbor was illuminated by a brilliant white light. The repercussion burst windows and caused late-night strollers to dash for cover. Two of the *World*'s correspondents ran to the harbor. Gazing across the water, they saw the *Maine* burning, its sinking hull lit by an exploding shell from the battleship's magazine. As it went off in the sky above, two ships circled below in search of survivors. There were fewer than ninety. Two-hundred-sixty-six men had died.

Later that night, the Associated Press bulletin of the disaster broke the predawn calm in the *World*'s city room in New York, where editors had just put the early editions to bed. The AP dispatch was soon followed by that of the paper's correspondents on the scene in Havana. Among those who got the news from the early edition of the *World* as it hit the streets was Arthur Brisbane, who by then had joined Carvalho and other *World* refugees at the *Journal*.

His boss already knew. An early-morning telephone call from the office had awakened Hearst.

"Have you put anything else on the front page?" Hearst asked the editor who called.

"Only the other big news," he replied.

"There is not any other big news. Please spread the story all over the page. This means war."

Within twenty-four hours, the *Journal* was blaming the Spaniards for the destruction of the *Maine* and the loss of life. DESTRUCTION OF THE WAR SHIP *MAINE* WAS THE WORK OF AN ENEMY . . . NAVAL OFFICIALS THINK *MAINE* WAS DESTROYED BY A SPANISH MINE, screamed its front page, above a drawing showing a Spanish mine. The *World* began its coverage in a more circumspect fashion. *MAINE* EXPLOSION CAUSED BY BOMB OR TORPEDO? asked its headline, above its illustration of the ship exploding. But soon, its editors sounded as shrill as Hearst's: WORLD'S LATEST DISCOVERIES INDICATE *MAINE* WAS BLOWN UP BY SUBMARINE MINE.

President McKinley begged the public to be patient while experts worked to determine the cause of the explosion. In the din, no one heard his pleas, especially on Park Row where the disaster released a pent-up war fever. The Cuban struggle, a dramatic and poignant fight for liberty so close to the American coast, was a story made for the newspapers. During the past two years, the *World* and the *Journal* had exploited every angle of the rebellion. It made for great reading, especially as the papers enlisted such writers as Stephen Crane and Richard Harding Davis. At times, the newspapers made their own news. The *Journal*, for instance, helped engineer the escape of an eighteen-year-old Spanish prisoner, described as Cuba's Joan of Arc, and brought her to New York.

All journalistic conventions were thrown aside. It was almost as if the pages were not wide enough to accommodate either the headlines or the incendiary drawings. From the start, Hearst rode at the head of the pack clamoring for war. He led his reporters like troops into battle, dispatching artists and reporters by the dozen to Cuba, engaging yachts to ferry politicians to the island, offering rewards to anyone who could prove how the Spanish had blown up the *Maine*, and hammering the president for resisting the call to war. Every day the *Journal* outdid the *World* in size, scope, and drama, and often in readers. The *Journal* became the first American newspaper to circulate more than 1 million copies of its morning and evening editions, a goal Pulitzer had long sought for the *World*.

There was an atmosphere of desperation under the gold dome of the Pulitzer Building as the publisher remained secluded on Jekyll Island, grieving over Lucille's death. The staff, from the editors at the top to the reporters on the beat, consisted of men and women whose loyalty ran so deep they had chosen to cast their lot with Pulitzer rather than Hearst. They were willing to do anything for their absent general, and not out of loyalty alone. Everyone knew that Pulitzer was pouring his own money into the paper to make up for the losses induced by Hearst. For those who remained at the *World*, losing to Hearst could mean the end to their careers.

The staff struggled to match the *Journal,* but lacked the resources to compete effectively with Hearst. Unhappy at the prospect of subsidizing his money-losing papers, Pulitzer had ordered widespread budget cuts before the excitement over the *Maine*. To pay for the *World's* new Hoe color presses, Pulitzer had to sell stock. He even ordered an audit of Kate's spending. It found only a $20 discrepancy among the 2,472 checks written the prior year to cover her $77,000 in expenses.

The epic battle did not pit Hearst against Pulitzer. Rather, it was Hearst against Pulitzer's leaderless troops in a helter-skelter twenty-four-hour-a-day competition. "An epoch of delirious journalism began the like of which newspaper readers had never known," said Charles

Chapin, who was beginning his tenure as one of Pulitzer's most famous city editors. Unable to match Hearst's corps of correspondents in Cuba, the *World* took to pilfering stories from the *Journal* to fill out its coverage, a sin with which the *Journal* was not entirely unacquainted.

No more stinging trap could have been laid than the one the *Journal* concocted for its rival. It was the same ruse Pulitzer had used to trick the *Star* when he was in St. Louis. The *Journal* printed a phony report about the heroics of a "Colonel Reflipe W. Thenuz," who was fatally wounded. After the *World* published its account of the good colonel's deeds, lifted entirely from the *Journal*, Hearst's headquarters gleefully announced that the colonel's name was an anagram that spelled "We pilfer the news."

In April, when Pulitzer returned to New York, he surveyed a wreck. The *World* was losing its battle with Hearst, and losing badly. The newspaper that had once set the news agenda for the city, and sometimes for the nation, was engaged in a futile game of catch-up. "It has been beaten on its own dunghill by the *Journal*, which has bigger type, bigger pictures, bigger war scares, and a bigger bluff," *Town Topics* gleefully reported. "If Mr. Pulitzer had his eyesight he would not be content to play second fiddle to the *Journal* and allow Mr. Hearst to set the tone."

From the command post of his house, Joseph again tried to fix what ailed the *World*. Ralph was also back in the city, having jumped on the first available ship in Cairo after receiving his father's recall order. He was bewildered and filled with anxiety about his father's command, but Joseph hardly noticed his arrival. "Mr. P. is solidly absorbed in the paper and the war times just now," Pulitzer's man George Ledlie reported to Kate, "and though I am forbidden to say so—looks and seems very well."

Trying once more to rearrange the hierarchy in his paper, Pulitzer decided that the triumvirate, which he called "the sacred college," was a failure. The *World* needed a captain, one among the men who would have more power than the others. He turned to Bradford Merrill, whom he had recruited from the *New York Press* two years earlier. Merrill was summoned to the house.

"You are to have general supervision over all editions of the *World*, subject only to my own instructions and that of the board of managers, of which you are a member," Pulitzer told him. "I want things done, and I don't want time wasted on consultations. I want men in charge to act, not wait for someone else."

Pulitzer was eager to put the brakes on the paper's outlandish journalistic practices. Under Merrill, each edition was to have one editor in charge. "But," said Pulitzer firmly, "this does not relieve you of your duty of reading the papers every day, criticizing, complaining, stopping bad tendencies, killing bad schemes, vetoing sensationalism, suggesting, proposing, curbing, stimulating."

Confident that Merrill would keep the staff in check, Pulitzer turned to the question of the day: should the United States go to war? There was no doubt that the *Journal* was champing at the bit for war. The *Sun* said war could not come soon enough. Almost every major metropolitan newspaper favored either war or the threat of one if Spain did not comply with American demands.

Pulitzer joined the chorus. But to do so he had to support war only as a last resort, in order not to contradict his support of international arbitration three years earlier during the Venezuelan crisis. He had not renounced the idea. Only the year before, he had instructed Seitz to publish a pamphlet on arbitration and send it to every member of the Senate "with compliments of the *World*."

"If we are on the brink of a conflict it is due to the deliberate policy of Spain—not to a desire for war by our people, by our President, or by our Congress. If Spain were to yield, even now, peace would be assured," Pulitzer began his signed editorial that appeared on his fifty-first birthday. "God forbid that the *World* should ever advocate an unnecessary war!" But, listing instigations ranging from the years of Spanish oppression in Cuba to the destruction of the *Maine,* he said the time had come for military intervention. "No lover of peace, no lover of justice, no lover of his country ought to hesitate in urging the government to strike one swift and decisive blow, now that the conflict is made inevitable by the mad folly of Spain."

The war would be short and thus merciful, Pulitzer concluded. The government ought to send the fleet to Cuba and Puerto Rico, where it would easily overcome the Spanish. "With these islands captured the affair will be over—and Cuba free. It would hardly be a war, but it would be magnificent."

On April 19, 1898, Congress gave President McKinley authority to use force against Spain. Three weeks later, Commodore George Dewey sailed his squadron into Manila Bay in the Philippines and in six hours overwhelmed the Spanish ships in the harbor. By then, Pulitzer was already miles from New York.

Upon completing his pro-war editorial, he left for England on the *Majestic*. Ledlie raised Kate's hopes that Joseph had overcome the grief he had felt on Jekyll Island and "that you will be greeted on the other side by a reasonable gentleman who I think begins to be anxious to get over where you are." It was a wishful prognosis. Joseph remained unsettled by Lucille's death and distracted by the mortal combat facing his cherished *World*. He wandered aimlessly in England and France for several weeks. His somber mood was not even lightened when he saw Kate and his youngest daughter in Aix-les-Bains. "When are we going to see you again?" Constance wrote plaintively after her father departed without leaving a word.

On his return to the United States, Pulitzer could not bring himself to open Chatwold for the summer so soon after Lucille's slow death there. Compounding his anguish were an Atlantic crossing marred by asthma attacks and a discouraging consultation with his eye doctor upon reaching New York. Instead, Pulitzer engaged a mansion at Narragansett Pier, Rhode Island, on a sea bluff overlooking a beach where he walked each day in the company of one of his men.

The "*Journal*'s war," as Hearst called it, or the "splendid little war," as a friend writing to Theodore Roosevelt described it, was a romp. Hundreds of thousands had volunteered for duty. Roosevelt gave up his post as assistant secretary of the navy to become a colonel of the U.S First Volunteer Cavalry, bound for Cuba. He sent a telegram to Brooks Brothers in New York to make him a uniform of blue cravenette. On the island, he led a regiment of Rough Riders in his famous charge up San Juan Hill. One of the most media-savvy politicians of the era, Roosevelt had made sure the press was along for the ride.

By the war's end in August, both the *Journal* and the *World* had achieved record heights of circulation but were drowning in an ocean of red ink. Pulitzer had no mother with profitable copper mines to pay for his deficits. The *World*'s executives were summoned to Narragansett. The pressure was on to cut expenses. Pulitzer punishingly lectured the business manager, John Norris, for excessive spending, at one point pinning him against a railing on the boardwalk.

Also coming to Narragansett were Winnie Davis, now thirty-three years old, and her mother, Varina, who took up quarters in its fashionable resort hotel. Since returning from her trip to Egypt with Kate, Winnie had basked in her new fame as a writer. Her new novel, set in a summer house at Bar Harbor, was earning praise, and she remained the darling of the South. Only a few days before arriving in Rhode Island, Confederate veterans attending their annual reunion in Atlanta had thrown their hats into the air when she entered the hall to a general's proclamation of "Comrades, behold our daughter!"

The trip through the South, however, was too taxing for Winnie, whose health was fragile. After riding in an open carriage through a heavy summertime Atlanta rain, she fell ill. Upon reaching Narragansett, she was confined to her hotel room. At first the gastritis from which the doctors concluded she suffered seemed like a surmountable problem, but as the days wore on she continued to decline. In early September, the Rockingham Hotel closed for the season but permitted her to remain in her room. A short time later, the Pulitzer home once again was in turmoil as a young woman died.

On September 21, 1898, dressed in white muslin with white satin trim, Davis lay in a casket in the hotel lobby. The following day an escort of Union veterans escorted the coffin carrying the "daughter of the confederacy" to the train station, where Kate Pulitzer and others joined it for the journey to Richmond. Thousands waited there for the funeral. Pulitzer, who still avoided funerals whenever he could, left for Europe, taking with him David Graham Phillips, his favorite at the paper, who was now working as an editorial writer and whom he continued to groom for bigger things. Their stay in London and Paris was short, and by the end of the month they were back in New York.

The *World* was desperate for Pulitzer's attention. It clung to a tenuous lead over the *Journal*. Before the war, the average combined daily and Sunday circulation of the *World* had been 419,000, to the *Journal's* 270,000. Since then, the *World* had lost more than 78,000 readers while the *Journal* had gained 46,000. "The circulation comparisons are menacing," Norris wrote to Pulitzer in a lengthy appraisal of the competitors' positions. On the advertising side, the situation was equally dire.

Norris, along with Seitz, worked assiduously to deduce Hearst's income. They estimated that Hearst had spent $4 million in his first three years and that he had access to another $5 million. The *Journal's* circulation revenue was easy to compute. But it took rulers to measure the advertising space and rate cards to calculate the revenue from advertising. They determined that the *Journal* was earning less than half of what the *World* took in. But the *Journal* was coming on strong. A buoyant Hearst predicted that his paper would be profitable in 1899. More ominous for Pulitzer was that Hearst's success could not entirely account for the decline of his own paper. The *World*'s decreases in circulation and advertising revenue exceeded the *Journal*'s gains. As Seitz succinctly put it to Pulitzer, "The *World* has lost more than the *Journal* has taken from it."

Fighting the *Journal* for readers on its terms had proved financially disastrous. The *World* was outmatched in every attempt to be more yellow than Hearst's editors and reporters. In the end, the effort left Pulitzer's reputation in tatters and his name inextricably linked to Hearst's. With the war—the main excuse for the excesses—at an end, Pulitzer decided that the time had come to try to restore some sanity to the *World*.

At eleven in the morning on November 28, 1898, the *World*'s reporters from all shifts and beats gathered in the city room under the gold dome. From the windows, they could look beyond the East River, across to Brooklyn, and out to sea. All of Manhattan was at their feet, giving reporters who watched over the city day and night a cocky sense of power. On this day, one could hardly see across the room. Though it stretched out 100 feet or more, there was not much space for this large a group. The place was already crammed with typewriter-topped desks of antique ash, standing back to back, side to side, creating a maze of aisles. Pasted on the walls and columns were large printed cards that read: "Accuracy, Accuracy!" "Who? What? When? How?" and "The Facts—the Color—the Facts."

The typewriters were still and the copy boys quiet as the men and women turned toward a platform at the end of the room, normally the city editor's perch, where Seitz; Merrill; William Van Benthuysen, the Sunday editor; and other managers stood. Never before had the reporters seen a meeting like this one. Each man took a turn speaking about the excesses of the past two years, confessing his own failings as if at an addiction meeting. "The great mistakes which have been made—I speak with modesty, because I have made a number of them myself—have been caused by an excess of zeal," said Merrill.

"There is and has been for two years, as you know, a fierce competition," Seitz told the group. "This has developed a tendency to rush things. It has not been to the advantage of any newspaper so doing. The *World* feels that it is time for the staff to learn definitely and finally that it must be a normal newspaper."

"Sensational? Yes, when the news is sensational," added Van Benthuysen. "But the demand is this, that every story which is sensational in itself must also be truthful."

In St. Louis, Pulitzer's old competitor Charles Knapp, who published the *Missouri Republican*, now renamed the *Republic*, decided to make a bid to dominate the city's newspaper market. Ever since Pulitzer had left the city, Knapp had longed for a chance to merge with the *Post-Dispatch* as his competitor, the *Missouri Democrat*, had done with the *Globe*. At first, Pulitzer had been uninterested in selling his paper. But Knapp figured that the well-known headaches arising from Jones's tenure at the *Post-Dispatch* and the losses incurred by the *World* might have changed Pulitzer's mind. His initial contact confirmed his hunch, and Knapp left for the East.

Pulitzer assigned the business manager, Norris, to meet with Knapp in Washington. After days of discussion, with some sessions lasting eleven hours, they had made little headway. Pulitzer was no help. He sent Norris new demands each time the two negotiators made any progress. Pulitzer was of two minds. He said he was not averse to disposing of the *Post-Dispatch*, but he couldn't go through with it when he was faced with the reality of such a proposition. Pulitzer sent Norris bewildering instructions. "You should drop it and not waste your time but concentrate on the *World* which needs you badly enough. But if Knapp should come back with something reasonable, you will communicate it. In fact, you will communicate to me anyhow what he says."

With Pulitzer blowing hot and cold, Knapp made a final effort. He went to Jekyll Island to meet Pulitzer directly. His timing was poor. Pulitzer was in a testy mood from frayed nerves and sleeplessness. A morning together and a lunch brought the two men no closer to an agreement than before. Knapp gave up and left.

Kate was also buffeted by Joseph's stormy temper. She made the mistake of writing him about a problem in New York involving a household servant. "Mr. P. wishes not to be bothered on this matter any further," Butes wrote back. "He read eight letters on the subject yesterday besides your own—which is an outrageous waste of time.

"He is sorry you have not been able to come down here," Butes continued. "And he asked you will *not telegraph* him as the expectation of telegrams keeps him in a very nervous condition. It is especially desirable that he should not get messages about sickness in the family unless really serious. They depress him and, of course, are unnecessary as he can be of no possible help."

By May 1899, when Pulitzer left for England in the company of his old partner Dillon and his son Ralph, he was in better spirits. A greater sense of calm had been restored at the *World,* and fiscally its house was being put in order. Although its circulation had dropped to prewar levels, so had its expenditures. It remained the best place in New York to advertise and the revenue now produced a profit rather than paying for far-flung war coverage, excessive press runs, and outlandish circulation campaigns.

Pulitzer told his staff to send no cables for a month, unless they were "supremely important." In Kensington he leased a different manor from the last one, and was sorely disappointed. "The barracks next door are just about as bad as they could possibly be, bugles at night, in the morning at six, there are four clocks or chimes, and peacocks in the neighborhood, all conspiring to spoil my much-needed repose."

In Britain, Pulitzer tested out several new secretarial candidates. The search for suitable companions remained an unsolvable problem for his aides. Pulitzer was impossible to please. Guests found being with him hard enough—they had to put up with his strictures against slurping soup or crunching on toast—but those who worked directly for him endured intolerable demands. One candidate, who quit after two weeks, told Pulitzer that one result of his having spent so many years bossing people was that he no longer knew how to relate to others. "You have therefore become so used to command that any other position with regard to those always with you became impossible to you.

"You must forgive me a further observation. Like all very successful men you have a degree of contempt for those whose lives have been to some extent failures," continued the very frank candidate. "You cannot help letting them feel that you regard them, through being in the necessity of taking such a position, an inferiority in life."

Pulitzer headed back to the United States without the hoped-for addition to his private staff. With the *World* past its crisis, he was eager to indulge his passion for presidential elections. Before sailing, Pulitzer told the British press that Bryan was likely to be the Democratic nominee in 1900 and hinted that the *World* might support his candidacy this time around. "That all depends upon his good sense or folly," said Pulitzer. If Bryan was willing to drop his support of free silver, he would have a united party behind him, Pulitzer predicted. If he refused, he would lose.

That summer Pulitzer reopened Chatwold, which had been unoccupied for more than a year and a half. His return to his hideaway in Maine was marred by his dissatisfaction with the remodeling of the "tower of silence." When he inspected his study he found that it was still not soundproof, and the lighting proved inadequate. The builder wanted $108,000, 250 percent more than the initial estimate. Pulitzer refused to pay the bill.

His house in New York also created unexpected expenses. The city's fire marshal warned Pulitzer that unless he made some alterations, the house's current condition might prove disastrous. He reminded Pulitzer that two fires had already occurred because of defective flues. Pulitzer, who had survived the deadly fire at the Southern Hotel in St. Louis, was not one to argue. He fixed the flues, constructed an enclosed fire escape in the rear of the building, repaired the electric lights, and installed a fire alarm in his valet's room.

Kate joined Joseph in Maine only briefly, preferring instead to divide her time between New York and Hot Springs, Virginia. Joseph's intolerant behavior had not abated since his grief-filled stay on Jekyll Island, and her patience with him was at a low point. It didn't help, either, that Joseph had instructed his cashier to cut $160 from her $6,000 monthly allowance, for customs duty he had paid on her behalf. Angus Shaw, the *World*'s cashier, who was used to being in the financial crossfire between the couple, warned her, "I suppose you will understand it, but I thought it best to let you know in case of any misunderstanding."

The relationship was getting back to normal.

Chapter Twenty-Five

THE GREAT GOD SUCCESS

O ne icy night in February 1891, firefighters responding to a call from the New York post office were told that cries could be heard coming from one of the ventilation shafts on the sidewalk. The tin vents led from an underground engine room where the fire was raging, and flames were coming up through them. When the firefighters toppled the vent, a thirteen-year-old boy scrambled out, mostly unhurt. Told that his friend was still inside, the rescuers saw what appeared to be a bundle of burning rags. They reached in and pulled out a seventeen-year-old newsboy, John Gardarino, his clothes on fire.

Gardarino was one of thousands of children on whose work the fortunes of Pulitzer and other newspaper barons rested. In cold or heat, in rain or shine, these boys stood on street corners; in front of theaters, restaurants, and clubs; in train stations; and on the docks hawking Park Row's newspapers. In the end, for all their high-speed color presses, telegraph lines connecting all points on the globe, and other technological marvels, the newspapers needed this army of street urchins to reach their readers.

The injured teenager had made the fatal mistake of curling up in the ventilation shaft for the night. He could not face his family, in a Crosby Street tenement, because he had failed to sell all his newspapers that day—or perhaps had gambled away his earnings in a crap game. Because of his shame, he lay dying in a New York hospital.

Newsies, as boys like Gardarino were called, played a particularly prominent role in the cutthroat competition between Pulitzer's *Evening World* and Hearst's *Evening Journal*. Despite their names, these editions began publishing in the morning and continued all day. When the news merited "extras," they might be on the streets every hour of the day and late into the night, numbered in bewildering fashion, and even printed on paper of different colors in order to gain a competitive edge. On any street corner, a New Yorker with a penny could buy a newspaper with news as fresh as the ink.

Since most copies of the evening papers were sold on the street, rather than delivered to homes like the morning paper, their sales depended greatly on a partnership between the headline writers and the newsies—almost like that of a playwright and an actor. The editors would craft an oversize attention-grabbing headline, and the newsies would work the street by calling it out. The right kind of headline—TINY TOT WITH PENNY CLUTCHED IN CHUBBY HAND DIES UNDER TRAM BEFORE MOTHER'S EYES—could clean out an entire run of the paper.

The Spanish-American War had been a boon for newsboys. They sold every copy of the *World* or *Journal* they could carry, even when the papers increased their press runs. Inside the Pulitzer building, however, the *World*'s managers desperately sought ways to comply with the publisher's order to stem its deficit. Raising its price was out of the question, because that would be a signal of defeat in the struggle against Hearst. Cutting salaries was also out of the question. Reporters would jump to the *Journal*, and the unionized compositors and printers were untouchable.

The newsies became the target of choice. The *World* raised the wholesale price of the paper from 50 cents per 100 to 60 cents. The *Journal* also raised its wholesale price, but all the other newspapers did not. Trimming a dime from a newsboy's take might not seem like much. But when this amount was spread over the paper's vast circulation, it could make up an entire annual deficit of nearly $1 million. Pulitzer's managers bet that the ragtag collection of immigrant children, who often didn't even speak the same language, could hardly put up much resistance.

They were wrong.

At first, the newsies tolerated the price increase. Selling sixty papers was easy during the wartime excitement. But in 1899, when newspaper sales decreased at the end of hostilities, the newsies grew anxious. Each day as they lined up on Park Row to get their bundles, the decision of how many papers to purchase weighed on their minds. Buy too few and miss out on profitable sales; buy too many and lose money.

The newsies demanded that the *World* and the *Journal* return to their prewar wholesale price, the same as other newspapers charged. Pulitzer and Hearst refused. On July 18, 1899, a delivery driver for the *World* in Long Island City stuffed his bundles with free sample copies of the paper and sold them to unsuspecting newsboys. When they figured out what had happened, they demanded their money back. He refused, and the boys tipped his wagon over and ran him off. Word of their action spread and soon all the newsies were on strike. Within a day, customers looking for their afternoon paper found newsboys without newspapers and signs pinned to their jackets such as "Please don't buy the *Evening Journal* and *World*, because the newboys has striked" or "I ain't a scab."

The strike exacted an immediate toll on the evening papers. "You could walk a mile without seeing one," one correspondent wrote home. Pulitzer got word of the strike just as he arrived in Bar Harbor after months in Europe. "Practically all the boys in New York and in many of the adjacent towns have quit selling," Seitz told his boss. "A call is out for a mass meeting of the boys in front of the Pulitzer Building and we have just been compelled to ask the police for assistance in the matter." The other newspapers were of no help. Except for the *Journal*, they were not targets of the boys' strike and were jubilantly running editorials in support of it.

But enemies with a common foe can find ground for cooperation. Two days after the newsboys began their action, Hearst's business manager Solomon Carvalho and Seitz got together. "I have just been over to see Carvalho in a long conference in the matter," Seitz told Pulitzer. "We have determined to hire as many men as possible Monday to man selling points in sufficient force to overwhelm any assault that could be made upon them and to force a representation of the paper on the streets."

Advertisers abandoned the papers in droves and demanded refunds as the circulation of the *Evening Journal* and the *Evening World* collapsed. "It is really a very extraordinary demonstration," Seitz told Pulitzer. "The people seem to be against us; they are encouraging the boys and tipping them and where they are not doing this, they are refraining from buying the papers for fear of having them snatched from their hands."

Using homeless men whom Seitz had recruited, many under protection of the police, the evening editions of the *Journal* and *World* returned to the streets on Monday and managed to remain for several days, but with far reduced sales. "Our policy of putting men out was not helpful," Seitz admitted to Pulitzer, "yet it was the only thing that could be done. We had to have representation and the absolute disappearance of the paper was appalling."

As the strike continued, Seitz kept Pulitzer informed at all times of the paper's hard-line policy, including the use of police to break up gatherings of the children. When they could, the boys attacked scabs, although, in a chivalrous gesture, they stayed clear of a few newsstands run by women. They did their best to continue their strike. "Ain't that ten cents worth as much as it is to Hearst and Pulitzer who are millionaires," Kid Blink, one of their leaders, told the thousands of newsies who came to a rally. But problems soon emerged. Blink was chased by strikers who thought he had been bought off when they spotted him near Park Row wearing new clothes and carrying a roll of bills. Other leaders were similarly accused of accepting bribes, and an increasing number of boys were seen selling the boycotted papers again.

A clever ruse brought an end to the strike. The *World* and the *Journal* told their agents and drivers to start permitting the newsboys to return unsold copies for credit. This modest improvement was enough to bring the boys back to work. However, 60 percent of the income would continue to remain with the newspapers. Absorbing the modest cost of some unsold papers was a small price for this victory. Furthermore, the credit scheme would create an incentive for the newsies to remain on the street longer, selling fresher editions of the newspaper.

Facing the resolute partnership of the *Journal* and the *World*, and weakened by the collapse of their leadership and by desertions among their ranks, the newsboys surrendered on the afternoon of July 26. "The leaders came in to me and threw up their hands," Seitz said. He immediately wired Pulitzer. "Strike broken. Much work required to restore circulation and rehabilitate the paper with the public." He then announced the strike's end to the newspapers.

It had taken the two powerful newspapers only a week to dispense with this publicly awkward and economically powerless challenge. All through it, Pulitzer had remained silent. Twenty years earlier, during his first months of running the *Post-Dispatch*, he had been similarly confronted by newsboys who wanted a higher share of the paper's sale price. He stood his ground then, without resorting to strike breakers or the police, and even expressing sympathy with the newsboys' demands.

At that time, however, as a struggling publisher trying to resurrect a bankrupt newspaper, he had limited financial options.

This was no longer an excuse. The *World* was the richest and most successful newspaper enterprise in the nation. At any time Pulitzer could have put an end to the strike by giving the boys a chance to sell the *World* at the same rate as they sold other papers. But he chose not to. Although he himself had once been a teenager living on the streets of New York, Pulitzer showed no mercy over a dime.

When David Graham Phillips completed his brief tour as the *World's* London correspondent, Pulitzer brought him back. First, Phillips worked on the news side of the paper. Then, at the suggestion of Brisbane (before he left to join Hearst), Pulitzer moved his protégé to the editorial page. This was the rarest of benedictions. The editorial page was the most important part of the *World* for Pulitzer. "As Mary Stuart said about her heart being left in France as she sailed for Scotland," he later confessed to Hosmer, my "heart was and still is in the editorial page and will be in spirit."

Phillips was one of four men assigned to William Merrill in charge of "the Page," as it was reverently called. The quartet included John Dillon, Pulitzer's original partner on the *Post-Dispatch*; George Eggleston, who had worked with Pulitzer on fighting Bryan in 1896; and James W. Clarke, known for his interviews. Housed in the dome, they worked in small cubbyholes. Phillips turned his into such a mess that the cleaning woman complained about the crumbled balls of paper—from false starts on editorials—strewn over the floor.

The pressure was immense. Not only were the opinions of the *World* read in the seats of government and widely reproduced by other newspapers, but they never escaped the attention of the boss. Every editorial of importance was read aloud twice to Pulitzer. He pushed the men to produce their best possible work, often admonishing them to write less but better. He wanted the paper to speak with one voice. "Indeed, you might talk to Dillon and Phillips and request them 'for the 400th time' to write in a similar vein," Pulitzer instructed Merrill.

One could never please Pulitzer. One moment he would ban comments on political subjects, only to complain later that the page was devoid of politics. In the summer of 1899, in the midst of the newsboys' strike, he unloaded his complaints. He telegraphed Merrill and instructed that his words be read aloud to Phillips and Eggleston. "It is dictated, as you see, angrily but yet deliberately for telegraphing," Pulitzer said. "Either the editors have opinions which they are afraid to express, or they have no opinions. In either case they do not do their duty. I am tired of being both a scapegoat and scarecrow; held responsible for the very things I dislike."

Despite the outburst, which most of his writers knew would pass like a summer storm, Pulitzer continued to view Phillips as his potential journalistic heir. He reserved personal guidance for Phillips that he gave no one else. Inviting him to Bar Harbor at the end of the summer, Pulitzer promised that together they would review his work and development since he had joined the *World*. "Promise me also to insist very emphatically—for I am so cowardly about criticizing sensitive and delicate, likeable persons, that I am sure to run away from it unless you use a club," Pulitzer continued. "Promise me further that you will use that club—with the understanding that it is for your own good, for the sake of your future. Mine is behind me, as you know."

Pulitzer, however, was unaware that Phillips had a different future in mind. Over drinks, Phillips told his friends that he would remain in journalism only as long as it taught him about writing and life. In the meantime, it was providing him with the material for his first novel. In his off-hours, holed up in his room at a Washington Square boarding house between Sullivan and MacDougal streets, Phillips was crafting a novel whose central character was an amalgam of Phillips's own experiences in journalism and his observations of Pulitzer. "I had a chance to see the truth, even if the editorials didn't permit me to tell it," Phillips said. "I was impressed with the awful failures among men who were avowed great worldly successes. How unhappy they were, how puerile in their motives, how unattainable happiness or contentment was to them."

In Phillips's novel, *The Great God Success*, a young man much like himself takes a job on a New York daily. The tone of the novel is set early. "Journalism is not a career," a seasoned reporter tells the central character, who is named Howard. "It is either a school or a cemetery. A man may use it as a stepping-stone to something else. But if he sticks to it, he finds himself an old man, dead and done for to all intents and purposes years before he's buried."

To avoid this fate, Phillips continued to work secretly on his book.

*   *   *

Following the settlement of the newsies' strike, complaints from distributors about the wholesale price of the papers brought Seitz and Carvalho back together. Carvalho told Seitz that the lesson from the past month was clear. "When I saw the advantage we had gained by co-operation during the newsboys strike," he said, "I went to Hearst and said that it seemed to me now was a good time to undertake an arrangement with the *World*."

The two managers first began working on a détente in 1897, when Hearst proposed that the *Journal* and the *World* might find it more profitable to divide the market rather than compete endlessly. The idea was compelling enough for the publishers to meet face-to-face for the first, and only, time in their lives. At the meeting, kept secret from the press, Hearst told Pulitzer that if they could come to an agreement he was willing to diminish the scope of his paper, freeing Pulitzer to raise the price of the *World*. "That is to say," said Seitz, who had been part of the negotiations, "Hearst was then willing to return to his original one-cent plan of a *real* one-cent paper, while the *World* could return to its class as a two-cent paper."

Proposals for a peace treaty ran into rough water as soon as the men tried to specify the details. One stumbling block was Pulitzer's continued effort to keep Hearst from using Associated Press wire copy. Ever since his days in St. Louis, Pulitzer had placed an inordinate value on such memberships. A few months before he and Hearst held their summit, a competitor of the AP's, United Press (unrelated to the present-day UPI), went out of business. Its subscribers in New York scrambled to apply for AP membership. The *Herald, Times,* and *Tribune* all were accepted, but Pulitzer used his position on the AP board to veto Hearst's application. Without any wire service, Hearst would be at an enormous competitive disadvantage. But he resorted to a trick Pulitzer had used in St. Louis. Hearst bought the *New York Morning Advertiser,* folded it into his own paper, and gained its AP membership for his morning edition.

Keenly aware of the early failures to broker a peace agreement and the continued hostility between their bosses, Seitz and Carvalho began talking in August 1899, to try again to work out some sort of agreement. Prior to the meeting, Seitz had been to Bar Harbor to receive his instructions for the negotiations. "We will consider any proposition on good faith, that we are and have been from the start, acting on the defensive and fully realizing about the absurdity, un-durability, and profligacy of this competition, which sooner or later must come to an end," Pulitzer told Seitz. "The natural common sense of the situation is to bring it to an end on terms mutually beneficial by combination instead of competition, and by a combination which if possible should be a radical parting of the ways, giving each a field to itself, rather than paralleling the identical ground."

Combination instead of competition. In short, Pulitzer was proposing a conspiracy to restrain trade, not unlike the trusts and monopolies that his paper attacked almost daily. "All trusts are not monstrous," Pulitzer later told Phillips. But even under the loosest interpretations of the Sherman Anti-Trust Act, passed nine years ago with his support, what Pulitzer sought was illegal. The idea was a betrayal of his avowed principles.

Remaining in Bar Harbor, Pulitzer dictated a memo summing up his discussions with Seitz. "Please don't mention my desire for peace any more than as a personal feeling," he said. "It is of supreme importance to show *no anxiety whatever.*" Pulitzer was worried his competitors might use his infirmity to their advantage. "They would quickly seize upon either anxiety or personal weakness and physical difficulties—on which they have already banked." He wanted Seitz to bargain from a position of power, not of necessity. "I will never negotiate under threats."

Pulitzer placed high hopes on the negotiations. As Seitz and Carvalho prepared to meet, he warned Seitz not to let the other side know that the *Post-Dispatch* was making money and that the penalty clause they devised for the treaty needed to be strong. "The point is simply to secure confidence in the scrupulous enforcement of the agreement, which is worthless unless both parties *have* confidence in it," Pulitzer said. "Probably both are afraid of each other."

Like a nervous suitor, Pulitzer became increasingly anxious as the two sides approached each other. He received a friendly personal message from Hearst and told Seitz to acknowledge it and to let Hearst know that while it might seem impolite not to reply personally, he wanted the negotiators to focus on potential penalties for breaking any final agreement. "Please deliver this in person to Hearst himself, but verbally—*not* giving it in writing but in Carvalho's presence if he desires," Pulitzer said. Hours later, he changed his mind. "Don't deliver Hearst message mailed yesterday till further notice," he urgently wired Seitz.

Upon finally sitting down with Carvalho once again, Seitz announced that Pulitzer was willing to consider any proposition, however radical, but had none in mind himself. "The burden of the negotiations, therefore," Seitz told Carvalho, "gets back to us, and, primarily, it seems to me that the first step is to devise some method of dividing the field."

"How would you do it?" asked Carvalho.

From the start, both agreed that any combination would have to include raising the price of both papers to two cents. "As I said at Bar Harbor," Seitz reminded Pulitzer, "I believe that we would get right up against the two cent proposition in very short order. I believe now that WE ARE THERE." But vexing details remained. They had to find a way to collude on advertising rates and develop business practices that kept the cooperation secret.

While the men negotiated, John Norris lunched with Adolph Ochs, who three years earlier had bought the money-losing *New York Times*. The paper was making large gains in circulation since it had dropped its price and adopted Ochs's style of objective reporting, expressed by the paper's new motto "All the News That's Fit to Print." (The motto of Ochs's paper in Chattanooga had been "It Does Not Soil the Breakfast Cloth.") Ochs told Norris in confidence that Carvalho had also approached him to see if the *Times* would go along with a price increase to two cents. Ochs favored the idea but told Carvalho he was worried that someone would start a penny paper and undercut those who had raised their prices. Carvalho assured him it couldn't happen, because the wholesalers and distributors would not handle any new paper in return for the lower price.

By September, Seitz and Carvalho had completed a draft of an agreement for their bosses.

Pulitzer pledged to sign a deal, although he remained doubtful that the negotiations could produce a suitable one. "It is difficult to direct a game by telegraph, from a distance, without seeing the gamesters' faces, or hearing their voices," he complained. The proposed contract that both newspapers raise their price to two cents, and only the evening editions would remain at a penny, that the papers would limit their size; and their advertising rates would be uniform. The publishers also would promise not to raid each other's staffs and not to engage in editorial warfare; and the *Evening Journal* would be permitted to have a membership in AP.

When Norris reviewed the proposed treaty, he told Pulitzer it was a dangerous and foolish plan. Bradford Merrill had an even worse interpretation. He believed the contract would benefit only Hearst. The struggle between the papers was not about making money, Merrill said. It was a battle for supremacy. "Now the fight can never be settled finally except by one or the other tacitly, at least, yielding the primacy. It cannot be settled by any contract or trust agreement to charge the same advertising rates or to advance the price to two cents. That would not settle the war. It would prolong it. It would give the enemy fresh sinews and fresh confidence. It would simply tie the two duelists together in an embrace so close that one could not for a long time tell the victor from the vanquished."

Pulitzer ignored both Norris's and Merrill's advice, and also that of Seitz, who, when asked, said he too opposed the plan. When the proposal was read to him, Pulitzer worked on strengthening the all-important enforcement clause. The draft suggested that if either side broke the terms, it would pay the other a sum of money. Pulitzer wanted to increase the size of the penalty to a minimum of $1 million. He told Seitz he would not sign any agreement unless it was "ironclad fireproof."

If the two publishers were to create a secret, illegal combination, Pulitzer was correct that the penalty clause would be the most important part of the deal. Without a private remedy, the contract would be worthless, since it could not be enforced in court. Pulitzer, who had steadily railed against monopolies and trusts for almost thirty years and whose *World* had championed the passage of the Sherman act, voiced no qualms. He was tired and beleaguered by the trouble besetting the *World* since Hearst had come to town. He was willing to make a pact with the devil if he had to.

As with crushing the newsies' strike, social and economic justice had become an abstract notion for Pulitzer, suitable for others but not for him. All he wanted, Pulitzer confessed to Seitz, was a truce. "That arrangement which will enable me to make the best possible paper in point of reputation and character, indulge my own inherent editorial and political tastes, and have no bother with business or other distractions. That is, *peace*."

The negotiations dragged on into the fall, stopping and starting as each publisher altered the work of his negotiators. Hearst frankly told Seitz, "In short, we are willing to adopt Mr. Pulitzer's phrase and substitute 'Combination for Competition.'" But in the end, neither side could figure out how to do it.

While the two sides negotiated, Pulitzer dispatched Phillips on a special assignment. The journalist put aside his novel and set off on a cross-country tour of numerous cities to assess the political strength of President McKinley and his probable opponent, the silver-tongued orator William Jennings Bryan. Though Pulitzer remained leery, Bryan had risen in his estimation by becoming a strong foe of American imperialism. The United States' victory in the Spanish-American War had given it authority over Cuba—and over the Philippines, where U.S. troops were trying to put down an insurrection using inhumane tactics like those of Spain.

"I cannot get over the fact that this man is rendering the most conspicuous service to the country, in his brilliant bold crusade against Imperialism," said Pulitzer, dictating detailed instructions to Phillips. "I think the work he has done in this cause is inestimable, simply in arousing and aligning the entire Democratic party against what is, after all, the burning danger and evil, the first step on the path to ruin."

Phillips was to end his reporting tour by visiting Bryan in Nebraska. "I want you to write up Bryan at home, the real man; his real force, his character, influence et cetera. At the same time I want you to be kind to him, tell all the truth possible, strictly and exactly, but from a kindly rather than antipathetic point of view." Phillips was already a Bryan man, and Pulitzer was becoming one.

With the arrival of winter and his travels at an end, Phillips resumed work on his novel *The Great God Success*. His protagonist Howard was rising to power and fame as an editor and then as a publisher, following the same principles Pulitzer had used; as Howard put it, "Catch the crowd, to interest it, to compel it to read, and so to lead it to think." Phillips based Howard's days as a reporter on his own life, but he modeled the character's time as a publisher on Pulitzer's. If there was anyone in Pulitzer's entourage who had been close enough to him to see the transformation in the onetime idealistic reformer, it was Phillips. Pulitzer—blind, in misery with real and imagined ailments, and incapable of acknowledging the suffering of others—had become entirely self-absorbed. His cause was himself. Phillips recognized the angst in Pulitzer and gave it to his fictional character.

"He could not deceive himself, nor can any man with the clearness of judgement necessary to great achievement," wrote Phillips about Howard. "He was well aware that he had shifted from the ideal of use *to* his fellow-beings to the ideal of use *of* his fellow-beings, from the ideal of character to the ideal of reputation. And he knew that the two ideals cannot be combined and that he not only was not attempting to combine them but had no desire so to do. He despised his former ideals; but also he despised himself for despising them."

Over time, Howard sells out—first to a coal trust and then for a political appointment. As the book draws to a close, melancholy envelops him. "And he fell to despising himself for the kind of exultation that filled him, its selfishness, its sordidness, the absence of all high enthusiasm," wrote Phillips. "Why was he denied the happiness of self-deception? Why could he not forget the means, blot it out, now that the end was attained?

"The answer came—because in those days, in the days of his youth, he had had beliefs, high principles; he had been incapable of slavery to appearances, to vain show, incapable of this passion for reputation regardless of character. His weaknesses were then weaknesses only, and not, as now, the laws of his being controlling his every act.

"He smiled cynically at the self of such a few years ago—yet he could not meet those honest, fearless eyes that looked out at him from the mirror of memory."

Chapter Twenty-Six

FLEEING HIS SHADOW

---◆---

M uffled sounds of screaming woke Kate in the late-night hours of January 8, 1900. They came from directly underneath the window of her second-floor bedroom in the house on East Fifty-Fifth Street in New York. Through glass and heavy draperies, she made out the terrifying word "Fire!" One of their nearly two dozen household servants had seen flames at the rear of the house and was yelling for everyone to get out of the building.

Kate jumped from her bed and ran into the adjacent bedrooms, where eleven-year-old Constance and thirteen-year-old Edith were sleeping. Draping them with blankets, she led the children down the smoke-filled stairs to safety on the street, where she consigned them to a neighbor.

Joseph was in Lakewood, New Jersey, where he had gone shortly after the new year with his son Joe. Ralph was back at Harvard. But three-year-old Herbert, the baby of the family, was still inside. Barefooted and clad only in her sleeping garment, Kate ran back into the burning house. Through the thickening smoke from flaming curtains, wall hangings, and paintings, she inched her way up the stairs to the third floor. There she found Herbert in the arms of his panicked nurse, who was standing on the windowsill preparing to jump. Kate held her back. Then, by alternately pushing and pulling them through blinding smoke down the hall and stairs, she guided them to safety on the first floor. The footman, who had sounded the alarm, tore a curtain off a rod and draped it over Kate's shoulders. With Herbert in her arms, she rejoined her two girls, who were safe in the house next door.

It took the firemen a full hour to contain the flames. The enclosed outside staircase, which Pulitzer had built at the suggestion of the fire marshal, had worked like a chimney in spreading the fire. As Kate and the children huddled in a neighboring house, the servants frantically tried to determine whether anyone was missing. Many of the staff members had fled from their top-floor bedrooms by climbing onto the roof and crossing over to adjacent houses.

One of the men said he had seen Morgan Jellett, Kate's personal secretary, turn back when she reached the roof, to retrieve from her room a satchel containing her Christmas presents. When firemen entered the house, they found Jellett's body on the third floor, the satchel in her hand. Near her lay the body of Elizabeth Montgomery, one of the governesses, dressed in her bathrobe and slippers. Also presumed dead was Rickey, a King Charles spaniel that had been a favorite of Lucille's.

A telephone call was placed to Lakewood. Pulitzer was told of the fire and that his family was safe. News of the deaths was initially kept from him, out of fear that it might upset him. When he learned of it, he paid for the funeral expenses and sent donations to the fire and police departments. The flames destroyed three portraits of Kate, one of Joseph, and a vast collection of other paintings, as well as bronzes—including a Buddha brought back from the Orient by James Creelman when he covered the Chinese-Japanese War—and four large antique Gobelin tapestries. Kate's diamond necklace from the French crown jewel collection and her famous $150,000 pearl necklace were never found. In all, the losses amounted to more than $500,000.

Kate and the children took rooms at the Hotel Netherland, while the servants were put up in a nearby rooming house. In the afternoon, Kate dispatched someone to obtain the measurements of all the servants so as to order new clothes for them. From Lakewood, Joseph arranged to rent the Henry T. Sloane mansion on East Seventy-Second Street for $17,500 a year. Built in French Renaissance style with a light granite exterior and white marble trim, it was, according to one newspaper, "considered to be one of the handsomest of all the newer New York residences."

As Pulitzer's fifty-third birthday neared, on April 10, 1900, he was hardly in a celebratory mood. He was bogged down in protracted negotiations with McKim, Mead, and White, the architectural firm he hired to design his new house on East Seventy-Third Street, where he had purchased a lot for $240,000. Like his neighbors, he wanted a mansion, but "an American home for comfort and use not for show or entertainment." It was to be without a ballroom, music room, or picture gallery, and he especially wanted it to be free of French design and furniture. He also set a limit of $250,000, including decorations, a low figure that no one around him took seriously.

Kate had not yet been consulted about the plans for the house. She was still recovering from the trauma of the fire. Her doctor urged her to go for a cure at Aix-les-Bains in southern France. "She is feeling the strain of all she went through at the time of the fire and needs very much to rest and the treatment at Aix," he wrote to Joseph. Persuaded, her husband authorized his financial officer, Angus Shaw, to give Kate $750 to pay for her passage to Europe. She in turn persuaded Shaw to give her $830 to cover the cost of her maid and taxes, and Shaw feared that Joseph might make him deduct the additional $80 from a future payment.

At the *World*, matters were no more settled than at home. Pulitzer continued to fret about the paper's sloppiness. In one story, a reporter erred in stating Standard Oil's stock value. "Accuracy! Accuracy!! Accuracy!!!" Pulitzer angrily telegraphed. Of greater concern was the restlessness among many of his key editors and managers.

Since January, the business manager, John Norris, had been hinting that he was preparing to leave. On April 2, he made his plans known. "Temperamentally, I am not equipped to get along with you," Norris wrote. To be sure that Pulitzer would not try to stop him, he added that nothing could be done to keep him on the paper. Pulitzer accepted his departure, and Norris went to work for Ochs at the *New York Times*. Even John Dillon, Pulitzer's original partner at the *St. Louis Post-Dispatch*, took another job. He joined the *Chicago Tribune* after laboring quietly in the *World*'s editorial shop for years.

Phillips was also feeling some wanderlust. Earlier in the winter, he had complained about his nerves and had requested a leave of absence. Pulitzer wanted to keep Phillips at all costs. He still believed the young writer might eventually take the helm of the paper. During a carriage ride around Lakewood, Pulitzer told Phillips he could have a two-month, all-expenses-paid trip to Europe. In late April, the young writer accepted the offer, picked up an advance on nine weeks of his salary, and left.

After more than a decade of on-and-off absentee ownership, Pulitzer could still not find a suitable way to run the *World* to his satisfaction.

Earlier, when Cockerill and Smith had been in charge, he felt that he had responsive alter egos at the helm. Now he had to beg his editors to follow his instructions. As he told them that year, "My being disabled from performing this duty, involves the necessity of your thinking, as nearly as possible, what you think I think."

To run his paper by remote control, Pulitzer contrived an intricate, even labyrinthine, means of communication. He kept his secretaries busy at all hours by dictating to his editors and managers a stream of telegrams filled with complaints about even the smallest mistakes in the paper—chastisement, praise (though rare), and incessant demands for every possible kind of up-to-date information about circulation and finances. The cable offices at Wiesbaden, Germany; Cap Martin, France; London, England; Bar Harbor; and Jekyll Island always knew when Pulitzer was in town.

The telegrams tested the patience of Pulitzer's personal staff. Once, on Jekyll Island, the duty of taking down and sending a telegram fell to Hosmer because Pulitzer's secretary, Butes, had remained in New York. After spending thirty minutes with Pulitzer as the latter composed a 300-word telegram, Hosmer retreated to his room and neatly transcribed the message so that the club's clerk could telephone it to Western Union. "But just as he is shirking off by the back door to place it beyond hope of recall," Billings wrote to Butes, "a messenger reaches him with instructions not to send it until Mr. P. has read it again and the circus begins afresh."

The public nature of the telegraph—one of the wonders of the nineteenth century—created a further challenge. Telegraph operators were privy to the content of any message and secrets were not safe. Furthermore, like in the children's game of "whisper down the lawn,"* repeated transmissions of a message could easily garble carefully worded instructions.

People in competitive businesses purchased secret codebooks designed for composing telegrams. The *Acme Commodity and Phrase Code*, for example, was a 902-page compendium of 100,000 five-letter codes. Pulitzer sent coded messages enthusiastically, but instead of using a commercially available codebook, he developed his own.

---

*Later replaced by the "telephone game."

The 5,000-entry book shed light on the concerns, interests, and ob-
sessions of its creator. Pulitzer developed a nomenclature for all the ele-
ments of his world. He had codes for politicians, rivals, business terms,
dates, amounts of money, family members, and even the weather. Wil-
liam Jennings Bryan became "Guilder," Theodore Roosevelt "Glutinous,"
and Hearst "Gush." The amount of business completed was "merciful,"
a gain was "piggery," and a discount—which Pulitzer loathed to grant—
was "menodus." Almost every telegram asked about "potash," the term
for advertising, including display ads, known as "memorials."

In constructing his coded world, Pulitzer went beyond hiding corpo-
rate and political communication from prying eyes. He devised codes
for his family and his fixation on sickness. The health of the children
and family alone merited thirty-seven terms. The weather on his voyages
was hardly an important secret, yet there were forty-eight codes for fog,
clouds, sun, and temperatures.

To stay out of trouble, staffers had to include the critically impor-
tant word "semaphore" in their reply. A veteran editor instructed those
who received a codebook to underline the word in the "reddest ink"
and understand its meaning: "I have read twice and fully, clearly, surely
understand and acknowledge your cable. I will do my best after consid-
eration and would certainly cable back and ask a question if I did not
understand or felt uncertain."

Each of Pulitzer's lieutenants possessed one of the six-by-nine-inch
books, about 300 pages long, with two alphabetically tabbed sections.
Owning one was an important mark of power at the *World*, as the code
was the sacred language of the inner court. Like high priests translat-
ing a religious text, the men sat each day at their desks under the gold
dome with their own annotated codebooks, carefully deciphering a new
stack of telegraphs and memos. Each man had his own code name. Don
Seitz was "Gulch"; Pulitzer's old partner Dillon was "Guess"; the edito-
rial writer and Pulitzer's protégé, Phillips, was "Gumboil"; the business
manager, Norris, was "Anfrancto"; and the financial adviser, Clarke, was
"Coin."

For himself, Pulitzer reserved the lofty name "Andes," after the high-
est mountain range in the Americas. It became so frequently used by
editors and reporters that the moniker no longer hid his identity. In fact,
aside from JP, "Andes" became the most common nickname for Pulitzer
at the *World* and at rival newspapers.

* * *

In late June 1900 the first of the Pulitzer children graduated from college. But when Ralph accepted his Harvard degree from President Charles Eliot, his parents were nowhere to be seen. They had not considered the event sufficiently important to alter their travel plans. Ralph's father was on the ocean, returning from a month spent in England, and his mother was undergoing a cure in Aix-les-Bains. Joseph did find time to bestow a graduation check large enough for Ralph to seek investment advice from his father's banker.

Like most of his 982 classmates, sons of America's wealthiest families, Ralph had passed his four years at Harvard in considerable luxury. Each month Shaw sent him $500 for living expenses, such as $30 for beer, $30 for theater tickets, $75 for meals at La Touraine restaurant, $25 for his boxing instructor, and $50 for clothes and presents. The amount had been increased by $60 in his last year, after his father suggested that Ralph should pay for the services of his manservant and a maid himself. "Not on your life!!!" Ralph had written to Butes. "When he said in London that he thought I must have a competent man to look after me, I am sure he had no notion of making me pay the man's wages."

Ralph's fifteen-year-old brother, Joe, who attended St. Mark's School, an exclusive boarding school west of Boston, possessed similar expectations. In the spring, he had asked his father to spend $1,300 for a sailboat. "I am afraid you will think that pretty steep but boats are pretty expensive things, as you know," he said. He also hoped his father would hire someone to take care of the boat, should it be purchased.

Neither Ralph nor Joe had much contact with the world beyond that of mansions in New York, manors in London, houses in a fashionable arrondissement of Paris, or summer cottages in Maine and Georgia. From their earliest years they had been cared for by nannies and educated by tutors until consigned to boarding schools for the finishing touches when they were as young as eight years old.

It was not until Joe was a teenager that he learned of his father's Jewish ancestry. In his first year at St. Mark's, which was Episcopalian, he heard boys making a hissing sound or calling him "sheeny" when he walked by. Joe confronted his Episcopalian mother about his heritage. She told him that he had nothing to be ashamed of, that the Jews were a great people, and she proceeded to list the names of prominent Jewish New Yorkers.

Pulitzer supervised the children's tutoring, training, and care—especially with Ralph, whose precarious health had required long stays in places like St. Moritz. Herbert, born late in the marriage, was still too young to be molded. To Pulitzer's immense frustration, both Ralph and Joe failed to show promise. The eldest was most willing to please his father, but was frail and more interested in the social world than the newspaper one. "I hardly know how to treat him, his ignorance is so terrible and my disappointment so great that I fear I discourage him," Pulitzer told Seitz when he sent Ralph to him for training at the *World* after graduation.

Pulitzer had even less hope for Joe, although Joe was robust and healthy. He was willing to stand up to his father, had little interest in his studies, and had a predilection for getting into trouble. His career at St. Mark's came to an abrupt end in 1901, when he and some friends sneaked into town to buy beer. Finding the school locked on their return, Joe led them up the ivy-covered walls and through an open window. Unfortunately, it led into the bedroom of the headmaster and his wife. "He has committed a crime against his father, his mother, his sisters and his own good name and future. This should be rubbed into him," Joseph wrote to Kate, blaming her for having spoiled the child.

Pulitzer took less interest in Constance and Edith. They spent far less time with him than the boys, including Herbert. This did not mean, however, that they were exempt from his supervision at a distance. Examining bills, he noticed some books by the French writer Alphonse Daudet that fourteen-year-old Edith had purchased. "I would as soon give her strychnine as let her read the average French novel at her formative impressionable age," Joseph told Kate. "You should watch this very sharply and tell the governess to do the same. I still cling to the hope that it must be a mistake."

With the sole exception of his departed Lucille, Joseph endlessly expressed his disappointment in his children to his secretaries, editors, and managers; to Davidson; and especially to Kate. Once, when his mail contained only a letter from Constance, he told Kate, "To all the rest of the children you can say I do not love them and they ought to be ashamed of themselves for not writing." Most who witnessed these harangues were cowed and lacked the courage to contradict him when he tore into his children. Only his distant cousin Adam Politzer, a distinguished professor of otology in Vienna, offered rare counsel.

"Do not forget, that they were born and brought up under quite different circumstances than we," Politzer wrote. "Self-made men like you and myself only come to maturity in that battle for existence—and who knows should we have been the sons of wealthy parents, if we were what we are now? Your children do not form any exception from those children who have grown up in similarly favorable conditions."

As her time in Aix-les-Bains drew to a close in June 1900, Kate assumed that she would rejoin her husband in London where he had rented a house, a coachhouse, and stables for the horses he brought from the United States. But without a word, Joseph boarded the *Oceanic* and sailed home, leaving young Herbert behind in London with a nanny. His rapid exit was not the first. Pulitzer increasingly refused to remain in one place. As soon as he reached a destination, he was ready to leave. He might sail across the ocean only to return by the next ship. "You always remind me of the gentleman in one of Horace's fables who ran and rode and sailed, thinking to flee from his cave and finally discovered that he was fleeing from his own shadow," Phillips told him. Phillips was one of the few in his employ who had the courage to be frank with Pulitzer.

When one of the governesses informed her of Joseph's sudden departure, Kate was furious. "You have surprised even me accustomed as I am to vertiginous movements," she wrote. "It looks queer to strangers that I should be ignorant of the sailing of my family." For several weeks there ensued a transatlantic battle between the two. Kate had run through her monthly $6,000 allowance and had no means of getting home. If Joseph did not wire her the money, she threatened to borrow it from the U.S. ambassador Joseph Choate in London. Pulitzer remained obstinate and refused. "Pray reconsider decision concerning passage else compelled to appeal to Ambassador," Kate wired from Paris, where she was staying in the luxurious Hotel Vendôme. After two days of back-and-forth telegrams, Joseph relented.

"Steamer tickets and $250," he said.

"Steamer tickets and $350 absolutely necessary to leave," she replied.

He caved in. "Very much obliged," she wired back.

On August 1, Kate and Herbert reached New York. Shaw paid her customs duties of $152.29 and anxiously wired Joseph in Maine to see if he should charge the amount to her personal account. Once again Shaw found himself in the midst of a spat between the two.

It was not a good time to arouse Joseph's ire. On September 14, 1900, his old friend and mentor Thomas Davidson died. Aside from Udo Brachvogel, who occasionally wrote (usually in hopes of getting money for his son's education), Davidson had been the one friend who had known Pulitzer since he was a teenager. About a year before his death, Davidson had come to Maine to visit Pulitzer. It had not been a good reunion. "He is extremely morbid about himself," Joseph complained to Kate, "talks about nothing except his unspeakable troubles, sighs and moans and probably undergoes some physical suffering with vastly more of a mental nervous kind." For Pulitzer, any competition with regard to woes was hard to bear.

After Davidson's death, the cause of his pain became known. When doctors operated on him, during the last months of his life, they discovered a huge bladder stone and a cancerous growth. It "must have been the main cause," wrote a friend, "of the frightful anguish our friend had been suffering for a long time." Despite his lifelong closeness to Davidson, Pulitzer could not overcome his aversion to funerals. Instead, he sent a $30 wreath of galax and orchids to Glenmore in the Adirondacks, where Davidson had chosen to be buried near a small house he owned.

In the fall of 1900, another presidential election loomed. Since the last one, the United States had become a colonial power. Although he had supported the Spanish-American War, Pulitzer remained opposed to imperialism. The fact that the imperialist power was the United States made no difference. After a brief flirtation with the potential candidacy of Admiral George Dewey, Pulitzer threw his lot in with William Jennings Bryan. Pulitzer's strong opposition to imperialism put him at odds with many of his old political allies. "Mr. Pulitzer is the keenest political observer I ever knew," said his friend William Whitney. "For once his judgment is at fault."

Backing Bryan put Pulitzer once again in the camp opposing Theodore Roosevelt, because Bryan's opponent, McKinley, selected the young New York governor for the vice-presidential nomination. Roosevelt traveled around the country, verbally assailing Bryan, while McKinley remained above the fray. According to Roosevelt, Bryan was espousing "communistic and socialist doctrine" and supporting him were "all the lunatics, all the idiots, all the knaves, all the cowards, and all the honest people who are slow-witted." Pulitzer had no interest in sticking around for the results at the polls. The election was a rerun of 1896, with the Republicans bound to make even more gains. For the first time ever, Pulitzer made sure he was a long way off by Election Day.

In the early morning of October 9, Pulitzer was asleep in his cabin on the *Oceanic*, bound for England and then to Wiesbaden to take baths and consult doctors. As the ship neared the coast of Ireland, it slowed its pace, feeling its way through a rain squall. At about four o'clock, when the ship was almost at a stop so as to take a sounding, the watch crew found themselves staring at looming Irish cliffs. The engines were thrown into reverse, shaking the ship and waking all the passengers. Before its progress could be halted, the hull struck part of the outcropping rock ledge, making a grinding, grating noise.

"In the few moments of doubt the watertight compartments had been closed and the life boats made ready," said Hosmer, who was in the cabin adjacent to Pulitzer's. Thinking that the ship's lurching indicated its arrival in port, Pulitzer had risen and dressed himself. "He came out in a state of perfect calm and self-possession," noted Hosmer. The two walked on the deck for an hour and then returned to bed. The ship continued safely to port in England.

This was not the last mishap before the end of their journey. A train wreck blocked the rails leading to Cologne, Germany. In the middle of the night, Pulitzer and his companions had to leave their train and walk through a field to board another one on the other side of the accident. It took thirty hours to finally reach Wiesbaden. Pulitzer, who had caught a cold in London, remained in bed for twenty-four of those hours. "Inevitably," Hosmer reported to Kate, "everything was wrong all the time and the world was full of damn fools."

The new century opened with greater promise for Pulitzer. More than half of the $524,600 he lent the *World* to keep it afloat in 1898 had been repaid as the paper regained profitability. The plan for a secret combination with Hearst, which had stalled in negotiations, lost its appeal now that money was to be made again. In fact, the paper's health was such that it withstood an advertising boycott by Bloomingdale's, Macy's, and other New York retailers who, thinking that the *World* was financially weak, had banded together to try to obtain a reduction in advertising rates. They miscalculated and found their sales plummeting when their large display advertisements were not printed.

An upturn in the economy also gave Pulitzer immense gains in the stock market. In fact, until the end of his life, his investment earnings frequently exceeded those from his two newspapers. He relied heavily on the banker Dumont Clarke to manage his investments; but, as with his newspaper managers and editors, Pulitzer rarely left Clarke alone to do his work. Instead, he regularly sent investment instructions based on inside information, sometimes obtained by his editors from their personal contacts.

Pulitzer invested in railroads, steel, and utilities, which were then the dominant industries in the stock market. Owning shares in these companies breached Pulitzer's political and moral views. He was putting his own personal wealth into companies he had long disdained because of their treatment of workers. Many were trusts and monopolies, as well. All were targets of the *World*'s editorials. Pulitzer fretted about this and on rare occasions asked Clarke to divest him of the most odious. Still, he wanted to safeguard his wealth, and he convinced himself that there were no other means. "I do not buy to sell," he told Clarke, "but to lock up assets for my children."

All the income from his newspapers and investments was put to use. Pulitzer was now spending almost $250,000 a year for household expenses and travel. This was more than 1,000 times what the average American earned. Though his newspaper made money by attacking wealth and privilege, Pulitzer's lifestyle had become indistinct from that of his neighbors on Fifth Avenue, in Bar Harbor, or at Jekyll Island who earned their fortunes on the backs of workers. When Pulitzer smoked cigars, they were Travita, among the finest made in Havana; when he drank, it was Perrier-Jouët Brut or Rüdesheimer Berg Orlean, which he imported by the hundreds of bottles; and when he ate, it was quail, duck, or goose.

The new mansion on the Upper East Side was taking shape on the drawing boards of McKim, Mead, and White and was the equal of those the firm had designed for its other wealthy clients. It included an indoor swimming pool and even the previously prohibited ballroom. It is doubtful, though, that the firm ever had a more demanding or difficult client. The partners made their artist work on Sundays, and then another artist would redraw the plans with large black lines, in hopes that Pulitzer could discern the shape. Additionally, scale models were built so he could feel the contours of the house. Frequently the work had to be rushed so as to catch a ship bound for Germany or England or wherever else Pulitzer might be at the time.

Just when matters seemed settled, Pulitzer would drive the architects to the end of their patience. "I was in despair when I got your letter," said Stanford White, in a typical moment of exasperation after receiving yet more alterations when construction was under way. "I will do whatever I can, but I do not see how it will be possible to have all you want done by Saturday," he warned. "I know one thing, and that is we have certainly made twice as many studies, and done twice as much work on this as we have ever done on any interior work before, and it is pretty hard where so many contrary orders are given, and so many changes made to know where we stand or what to do."

On September 6, 1901, the anarchist Leon Czolgosz shot two bullets into President William McKinley, who had been touring the Pan-American Exposition in Buffalo, New York. For six days McKinley lingered close to death as Americans feared that an assassin had taken a president's life for the third time in less than four decades. Pulitzer was so anxious that even though the *World* had reporters on the scene, he sent Hosmer, who was a medical doctor, to Buffalo to provide him with up-to-date reports. Hosmer's telegrams back to Chatwold forecast the worst. Indeed, on September 14, McKinley died, and Pulitzer's archenemy Theodore Roosevelt became president.

In the circulation war between the *World* and the *Journal*, McKinley's death provided an unexpected boon for Pulitzer's paper. Among the raft of anti-McKinley articles that had appeared in the *Journal*, there had been two unfortunate ones that appeared to suggest an assassination was in order. An outcry erupted against Hearst. He was hanged in effigy in a number of cities, and boycotts of the *Journal* were undertaken. "Large piles remain unsold on the stands and it is being execrated popularly," Seitz told Pulitzer a few days after McKinley's death. "You hear little groups discussing it and offensive remarks being made in cars about people who have it in their possession."

For the first time since his arrival in New York, Pulitzer's competitor was on the ropes. Hearst changed the name of his paper to the *American and Journal*, later dropping "Journal," and lay low. His circulation dropped calamitously and fell 75,000 behind that of the *World*. Pulitzer's editors wanted to join the lynch mob. "For the first time in five years, we now have the chance to part company with the *Journal* in the public mind," Seitz told Pulitzer. But Pulitzer declined the opportunity. He ordered that Hearst be ignored in the pages of the *World* except when events occurred that were newsworthy, such as the burnings in effigy, or prominent figures mentioning him in speeches. Even then, he added, Hearst's name should come up only "if facts absolutely correct, true, and the thing is not displayed maliciously."

In his earliest days as a publisher, Pulitzer had once been offered a similar opportunity. Edward Augustine, the lobbyist with whom he had done battle in Jefferson City, who committed suicide after a financial failure. Other newspaper editors in St. Louis played up the ignominy of his end, but not Pulitzer. He resisted the chance to get even and treated Augustine's death with decorum. He was not going to alter his sense of gentlemanly restraint now just because it was Hearst's turn at bad luck.

On the other hand, there was no need for spite. "This McKinley business has rebounded hard against the *Journal*," one of Pulitzer's editors reported in a confidential memo. "It is a notable fact that in the storm of criticism directed against the *Journal* since the shooting, the *World* has scarcely once been coupled with it, although the main object of the attack throughout has been so-called 'Yellow Journalism.'"

The combination of the editorial reforms at the *World* and Hearst's perceived complicity in McKinley's death in the public's mind accomplished what Pulitzer had sought since the Spanish-American War. Words he had longed to hear came in the confidential memo: "The result is that people do not THINK of the *World* and *Journal* together as they did, and were perhaps justified in doing some time back."

The calm that Pulitzer sought at Jekyll Island was missing during the early months of 1902. He was infuriated by the rising cost of his house in New York. Instead of the $250,000 he had agreed to pay, the price was now $644,000. And on top of this, he had authorized $165,000 in renovations at Chatwold. When he wasn't worrying about the money, he was lamenting the decisions that he believed he had to make about decorating, never mind that Kate remained in New York, bearing the brunt of the work.

In choosing art, Joseph became so frustrated that he considered simply buying an entire collection from someone who had taste. George Ledlie, his advance man, discouraged this idea. "You may say you have no-one to advise you," wrote Ledlie. "On the contrary, and I say this, not because Mrs. Pulitzer is Mrs. Pulitzer, but from knowledge I have obtained in various shopping expeditions with her, that I fully believe you can without hesitation, leave the final decision in any matter requiring artistic senses to her."

Kate was willing in mind and spirit but not in body. She became increasingly weak and ill that spring. Pulitzer, whose list of ailments could fill a page, was not sympathetic. On board the *Majestic* as it approached the coast of England, he wrote to Kate that his doctor was positive there was nothing wrong with her that a little rest couldn't cure. "I am perfectly confident that all you need is a little self-restraint and philosophy. Never mind about carpets or furniture or hangings. You will get them all quickly enough when you are well." He added that he had slept better on this voyage than on any before.

Kate, however, did not improve with rest. Her condition worsened after Joseph had sailed. Her doctors decided she needed to leave the city, and they gave her their usual prescription: a cure at Aix-les-Bains. With this in mind, she began to feel better, until she received a letter from Joseph, who had already traveled from England to southern France, forbidding her to bring Herbert. "The result," said Ledlie, "was that she had a bad crying spell, followed by a fainting time, declared if the baby did not go, she would not go, and we had a very bad time of it." Since the doctors had instructed the staff to humor Kate, Ledlie and the others decided to tell her that she could take the child along. Ledlie then craftily explained the situation in a private letter to Butes, who was with Joseph. They both agreed Joseph would not be informed until the morning of her arrival.

Fortunately, Kate and the baby hardly weighed on Joseph's mind when they finally came together. Rather, he was recovering from listening to a reading of Phillips's novel, which had been published under the pseudonym John Graham. Phillips had to use another name because in bringing out the book, he had violated one of the *World*'s cardinal rules, included in his contract: that publishing any work outside the paper was prohibited. The breaking of this rule, however, paled in comparison with the accusation in the novel that Pulitzer had sold out his ideals.

"I not only read it but enjoyed it very much with one single reservation," Pulitzer told Phillips, without further elaboration. "The book showed undoubted talent, imagination, and skill in constructing dialogue." To Pulitzer's mind, it also showed treachery. "Mr. Pulitzer was keenly hurt when he discovered that the author of the novel was Mr. Phillips," said Seitz. He had trusted Phillips and treated him at times like a son. Pulitzer asked if Phillips had read *Crime and Punishment*. "If not, don't let twenty-four hours pass before you do so."

In selecting Dostoyevsky's novel from the countless ones he had read, Pulitzer chose a work in which a murderer is racked by guilt. His implication would not be lost on Phillips. The *Great God Success* did not end their friendship, but it would never be the same again. Not long after the book's publication, Phillips resigned from the *World*.

Joseph left Kate and the children in Aix-les-Bains and went to spend the summer of 1902 at Chatwold. Kate's French doctor warned him to send her as few letters or telegrams as possible and said that those he did send must be bright and cheery. "She is suffering from one great nervous depression which causes gastric trouble and loss of weight," reported the doctor. "It is necessary for her cure to take a *very severe treatment* for two months." By late summer Kate's health improved. "I am better but it takes very little to throw me back again," she wrote. "I am not yet permitted to take the douches, and the doctor does not tell me when I can do so. He says that in my condition they would be dangerous."

Alone in Maine, except for his staff, Joseph mostly obeyed the doctor's orders regarding correspondence with Kate. Yet he was, once again, furious over Kate's spending. Since he could not complain to her, Joseph decided to turn over her allowance to Ledlie and have him pay the bills. This put Ledlie, who was close to Kate, in an impossible position. If Kate were to order him not to pay a bill because she felt it was Joseph's responsibility, then Ledlie would have to do battle with his boss. He and Butes, Pulitzer's main personal secretary, quickly consulted with each other behind their boss's back and decided they were both in a hopeless position as long as Joseph and Kate continued their fiscal war.

In September, John Dillon, who was now fifty-nine, came to Maine for an overdue reunion with Pulitzer. After quitting the *World* in 1900, he had soon regretted his decision and had come back to work for his old partner. As was customary when one visited Pulitzer, the two men went out for a horseback ride, accompanied by at least one of Pulitzer's companions, who minded the horse for him. During the ride, Dillon was thrown from his mount. When they managed to get him back to the house, doctors said that he had suffered two broken ribs and some undetermined internal injuries.

Telegrams to Dillon's family assured them there was no cause for alarm. "Excellent care by two nurses. Takes nourishment. Must wait healing and subsidence of inflammatory condition resulting from fall." The healing did not come. Rather, pneumonia set in, and Dillon's heart grew weak. Pulitzer called to the house the noted doctors S. Weir Mitchell and William Sydner Thayer, both of whom had treated Joseph and Kate. There was little they could do, and once again Chatwold became the scene of a deathwatch. On October 15, Dillon died with his wife and two of his children by his side. The family returned to New York with the body, and several days later Dillon was buried in St. Louis.

"Am all broken up by Dillon," Pulitzer telegraphed to Florence White, who had begun his working life as a cub reporter for Dillon and Pulitzer years earlier. "Wish you would attend service . . . specially representing me and papers." Instead of heading west for the funeral, Pulitzer gathered up his entourage of seven employees and two servants and boarded the eastbound *Celtic,* leaving New York on October 31.

For an additional $394.29 above the price of a first-class ticket, the White Star line had made the usual preparations for its notoriously noise-sensitive customer. Piano playing in the bars ceased at ten o'clock in the evening rather than at eleven. A custom-made green baize door was installed to close off the hall leading to Pulitzer's quarters. "The slamming of a door is most penetrating, it can be heard a half-mile off, especially along a straight corridor," Pulitzer warned the ship's owners. Portions of the deck above his room were cordoned off to redirect promenading passengers, and those who had to cross the area walked on heavy mats. "It is not a question of pleasure, luxury," Pulitzer explained when making his demands. "It is an absolute, indispensable necessity."

Leaving New York for Jekyll Island in January 1903, Pulitzer instructed Seitz to ride the train with him as far as Washington. When the train pulled out of the Jersey City station, Hosmer handed Seitz a sheath of papers and told him to be prepared soon to render an opinion on its contents. Settling into an isolated compartment, Seitz dived into the file. It revealed, in a sharply condensed form, an idea Pulitzer had been mulling over for years. He wanted to use his wealth, upon his death, to create a school to train journalists and endow a prize to reward excellence among working journalists.

Years before, while running the *Post-Dispatch,* Pulitzer had poked fun at publishers meeting in Columbia, Missouri, for wanting to create a professorship of journalism. "It is as absurd to talk of it as to talk of a professorship of matrimony, it being one of those things of which nothing can be learned by those who have never tried it." A decade later, Pulitzer began to change his mind. He conceded that a professor of journalism might be able to teach some of the technical aspects of the trade. "Of course," Pulitzer added, "the highest order of talent or capacity could no more be taught by a professor of journalism than could the military genius of a Hannibal, Caesar, or Bonaparte be taught in military academies."

By the 1890s, the idea had become a central part of Pulitzer's plan on how to use his wealth. Next to power, Pulitzer most sought respectability. Much of the public thought his profession lacked dignity. The competition with Hearst had, at least for a while, bound the two men together as purveyors of the crass, sensational, and prurient fare of Yellow Journalism. Two years earlier, for instance, *Life* magazine had published a drawing of Pulitzer as a bird on a perch labeled *Pulitzus Nundanus,* listing its characteristics as "Scavenger. Eats anything, and grows fat on filth. Vindictive and noisy, but harmless." A school and the respect that might come with it would go a long way toward ennobling the profession and its most famous member.

While he was at rest in Europe, Pulitzer shared his thoughts with others. One in particular was his friend Seth Low, president of what was then called Columbia College in New York. In 1892, Pulitzer's scheme was considered by Columbia's trustees. They rejected the idea. Now, a decade later, Pulitzer resurrected the plan as he contemplated the end of his life while summering at Chatwold. He revised his will and, at last, laid out his thinking about his legacy in a memo for George Hosmer, his faithful companion of many years, marking it "strictly confidential."

"My idea is to recognize that journalism is, or ought to be, one of the great and intellectual professions," he said. To that end, Pulitzer proposed that journalists receive training on a par with that given to lawyers and doctors. He decided he was prepared to give Columbia University as much as $2 million—a gift almost three times the size of the institution's annual operating budget—if it was willing to create and run a journalism school. Pulitzer then added that his gift should also be used to award annual prizes to working journalists, newspapers, or writers, for achievement, excellence, and public service. This money would eventually create what became known as the Pulitzer prizes, perhaps the most highly recognized and coveted award except for those created by Alfred Nobel the previous year.

Although his idea for journalism prizes may have seemed like an afterthought to the officials at Columbia, Pulitzer had long used the technique to motivate his own reporters. As early as 1887, reporters on the *World* competed for annual monetary awards in a number of categories such as best news story and best writing. Editors were not excluded. Pulitzer held competitions for best headline and best copyediting, as well.

Pulitzer selected Columbia for his munificence because of its location in the capital of newspaper publishing and because it already had a School of Mines. ("Why not also have a School of Journalism," he said.) But if Columbia seemed uninterested, Pulitzer said he would try Yale.

"My own ideas are positive enough about the general scheme, the general provisions and the general object, but when it comes to the vital details of a working plan I am quite at sea," he continued. "I cannot help thinking that there is no profession in which every student of the United States has a more direct interest, or which represents, for good or for evil, the moral forces and moral sense of a nation."

Pulitzer assigned Hosmer to work secretly on the plan. He wanted it ready by his fifty-sixth birthday on April 10, 1903. For the first time since making a success of the *World*, Pulitzer felt the thrill of engaging in work that could outlast him. The journalism school, with its accompanying prizes for journalists from all over the country, represented an immense hope. "I don't believe I have ever done anything that will give the children and their children a better name, and that—after all—is something," he later wrote to Kate.

On the train heading south on this January day, Seitz held the finished proposal in his hands. It stipulated that Pulitzer would provide Columbia with the $2 million in three installments. In return, the university would construct a building, invest the money, and use the income to pay salaries for the instructors and award the annual prizes. Before Seitz had a chance to take it all in, Pulitzer had groped his way down the hall of the train and was at his door.

"You don't think much of it," he said.

"I do not," replied Seitz.

"Well, what should I do? I want to do something."

"Endow the *World*. Make it foolproof."

"I am going to do something for it, in giving it a new building."

Ignoring Seitz's opinion after asking for it, as he often did, Pulitzer instructed Hosmer to approach Columbia and Harvard universities with the idea, without revealing who was backing it. At Columbia, President Nicholas Murray Butler, who had taken over from Low, certainly knew whose money was being offered. By summer, he had won the trustees' approval. When the agreement was signed, it was backdated to April 10, Pulitzer's birthday.

On Jekyll Island the following winter, Pulitzer devoted a part of each day to listening while one of his secretaries read aloud from the *World*. This was, by now, a well-rehearsed ritual. Pulitzer was extraordinarily attentive. A seasoned secretary knew enough to carefully read the *World*, as well as other newspapers, before the appointed time and to be prepared to describe the layout, size of type, and illustrations used in each story. What Pulitzer heard during one of these readings made him erupt in anger.

On Sunday, February 22, the *World* published an article about Katherine Mackay, a socially prominent New Yorker. It made mention of the decorations in a nursery that had been prepared for the birth of Mrs. Mackay's child. Although the article did not use the word "pregnant," it offended Pulitzer's Victorian sentiments to the core. Pregnancy was a reminder of a taboo subject: sex. Upper-class women did all they could to hide their condition during pregnancy, including remaining indoors during the final months.

Pulitzer let loose a barrage of invective that was immediately telegraphed to New York. "I own the paper and am responsible for its honor and consider lies, falsehoods, gross exaggeration, puffery, yellow plushism, flunkeyism as a crime inexcusable by any direction or any circulation," he said. "Telegraph me who wrote it. See he quits office today." The editors were flabbergasted. The photographs used had been supplied by Katherine Mackay herself and no one, including the Mackay family, had objected to the article. One editor said even his sixteen-year-old daughter liked it. Another said he had heard many expectant women discussing their condition in the presence of both sexes without any objection.

Pulitzer replied that it was entirely possible that the Mackays, who were his friends, were not shocked. Nonetheless, he would not tolerate this kind of story, because it represented a drift in an abhorrent direction pioneered by the *Journal*, which featured "well-known ladies in an interesting condition," he said, still avoiding the word "pregnant." "If that is not disgusting and sickening," he continued, "I don't know what is."

Seitz identified the reporter who had written the piece. It was not a man but a woman, Zona Gale, and he promised Pulitzer she would be dropped. Gale was then a struggling freelance writer working mostly for the *Evening World* while creating novels in her spare time. Years later, she would win a Pulitzer prize as a playwright.

On May 10, 1903, the *World* celebrated its twentieth anniversary under Pulitzer's ownership with a 136-page issue, the largest newspaper ever printed. A few days later, Pulitzer's daughter Edith, who attended Miss Vinton's School for Girls in Connecticut, was summoned to her headmistress's study. Such invitations usually were reserved for reprimands, so Edith was panic-stricken.

When Edith arrived, Miss Vinton began reading aloud from the *New York Times*, the only newspaper permitted in the school. In it was an editorial written by Adolph Ochs on the anniversary of the *World*. In most flattering terms, it spoke about Edith's father and the accomplishments of his paper. "Whatever may be said of the ways of the *World*," Ochs had written, "it will be universally admitted that it has 'done the State some service,' and has fought with notable vigor and unflagging zeal for the triumph of many good causes."

Pulitzer took great joy in hearing Edith's story. He was in Bad Homburg, Germany, where he had gone to try its baths, having tested the curative powers of those in Carlsbad, Wiesbaden, and Baden-Baden. But his rest was disturbed when one of his male personal assistants was caught soliciting sex from a man. The ax fell quickly. "Mr. Pulitzer wishes me to tell you that this incident has given him great pain and that he is much distressed with the duty and sorrow at the necessity of terminating your recent personal relation with him," one of the other secretaries wrote to the man. Perhaps because of his own intimate friendship as a teenager with Davidson, though, Pulitzer was unwilling to be as cruel as others might have been at the time toward a homosexual man. He arranged for him to have a job helping in the London office of the *World*.

The forty-three-year-old, Irish-born James Tuohy, who served as the London bureau chief, was well used to doing personal services for Pulitzer. In fact, for years he had orchestrated the search for British companions, which Pulitzer preferred over Americans. This new assignment, however, seemed unlikely to succeed because London was as intolerant toward homosexuals as most other places. He warned his boss: "I note your instructions. . . . The difficulty is how am I to know what he is doing? If I tell him that a repetition of anything like the Homburg incident means a termination of his engagement, he simply won't tell me."

In fact, not long after arriving in London, the man was propositioned in a Piccadilly restaurant by Grenadier Guardsmen who, according to Tuohy, "have a reputation, by the way, of augmenting their pay considerably by this avocation." It seemed unlikely that Pulitzer's solution for the man would work. "I am afraid that ———'s fatal attraction will get him into trouble, in spite of himself, before long."

From Bad Homburg, Pulitzer migrated to Étretat on the northern coast of France, and then to London for the fall. He had little interest in the mayoral race back in New York. In fact, his passion for politics was diminishing. The change was evident to careful readers of the editorial page.

One reader in particular was Pulitzer's editor James W. Clarke. In preparation for the paper's twentieth anniversary earlier in the year, he had examined the state of the editorial page. Clarke's report read like a nonfiction version of Phillips's novel. He found that over the years since Pulitzer had ceased being present at the paper, the page had lost its soul and the fires of reform had dimmed to a flicker. In its first years, when Pulitzer himself wrote the editorials, "politics, politics, politics dominated the page," Clarke said. "They were hot, partisan politics, too. The tone was radical and at times violent. The masses were steadily championed, the millionaires and money power constantly denounced.

"There was no mincing of words in denouncing Republican Presidents and statesmen," Clarke continued. "The page was sprinkled liberally with attacks upon other papers and upon men. . . . Plenty of epithets and personalities. Plenty of first-class invectives, some good satire—but humor very light. It was mostly hard pounding and expounding."

This was a grim verdict for Pulitzer. His cherished editorial page had become like him, old and stodgy. He was bereft of friends, and the companions with whom he spent his days were paid to be with him. His most important connections to his beginnings in St. Louis—Davidson and Dillon—were dead. He was estranged from his only living sibling, who was also his last tie to his childhood in Hungary. Since their fights in 1883, Albert had gone to Europe, and neither man had written to the other after that. Joseph's children were a disappointment and his family provided no comfort, broken up as it was on two continents. His stoic wife, Kate, remained willing at all times to fill the void, but Joseph had spurned her offers of companionship so frequently that she ceased to ask.

Writing to Joseph from Aix-les-Bains, Kate marked the moment. "Twenty-five years married, how strange it seems," she said. "When we think that, a hundred years hence, not one of us now living will be alive to care or to know, to enjoy or to suffer, what does it all amount to? To a puff of smoke which makes a few rings and then disappears into nothingness and yet we make tragedies of our lives, most of us not even making them serious comedies."

Chapter Twenty-Seven

CAPTURED FOR THE AGES

◆

In early 1904, the *New York World*'s writer Samuel L. Williams stepped down from a train in Detroit, Michigan. Williams, who had been afforded a rare honor for a staffer—riding and swimming with Pulitzer at Chatwold—was on a secret scouting mission. William Merrill, the dean of the *World*'s editorial page, was getting old, and his editorials were getting stale. Pulitzer wanted a young man in the shop who could write with a passion and verve equal to those of Phillips before he abandoned his editorial cubbyhole for fiction.

"I knew pretty well what JP wanted," Williams recalled. "His young men had to know history, biography, have keen perception, and a concise, direct, simple, forceful style. In editorials he especially wanted clarity, brevity, and a punch in the last paragraph." To find the right man, Williams had traveled from city to city, reading yards and yards of ponderous editorials. "Finally," he said, "I discovered some editorials in the *Detroit Free Press* which seemed to meet Pulitzer's specifications." He read and reread these, and culled those he thought had been written by the same person. An old friend, a newspaperman in Detroit, identified the author as Frank Cobb and arranged for Williams to meet him at dinner.

Williams took an immediate liking to the tall, broad-shouldered thirty-four-year-old Cobb. He had a mop of hair that hung down his forehead, sparkling eyes, and powerful hands and arms from working for years in a sawmill. "At the table, Cobb proved himself a brilliant conversationalist, an omnivorous reader, a shrewd observer, a forceful talker, and a keen analyzer of men and affairs. He had vitality of brain and body, yet was so simple in manner, so modest, so lovable, that I knew immediately I had found the Ideal Editor."

After dinner, Williams telegraphed Pulitzer. In the morning, he received his instructions from the publisher. He was to learn everything he could about Cobb and to provide a complete account, including the color of Cobb's eyes, shape of his forehead, and his table manners. Williams grilled Cobb, who by now realized he was being considered for some post. He had read the right books, he opposed Bryan and free silver, and liked Roosevelt but had attacked him editorially, Williams reported. "As to personal appearance, cheerfulness, tone of voice and table manners—highly commendable! He ate soup without a gurgle."

Cobb was not entirely sure he wanted to leave his job at the *Detroit Free Press*. But after a visit with Pulitzer on Jekyll Island, he was persuaded to join the *World*. In the spring, he reported to Merrill. In no time his crisp writing and his persistent requests for information from others drew the attention of the editorial staff. "He would end each inquiry with a sort of grunt that sounded like *ubn* but was really a question mark," Williams said.

Once again Pulitzer had a young man to mold, and this time one who would not leave him or betray him. Over time, the relationship between the older publisher and the young writer grew into the kind of collaborative, though tumultuous, partnership Pulitzer had long sought. Cobb became the most trusted, most loyal, most effective, and longest-serving among Pulitzer's editorial lieutenants. His tenure was exceeded only by that of John Cockerill, Pulitzer's first adjutant for twelve years.

For Kate, the winter of 1903–1904 had been especially depressing. She was sick for most of January, and many of their friends had died during the cold months. She felt that all she had done was send notes and cards of condolence. Though she despised Jekyll Island and had not been there in eight years, she tentatively asked Joseph if she could come for a visit. "I shall not be the least offended," she wrote, "if you think you have not room enough."

Her plea reflected a change of heart. Though the pair continued to squabble over money, Kate increasingly took pity on her husband. She had grown to accept his ailments, phobias, and eccentricities as permanent attributes. The Joseph she had fallen in love with was gone.

She occasionally spoke wistfully about the early years of their marriage. Gazing at a photo from many, many years ago, she remarked to a visitor about the sweet expression her husband had in the picture.

"Shall be engrossed with work and the quarters are not comfortable but I shall be glad to see you if you come," Joseph replied. As if this were a courtship and she had won her prey too quickly, Kate held back. "Am very sorry but think it best not to go Jekyll," she wired, "as sure should be in your way you being engrossed in work would be an irritation to you feeling you must give me time. I quite understand and appreciate condition." Her message forced Joseph to be more emphatic in asking her to come. As soon as he was, Kate replied with alacrity that she consented. "Expect you to welcome me with joy or will leave on first raft," she teased.

Remaining in New York was nineteen-year-old Joe. "The house seems very empty just at present," he wrote to his father. Since being thrown out of St. Mark's School for his nighttime escapade, he had worked at the *Post-Dispatch* and the *World* while being tutored. Unbeknownst to Joe, his father instructed Butes to check quietly to see if Harvard would take him. "Keep secret from Joe as don't want him to know," wrote Pulitzer.

Harvard decided that if Joe passed a set of entrance exams, it would accept him. He was ecstatic upon getting the news and pledged to redouble his efforts with his tutor. The gift, however, did not come without strings attached. His father stipulated that Joe would have to promise to study hard in order to win admission without conditions, to work hard in college, to be satisfied with an allowance that was small by Pulitzer's standards, and not to come to New York except during vacations.

After her time with Joseph on Jekyll Island, a rare interlude of comity between them, Kate returned to New York to cope with the finishing touches at their new house on East Seventy-Third Street. Joseph left for Aix-les-Bains. "I wish there was more sunshine in your life—worry and wearisome work are dull companions," Kate wrote to him when he was settled in Aix. "If you could only take pleasures in things outside your work it would be a Godsend." In his absence, the *World* marked the anniversary of his ownership quietly. Kate, however, couldn't let it go unnoticed. She wrote to Joseph, "We will pass over what it has been to me, and my heart was so full of the conflicting elements of pride and pain that I could not speak of it."

* * *

In May 1904, George Harvey, Pulitzer's former managing editor, who was now president of Harper & Brothers, brought out a work dictated by Pulitzer describing his plans for the journalism college, as the main article in the company's *North American Review*, a highly regarded magazine. At length, Pulitzer explained the need for professional training and what kind of training he envisioned. But he laid out a grander vision for the school's purpose than simply churning out well-trained reporters and editors.

"In all my planning the chief end I had in view was the welfare of the Republic," he wrote. Better-trained journalists would make for better newspapers that would better serve the public good. "Our republic and its press will rise or fall together," he continued, in words that would later be mounted on the walls of his school. "An able, disinterested, public-spirited press, with trained intelligence to know the right and the courage to do it, can preserve that public virtue without which popular government is a shame and a mockery. A cynical, mercenary, demagogic press will produce in time a people as base as itself."

However, in the year since inking the agreement to create the journalism school, Columbia University's officials had been exposed to Pulitzer's less lofty side and had suffered from his irascibility. At first, he insisted that Columbia take the lead on the project, only to subsequently threaten to kill it if his choices—including the presidents of Cornell and Harvard—were not appointed to the advisory board. When Columbia's president, Butler, objected to the appointment of presidents from rival institutions, he was rebuked. "Understand jealousy," Pulitzer wired from St. Moritz to Bradford Merrill, into whose hands Pulitzer had entrusted the final arrangements. "Telegraph Butler my insistence. Unalterable. Final."

Butler consented but counseled that the public announcement of the gift be delayed until the entire advisory board had been selected and approved by the trustees. He also believed that a board comprising illustrious men would defuse charges that Pulitzer was building a monument to himself. Pulitzer would have none of it. He ordered that the *World* break the news. Merrill, however, defied his boss and acquiesced to Butler's wishes. It took him less than twenty-four hours to learn what his boss thought of that decision. Pulitzer ordered Merrill off the project, forbade any further meetings with Butler, and demanded once again that the news be published. "We are certainly dealing with a wild man," Butler told an associate.

Realizing that the story would soon break, Butler had his staff cobble together an announcement. In late August 1903 Pulitzer's plan finally became public. Every major newspaper in the nation gave it great prominence. Even his rivals in the press praised the idea. "By this benefaction," noted Ochs at the *New York Times*, "Mr. Pulitzer wins a new distinction in the history of the art he has himself so successfully practiced." Pulitzer's political opponent Theodore Roosevelt was not among the cheering crowd, telling a friend, "I share your indignation at Columbia College having accepted such money for such a purpose from such a knave."

None of the public praise assuaged Pulitzer. The day after the announcement, he forbade Seitz to send him any more telegrams concerning Butler. He didn't want to hear anything more about the project until he returned to the United States in the fall. Pulitzer further ordered Seitz to inform Columbia's president that unless Butler complied with all his wishes, he would expect Columbia's trustees to have a sense of honor and return the donation. "Again: All disagreeable cables forbidden." Like Merrill, Seitz disobeyed Pulitzer, but unlike Merrill, he got away with it. "He later took me to task for not delivering his ultimatum," said Seitz. "My reply was that I did not want to spoil all the applause."

In Aix-les-Bains, having just concluded his last tantrum about the journalism school, Joseph spiraled down into one of his periodic episodes of depression. The weather was insufferably hot and humid after a week of rain, and he had not slept well in ten days. Kate let Joseph know that two of the girls were back at their boarding school in Connecticut, and this news gave him a chance to pick up his favorite theme of abandonment. "I am sorry the children are at Ridgefield again in the hands of—well, whatever these women are," he said. "You know my views about the way children should be brought up, and they certainly have not had a mother in any sense in which I have been used to understand and value that idea," he continued. "I wish you could have made it possible to go with them or be with them, and almost deplore my so-called success or prosperity, which alone enable you not to do so."

Joseph didn't rest after launching this volley. He continued his assault on Kate by taking up the issue of her mothering with their seven-year-old, Herbert. "Now be a good boy," Pulitzer wrote, "love your father and tell your Mother and Edith that I think it is a perfect shame having turned you away from them, that one of them ought to be with you all the time, that you ought to have a Mother or a sister to take care of you constantly as your father would so much like to do himself."

When Pulitzer's mood was this somber, none of the family escaped his vengeful wrath. His son Joe, who had stoically endured a drought of letters from his father, found himself summarily judged guilty of filial disrespect. "Thirty-five days since I sailed and not one word from you," Joseph wrote to him. "Thirty-five times I have told you with pain how much pain you give me when you don't write simply as evidence of neglect—and that you do not think of."

None of Pulitzer's secretaries, with the possible exception of Butes, could temper these outbursts. They recorded, typed, and mailed the venom he spewed. The most common refrain in his complaints was that his family had abandoned him and that he never received any words of appreciation. "Instead of getting them I have received only blows, and hurts and injuries," he wrote to Kate on one occasion when he threatened to withhold payment for an expense they had agreed on. "Promises of affection and kindness not appreciated are not obligatory, the consideration failing," he said.

His cruelty stung a bewildered Kate, exacerbating her precarious struggle with her own mysterious ailments. When she reached Paris, her doctor convinced her that she had arrived in the nick of time. If she had a breakdown now, it would be harder for her to recover from this one than the last one, he told her. She repacked her bags and left immediately for the French baths.

The elections of 1904 woke Pulitzer from his political slumber. One of his three archenemies—Hearst, Bryan, and Roosevelt—could end up occupying the White House for the next four years unless he did something about it. The year was only a few hours old when Pulitzer, in bed with a cold in New York, began to resume political command of the *World*, dictating memos laying out the kind of coverage he wanted and even assigning specific stories. Merrill, Cobb, and others on the editorial page of the paper awaited their instructions from the reinvigorated Pulitzer.

President Roosevelt also wanted to know what was on Pulitzer's mind. Nine years after Hearst's assault on its dominance and six years after its disgrace in the Spanish-American War, the *World* still remained the most politically powerful newspaper. The president sent his inquiry by circuitous means. One night in January, Ralph Pulitzer, twenty-four years old and acting like an heir apparent, went out with George Harvey, Katherine Mackay (the subject of Zona Gale's article that upset Pulitzer), and Grace Vanderbilt (wife of Cornelius Vanderbilt III). After seeing the two women to their carriages, Harvey asked Ralph to take a drink with him at the Waldorf Hotel.

Ralph dutifully reported to his father that Harvey drank "a monstrous Scotch and Soda" while he stuck to a "modest glass of sherry." Harvey had come from seeing the president at the White House. "Roosevelt had said he was very anxious to meet you," Ralph wrote to his father on Jekyll Island, "and had asked Harvey to ask you if you would not come and see him at anytime to suit your convenience, either lunch or dinner." Peeved at Roosevelt's indirect manner, Joseph wired back, "Tell Harvey impossible for me to answer Roosevelt's invitation received in such a round-about accidental way." He then added disingenuously, "My health forbids Washington as you know." In fact, the train that would carry him north in a few weeks ran through the nation's capital.

Roosevelt extended his invitation to the White House because there had been a fragile cease-fire between the two men for several years. It began in 1899, when Roosevelt was sworn in as governor of New York. One day, early in his term, Roosevelt took aside one of the *World*'s reporters. "Say to Mr. Pulitzer for me," he said, "that I appreciate very highly the fairness with which the *World* has treated me. When I was Police Commissioner I felt I was unjustly treated and resented it, but I have noticed lately a much more conservative policy, and personally, I am grateful for the attitude of the paper toward me."

After Roosevelt assumed the presidency on the death of McKinley, the *World* had continued its self-restraint and at times had even complimented the president for his judicial appointments, his handling of a coal strike, and his enforcement of antimonopoly laws. The paper's new attitude, however, was deceptive. It had more to do with its publisher's diminished interest in politics, his work on his journalism school, and his obsessive preoccupation with building his new house in Manhattan than with any real change of heart, as Roosevelt soon learned.

Even if his paper remained quiet, Pulitzer had shed none of his misgivings about Roosevelt. But he saw no prospect of preventing Roosevelt from winning a term of office on his own. Although Bryan remained popular among Democrats, he couldn't win. More frightening to Pulitzer was the prospect of Hearst's candidacy. Hearst had been elected a U.S. representative and, unlike Pulitzer, had served out his term; he was also the owner of eight newspapers and was spending millions to win the nomination. To block these two men, Pulitzer put his hopes on Alton B. Parker, a New York judge who was a protégé of New York's governor, David Hill.

Pulitzer sent Williams to Nebraska to determine Bryan's intentions. If he had expected a cordial reception for his emissary, Pulitzer was in for a surprise. Bryan had waited years for a chance to vent his disappointment in Pulitzer. He gave Williams an earful. "Tell Mr. Pulitzer that the trouble with him is that he has too much money," he said. "He used to be a socialist when he was poor but now that he has acquired wealth he is just like the rest of the capitalists.

"I have discovered the secret of Mr. Pulitzer's opposition to me," Bryan continued. It had become clear to him when he watched how Pulitzer forced President Cleveland to accept the public sale of bonds. "That is the secret. Mr. Pulitzer and the *World* can rule Cleveland. They can make him do as they want. But they cannot rule Bryan. They cannot make me bow to their will." He said he would not be a candidate and would turn down the nomination, clearing one hurdle for Pulitzer's chosen man, Parker. But he raised another by promising to "resist any attempt to hand the Democratic Party over to the corporations and capitalists as the re-organizers are trying to do.

"I want to be a Cincinnatus, I do not want the cares of millions of dollars," he said, ending his hours-long meeting with Williams. "Tell Mr. Pulitzer to come out to my farm and I will make a farmer of him. I will show him how to be free from cares and worries about investments, stocks, bonds and guarding accumulations of wealth."

Toward the end of the interview, Bryan recalled the first time he and Pulitzer met. It was in Washington, after Bryan's loss in the election of 1896. "He tried to see my face and feel my bumps." Bryan said. "He felt my chin and jaw and commented on it. Tell him this jaw is stronger and firmer than ever."

The Republicans enthusiastically gave their nomination to Roosevelt in June 1904 while the Democrats continued to squabble. When the Democratic Party gathered in St. Louis, Bryan's plans were still undisclosed. If he backed Hearst, who had courageously supported his bids in 1896 and 1900, Bryan could split the convention. It seemed likely that this was his plan. His opening speech drew cheers of "Bryan, Bryan!" and Governor Hill agreed to omit any reference to the gold standard in the platform to appease Bryan's supporters. As dawn approached, after a long night of speeches, Bryan made his intentions known. He declined to support Hearst and instead seconded the nomination of a free silver candidate. Parker won the nomination on the first ballot and Hearst was left out in the cold.

As the Democrats settled on their nominee, Pulitzer returned to New York from Aix-les-Bains. He sailed home on the *Baltic,* along with J. P. Morgan, who continued to give him wide berth, especially after suffering through a monthlong rehash of the gold bond affair in the *World* that May. The articles, which also appeared in 2 million pamphlets, were Pulitzer's handiwork. As he told his staff, he wanted the history of how Morgan and his cronies "swindled Cleveland, government, nation," to be told "so that every child can understand.

Pulitzer was elated that his man was the choice of the Democratic convention. But his obsession with cleansing the party of Bryanism soon crippled the nominee's prospects. William Speer, a reporter for the *World,* was on leave to serve as Parker's secretary. Working through Speer, Pulitzer insisted that Parker force the party to swear allegiance to the gold standard. Parker acquiesced and sent a telegram from his Hudson River estate to St. Louis, saying that he regarded the gold standard as sacred and that he would decline the nomination if the party didn't agree. Riled but exhausted, the delegates complied by giving him the nomination on his terms, and returned home still deeply divided on the currency issue.

Although Bryan and Hearst were beaten and he had his man as the party's standard-bearer, Pulitzer was not complacent. He knew how to read an electoral map. Parker ran a lackluster campaign, modeled on those of the past, when a candidate did not sully himself with speeches or touring. But Bryan and Roosevelt, with their stirring stump speeches and national tours, had so altered the political landscape that such antiquated behavior was a prescription for defeat. If Parker wouldn't take on Roosevelt, Pulitzer would.

From Bar Harbor, Pulitzer ordered Merrill to go after George Cortelyou, Roosevelt's former secretary of commerce and labor. As chairman of the Republican Party, Cortelyou supervised the collection of funds from corporate leaders and financiers for the president's election campaign. Pulitzer told Merrill to compare the party chief to the nefarious Boss Tweed, and to demand that Republicans open their books so that the public could see how much money was coming into the president's coffers from trust, monopolies, and corporations facing possible federal prosecution.

Pulitzer had long sought to end corporate campaign donations, but the government was still three years away from imposing a ban. "Roosevelt is very culpable, or at least, under suspicion for not having put through bills to prevent it in Washington. All the more because he consented to the amazing impropriety of making his Secretary of Commerce, collector of these very contributions and making him afterwards Postmaster General."

Merrill did his best as the fall campaign got under way, but his efforts paled in comparison with Pulitzer's own editorial, which appeared on October 1, 1904. Written as an open letter to the president, it was vintage Pulitzer, of the kind readers had not seen in years. Pulitzer castigated Roosevelt for failing to keep his pledge to remove the veil of secrecy from the affairs of corporations.

Stretching across two pages, the editorial sustained its intensity to the end. Pulitzer reminded readers that Roosevelt had created a special government agency to "get the facts" on corporations but had done nothing with it. "The Bureau of Corporations was organized February 26, 1903—more than 19 months, more than 80 weeks—exactly 583 days ago—yes, exactly 583 days ago," wrote Pulitzer. Line after line, Pulitzer pointed out that the agency had obtained no documents, subpoenaed no witness, and exposed no restraint of trade or corporate misdoing, repeating the refrain "after these 583 days" with each accusation.

Returning to his bête noire, Pulitzer charged that Cortelyou was collecting tribute from corporations in return for a promise of protection. Then, he posed ten repetitive questions, set in boldface type. They began with "How much has the beef trust contributed to Mr. Cortelyou?" and continued through each important trust—paper, coal, oil, steel, etc.— until the last one: "How much have the six great railroads contributed to Mr. Cortelyou?"

The ten questions became an instant hit with Democrats, who were desperate for a weapon to use against their foe. It wasn't long before

Democratic speakers began to lead their audiences into chants of "How much? How much? How much?" The actual answer was far less than Pulitzer surmised, especially as corporate leaders had little doubt that Roosevelt would win. Cortleyou declined to respond publicly, but sent a private message to Pulitzer. He took one of the *World's* reporters by the arm in a hotel lobby in Washington. "As God is my witness," he said, "I am conducting an absolutely clean campaign. I have not coerced a penny out of anyone, and my order from the start has been to accept no money on a pledge of any sort whatsoever." The message fell on deaf ears. Pulitzer continued his attacks.

Roosevelt considered the attacks an attempt to divert attention from the Democrats' equally odious money-raising tactics. In the end, he easily dispatched Parker, who took a drubbing even in his home state. The results did little to change Pulitzer's antipathy toward Roosevelt. He promised that the *World* would remain a thorn in Roosevelt's side as he began his first full term as president. "The *World*," Pulitzer wrote, "thinks no more of his military megalomania and his swashbuckler tendencies than it did before; but the returns prove that an overwhelming majority of voters had no such misgiving."

As 1905 began, Pulitzer once again considered an offer by Charles Knapp, the publisher of the *St. Louis Republic*, to buy the *Post-Dispatch*. Knapp had not lost his desire to acquire the *Post-Dispatch*, despite the discordant end to his last round of negotiations with Pulitzer several years earlier. This time he teamed up with Pulitzer's friend David Francis, who had been governor of Missouri and a member of Cleveland's cabinet. In February, during a carriage ride around Jekyll Island, Francis laid out his plan. Essentially, Pulitzer would get $2.5 million in long-term bonds at 8 percent interest. Since Pulitzer did not decline the proposal, Francis left believing he had a deal.

When Francis returned to St. Louis he was shocked to learn that Pulitzer was seeking more cash and fewer loans. He protested that the publisher was changing the terms of their agreement. "Answering your telegram," replied Pulitzer, "you accepted nothing except your own imagination." In the end, the unsigned documents that had been drawn up were forwarded to Seitz in New York; he locked them away in a safe-deposit box. It was the last time Pulitzer would toy with the idea of giving up the newspaper that had launched his career as a publisher.

Francis was not the only one to suffer from Pulitzer's fickleness that winter. President Butler of Columbia University was astonished to learn that his new benefactor no longer wanted to proceed with the plan to build a journalism school. The university had custody of half of the promised $2 million and was ready to proceed. But the fight over the advisory board had left bruised feelings on both sides and Pulitzer altered the terms of his gift. He left it to Merrill to explain his actions.

"Mr. Pulitzer is alone responsible for the present delay," Merrill told reporters. "His present determination is that actual establishment of the college of journalism shall be postponed until his death." He explained that Pulitzer's fragile health prevented him from devoting the necessary time to the project, that a suitable leader for the college had not been located, and that waiting until his death would remove any suggestion that Pulitzer was unduly interfering with Columbia's decisions on how to set up the college, although in fact he was.

"To avoid all uncertainties or misconceptions," Merrill said, "I may add that the endowment of this college is absolutely irrevocable, and its establishment beyond a shadow of doubts." All would have to wait, however, for Pulitzer's death. Columbia would pay him the income from the $1 million it held, and Butler began a deathwatch.

On April 10, 1905, Joseph turned fifty-eight. Kate sent birthday wishes from London. "At least you have the consolation of feeling that your life, though full of worries and much unhappiness, has been full of achievement too, that you will have left your mark in your generation," she wrote. But the birthday reminded Joseph of his mortality and his ever-present fear that his achievement—the *World*—would die with him. In his eyes, neither Ralph nor Joe was preparing for a future role as a newspaper owner. He reminded Ralph that heirs, such as those in the Gould family, were often forced to sell their inherited businesses. "I wish I could still more strongly impress upon you, and above all on Joe, and your mind the necessity of the proprietor's ability to manage his property," he said.

Newspaper management was not foremost on Ralph's mind. He had been courting Frederica Webb, who was the great-granddaughter of Commodore Cornelius Vanderbilt and thus a member of a family the *World* routinely assailed and ridiculed. He was getting up the courage to tell his controlling father that he had asked her to marry him. Ralph had cause to worry. For Joseph's children, any encounter with their father could go wrong. One night at dinner the prior fall, Joseph had told Edith that she must cease riding Constance's horse, which was recuperating from an injury. Edith began to defend herself, but her father cut her off. When she complained, he laughingly said he would probably interrupt her again but that she should continue.

"Oh dear!" exclaimed Edith on the verge of tears. "If anything happens to any horse everybody comes to me about it and everybody says I am to blame. It is not fair. I am tired of this. I will not have it."

"What do you say?" a startled Joseph asked.

"I say I am tired of these accusations," Edith replied.

"Please remember you are talking to your father."

"Certainly, but I must defend myself. It is not fair."

"Fair or not fair, don't forget that you are talking to your father. If you are going to talk that way, I wish you would leave the table."

"I was going when you came, but I came back to talk to you."

"I don't want you to talk to me in that way. I don't want you at the table if you intend to talk that way. Don't come to the table. Don't come back to the table at all."

Kate had mailed her birthday greeting to Joseph from London because the celebrated artist John Singer Sargent was painting her portrait there. Both she and Joseph had long sought a chance to sit for Sargent. James Tuohy, the *World's* London bureau chief, was given the assignment to procure the sittings. Like most emissaries, Tuohy had found it hard to meet with Sargent. "He requires very delicate handling, and is absolutely overwhelmed with commissions," he had reported two years earlier. Pulitzer's longtime friend and companion George Hosmer was also enlisted in the effort and tried to chase down Sargent when he came to Boston. "Will pay anything he wants," Pulitzer telegraphed Hosmer.

Finally the painter consented to having Kate sit for him. "He seems greatly interested in the portrait," Kate excitedly wrote to Joseph after her first day with Sargent. "He is a wonderful artist. I think a genius, his portraits haunt one, he has two or three in his studio now which are quite wonderful." As he sketched her, Sargent told Kate stories of other sittings, describing one of his subjects as "the most objectionable type of a money-grasping, vulgar, Sixth Avenue Jew," oblivious of the fact that Kate had married a Jew.

By mid-May, the sittings came to an end. The completed painting showed Kate in a beguiling pose, standing by a table, her hair coiffed toward the back of her head, her arms to her side, wearing a low-cut dress with many folds and ruffles. She looks demurely outward as if watching someone. In Aix-les-Bains, Joseph received a firsthand report on the portrait from Edith, who wired him an excited appraisal upon its completion. Joseph sent his thanks to the painter. "Sincere thanks on behalf of future generations," he wrote. "Alas, alas that I cannot see it myself." After much inveigling by Kate, Sargent agreed to paint Joseph as well. "I feared it was a hopeless task when I broached the subject as he had refused so many," Kate wrote to Joseph, "but a woman can coax a really great man into any halfway reasonable thing."

Her portrait complete, Kate left England for a cure in France in the company of Constance and Edith. Instead of joining Joseph in Aix-les-Bains, she went to Divonne-les-Bains. There Kate was told that Catherine Davis, her ninety-year-old mother, who had fallen ill a few weeks earlier, was dead. Although the news was not unexpected, its arrival hit Kate hard. "She collapsed entirely and has been neither able to eat nor sleep since, even with very large doses of medicine each night," Maud Alice Macarow, her faithful companion, wrote to Joseph.

Kate wanted to leave and return immediately to the United States. Her doctor, however, insisted that she remain in Divonne-les-Bains. Joseph concurred. "I forbid your mother sailing," he wired Edith. "Both you and Constance must do your utmost to comfort your mother." He instructed Joe, who was in New York, and his secretary George Ledlie to attend the funeral in Washington, where Catherine Davis had lived with her other daughter, Clara. But a day later, Joseph changed his mind. "If you are feeling strongly to sailing, upon reflection, I withdraw my objection." By then, Kate had reconciled herself to missing the funeral.

Almost in a pique of jealousy that Kate's illness outranked his, Joseph sent her one of the angry, spiteful letters he was so capable of writing. Fortunately for Kate, neither Macarow nor Edith had the courage to give her the letter. When he returned to his senses, Joseph asked to have it back. "I am glad you wish your letter to Mother returned as it will be a long time, I fear, before she is in a fit condition to read it. She, of course, knows *nothing* at all about it," said nineteen-year-old Edith, well accustomed to her father's volatile moods.

Unaware of her husband's intercepted missive, Kate completed a long-planned, loving gesture for Joseph. Since before their marriage, he had carried a watch in which was encased a photograph of his late mother. It survived the house fire but was damaged. Kate had brought the watch to London to be repaired. Her consideration extended farther. She had hired an artist to reproduce the miniature portrait of her husband's mother on a large scale. The finished reproduction disappointed her but she sent it on anyway. "I fear it is too small for you to see but at least you can feel that you have a picture of your mother," she wrote, adding that she would have an even larger one made.

Pulitzer took his turn before Sargent in June 1905. Tuohy, the London bureau chief, put aside his regular duties to prepare for Pulitzer's arrival. By now he was used to doing the personal jobs that came with the post. In this case, he made sure that the bedroom windows in the London house Pulitzer rented were refitted with thick plate glass and that Pulitzer's horse, which had been sent ahead of time, was getting acclimatized.

Accompanying Pulitzer to London was Norman G. Thwaites, the thirty-two-year-old son of a British parson. A veteran of the Boer War, Thwaites had joined the cadre of secretaries in 1902. He had been recruited by Tuohy, who referred to the hunt for secretaries as the "pursuit of white mice." Pleasing Pulitzer was nearly impossible. He insisted on hiring unmarried men who could freely travel anywhere in the world. He even dictated that he would hire no short men. "As I have to walk with my companion," the six-foot two-inch Pulitzer explained, "I don't like to stoop too low." To find a suitable candidate Tuohy and Butes had to parse as many as 100 applicants responding to discreet advertisements placed in British newspapers.

When Thwaites first called on Pulitzer, he was brought into a room where Butes was furiously sorting out stacks of applications. Overwhelmed by their number, Butes was preparing to send Thwaites away when Pulitzer suddenly walked in. After introductions were made, Pulitzer brought Thwaites over to the window. He ran his long tapered fingers over the man's head and face and then asked Thwaites to take him by his arm for a walk in the garden. In stronger light, Pulitzer could still distinguish contours of people and objects, but not much more.

The two strolled about for an hour discussing books and plays; this gave Thwaites, a consummate London theatergoer, a chance to impress

Pulitzer. It also bode well that he spoke German, could write shorthand, and knew how to ride horses. His soothing reading voice tipped the balance in his favor, and Pulitzer offered him a trial. In the three years since, Thwaites had become one of Pulitzer's most trusted men.

On this trip, Thwaites had the task of taking Pulitzer for a ride in the park each day before the sittings at Sargent's legendary studio on Tite Street. The painter was a stickler for punctuality, and Kate had warned Joseph, "You will have to be on time as he gets very nervous and out of sorts if one is at all late." Pulitzer assumed that at their first meeting Sargent would want to talk and maybe, at best, execute a few sketches. The painter, however, was in no mood to chat. He immediately placed a canvas on his easel and went to work. "Sometimes I get a good likeness, so much the better for both of us," he said. "Sometimes I don't—so much the worse for my subject but I make no attempt to represent anything but what the outward appearance of a man or woman indicates."

As he said this, Sargent rapidly sketched a perfect charcoal likeness of Pulitzer on the canvas before him. Over the coming days he worked to turn the outline into a portrait. "He worked at a great pace," observed Thwaites, "advancing upon his canvas and retiring much in the manner of a boxer sparring for an opening." Sargent smoked continuously as he worked, filling the studio with the odor of Egyptian cigarettes. Although Pulitzer was a cigar smoker, he despised the smell of cigarettes. "None of us dared smoke them when near him," said Thwaites. Yet now he made no objection. "For three sittings, Pulitzer behaved with singular sweetness."

On the fourth visit to the studio, the painting neared completion. When Thwaites studied it, he thought it showed a genial, aging man with a beneficent countenance. But on this day Pulitzer was followed into the studio by a man who wanted an appointment with him. "Tell him to go away," Pulitzer shouted. "A look of fury and impatience entirely changed the face of the subject, and Sargent contemplated the scene with keen interest, while making a dab or two on the canvas."

In the end, with his final brushstrokes, Sargent captured the dual personalities of Pulitzer. "Hide, with a sheet of paper, one-half the face and you have a benevolent middle-aged gentleman," said Thwaites. "Observe, now, the other half, and you have the malevolent, sinister and cruel expression of a Mephisto. Unconsciously, the painter had presented what he saw."

Chapter Twenty-Eight

FOREVER UNSATISFIED

———————————◆———————————

His image preserved for posterity by one of the great portrait artists of the era, Pulitzer boarded the homebound *Cedric* on July 5, 1905. As he crossed the Atlantic, his secretaries read to him from stacks of accumulated copies of the *World*, a habit he rarely shed. The paper was dominated by front-page stories about an insurance scandal rocking New York.

The story had surfaced several months earlier, when twenty-nine-year-old James Hazen Hyde, heir to a vast insurance fortune, put on a costume ball for the cream of New York society. The event was held at Sherry's, in a building on Fifth Avenue designed by Stanford White, with dining and reception rooms resembling those of French palaces. Actors, dancers, and musicians were hired. Waiters were costumed and wore makeup applied by the staff of the Metropolitan Opera. And even though it was the dead of winter, the rooms were decorated with wisteria, rosebushes, and heather to replicate the gardens of Versailles.

Many of Pulitzer's friends and acquaintances attended the ball, as well as his son Ralph. Katherine Mackay was dressed as Phèdre, a queen of ancient Greece whose love affair and its murderous consequences were a popular subject in French theater. Her silvery costume had a train carried by two black children. The press feasted on every aspect of the event, providing readers with pages of details and illustrations. The party, *Town Topics* said, "rivaled in splendor all the celebrated fancy dress affairs that have been given in the history of New York."

Under normal circumstance, the event would have receded from the front pages after a few days, and into New York lore. But the outlandish cost of the event—said to be around $50,000—provided Hyde's business opponents with evidence they sought to prove his unsuitability to run his father's Equitable Life Insurance Society. The ensuing corporate battle, which eventually embroiled all three of the nation's largest life insurance firms, lifted a veil of secrecy hiding extensive corruption and misuse of funds. The revelations were milked for all they were worth by the press. They shocked readers because the money had been entrusted to the firms to protect working-class families from destitution in the event their provider died.

The *World* aggressively followed every lead in the scandal, and by the time Pulitzer boarded the *Cedric* it had run 122 front-page stories. As the ship's engines drove the liner across the ocean, his secretaries droned on about the Equitable affair. He grew unhappy. When he first heard of the scandal, he had urged his staff to pursue the story. Now he thought the paper had gone too far, and he dictated nearly 100 pages of severe criticism, unloading buckets of complaints on Frank Cobb about Cobb's work on the editorial page. When Pulitzer disembarked in New York, he gave orders that temporarily checked the *World*'s determined pursuit. Several days later, as he traveled north to his retreat in Maine and reviewed a new batch of papers, Pulitzer changed his mind yet again. "Keep up the headline of Equitable Corruption," he ordered. "Mistake to drop 'Equitable Corruption.'"

The staff usually tried to ignore Pulitzer at these moments—especially Cobb, who this time was suspended and then earned a bonus as his boss's enthusiasm for scandal-mongering returned. Back in Pulitzer's good graces, Cobb learned that he could earn even more if he could keep his publisher happy. "And you could not possibly please me more than by swearing to accept my criticism in the future without feeling hurt, even if it should seem to you to be wrong," Pulitzer wrote. "Will you remember this? Swear!"

How to please Pulitzer eluded those who worked for him. One reporter, who had considerable tenure at the *World*, finally had the temerity to sum up the frustration in a note to the boss. "To the mottos of 'Accuracy, terseness, accuracy' that are now on the office walls," he wrote to Pulitzer, "I would add another line—'Forever Unsatisfied.'"

Within a month of his return to the United States, Pulitzer persuaded sixty-four-year-old William Merrill to retire and turn the editorial page over to Cobb. As soon as Merrill had packed up and left, Seitz received a telegram from Bar Harbor. "Please remove from door on the fourteenth floor the name and title of William Merrill and put on it the words: Mr. Ralph Pulitzer, Assistant Vice President."

Merrill was wounded by Pulitzer's callous treatment. At his desk in the Dakota, a famous gabled apartment building on the Upper West Side, he thought back to a time when Pulitzer had held a dinner for his editors at the house on Fifty-Fifth Street. "Don't remember me, I pray you, by anything I may have done in anger," Pulitzer had told them. Then, placing his hand on Merrill's shoulder, he had continued, "There may have been a little difference between Merrill, here, and me, but we are now just as good friends as ever."

Worried that he might not get a pension after nearly twenty years of working for Pulitzer, Merrill returned to the *Boston Herald*, from whence Pulitzer had plucked him years before. A few months later, he at last received a communication from his former employer, although it was indirect, as usual. Pulitzer, Butes wrote to Merrill, "never quite realized that he had lost a friend until he returned to New York, resumed his drives though the Park, recognized the Dakota and remembered that you were no longer there. It still seems impossible to him; he still cannot understand how such a thing could have happened."

Before Merrill could feel sentimental, the next paragraph announced the true purpose of the correspondence. Merrill was asked to return the letters Pulitzer had written to him over the years. Pulitzer was worried that, should something happen to Merrill or Merrill's wife, "there is no telling into whose hands those papers might fall, and how they might be misused." Merrill complied but added that the severance of their friendship remained a mystery to him.

Ralph finally screwed up his courage and informed his parents of his intention to marry Frederica Webb. His selection of a member of one of New York City's elite families was no surprise. Though Ralph worked at the *World*, he shared none of his father's passion for politics or social causes. Tellingly, Ralph kept a photograph of J. P. Morgan on the bureau of his bedroom. In this regard, he was far more like his mother, particularly in his interest in high society. To the public, Ralph was a typical spoiled, protected scion of wealth. Two summers earlier, he had spent three weeks hunting and floating down the Missouri River in Montana in the company of a well-known guide. He proudly sent home a photograph of three bighorn sheep he had killed. Unfortunately, he had violated Montana's game laws, and the game warden found the beheaded carcasses. The state brought charges against Ralph and threatened to have him extradited from New York if he didn't come back on his own accord. In the end, he pleaded guilty to two separate charges and paid $1,000 in fines, and his father paid the $2,000 in bills from a law firm in Montana.

Money was of little concern to Ralph. When he shopped for his fiancée's engagement ring, he felt compelled to buy one costing $5,300. He told his father that the only other choice, which was half the price, "was a very commonplace emerald which would not have born a triumphant comparison with the rings she already has." Both parents made plans to attend the wedding, unlike Ralph's college graduation. At the end of September, Kate returned to the United States after a long stay at the French baths. She felt disconnected. "With the world in which we must live," she wrote to a friend, "the longer we stay out of it the harder it is for one to pick up the broken strands."

On October 14, 1905, on one of the few occasions since Lucille's death seven years earlier, the entire Pulitzer family gathered to celebrate Ralph's wedding to Frederica Webb in Shelburne, Vermont. The Webbs' plans for the wedding—a union of two of New York's most prominent families—were all that one might expect. The hamlet of Shelburne had seen nothing like it before. A few lucky locals received coveted invitations. In nearby Burlington, reported one newspaper, "every dressmaker in the city is busy into the night preparing the costumes of the favored one."

On the morning of the ceremony, a special train, ten cars long, brought guests from New York. Those attending the ceremony reached the little Trinity Episcopal Church in carriages with horses festooned in white chrysanthemums. Kate and the bride's mother, both dressed in white satin with white hats, entered together. Ralph stood at the altar with Joe, who was his best man, while their father sat in a pew. Boys from New York's St. Thomas Church sang as the bridal party processed.

For a brief moment the wedding purged Joseph of his pained complaints about his children, particularly his boys. He became teary-eyed as Ralph and Frederica exchanged vows. It was a rare moment of sentimentality and affection for him. Ralph was similarly ashamed to show emotion in public. "I looked at you as we walked down the aisle," Ralph later told his father, "in fact, yours was the only face I saw, and I felt a lot of things that I probably would not have been able to express to you." This was as close as the Pulitzer men came to expressing affection.

The father expressed his pleasure in the only way he knew. He bought Ralph a house—adjacent to his own in New York—and wrote a large check for the honeymoon. But by the end of Ralph and Frederica's tour of Europe, Joseph was his normal self again. "Your allowance has been stopped," he wrote to Ralph, "and the only thing you will get is your salary. Salaries, by the way, are not paid in advance."

Early in 1906, Pulitzer learned that after all the effort to get Joe into Harvard, the school and his son were a poor match. Joe cut classes, idled away hours enjoying lunches and quiet spells by the fireplace of a fraternity house, and overspent his allowance. Summoned to New York in February, Joseph threatened to pull Joe out of Harvard unless he changed his ways. He didn't, and his father was true to his word.

Joseph decided that Joe's lessons would be better taught in the newsroom and that his new teacher would be Charles Chapin of the *Evening World*, the most accomplished and feared city editor who had ever worked on Park Row. Chapin was already legendary by 1906; a dozen years later he would murder his wife, and thereafter he would spend the rest of his life in Sing Sing prison, tending acres of magnificent rose gardens of his own making. At Pulitzer's *Evening World*, Chapin was unbeatable in the guerrilla warfare of Yellow Journalism; he was also a newsroom tyrant who fired reporters for even the slightest mistake. Journalists put up with Chapin's despotism because he was one of the most innovative and daring editors in New York. "Quite possibly, viewed as a machine, he was the ablest city editor who ever lived," said Stanley Walker, the venerable city editor of the *Herald Tribune*.

In April, Joseph called Chapin. "I am sailing for Europe in the morning, and I am sending Joe down to work under you," he said. "Treat him exactly as you would any other beginner and don't hesitate to discipline him should he need it. There is to be no partiality shown because he is my son." Under Chapin's tutelage, Joe worked assiduously at improving the writing and reporting skills he had learned at the *St. Louis Post-Dispatch*. But he could not resist behaving like the owner's son. He began to take leave from work and was soon absent for an entire week without permission.

When he returned, Chapin fired him on the spot. "The office gasped with astonishment when it got noised about that I discharged 'Prince Joe,' as they called him," recalled Chapin, "but Joe good-naturedly treated it as a joke and took the night train to Bar Harbor, where he fitted out his yacht and sailed in all the regattas that summer, or until his father returned from Europe and sent him out to St. Louis."

His father's continued harshness inflicted great pain on Joe. Only a few months earlier, during a carriage ride and in front of Ralph, Joseph had dressed Joe down as "utterly worthless, ignorant, and incompetent." But in St. Louis, far from his father, Joe found the home he needed at the *Post-Dispatch*. He eventually developed into the most successful editor and publisher among the Pulitzers' children. Despite having named Joe after himself, Joseph would always remain to his death blind to Joe's innate journalistic talents, which matched his own. Temperament separated the two men. Later in the year, after one of their periodic dustups, Joe wisely grasped their distinctness but unwisely shared it with his father. "One of the strange differences between us two, to my mind, is the fact that you have never come near learning how to enjoy life, whereas, I, I fear, have learned the lesson only too well."

After Joe was banished to St. Louis, one of Pulitzer's last remaining connections to his own years there ended. At age seventy-seven, Carl Schurz died. The German-American had inspired Pulitzer to enter politics and—although, curiously, he never mentioned Pulitzer in his memoirs—had remained fond of him, even after their harsh political confrontations in the 1870s. Shortly before his death, Schurz showed a visitor a photograph of Pulitzer that he kept on his desk. Pulitzer instructed Butes to send a wreath with his card, and instructed Kate to represent him at the memorial service. "You would have been proud of your chief," she said, after detailing the many tributes paid to Schurz.

Kate, her companion Maud Alice Macarow, and Edith spent the summer in Europe, as Kate was under doctor's orders to rest at Divonne-les-Bains. Her departure was marred by another quarrel with Joseph. After a prolonged silence, Kate wrote, "Now, don't worry. Understand I have learned to make all allowances for the tricks your nerves play on you and stop being cross with me for it does you no good and does much harm."

In London, Kate returned to Sargent's studio to have tea with the artist. In a pained voice, he told her, "I did not do you all justice in your portrait—you are much better looking than I painted you." It was a compliment that she immediately shared with Joseph, sparking momentary jealousy. But, Kate graciously added, "he spoke nicely of you, said you had such a splendid forehead and were a wonderful type for an artist."

From London, the group went to Paris. Between stops at the salons of her favorite couturiers, on whom she dropped $15,000 that year, Kate toured the sculptor Auguste Rodin's studio. Stephen MacKenna, the *World*'s Paris bureau chief, was a good friend of Rodin and arranged the visit. Rodin, who had begun his career as a controversial artist, had become immensely popular, and his busts were sought after by the wealthy. "He is in sculpture, as Sargent is in painting," Kate said. "There is such soul, poetry, and mystery in his work that in looking at them you feel that you are sensing his touch." The artist, donning his trademark cap, took Edith and Kate on a tour of his studio and his country estate outside Paris. "I wish he could do a bust of you," Kate wrote to Joseph, "it would be just as wonderful as the Sargent portrait."

After Paris, the group moved on to Divonne-les-Bains. One night, when they came down from their hotel rooms for dinner, the waiter took them to a table right next to one where J. P. Morgan was sitting alone. As they passed by, Kate bowed slightly, and Morgan jumped up to shake her hand. During dinner, Edith noticed that whenever her mother glanced in Morgan's direction she would catch his eye and he would smile at her. Small talk soon ensued, and Morgan chatted about his farm in England, which Kate had visited when Morgan's father was living there. When he rose to leave the dining room, Morgan offered Kate a large box filled with fresh strawberries.

"Isn't he hideous," Edith said to her tablemates as Morgan exited the room.

"I don't think he is repulsive," replied Kate, unwilling to indulge her daughter in cattiness.

Macarow, her eyes following Morgan out of the room, murmured, "Well, the back of his head isn't so bad."

Later that night, before retiring, Edith wrote to her father. "Oh dear, I have never seen such a hideous face," she said. "It isn't only the nose—

even with a decent nose he'd be ugly—and he had the ugliest little bits of pig's eyes."

Kate returned to the United States in order to be there in time for the birth of their first grandchild, Ralph Pulitzer Jr. "I am as happy as when Ralph was born," Kate wrote to Joseph. "The baby is a darling. Terrible temper just like yours."

After consecutive failed bids to become president of the United States or mayor of New York City, Hearst rose like a political phoenix in the summer of 1906. He won the Democratic Party's nomination for governor of New York. The press went wild with excitement, covering what otherwise would have been a dull campaign. Kate, who was in New York, accompanied Ralph and his bride to a rally for Hearst at Madison Square Garden. In the White House, Roosevelt could not tolerate the idea that Hearst, whom he despised almost as much as he hated Pulitzer, might hold the post he himself had held before becoming president. He worked to spread rumors of Hearst's immoral behavior. When those charges did not gain enough traction, Roosevelt, resurrecting a hurtful charge, instructed his secretary of state to let it be known that the president believed Hearst had been partially responsible for the assassination of McKinley.

Of all of Hearst's enemies, Pulitzer was the one who remained fair. He issued strict instructions to his staff that his view of Hearst should not color the paper's coverage of the candidate. "Treat Hearst without a particle of feeling of prejudice, if this is possible," he wrote. Two years earlier, when Hearst had run for president, Pulitzer had similarly restrained his editorial staff. "Never for a moment fail to admit that Hearst is a very clever politician, and able man," Pulitzer wrote, ordering that he "should be treated with, at least, that respect which is due to his following." While continuing to oppose Hearst, Pulitzer privately admitted admiration for his rival's allegiance to his principles.

Hearst, however, knew none of this. During his campaign, he made Pulitzer a frequent target. Over the course of seven speeches in New York and Brooklyn, Hearst damned the man he had once admired. "When Mr. Pulitzer was building up his paper he had principles, or at least he professed principles," Hearst said. "When he was appealing for the pennies of the people he proclaimed himself the champion of the people. In his old age, when he has amassed his fortune and has invested it in gas stocks and railroad stocks and other Wall Street securities, he repudiates the principles that made him and betrays the people that supported him.

"False to his principles, false to his own people, he fawns and truckles to a class that uses him while it despises him.

In the end, Hearst lost the election to the Republican, Charles Evans Hughes, though by only a slim margin. Exhausted, Hearst and his family left New York for a vacation in Mexico. Stopping in St. Louis, the defeated candidate went to the *Post-Dispatch* building in order to use the Associated Press facilities to send some business messages. As he entered the building, Joe Pulitzer, who was in exile at the *Post-Dispatch*, saw Hearst and followed him up to the AP office.

"I want to know if you realize what you said in your speeches about my father and I want to know if you believe it," Joe said in a low tone when he caught up with Hearst.

"Many things are said in a political campaign that are regrettable," replied Hearst.

"That won't do," said Joe, interrupting Hearst. "I intend that you shall say whether you believe it or not."

"I usually mean what I say," Hearst said. Then, noticing the young man's rising temper, he crossed his arms in front of his chest, a defensive boxing stance that Joe would have recognized as the "Harvard guard." It was done just in time. Joe struck at Hearst, who warded off the blow. The young Pulitzer tried again, but others in the office held him back while Hearst's wife, who had been seated nearby, grabbed her husband by the arm. Hearst escaped unscathed.

Three decades after his father had shot at a lobbyist and brawled with an editor, St. Louis had another fighting Pulitzer on its hands. "Alas, the punch didn't land," Joe admitted nearly fifty years later, adding, "that's always been one of my regrets."

Kate was proud of Joe and told her husband, "You should feel happy at Joe's feelings for you." Joseph, however, was in no mood to hear about his pugilistic son standing up for him. He had just disembarked from a grim Mediterranean cruise. Hosmer had been ill the entire voyage and had thus deprived Joseph of conversation; and the backup, a loyal secretary, was seasick. Kate tried to comfort Joseph and offered to come to Cap Martin, where he was settling in for the winter. "Whenever I hear that you are lonely and miserable and forlorn, I always want to help and shelter you." But he refused her entreaties, telling her to stay away. "If it is any comfort to you," she wrote back, "I should like you to know I think of you constantly and feel most sorry for you."

Reaching age seventy-five, Hosmer decided that his health would no longer permit him to be in Pulitzer's company. After sixteen years of providing companionship to the publisher, Hosmer told Butes, "I am going home for a rest as I am too much used up by recent illness to be of any good here." He reached New York a few days before Christmas. After completing some errands for Pulitzer, he went uptown to see Kate. When he reached the house, he found Edith and Constance at the lunch table with Kate's personal companion Macarow and another guest. Kate was eating alone in her room.

At length, Hosmer explained that Joseph was depressed, filled with melancholy, lonely, and without any companionship "or any sense just at the present of intimate or pleasant association with any human creature." Kate wanted to leave immediately for France. In 1890, she and Hosmer had rushed across the ocean to rescue Joseph from a similar descent into darkness. This time, though, the two decided that it might make matters worse if Kate went without her husband's consent.

She stayed in New York. "I wish I could give you happiness or least contentment," she wrote to Joseph on Christmas Eve. "As one grows older, peace almost seems happiness. I wonder if that restless spirit of yours will ever accept peace as a substitute for active happiness?" On board the *Honor,* a yacht he had leased to take him to Greece, Pulitzer asked Thwaites to send a note to Butes in New York. "I shall eat my Christmas dinner in solitary grandeur, I suppose."

Shortly after New Year's Day, 1907, Kate's trunks stood packed in her bedroom in New York. Joseph had admitted that he could use her company, and Kate had booked passage to France. But then a telegram arrived. It announced that he was out of his depression and had no need for her care. Although she was pleased that he was better, Kate's anger flared. "There is one thing you must never in your life do again," Kate told him, "that is complain that your family has neglected and deserted you. For I have kept copies of my telegrams urging and telling you to let me join you and also urging you to let the children join you, both of whom were only too willing to go. So you must get that morbidly false idea out of your mind." It was advice he would continue to ignore.

"You would be so much happier, dear," Kate insisted, having regained her composure, "if you would only give people the benefit of the doubt and not assume they must necessarily be always in the wrong and that they intend either way to hurt or to injure you."

To her pleasure, the *World*'s bureau chief in Paris, Stephen MacKenna, persuaded Rodin to travel to Menton in southern France, where Joseph was staying, to execute a bust for the princely sum of 35,000 francs. Joseph, who had taken to the idea, wanted the finished work to be displayed in the Pulitzer Building in New York. But he remained his prickly self as the day neared for the sculptor's arrival. "I can't adapt myself to his pleasure, he must adapt himself to mine, come with me on my ride, not touch me in the afternoon," Pulitzer demanded. "Also, he should definitely have some idea of my character and moods and should make allowances for them. I don't care a damn how ugly he makes me, but he shouldn't misrepresent me. There are elements of romance and tragedy."

"As to the sittings," Pulitzer informed MacKenna, "I cannot possibly give him more than one sitting a day as I am an invalid suffering from insomnia, usually tired." When Rodin arrived in mid-March, Pulitzer found him charming—until the artist asked him to remove his shirt, as he did with every male subject. Pulitzer, who possessed an exaggerated Victorian prudishness, refused. Rodin threatened to leave. He said he could not even begin to do a bust without studying the neck and torso of a subject. With the room cleared of everyone save Rodin's assistant, the sitting began with a shirtless Pulitzer.

Pulitzer's French had grown rusty and Rodin spoke no English, so the two conversed through an interpreter. "But his great personality was easily seen," said Rodin. "His head was that of a master of destiny who by sheer will had risen from a humble beginning to the level of more fortunate fellowmen; then by same force had [reached] one still higher beyond them, where they could not follow because they lacked his character."

Pulitzer asked Rodin to show him as a sighted person. "What I see in your face I will show, and not what you see," Rodin curtly replied. "Blind though he was," the sculptor recalled years later, "he was a great dominant force, and this characteristic I tried to express in my bust of him." Rodin returned to Paris, after three weeks in Menton, convinced that Pulitzer did not have long to live. He told his atelier to lose no time in making the marble bust and the bronze casts.

The sittings with Rodin were the final personal service that Mac-Kenna, who had run the Paris bureau since 1903, rendered for his boss. Unlike Tuohy in London, MacKenna resented doing errands for Pulitzer. Back in Paris, he received a telegram from Pulitzer ordering him to buy six chickens and six ducklings and deliver them to the Gare de Lyon for shipment to Menton. "Refuse de vous acheter six poulets et six canetons; ceci est ma demission," MacKenna wired back. "Refuse to buy you six chickens and six ducklings; this is my resignation."

On April 10, 1907, Pulitzer turned sixty. From southern France, he sent orders for his staff in New York and St. Louis to celebrate the occasion. Sixty editors from the *World* and sixty from the *Post-Dispatch* came together for sumptuous meals at Delmonico's restaurant in New York and at Planter's Hotel in St. Louis, respectively. At an appointed hour, a long-distance telephone line was opened, connecting the two celebrations. Toasts were made late into the night and duly wired to Pulitzer. During the meals, a cable from Joseph, filled with lofty declarations of principle—like those usually chiseled on walls—announced that Ralph would become president of the Pulitzer Publishing Company. Joseph's cable also included a declaration of his retirement, a sequel to the one announced in 1890. But those who worked for him discounted it. Pointedly, no mention was made of any new responsibilities for Joe, who was hosting the dinner in St. Louis.

There still was no truce between the father and his son in exile, despite Joe's endless apologies for any unintended slights. The exile would continue. "There is not one scintilla of a shadow of a shadow, or one shade of a scintilla of a shadow of reason for the thought that I even contemplated your coming to New York last year, this year or next year," Joseph wrote Joe a month after the dinner.

"I do not expect perfection and Lord knows I am indulgent enough and affectionate enough and weak enough in my children," he continued. "But I leave you under no delusion; I must say that if you should work ten times as hard with a hundred times the talent you possess, it would still be no equivalent or recompense for the constant pain and suffering and distress, mental, moral and consequently physical, by day and by night, and almost every waking hour of the night and day, you have caused me this winter before and certainly one winter before that."

Joseph's somber mood had worsened by the time he reached Maine in July. After giving thirteen years of selfless service to an impossible boss, Alfred Butes told Pulitzer he had accepted an offer to work for the British newspaper magnate Alfred Harmsworth, who recently had been given the title Baron Northcliffe. Pulitzer had known the British publisher since first renting houses in England in the 1890s. The two had much in common. Northcliffe, like Pulitzer, had begun his working life as a reporter. By his thirties, he had become his nation's preeminent newspaper publisher. Also, they both discovered that gaining power took a toll on friendships. "I am the loneliest man in the world," Pulitzer once told Northcliffe. "I cannot afford to have friends. People who dine at my table one night find themselves arraigned in my newspaper the next morning."

That Butes went to work for Northcliffe made the desertion all the more painful. Pulitzer had assumed Butes would always remain with him, but signs of trouble had been long evident and might have been noticed by a boss who was sensitive to the feelings of those surrounding him. Butes, who was English, had a wife and child he hardly ever saw. Instead, he accompanied Pulitzer to Europe in the spring, Chatwold in the summer, Jekyll Island in the winter, and New York for occasional stays. "I am a miserable alien," he had told Seitz several years before.

The break cost Butes an inheritance his boss had intended for him, and it destroyed Northcliffe's friendship with Pulitzer. Norman Thwaites was given the unfortunate task of consoling Pulitzer. The two went for a horseback ride in the woods at Bar Harbor. "I sought to keep his mind engaged by bits of news from the day's papers," Thwaites said. But Pulitzer didn't respond, so Thwaites became silent.

"Well, why don't you talk?" Pulitzer suddenly said, swinging at Thwaites with his riding crop. "Is there no news in the paper? Dammit, man, talk, talk!"

When Thwaites explained that he had been talking for an hour, Pulitzer "relented at once and, after apologizing, he bade me to tell him why he was treated so cruelly."

In the fall, Harold Stanley Pollard, who had joined Pulitzer's cadre of assistants in 1905 after a brief tenure at the *New York Times*, went to Paris on a mission to determine what progress Rodin had made on the bust. At first he was turned away from the studio because Rodin was not there, but Pollard persuaded the concierge to let him have a peek at the work. Inside the studio, the man lifted the cloth off the bust. Pollard was struck at once by the resemblance that Rodin had achieved. "My mind flashed over the pictures by Bonnat, Sargent, and even the old-time photographs," he reported to Pulitzer. "He has seen in you the thoughtful mature man. He has depicted in his marble, an expression of mental introspection, a face outward quiet, immobile, gentle, and almost sad in his smooth soft lines, not a feature is harsh, aggressive or combative, but over all there is a wonderful glow of thought, of a brain studying, thinking, planning, pondering, deeply, earnestly, constantly.

"He had neither made the eyes perfect nor sightless. He has given one the slight dropping difference we notice in comparison with the other," Pollard said. The concierge slowly turned the white marble bust. "I caught a sudden view, half profile, half full front. It was you as I have seen you in the quiet of the study when everything around you was quiet and peaceful, when you were thinking and planning those things that have made both history and success."

At last, the attendant threw the cover back over the bust.

"Is it finished?" asked Pollard.

"Yes, it is finished," he replied.

Pollard was not the only man on a mission for Pulitzer. In early December, the London bureau chief James Tuohy and his family traveled to Leith—in Scotland, north of Edinburgh—to join Arthur Billings for the launch of Pulitzer's new yacht. For more than a year, Billings, who had taken leave from his post at the *World*, had supervised the building of the yacht at the famous Ramage and Ferguson shipyard. Painted white, and christened the *Liberty*, the 300-hundred-foot yacht lacked only its engines, funnels, and mast. With a bottle of champagne, Tuohy's daughter Jane launched the ship down the ramp of its dry dock and into the water.

The $1.5 million *Liberty* was the culmination of a long search for a suitable oceangoing vessel. Pulitzer had wanted to own a yacht ever since his days on Jay Gould's in 1883. After he became blind and infirm, Kate had pressed him to find one. His earlier discouraging episode as a yacht owner almost cured him of his desire. But in 1905, at Kate's urging, he began the search in earnest. He considered half a dozen yachts but none seemed suitable. "The great difficulty is that a vessel which would seem very silent to others may be very noisy to me—because of my excessive sensibility to noise," Pulitzer wrote to one seller.

As a result, the *Liberty* had been specially designed to minimize noise, from its bulkhead to its every door and porthole. Once it passed its sea trials, Pulitzer anticipated being able to travel around the globe in a cocoon of silence, served by a forty-five-man crew and a twelve-man staff of personal assistants to read aloud, play music, or provide conversation. "I certainly expect to spend a large part of life-remains I have on the sea," Pulitzer wrote to Hosmer, who had logged more miserable nautical miles traveling with him than any other man. "You know Pulitzer's sea-ways are very far from safe," he joked about himself.

On a Sunday morning in July 1908, the *New York World*'s editor Arthur Clarke was silently sorting papers at his desk on the dais in the twelfth-floor newsroom when the telegraph editor came running in.

"Arthur, Joseph Pulitzer is in the reception room!" he exclaimed.

Clarke smiled but said nothing. Since the opening of the Pulitzer Building in 1890, its owner had been there only twice. If there was to be an apparition, Sunday morning was an unlikely time.

"Arthur, I'm not kidding you," the editor begged. "Joseph Pulitzer is outside. I saw him when I got off the elevator. He's resting on the couch. Seitz, Lyman, Arthur Billings, and a swarm of secretaries are with him. In one minute the whole crowd will be in here."

Clarke remained unmoved, ignoring the frantic excitement of the editor. Then he heard Pulitzer's unmistakable voice. "I'll go to Van Hamm's office, if you say so, but I won't go any damned roundabout way."

He looked up and in came Pulitzer, inappropriately dressed for the summer in a tightly buttoned dark suit and with his eyes hidden by his usual goggle-like dark lenses. The publisher was crossing the cavernous newsroom, a maze of desks normally filled with reporters, editors, and copy boys running between them. Being guided by a secretary just barely prevented Pulitzer from striking a phone booth but caused the secretary a bruise as he, instead of his boss, smacked into it. "Clumsy!" said Pulitzer when he heard the impact.

The group reached the empty office of Caleb Van Hamm, the managing editor. Sitting in Van Hamm's desk chair, Pulitzer asked Seitz how many windows there were in the room. "Three," Seitz replied. Then the party moved to the office of Robert Lyman, the night editor. Pulitzer now asked how far it was from the copy desk. When he was told that fifty feet separated the two, he became agitated. "Idiotic," he said. "Why not put it over in City Hall Park? The night editor must be near the copy desk. No nonsense about it. Swear you will change it!" All took an oath, but as with most of Pulitzer's instructions of this sort, they ignored the directive later, when he was gone.

Pulitzer's irritation was exacerbated by an interview with George Carteret, the night editor. Running his hands over the head of the six-foot-tall, 250-pound editor, Pulitzer exclaimed, "God, you have a big head, Mr. Carteret!"

"You are right, Mr. Pulitzer. I guess I have a big head," replied Carteret.

"You can't deny it. Now tell me, Mr. Carteret, what is in that big head for tomorrow's paper?"

Unfortunately, the editor had come in late and hardly knew what was in that day's edition. "My God! Only half-past eleven! And you haven't read the morning papers! Great God! What kinds of editors are running this paper?" Angry, Pulitzer rose, and his entourage followed. He paused at the city desk before beginning his trek back across the newsroom to the elevators.

"I want to say a word to Arthur Clarke," said Pulitzer. The two men shook hands and, as was usual with Pulitzer, discussed their various health ailments.

"Now tell me, my boy, what are you preparing for tomorrow's morning paper?"

Clarke listed the various anticipated stories and the leads that reporters were following.

"There isn't a good, bright Monday morning feature on the whole schedule," said Pulitzer. Putting his hands on Clarke's head, he added, "What have you in there, Mr. Clarke? That is where your Monday morning feature should be. You must cudgel your brain all week for it." Clarke promised he would.

"I know you will have a good paper tomorrow, Mr. Clarke," finished Pulitzer, who then turned and was escorted from the room, never to return again.

The truth was that the *World* functioned smoothly and successfully without Pulitzer. He had become a figurehead, an aging ruler whose only domain at the paper remained the editorial page. Even there, his hold was tenuous. He complained about its pessimistic tenor. "I am tired of this pitching into everything in this county," he told one of his editors. "I am tired of graft and corruption stories, as if the country were going to the dogs and everything corrupt."

Two months before his surprise visit, the *World* had celebrated its twenty-fifth anniversary under his ownership. Two thousand guests, including dignitaries from Washington traveling in a specially chartered train, gathered at the foot of the building for a spectacular shower of fireworks that bathed all seventeen stories in flickering light for hours. As he had been when the cornerstone was laid, and then when the building was dedicated, Pulitzer was oceans away. Ralph, who presided over the ceremonies, read a cable sent by his father from Nice, where he was testing his new yacht *Liberty*, which the secretarial staff was already calling *The Liberty, Ha! Ha!!*

"Without public approval a newspaper cannot live; the people can destroy it any day by merely refusing it," Ralph said, reading the telegram aloud while standing in front of a portrait of his father draped with flags. "In its last analysis, nay, in its first and every analysis, step by step, day after day, the existence of a newspaper is dependent upon the approval of the public." That the *World* possessed. On an average day that month, the paper sold 707,432 copies and mailed thousands of copies to readers in every state and territory of the union.

At midnight, everyone who could find space crowded into the cavernous underground press room to watch the largest Hoe presses on earth, the size of locomotives, stir to life, rhythmically stamping out a 200-page anniversary issue with eight sections in color.

In August, Pulitzer sailed back across the Atlantic and summoned Seitz to his yacht to discuss coverage of the presidential election. Pulitzer's old Democratic antagonist was back. At the beginning of the year, Pulitzer had done everything in his power to discourage Democrats from turning to William Jennings Bryan for a third time. The *World* even printed, and distributed widely, a pamphlet called "The Map of Bryanism: Twelve Years of Demagogy and Defeat—An Appeal to Independent Democratic Thought, by the *New York World*." It hit its mark. "Mr. Bryan has formally and officially cussed the pamphlet from hell to Harlem," Frank Cobb told Pulitzer.

In fact, Bryan's day had come and gone. Cobb, who had not heard the politician speak since he gave his famous "cross of gold" speech at the convention in 1896, was saddened after attending a New York rally. "He is fat and heavy and bald," Cobb told Pulitzer. "He looks like a traveling evangelist, who had failed as an actor, and then got religion. He speaks slowly and deliberately. He has lost all the sacred fire that made him the greatest orator I ever heard."

Pulitzer instructed Cobb to promote alternative candidates. Cobb was impressed by the president of Princeton University, Woodrow Wilson, and Pulitzer urged him to draft an editorial promoting Wilson as an alternative to Bryan. "What better candidate could they present who would have a better chance to carry New York and New Jersey than anybody I can think of now," the publisher wrote.

Pulitzer's efforts were of no use. Bryan easily won the nomination. Although he was convinced that Bryan would lose to Roosevelt's hand-picked successor, William Howard Taft, Pulitzer ordered Cobb to support the Democratic nominee. "Bryan is as dead as a door nail," Pulitzer told Cobb when they met on the *Liberty*. "A vote for Bryan is not a practical living vote, but a protest; a protest against the tendencies of the party in power; a check and rebuke to stop those tendencies; an exceedingly important rebuke and check if the vote is large enough to keep the party in power after elections on the anxious seat."

Without knowing Pulitzer's motives, Bryan was grateful for the *World*'s support. In 1904 he had privately denounced Pulitzer as a slave to wealth, but now he sent a message of thanks. Pulitzer passed it on to Cobb. "It is a sign of forgiveness which might amuse you," he wrote in an accompanying note.

Pulitzer believed that the *World* could increase its credibility and power if it mounted a campaign to resist Roosevelt's plans to create a legacy for himself as a great president. "The country has gone crazy under Roosevelt's leadership in extravagance for the war idea," Pulitzer said. "All my life I have been opposed to that so-called militarism. I may be crazy in thinking the country crazy, but the fact remains we have increased our war expenditures over one hundred millions a year." As far as Pulitzer was concerned, Roosevelt had set the nation on a course of unbridled, unneeded, and unwise military growth. "The logic of jingo-ism, Rooseveltism, seems to be that the greater we are in population and strength, the more afraid we must be of foreign attack and war."

Roosevelt might be a lame duck, but Rooseveltism was an enemy yet to be vanquished.

Chapter Twenty-Nine

CLASH OF TITANS

◆

On the evening of October 2, 1908, William Speer, the editor whom Pulitzer had detailed to work for the Democratic presidential nominee in 1904, was at his desk in the editorial offices under the gold-leaf dome of the Pulitzer Building. As usual, the publisher was overseas and the editorial department was doing its best to carry on. But waging Pulitzer's fight against Roosevelt seemed a futile exercise for those, like Speer, who wrote the *World*'s editorials. Neither its relentless attacks on the president—and thus on his successor, William Howard Taft—nor its support of Bryan was having much effect on the electorate. The day before, when Taft proclaimed in Bryan's home state of Nebraska, "I am going to be elected," few doubted his prediction.

The one promising bit of hard news on this otherwise slow day was a tip that Speer received from an acquaintance. Reportedly, a group of Panamanians, disgruntled because they were not among those who profited from the canal now under construction in their new nation, had arrived in New York. If these men could be located, they might confirm a story that the *World*'s reporters had doggedly pursued for years.

According to rumors, when President Roosevelt concluded his deal in 1902 to build the canal, $40 million earmarked by the U.S. government to purchase a French company's holdings in Panama had gone to an American syndicate created by William Nelson Cromwell, the project's main lobbyist. Indeed, the transaction, along with the money, had been entrusted to J.P. Morgan & Co. which seemed short on proof that it had been used to pay off the French. Rather, the *World*'s reporters believed, the syndicate had earlier bought out the French bondholders and then pocketed the money. Cromwell's own behavior did nothing to dampen speculation about who got the money. In 1906, when testifying before a U.S. Senate committee, he refused to discuss his part in the canal transaction, claiming it was protected by attorney-client privilege.

The story had immense appeal in the anti-Roosevelt *World*'s newsroom, which was well aware of Pulitzer's long-running battle with the one time boy wonder of New York politics. On the other hand, Roosevelt held nothing more sacrosanct than the building of the canal. He considered it one of his crowning achievements and would tolerate no questioning of his motives or actions in obtaining it—to do so meant impugning his character.

Speer left his office, went down a flight of stairs to the newsroom and located the night editor. Under Pulitzer's ownership, the paper had assembled a vaunted news-gathering team and was enjoying a renaissance in prestige and power after distancing itself from its association with Hearst's *American*. (The *Herald* and the *Tribune* were growing progressively weaker; later, they would merge, but now the union was nearly twelve years in the future. By contrast, the once anemic *New York Times* was gaining strength. Among its admirers was Pulitzer himself. "You may not know that I have the *Times* sent to me abroad when the *World* is forbidden," he had written to Adolph Ochs earlier in the year, "and that most of my news I really receive from your paper.")

After listening to Speer, the night editor sent out one of his best men to hunt down the rumored Panamanians. The man checked all his sources, including some among those who had participated in financing the canal. But it was to no avail. The Panamanians could not be found, if they existed at all. Meanwhile, though, his snooping was noticed.

Around ten o'clock that night, Jonas Whitley, a former reporter for the *World* who now did publicity work for Cromwell, came into the newsroom. He confronted the managing editor, Caleb Van Hamm, about pursuing a story concerning Cromwell without checking with him. As Whitley talked, Van Hamm realized he knew nothing about it but saw an opportunity. "Dear, dear, Jonas, sorry to hear that," he said. "Tell us all about it."

Whitley sat down and spewed a remarkable story that he thought wrongly the *World* already knew. Cromwell, he said, was being blackmailed by men who threatened to turn over evidence of his wrongdoing in the Panama affair to the Democratic Party unless he paid them off.

When Whitley was done, Van Hamm promised to locate the article supposedly being written and told him to return in an hour, when he would be given a chance to review it before it appeared.

As soon as Whitley left, Van Hamm hurriedly dictated an account from his notes. When Whitley came back, Van Hamm showed him proofs of the story. The public relations man made some minor corrections, picked up a telephone, and read the story to Cromwell. A few hours later it appeared in the early edition of the *World*. The rumors—founded or unfounded—that Cromwell and his cohorts had profited from the canal deal were in print. Among the alleged profiteers were Douglas Robinson, the president's brother-in-law; and Charles P. Taft, the brother of the presidential candidate.

"But for Mr. Cromwell it is probable that no Panama story of any kind would have been printed during the campaign," said Speer's boss, Frank Cobb, "and it is certain that the names of Charles P. Taft and Douglas Robinson would not have been published in connection with the affair."

After years of dormancy, the story of corruption involving the canal was back on page one.

Over the next few weeks, as Taft successfully concluded his presidential campaign against Bryan, the *World*'s reporters did everything they could to keep this story alive. Pulitzer urged them on. "Examine the record, especially his [Cromwell's] Panama record and his relations with corporations and trusts," he wired from Wiesbaden. The paper ran a long profile of the lobbyist, reported the firing of the Canal Zone governor because he had uncovered evidence of the alleged fraud, published copyrighted reports from its Paris correspondent on his efforts to solve the mystery, and even hired a prominent British lawyer and member of Parliament to dig into the French records. Finally, the paper admitted defeat. "Every source of official information as to the identity of who got the $40,000,000 is not only closed, but wiped out, obliterated, as a result of an agreement between the United States Government and the new Panama Canal Company," reported the *World*'s Paris correspondent.

The articles, while conceding that there was no evidence tying Cromwell to an illegal scheme, resurrected the public's doubts about the murky means by which the United States had acquired the Canal Zone when Roosevelt, in his words, "took the isthmus." The temerity of the *World* in raising these issues again at the close of his reign caught Roosevelt's attention. He had expected the worst from Pulitzer's paper, but his anger grew when other newspapers picked up on the *World*'s reporting as if the malfeasance had been proved. "Who got the money?" asked the *Indianapolis News* on the eve of the election. "For weeks this scandal has been before the people," it continued. "The records are in Washington, and they are public records. But the people are not to see them—till after the election, if then."

Pulitzer was sailing across the ocean in blissful ignorance of the tempest his newspaper was stirring up. He had been on course for Bermuda, but he changed his mind and arrived in New York a few days before the election. He went to bed in his house there by ten o'clock in the evening. "What is the use of sitting up for a foregone conclusion?" he told Seitz. Taft won handily, as the public endorsed Roosevelt's selection of his successor.

With the election over and his man triumphant, Roosevelt vented his anger in a private letter to a friend in Indiana, where the *World*'s accusations had received prominent attention in the press. The president charged that the men behind the articles on the Panama Canal were liars for hire or were seeking to boost circulation. "The most corrupt financiers, the most corrupt politicians are no greater menace to this country than the newspaper men of the type I have above discussed," he wrote. "Whether they belong to the yellow press or to the purchased press, whatever may be the stimulating cause of their slanderous mendacity, and whatever the cloak it may wear matters but little. In any event they represent one of the potent forces for evil in the community."

By the time Roosevelt's reaction became public, Pulitzer had left New York for a postelection cruise in southern waters. Seitz jumped onto a train and caught up with the *Liberty* as it docked in Charleston. Roosevelt's letter, which had focused on the *Indianapolis News,* was on the front page of the local paper in Charleston, along with an interview with Delavan Smith, publisher of the besieged newspaper in Indiana. The two items were read to Pulitzer, who knew little of what had happened since he left New York.

An astonished Pulitzer listened as his secretary read on. Smith was backpedaling as fast as he could. "The President's comments on the Panama editorial are based on statements made by a prominent New

York paper, not the New York *Sun*," Smith told reporters who caught up with him on a train leaving Chicago. He claimed that the *Indianapolis News* had credited the information to "the New York newspaper making the charge and distinctly disclaimed any responsibility for its accuracy."

"What New York paper does Smith mean?" asked Pulitzer.

"The *World*," replied Seitz.

"I knew damned well it must be."

Roosevelt had not mentioned the *World*. It was entirely possible that the matter might blow over, now that he had let off steam with his attack on the *Indianapolis News*. But Speer was in no mood to let the president's comment pass unchallenged. He and Cobb conferred. "Up to this time the *World* had not discussed the Panama matter editorially," Cobb said. "But when Mr. Roosevelt went so far as to tell the American people that the United States government 'paid the $40,000,000 direct to the French government,' it seemed to the *World* that the time had arrived when the country was entitled to the truth and the whole truth."

By the time the *Liberty* reached New York, Speer had published an unusually long editorial that meticulously demonstrated how Roosevelt's statement contradicted the public record. In blunt terms, he accused the president of knowingly lying. "The fact that Theodore Roosevelt as President of the United States issues a public statement about such an important matter full of flagrant untruths, reeking with misstatements, challenging line by line the testimony of his associate Cromwell and the official records, makes it imperative that full publicity come at once through the authority and action of Congress."

Pulitzer did not know of Speer's remonstrations against the president. Whether Pulitzer wanted a fight with the president or not, he now had one.

Roosevelt still had three months left in office, and the power to pursue his quarry. On December 9, the day after the *World*'s editorial appeared, Roosevelt contacted Henry Stimson, the U.S. attorney for the Southern District of New York. Two years earlier, Roosevelt had selected the thirty-eight-year-old Republican corporate lawyer—who shared the president's love of hunting and the outdoors—over other, more prominent candidates for the post. The appointment put Stimson on a road that would eventually take him to the highest level of national government. Already, he was being touted as a candidate for governor, and he remained deeply grateful to the president for his good fortune.

"I do not know anything about the law of criminal libel, but I should dearly like to have it invoked about Pulitzer, of the *World*," Roosevelt told Stimson. "If he can be reached by proceeding on the part of the Government for criminal libel in connection with his assertions about the Panama Canal, I should like to do it," Roosevelt said, frankly confessing the depth of his enmity toward Pulitzer and setting Stimson on the publisher's trail.

"When I was Police Commissioner I once and for all summed him up by quoting the close of Macaulay's article about Barère* as applying to him." The fights of 1895 between the *World* and Roosevelt, especially those when he sought to enforce the city's blue laws, were never far from Pulitzer's thoughts either. "Roosevelt as Police Commissioner was very much like he is in the present time," Pulitzer had warned Cobb earlier in the year. "The child is father of the man."

Roosevelt wanted revenge for years of abuse from the *World*, and he was willing to use the federal government's prosecutorial powers in his personal vendetta. But to do so would require invoking a rule of law that had its roots in the notorious fifteenth-century English Star Chamber. Even though American common law was based in great part on that of England, the use of criminal proceedings for libel had long fallen into disfavor except in cases that involved a breach of peace. Not since the discredited Alien and Sedition Acts of 1798 had a president so brazenly sought to stifle criticism of the government. If Roosevelt had his way, Pulitzer would spend his final years behind bars.

Stimson found the envelope from the White House on his desk the next day. A highly competent attorney, though one with political ambitions, he knew that the president was overreaching his powers. "Without

---

*Roosevelt, insultingly, was comparing Pulitzer to Bertrand Barère de Vieuzac, the historian Thomas Macaulay's favorite whipping boy. Barère was an advocate of the guillotine during the French Revolution. Typical of the comments made by Macaulay was one in an essay of 1844. "Barère approached nearer than any person mentioned in history or fiction, whether man or devil, to the idea of consummate and universal depravity. In him the qualities which are the proper objects of hatred, and the qualities which are the proper object of contempt, preserve an exquisite and absolute harmony." (Thomas Babington Macaulay, *Complete Works of Lord Macaulay* [London: Longmans, Green, 1898], 170.)

having yet had the time to look it up in connection with this case I am of the very strong impression that there is no Federal law punishing criminal libel," he told Roosevelt, in a letter marked "Personal." In an earlier case involving attacks against a federal judge, Stimson explained, the only remedy that could be found was in state courts. "But as I said before, I will have the matter thoroughly investigated and will report to you."

Impatient, Roosevelt looked for other ways to bring the might of the federal government down on Pulitzer. In hopes of getting a congressional committee to pursue the matter, the president contacted a Republican senator, Philander Chase Knox, who had served as his attorney general when the United States fostered a revolution in Panama so as to gain control of the Canal Zone. "Oh Mr. President," Knox had said at the time, "do not let so great an achievement suffer from any taint of legality."

"It seems to me," Roosevelt told Knox, "at least well worth considering whether it would not be wise once and for all to nail the infamous and slandering falsehoods of Mr. Pulitzer, published in his paper, the New York *World*, and of those who have taken their cue from the Pulitzer publications."

Next, Roosevelt composed a 4,800-word "special message" to the Senate and the House, attached a stack of documents, and sent the packet to Capitol Hill. When members of the Lake to Gulf Waterways Association visited the White House, Roosevelt publicly tipped his hand. "We have cause to be ashamed of a certain set of Americans in connection with the canal, and that is of those Americans who have been guilty of infamous falsehood concerning the acquisition of the property and the construction of the canal itself," he told the group. "If they can be reached for criminal libel, I shall try to have them reached."

On December 15, 1908, the secretaries of the Senate and the House began reading the president's message to their respective chambers. Because accusations of corruption surrounding the canal had once again surfaced, Roosevelt told the lawmakers, he was submitting to them a complete rebuttal. At that, the few senators who were on the floor broke into laughter. The merriment grew when Roosevelt added that no one believed anything published in Pulitzer's newspaper. The House was more circumspect, especially as one of its members had introduced a motion to investigate the canal matter.

Two minutes into the message, it became clear that Roosevelt had far more in mind than a simple refutation of the accusations. "The real offender is Mr. Joseph Pulitzer, editor and proprietor of the *World*," Roosevelt said. These libelous actions, he claimed, were so egregious that Pulitzer should be prosecuted by the government. "It is therefore a high national duty to bring to justice this vilifier of the American people, this man who wantonly and wickedly and without one shadow of justification seeks to blacken the character of reputable private citizens and to convict the Government of his own country in the eyes of the civilized world of wrongdoing of the basest and foulest kind, when he had not one shadow of justification of any sort of description for the charge he had made." To that end, Roosevelt announced that the attorney general was considering by what means to prosecute Pulitzer.

Roosevelt did not mention Stimson's estimation that there were no applicable federal laws. In state court, both the president's brother-in-law and the brother of the president-elect had grounds to pursue a civil libel case. For that matter, so would Cromwell, if he were willing to have a court examine his conduct during the acquisition of the canal. The president, as a public figure, would have a harder time winning a libel case. But that was not his goal. By his public declaration and his behind-the-scenes orders to the Justice Department, Roosevelt made it clear he wanted to use the Federal Government as a club to silence Pulitzer.

Congress returned the documents without comment. Its silent but mocking response only further aggravated the president. If the legislature didn't care about his reputation, he would make sure those who worked for him did.

While Roosevelt was seeking help from Congress in punishing Pulitzer for his affront to the presidency, the *Liberty* docked in New York. In the soundproof underground room of Pulitzer's house on East Seventy-Third Street, it fell to Norman Thwaites to read aloud an account of Roosevelt's message appearing in the evening papers. The secretary steeled himself for an angry outburst, but none came. "Go on," Pulitzer said quietly, and Thwaites continued reading. "Suddenly," Thwaites said, "he rose from the couch on which he was taking his afternoon rest and smote the coverlet with clenched fist."

"The *World* cannot be muzzled! That's the headline," Pulitzer burst out. Then, dictating at a clip that strained the capacity of Thwaites's shorthand, he dictated an editorial. "Send for Cobb. Tell him to be here in a half-hour." Pulitzer also summoned his managing editor, Van Hamm. They took a carriage ride around Central Park. Van Hamm brought Pulitzer unwelcome news. "We have no conclusive evidence to establish those statements which the President charges us with making," he told Pulitzer. Reviewing the course of events, he insisted that the *World* was not at fault. Robinson and Taft were linked to the scandal by Cromwell's public relations man, who had named them in his statement about the alleged blackmail that triggered the whole affair.

This didn't satisfy Pulitzer. He ordered the paper to stop printing any more articles about Panama and the missing money. "It is idiotic, as we have no proof whatever of any of these charges. Impress this upon Mr. Van Hamm. I want accuracy, truth, and restraint," he told Seitz. "The honor and truthfulness of the paper is my honor. Much of what Roosevelt says is true. The *World* ought not have made that charge."

There was nothing Pulitzer could do about that now. Instead, he talked with Cobb about mounting the paper's defense. Pulitzer wanted to follow up his editorial with a selection of Roosevelt's previous denunciations to illustrate the president's extreme verbal intemperance. "Now, I hope this is clear and that you will put every single one of the editorial writers to work," he told Cobb. "Tell the editorial gentlemen to dine downtown at my expense and have a good bottle of wine. Let them stay down till midnight. I consider this an emergency."

By nightfall, Pulitzer also released a statement for the reporters, who had been calling all day. "So far as I am personally concerned," he said, "I was at sea during the whole of October, and, in fact, practically for two years I have been yachting on account of my health." He claimed never to have read any of the offending articles and said he had nothing to do with them. "Mr. Roosevelt knows all this perfectly well. He knows I am a chronic invalid and mostly abroad yachting on account of my health."

It was a half-truth. Although Pulitzer had been unaware of the escalation of the stories about Panama, he knew that the paper was pursuing the matter. In fact, as early as June he had discussed it with Cobb. He liked to claim that his only domain was the editorial page, but he frequently called for news coverage of issues that interested him. In September, for instance, he had provided lengthy instructions for the *World* to go after Roosevelt's moneyman Cortelyou.

Yet Pulitzer did not choose to escape blame entirely. He said that the paper was his and he took general responsibility for its continual attacks on Roosevelt and the president's policies. "I am really sorry he should be so very angry but the *World* will continue to criticize him without a shadow of fear even if he should succeed in compelling me to edit the paper from jail."

Aid came from a surprising quarter. In Lincoln, Nebraska, William Jennings Bryan published a defense of Pulitzer in his newspaper, the *Commoner*. "Mr. Pulitzer is on solid ground when he resists the President's attempt to convert newspaper criticism of officials into criticism against the government itself," said Bryan. "The President's message is indefensible in so far as it asserts the right of the government to prosecute the *World* or Mr. Pulitzer."

Pulitzer believed prison was a real possibility, and he said so to his friends, though he put on a brave face. "We are treating the thing with some hilarity," he wrote to one friend a few hours after Roosevelt's intentions became known. "I think it simply an effort to shut up the paper's criticism just as Congress and Senate have been shut up." Still, Pulitzer wanted to escape New York as soon as he could. But as the object of a possible government prosecution, he couldn't make a move without checking with the U.S. attorney. The next day, Pulitzer sent Seitz to see Stimson.

"How long will Mr. Pulitzer be away?" Stimson asked Seitz.

"A few days," he replied.

"I will not need Mr. Pulitzer for a few days," Stimson said ominously, concluding the conversation.

On December 16, 1908, as the *Liberty* sailed out of New York harbor, Pulitzer's editorial appeared in the *World*. Greatly massaged by Cobb, and improved by research, it was an eloquent defense of the newspaper and the rights of the press. "Mr. Roosevelt is mistaken. He cannot muzzle the *World*," the editorial began. It urged Congress to investigate the transactions involving the Panama Canal and cheekily said that the *World* felt complimented by the president's prosecution.

"This is the first time a President ever asserted the doctrine of lèse-majesté, or proposed, in the absence of specific legislation, the criminal prosecution by the Government of citizens who criticized the conduct of the Government or the conduct of individuals who may have had business dealings with the Government." Neither the king of England nor the German emperor, the editorial noted, had such power. "Yet Mr. Roosevelt, in the absence of law, officially proposes to use all the power of the greatest government on earth to cripple the freedom of the press on the pretext that the Government itself has been libeled—and he is the Government.

"So far as the *World* is concerned, its proprietor may go to jail, if Mr. Roosevelt succeeds, as he threatens; but even in jail the *World* will not cease to be a fearless champion of free speech, a free press and a free people. It cannot be muzzled."

The *Liberty*'s southerly course prompted unfounded rumors that Pulitzer was on his way to Panama to obtain vindicating evidence. A blind publisher was hardly the person to conduct the necessary research. From Norfolk, Virginia, where the *Liberty* paused briefly, Pulitzer ordered a reporter for the *World* in England to leave for Paris and "dig twelve hours a day on who really got the money"; he also told Scitz to hire Wall Street investigators to conduct a similar investigation on this side of the Atlantic. All the work had to be coordinated by one editor, said Pulitzer. "Tell him to be scrupulously careful weighing every word," he said, repeating his old refrain. "But accuracy, accuracy, accuracy."

Summoned, Cobb raced by train to meet the yacht at Old Point Comfort at Norfolk. On board he found a highly disquieted Pulitzer, worried about the possibility of prison but still capable of seeing the irony of his potential fate. "For years we have asked Roosevelt to send somebody to jail, so he begins on the editors of the *World*," Pulitzer said. He now believed that Roosevelt would seek to prosecute him in state court.

"My opinion is that if anything comes out of this Roosevelt Panama matter it will be through Jerome," he told Cobb, referring to New York's district attorney William Jerome. The *World* had long supported Jerome but had recently aroused his ire by criticizing his prosecutorial decisions. It was an attack that now seemed ill-timed. "We pitched into Jerome because he did not do anything about wealthy lawbreakers; now he turns against the *World*." Pulitzer asked Cobb to convey a private message to Jerome that though he took responsibility for everything in his newspaper, he had known nothing of the articles and had been out of touch when they appeared. In effect, he was throwing his editors to the wolves.

Legally, Pulitzer's guess was on the mark. Stimson had already told Attorney General Charles Bonaparte that he had found no law, precedent, or means to charge Pulitzer in federal courts. Stimson met at his house with Jerome. "He is ready and anxious to cooperate in any way, and he has told me he considers the movement of the utmost importance," Stimson said, adding that such an approach would benefit the president. "This would tend to minimize the danger of the Panama prosecution being criticized as personal to President Roosevelt."

Despite Stimson's hesitance to pursue the president's plan to prosecute Pulitzer in federal court, Roosevelt felt confident. On January 30, 1909, he lunched with Douglas Robinson, one of the supposed victims of the libel; his sister Corinne Roosevelt Robinson; and the treasurer of the Republican Party. Roosevelt and his brother-in-law reviewed the case. "Both the President and Mr. Robinson," said an aide who sat in on the lunch, "think they will put Pulitzer in prison for criminal libel."

Later that night, Roosevelt attended the Gridiron dinner—an annual press gathering, characterized by bawdy humor and skits—in Washington's Willard Hotel. The one representative of the *World* who attended reported privately to New York that he had overheard the president promising to make an example of Pulitzer for crooked journalism in deceiving people about government. "I mean to cinch these men, the ringleaders and not their hired men or agents for the damage they have done."

With the clock ticking on his term of office, Roosevelt stepped up the pressure on the Justice Department to get Pulitzer. The intensity of the investigation was felt at the *World*. Pulitzer and others on the paper became convinced that federal agents were snooping through the mail and examining the documents carried by hired messengers between Washington and New York. The fear made the use of Pulitzer's codebooks an even greater imperative. Soon a new code word, "Charlotte," was added to the 5,000 entries already in the book. It meant extradition, and Pulitzer wanted to know if he could be extradited from Bermuda should he go there.

Pulitzer could not restrain his anxiety. He repeatedly asked Cobb to play up his infirmities to "dispel the general myth and assumption that a totally blind man and confirmed invalid can be the editor of a paper like the *World* in any responsible sense whatsoever." At the same time, Pulitzer knew that the stakes were more than personal. If Roosevelt were to win, he told his editors, "it will stop all criticism and free thought in the majority of papers and absolutely abolish opposition of any kind—and it will give the government—nay not the government but the administration—the party in power—complete license and make it more powerful than even Roosevelt has been."

The Justice Department's attorneys convened two grand juries—one in Washington, D.C., and another in New York City—and began issuing subpoenas to a wide cast of characters that included editors in New York and a boy who sold newspapers on the streets of Washington. Government lawyers, however, remained mum on the purpose of the proceedings. Attorney General Bonaparte refused all comment when reporters caught up with him in Baltimore. "I must, therefore, ask my good friends of the press to exercise the great virtue of patience just now, promising to soon let them know all there is to be known or at all events all that I can tell them," he said.

Stimson was convinced that this approach was a mistake. If the government remained silent, he told Bonaparte, newspapers would use the secrecy surrounding the case as proof that it was on a fishing expedition. He was right. "This action by the Government is said to be without precedent in the history of American jurisprudence and lawyers regarded as authorities in libel actions are puzzled as to the exact course the Government will adopt," reported the *New York Times*, a newspaper not known for hyperbole, even then. "It is said that all the proceedings are being personally supervised by President Roosevelt." The secrecy even prompted a U.S. senator to seek a resolution to compel Bonaparte to disclose whether the president had ordered the prosecution and, if so, under what statute.

Ralph, who feared he might also be indicted, met with his father's legal team. It consisted of the reform-minded lawyer De Lancey Nicoll, who had remained loyal since 1887, when Pulitzer had backed him in a contentious election; and John Bowers. Reviewing the subpoenas and other documents, the two lawyers noticed a pattern that led them to consult a federal law book so old that it was musty and its typeface used what looked like an "s" for an "f." There they at last uncovered the legal strategy that Roosevelt's lawyers planned to use in the government's pursuit of Pulitzer.

* * *

Since there was no current applicable law, the Justice Department was dusting off an obscure law of 1825. Under its terms, the federal government retained the right to prosecute a crime committed on federal property, such as West Point, using state law in the absence of a federal criminal statute. Astonishingly to the lawyers, this law required that the prosecution be based on state laws that existed prior to 1825. In other words, the government was planning to prosecute Pulitzer by using century-old state laws that might no longer be in force.

Everything became clear. The two grand jury proceedings were held so that the prosecutors could use a Maryland law of 1802 (the District of Columbia had, in its early days, adopted Maryland's laws) and a New York law of 1805. If one effort failed, the other might prevail. The discovery also solved the puzzle of why Jerome had participated in the investigation by the New York federal grand jury. If this plan succeeded, Jerome would try the case jointly with Stimson.

Nothing like this had ever been attempted before by federal prosecutors. Pulitzer's lawyers knew that if it was made public, the government's case would appear to be on shaky ground. To make the best use of their discovery, Nicoll and Bowers gave the story to all the press, rather than holding it for the *World* alone. The strategy worked. Newspapers such as the *New York Times* reported it on the front page. The headline in the *Times* read, LIBEL PROSECUTION SECRET COMES OUT: HALF-FORGOTTEN LAW USED.

Stimson was infuriated. He telephoned Bonaparte and, failing to reach him, sent an angry telegram. Later, a bit calmer, Stimson explained his actions to his boss. "I was anxious," he said, "that a statement of the real ground of my investigation should be issued by the Government before a biased and perverted account should be issued by the other side." Now it was too late. Pulitzer had won the first round in the court of public opinion.

Cobb seized the high ground. "To prosecute the *World* under the antiquated statute of 1825," he wrote, "would represent the last word in the prostitution of the Federal machinery of justice to gratify the personal malice of an autocratic President."

In the legal proceedings, the news was no better for the president. All the witnesses brought before the New York grand jury had invoked their Fifth Amendment right not to testify. One after another, the *World*'s treasurer, J. Angus Shaw; Pulitzer's banker Dumont Clarke; the editor Florence White; and others remained closemouthed in front of the jury. If Stimson wanted to force them to answer his questions, he would have to bring them before a judge in an open court, and the questions the government wanted to keep secret would become public. He was getting nowhere.

"Thus far, we have not connected either of the Pulitzers with the commission of the offense, and in my opinion, have not evidence to indict either," Stimson reported. This was not what the president wanted to hear. Roosevelt sent a terse note to Stimson, dropping the usual "Dear Harry," demanding that he come to the White House.

The following morning, before meeting with his cabinet, the president sat down with Stimson and Bonaparte at the White House. Also present was Roosevelt's brother-in-law Douglas Robinson; he had just returned from seeing Jerome, the district attorney in New York, who had not ruled out bringing his own case against the *World*. When this gathering broke up, Stimson and Bonaparte returned to the Justice Department, where they conferred with the U.S. attorney for Washington and his assistant. The message was clear. Roosevelt wanted Pulitzer in the dock.

Like most lawyers who examined the case, Jerome had doubts about it, but he enjoyed having a chance to torment Pulitzer. As Stimson spun his wheels, Jerome remained mostly mum about his intentions. The *World* assigned reporters to tail Jerome and to try to get his assistants to leak his plans. But nothing could be learned. When Pulitzer returned from his cruise, confounding those who thought he had gone to Panama, he told Seitz to find out what Jerome was planning. Seitz turned to a star writer from the *Evening World*, Irvin Cobb (not related to Pulitzer's editorial writer Frank Cobb). Cobb had gotten to know the district attorney when he covered the famous trial of Harry K. Thaw, who murdered Stanford White. Seitz hoped he might use this friendship to determine Jerome's plans.

"To put it badly," Seitz said when he brought Cobb into his office, "we've exhausted practically every expedient, every available resource we could think of—we and our lawyers and other representatives—and without success. A grave emergency exists. Mr. Pulitzer is in a very depressed, very harassed state. The possible consequences to his health are dangerous—most dangerous. So as a last resort we are asking your cooperation."

Cobb agreed and was told he could use as much money and man-power as he needed to get the job done. However, he simply hopped onto a trolley and rode down to Pontin's Restaurant, a popular hangout for lawyers. There he found Jerome having a drink. "I don't like a hair in that man's head," said Jerome when Cobb asked him about Pulitzer. "He has attacked me viciously, violently, and without due provocation.

"Even so," Jerome continued, "I never intended to make either a burnt offering or a martyr out of him." In fact, Jerome said that within forty-eight hours of meeting with Stimson he had made up his own mind not to pursue the case. But because he had been annoyed by the *World's* behavior toward him, he admitted, "I've let King Pulitzer—and his gang of sycophants—stew in their own juice."

Cobb returned to the office and reported what he had found out. Seitz put him on a telephone to Pulitzer's house and asked him to repeat this to Norman Thwaites. After hearing it, Thwaites said that Pulitzer was sitting with him and wanted to know how Cobb had obtained the information so quickly.

"Well, it's like this," said Cobb, who then recounted his trolley ride and the alcohol-laced interview with Jerome.

"Well, I wish I might be God-damned," said Pulitzer, loud enough to be heard over the telephone, when Thwaites had repeated the tale. Cobb turned in his expense report of ten cents for his trolley rides and returned to work.

Stimson remained firmly convinced that Pulitzer was beyond his reach. In February he instructed the grand jury that there was not enough evidence to indict Joseph and Ralph Pulitzer. "I am sorry for the President's disappointment," Stimson wrote to Bonaparte, carefully choosing his words, "but feel sure he appreciates the impossibility of my allowing the grand jury to indict a man without legal evidence, no matter how much reason there might be to imagine he was also probably responsible." Further, he warned that the case in New York against the *World* would be endangered if the grand jury in Washington made the mistake of indicting the Pulitzers. Once they were indicted, their lawyers would be able to make public evidence revealing the weakness of the government's case. "It will also go a long way," Stimson said, "towards confirming the impression that an indictment was obtained by use of the overwhelming influence of the Government where it would not have been otherwise obtained."

Bonaparte brought the U.S. attorney's letter to the White House. Roosevelt was none too happy when he read it. He told Bonaparte that if Stimson was unwilling to go after Pulitzer in New York, he himself would insist that the U.S. attorney in Washington do so. At his desk the next day, Roosevelt rebuked Stimson. "This letter is purely private and is merely to explain why I agree with Bonaparte that no effort should be made to get the District Attorney here to abandon his position, as you suggest," Roosevelt told Stimson. If the Pulitzers were not indicted, then the lesson he wanted to teach the press would be lost, he continued. "I think that much more service would be rendered by indicting the two Pulitzers with only one chance in three of convicting them, than by indicting their subordinates with three chances out of four of convicting them."

Stimson did not cower. "If you had been sitting on the Grand Jury I feel perfectly confident that you would have agreed with me," he told Roosevelt. The evidence was insufficient and the law unsupportive. "But in the second place, as a matter of policy and expediency, and not of official duty, I have a very strong conviction against pulling the trigger unless I have a ball-cartridge in the gun," said Stimson, appealing to Roosevelt the hunter. In New York, as "there has been sedulously nursed a belief that the government is doing something unusual in this prosecution under pressure of your personal desires, there is more than ever before, in my opinion, the absolute necessity that the bullet discharged should be true to the mark."

Roosevelt ignored Stimson's warning. If he couldn't get the U.S. attorney in New York to do his bidding, the one in Washington would. The prosecution in the capital was actually led by two men: Daniel W. Baker, who was the city's U.S. attorney; and Stewart McNamara, his assistant. Most of the work fell to McNamara, whom Bonaparte elevated to special assistant to the attorney general to show the importance the administration attached to the prosecutions.

On his yacht, Pulitzer prepared for the indictment. The *World*'s reporters were watching the proceedings in Washington carefully, even compiling biographies of the grand jury members in hopes of predicting their behavior. Pulitzer told his editors that if he was indicted, they were to prominently publish a disclaimer saying that he had been away and that he had known nothing of the stories until Roosevelt lodged the complaint. They were also to drop all editorials on Panama.

On February 17, 1909, the twenty-three grand jurors in Washington indicted Pulitzer, his company, and the editors Van Hamm and Lyman on five counts of criminal libel. The indictment charged, among other things, that the men and the *World* had libeled President Roosevelt, Roosevelt's brother-in law Robinson, President-Elect Taft, Taft's brother Charles, the financier J. Pierpont Morgan, Secretary of State Elihu Root, and the lobbyist Cromwell. The grand jury also indicted Delavan Smith and Charles Williams of the *Indianapolis News*, which had used the *World's* articles on the Panama Canal.

Frank Cobb was ready for this moment. He published an editorial ringing with defiance. "Mr. Roosevelt is an episode," wrote Cobb. "The *World* is an institution. Long after Mr. Roosevelt is dead, long after Mr. Pulitzer is dead, long after all the present editors of this paper are dead, the *World* will still go on as a great independent newspaper, unmuzzled, undaunted, and unterrorized."

Arrest warrants were brought to New York. McNamara was champing at the bit to put Pulitzer in custody. New York, however, would be a hard place to do so. The city's judges were known to be reluctant to permit an extradition to Washington for this sort of indictment, as a previous case had shown. In 1895, they had refused to send the editor Charles Dana to the capital when he had been indicted for libel in a case that involved neither the federal government nor unusual applications of law. (Ironically, Dana's defense attorney, Elihu Root, was now Roosevelt's secretary of state.) "Menacing as was the Dana case to the liberty of the press, it was far less serious than this Roosevelt persecution, for the complaint against Mr. Dana was made by a bona fide resident of the District of Columbia," Pulitzer told Cobb. "The President of the United States did not instigate the proceedings and direct the persecution thereby perverting the powers of the government to the gratification of personal revenge."

McNamara consulted the attorney general about the feasibility of arresting Pulitzer in Norfolk, where his yacht was to dock on its way back from a cruise to Havana. They believed it would be easier to extradite him from Virginia than from New York. But sloppy paperwork on McNamara's part thwarted the plan, and the *Liberty* sailed as fast as it could toward New York. Stimson was of no help to the case in Washington, either. Convinced that it was a waste of time, he ignored it while working on his own indictments in New York. The rush to arrest Pulitzer came to a standstill. Florence White sent word to Pulitzer that the attorney Nicoll had said an arrest was no longer imminent. "He also says he believes there is no danger of arrest in Charleston, and that Mr. Andes [Pulitzer] might cruise in that vicinity and return to New York when he heard from Mr. Nicoll."

Meanwhile, the grand jury in New York continued gathering evidence. Only the president and his lawyers knew that Pulitzer himself was no longer a target in Stimson's planned prosecution. Half an hour after Roosevelt left office on March 4, 1909, the jury in New York issued indictments containing fourteen counts of libel against the Press Publishing company (the corporation that published the *World*), and Van Hamm. Despite his growing opposition to Roosevelt's vendetta, Stimson had purposely delayed the issuing of the indictments in order to protect his political patron. He was worried that Pulitzer's lawyers might try to embarrass Roosevelt by serving him with a subpoena as he prepared to sail for a well-publicized trip to Africa. "I am trying to engineer my indictments," he told the attorney general, "so there will be no issue of fact pending at the time of his departure, or if there is such an issue, I will be in a position to call the bluff and bring it on for immediate trial."

These indictments, like those in Washington, were based on an unusual interpretation of law. In this case, the old federal law brought to bear was an "Act to Protect the Harbor Defense and Fortifications Constructed or Used by the United States from Malicious Injury, and for Other Purposes." Stimson reasoned that the paper could be charged under federal law for its allegedly libelous actions because twenty-nine copies of the *World* had been mailed to West Point and one had been delivered to the city's federal building. Noticeably absent from the indictment was Pulitzer's name.

By the time the *Liberty* steamed into Brooklyn's Gravesend Bay, other fissures had appeared in Roosevelt's strategy. Joseph Kealing, the U.S. attorney in Indianapolis, resigned in protest after eight years on the job, rather than pursue the case. Kealing told Bonaparte he believed the government was overreaching in trying to drag the defendants in Indianapolis to trial in Washington. "I believe the principle involved is a dangerous one," he said, "striking at the very foundation of our form of government. I cannot, therefore, honestly and conscientiously insist to the court that such is the law."

His nerves agitated, Pulitzer remained apprehensive. "Never was the time more propitious than now to treat judges and courts and all forms of justice with respect," he instructed his editors. He had cause to be anxious. Even after issuing its indictments, the grand jury in New York continued its probe. Hosmer was called to testify, and he sent Pulitzer a long description of his ordeal in the closed chambers. Unaware of how Stimson had stood up to Roosevelt, Hosmer insultingly compared Stimson to Lepidus in Shakespeare's *Julius Caesar*, described by Mark Antony as "a slight unmeritable man, meet to be sent on errands."

Over time, it became clear that neither the case in Washington nor the one in New York had much traction. "Panama matter at this end apparently making no progress," reported one of Pulitzer's men in New York. Roosevelt was now in Africa chasing big game, and Stimson had returned to private law practice and was rumored to be planning to run for higher office. The matter fell into the hands of President Taft's appointees, who dutifully pressed on, out of loyalty to the man who had picked their boss for the presidency. With no prospect of any trials soon, Pulitzer was granted permission to leave the country.

Clearing Sandy Point, the *Liberty* went south, as usual. During breakfast, off the coast of southern Virginia, Pulitzer asked the captain which way the yacht was heading that morning.

"Due east, sir," he replied.

"If we keep on 'due east,' where will we fetch up?" asked Pulitzer.

"Lisbon, sir."

"Keep on, due east."

It was a bad decision. The crossing took them into a severe spring gale, followed by long days of heavy swells. By the time the group reached Lisbon, they were sick and exhausted, and Pulitzer had whooping cough. Life on board worsened. A new secretary who had joined the bedraggled group came down with smallpox. The yacht had to be fumigated and everyone vaccinated before authorities allowed the *Liberty* to move on. The voyage was hardly an escape from Pulitzer's persecution back home.

Pulitzer spent the summer and fall of 1909 on the *Liberty* cruising from northern Europe to the area around Gibraltar, with short stays in port cities and one in Carlsbad for another cure. Back in the United States, the legal proceedings against him and his newspaper ground on. The government prepared to prove the articles untrue by tapping into its huge archive of documents relating to the acquisition of the canal and even deposing all the members of the junta in Panama.

Although they felt they had the upper hand when it came to the law, Pulitzer's lawyers took no chances. They dispatched their own investigators to Washington, Paris, and Panama to uncover proof confirming charges of corruption involving the canal. If they succeeded, not only would they have an irrefutable defense, but the *World* would have the scoop of the century. This undertaking, however, became increasingly expensive when Pulitzer's lawyers decided to use rogatory commissions that would permit the taking of testimony usable in a U.S. court. The Justice Department insisted that Pulitzer pay the travel and lodging costs of its attorneys who had to witness the hearings.

Each side believed its foreign research benefited its case. From Paris, McNamara wrote to George W. Wickersham, Taft's attorney general, that "the witnesses who had testified have not only not substantiated in the smallest degree the contentions of the *World*, but have rejected their allegations in toto and have established more thoroughly the utter falsity of the libels." On the other hand, the *World*'s reporter Earl Harding, who accompanied the lawyers to Paris, was convinced that a ledger he obtained showed the collusion of American investors in acquiring French canal stock to benefit from the U.S. payment.

Harding was among those at the *World* who believed Cromwell and his associates had made an immense, illegal profit from the canal deal and that the truth could set Pulitzer free. On June 3, 1909, he went to the docks of New York to see off Pulitzer's attorneys, who were leaving for Panama. He saw Cromwell's law partner, Edward B. Hill, accompanying the Justice Department's attorney. "Every bit of telltale evidence in Panama would be bottled up," Harding concluded. "It was three in the afternoon. I hurried back to the *World*, told my misgivings to Don Seitz, and instantly got his clearance to take the next train to New Orleans, leaving at 4:40 PM." In New Orleans he boarded a Panama-bound United Fruit cargo ship.

The Canal Zone was a beehive of activity and teeming with thousands of Americans. In the five years since the United States had resumed work on the canal, a large trench had begun to take shape. Despite the region's heavy rainy season, landslides, and malaria, workers were excavating 3 million cubic yards of dirt a month, creating a ditch large enough to lay down two Empire State Buildings on their sides, end to end. But it would be still five more years before the first ship would pass through the canal.

Harding caught up with Pulitzer's attorney, who was quite surprised to find him in Panama. Harding determined that, as he had feared, Cromwell's men and Panamanian conspirators were obstructing the legal investigation, preventing the investigation from getting to the bottom of the story. In fact, the attorney had already been convinced that there had been no corruption. "The *World* has been misled," he told Harding. "We haven't a leg to stand on."

Harding decided that if Panama would not yield the secrets, then they could be found in the capital of the country which once ruled Panama. Before leaving for the Colombian capital of Bogotá, he hired Edwin Warren Guyol, a native of New Orleans who spoke Spanish and had worked as a reporter in Cuba. Nicknamed "M'sié Manqueau" for having lost his arm in an accident, Guyol had a rough-and-tumble reputation. But he proved loyal to the end. When men tied to Cromwell attempted to bribe him, he told Harding. They, Guyol said, wanted him to spy on Harding and impede the research. In particular, he was to work closely with Marquis Alexander de St. Croix, a French wine salesman who was leaving for Bogotá ahead of them. The pair decided to play along as if Guyol had agreed to double-cross Harding.

When Harding and Guyol reached Bogotá in August, they made their arrival conspicuous. They published an open letter in the main newspaper asking for help from Colombians, who were still smarting after the forced separation of Panama from their own territory. Officials at the U.S. legation warily watched Guyol and Harding. As it turned out, they had reason to.

Harding concluded that it was time to resort to extreme means to find the documents they were looking for. "In short," he said, "it was a case, as far as we were concerned, of fighting the devil with his own tools." They selected St. Croix, the wine merchant whom they believed to be a spy for Cromwell, as their first target. Continuing to pretend that he himself had been bribed, Guyol tried to get St. Croix to let him know what Cromwell was covering up. After this effort failed to produce any results, Guyol obtained Harding's permission to spike St. Croix's brandy with chloral hydrate (a hypnotic and sedative) in order to search his luggage. To ward off any effect on himself when he drank brandy with St. Croix, Guyol drank a cup of olive oil beforehand. The luggage contained nothing incriminating.

Next they turned to the U.S. legation. Harding was convinced that it held documents dating from when the United States engineered Panama's revolution, and that these would be the proof he sought. A U.S. official, who regularly indulged a passion for drink and gambling, particularly high-stakes stud poker, gave them their first opportunity. Using the *World*'s money to pay his gambling debts at a club in Bogotá, Guyol befriended this official. One night, when the man napped on a sofa at the club, Guyol stole his keys and then unlocked and propped open a door to the legation. Twice, he repeated the maneuver, once almost getting caught and being forced to hide in the saddle room for two hours. By the end, Guyol had managed to read all the official correspondence for 1902, but he failed to find any proof of wrongdoing.

Harding took matters in his own hands. On October 23, he made his own nighttime trip into the U.S. legation while the minister was dining at the presidential palace. A young clerk, who claimed he knew where an incriminating letter by John Hay was, agreed to take Harding to the file room. As they began opening document folders, the minister's son discovered them and sounded the alarm. Luckily for Harding, he was not prosecuted. The Colombians were unlikely to care, and putting Harding into custody to return him to the United States would be nearly impossible. Instead, the clerk was fired, Harding and Guyol were declared persona non grata, and a letter of complaint was sent to the *World*.

Not one to give up, Guyol made one last attempt to discover their Holy Grail. He spotted the official whose keys he had borrowed leaving the legation with a valise in the company of St. Croix. He followed them across Colombia, plotting all the way how to steal the valise, convinced it held the wanted documents. His first plan was to grab it when they boarded a riverboat and then jump into the river and make for shore, but since he had only one arm, this plan seemed doomed from the start. Luckily, he had a better opportunity when the locked leather duffel bag was unloaded from a train. Finally alone with the bag, he broke it open, to discover that it held nothing of value. All he brought back with him to

Harding were broken ribs from falling off a horse during his pursuit of the two men.

With that, the far-flung search for evidence of corruption involving the canal came up empty-handed. Keeping their boss from prison would now rest solely on the legal skills of his lawyers.

Chapter Thirty

A SHORT REMAINING SPAN

———————————◆———————————

I n late September 1909, Pulitzer and his personal staff of sixteen settled for the autumn in one of the fashionable districts of Berlin, near the famous Tiergarten park and the city's elegant opera house. As usual, the landlord had been required to make numerous alterations to please his tenant. Thick plate glass was added to the bedroom windows, heavy carpets were laid down, and all the windows and door hinges were well oiled.

After disagreeable stays in Paris and London over many years, Pulitzer found Berlin to be just right. For once he managed to shed his woes, attend concerts and operas, and eat out with friends. He was the most content he had been in a long time. "With due reserve," Thwaites wrote to Seitz in New York, "I may say that Berlin is a great success and serenity of our daily tenor is positively uncanny." Over the past three years, Europe had become Pulitzer's new home. If he was not at sea, he was in Aix-les-Bains, Cap Martin, London, or, now, Berlin.

Europe had also become the home of Joseph's brother Albert. Since his departure from New York fourteen years earlier, Albert had wandered around the continent, staying in fashionable hotels, occasionally returning to the United States, and living from the proceeds of the sale of his *Morning Journal*. He and Joseph had not spoken or written to each other since their confrontation over Albert's refusal to merge his newspaper with Joseph's. In a way, Albert had been revenged. Each day, as Joseph waged a life-and-death struggle with Hearst, he had been competing with the newspaper that Albert created.

Albert had also cut his ties with his former wife, Fanny, years before her death that summer, and his son Walter, who was trying to make a living as a writer in New York. At the *World*, Walter was persona non grata because of his father. "There were strict orders that under no circumstances was he to be identified as related to or connected with the Joseph Pulitzer family in any way, shape or manner," recalled one editor.

During the years after he gave up journalism, Albert wrote a romantic novel about a Napoleonic prince, Eugène de Beauharnais; toyed briefly with starting another newspaper in New York; and eventually settled down in Vienna, taking as a companion a young woman with whom he had a son. Like his brother, Albert suffered intensively from insomnia and depression—which doctors treating the wealthy called "neurasthenia"—and from other, undiagnosed ailments. For Joseph, it was sound that caused him great suffering. For Albert, it was changes in temperature and light.

Over time, Albert's behavior grew increasingly odd and unpredictable. Earlier in the year, he had abruptly left Vienna and taken up residence in San Francisco, at the Fairmont Hotel. His demands on its staff and his unusual eating habits were the talk of the town. A newspaper in San Francisco published on its front page a one-day sample of what the Fairmont's kitchen fed its eccentric guest. Rising before dawn, the corpulent gourmand consumed shredded wheat and two to eight baked apples with cream. A midday plate of Corinth raisins and vegetables would hold him over until a five-o'clock glass of lemon squash, effervescent with bicarbonate of soda. At seven, he sat down for a dinner of San Francisco oysters, clam chowder, veal, chicken, and sweet russet pears, all washed down with a bottle of Moselle wine.

While he was in San Francisco, Albert worked feverishly on his memoirs. He left the Fairmont and hid himself away in the remote Tavern Resort on the top of nearby Mount Tamalpais. There he drew the ire of other guests by rising before the sun to begin typing, knocking over chairs in his room, and requesting special trains when the scheduled ones had ceased running up the mountain. The novelist Gertrude Atherton claimed that at one point he burst uninvited into her rooms while showing friends around.

By fall, his memoir complete, Albert returned to Vienna. He was despondent. He called on Dr. Max Neuda, his physician and friend. The two discussed the works of Baruch Spinoza, Albert's favorite philosopher. On the morning of October 4, as was his practice, his companion read to Albert from the morning newspapers. Among the stories was one of a man afflicted with insomnia who had committed suicide. *"Wenn ich nur Mut dazu hätte,"* Albert said. "If only I had the courage." He asked his companion to leave him alone. When she departed, he went to the druggist and purchased a poisonous substance, probably a diluted form of prussic acid then used for the treatment of neuralgia.

There are two kinds of suicides: one in which the person is crying for help; the other in which death is sought. Albert wanted the latter. After drinking the potion, he took up his revolver, pressed the barrel to his right temple, and pulled the trigger.

Joseph learned of his brother's death from a reporter who called on him at his house in Berlin. Though only a 325-mile train ride separated him from where his brother lay in a morgue in Vienna, Joseph did not go. Instead he sent Thwaites, with several thousand German marks.

Reaching Vienna, Thwaites drove out to the Zentralfriedhof, the final resting place for many of the city's most famous residents. There, in the mortuary of the Old Jewish section, he found Albert, covered with a white cloth, in a cheap wooden box. "No money having been traced, the millionaire was about to be buried as a pauper," Thwaites said. "The face was quite unmarred. The bullet had ranged upward through the temple, making the exit at the back of the head on the left side. A terrible wound."

Using Joseph's money, Thwaites purchased a better casket and paid for flowers. The following day, led in song by a Jewish male chorus, a small group accompanied the casket in a long procession to the burial plot that Neuda had purchased for Albert. At the graveside, it was left to the doctor to provide a eulogy. Recalling Albert's visit to him and their philosophical chat a few days prior, he said, "It little occurred to me then, that this visit and this discussion were prompted by your decision to take leave of this earthly life, and so to say a word of farewell to me."

Several days later, Joseph's cousin Adam Politzer, who lived in Vienna, met with Neuda. As executor of the estate, Neuda had carefully examined all the items in Albert's possession. "Alongside numerous love letters of extremely diverse provenance, which Neuda destroyed immediately, only credit letters and other insignificant papers were found," Politzer told Joseph. "A letter for you was not present. Nor was any other note that referenced you."

Of the nine children born to Fülöp and Elize Pulitzer, only Joseph remained alive.

As winter set in, Pulitzer abandoned Berlin for the warmth of Cap Martin. He was slowing down. Even those around him who discounted his continual health crises detected a change. One evening, while Pulitzer was cruising in Mediterranean waters on the *Liberty*, Harold Pollard brought him out on deck to see a full moon. After looking up into the night sky for a while, Pulitzer gave up. "It's no use, my dear boy," he said, "I cannot even get a glimmer of its light."

Seitz, who came from New York for his usual business consultations with Pulitzer, encountered a calmer, reflective, more philosophical boss. On a car ride through the countryside, Seitz and Pulitzer were left alone for a while when the engine stalled and Pollard went for help. "You see how quiet I am," Pulitzer said. "Real troubles never bother me. It's only the small annoyances that upset me." In the silence of the parked automobile, Seitz described the view of Cap Martin below them. "You know I was here thirty-five years ago for the first time and the sight is always with me," Pulitzer remarked.

Suddenly, Pulitzer changed the subject. "We will not have many rows," he told a disbelieving Seitz, who had been buffeted by Pulitzer's infamous temper for eighteen years. "No, I am serious," he continued. "I am not going to live long. I have had warnings. Besides I am no longer equal to thinking or deciding. You will have to get along without me more and more from now on and see less and less of me."

Contributing to Pulitzer's melancholy was his increasing loneliness. He had entered into a time of life marked by frequent deaths. Two days after Christmas 1909, Angus Shaw "sorrowfully and faithfully" telegraphed the news that Dumont Clarke, Pulitzer's sixty-nine-year-old banker and trusted adviser, had died of pneumonia. The flags on the Pulitzer Building were lowered to half-mast. "Coin," as he was known in the codebook, had been at Pulitzer's side since the *World* began making him rich. The two had, in Pulitzer's words, "implicitly trustful, irregular relations in money matters." Every dollar of Pulitzer's income was funneled to Clarke's bank. Without any paperwork or signatures, Clarke had invested, transferred, or wired money as Pulitzer saw fit. He had also provided wise counsel on everything from personnel issues at the *World* to coping with children at home. Although Clarke's son promised to provide Pulitzer with the same service, he could not replace his father.

Pulitzer's loneliness was also an unescapable consequence of the years when he had spurned Kate's tenderness and alienated his children. The unreliability of Pulitzer's affection and his unpredictable cruelty left them little choice. Though they held him in great affection, they had defensively created lives apart, accentuating his isolation. "I want some love and affection from my children in the closing short span of life that still remains," he wrote to Joe after receiving a complaining note from his son, still chafing under Pulitzer's strictures. "If I cannot have that love and affection, I may at least expect to be spared willful, deliberate disrespect disobedience, and insult."

Kate did her best to try to end her husband's self-imposed exile from the family. "Pray realize that you would be so much happier yourself if you have light hearts and happy faces around you," she had written several years earlier. "Love served is always so much better than that which is bought. You cannot either buy or beat love from anyone, you can only earn it and you can, for no one can be more tender or charming than you when you wish to be."

His twenty-nine-year-old son, Ralph, who came to visit in January, limited most communications with his father to matters of business relating to the *World*, of which he was now ostensibly the president. Twenty-four-year-old Joe was trying to build a life for himself in St. Louis, working at the *Post-Dispatch*. He felt certain that nothing he did could measure up to his father's expectations, and he understood his place among the sons. "I realize what a loss Mr. Clarke's death had been for you and how necessary it is for you to see Ralph," Joe wrote to his father while his older brother was in Cap Martin. "It has given me a good deal of pleasure to feel you attach at least enough importance to me and have enough confidence in me to want me here in New York when Ralph is away."

Pulitzer's two daughters—twenty-three-year-old Edith and the twenty-one-year-old Constance, saw more of New York high society than of their father. Kate spent almost as much time in Europe as Joseph, but only in the rarest of circumstances were they in the same place at the same time. Little Herbert was, at thirteen, still too young to have given offense.

Once again, Pulitzer revised his will. He had written his first one in 1892 and had altered it substantially in 1904 to provide instructions for the creation of the journalism school and prizes. As he cruised on the *Liberty*, he fretted over who would best carry out his wishes. He replaced Clarke with Governor Charles Hughes of New York as one of the trustees. The lugubrious voyage, complete with rough seas, gave Pollard cause to rename Pulitzer's entourage the "sea-sickophants."

In the United States, Roosevelt's prosecutions were still working their way through the courts. In October, Pulitzer had his first victory. It came when his lawyers appeared before a federal judge in Indiana in whose courtroom the Indianapolis portion of the case had landed. Calling the case "political," the judge questioned the U.S. attorney's right to try it in Washington, suggesting that this venue would set a precedent subjecting newspapers to hundreds of libel trials. The following day he dismissed the case.

"I am of the opinion," said the judge, "that the fact that certain persons were called 'thieves' and 'swindlers' does not constitute libel per se," he said. Citing a newspaper's duty to report the facts and draw inferences for its readers, the judge said the issue of the canal could use some public scrutiny. "The revolution in Panama, the circumstances concerning it, were unusual and peculiar."

The ruling effectively killed the indictments in Washington. Pulitzer no longer faced any prospect of prison. But the pleasure of the victory was muted by the knowledge that the stronger legal case, the one in New York assembled by Stimson against the *World* before he left office, remained to be tried.

On January 25, 1910, Pulitzer's attorney De Lancey Nicoll arrived at the U.S. district court in Manhattan. The day before that, a jury had been seated to hear, at long last, the criminal libel charges brought against the *World* and its editor Van Hamm. The case, built by Stimson, was the only remaining legal bullet from the chamber loaded by Roosevelt while he was still president.

Nicoll was fully prepared to present the evidence gathered by Pulitzer's team of investigators and reporters to prove the truth of the corruption charges made against Cromwell and Roosevelt. But to go that route was to concede the federal government's power to prosecute. Instead, Pulitzer wanted Roosevelt's right to prosecute to be on trial. Thus, on the first day, Nicoll made a motion to quash the indictment on constitutional grounds. Judge Charles Hough, who owed his job to Roosevelt, surprised Nicoll by agreeing to hear him out the next day.

As Nicoll began his argument, it sounded like a lecture in law school. He traced the history of libel laws in English law and demonstrated that the United States' brief experience with the Alien and Sedition Acts had given the nation an aversion to laws permitting the national government to prosecute libel. Then, turning to the old federal law being used by the prosecution, Nicoll made his case.

The law was intended to punish assault and murder on the high seas, which were beyond the reach of state laws, and was never intended to be used to prosecute an offense that could easily be tried in a state court. "The curious and ingenious mind, which for the first time in eighty-five years, twisted the statute to meet the ends of this prosecution has retired, and this case has been left to the present Attorney General to press as a matter of department routine," Nicoll told Judge Hough. "You might as well revive the sedition laws, or pass another one like it. They would be a better law than this one."

The U.S. attorney Henry Wise, who had taken over for Stimson, rose to challenge Nicoll's interpretation and argued that the law as amended covered libel as well. But Judge Hough had little patience with this view. "I am clear," he said interrupting the two bickering lawyers, "that the construction of the act of 1808 proposed by the prosecution in this case is contrary to the spirit which actuated the members of Congress in passing this law." Hough granted Nicoll's motion to quash the indictment and suggested strongly that the jurisdictional issue be settled not by him but by the Supreme Court.

"I am naturally somewhat surprised," said Wise when reporters surrounded him outside the courtroom. "If any further action is to be taken it will rest with the Attorney General of the United States."

The only party on the winning side still unhappy was Pulitzer. Anxious until the day of the trial, he now wanted to win his argument before the Supreme Court. "If there still remains the likelihood that someday another Roosevelt will prostitute his power by invoking the act to protect harbor defenses in order to prosecute newspapers that have offended him, the sooner there is a final decision of the Supreme Court of the United States the better," Frank Cobb wrote in the *World* the morning after the decision. As the victor, however, Pulitzer could not appeal.

Only the administration could. One day before the time for an appeal would have run out, Taft's cabinet decided to take the case to the Supreme Court.

In March, Joe came to Cap Martin on an important mission. In January he had pleaded with his father to grant his long-standing wish to marry Elinor Wickham, a fetching dark-haired daughter of an old family in St. Louis. "We are anxious to end the demoralizing suspense of this long three years of waiting *this spring*," he said, "and I beg to you to end it by giving your consent."

Even Wickham had written to Joseph in hopes of softening his heart. Her letter only gave him a chance to vent. "Try your moral sense and get him to tell you the truth what his conduct toward me has been for the last ten years," Joseph wrote back, "and see whether you cannot influence him toward a father who is already old and broken, totally blind, cannot sleep, has an infinite variety of infirmities with one foot and half in the grave, and expects nothing from his children except a little less intense selfishness and some sympathy."

In person, Joseph was rarely the ogre who dictated the letters. When Joe arrived, Joseph gave him a gift of $1,000 for his twenty-fifth birthday and consented to the marriage. His father's kindness, once again, had the effect of inducing guilt in Joe. As the train left, he looked back at Cap Martin and saw his father's villa. "It made me realize more keenly than I have realized in all my life under what deep obligation I am to you and how very much at fault I have been in the past in not feeling this obligation," Joe wrote to his father. "In a way I hated to leave you back there, even now, with the happy prospect that I have before me I feel very selfish in going away."

The children gone, Pulitzer once again fiddled with his will. He decided to include a warning along with the ample funds he was planning to leave them. "They should never forget the dangers which unfortunately attend the inheritance of large fortunes, even though the money came from the painstaking affections of a father," he wrote. "I beg them to remember that such danger lies not only in the obvious temptation to enervating luxury but in the inducement which a fortune coming from another carries to the recipients to withdraw from the wholesome duty of vigorous, serious, useful work."

* * *

After several more cruises in the Mediterranean, Pulitzer spent the summer in Chatwold and returned to roam Europe in the fall. Roosevelt's prosecution of the *World* played its last inning on October 24, 1910, when the government asked the Supreme Court, a majority of whose members had been appointed by Roosevelt and Taft, to overturn the lower court's decision throwing out the case. James McReynolds, appearing on behalf of the Justice Department, said the government only sought to protect those that were in the federal enclaves where the *World* had circulated. It didn't matter, he said, where the paper was printed. Rather, the crime of libel could occur where the paper was read, as well. Justice Holmes and others questioned him at length and pointedly asked if New York's laws had not been sufficient.

Pulitzer's attorney once again presented his elaborate, theatrical history of libel, which now included a long excerpt from Roosevelt's message to Congress holding it to be a "high national duty" to prosecute Pulitzer. This time Nicoll hammered away at the pernicious nature of Roosevelt's action. With more than 2,000 federal enclaves, a president could bring simultaneous grand jury proceedings in all parts of the country, financially crippling most newspapers, Nicoll said. "Whenever the President of the United States wished to destroy a newspaper that had offended him by political criticism he would have had only to compel it to match its scanty resources against the vast resources of the United States government.

"This was the real issue involved in the Roosevelt proceedings," Nicoll continued, "and in resisting the claim of Federal jurisdiction the *World* was fighting to preserve not only its own constitutional rights but the constitutional rights of every newspaper published in the United States."

Ten weeks later, on January 3, 1911, the court ruled unanimously in favor of the *World*. It concluded that the federal government had no right to prosecute the case. Reading the decision from the bench, Chief Justice White said the federal government could not claim that just because a newspaper circulated on its property it could pursue a federal libel case, especially when ample state remedies existed. He placed the decision on the desk before him. "It would be impossible to sustain this prosecution without overthrowing the very State law by the authority of which the prosecution can be alone maintained," White said.

In short, Roosevelt's stubborn refusal to listen to Stimson and his insistence on pursuing Pulitzer using federal powers had fatally flawed his effort from the start. By challenging a well-accepted division of prosecutorial power between the states and the national government, Roosevelt missed his mark.

Pulitzer got word of the Supreme Court's decision in Cap Martin. It was one of the sweetest victories of his life. Though the Supreme Court's ruling was narrow, covering only a jurisdictional issue, Pulitzer believed he had rebuffed a wider assault on the nation's independent press. He left it to Frank Cobb to put this into words. The Court's action, Cobb wrote, meant that "freedom of the press does not exist at the whim or pleasure of the United States. It is the most sweeping victory won for freedom of speech and of the press in this country since the American people destroyed the Federalist Party more than a century ago for enacting the infamous sedition law." Pulitzer's vanquished foe was speechless. "I have nothing to say," Roosevelt told a reporter for the *World* who took a train out to Oyster Bay.

The pleasure of the victory, however, was muted by other news from New York. On January 23, 1911, Pulitzer's onetime journalistic heir apparent, David Graham Phillips, was walking toward the Princeton Club in New York City to pick up his mail. Almost a decade had elapsed since he had worked for Pulitzer. In the intervening years he had established himself both as a successful author of socially conscious fiction and as a leading muckraking journalist. In fact, when Theodore Roosevelt in a speech coined the term "muckraking" to disparage the work of reform-minded writers, he had Phillips in mind. As Phillips neared the club, a well-dressed young man approached him.

"There you go," said the man, as he pulled out a .32 caliber automatic pistol and opened fire, sending six bullets into Phillips.

"Here I go," he said, firing a final round into his own head. The deranged assailant, the son of a prominent family in Washington, D.C., believed that his family, and especially his sister, had been defamed in Phillips's books. A policeman rushed over from the park and three of Phillips friends came bounding out from the club.

"Graham, what happened?" asked the first friend to reach Phillips.

"He shot me in the bowels, " Phillips replied, referring to the dead assailant lying on the pavement. "Don't bother with him. For God's sakes get a doctor."

An ambulance rushed Phillips to the hospital. At first the doctors believed he would recover from his wounds, but the hemorrhaging could not be stopped. The following evening, Phillips declined rapidly. "I could have won against two bullets, but not against six," Phillips murmured a few minutes before dying at eleven-thirty that night.

Funeral services were held two days later at St. George's Episcopal Church, at East Seventeenth Street and Stuyvesant Place. Many of Phillips's former colleagues from the *World* packed into the church, along with admirers of the writer. Even if it had not been for Pulitzer's aversion to funerals, this was one for which distance was a legitimate excuse— not to mention that Pulitzer was beset by an increasing number of ailments. "I have been extraordinarily tired, fatigued and exhausted ever since you left," he wrote to Ralph in early March. "I am not fit for business, cannot attend to it in a perpetual state of headaches and pains." A cure in Wiesbaden brought no relief. In May, Pulitzer's men told Kate that though Joseph's blood sugar was down from a dangerous level, his nerves were shot and he was plagued with continual indigestion.

One of Pulitzer's many doctors reviewed medications with him. He urged his patient to take Veronal, a relatively new sedative. "It induces a thoroughly normal sleep and, for most people, causes absolutely no side effects," he told Pulitzer. "Even over the course of multiple years, Veronal taken in doses of 8–12 grains is totally harmless, and the fear of Veronal poisoning wholly unfounded." However, patients built up tolerance to this drug and required increasingly higher dosages. Several years later, experts would warn patients of its dangerous side effects. "Veronal must be ranked among the treacherous somnifacients," reported one of the main medical manuals. "The number of serious and fatal cases of poisoning is so large that great care should be employed in its use." Neither Pulitzer nor his doctor knew this when he began taking the drug.

In the summer of 1911, Republicans nervously faced the prospect that Theodore Roosevelt would challenge President Taft's renomination, and Democrats were stirred by the belief that Taft could be defeated. Presidential elections could still ignite Pulitzer's passion, and he sailed home to confer with his editorial page writers. Pulitzer's interest in "the Page," as it was called, remained strong, although he was becoming uninterested in the operation of the paper. As he told one correspondent that spring, "My whole aim and end in life is to know nothing of the affairs of the *World*."

Pulitzer and Cobb met on board the *Liberty* off the shore of New York at the end of June. Pulitzer wanted the *World* to promote Woodrow Wilson for the presidency. With the backing of the *World*, Wilson had become governor of New Jersey after serving as president of Princeton University. But Pulitzer worried that Wilson's attacks on the money trust were a revival of Bryanism, which Pulitzer feared could doom his chances. Cobb disagreed but consented to follow Pulitzer's instructions to publicly chastise Wilson. "Remember I have the highest respect and regard for him," Pulitzer told Cobb. "This man is a great artist, a great genius, but he is leading himself astray and should be brought back to his senses. This should be done kindly and sympathetically and as a friend and admirer."

Concluding his meeting with Cobb, Pulitzer picked up his family in New York—all except Joe and Elinor, who were traveling by train from St. Louis—and sailed north to spend the summer in Bar Harbor. Chatwold was at its best. After years of remodeling, the summer mansion at last provided the quiet refuge for which Pulitzer yearned. He slept in the upper floors of his unconventional, eccentric "tower of silence." He could swim in a pool of heated seawater in the basement and spend his days on a large veranda facing the ocean. Whereas Joseph craved solitude, Kate and their daughters thrived on the summer social whirl, which as the *New York Times* predicted, "will decidedly outshine that of 1910 in every way."

Joseph spent time with his family at intervals. On most days he ate lunch or dinner with Kate, one of their daughters, or Herbert, and a secretary, at a table set for four in the magnificent main floor library. Visits with Ralph and Joe were mostly confined to boat rides. Joseph was exhausted by the contact with the family. "The intensity of his family emotions was such," noted Alleyne Ireland, Pulitzer's newest secretary, "that they could only be given rein at the price of sleepless nights, savage pain, and desperate weariness." Nonetheless, he remained intensely curious about his children. "Everybody had to be described over and over again, but especially young Master Ralph, a bright and handsome child, born long after his grandfather had become totally blind," Ireland said.

Joseph's favorite indulgence was a ride on his large electric launch boat. He would sit in an armchair at the center of the vessel, with two companions nearby, as the boat navigated the calm waters of Frenchman Bay. In early August, Clark B. Firestone, recently hired at the *World*, joined Pulitzer for one of the rides, and for his requisite education as an editorial writer at the hands of the master. As the men rode about, Pulitzer began, as always, with his belief that independence was a paper's most valuable attribute. No political, financial, social, or personal influence could be brought to bear on the *World*'s editorial positions. He warned Firestone, who only recently had been hired away from the *Evening Mail*, that he should not let any friendship influence his editorials, now that he was a writer for the *World*. "I wish," Pulitzer said, "that these writers would realize far more fully than they do the immense asset of their independence and exercise to the full their right to say anything they please, fearless of naught save overstatement and untruth."

Next to independence, the most important criterion was that the editorials should be readable, Pulitzer said. To succeed in this regard, they should be on a theme of popular interest, be free of unfamiliar terms and phrases, and be trimmed to the tightest possible construction. Pulitzer recalled that when Cobb came to the paper after working in Detroit, he believed that the leading editorial should run as long as half a column. Pulitzer rapidly disabused him of that idea. In order to win Cobb over to a more terse style, Pulitzer told Firestone, he summoned as "gems of compact and telling expressions" the ten- to twelve-line editorials the *Sun* used to publish.

The point, Pulitzer said, was to make an impression on the readers that they could not shake off. "Every day *The World* should contain some striking utterance, something out of the ordinary, something so independent that no other newspaper could print it; something unexpected and yet of the sort to capture the reader's conviction.

"I dislike the word 'sensational' and never use it, but I want striking things to appear on the editorial page. Of course, it cannot compete with the news columns in effects of novelty, but can approach them."

Pulitzer concluded his lesson with a reminder to use humor. "He urged me to exploit all my latent possibilities in the line of sarcasm and satire," Firestone said. Before they parted, Pulitzer promised that he would never ask Firestone to write an editorial on a position he opposed. Better that certain opinions of his own not be published, Pulitzer added, than that they might appear through the medium of a writer who did not honestly share them.

After a full summer in Chatwold, Pulitzer was no better than he had been when he sailed back from Europe in June. "I have dreadful headaches, dyspepsia, nearly everything bad, sleep horribly and on brink of collapse," he wired to Ralph in September. As the leaves turned and the fall winds heralded the oncoming winter, Pulitzer abandoned his much-loved Maine retreat for New York. That made matters worse. In the eight years since the house on East Seventy-Third Street was built, it had defied all the work by architects and experts, and all the money spent, to make it soundproof. The failure was not for lack of effort. When the house was first built, Pulitzer's personal staff took turns sleeping in his bedroom. George Ledlie reached a point where he wasn't sure if he might be imaging sounds.

Wallace C. Sabine, a renowned professor of acoustical engineering at Harvard, was enlisted. It was decided to build a new, almost windowless bedroom off the back of the house, using the firm of Foster, Gade, and Graham. When this room was completed, the contractor and Pulitzer's aide Arthur Billings closed themselves off in it while half a dozen assistants banged on pipes in the basement and around the swimming pool as well as on rooftop vents while others ran the elevators up and down. "Foster is satisfied and so am I," Billings reported to Pulitzer, "although the final success can only be assured after your acute hearing has put the room to a test." It failed.

The house's proximity to the *World* also permitted Pulitzer's managers and editors to pester him with their business and editorial plans. It was a curse he had brought on himself by refusing to renounce power and turn decision making over to Ralph. Foremost on Seitz's mind was moving ahead with a plan to purchase a paper mill so as to wean the *World* from the paper trusts, which were increasing their prices by a rate 30 to 40 percent a year. Pulitzer said he almost fainted when he heard that Ralph was going to leave on vacation without concluding the deal. The time spent with Joe, who came to visit, was no better. Joseph now wanted his son to be in New York and said he had consented to let him remain in St. Louis up till now only because of his wife's family. The conversation ended when Joseph said that returning to New York was against his wishes.

If his employees and his children were not making demands on him, the politicians were. The reform-minded mayor William J. Gaynor, who had just survived an assassination attempt captured in an iconic photograph in the *World*, told Pulitzer he was frustrated with the paper. After supporting his election, Gaynor claimed, it was now siding with Hearst in attacking him on a proposal for building a subway. "You can hear it everywhere that the *World* that used to be a great power is now merely an echo of Hearst. Whatever Hearst wants or stands for, the *World* trails along afterwards as meekly as if it had no principles," Gaynor said. "The *World* has done more to promote the political schemes of Hearst than all his own newspapers. Without the *World*, Hearst would not amount to anything."

In his twenty-eight years at the helm of the nation's most important newspaper, Pulitzer had built up immunity to the complaints of his allies and to vilification by enemies. His attitude toward his greatest public opponents, William Randolph Hearst, William Jennings Bryan, and Theodore Roosevelt—unlike his attitude toward his family—was open-minded and uncommonly charitable.

Roosevelt never let up on his attacks on Pulitzer after losing his court battles. In fact, in a letter to a British friend that summer, Roosevelt compared Pulitzer to Charles Dickens's Jefferson Brick. Pulitzer, on the other hand, told Cobb that it was time to give Roosevelt his due. "Personally," Pulitzer said, "I believe that the Panama work is a monumental achievement and that the paper must give Roosevelt the credit for the work and we must draw the biggest kind of line between that phase and the mere incident of his personal attack upon the paper on account of charges it made of corruption specifically and personally which it certainly could not substantiate—never did and never will."

Of the three men, only Hearst noticed this generous trait in Pulitzer. Though the two had spent years in a competitive struggle that could have ended with one destroying the other, Pulitzer had always restrained his staff's spitefulness and had urged his editorial writers to recognize Hearst's strength. In October, when the *World* published a complimentary article about Hearst, its longtime competitor assumed that the idea had been Pulitzer's and sent his thanks.

Chapter Thirty-One

SOFTLY, VERY SOFTLY

On October 18, 1911, the *Liberty* pulled up anchor and sailed from New York. On board were Pulitzer; Herbert and his tutor and nanny; five secretaries; and Pulitzer's English valet Jabez Dunningham, who had been with him since 1896. They were bound for Jekyll Island but got only as far as Charleston, where the captain anchored the yacht to wait until the course of a West Indian hurricane became clearer. Aside from a bad cold, which had confined him to his home while he was in New York, Pulitzer's health was as it always had been—a source of endless complaints but not so many as to cause alarm among his companions, or in his new traveling physician.

On the second day in the harbor, Pulitzer complained of severe stomach pains. Since his physician was untested, the staff called Dr. Robert Wilson Jr., a prominent doctor in Charleston. After diagnosing the problem as severe indigestion, he gave Pulitzer a dose of Veronal. Pulitzer rallied and was well enough several days later to lunch on board with Robert Lathan, the editor of the *Charleston News & Courier*. The two men buoyantly shared their predictions for a Democratic victory in 1912. "I had never seen J.P. in a more genial mood or in higher spirits," Alleyne Ireland noted.

The following day, however, Pulitzer felt ill again and remained below deck all day and night. In the morning, Thwaites sent a telegram to Kate in New York. Over the years, she had received dozens of similarly alarming messages, many of which she had wisely chosen to ignore. In this case, however, she ordered a private railcar. By four o'clock that afternoon, she was on her way south.

At about three in the morning, as Kate's train entered the Carolinas, Joseph woke up. He asked Dunningham to send for Ireland. Rapidly putting on a dressing gown, Ireland grabbed a dozen books and headed to Pulitzer's cabin. "He was evidently suffering a good deal of pain," Ireland noted, "for he turned from side to side, and once or twice got out of bed and sat in an easy chair."

Ireland tried reading from several of the books he brought. He had little success engaging Pulitzer until he happened upon the historian Macaulay's essay on Hallam's *Constitutional History*, written when Macaulay was very young. "I read steadily until about five o'clock," Ireland said, "and J.P. listened attentively, interrupting me from time to time with a direction to go back and read over a passage." Around five-thirty Pulitzer began to suffer again. The ship's doctor as well as Dr. Wilson was summoned. Wilson gave Pulitzer Veronal, the sedative he had been taking for six months. Resting more comfortably, Pulitzer dismissed Ireland as the sun began to rise. "You'd better go and get some sleep," Pulitzer said, "we will finish that this afternoon."

Pulitzer's German reader and pianist Friedrich Mann took over for Ireland. He read from Christopher Hare's *The Life of Louis XI*. By mid-morning, Mann reached the chapter portraying the death of the French king. Louis XI was sixty-three and had ruled for twenty-three years. Pulitzer was sixty-four and had ruled the *World* for twenty-eight years. As had been his habit, Pulitzer quietly murmured, when the reading began to help him doze off. "*Leise, ganz leise*," he said. "Softly, very softly."

At one o'clock, Pulitzer awoke with a sharp pain in his chest and then fainted. Several minutes later, Kate arrived. She entered the cabin with Herbert. For about twenty minutes, they remained at the bedside as her husband of thirty-three years drew his last breaths.

The following day, a coffin of silver-mounted Spanish cedar containing Joseph's body was brought to the Charleston train station and placed in a railcar lined with mourning cloth. Kate, Herbert, and four of Joseph's men boarded a second private car, the one Kate had ridden from New York. The train pulled out at four-thirty in the afternoon for the overnight ride to New York. Joe and Ralph came from St. Louis and New York, respectively, to meet the train on its route north. Constance, who was living in Colorado Springs, and Edith, who was in France, both made hurried plans to go to New York.

When the train reached the city at five past two on the afternoon of October 31, 1911, flags at the *World*, as well as at the *Tribune* and other newspapers, were flying at half-mast. Pulitzer's death was on the front page of almost every newspaper in the land. The obituaries uniformly focused on Pulitzer's achievement in making the *World* a dominant newspaper, on his innovations in journalism, and on his financial success. It would have disappointed the subject of the stories. "I hate the idea of passing away known only as the proprietor of the paper," Pulitzer wrote a few months before his death. "Not property but politics was my passion, and not politics even in a general, selfish sense, but politics in the sense of liberty and freedom and ideals of justice." His rival Hearst understood. "In his conception, the newspaper was not merely a money-making machine," Hearst told his readers. "It was the instrument of the will and power of its hundreds of thousands of readers, the fulcrum upon which that power could be exerted in the accomplishment of broad and beneficial results."

Pulitzer's death was publicly attributed to heart troubles: Dr. Wilson, who completed the death certificate, listed angina as the cause and gallstones as a contributing factor. No mention was made of Veronal or any of the other medications. The press charitably avoided comment on Pulitzer's well-known two-decade struggle with depression and other maladies.

The body was brought to the family home on East Seventy-Third Street and placed in the library, which was filled with flowers and wreaths. The next morning, hundreds of the *World*'s staffers came uptown to pay their final respects. At noon, representatives of the Grand Army of the Republic held a service for their former member and placed a flag on the coffin. Pallbearers, including President Butler of Columbia University, the former managing editor George Harvey, the former mayor Seth Low, Pulitzer's doctor James W. McLane, and the business manager Angus Shaw escorted Pulitzer's coffin to a waiting cortege of carriages. The procession made its way twenty blocks south down Fifth Avenue to St. Thomas Episcopal Church, where more than two dozen policemen did their best to keep order as a crowd of thousands gathered on the street in front.

So many former editors and reporters of the *World* had been summoned that they were instructed to gather in the Gotham Hotel two blocks away. At the appointed time, the alumni were to emerge and join the funeral procession. However, the plan went awry. "Happy pairs, reunited after decades, danced together on the pavement," said Elizabeth Jordan, a former writer for the editorial page. "The orderly line, held for a moment, broke up in confusion. Reminiscences were yelped from one editor to another. Men ran up and down the line, seeking someone they hadn't found."

The boisterous merriment continued until the group saw the casket being carried into the church and heard the ponderous notes of the organ. "Something like an electric shock swept the ranks of the former employees," said Jordan. "Every pair of shoulders straightened, every smile disappeared. The line formed as if by magic. Reverently, two by two, with bent heads and lowered eyes, and hearts full of memories, the editors who had helped Joseph Pulitzer to build his *World* followed their dead chief into the crowded church."

A choir of forty-five men sang "Abide with Me" as Pulitzer's coffin made its way past pews filled with politicians, judges, newspapermen, and his old guard. Among them were John Norris, his longtime business manager, now with the *Times*; former reporters and editors such as James Creelman, Caleb Van Hamm, and Bradford Merrill; and members of Pulitzer's personal staff such as George Ledlie, Arthur Billings, Norman Thwaites, and Friedrich Mann.

The flag-draped coffin was covered with a blanket of lilies of the valley and orchids. It was brought to a rest in front of the altar amid more than 100 floral pieces including a wreath of roses from the republic of Colombia bearing a card engraved "To Her Friend." Reverend Ernest Stires read from chapter 15 of the First Epistle to the Corinthians. As he began, elevator motors, ventilators, and presses were shut down, and telegraph machines and telephones were disconnected at the *World* and *Post-Dispatch* buildings. For five minutes, with all the lights extinguished, Pulitzer's staff on duty that day stood at silent attention.

"For man walketh in a vain shadow, and disquieteth himself in vain: he heapeth up riches, and cannot tell who shall gather them," Stires read on, following the traditional Episcopal burial service and eschewing a eulogy. As a second hymn was sung, Stires brought two wreaths down from the altar and placed them on the flower-draped coffin. After a moment of silent prayer, the chorus burst into song again. "Hark! hark, my soul! Angelic songs are swelling," the men sang as the coffin was brought out from the church.

A special train took Pulitzer's body and his family—except for

Constance and Edith, who had not yet arrived—as well as a select group of editors, members of his personal staff, and a few friends to Woodlawn Cemetery in the Bronx. At the grave, Stires gave the final invocation before an improvised pulpit of canvas. As they all stood before the grave, the booming of guns from a naval fleet coincidentally visiting New York could be heard in the distance.

With the approach of dusk, Joseph's body was lowered into a grave next to that of his beloved daughter Lucille Irma. Inside the casket, Pulitzer's right arm lay across his chest and in his hand he clasped a copy of the *World*.

In the days following his burial, his astonished family read Joseph's will. He left the *World* and the *Post-Dispatch* in the hands of four trustees who, in time, would turn control over to his sons. Twenty-seven-year-old Joe would have to wait until he was thirty and fifteen-year-old Herbert would have to wait until he was twenty-one to assume a seat on the board. In an unintended error, Joseph failed to give thirty-two-year-old Ralph a seat in his last revision of the will. Acting on the advice of Joseph's lawyer, one of the trustees resigned and gave his place to Ralph.

But what dumbfounded the brothers was their father's division of the stock. Herbert, the youngest, who had done hardly more than visit one of the newspapers, was given 60 percent of the stock. Ralph, who had practically been running the *World*, was given 20 percent; and Joseph, the most talented of the three, received only 10 percent. The remaining 10 percent of the shares were to be used to produce an income to be divided among editors and managers.

When it came to power, Joseph provided for a more equal distribution. Each member of the board, on which each son would eventually have a seat, had only one vote. The board members in turn would select the directors for the two newspapers. In crafting the convoluted distribution of his newspaper assets and in devising his board, Joseph had had one goal in mind, and he made it clear in his final instructions.

"I particularly enjoin upon my sons and my descendants," Pulitzer wrote, "the duty of preserving, perfecting, and perpetuating the *World* newspaper, to the maintenance and publishing of which I have sacrificed my health and strength, in the same spirit in which I have striven to create and conduct it as a public institution, from motives higher than mere gain, and it having been my desire that it should be at all times conducted in a spirit of independence and with a view of inculcating high standards and public spirit among the people and their official representatives, and it is my earnest wish that said newspapers shall hereafter be conducted upon the same principles."

In addition to specifying his plans for his newspapers, Pulitzer disposed of his personal assets. For Kate, he set up a $2.5 million trust and the use of the houses in New York and Maine. His daughters, Constance and Edith, would share the income from a $1.5 million trust. Columbia University at long last received its promised gift to create the journalism school. Irascible until the end, Pulitzer also included a provision that would give the money to Harvard if Columbia failed to live up to its promises. He also left $250,000 for the Pulitzer prize and scholarships.

The remainder of his money was assigned for donations to the Metropolitan Museum of Art; to the Philharmonic Society; and to the city, for a fountain—which was eventually built on the Grand Army Plaza there—and for a statue of Thomas Jefferson. Also, gifts of $100,000 were to be shared among certain of the *World*'s writers and personal secretaries. There was an equally large sum for his valet Dunningham, and a smaller sum for George Hosmer.

Kate outlived her husband by almost sixteen years. Residing mostly in Europe, she spent her time helping young artists and musicians and supporting charities such as the Red Cross. She died in Deauville, France, in 1927. For years after her death, the family brought John Singer Sargent's portrait of her to Chatwold to be with them during the summer. The portrait of Joseph remained in St. Louis.

Ralph divorced Frederica and later married Margaret Leech, a talented writer who won two Pulitzer prizes for history. For a number of years Ralph took the helm of the *World*, although his youngest brother, Herbert, earned the largest share of its income while doing little or nothing in the way of work. Ralph died in 1939. Herbert had his opportunity to manage the *World* for a brief time in 1930, but it held little interest for him. Rather than journalism, his main passions were hunting big game in Africa and fishing near his home in Palm Beach. He died in 1957.

Joseph, the one brother to inherit his father's journalistic talent, remained in St. Louis, where he guided the *Post-Dispatch*. Under his rule, his father's original paper flourished as one of the nation's most important and profitable newspapers. His wife, Elinor, died in 1925 in an automobile accident. He later was remarried to Elizabeth Edgar. He died in 1955. In 2005, the descendants sold the *Post-Dispatch*. It continues today as a shell of its once distinguished self.

Edith married William Scoville Moore, grandson of the author of "Twas the Night before Christmas." Constance married William Gray Elmslie, who had once been Herbert's tutor. She died in 1938 after spending most of her life in Colorado Springs. Edith was the last living child of Kate and Joseph when she died in 1975.

In the early morning of February 27, 1931, a group of the *World*'s editors and writers gathered around the city desk. The news was glum. Nineteen years after Pulitzer's death, the paper was facing its own mortality. With its circulation getting hammered by new morning tabloids on the one hand, and losing the battle as a news leader to Ochs's invigorated *New York Times* and the newly merged *Herald-Tribune* on the other, the *World* seemed at a loss as to where to find a place for itself on the newsstands. Briefly in the 1920s, it had flared like a comet when the editor Herbert Bayard Swope filled its pages with the writing of men like Walter Lippmann, Heywood Broun, and Franklin P. Adams.

But without Joseph and his brilliant editor Frank Cobb, who died in 1923, Ralph and Herbert were ill-equipped to run the newspaper. The blame rested as much on their father as on the two sons. As an absentee owner, Joseph had refused to cede sufficient control so that a corporate management structure could be built. The internal disunion at the paper was aggravated by his system of keeping his managers competing and spying on each other. Until the end, Joseph had remained the keystone in the arch of management. After 1911, "the Pulitzer building was a haunted house," said one of the *World*'s writers. When the Depression came in 1929, the *World*'s losses mounted. Ralph, Herbert, and Joe agreed that maintaining the paper was a lost cause.

The reporters and editors at the city desk that morning had taken part in a last-ditch effort to persuade the brothers to sell the paper to the staff. Instead, the three sons surrendered the *World* and *Evening World* to Scripps-Howard for $5 million after obtaining a judge's consent to break their father's enjoinment that the paper never be sold. The resulting *New York World-Telegram* carried only the name of the paper. Joseph Pulitzer's *World* was gone.

The city editor James Barrett had just put the final edition carrying the announcement of the sale to bed. "Everyone found a paper cup, or two," said one of the reporters. "And the bottles weren't filled with water, because what they were filled with took the wax off the cups and curdled." Suddenly, Barrett slapped the desk and burst into song. To the tune of the "Battle Hymn of the Republic," the men belted out, "J.P.'s body lies a-mouldering in the grave, but the staff goes marching on." At three in the morning, they decided to move their wake to Daly's, a speakeasy popular with newspapermen. They left the Pulitzer Building, went into the chilly night, and marched down Park Row singing.

ACKNOWLEDGMENTS

The idea for this book belongs to my editor Tim Duggan. At first, I was unconvinced there was a need for a new biography of Joseph Pulitzer. The last serious one had been written in 1967 by W. A. Swanberg, whose books first got me interested in biography. However, after some modest research, I found that Swanberg had missed a great deal and that a new look at Pulitzer was long overdue. So, I remain thankful to Duggan for his clairvoyance and to the literary agent Mark Reiter, then with PFD New York, who negotiated the contract and supported the project from the start.

At HarperCollins, I also owe thanks to assistant editor Allison Lorentzen and copyeditor Susan Gamer for shepherding the manuscript to publication.

Like most authors, I live in fear of not properly thanking the many who made this book possible. But, here to the best of my ability, is my supporting cast.

The description of the Pulitzer family genealogy and of their life in Makó would not be so complete were it not for the work of historian András Csillag, a professor of American Civilization at Szeged University, Szeged, Hungary. Since the 1980s, he has doggedly pursued research into the family's history. The tour he provided me of Makó, Pulitzer's birthplace, was of enormous help. I was also assisted in Makó by Laszlo Molnar, Adrienn Nagy, and Marton Eacsedi, caretaker of the Jewish Cemeteries. In Budapest, Gyorgyi Haraszti, of the Institute of History of the Hungarian Academy of Sciences, Victor Karady, in the Jewish Studies Department of Central European University, and Mátyás

Gödölle, of the Hungarian National Museum answered my many questions about Pest when Pulitzer lived there as a child. Istvan Deak, at Columbia University, also provided helpful guidance.

The bulk of Pulitzer's papers and those of the *World* are kept at the Rare Book and Manuscript Library of Columbia University. Director Michael Ryan, Jennifer B. Lee, Tara C. Craig, Kevin O'Connor, and the entire staff provided exceptional assistance. The second largest holding of Pulitzer papers is the Manuscript Division of the Library of Congress, where Jeffrey M. Flannery was a constant help. At the Missouri Historical Society, Jason D. Stratman not only assisted me during my many visits but responded for years to my e-mail queries.

Eric P. Newman, founder of the Eric P. Newman Numismatic Education Society in St. Louis, graciously made me a copy of a loan from Preetorius to Pulitzer to buy shares of the *Westliche Post*. Pat and Leslie Fogarty, who discovered a cache of previously unknown Pulitzer documents, kindly let me examine them for the preparation of this book. Journalist Eric Fettmann shared with me a letter from Nannie Tunstall to Pulitzer. It played a pivotal role in being able to properly date the romantic relationship between the two. The late Muriel Pulitzer, a remarkable artist, permitted me to use her grandfather's memoirs. Her nephew Nicholas W. Wood, of Arlington, Texas, made it possible for me to meet Muriel. I also owe a great deal of thanks to Emily Rauh Pulitzer and James V. Maloney, Chief Financial Officer of the Pulitzer Foundation for the Arts, for their assistance and interest in the project.

Roman scholar Susanna Braund helped me try to track down an important allusion made by David Graham Phillips. Alexandra Villard de Borchgrave permitted me to use her files relating to Henry Villard. Dr. Edward Okum, who had treated Joseph Pulitzer's grandson for eye troubles, sorted out important questions regarding Pulitzer's blindness. Dr. Edwin Carter once again provided me with important psychological insights into my subject. Eric Homberger, author of *Mrs. Astor's New York: Money and Social Power in a Gilded Age*, gave me important advice on dealing with the anti-Semitism that confronted Pulitzer in New York City.

Jason Baker did yeoman's work in translating German documents for me. I am also grateful for his insights about Pulitzer's work at the *Westliche Post*. Baker was assisted by Rick Strudell, who managed to decipher nineteenth-century German penmanship. Cornelia Brooke Gilder helped me with research in the Berkshires. Jude Webre completed important fact-checking in the Columbia University holdings of Pulitzer papers. Elizabeth Elliott chased down elusive information on Tunstall in Lynchburg, Virginia. Charles Litchfield and Nancy Ross, two high school students, served as editorial interns in 2004 and 2005.

Tripp Jones, archivist, the Church of the Epiphany, went out of his way to provide me with insights into both the role of his church at Joseph and Kate's wedding as well as that of Joseph's relationship with the Episcopal Church as a whole. David G. Hardin and Keitha Leonard, both attorneys, assisted me in interpreting estate and business matters. The law firm of Ropes & Gray represented me pro bono in my Freedom of Information dispute with the Department of Justice, and Stephen M. Underhill, a graduate student from the University of Maryland working at the National Archives, helped locate the 1909–1910 Pulitzer prosecution records.

A large cast of people in libraries, archives, and universities from Budapest to St. Louis went out of their way to assist me. Specific individuals include: Jill Abraham, at the National Archives, who helped locate military records on Pulitzer, whose name was spelled several different ways, making it hard to locate some of the items; Wanda Adams, Leavenworth Public Library; Marisa Bourgoin of the Corcoran Art Gallery; Christine M. Beauregard, New York State Library; Joseph Fred Benson, Supreme Court of Missouri; Stephen Bolhafner, *St. Louis Post-Dispatch*; Frederick W. Brunello, New York Times Corporate Records; Michael DeArmey, University of Southern Mississippi; Jill Gage, Newberry Library; Judy Garrett, Berkshire Historical Society; James Good, Lone Star College–North Harris; Suzanne Hahn, Indiana Historical Society; Linda Hartman, Santa Fe Public Library; Mike Klein, Library of Congress; Shaun J. Kirkpatrick, United States Army War College and Carlisle Barracks; William Massa, Sterling Library, Yale University; Shirley McGrath, Greene County Historical Society; Katie McMahon, Newberry Library; Barbara Miksicek, St. Louis Police Library; Janie Morris, Duke University Library; James P. Niessen, Alexander Library, Rutgers University; Jenny Olmsted, Jekyll Island Museum; Janet Parks, Avery Architectural and Fine Arts Library, Columbia University; Donald Ritchie, U.S. Senate Historical Office; Nicholas B. Scheetz, Georgetown University Library; Wendy Schnur, G. W. Blunt Library of the Mystic Seaport Museum; Christina Shedlock, Charleston County Public

Library; David A. Smith, New York Public Library; James M. Smith, Rare Books and Manuscript Library, Ohio State University; William T. Stolz, Senior Manuscript Specialist, Western Historical Manuscript Collection, Columbia; Allen E. Wagner, University of Missouri–St. Louis; Andrew Walker, St. Louis Art Museum; Travis Westly, Library of Congress; Clive Wilmer, Cambridge University, England; Kenneth H. Winn, Missouri State Archives.

I also want to acknowledge the permitted use of materials from the Rare Book and Manuscript Library of Columbia University; Columbia University Oral History Research Office Collection; Midwest Manuscript Collection at the Newberry Library; Special Collections, Georgetown University Library; Special Collections Research Center, Syracuse University; and other institutions in the United States, Great Britain, and Hungary.

David O. Stewart, author of *Impeached*, was my constant literary companion during this project. He read every word I wrote and his comments greatly improved the manuscript. Editor Veronika Hass diligently reviewed my final drafts, frequently saving me from mortifying errors. David Garrow, author of *Bearing the Cross*, read large sections of the manuscript and provided valuable guidance. Others who read portions of the work include author Kenneth Ackerman; Zohar Kadman Sella, a student at Columbia University Graduate School of Journalism; Howard N. Lupovitch, of Colby College; Robert Priddy, broadcaster and independent historian in Missouri; and Richard Zacks, author of a forthcoming book on Theodore Roosevelt as police commissioner.

Friends Jim Percoco and Dean Sagar helped me sort out Pulitzer's role in the Civil War and worked to help me overcome my prejudices about the war. Friend and author Linda Lear gave me the idea for the subtitle to this book.

A research fellowship provided by Gilder Lehrman Institute of American History greatly defrayed my travel costs to New York City. A grant from the Richard S. Brownlee Fund of the Missouri State Historical Society helped fund my travels to Missouri. Its executive director Gary Kremer also provided useful guidance on Jefferson City in the 1870s. I am especially honored by support I received from the T/EL&DS, especially from its 2008 director J. Revell Carr, who was busy supervising the construction of the society's new headquarters.

Last, members of my family in New York—Christopher and Elissa

Morris and Helen and Martin Scorsese—gave me lodging and meals during my many research trips. My children, Stephanie, Benjamin, and Alexander, probably wondered if their father would ever finish this project and my wife, Patty, put up with long absences while I conducted my research and with long absences when I was home but locked away in my office.

Notes

To conserve space, the endnotes contain abbreviations for frequently cited sources and a more numeric dating system.

ARCHIVAL COLLECTIONS OR REPOSITORIES

ABF	Brisbane Family. Special Collections Research Center, Syracuse University
ABF–2001	2001 Addition to Brisbane Family, Special Collections Research Center, Syracuse University
AB-LC	Arthur Brisbane File, Lake County Historical Society, OH
AJHS	American Jewish Historical Society, New York, NY
BLMC	British Library Manuscript Collection, London
CAG	Corcoran Art Galley, Washington, DC
CDP	Chauncey Depew Papers, Sterling Library, Yale University
CJB	Charles Joseph Bonaparte Papers, Manuscript Division, Library of Congress
CS	Carl Schurz Papers, Manuscript Division, Library of Congress
DCS-NYPL	Don Carlos Seitz Papers, New York Public Library
EBW	E. B. Washburne Papers, Manuscript Division, Library of Congress
EFJC	Eric Fettmann Journalism Collection (privately held)
EHP	Earl Harding Papers, Special Collection, Georgetown University Library
HR	Hermann Raster Papers, Newberry Library, Chicago, IL
HSP	Henry Stimson, Manuscript and Archive, Sterling Library, Yale University
HW	Henry Watterson, Manuscript Division, Library of Congress
JA	Julian Allen Scrapbook, #13-z, Southern Historical Collection, Wilson Library, University of North Carolina at Chapel Hill
JB	James Broadhead Papers, Missouri Historical Society, St. Louis
JBE	J. B. Eads Papers, Missouri Historical Society
JC	James Creelman, Rare Books and Manuscript Library, Ohio State University
JJJ	John Joseph Jennings Collection, Beinecke Library, Yale University
JNP-MHS	John W. Norton Papers, Missouri Historical Society, St. Louis
JP-CU	Joseph Pulitzer, Rare Book and Manuscript Library, Columbia University
JP-LC	Joseph Pulitzer, Manuscript Division, Library of Congress
JPII-LC	Joseph Pulitzer Jr. (1885–1955), Manuscript Division, Library of Congress
JP-MHS	Joseph Pulitzer Collection, Missouri Historical Society, St. Louis
JP-NYSL	Joseph Pulitzer, correspondence, New York State Library, Albany
LB	Louis Benecke Family Papers, 1816–1989, Western Historical Manuscript Collection, Columbia, MO
LS	Louis Starr Papers, Rare Book and Manuscript Library, Columbia University
MHS	Missouri Historical Society, St. Louis
MSA	Missouri State Archives, Jefferson City, MO
MMW	McKim, Mead, and White Collection, New-York Historical Society
NARA	National Archives, Washington, DC

NARA-MD	Department of Justice, Record Group 60, file #10963–02, National Archives, College Park, MD
NARA-NY	US v. Press Publishing Files, National Archives, New York City
NT-DU	Nannie Tunstall Papers, Duke University Library
N-YHS	New-York Historical Society
NYTA	New York Times Corporate Archives
PDA	Archival material on file in the library of the *Post-Dispatch*, St. Louis, MO. The paper held files of miscellaneous letters, articles, and photographs all mixed in with personal affairs of Joseph Pulitzer II and Joseph Pulitzer III.
PLFC	Pat and Leslie Fogarty Collection (privately held)
SB	Samuel Bowles Papers, Manuscript and Archive, Sterling Library, Yale University
SSMHS	Sylvester Scovel Papers, Missouri Historical Society, St. Louis
SLPA	Microfilms made by the *St. Louis Post-Dispatch* containing miscellaneous Pulitzer correspondence. One copy is owned by the paper; the other is on file at the St. Louis Public Library.
SLPDL	St. Louis Police Department Library, St. Louis
StLi	American Committee of the Statue of Liberty, New York Public Library
TD	Thomas Davidson. Manuscript and Archive, Yale University
TRP	Theodore Roosevelt Papers, Manuscript Division, Library of Congress
UB	Udo Brachvogel Papers, New York Public Library
WCP-DU	William W. Corcoran Papers, Special Collection Library, Duke University
WHMC	Western Historical Manuscript Collection, Columbia, MO
WHS-IHS	William H. Smith Papers, Indiana Historical Society
WG-CU	William Grosvenor. Rare Book and Manuscript Library, Columbia University
WP-CU	*World* Papers, Rare Book and Manuscript Library, Columbia University
WR-LC	Whitelaw Reid Papers, Manuscript Division, Library of Congress
WSP	William Speer Papers, Rare Book and Manuscript Library, Columbia University

PERSONAL NAMES

AB	Alfred Butes
ABi	Arthur Billings
BM	Bradford Merrill
DC	Dumont Clarke
DCS	Don Carlos Seitz
DGP	David Graham Phillips
FC	Frank Cobb
FDW	Florence D. White
GHL	George H. Ledlie
GWH	George W. Hosmer
HS	Henry Stimson
JAS	J. Angus Shaw
JN	John Norris
JP	Joseph Pulitzer
JPII	Joseph Pulitzer Jr.
JWC	James W. Clarke
KP	Kate Pulitzer
MAM	Maud Alice Macarow
NT	Norman Thwaites

PB	Pomeroy Burton
RHL	Robert H. Lyman
RP	Ralph Pulitzer
TR	Theodore Roosevelt
WHM	William H. Merrill

FREQUENTLY CITED BOOKS OR MANUSCRIPTS

AI	Alleyne Ireland. *Joseph Pulitzer: Reminiscence of a Secretary.* New York: Mitchell Kennerley, 1914.
APM	Albert Pulitzer. "Memoirs." Unpublished memoir written by Albert Pulitzer in 1909 and edited and annotated by his son Walter Pulitzer between 1909 and probably 1913. In author's possession. On deposit in the Rare Book and Manuscript Library, Columbia University.
DCS-JP	Don C. Seitz. *Joseph Pulitzer: His Life and Letters.* New York: Simon and Schuster, 1924.
GJ	George Juergens. *Joseph Pulitzer and the New York World.* Princeton, NJ: Princeton University Press, 1966.
JLH	John L. Heaton. *The Story of a Page: Thirty Years of Public Service and Public Discussion in the Editorial Columns of the New York World.* New York: Harper, 1913.
JSR	Julian S. Rammelkamp. *Pulitzer's Post-Dispatch, 1878–1883.* Princeton, NJ: Princeton University Press, 1967.
JWB	James Wyman Barrett. *Joseph Pulitzer and His World.* New York: Vanguard, 1941.
WRR	William Robinson Reynolds. "Joseph Pulitzer." PhD diss., Columbia University, 1950.
WAS	W. A. Swanberg, *Pulitzer.* New York: Scribner, 1967.

NEWSPAPERS

Readers may note the appearance of smaller newspapers in some of the endnotes. This is because they made extensive use of wire copy and often contained valued reports about New York journalism and politics.

AtCo	*Atlanta Constitution*
BoGl	*Boston Globe*
BrEa	*Brooklyn Eagle*
ChTr	*Chicago Tribune*
DeFr	*Detroit Free Press*
EvPo	*St. Louis Evening Post*
GlDe	*St. Louis Globe-Democrat* (including issues when it was the *St. Louis Globe*)
LAT	*Los Angeles Times*
MoDe	*Missouri Democrat*
MoRe	*Missouri Republican*
NYA	*New York American*
NYH	*New York Herald*
NYEJ	*New York Evening Journal*
NYEW	*New York Evening World*
NYMJ	*New York Morning Journal* (later succeeded by the *New York American*)

NYS	*New York Sun*
NYT	*New York Times*
NYTr	*New York Tribune*
NYW	*New York World*
SeDe	*Sedalia Democrat*
StLoDi	*St. Louis Dispatch*
PD	*St. Louis Post-Dispatch*
StLoPo	*St. Louis Post*
ThJo	*The Journalist*
TT	*Town Topics*
WaPo	*Washington Post*
WP	*Westliche Post*
WSJ	*Wall Street Journal*

Note: When citing Pulitzer letters and other documents located at either Columbia University or the Library of Congress, I have chosen to limit the citation to the date of item and collection, unless more information would be needed for its retrieval. For instance, some correspondence and other items were not filed chronologically or sometimes are incorrectly filed. In those cases, I have provided the box and file folder information.

Additionally, finding aids I developed in conjunction with the research for this book have been deposited at the Rare Book and Manuscript Room of Columbia University and the Manuscript Room of the Library of Congress.

Last, the endnote appears at the point at which I begin using the source. So quotations in subsequent paragraphs stem from the same source unless otherwise specified.

PROLOGUE: HAVANA 1909

1. **On the afternoon:** Descriptions of Havana harbor are drawn from Robert T. Hill, *Cuba and Porto Rico with the Other Islands of the West Indies* (New York: The Century Co., 1898) and photographs in the G. W. Blunt Library of Mystic Seaport.
1. **The length of:** AI, 28. Sarawak is today one of the two Malaysian states on the island of Borneo.
2. **And it was talked about:** Data calculated using data from the twenty-fifth anniversary issue of *World*, 5/10/1903, copy contained in May 1903 Folder, WP-CU.
3. **"*The World* should":** JP and Clark B. Firestone conversation, transcript, undated, undated folder 1910, JP-LC, Box 9.
4. **"I think God":** JP and Firestone conversation, transcript, 8/5/1908, WP-CU.
5. **At last the small boat:** WRR, 711.

CHAPTER 1: HUNGARY

A note about family names: I have chosen to keep Joseph Pulitzer's ancestors and family names in their original spelling, such as Mihály (instead of Michael), Fülöp (instead of Phillip). But as Jószef Pulitzer would become known by the American spelling of his name, I instead refer to him as "Joseph."

9. **By the time:** Moravia is now located in the eastern third of the modern Czech Republic. When I visited the Jewish cemetery in Makó in 2006, I found graves for Pulitzers with all three spellings: "Politzer," "Puliczer," and "Pulitzer." András Csillag, "The Hungarian Origins of Joseph Pulitzer," *Hungarian Studies*, Vol. 3, No. 1–2 (1987), 193; Peter I. Hidas, "A Brief Outline of the History of Jews of Hungary," delivered December 13, 1992 at the Temple Emanu-El-Beth Sholom, Westmount, Canada (un-

published, in author's possession); Lupovitch, *Jews at the Crossroads*, xviii–xix; András Csillag, *Pulitzer József makói származásáról* (Makó: Makó Múseum, 1985), 13–14.

10. **In Makó, the Pulitzers:** Csillag, "Hungarian Origins," 194–196.

10. **When Joseph's father:** Ibid., 198; APM, 16; Csillag, *Pulitzer József makói származásáról*, 13.

10. **Following Jewish custom:** Birth Recorders Book, Makó, Israelitic Religious Birth Registrar's Office, Vol. 36.16, JPII-LC. The copy is accompanied by a translation, which, however, fails to translate the Hungarian word *körülmetélö* (circumcision.) The translation was done for the Pulitzer family in 1937 (possibly later). The birth of Pulitzer is also noted in the listing of Jewish births in Makó on microfilm #0642780 of the Family History Center for the Mormon Church.

11. **Nonetheless, as Jews:** The percentage was determined using estimated population figures but it matched that provided by Marton Eacsedi, caretaker of the Jewish Cemeteries in Makó, in an interview with the author, January 21, 2006. A city plan of 1815 described the crooked streets of the Jewish settlement: Toth, "History," 4.

12. **Despite the revolution's:** The strength of Hungarian nationalism among Jews is described in Alexander Maxwell, "From Wild Carpathians to the Puszta: The Evolution of Hungarian National Landscapes," in Ruth Buettner and Judith Peltz, eds., *Mythical Landscapes Then and Now* (Yerevan, Macmillan, 2006); Gyorgyi Haraszti, of the Institute of History of the Hungarian Academy of Sciences, interview with author, January 24, 2006; APM, 4.

12. **The end of:** *Jewish Encyclopedia*, Vol. 8 (New York: Funk and Wagnalls, 1901), 273. Pulitzer attended the Hebrew school in Makó, according to his childhood friend Adolph Reiner, *The Journal of Temesvar*, June 21, 1913 (translation in JPII-LC.); Patai, *The Jews of Hungary*, 284–285; Lopovitch, *Jews at the Crossroads*, 240–243.

12. **There was nothing modern:** APM, 12.

12. **In the spring:** Csillag, *Pulitzer József makói származásáról*, 19; McCagg, *Habsburg Jews*, 135.

13. **Unlike Buda, which:** The descriptions of Pest and Buda are drawn from prints in the Hungarian National Museum and from Beattie, *The Danube*; and Parsons, *The City of Magyar*.

13. **The Pulitzers' wagon:** Komoróczy, ed., *Jewish Budapest*; Csillag, "Hungarian Origins," #199. Fülöp was no stranger to the Jewish quarter. On his business journeys he had lodged in the enormous Orczy House, which was so immense it was regarded as a kind of shtetl, or little Jewish town, in and of itself.

13. **The move to Pest:** Csillag, "Hungarian Origins," 199–201; Victor Karady, professor in the Department of History and Nationalism Studies Program at Central European University, interview with author, January 17, 2006.

13. **Because of the family's:** APM, 11–12. This tale has all the markings of a family legend and may be only an exaggeration. Years later, though, one of Joseph's childhood friends cryptically reported that he "did beat his teacher."

14. **If Joseph didn't:** APM, 20, 46; Less than six years later, Joseph Pulitzer would meet the American philosopher Denton J. Snider. Upon learning that Snider was teaching a course in philosophy, Pulitzer said, "What good can you get from that?" (Denton J. Snider, *The St. Louis Movement*, 163.)

14. **For Joseph, Pest:** Kósa, *The Old Jewish Quarter of Budapest*, 14.

14. **Leaving the market:** APM, 16.

15. **Any exploration of:** Beattie, *The Danube*, 181–182. See also Paget, *Hungary and Transylvania*; and Parsons, *The City of Magyar*.

15. **The wealth, success:** Today Temple Emanu-El in New York City is larger than this synagogue but does not seat more people; Komoróczy, *Jewish Budapest*, 110; Patai,

The Jews of Hungary, 298–301. Most, if not all, of the Pulitzer death records and gravestones in Hungary recognize the family as Neologs.

15. **Despite having secured:** In all the couple had nine children. Lajos, born in 1840, lived sixteen years; Borbála, born in 1842, five years; Breindel, born in 1845, one year; Anna, born in 1849, eleven years; Gábor, born in 1853, two years; and Arnold, born in 1856, less than one year. The birth and death dates of one child, Helene, are not known, but she died before 1858. Only Joseph and his brother Albert, who was born on July 10, 1851, lived into adulthood. (Csillag, "Hungarian Origins," 197.)

16. **Four years older than Albert:** See John Bowlby, *Attachment and Loss*; Wass and Corr, eds., *Childhood and Death*; Silverman, *Never Too Young to Know: Death in Children's Lives*.

16. **As an additional:** Fülöp's will was probated in Pest, and an account of its contents is found in Csillag, "Hungarian Origins," 202–203 (a portion of the will is reproduced on 201).

16. **"Thus was my mother":** APM, 16.

16. **Financial relief appeared:** JP to Nannie Tunstall, May 2, 1878, EFJC. Albert never mentions Frey in his memoir, and Joseph seems never to have talked about Frey to his friends or family. His absence from their recollections is striking, especially in comparison with how much they both discussed their affection for their mother.

17. **The deaths and:** APM, 19; *Temesvar Hirlap*, June 21, 1913, translation in JP-LC, Box 12, folder 3.

17. **Going to the:** Komoróczy, *Jewish Budapest*; 104; Patai, *The Jews of Hungary*, 286.

18. **Pulitzer had grown:** Pulitzer later told friends that he traveled to Paris and London in hopes of joining an army; but this seems doubtful, considering the cost of such travel and his family's financial condition at the time.

18. **Events in the:** Geary, *We Need Men*, 103; *Boston Daily Courier*, September 1, 1864, 1; Murdock, *One Million Men*, 188; *Papers Relating to Foreign Affairs* (38, Congress, 2nd Session, House Executive Document No. 1, vol. 3, Serial 1218, Washington, 1865), 177. Allen was established in Hamburg in early March: Julian Allen Scrapbook, #13-z, Southern Historical Collection, Wilson Library, University of North Carolina at Chapel Hill.

18. **Allen set up:** *Foreign Affairs*, 184–185; *Boston Courier*, 9/1/1864, 1. The contract the recruits signed required turning over any bonus they received to Allen. His promise to pay all travel expenses from the recruit's home is one of the reasons I believe that Pulitzer did not come to Hamburg by happenstance but rather responded to Allen's advertisements. It was unlikely, considering the financial condition of his family, that Pulitzer would have embarked on a three-capital tour of Europe; *Foreign Affairs*, 178.

18. **In early summer:** Adolf Zedlinski to JP, 8/13/1903, JP-CU. Among those who once frequented the restaurant was the poet Joseph von Eichendorff, who had died in 1857.

18. **There Pulitzer located:** *Boston Courier*, 9/1/1864; *New York Evening Post*, 8/10/1864 and *New York Evening Express*, 8/10/1864 (copies of both are in Allen's scrapbook). A copy of the contract is reproduced in *Foreign Affairs*, 185. See also *ChTr*, 8/16/1864, 3. An article also appeared in the *Springfield Republican* that was reprinted in *NYT*, 8/19/1864; *ChTr*, 8/11/1864, 1.

19. **Pulitzer was among:** "Copy of report and list of passengers taken on board the *Garland* of Hamburg," National Archives, Washington, DC. Pulitzer was among the last two dozen to board; *Galignani's Messenger*, date unknown, in Allen's scrapbook; *Foreign Affairs*, 179.

CHAPTER 2: BOOTS AND SADDLES

Pulitzer remained closemouthed about the details of his service. Unlike other Civil War veterans, he never participated in commemorative events and never even told battle tales. The official records are also incomplete. There is, for instance, no information in his military service file to account for his whereabouts between January and May 1865. All the muster calls for these months are missing. Many such records were lost, so the disappearance of Pulitzer's is not suspicious; but it is nevertheless frustrating to historians.

20. **After nearly six:** The *Lizzie Homans*, the *City of Limerick*, and the *Etna* all reported seeing icebergs on their voyages across the Atlantic from Liverpool, England. Even as late as August, while Pulitzer was seaborne, a ship reached Boston with tales of seeing large quantities of ice in Iceberg Alley. *NYT*, 8/16/1864, 8; 8/22/1864, 8; 8/23/1864, 8; 9/1/1864, 8.

20. **Boats bearing federal:** Article in *Courier de Lyon*, which was sent to Secretary of State William Seward by Consul William L. Dayton in Paris, 10/17/1864. It appears, translated, in *Foreign Affairs*, 165.

20. **Pulitzer knew the:** Pulitzer later told friends that he slipped over the ship's railing at night and swam ashore so as to collect his own bounty. This tale has long been considered a myth. The ship never came close to a Boston dock. But the discovery that Pulitzer was among those in Allen's recruiting scheme gives the tale new credibility. In fact, the waterway separating Deer Island from the mainland was only about 300 feet wide at its narrowest point and a dozen feet deep. In the end, it may be that Pulitzer only embellished his escape from the clutches of the Massachusetts recruiters. Instead of thrashing about in the polluted harbor water of the docks, leaving all his personal belongings behind, he and a dozen or two dozen men probably easily traversed the channel at low tide. I compared the ship's manifest with the rolls of Massachusetts regiments and found that almost all the men I looked up did, in the end, join the Union forces. The channel between Deer Island and the mainland was filled in by a hurricane during the twentieth century. The width and depth of the channel when Pulitzer arrived were estimated from nautical charts on deposit at the Library of Congress.

21. **Reaching New York:** One could earn $300 from the county, $75 from the state, and $300 from the federal government (*Frank Leslie's Illustrated Newspaper*, 3/19/1864, 404). Advertisements in *NYH* listed bounties of $400 for aliens and $600 for men willing to be substitutes. See *NYH*, 5/27/1864, 6/3/1864, 6/7/1864; *NYT*, 1/30/1864, 8.

21. **Despite such efforts:** *NYT*, 8/2/1864, 3. Lieutenant Colonel R. W. Winfield Simpson and Captain R. McNichol, from Kingston, ran a regular advertisement in New York newspapers. Typical of them was one that can be found in *NYT*, 9/29/1864, when Pulitzer was in the city; *NYT*, 8/ 7/1864. *NYT*, 2/4/1865, 8; *NYT*, 9/24/1864, 1. Information on Henry Vosburgh drawn from *Descriptive Book of Drafted, Draft Register for the 13th District Headquarters in Kingston*, National Archives, 159, as well as cemetery and census records provided by the Greene County (NY) Historical Society.

21. **At the Kingston tent:** Pulitzer's military service record, NARA. (Note: His service records are sometimes hard to locate because his name is variously spelled as "Pullitzer" and "Politzer.") Geary, *We Need Men*, 145. Ironically, Vosburgh's luck in obtaining Pulitzer's services as a substitute did not ward off an early death. He died within a year of natural causes. (Headstone at Colleburgh Cemetery, headstone inventory, Greene County Historical Society, Coxsackie, NY.)

21. **With money in:** The ring, along with letters telling its story, is stored in the Library of Congress among the collection of Joseph Pulitzer II papers. The younger Pulitzer acquired the coin in 1938, when relatives in Hungary mailed it to him. (Polgar Gyulane to JPII, 4/18/1938.)

22. **A few days:** Bill Twoney, "Hart Island—Part 1" *Bronx Times Reporter*, 11/24/1994; *NYT*, 12/12/1867, 7; *NYT*, 8/7/1864, 2; *NYT*, 1/10/1865, 4.

22. **Pulitzer also avoided:** *NYT*, 8/27/1864, 3 and 11/20/1864, 5. Pulitzer's story is consistent with the fact that the cavalries were also becoming less selective about recruits. See, for instance, the poster with five charging cavalrymen in New-York Historical Society Civil War Treasures Collection, PR–055–3–207; DCS-JP, 43.

22. **On November 12, 1864:** Starr, *The Union Cavalry in the Civil War*, Vol., 2, 322–333.

23. **Pulitzer was assigned:** Descriptive Book, Companies B-M, 1st New York Lincoln Cavalry, NARA. Stevenson, *Boots and Saddles*, 320. Later in Pulitzer's life, when he was famous, several of his wartime acquaintances contacted him. One of them, the German-born John See, who recalled being his tent mate, was seeking financial assistance in 1910. One of Pulitzer's staff members checked to make sure this was the case before Pulitzer sent a check. (Witherbee memo to Seitz, undated but in May–June, 1910, folder, JP-LC, Box 9.)

23. **Although it was a relief:** McPherson, *For Cause and Comrades*, 115.

23. **A less significant:** *NYT*, 11/11/1864, 5, and 11/12/1864, 1; Beach, *The First New York (Lincoln) Cavalry*, 453. President Lincoln proclaimed the last Thursday of each November as Thanksgiving Day in the fall of 1863.

23. **For the remainder:** Beach, *The First New York (Lincoln) Cavalry*, 452; *Illustrated London News*, Vol. 45, No. 1291 12/10/1864, 574.

24. **Pulitzer's pain and:** Beach, *The First New York (Lincoln) Cavalry*, 456–457

24. **Warfare resumed with:** John G. Steele to JP, 9/8/1885, JP-CU. Previous biographies of Pulitzer placed him in Sheridan's raids when they resumed in late February, specifically attacks on Waynesboro on March 2 and Beaver Dam Station on March 15. Afterward it was believed that Pulitzer escaped hazardous duty by being assigned as an orderly to Major Richard J. Hinton, who was in the valley on special duty. But the records do not bear out this account. Hinton was a British-born American journalist whose strong abolitionist sentiments led him to move to Kansas, where he became a leading advocate of a slave-free state and a follower of John Brown. For most of the war he served as a recruiter and an officer of black soldiers in Kansas. His military records do not include service in the Shenandoah Valley. But one cannot be certain that he didn't come east, because at the beginning of the war he conducted some secret missions to the South (significant enough so that he was thanked by President Lincoln). Yet, if he had been conducting secret work, one would think that he would hardly select a soldier who took orders only in German. Furthermore, Hinton spent the remainder of his life as a journalist, writer, and public official; and his limited correspondence with Pulitzer, when the latter became a well-known publisher, made no reference to having known him before: (DCS-JP, 46; JWB, 14; WRR, 5; *WAS*, 4). What may have occurred is that Pulitzer's first biographer confused two Hintons. This biographer wrongly assumed, when Pulitzer said that he had served under a Major Hinton, that this was the better-known Richard, unaware of Chalmers A. Hinton, a captain in the First Lincoln. Chalmers Hinton was detached and assigned to tend prisoners of war at City Point, Virginia. There is, however, no record that Pulitzer was detached to work for this Hinton, either.

What other military records and a fragment of correspondence dating from many years after the war do reveal is that Pulitzer remained far from harm's way during the final months of the war. When his name surfaces in the records of June 1865, it is on a muster-out roll of a detachment from Company L in the First Regiment of the New York Cavalry. The group of six was under the command of Franz Passeger, a Viennese major. During January, February, March, and possibly April, Passeger served as a bodyguard for and then on the staff of General H. Chapman. The general had just returned to service after being wounded in the fall of 1864 and was assigned to Camp Averell, near Winchester.

24. **April 1865 brought:** Beach, *The First New York (Lincoln) Cavalry*, 511–512.

25. **Promptly at nine:** NYT and ChTr, 5/24/1864; DCS-JP, 47. For years Pulitzer apparently believed that he had seen Lincoln, but he realized, after considering the facts, that he could never have.

26. **The reviews over:** NYT, 6/1/1865, 1.

26. **When Pulitzer's turn:** Pulitzer's military service record, NARA; Pulitzer's discharge, JP-MHS.

27. **On June 26:** NYH, 6/29/1865, 3.

27. **Peace had its:** In June and July, alone, the city provided meals, lodging, and what the newspapers called "extra delicacies" to 60,000 men. *Illustrated London News*, 8/12/1865, 128; NYT, 10/1/1865, 5; Ida Tarbel, "Disbanding Union Army at the End of the Civil War," BoGl, 5/26/1907, 5; NYT, 7/16/1865, 5, 8/9/1865, 3, 8/12/1865, 8, 9/13/1865, 9, 9/28/1865, 2.

27. **Bewildered, alone, and:** WaPo, 9/28/1890, 9.

27. **One day, as:** James Barnes, "Joseph Pulitzer, a Dominant Personality: Some Personal Reminiscences," *Colliers*, 11/18/1911. Pulitzer shared similar details with *New York Graphic*, reprinted in *Evening Gazette* (Cedar Falls, IA), 1/20/1887, 3.

28. **At last, the:** Various biographers have offered differing reasons for Pulitzer's move to St. Louis but none have been backed by any evidence. One version often repeated, but certainly not true, appeared in *American Heritage*. "Mustered out, Pulitzer asked around about where he might settle in the United States: he wanted a place where German was not spoken, so that he could improve his English. A practical joker, it is said, sent him to St. Louis, which had a colony large enough to make a sizable town in Germany." (David Davidson "What Made the 'World' Great?" *American Heritage*, Vol. 33, No. 6 [Oct/Nov 1982]); Henry Charles Hummel, who joined the Lincoln Cavalry on the same day as Pulitzer and served on the same detachment, may have moved to St. Louis with him. A river man named Charles Hummel begins appearing in the St. Louis city directory the same year as Pulitzer does: Pulszky and Pulszky, *White, Red, Black*, 167–174. During the fall, when Pulitzer was vainly seeking work in New York, a newspaper reporter watched Germans debark from ships including, in particular, a "phlegmatic Teuton who paid for 'ten through tickets to St. Louis by the 5 o'clock train." As a rule, concluded the reporter, German immigrants arrived with a plan of operation. "They strike at once for the West. . . . their first query is for the ticket office, where they purchase the necessary documents, and then wait anxiously for the departure of the train." (NYT, 9/12/1865, 1.) Certainly Pulitzer would have learned about the large German communities in St. Louis, Cincinnati, and Milwaukee from other German-speaking soldiers in his regiment, especially during the two-week encampment outside Washington, when they discussed plans for civilian life.

CHAPTER 3: THE PROMISED LAND

29. **When Pulitzer got:** The exact date of his arrival is unknown. Previous biographers accepted October 10, 1865, a date Pulitzer himself probably used. At the same time Seitz claimed Pulitzer was superstitious when it came to numbers and attributed special significance to the number 10, the date of his birth. "He made the superstition

something of a fad and used the numerals always when he could," said Seitz, (DCS, 11). Pulitzer's superstition about the number also makes the dating of his arrival suspicious. In fact, his description of the cold weather did not match weather records for the day. Nor do the facts in another recollection related to his arrival bear up under scrutiny. So while it is unlikely that an exact date can be determined, it seems certain that Pulitzer arrived sometime in the fall of 1865. The data on ferry traffic are drawn from Scharf, *History of Saint Louis City and County*, Vol. 2; DCS-JP, 50.

29. **Through the darkness:** DCS-JP, 51.

30. **It was like coming home:** The similarities between the Pest riverbank and that of St. Louis struck me while I was examining nineteenth-century prints in the Hungarian National Museum. Except for minor differences I thought I was looking at the photo *St. Louis Levee* by Thomas Easterly in the collection of the Missouri Historical Society. Ernst D. Kargau's 1893 work *St. Louis in früheren jahren. Ein gedenkbuch für das deutschthum* was translated and published as *The German Element in St. Louis*, 9. The names of the establishments, however, are taken from the original German edition (St. Louis, MO: A. Wiebusch, 1893), 12.

30. **St. Louis was:** Twain, *Life on the Mississippi*, 525; Thérèse Yelverston, *Teresina in America*, 115.

30. **Despite its foul:** "In no American city, not even in Cincinnati, although more Germans, in proportion, live there than in St. Louis, have I found the German element so preponderant," noted Friedrich Gerstäker, a German traveler: Friedrich Gerstäcker, *Gerstäcker's Travels*. Olson, "St. Louis Germans, 1850–1920."

30. **He found work:** Kargau, *German Element*, 124–125; Snider, *St. Louis Movement*, 145.

31. **For the first:** *MoRe*, 9/5/1865, 3; DCS-JP, 52; *ChTr*, 5/24/1883, 10; *MoRe*, 1/1/1877, 6. A "Joseph P. Pullitzer" was listed in the 1866 city directory as a coachman; the family that employed Pulitzer as a coachman may have been the Weinhagens.

31. **In 1866 Pulitzer:** WRR, 6.

31. **Despite Pulitzer's inability:** Udo Brachvogel, "Episoden aus Joseph Pulitzers St. Louis Jahren," *Rundschau zweier welten*, January 1912. As with his experiences in the Civil War, Pulitzer almost never talked about his first years in St. Louis. When he did tell tales, he would invariably cut them short and complain that the listener had unfairly countenanced the reminiscence. "As soon as a man gets in the habit of talking about his past adventures," Pulitzer said on one such occasion, "he might as well make up his mind that he is growing old and that his intellect is giving way." But in a rare moment late in life, Pulitzer did recount several stories from this time. While cruising the Mediterranean in 1911, Pulitzer shared some with Alleyne Ireland, who was one of the last in a long string of personal secretaries and who would later serve as his companion. "He was generally more willing to talk when we took our meals at the large round table on deck, for he loved the sea breeze and was soothed by it," Ireland recalled (AI, 168, 174–175).

32. **One time Pulitzer:** AI, 171–172.

32. **The various jobs:** DCS-JP, 53. The services provided by the organization were sorely needed. Six thousand German immigrants arrived in St. Louis in 1866 (Kargau, *German Element*, 206–208).

32. **In Pulitzer's case:** Adalbert Strauss to Joseph Pulitzer Jr., 6/11/1913, JPII-LC. Strauss was not alone in being "introduced" to Elize. Charles P. Johnson, who met Pulitzer around this time, had a similar experience. "One of the most attractive traits of his character to me was his admiration and abiding love for his mother," said Johnson. "She was his guiding star" ("Remarks of Gov. Chas. P. Johnson, Birthday Anniversary Dinner," April 10, 1907, PDA).

33. **Pulitzer paid the $2:** Pulitzer's entry is written in his own hand in the July 18, 1866, membership ledger. He listed his occupation as clerk at "Theo Strauss & Co, 19th & Franklin." The occupations of other members were determined by examining the pages adjoining Pulitzer's entry. Record Group 12—membership, Mercantile Library Archives, St. Louis, MO; Annual Report of the St. Louis Mercantile Library Association, 1866, 12–13; Taylor and Crooks, *Sketch Book of Saint Louis,* 66–67.

33. **He approached the:** JP to RP, 3/23/1903 JP-CU; Annual Report of the St. Louis Mercantile Library Association, 1866, 14; Clarence Miller, "Exit Smiling, Part II," *Missouri Historical Society Bulletin,* Vol. 6, No. 2 (January 1950), 188.

33. **His hours in:** Leidecker, *Yankee Teacher,* 317–320; Snider, *The St. Louis Movement in Philosophy,* 7, 139. The men who formed the society also ended up as characters in a novel, *The Rebel's Daughter,* by John Gabriel Woerner. Professor Altrue is a representation of Harris, Dr. Taylor is Dr. Schneider (a play on the German word *Schneider,* "tailor"), and Brockmeyer appears as Rauhenfels. See Woerner, *Woerner,* 103.

34. **When he wasn't studying:** Clarence Miller, "Exit Smiling, Part II," *Missouri Historical Society Bulletin,* Vol. VI, 2, Jan. 1950, 188; E. F. Osborn to JPII, 6/15/1913, PD. Chess was a popular game in Hungary. In fact, victories by a Hungarian in a correspondence match between Pest and Paris in the 1840s had created a popular opening strategy called the "Hungarian defense."

34. **Pulitzer quit his post:** William Kelsoe to Carlos Seitz, undated but part of series of correspondence in 1921–1922, PDA; A. S. Walsh to JPII, June 1913, PDA. According to A. S. Walsh, the teenager who worked in the drugstore, "Joe used to often come into the store to have a chat and compare notes and during the epidemic his visits seems to be more frequent than usual" (A. S. Walsh to JP II, June 1913. PD). In late summer cholera returned to St. Louis. Twice before, the disease had ravaged the city; this time its destruction was far less, though still considerable. In its fourth week as many as 140 people were dying each day. The drugstore remained open twenty-four hours a day. Joseph Nash McDowell, an eminent doctor and founder of a medical school, had an office above the drugstore. When the city turned to him for help in managing the epidemic, he reportedly hired Pulitzer to work at Arsenal Island, where the sick were quarantined and the dead were buried. The epidemic subsided after September. By November the number of reported deaths was down to four, and Pulitzer returned to work in Patrick's office. I made an extensive search in St. Louis records for any information about Pulitzer's service on Arsenal Island, but I failed to uncover anything.

35. **By the spring of 1867:** Pulitzer's notary public certificate, JPII-LC; W. A. Kelsoe to Seitz, undated (written between 1913 and 1920), PDA.

35. **Pulitzer continued working:** DCS-JP, 55; AI, 221; JP to William James, 6/21/1867, 7/13/1867, Wortham James Collection, 1820–1891, folder 2211, WHMC. Surviving correspondence—which are his earliest existing letters—while routine and historically insignificant reveals that Pulitzer had begun to acquire some command of English. He may have used form letters, but the transactions could not have been completed by someone lacking understanding of the language.

35. **After a few months:** See White, *The German-Language Press in America;* Trefousse, *Carl Schurz,* 162. Schurz to Margarethe Schurz, 7/16/1867, *Intimate Letters of Carl Schurz;* DCS-JP, 61. Circulation figures are notoriously inaccurate in this period. But to bid for the city's legal advertising and printing, the owners of the newspapers had to submit circulation statements signed under oath. These "official" circulation figures for 1867 were published in *ChTr,* 6/5/1867, 2.

35. **Prosperous and growing:** Trefousse, *Schurz,* 162. Seitz suggests that Pulitzer was hired through his acquaintance with Preetorius and Willich. One Associated Press

dispatch from St. Louis, published at the time of Pulitzer's death, makes mention of the connection between the paper and the immigration society: "Willich found Mr. Pulitzer's methods of obtaining information unique, likewise his treatment of individual cases, and a word from his obtained for Pulitzer a place as a reporter on the *Westliche Post,* a German daily." AP dispatch, 10/29/1911, JP-LC, Box 12.

Just how Pulitzer, with no training or experience in journalism, obtained a job as a reporter on the *Westliche Post* is shrouded in mystery and legend. Pulitzer knew Preetorius through the Mercantile Library. Perhaps he had also met another owner, but he probably had not met Schurz. Pulitzer is said to have credited his experience when he and forty other men were bamboozled by the dishonest employment agent promising work downriver. A reporter got wind of the tale and persuaded Pulitzer to write it up for the *Westliche Post,* according to Ireland. The resulting work attracted Preetorius's eye and earned his admiration, and Pulitzer was offered a position on the paper. However, the article itself has never surfaced.

Numerous remembrances of Pulitzer at this time offer an alternative scenario, crediting chess with introducing him to men who would provide him with his first newspaper job. Unfortunately, the accounts vary considerably in consistency and reliability, often reducing the tale to one epic match. As with reports of Pulitzer's swim in Boston harbor, it is hard to discern the actual contours of what happened. Typical of the accounts told when Pulitzer was still alive was one that appeared in the magazine *Current Literature* in 1909: "After performing various sorts of work he found himself one day in a restaurant looking on at a game of chess, a game in which he was said to have genius. A suggestion that he made to one of the players proved to be the little pivot on which his whole subsequent career turned. The player was Dr. Emil Preetorius, who with Carl Schurz was directing the *Westliche Post.* The acquaintance thus begun led to Pulitzer's entry upon the stage which he has never left."

A decade after Pulitzer's death, the *St. Louis Post-Dispatch*'s editor William A. Kelsoe sought out a few St. Louisans who were still alive and who might have remembered such a game. "I have found no one who can locate positively the saloon or restaurant in which that historic game was played," Kelsoe said. Two or three old-timers told Kelsoe they thought it might have been played in the Rheinische Weinhalle. Others mentioned Wagner's Restaurant, a meeting place popular with both German and non-German politicians, businessmen, and lawyers. Even if there was no single match, it could well have been that Pulitzer's chess skills, which had served him in Civil War camps, helped him gain attention at the Mercantile Library and other gathering places (AI, 171–172). The inclusion of Schurz's name in the anecdote suggests that if the chess game was actually played, it occurred in 1867, when Schurz had joined the *Westliche Post.* It is the same year Pulitzer began working for the newspaper: Kelsoe to Seitz, undated, PDA.

36. **"I could not":** DCS-JP, 58.

36. **Preetorius and Willich:** Saalberg, "The Westliche Post of St. Louis," 195.

36. **It wasn't long:** DCS-JP, 58–60. In fact, reporters for English-language newspapers referred to German reporters derogatorily as "Schnorrers," a humorous Yiddish term for a type of beggar who, in contrast to an ordinary beggar, disguises his purpose, has pretensions at being a gentleman, and acts indignant when offered the assistance he seeks.

36. **If Pulitzer believed:** *MoRe,* 10/30/1911.

36. **While Pulitzer honed:** APM, 26.

37. **Reaching the United States:** Built in 1865, the 2,695-ton *Allemannia* was capable of a speed of twelve knots: APM, 27–31.

37. **Although the reunion:** The *Chicago Tribune* reported that "the city is full of men

out of employ, most of them young men from the East, who have white hands and want some clerical work to do" (*ChTr*, 4/23/1867, 2); APM, 36.

39. **Settled at last:** APM, 33, 39.

39. **For Joseph the:** According to his friend Anthony Ittner, Pulitzer regarded Anna Preetorius as "one of the most kind-hearted, agreeable accompanied ladies that it was his good fortune to have ever met" (Anthony Ittner to JPII, June 11, 1913, PD). Edward Preetorius recalled that when he was a baby, Pulitzer "was a frequent and welcomed visitor at my parents' house and they have told me of the numerous kindnesses [Pulitzer] visited upon me" (Edward Preetorius to JP, March 4, 1903, JP-CU).

39. **Pulitzer was comfortable:** Snider, *St. Louis Movement*, 167.

39. **Pulitzer attended a few:** Ibid., 118; The significance of the *Journal of Speculative Philosophy* in the history of American philosophy has been widely described. Perry, *The St. Louis Movement in Philosophy*, 10; James A. Good,"'A World-Historical Idea': The St. Louis Hegelians and the Civil War," *Journal of American Studies*, Vol. 34, No. 1 (December 2000), 447–464; Snider, *St. Louis Movement*, 32.

40. **A nomadic philosopher:** Record Book of the St. Louis Philosophical Society, MHS.

40. **In contrast to:** Knight, *Memorials of Thomas Davidson*, 107–108. See also Fagan, "Thomas Davidson: Dramatist of the Life of Learning." It's not clear when and how Pulitzer met Davidson. Considering Pulitzer's avowed pursuit of education, he may well have attended one of Davidson's popular meetings.

40. **The Scot's charms:** Thomas Davidson to Kate Bindernagel, 8/10/1870, TD. The eight-year engagement came to an end when Davidson was in St. Louis. Davidson never did marry. After his death, his friend William James offered an explanation. He said Davidson told him that he had been tempted twice to marry but he demurred because of his first relationship. "'When two persons have known each other as we did,' he said, 'neither can ever fully belong to a stranger, so it wouldn't do! It wouldn't do! It wouldn't do!' He repeated as we lay on the hillside in a tone so musically tender that it chimes in my ears still, as I write down his confession" (Knight, *Memorials of Thomas Davidson*, 118). See also *The National Cyclopaedia of American Biography*, 312. The same kind of allusion was made at a commemorative service for the St. Louis Movement: "Davidson had an exceptional sympathy with young fellows who seemed to be moving along a path that beckoned toward social renovation," said one of the speakers. *A Brief Report of the Meeting Commemorative of the Early Saint Louis Movement, January 14, 15, 1921, Vanderweart's Music Hall, St. Louis, Missouri*, 60, MHS.

41. **If Davidson was:** Homosexuality was not kept hidden from shame or fear, though each played a role. Rather, in a world devoid of discussions of sex, one's sexuality preference would have not been considered an element of identity that one could or should divulge. "Sexuality was not considered a determining feature of social identity," explained the historian Graham Robb. Further, the intimate relationships that men and women often had with their friends of the same gender could mask something that in retrospect seemed evident. "Many people," said Robb, "discovered their homosexuality only when the person they had loved had gone away or died" (Robb, *Strangers*, 127–139). Also Isaac Rossetti to Thomas Davidson, June 12, 1867, TD.

41. **Five years earlier:** Samuel Rowell to Thomas Davidson, January 1862, TD.

41. **Davidson himself confessed:** Thomas Davidson to Kate Bindernagel, 8/14/1870, TD. It's obviously hard to determine what emotional state Davidson may have been in during those years. But one man who was a student recalled that his fellow students used to recount finding Davidson walking the halls, glassy-eyed, in an apparent "drugged condition, spouting Greek." The student's conclusion was "that he was a

secret or perhaps periodic drinker" (William Clark Breckenridge to Robert L. Calhoun, 8/25/1871, MHS).

41. **Pulitzer fell under:** DCS, 56, 38. James Barrett, who wrote an unreliable biography in 1941—with which the family did not cooperate—expanded Seitz's description of Pulitzer and Davidson sharing quarters. "The fact that JP dressed and undressed complacently in the presence of his learned friend was proof enough of the serenity of his life with Davidson. . . . No other man ever won from him so warm a token of regard. The mere thought of being even without a collar in the presence of other men was enough to throw JP into paroxysm of annoyance" (JWB, 32).

41. **As when Davidson:** JP to Davidson, undated but certainly from June 1874, TD.

42. **Davidson ignored this:** JP to Davidson, 7/11/1874, TD.

42. **Ten days later:** JP to Davidson, 7/21/1874, TD. Fascinatingly, Pulitzer embellishes his letters with an increasing number of exclamation marks that match their chronological progression. Specifically the first letter in the series opens with "Tom!"; the next with "Tom!!"; and the last with "Tom!!!"

42. **In the end:** Without doubt, men of the era expressed friendship through words and gestures that a century later would be interpreted as homosexual. Men were permitted a kind of romantic friendship that is no longer possible. The only surviving letters from Davidson to Pulitzer offer little help in gauging the scope of their friendship. They date from years after Pulitzer was married. The letters say nothing about the pair's time together in St. Louis, though they do offer a small hint of past intimacy. In New York society, laced with formality, Pulitzer was addressed even by his closest friends as "My dear Pulitzer." Davidson was among only one or two correspondents who wrote to him as "Dear Joe." On his part, Pulitzer closed his letters "Your affectionate friend," "As ever your friend," and "Your old friend." But, as he was blind by then and dictated his letters, Pulitzer might have felt restrained in what he could say, though the closings he did use were very untypical. "The friendship with Davidson," said Seitz, "remained Mr. Pulitzer's closest relationship until the wise and kindly Professor left life at Cambridge, Mass., September 14, 1900" (DCS-JP, 56).

CHAPTER 4: POLITICS AND JOURNALISM

43. **Politics and journalism:** Johnson, "Birthday Anniversary Dinner," 4/10/1907, PDA.

43. **The keystone of:** Foner, *Reconstruction*, 41–42; Peterson, *Freedom and Franchise*, 191; Primm, *Lion of the Valley*, 261–268.

44. **Schurz placed the:** Memorial service for Schurz, 10/10/1906, JP-CU.

44. **Pulitzer not only:** Johnson, "Birthday Anniversary Dinner"; 4/10/1907, PDA; WP, 8/10/1868, 3; Saalberg, *"The Westliche Post,"* 196.

45. **A New Englander of:** NYH, 4/29/1872; NYT, 7/21/1900, 7.

45. **His maneuver gave:** Trefousse, *Schurz*, 173.

46. **Preetorius and Pulitzer:** WP, 1/13/1869 (weekly edition), 3.

46. **Schurz's election altered:** Schurz to Preetorius, 3/12/1869, *Intimate Letters*, 473.

46. **The vacuum at:** Charles E. Weller letter, 7/28/1919, PDA. Weller, who was one of the first people in St. Louis to own a typewriter, is sometimes wrongly credited with having composed the phrase "Now is the time for all good men to come to the aid of their party," known to anyone who has taken a typing course.

47. **Pulitzer even took:** William Fayel remembrance, reprinted in DCS-JP, 60–61.

47. **It wasn't long:** Charles E. Weller letter, 7/28/1919; and A. S. Walsh to JPII, June 1913, PDA.

47. **Reporters poked fun:** Fayel in DCS-JP, 60–61.

47. **For good reason:** Johnson, "Birthday Anniversary Dinner," 4/10/1907, PDA.

48. **Although Johnson admired:** Anthony Ittner to JPII, 6/11/1913, PDA.

48. **In the summer:** Hyde and Conrad, *Encyclopedia of the History of St. Louis*, Vol. 2 (New York: Southern History, 1899), 1097; *PD*, 4/21/1879, 4.

49. **From the pages:** *WP*, 7/21/1869, 3.

49. **Under this withering:** *WP*, 7/23/1869, 3.

50. **In battling the:** Theodore Welge to JPII, 6/6/1913. PDA.

50. **In October 1869:** Saalberg, *"The Westliche Post,"* 200.

50. **Despite the interminable:** Weller letter, 7/28/1919, PDA; unknown author to JPII, 6/11/1913, PDA.

50. **At night, Pulitzer:** Kargau, *The German Element*, 53–54.

51. **Joseph's brother Albert:** Albert's name appears in a list of German teachers in the *14th Annual Report of the Public School Board of St. Louis* (St. Louis, MO: Plate, Olshausen, 1868), lxiii; *APM*, 41–42, 48–49, 59–60.

52. **In November 1869:** The election call was made on November 10, 1869: Writ of Elections, Gov. McClurg, Missouri State Archives, Jefferson City, MO. The *Missouri Republican* supported John Daily; the *St. Louis Times* pushed it own editor, Stilson Hutchins, for the nomination: *MoDe*, 12/14/1869, 2.

52. **The Republicans held:** Eichhorst, "Representative and Reporter: Joseph Pulitzer as a Missouri State Representative," 20; *WP*, 12/14/1869, 3.

53. **The next morning:** *WP*, 12/14/1869, 3; *MoDe*, 12/15/1869, 4.

53. **The wishful thinking:** *MoRe*, 12/19 and 12/21/1869, 2; Constitution of the State of Missouri, 1865, Art. IV, Sec. 3. The *Democrat* picked up Pulitzer's charge; the *Republican* and the *Times* defended their candidate and accused Pulitzer of failing to pay taxes, one of the requirements for being a candidate. But in the end, the difficulty in fielding a candidate, lingering questions about the latest candidate's eligibility, and squabbling between the *Republican* and the *Times* left the Democratic Party ill-prepared for the election. *MoRe*, 12/21/1869, 2; *MoDe*, 12/20/1869, 3; *StLoTi*, 12/21/1869, 1.

53. **With three days:** Original in Oaths of Loyalty 1869, Series XIV, Sub Series B, Dexter Tiffany Collection. MHS; *WP*, 12/18/1869, 3. According to Jason Baker, who assisted the author in translating German documents, "At no point in the letter does he claim to be anyone other than Pulitzer, but referring to himself in the third person allows the reader to think so. He never perjures himself, but there is a certain level of deception at play." Further, Baker said, the rhetorical devices and phrases as well as a trademark comical note leave little doubt that the letter is the work of Pulitzer.

54. **Not a day:** *WP*, 12/19 and 12/20/1869, 3.

54. **On election day:** The election results were published in all the newspapers, as well as the weather conditions. Turnout was estimated by using election results from other years.

54. **"We doubt that":** *WP*, 12/22/1869, 3.

CHAPTER 5: POLITICS AND GUNPOWDER

56. **Shortly after New Year's Day:** *PD*, 2/15/1870, 2. Advertisements announcing that Missouri Pacific and other railroads were honoring passes for legislators traveling to Jefferson City for the legislative session were published in newspapers. For a reference to this practice see *PD*, 2/8/1870, 2; and Eichhorst, "Representative and Reporter," 31. The state paid $50 for a round trip from St. Louis. Copies of Pulitzer's per diem forms are on file in the MSA, General Assembly Records for 1870 Adjournment Session, Record Group 550, Box 94, folder 28, Jefferson City, MO.

56. **The state capital:** A measure to move the capital to St. Louis was introduced on January 18, 1870. *NYT*, 1/20/1870: 1. Pulitzer, who was still imbued with the ideals

of the "St. Louis movement," offered a bill to set aside land in St. Louis for the national capitol: *Twenty-Fifth General Assembly House Journal, Adjournment Session, 1870*, 72. (Hereafter cited as *House Journal*.)

56. **Bringing with them:** Anthony Ittner to JPII, 6/11/1913, PDA; Kremer, *Heartland History,* 69; Bruns, *Hold Dear, as Always,* 14–15.

56. **On January 5:** *House Journal,* 4. Pulitzer was assigned to the Committee on Banks and Corporations.

57. **In Jefferson City:** *ChTr,* 1/15/1870, 4; *House Journal,* 49.

57. **Pulitzer's fellow Radical Republicans:** Peterson, *Freedom and Franchise,* 170; Tusa, "Power, Priorities, and Political Insurgency," 133. A Democrat and former state official writing to a friend in the summer of 1869 asked, "What the devil is this generally abnormal condition of things, politically, to result in? My opinion is it can't stand at what it is." (B. F. Massey to J. F. Snyder, July 15, 1869, quoted in Barclay, *The Liberal Republican Movement in Missouri,* 183.)

57. **Suffrage was the:** The legislature had ratified the Fifteenth Amendment during its prior session but had failed to include in its vote the second portion of the amendment; accordingly, the secretary of state had not issued a formal notification to the federal government. Its passage in this session was a foregone conclusion: *ChTr,* 1/7/1870, 1 and 1/10/1870, 4. See also Barclay, *Liberal Republican Movement in Missouri*; and Tusa "Power, Priorities, and Political Insurgency," 133.

58. **The state's constitution:** Barclay, *Liberal Republican Movement in Missouri,* 186–187.

58. **From the start:** Walter Gruelle in *StLoDi,* 1/6/1870, 2.

58. **On a Sunday:** *MoRe,* 1/26/1869, 2; *WP,* 1/26/1869, 3.

59. **The new week:** *Kansas City Daily Journal of Commerce,* 3/8/1870, 2.

59. **In Pulitzer's eyes:** *WP,* January 25, 1870, 3.

59. **Among the arriving:** Kargau, *German Element,* 139; *One Hundred Years in Medicine and Surgery in Missouri* (St. Louis, MO: St. Louis Star, 1900), 79–80; *PD,* 4/21/1879, 4; *MoDe,* 4/24/1869; *StLoTi,* 2/28/1870, 1; Ittner to JPII 6/13/1913, PDA.

60. **Before boarding the:** Theodore Welge to JPII, 6/6/1913, PDA.

60. **The city-county:** *MoRe,* 11/26/1869; William N. Cassella Jr., "City-County Separation: The 'Great Divorce' of 1876," *Missouri Historical Society Bulletin,* Vol. 15, No. 2 (January 1959), 88.

60. **Specifically, Pulitzer's bill:** Saalberg, "The *Westliche Post,*" 197–198; *WP,* 9/24/1869. A summary of Pulitzer's bill appeared in *MoRe,* 3/11/1870, 2. See also Thomas Eichhorst, "Representative and Reporter," 49. The critics weren't entirely wrong. It was a common practice for politicians to steer both official advertising and printing business to papers that favored them.

61. **Although Pulitzer's bill:** *MoDe,* 1/27/1870, 1; *WP,* 1/30/1870, 3.

61. **The next morning:** *WP,* 2/28/1870, 3. Pulitzer also described the passage in the Missouri House of the Richland County project, a kind of redistricting scheme to create a new county. "The land wildcatters, lobbyists, and other gentlemen interested in the project held a banquet that same evening to celebrate the House's passage of the bill, in Schmidt's new hotel, at which almost all legislators who voted for the project were in attendance, and the champagne, whiskey, and so forth flowed in streams until late in the evening, or better, early in the morning. It is being said that the passage of the bill 'cost' $35,000."

61. **That evening the:** The description of the events in Schmidt's Hotel on January 27, 1870, is drawn from the following newspapers: *StLoTi, MoDe, MoRe,* and *PD,* published on 1/28/1870. Other sources are noted separately. See also *WP,* 1/30/1870, 3; *MoDe,* 1/31/1870, 3.

62. **Back at the boardinghouse:** Ittner to JPII, 6/11/1913, PDA.
63. **"I want to":** There is little doubt Augustine used the word. Judge Cady, who was standing by his side, said Augustine called Pulitzer a "pup."
64. **Ittner, who was:** Ittner to JPII, 6/11/1913, PDA; *St. Louis Times*, 1/28/1870, 1.
64. **By the time:** *MoRe*, 1/29/1870, 2.
65. **Seizing the moment:** *MoRe*, 1/28/1870; *House Journal*, 305–306; *StLoT*, 1/28/1870, 1. The papers often ran verbatim accounts of the speeches but did not put quotation marks around the words and sometimes changed first person to third person. The quotations from this debate were compared with those appearing in several newspapers.
65. **The House probe:** *MoDe*, 1/29/1870, 1 and 2/2/1870, 1; *Kansas City Daily Journal of Commerce*, 1/30/1870, 2; *ChTr*, 1/29/1870, 4.
66. **The clamor impelled:** *WP*, 1/30/1870, 3.
66. **He called Augustine:** Late in life, Pulitzer pulled back his hair to show what he claimed were the scars from Augustine's brass knuckles.
66. **The Cole County grand jury:** *State of Missouri v. Joseph Pulitzer*, No. 1182 P.H., No. 16, Circuit Court of Cole County, MO, MSA. Pulitzer's arrest was also noted in newspapers such as the *Kansas City Daily Journal of Commerce*, 2/19/1870, 2; *MoDe*, 1/21/1870, 1 and 2/4/1870, 2.
67. **This was not:** *MoRe*, 2/11/1870, 1; *House Journal*, 431–432.
67. **Pulitzer's choice of:** Since 1864, German language instruction for all students had been part of the public school curriculum, and it would remain so until 1887, when the German faction lost control of the school board: *MoDe*, 3/1/1870, 1; Eichhorst, "Representative and Reporter," 59; *Kansas City Daily Journal of Commerce*, 3/2/1870, 2.
68. **Pulitzer immediately moved:** *MoDe*, 3/11/1870, 1; *House Journal*, 821. The debate created a problem for Pulitzer the reporter. While arguing over the fate of the accused legislator, the House adopted a resolution prohibiting members of the press from publishing any part of the plan until it granted permission. Since the measure was adopted on a voice vote, the view of the future press lord on freedom of the press was not recorded.
68. **The legislative session:** *MoRe*, 2/25/1870, 2; *House Journal*, 577.
68. **On March 10:** *MoRe*, 3/11/1870, 2. Seven of the eleven representatives at the meeting were opposed to the measure.
68. **The plan almost worked:** *MoDe*, 3/17 and 3/18/1870.
68. **As the first:** *Kansas City Daily Journal of Commerce*, 3/15/1870, 2; *St.LoDi*, 3/15/1870, 2.

CHAPTER 6: LEFT BEHIND

Pulitzer's tenure as an elected state representative is an important component of the "making" of Pulitzer the newspaper publisher. Remarkably even his two most scrupulous biographers did not explore why his tenure in the Missouri general assembly ended. Swanberg closed his chapter on the episode with the phrase "on March 24 his lone term in the legislature ended" (19). Reynolds wrote, "Thus his experience as a state legislator ended, an experience to which he often looked back with satisfaction" (23). Maybe my own experience as a journalist made me skeptical that Pulitzer would simply walk away from a prized elective office. A quick look at Missouri newspapers that fall revealed that his retirement was not voluntary at all.

Among the serendipitous joys of research are the odd little connections one finds between figures in history. In researching the life of Gratz Brown for this chapter, I found that he was the grandfather of Margaret Wise Brown, an author familiar to all twentieth-century parents: she wrote *Goodnight Moon* and other classics of children's literature.

70. **The prospect of:** Theodore Welge to JPII, 6/6/1913, PDA.

71. **The trial was:** General Assembly Records for 1870 Adjournment Session, Record Group 550, Box 94, folder 28, MSA; *NYT*, 5/25/1870; JP passport application, NARA. While in the mayor's office Pulitzer met Julian Kune, a Hungarian who had fled to the United States following the revolution of 1848 and was also back on his first visit home: Kune, *Reminiscences*, 130.

71. **By mid-July:** *Ciberia* passenger manifest, 7/13/1870, NARA.

71. **A former U.S. senator:** Peterson, *Freedom and Franchise,* 176; *NYH*, 4/29/1872; *NYT*, 7/21/1900, 7. Though it remained the state's premier Republican newspaper, the *Democrat* had already turned against President Grant after he ignored the owner William McKee's candidates for federal patronage jobs. Now it was ready to turn against the state's governor.

72. **Five days following:** *MoDe*, 8/31/1870, and *MoRe*, 9/1/1870, both quoted in Barclay, *Liberal Republican Movement in Missouri*, 234–235 (footnotes).

72. **"Upon this question":** Barclay, *Liberal Republican Movement in Missouri*, 243; The actual vote was 439 2/3 to 342 5/6, according to the convention's method of counting.

72. **Once resettled on:** Pulitzer's dispatches in the *Westliche Post* revealed clearly that he had moved into the inner circle of the renegades. His pieces predicted each move of the party split with the clarity only an insider could have. See, for instance, *WP*, 9/2/1870, 3.

72. **Meanwhile, in the House:** *ChTr*, 9/5/1870, 2; *Mountain Democrat*, 9/17/1870, 2.

73. **With the conventions:** *MoDe*, 9/21/1870, 4.

73. **As exciting as:** *MoDe*, 11/8/1870, 1; Christensen, "Black St. Louis," 205–206; *WP*, 9/3/1870, 3.

73. **On their side:** *MoDe*, 2/19/1870; *ChTr*, 7/4/1872, 4.

73. **Grosvenor did his**: *MoDe*, 11/5/1870, 2, and 11/ 8/1870, 2.

74. **On November 3**: *MoDe*, 11/3/1870, 4; original in Oaths of Loyalty 1869, Series XIV, Sub Series B, Dexter Tiffany Collection, MHS. See also *MoDe*, 11/8/1870, 1.

74. **All the rhetoric:** *MoRe*, 11/8/1870, 2.

74. **In the morning:** Peterson, *Freedom and Franchise*, 188.

74. **In Pulitzer's ward:** *MoRe*, 11/11/1870, 2; *WP*, 11/10/1870, 3. The *Anzeiger des Westens* had a different take on the results. It attributed the Democratic victory to the split in the Republican Party. Pulitzer asked if the editor didn't realize that this was a loss for Germans. "Is he not aware that it was German-haters, the dyed-in-the-wool McClurgians, the French, and the Negroes that defeated the Liberal Republican county ticket, which was supported by the majority of Germans, through their total defections and in some cases desertion to the Democrats?" The vote totals, particularly in the Third and Fifth wards, the latter being Pulitzer's, show that it was not the Germans who elected the Democrats. It was the Irish, said Pulitzer. "They, the Irish, played this role in the Tuesday election as well, and the entire glory in which the *Anzeiger* may sun itself is an Irish-French-Negro victory. He may do this if he wishes, but he should call a spade a spade" (*WP*, 11/11/1870, 3).

75. **Pulitzer's friend Joseph Keppler:** *Frau und Frei* (St. Louis, MO: undated but certainly November 1870), MHS.

75. **Out of office:** Avery and Shomemaker, *Messages and Proclamations of the Governors of the State of Missouri*, Vol. 15, 14.

75. **Not quite. Schurz:** Peterson, *Freedom and Franchise*, 207.

75. **Pulitzer did not share:** Hutchins declined to be the Democratic candidate against Pulitzer in the 1869 election. I suspect it was his friendship with Pulitzer that caused

him to wait for another year to run. He did run eventually, and won a seat in the legislature.

75. **Any concern about:** *ChTr*, 2/2/1871, 2; Peterson, *Freedom and Franchise*, 191–197; Grosvenor to Schurz, 2/16/1871, CS.

76. **The growing movement:** Receipts for payments to Pulitzer for service to the committee from January 11 until March 1 and signed by Benecke may be found in the Accounts of the Twenty-Sixth General Assembly, First Session, MSA.

76. **When the legislative session:** Quoted in Peterson, *Freedom and Franchise*, 198.

76. **But that too:** *ChTr*, 4/22/1871, 2; *Every Saturday*, 10/28/1871, 418.

77. **Members of the:** *Missouri Staats-Zeitung*, undated clipping, WG-CU, Box 2.

77. **Pulitzer's patron, State Senator Benecke:** Louis Benecke to Pulitzer, 10/26/1871, LB. One wonders if Benecke harbored some doubt about how Pulitzer had handled the committee vote. "If I understand and remember that proxy rule right," Benecke said to Pulitzer, "you were simply authorized to act as this proxy in order to have a quorum and did not attempt to cast a vote for this till all members present voted. Am I correct?"

77. **Charles Johnson came:** Hill was a colorful fellow and was loved by the press for that reason. By the time of Pulitzer's trial he had been married twice; his second marriage was in a divorce court when his wife drowned while in Europe. A few years later he arranged for the division of Peter Lindell's $6 million land estate by inviting in from the streets a crippled boy beggar. He had the boy draw lots of equal size from a hat. "The blindfolded boy was released, and bright tears glistened in his eyes as 10 golden half-eagles were dropped into his hands, and he was told that he completed the division of the great Lindell estate to the satisfaction of all the heirs then present": *ChTr*, 2/13/1879, 2.

78. **The charge was:** It's not clear to what offense Pulitzer may have pleaded guilty, or if he did plead guilty at all. The court records do not reveal the case's final disposition. Johnson's diary is no help, either, recording only the cryptic note, "Settled case $100 fine" (Johnson, *Diary*, 11/20/1871, WRR, 19), 11/18/1871, WRR, 19. Pulitzer borrowed money to pay for legal fees and the fine from Henry C. Yaeger, a miller in St. Louis. Others—such as Daniel G. Taylor, a former mayor of St. Louis; and Edwin O. Standard, who was lieutenant governor when Pulitzer served in the legislature—may also have loaned money. Why Yaeger was so generous is not really known. But at some point that year or the following year, Pulitzer rendered him a personal favor. Yaeger wanted Governor Brown to pardon a friend. "Joe Pulitzer assisted me in the matter, and the very day the Governor received my letter, I received a telegram that my request had been granted," Yaeger recalled many years later. (Henry C. Yaeger to Governor David R. Francis, 4/25/1892, Francis Papers, MHS.) Yaeger's name is misspelled "Yeager" in some records, but clearly the same person is meant.

78. **A seat on:** Johnson, *Diary*, 1/15/1872, WRR, 23. Amazingly, as of 2006, the governor of Missouri still appointed the police commissioners in St. Louis; and even more remarkably, they still earned $1,000 a year for their service.

79. **The conservative *Anzeiger*:** *Anzeiger Des Westens*, 1/18/1872, translated in *MoDe*, 1/23/1872, 3; *Western Celt* quoted in *MoDe*, 1/18/1872, 2.

79. **The grumbling by the press:** *MoDe*, 1/19/1872, 1. One of the five senators from St. Louis voted against Pulitzer. His identity was not publicly disclosed, because only the delegation's total vote was leaked to the press, but certainly Pulitzer knew who it was.

CHAPTER 7: POLITICS AND REBELLION

In writing about the 1872 convention there is a danger of adopting Henry Watterson's view that it was a gathering of cranks with little chance of succeeding against Grant. The reality of politics at the time probably did doom the Liberal Republican effort no matter who it nominated, but to the conventiongoers it was a serious affair, an act of rebellion against what they perceived as crimes against democracy. That said, the convention did generate some wonderfully hilarious coverage. My favorite is a little book called *That Convention; Or Five Days a Politician* self-published by Fletcher G. Welch and illustrated (profusely) by Frank Beard.

80. **In late January:** *MoDe*, 12/18/1871, 2.

80. **As these:** Peterson, *Freedom and Franchise*, 206; Grand Duke Alexis's arrival in New York City a few months earlier was covered by Albert Pulitzer, who was then working for the *New York Sun*.

80. **As Liberal Republican:** *MoDe*, 12/18/1871, 2, and 1/24/1872, 1.

80. **McCullagh was among:** Dreiser, *Newspaper Days*, 107. McCullagh also became the subject of a poem by Eugene Field called "Little Mack."

81. **On his first:** *MoDe*, 1/25/1872, 1. The microfilm for this edition is almost unreadable. Copies of the original paper at the Library of Congress don't include this particular date, but a clipping from the edition may be found in the Grosvenor Papers, Columbia University.

81. **That night Pulitzer:** Grosvenor's remark was contained in a letter published in an unidentified newspaper, 2/15/1872, WG-CU, Box II.

81. **Grosvenor ascended the**: *SeDe*, 2/27/1872, 2. Benecke was given a seat on the committee for a permanent organization, and he and Johnson were assigned to the resolutions committee. (*People's Tribune*, 1/31/1872, 3.)

82. **Their work complete:** *MoDe*, 1/25/1872, 1.

82. **Grosvenor and Pulitzer were keenly:** *NYT*, 4/24/1872, 1. The *New York Times*'s effort to "correct" the Associated Press's coverage of the convention was a dispatch from St. Louis that appeared on 1/27/1872, 3. "The Associated Press report of the so-called Liberal Republican Convention, at Jefferson City, on the 24th, was a gross exaggeration of the importance of the whole affair," it read in part. See Ross, *The Liberal Republican Movement*, 151–152, for a discussion of personal abuse and misrepresentation in the press during the 1872 campaign. The *Times*'s articles on Liberal Republicans were so poisonous that the paper lost much of the reputation it had gained in 1871 when it brought down Boss Tweed by publishing evidence of his corruption.

82. **In the short span:** Unidentified 1872 newspaper clipping in WG-CU, Box II; *MoDe*, 1/26/1872, WG-CU. Pulitzer's public profile was sufficient that he was among the targets of a fraudulent telegram supposedly from President Grant but concocted by Grant's opponents. Printed on the front page of the *Sedalia Daily Democrat*, the telegram, purportedly to the chair of the Radical Convention, read: "Return my thanks to the Republicans of Missouri for the confidence reposed in me. Will defeat the plans of Sumner and Schurz. Show this to Brown, Pulitzer and Charley Johnson." (*SeDe*, 2/27/1872, 1.)

83. **When he got back:** Scharf, *History of Saint Louis City and County*, Vol. 1, 743–744; Morris, *The Police Department of St. Louis*.

83. **The police commission:** Minutes of the St. Louis Police Commission, 8/30/1872, 347–352, SLPDL.

83. **For the first few months:** Minutes, 3/5/1872, 287–290, SLPDL. Pulitzer's association with this led to two myths about him. His biographer Seitz claimed that Pulitzer "warred with the local gambling ring," but an anonymous biographer, who published a political tract intended on thwarting Pulitzer's bid for the U.S. Senate, claimed that he had been on the take: Tusa, "Power, Priorities, and Political Insurgency," 188. Pulitzer was absent from the police commission meetings for the first time on 3/30/1872 (Minutes); Brown to Grosvenor, 2/17/1782 WG-CU. Pulitzer's March trip to the East is mentioned in *MoDe*, 3/13/1872, 2.

83. **As the Cincinnati convention:** *MoDe*, undated but weeks before the convention, Clippings files, Box II, WG-CU.
84. **On an April evening:** Johnson, undated April diary entry, WRR, 26.
84. **Pulitzer and Grosvenor left:** Croffut, *An American Procession*, 142. Pulitzer was actually twenty-five at the time.
84. **Reaching Cincinnati in:** Chamberlin, *The Struggle of '72*, 334.
85. **Not only did the convention put Pulitzer:** King, *Pulitzer's Prize Editor*, 77.
85. **The group agreed:** Henry Watterson, "The Humor and Tragedy of the Greeley Campaign," *Century Magazine*, Vol. 85 (November 1912), 29–33. This account also appears in Watterson's memoirs, but the version published by *Century* is of greater value because it is accompanied by letters from Horace White and Whitelaw Reid, who read and commented on it. See also *NYT*, 5/1/1872, 1.
86. **On May 1:** Watterson, *Henry Marse: An Autobiography*, Vol. 1, 242–243. Appropriately, the hall to which the delegates made their way was built over a potter's field that had been used by the Commercial Hospital and Lunatic Asylum.
86. **At noon, Grosvenor:** The *Philadelphia Inquirer* erroneously reported his appointment as "Joseph Pulitzer, of Wisconsin." Evidently Pulitzer's fame as a warrior in the Liberal Republican cause had not yet reached the City of Brotherly Love. (*Philadelphia Inquirer*, 5/3/1872, 8.)
87. **The next day:** *Proceedings of the Liberal Republican Convention*, 9–10.
87. **Schurz's speech concluded:** Newspaper clipping, unknown paper and undated, Box II, WG-CU.
87. **When the bleary-eyed delegates:** Lena C. Logan, "Henry Watterson and the Liberal Convention of 1872," *Indiana Magazine of History*, Vol. 40, No. 4 (December 1944), 335.
88. **Watterson, who had:** Watterson, "The Humor and Tragedy," 39.
88. **The contest narrowed:** An excellent account of the convention may be found in Matthew T. Downey, "Horace Greeley and the Politicians: The Liberal Republican Convention in 1872," *Journal of American History*, Vol. 53, No. 4 (March 1967), 727–750.
89. **Despite all of:** Watterson, "The Humor and Tragedy," 39.
89. **Back in St. Louis:** Looking back at the convention at the end of the year, Schurz called it "the 'slaughter house' of the most splendid opportunities of our time." (Schurz to Grosvenor, December 25, 1872, WG-CU.) "Schurz about an hour ago finally agreed to recede from his Cincinnati speech and adopt the popular word of 'anybody to beat Grant.'" And, in fact, Schurz wrote an editorial in which he repudiated or, in the words of the *Missouri Democrat*, "ate" his previous condemnation.
90. **Of concern to:** JP to Reid, 6/12/1872 and Reid to JP 6/17/1872, WR-LC.
90. **A sense of optimism:** *ChTr*, 6/22/1872, 4.
90. **But Pulitzer's work:** *ChTr*, 7/15/1872, 6.
91. **After New York:** Minutes of the St. Louis Police Board, August 14–December 3, 1872, SLPDL; DCS-JP, 74; *ChTr*, 7/22/1872, 2; *MoDe*, 9/20/1872, 2.
91. **Police commission work:** JP to Schurz, 9/24/1872, CS.
92. **As fall approached:** Wolf, *The Presidents I Have Known*, 84–85.
92. **The campaign produced:** Schurz mentioned acquiring a larger number of shares in the paper at about this time, in a letter to his parents. (Schurz to parents, 11/14/1872, CS; JP to St. Clair McKelway, *NYW*, 11/7/1913.)
92. **The potential changes:** *MoDe*, 9/19/1872.
93. **Within a week:** The original note is in the possession of Eric P. Newman of St. Louis: Pulitzer to Schurz, 9/24/1872, CS. Typically, Pulitzer also claims that because of his efforts "our newspaper is already much better!" The *Indianapolis Sentinel* saw Pulitzer's purchase as "evidence that he will continue on that journal the fine service,

which has heretofore been the strong point of his reputation": JP to St. Clair McKelway, *NYW*, 11/7/1913. The evidence suggests that the "proprietors" to whom Pulitzer refers did not include Schurz. He did not believe that the election had damaged the paper. "We did not suffer during the campaign," Schurz wrote to his parents after its disastrous conclusion. (Schurz to parents, 11/14/1872, CS.)

93. **While Pulitzer's stock:** JP to Schurz, 9/24/1872, CS.

CHAPTER 8: POLITICS AND PRINCIPLE

95. **Pulitzer mounted a campaign:** Letters of support quoted in subsequent paragraphs may be found in Woodson Governor, Box 25, Folder 6, MSA, unless otherwise indicated.

96. **Preetorius was opposed:** Preetorius to Grosvenor, 2/27/1873. WG-CU.

96. **Woodson's appointments:** JP to Louis Benecke, 3/5/1873, LB.

97. **Pulitzer's career in journalism:** One assumes some inflation in the price paid to Pulitzer from the retelling of the tale over the years. But the paper itself was certainly worth hundreds of thousands of dollars. The *Missouri Democrat*, with a circulation only slightly higher than that of *Westliche Post*, changed hands the same week for $456,100. Date of note redemption is marked on the note itself. Note in private possession of Edwin P. Newman.

97. **Pulitzer immediately sought:** Weldge to JPII, 6/6/1913, PDA.

97. **Freed from the:** *MoDe*, 9/19/1872; *Unser Blatt*, 12/7/1872, also cited in WRR, 103–104; "Remarks of Gov. Chas. P. Johnson, Birthday Anniversary Dinner," 4/10/1907, PDA. In December his friend Keppler had drawn a cartoon of Pulitzer's shadow falling on a map of New York, with the caption "Coming Events Cast Their Shadows before Them."

98. **On his way:** APM, 61–62.

98. **Albert arrived in:** Ibid., 82–83.

98. **At the time:** To come up with the necessary $175,000 to purchase the *Sun* Dana enlisted several friends, including Senator Roscoe Conkling, who would later become one of Joseph Pulitzer's close friends, and Senator Edwin D. Morgan. See Turner, *When Giants Ruled*, 84; *Sun* editorial quoted in Emery and Emery, *The Press and America*, 217. By 1876 the newspaper had a circulation of more than 130,000 copies.

99. **Under Dana's regime:** APM, 84–85. The editor was John B. Wood, who was called the "great condenser." Walter Rosebault, a Jewish reporter from Savannah, who like Albert was only twenty, remembered that Albert "spoke with a slight, but not unpleasant, foreign accent." (APM, 88.)

99. **The editor decided:** *NYS*, 8/24/1871, 2. It is also quoted in WAS, 22. One wonders if the "friend in New York" referred to in the article might have been Albert.

99. **Albert rose rapidly:** APM, 90–93; *NYT*, 7/7/1871, 5. "The work Pulitzer did on that trial gave him a big reputation among Newark reporters of the seventies, and put him in the class with Julian Ralph, Frank Patten, Johnnie Green and other talented New York reporters of the day." (*Newark Advertiser,* quoted in APM, 92.)

100. **The fit was:** APM, 128, 130.

100. **After the brotherly:** Watterson, *Marse Henry*, Vol. 1, 210–211.

100. **In the fall:** A copy of the menu may be found at the MHS. It was printed, with the paper's compliments, by the *Missouri Democrat*, which had so strongly opposed Pulitzer and Grosvenor's efforts with the Liberal Republicans a year earlier.

101. **Pulitzer resumed his:** Interview with John Johnson, in Kelsoe, undated letter, PDA; "Birthday Anniversary Dinner," 4/10/1907, PDA.

102. **Membership in AP gave:** The third owner, George Fishback, won the auction by

bidding $456,100, or $100 more than the pair's final offer. (Hart, *A History of the St. Louis Globe-Democrat*, 113.) McCullagh, who remained with the *Missouri Democrat*, attacked the new rival paper, dubbing it "Robbers' Roost" for supposedly stealing news items from the Western Associated Press.

102. **Neither McKee nor Houser:** *GlDe*, 1/ 8/1874, 4.

102. **The owner of the *Democrat*:** The papers loved insulting each other. Responding to an item in the *Democrat* that factiously suggested the *Globe* was published in German, McKee and Houser wrote, "For all the influence it has, the *Democrat* might as well be printed in Scandinavian." (*GlDe*, 1/8/1874, 4.)

103. **The legal maneuvering:** One person recalled that Pulitzer earned $47,500 from the deal, but this figure seems high. (Rosewater, *History of Cooperative News-Gathering*, 181.)

103. **In the spring:** *ChTr*, 7/5/1874, 1. Built at a cost of more than $10 million, the bridge rested on a masonry foundation sunk deep into the riverbed, using caissons filled with pressurized air. A dozen of the 352 men who worked in these underwater air chambers died.

103. **Pulitzer confessed that he:** Eads to JP, 1/19/1885, JP-CU. Pulitzer's friend White-law Reid declined Eads's invitation to invest in the Mississippi project. Reid to Eads, 3/2/1875. JBE.

103. **After turning the money**: It was Papin Street, off Chouteau Avenue, DCS-JP, 77; *Dubuque Herald*, 10/28/1873, 1; *Freeborn County Standard*, 8/17/1892, 2; A. S. Walsh to JPII, undated but probably June 1913, PDA. T. Saunders Foster, who knew Pulitzer around this time, recalled that "he was very fond of riding, and owned a fine saddle horse on which he took long morning rides." (George S. Johns, "Joseph Pulitzer in St. Louis," *Missouri Historical Review*, XXV, No. 3. April 1931, 415.) Also JP to Schurz, 6/3/1874, CS; Ed Harris, memo to JPII, 2/29/1942, JPII.

104. **Financial freedom also:** JP to EP, 5/25/1905, JP-CU. A copy of the illustration reproduced in early editions of DCS-JP, between 78–79; Charles Nagel, *A Boy's Civil War Story*, 397. Nagel eventually becomes a cabinet member in the Taft administration. Katherine Lindsay Franciscus, "Social Customs of Old St. Louis," originally published in *PD*, 12/9/1928, and reprinted in *Bulletin of Missouri Historical Society*, Vol. 10, No. 2, 157–166; JP to Davidson, 1/15/1875, TD. Playing Mephistopheles was a minor frivolity for Pulitzer. But interestingly, in his life yet to come Pulitzer would be repeatedly identified publicly and privately with this character. Those who were present when his anger rapidly surged, or who felt his hot temper or listened as he eviscerated an editor, would more often than not reach for Mephistophelian metaphors to describe what they witnessed.

104. **Finally feeling prepared:** Pulitzer took his bar exam before Judge Napton; *MoRe*, 7/2/1874, 8.

104. **The treatment the bolters received:** *Galveston Daily News*, 8/28/1874, 1.

105. **On September 2:** The interview, real or not, was the work of McCullagh, who had left the *Missouri Democrat* to join his old bosses at the *St. Louis Globe*. McCullagh had probably learned of Pulitzer's disillusionment with the People's Party directly from him and chose to report it as a reconstructed interview; *GlDe*, 9/6/1874, 1.

106. **For Pulitzer, the:** *MoRe*, 9/7/1874, 2.

106. **Drawn into civic life:** Undated clipping, *GlDe*, 9/1873, WG-CU.

106. **The Missouri Democratic Party:** *SeDe*, 10/9/1874, 4.

108. **Not an eyebrow:** Liberal Republicans also failed to recognize the threat to Black Americans. Grosvenor referred to the "phantom of a Ku-Klux excitement" and Brown said, "The Ku Klux Klan has been magnified a hundredfold in order to furnish capital for the hungry carpetbaggers that infest the South." (*ChTr*, 4/22/1871, 2; Peterson, *Freedom and Franchise*, 201.)

108. **After Sedalia, it:** *Versailles Weekly Gazette*, 10/14/1874, 3; *Warrensburg Standard*, October 9, 1874, 2; *Kansas City Journal of Commerce*, 10/16/1874. Pulitzer's nose, ridiculed by the reporter, became an object of admiration among his supporters. One reader of the *Sedalia Daily Democrat* complained of criticism about Pulitzer's nose. Claiming it had "perfect Grecian symmetry," the letter writer said he would prefer to have "one like Pulitzer's than a dozen such purple-hued smellers" as that found on the face of a particular critic. (*SeDe*, 10/16/1874, 2.)

108. **The highlighting of:** *MoDe*, 9/20/1872, 2; Twain, *The Adventures of Tom Sawyer*, 14. It was reported that when Pulitzer and Keppler used to while away the hours at cafés in St. Louis, Keppler would end the evening with the comment, "Well, Joey, there's only one thing left to do. I'll go back to the office and draw your nose." (DCS-JP, 2–3).

108. **The nose became:** The nose, according to the historian Sander Gilman, became "the central [locus] of difference in seeing the Jew"; Gilman, *The Jew's Body*, 169–193.

109. **From Knob Noster:** *Boonville Advertiser*, 10/16/1874, 2; *Boonville Weekly Eagle*, 10/23/1874, 3.

109. **A few weeks:** *WP*, 1/27/1875.

C H A P T E R 9 : F O U N D I N G F A T H E R

111. **On the evening:** *ChTr*, 2/22/1875.

112. **Hesing's words were:** JP to Governor Hardin, 1/14/1875, Folder 15402, Charles Hardin Papers, MSA.

112. **With his political fortunes:** *MoRe*, 3/10/1875, 5. Actually, Pulitzer was wrong. The only recorded monument to Eads in St. Louis is a medallion on a pedestal in Forest Park. Eads's bridge, however, was designated a national monument and still stands.

112. **Leaving the committee:** DCS-JP, 87.

112. **By the 1870s:** Wharton, *Old New York*, 240.

113. **Two of the:** "When others abandoned a cause as hopeless, when the last ray had been extinguished, then it was that Bowman would clench his hand, bring all the devious methods of his intellect to bear, and ultimately triumph over his enemies." *ChTr*, 10/22/1883, 1.

114. **After setting down:** *MoRe*, 3/23/1875, 8.

114. **"Just returning from":** The press in St. Louis got wise to Pulitzer's dishonesty. By 1879, one reporter referred to this habit as "old tactics that have puzzled many a news-gatherer." (*GlDe*, 8/19/1879, 5.)

114. **The paper was correct:** Hutchins also offered misinformation at the trial. Speaking of Pulitzer's appointment to the police board, he said, "I know that Joseph Pulitzer was, to my surprise, appointed police commissioner, without any agency of mine and without my knowledge that he was an applicant." As the two worked closely on Liberal Republican affairs and spent time together with Charles Johnson, who helped Pulitzer get the seat on the commission, Hutchins's testimony was hardly credible. But Bowman did not challenge it. Testimony was published in *MoRe*, 3/12/1875, 8.

114. **The seats in the courtroom:** *MoDe*, 3/24/75, 2; *MoRe*, 3/24/1875, 1; *GlDe*, 3/24/1875, 4.

115. **"Not for everybody":** Two weeks later, Bowman sued Hutchins for libel, for comments about the trial published in the *Dispatch*, a struggling afternoon newspaper that Hutchins ran in addition to the *St. Louis Times*.

115. **Hard feelings put aside:** *NYT*, 3/29/1875, 7.

116. **In early May:** *SeDe*, 5/6/1875, 1; Isidor Loeb, Introduction, *Missouri Constitutional Convention*, Vol. 1, 60–67; biographical account of the personnel of the convention by Floyd C. Shoemaker, *Missouri Constitutional Convention*, Vol. 1; Gary Kremmer, "Life in Post-Civil War Missouri" presented at Arrow Rock, Missouri, on 9/17/2000.

116. **At age twenty-eight:** The style of hat Pulitzer wore is a later variation of the slouch, known as an Antietam, with a higher, flatter crown.

116. **Pulitzer had done:** Loeb and Shoemaker, *Debates of the Missouri Constitutional Convention of 1875*, Vol. 1, 245, 249.

117. **The war of words:** Ibid., 94–96.

117. **As the summer heat**: Broadhead to his wife, 7/4/1875, JB.

117. **Pulitzer's style:** *Debates*, Vol. 1, 402–403.

118. **Behind closed doors:** Ibid., Vol. 5, 412.

118. **In the end:** In defense of Pulitzer, it should be noted that not until long after his lifetime would the detrimental effects of home rule in St. Louis become apparent. For a complete history of the issue, see William N. Cassella Jr., "City-County Separation: The 'Great Divorce' of 1876," *Missouri Historical Society Bulletin*, Vol. 15, No. 2 (January 1959).

118. **As the convention:** *Debates*, Vol. 5, 86–87.

119. **In July the:** On October 30, 1875, voters gave their approval. The constitution would remain the state's highest law until 1945.

120. **A sense of failure:** JP to Hermann Raster, 9/27/1875 and 6/24/1875, HR.

120. **The only good news:** See Timothy Rives, "Grant, Babcock, and the Whiskey Ring," *Prologue* Vol. 32, No. 3 (Fall 2000).

121. **In December a grand jury:** Ibid.; and *ChTr*, 2/8/1876, 1 and 2/11/1876, 5.

121. **During his first year:** APM, 142, 135–138.

121. **At the *Herald*:** Ibid., 104, 142, 148: *Helena Independent*, 12/12/1883, 6.

122. **When he received:** "Testimony before the Select Committee Concerning the Whisky Frauds," 7/25/1876, House of Representatives, 44th Congress, 1st Session, Mis. Doc. 186, 43.

122. **In April, Pulitzer's:** John Henderson to Elihu Washburne, 4/12/1876; JP to Elihu Washburne, 5/9/1876, EBW.

123. **In Germany, Pulitzer:** *Indianapolis Daily Sentinel*, 9/4/1876, 2.

CHAPTER 10: FRAUD AND HIS FRAUDULENCY

124. **The presidential campaign:** NYT, 7/26/1876, 8.

124. **By his absence:** *Official Proceedings of the National Democratic Convention*, St. Louis, MO, June 27, 28, 29, 1876, 21. The Democrats were the first party to hold a national convention west of the Mississippi.

124. **Pulitzer was elated:** The campaign plans of leading Democrats were carried in newspapers. See, for instance, *SeDe*, 10/6/1876, 2. After 1885 only a few small states, such as Maine, continued to hold elections in October.

125. **In early September:** *Indianapolis Daily Sentinel*, 9/4/1876, 2.

125. **For more than:** DCS, 29; *Galveston Daily News*, 9/14/1876, 1. Several newspapers commented on Pulitzer's English and his way of talking. Typical was one in Zanesville, Ohio, which said, "Mr. Pulitzer, though of German birth, has in his speech little or no foreign accent." ("Schurz Shattered," Mesker Scrapbook, Vol. 3, 45, MHS.)

126. **Fresh from his:** "Schurz Shattered," 45; *Portsmouth Times*, 9/9/1876, 3; JP to George Alfred Townsend, 9/19/1876. PDA; *Cincinnati Enquirer*, 11/2/1876, 2, quoted in King, *Pulitzer's Prize Editor*, 81.

126. **In mid-September:** JP to George Alfred Townsend, 9/19/1876, PDA.

126. **The next day:** "Schurz Shattered," 47. In another article, from an unidentified newspaper, Pulitzer compares the alliance of Morton and Schurz to the Mississippi and Missouri rivers. "As the muddy waters of the Mississippi absorb the clear waters of the Missouri, Morton will soon enough have entirely absorbed the spirit of Schurz. And they will both be as muddy as the Mississippi."

127. **To the delight:** *NYT*, 9/13/1876, 1; *StLoTi*, 9/4/1876, quoted in *WAS*, 40. Though he did not consent to meet Pulitzer, Schurz wrote a five-column rebuttal that was published in the *New York Staats-Zeitung.* The sympathetic *New York Sun* gave Pulitzer space to respond. (*Edwardsville Intelligencer*, 8/20/1876, 2.)

127. **Although Schurz remained:** *WP*, translated in *Decatur Daily Republican*, 9/28/1876, 1; *NYT*, 8/7/1876, 4.

127. **Pulitzer sought to:** "Schurz Shattered," 46.

128. **As in his other speeches:** *DeFr*, 10/18/1876, 1.

128. **At the end:** *NYT*, 10/26/1876, 5 and 10/31/1876, 10; *WaPo*, 12/24/1885, 4. Pulitzer's work in the campaign not only pleased the Democratic Party but also, as he had hoped, attracted attention. The following year the *New York Tribune* said that Pulitzer was so frenetic as a campaigner "that old Mr. Tilden couldn't make out for a while whether he or Pulitzer was running for the Presidency, and never has been entirely clear about it since Pulitzer first burst on the scene." (*NYTr*, 3/14/1877, 4.)

129. **Bringing his assault:** *NYS*, 11/1/1876, 1. Almost thirty years later, Pulitzer wrote to a friend that his speeches during the campaign "attracted a good deal of attention and gave me a greater reputation than that I have now." (JP to FDW, 10/13/1903, SLPA.)

129. **The *New York Sun*:** Turner, *When Giants Ruled*, 95; Allen Churchill, *Park Row* (New York: Rinehart, 1958), 12.

129. **The famous editor's office:** Don Carlos Seitz, *Newspaper Row: Some Account of a Journey along the Main Street of American Journalism* (unpublished, American Heritage Center), 98; Smythe, *The Gilded Age Press*, 10.

130. **Pulitzer told the men:** Mitchell, *Memoirs of an Editor*, 264; John Schumaker to JP, 10/29/1887, JP-CU.

131. **The nation's partisan press:** *StLoTi*, 11/11/1876, 4 and 11/16/1876, 4.

131. **In New York:** Mitchell, *Memoirs of an Editor*, 265; *Harper's Weekly*, 12/30/1876, 1055; Young, *The American Statesman*, 1593.

131. **As a member:** *NYS*, 12/30/1876, 3.

132. **By this point:** *NYS*, 12/29/1876, 3.

132. **Pulitzer did not limit:** *ChTr*, 1/9/1877, 1. The *New York Times* described Pulitzer's "fiery talk" as being "on the order which was current among German students of 1848" (*NYT*, 1/9/1877, 1). Watterson found his speech hard to live down. "I became the target for every kind of ridicule and abuse. Nast drew a grotesque cartoon of me, distorting my suggestion for the assembling of 100,000 citizens, which was both offensive and libelous. . . . For many years afterward I was pursued by this unlucky speech, or rather by the misinterpretation given to it alike by friend and foe. Nast's first cartoon was accepted as a faithful portrait, and I was accordingly satirized and stigmatized, though no thought of violence ever had entered my mind, and in the final proceedings I had voted for the Electoral Commission Bill and faithfully stood by its decisions. Joseph Pulitzer, who immediately followed me on the occasion named, declared that he wanted my 'one hundred thousand' to come fully armed and ready for business; yet he never was taken to task or reminded of his temerity." (Watterson, *Henry Marse*, 303.)

133. **On March 2:** The end of Reconstruction was not, of course, such a simple matter. For a more complete story, see Foner, *Reconstruction*; or Lemann, *Redemption*. See also Turner, *When Giants Ruled*, 96.

133. **The loss stung:** *Galveston Daily News*, 3/10/1877, 1.

133. **In St. Louis:** *ChTr*, 4/12/1877, 1; *NYT*, 4/12/1877, 1.

133. **On April 10:** *MoRe*, 4/12/1877, 4. Reynolds, in "Joseph Pulitzer," believed it was a "tea party," given by Mrs. Dan Morrison, that Pulitzer attended. The only thing known with certainty is that Pulitzer returned to his hotel at midnight.

134. **The fire engines:** *ChTr*, 4/12/1877, 1. One fireman, Phelim O'Toole, saved a dozen people from the fire and inspired a song, the second stanza of which is: "To save help-less women, at the word of command,/He bravely came forward, for duty he strives;/Ascending the ladder, his life in his hand,/Defying the fire fiend, while hope now survives./Brave Phelim O'Toole mounts higher and higher,/And reaches the high elevation at last;/He bears fainting women from torturing fire/Down the perilous ladder the danger is past."

135. **Pulitzer was the first witness:** *MoRe*, 4/17/1877, 4.

135. **On April 27:** *ChTr*, 4/28/1877, 2; *NYT*, 4/28/1877, 5.

135. **A month later:** *NYT*, 4/27/1877, 8. Albert's itinerary is reprinted in APM, 152–153. The letter from Fannie Pulitzer is reprinted in APM, 154–157.

136. **Pulitzer found the aging editor:** *Ohio Democrat*, New Philadelphia, OH, 7/12/1877.

137. **With a flourish:** The article in the *Sun*, which appeared during August, was re-printed in the *Washington Post*, 1/22/1878, 2, shortly after Bowles's death. It carried the byline "J. P."

137. **Pulitzer sprained his ankle:** *WRR*, 54–55. The account of this month is based on Johnson's diary.

CHAPTER 11: NANNIE AND KATE

Much of this chapter revolves around the story told in six surviving love letters by Pulitzer. Three of them have been long known because they are reprinted in full in Seitz's 1924 biography. The originals seem to have been lost in the years since then. They are remarkable in how honest and prescient Pulitzer was in warning Davis of the kind of life they would lead after their marriage.

Two of the other three letters, the ones to Tunstall, have also been publicly avail-able since they were donated to the American Jewish Historical Society. But as they were undated, and in fact incorrectly cataloged, anyone examining them would not have known that they were written during the same time period when Pulitzer was courting Davis. Fortunately, I was able to date them because Eric Fettmann, a re-markable collector of artifacts of American journalism, had purchased a letter from Pulitzer to Tunstall dated May 2, 1878. With this letter, one is able to correctly date the other two as having been written between February and May 1878.

138. **As 1877 ended:** JP to KP, DCS-JP, 91.

138. **St. Louis grew:** Quoted in Roberts, *The Washington Post*, 1.

138. **Field was not:** Ibid., 7. It's unclear to what extent, if any, Pulitzer participated in the launching of the *Post*. He had been a regular contributor to the *St. Louis Times* when Hutchins ran it. But a search of early editions of the *Washington Post* turns up only one article clearly written by Pulitzer, a reprint of one from the *New York Sun* in the summer of 1877.

138. **Journalism, however, was:** *GlDe*, 1/03/1878, 3; *ChTr*, 11/19/1876, 2, 11/22/1876, 1, 11/18/1876, 1, 10/31/1877, 2. Seitz claims that Pulitzer studied for and passed the bar examination in the District of Columbia. A check of the record of the bar, now in the archives of the University of District of Columbia, found no attorneys standing for the bar in 1877 or 1878, so there was no way to determine if Pulitzer was admitted to practice in Washington. It would not, however, have been a requirement for ap-pearing before the elections committee. Pulitzer was still ambiguous about his career

path. He listed himself in the Washington city directory as a correspondent, probably because of his loose connection with the *New York Sun.*

139. **The Committee on Elections:** Minute Book, *Records of Committee on Elections,* 45th Congress, 1/30/1878, NARA; *WaPo,* 1/30/1878, 1; *BoGl,* 2/14/1878, 1. Though at first glance this might seem like a late date to decide an election of 1876, it was not. During the nineteenth century Congress often took a year before holding its first session, so only a few days of lawmaking had elapsed when the case of who should represent the Third District of Missouri came before the House.

139. **If the Committee:** *WuPo,* 2/12/1878, 2.

139. **The editorial had:** Minute Book, *Records of Committee on Elections,* 45th Congress, 2/20 and 2/21/1878, NARA.

140. **Despite this loss:** *WaPo,* 1/24/1878, 1; 1/29/1878, 4; 2/25/1878, 4; 2/26/1878, 4.

140. **Pulitzer did not lack:** *WaPo,* 1/24/1878, 1, and 1/30/1878, 4; Gallagher, *Stilson Hutchins,* 26.

140. **On January 12:** *WaPo,* 1/14/1878, 4; *Washington Star,* 6/20/1878; *Stevens Point Journal,* Stevens Point, WI, 6/29/1878, 1.

141. **But to Davis's parents:** *Pitzman's New Atlas of the City and County of Saint Louis, Missouri, 1878* shows Pulitzer, Hutchins, and Brockmeyer's lots. Pulitzer owned 3.4 acres of land; Hutchins owned an adjacent acre; and Brockmeyer had almost four acres nearby.

141. **Trying to hide:** The Jewish practice of circumcision was not introduced as a medical practice in the United States until 1870 and did not become widely practiced among Christians until the 1900s. See David L. Gollaher, "From Ritual to Science: The Medical Transformation of Circumcision in America," *Journal of Social History,* Vol. 28, No. 1 (1994). Throughout his life, and long into the twentieth century, Pulitzer's contention that his mother was not Jewish remained unchallenged. For instance, *The Hebrews in America,* published in 1888, reported, "The Messrs. Pulitzer, however, are not being classed among the chosen people, their father being a Hebrew and their mother a Christian lady of Vienna." Ironically, Kate Davis was a strong-willed, independent-minded woman and might not have been deterred if Pulitzer had been honest.

141. **Davis was not:** *WaPo,* 1/14/1878, 4.

141. **Born in a:** Morris, *The First Tunstalls.*

142. **William Corcoran, one:** Corcoran wrote to Tunstall that she was expected in January 1878. Corcoran to Tunstall, 12/14/1877, WCP-DU; *WaPo,* 2/24/1888, 2; Corcoran, *A Grandfather's Legacy,* 490.

142. **Tunstall certainly filled:** William MacLeod, Private Journal, 4/16/1888, CAG; Corcoran to Tunstall, 12/22/1885, WCP-DU. Governor Kemper of Virginia, a distant cousin, once sent her a bouquet for the New Year, writing, "If these flowers were all gold and diamonds, they would more worthily express your merits and my appreciation": (James Lawson Kemper to Nannie Tunstall, 1/1/1876, NT-DU.)

142. **Tunstall was well-educated:** Nannie Tunstall to Virginia Tunstall Clay, 3/21/1884, NT-DU.

142. **In February, while:** *NYT,* 2/17/1878, 2. Unless otherwise indicated, the quotations from the letters of JP to Tunstall are drawn from the Joseph Pulitzer Letters, AJHS.

143. **"Is there no":** JP to Tunstall, 5/2/1878, EFJC.

143. **On a spring day:** *WaPo,* 3/6/1878, 4, and 3/22/1878, 2.

143. **Indeed, Pulitzer was:** *House Journal,* March 3, 731; Constitutional Convention, Vol. 4, 123; *SeDe,* 6/5/1875, 3.

144. **Pulitzer longed not:** JP to KP, undated but probably April 1878, reprinted in DCS-JP, 91–92.

144. **"You can now see":** JP to KP, undated but probably June 1878, reprinted in DCS-

JP, 93. McCullough was in Washington, appearing in the theater, in early June. He was also, indeed, scheduled to sail to Europe on June 15 (*WaPo*, 5/31/1878, 2) as Pulitzer noted in his letter. Thus this letter to Davis was written in the first week of June 1878.

145. **"I must have business":** JP to KP, June 1878, reprinted in DCS-JP, 94–95.

145. **The ceremony actually:** "Large, roomy and with an air of sober reliability about it, one feels the sentiment of respect for it," wrote a newspaper reporter who had passed through its iron gates in search of newsworthy items only a month before; Tripp Jones, archivist, interview with author, Church of the Epiphany, Washington, DC, August 4, 2005. Examples of Washington luminaries who were members of the parish in 1878 would include Secretary of the Treasury John Sherman and Chief Justice Morrison Waite. "A Notable Church," *WaPo*, 5/11/1878, 2.

146. **The newlyweds, whose union:** Pulitzer told this tale to a neighbor in St. Louis. George S. John, "Joseph Pulitzer: Early Life in St. Louis and His Founding and Conduct of the Post-Dispatch up to 1883," *Missouri Historical Review* (January 1931), 67.

146. **The Reverend John H. Chew:** As H. L. Mencken observed, "Most Americans when they accumulate money climb the golden spires of the nearest Episcopal Church." Quoted in Collier, *The Rockefellers*, 36–37. The stained-glass window has since been moved to the front wall of the church: Jones, interview.

CHAPTER 12: A PAPER OF HIS OWN

This chapter, as well as subsequent ones, benefits greatly from internal *Post-Dispatch* documents that came to light in 2008, when the Fogarty Papers became known. For more information, see page 12.

149. **In the early morning:** At Hudnut's pharmacy downtown, the temperature had hit ninety-two degrees the afternoon before. The Pulitzers may have been lucky and avoided much of the heat by staying for several days along the ocean at Long Branch, New Jersey, where Joseph held reservations at the West End hotel, which opened for the summer season the day following their wedding. With each passing year, Long Branch was becoming an increasingly popular destination for the wealthy seeking a cool spot for the summer. It had a safe blue-blooded pedigree. As one hotel operator told the *New York Times* that June, he had "not received a single application for rooms from a Jew this year, while at the same time last year he had many." (*NYT*, 6/11/1878, 1.)

149. **Having spent all:** NYS, 10/20/1878, 3.

150. **When Joseph and Kate:** NYS, 10/6/1878, 3. The socialists were the demagogues and were dangerous, admitted Pulitzer. But the despotic solution chosen by Bismarck was equally, if not more, dangerous. "To Germany it is a choice between the Scylla and the Charybdis," said Pulitzer, referring to a mythical Greek sea monster and a whirlpool whose positions in a narrow channel meant that fleeing from one put one in danger of the other.

150. **In Paris, Kate:** KP to JP, 10/2/1904, JP-CU.

151. **The two-month honeymoon:** NYT, 9/12/1878, 2.

151. **The Pulitzers' European:** NYS, 9/6/1878.

151. **Because Pulitzer hated:** Ibid., 3. Pulitzer's friends Hutchins and Cockerill, at the *Washington Post*, likewise viewed the incident as further evidence of the illegitimacy of the administration and found it sufficiently noteworthy for an editorial. (*WaPo*, 10/7/1878, 2.)

151. **At the *Sun*:** NYS, 9/22, 10/6, 10/13. 10/19, 10/20, and 10/27/1878.

152. **The most singular:** NYS, 10/27/1878, 3.

152. **Although long-winded:** *NYS*, 9/22/1878, 3.

153. **The St. Louis:** W. H. Bishop, "St. Louis," *Harper's New Monthly Magazine*, quoted in JSR, 21; "Remarks of Gov. Chas. P. Johnson," Birthday Anniversary Dinner," 4/10/1907, 20–21, PDA.

153. **Encouraged, Pulitzer went:** JN to JP, 3/10/1900, JP-CU.

153. **In the early morning:** It was so cold that winter that ice closed the Mississippi River for forty-six days. The account of the auction and Pulitzer's taking possession of the *Dispatch* is based on reports in the *GlDe*, 12/10/1878, 1; *MoRe*, 12/10/1878, 1; and *Evening Post*, 12/09/1878, 1 and 12/10/1878, 4.

155. **Arnold raised his bid:** The receipt for $2,500 for the purchase of the *Dispatch* was made out to Arnold. (PLFC) It is not inconceivable that the unknown bidder, like Arnold, was working for Pulitzer, who was far wilier in business than he ever let on.

155. **During the confusion:** *GlDe*, 12/10/1878, 1. McCullagh may have had a hand in writing the comment.

156. **The following day:** *Evening Post*, 12/10/1878, 1; Clayton, *Little Mack*, 132.

157. **The answer was:** Pulitzer continued this strategy of deception for so long that later a reporter for the *Globe-Democrat* complained about "his old tactics that have puzzled many a news-gatherer": *GlDe*, 8/19/1879, 5.

157. **Pulitzer's antics gained:** *GlDe*, 12/11/1878, 4.

157. **St. Louisans already:** The size of Allen's investment was disclosed when the paper went bankrupt five months later. See *PD*, 5/10/1879, 1.

158. **Dillon's *Evening Post*:** Further, the *Post* was wrongly perceived as a pawn of the *Globe-Democrat* because of Dillon's identification with McCullagh and his use of the *Globe-Democrat*'s presses. The *Post* did have a similar look, but it hardly deserved to be called an "illegitimate offspring," the description given to it by the unfriendly *Republican*. For these and other reasons, the *Post* had not yet found a readership large enough to sustain it.

159. **Although the flagging:** For the first time since the panic of 1873, being a newspaper publisher was looking again financially attractive. There were 718 daily newspapers published that year in the United States, a number that had remained relatively stable for four years. With improved economic conditions, the number was beginning to rise again. Nearly 100 new dailies were being launched, a 13 percent increase in the number of papers. This was part of an upward trend. Within a decade the total number of papers would more than double: George P. Rowell & Company Data on the Number of Newspapers and Periodicals: 1868–1908, reprinted in Lee, *The Daily Newspaper in America*, app., table X, 720–721; Douglas, *The Golden Age of the Newspaper*, 132.

159. **Pulitzer openly professed:** *PD*, 12/21/1878, 2.

159. **Pulitzer's timing was:** *ChTr*, 9/13/1872, 4.

160. **The two men:** The merger agreement and accompanying documents, PLFC.

161. **The new paper:** *PD*, 12/13/1878, 2; JSR, 65.

161. **The declaration was:** Merger agreement, PLFC.

161. **Anyone who knew:** *GlDe*, 12/13/78, 4.

CHAPTER 13: SUCCESS

162. **Before the *Post and Dispatch*:** Figures for the actual press runs are contained in the Fogarty Collection.

162. **In the following weeks:** The purchase from Hoe marked the beginning of a long and important relationship between Pulitzer and this manufacturer of printing presses. Within a few years, Hoe would push his engineers to their limits in creating larger and faster presses to meet Pulitzer's demands at the *New York World*.

162. **Years before, when:** *PD*, 12/19/1878, 2, quoted in JSR, 45.

163. **He was on to something:** Pulitzer's return to St. Louis coincided with a period when the leadership of the city was changing from an older, conservative group to a younger, more progressive one. See Moehle, "History of St. Louis, 1878–1882."

163. **Like an editorial Paul Revere:** *PD*, 1/30/1879, and 1/31/1879, 2.

164. **As the campaign:** The series began in *PD*, 2/15/1879, 1. McCullagh, in particular, was singled out because he earned $30,000 in stock in addition to his salary, and owned diamonds and watches.

164. **When citizens file:** *PD*, 3/1/1879, 8 and 3/21/1879, 2, for an example of the tax oath; *PD*, 2/17/1879, 2; JSR, 52.

165. **Pulitzer concluded that:** *PD*, 2/24/1879, 2; JSR, 55. Documents in the Fogarty Collection confirm the increases in circulation claimed publicly by the paper. Pulitzer was a rare publisher in that the circulation figures he announced matched those kept in the actual books.

165. **There was hardly anything:** *PD*, 1/2/1879, 1 and 2. Pulitzer's staff would fall prey to the same journalistic prank twenty years later, when he was competing with William Randolph Hearst.

166. **The *Post and Dispatch*:** PD, 3/28/1879, 2 and 2/21/1879, 1.

166. **Pulitzer was not easily:** JSR, 55–56.

167. **On Tuesday:** *PD*, 2/18/1879, 1.

167. **For days, the:** *PD*, 2/19/1879, 1.

167. **After weeks of delay:** *PD*, 05/26/1879, 2; *PD*, 3/11/1879; JSR, 63.

168. **Despite the paper's:** DCS-JP, 197.

168. **After concluding his:** Stealey, *130 Pen Pictures of Live Men*, 345–347.

169. **The street urchins:** William Smith to JP, 10/26/1902, JP-CU.

169. **On April 21, 1879:** *PD*, 4/21/1879, 4, and 4/22/1879, 4.

170. **Pulitzer didn't have time:** *WAS*, 60.

170. **Neither Dillon nor:** The terms of the loan were cleverly written. There were three parties to the agreement. The *Post-Dispatch* turned over title to its property to Gottschalk for $1. In turn, he lent the money to Pulitzer, who provided it to the paper. Then a series of postdated checks were written for the interest on the loan, to be cashed at intervals, and for the final balance. Should the checks not clear, Gottschalk would have recourse to sell the assets of the corporation. PLFC.

171. **Lawyers who researched:** William Smith to Joseph Medill, 2/18/1880, M 0258, Box 3, Folder 2, WHS-IHS.

171. **With his new:** *PD*, 3/5/1879, quoted in JSR, 69.

171. **Nothing was too:** JSR, 70.

172. **Watching with dismay:** *PD*, 5/14/1879, 1; *GlDe*, 5/14/1879, 8. The original sale agreement with the name of Theodore Lemon, PLPC.

172. **Joseph settled the pregnant Kate:** Corbett and Miller, *Saint Louis in the Gilded Age*, 72; Eberle, *Midtown*, 13. See JSR, 292, and WRR, 102, for discussion of whether Kate Pulitzer was snubbed by St. Louis society.

172. **Usually Kate, with:** *Galveston Daily News*, 5/31/1883, 7; Stealey and Johnson diary entries, quoted in WRR, 103.

173. **Dillon agreed to sell:** *GlDe*, 11/30/1879, also reprinted in *PD*, 12/05/1879, 4. The actual cost of buying out Dillon is unknown, although several sources cite $40,000.

173. **Joseph reorganized the:** JP to Dillon, Reel II, SLPA, 3/21/1905.

173. **That night, Cockerill:** WP, 12/22/1879, 2; King, *Pulitzer's Prize Editor*, 92–93.

174. **The challenge that:** In fact, the postage bill for mailing the *Globe Democrat* to out-of-town newspapers exceeded that of all other St. Louis papers combined; Clayton, *Little Mack*, 106–107.

CHAPTER 14: DARK LANTERN

175. **Chambers put his:** *PD*, 12/17/1879, 4; *MoRe*, 12/12/1879, 3.
176. **After a week's:** On the day appointed for the auction, about 150 curious onlookers and newspapermen gathered at the courthouse. After waiting thirty minutes past the announced starting time, a man showed up and announced that the sale had been postponed: *MR*, 1/1/1880, 8, and 1/7/1880, 5; *PD*, 1/7/1880, 4; *ChTr*, 1/8/1880, 5.
176. **Rather than a funeral:** William Henry Smith, the general agent for the Western Associated Press, acquitted Pulitzer of any deception and ruled that the certificate could not rightfully belong to the mortgage holders. (W. Henry Smith to Joseph Medill, 2/18/1880, WHS-IHS.)
176. **His exuberance stemmed:** *PD*, 1/7/1880, 4.
176. **At home, his:** Information about servants obtained from 1880 census records. Two of the women who worked for the Pulitzers were Irish-born; *MoRe*, 12/16/1880, 3.
176. **Unencumbered by financial:** *SeDe*, 1/8/1880, 1.
177. **By one o'clock:** *WaPo*, 1/13/1880, 4; *GlDe*, 1/23/1880, 1.
177. **Awakened with the news:** *PD*, 1/23/1880, 1 and 4; *GlDe*, 1/23/1880, 1.
178. **In New York:** *ChTr*, 1/28/1880, 11; *WaPo*, 1/26/1880, 2.
178. **Reports from Cockerill:** Church records on file at the Diocesan Archive at Washington Episcopal Cathedral.
179. **"Now damn you":** *GlDe*, 3/2/1880, 4; *PD*, 3/2/1880. Pulitzer admitted the following day that he had drawn a gun but said he was so blind without his glasses that he could have done no damage. One of the bystanders picked up the weapon and placed a notice in the newspaper that if the owner wanted to retrieve it, he could do so at the bystander's house.
179. **Early in the race:** *PD*, 2/15/1879, 4. Pulitzer stuck fast to his opposition to Tilden. See, for instance, *PD*, 2/12/1881, 4. Pulitzer's early interest in determining the Democrats' 1880 candidate led Hutchins at the *Washington Post* to suggest that Pulitzer's efforts could save the expense and trouble of a convention. (*WaPo*, 7/14/1879, 2.)
180. **If Pulitzer could:** *PD*, 4/28/1880, 4.
181. **Missouri Democrats gathered:** Stealey, *130 Pen Pictures*, 347; *WaPo*, 5/28/1878, 1.
181. **The convention, which:** See *Official Proceedings of the National Democratic Convention, 1880*; Watterson, *Marse Henry*, Vol. 2, 249–250.
182. **Pulitzer face a quandary:** *WaPo*, 6/25/1880, 1; JP to English, 6/27/1880, N-YHS.
183. **The Democrats' choice:** JSR, 133–134
183. **On his return:** *ChTr*, 6/27/1880, 2; JP to Smith, 6/27/1880, N-YHS.
183. **The *Evening Chronicle's*:** JSR, 110–111.
184. **Pulitzer was comforted:** Ibid., 105–106; *PD*, 4/30/1880, 4.
184. **On August 8:** Johnson, *Diary*, 8/8/1880, and subsequent entries, WRR 98–99.
184. **To get the nomination:** Edward C. Rafferty, "The Boss Who Never Was: Colonel Ed Butler and the Limits of Practical Politics in St. Louis, 1875–1904," *Gateway Heritage* (Winter 1992), 54–73.
184. **Butler had a simple:** For a discussion of Pulitzer's payment of the fee, see JSR, footnote 36, 151. Rammelkamp believed that there was some dispute over whether Pulitzer actually paid a fee. It was, however, a common practice and was required of all candidates at the time. Furthermore the *Globe-Democrat*, edited by the rather scrupulous McCullagh, said that Pulitzer had paid. (*GlDe*, 9/26/1880, 6.)
184. **Believing that his nomination:** JP to Smith, 7/21/1880, N-YHS.
185. **Pulitzer was pleased:** Ibid.

185. **On the evening of August 14:** *Indiana Sentinel*, 8/15/1880. "A masterly effort," said the *Washington Post*; "a disheartening failure," said the *New York Times*. Late in life, Pulitzer thought it one of the best speeches he ever delivered. (JP to FDW, 10/13/1903, SLP.)

186. **As the primary:** *PD*, January 10, 1879, 2. Pulitzer even went so far as to cancel a speech in Indiana so as to see to his own election. (*Fort Wayne Daily Sentinel*, 9/14/1880, 4.)

187. **With Allen's entry:** *GlDe*, 9/26/1880, 6.

187. **Calling Pulitzer a demagogue:** For a description of the 1879 Senate race, see JSR, 45–47; *PD*, 9/24/1880, 4; *MoRe*, 9/24/1880, 1, 4.

187. **The *Republican* greeted:** MR, 9/25/1880, 4; results from *GlDe*, 9/26/1880, 6; Johnson, *Diary*, 9/25/1880; WRR, 99.

187. **When Pulitzer lost:** Johnson, *Diary*, 9/27/1880, WRR, 99.

188. **Pulitzer wasted no time:** DCS-JP gives Lucille's birth date as September 30, 1880, but St. Louis's birth records give it as October 3. In either case, Joseph was in New York at the time: *NYT*, 9/30/1881, 5; *BrEa*, 9/30/1880, 4.

188. **Following the party leaders':** *AtCo*, 10/5/1880, 1; *BoGl*, 10/01/1880, 1.

188. **Pulitzer had one:** *Indianapolis Sentinel*, 10/8/1880, copy in JP-LOC, Box 1, October 1880 folder.

189. **Despite the size:** *Ohio Democrat*, 10/28/1880, 2.

189. **Pulitzer the journalist:** JSR, 138.

189. **When Election Day came:** Not all the elections that year were unfavorable. On November 23, Pulitzer was elected vice president of the Western Associated Press: *NYT*, 11/24/1880, 5.

CHAPTER 15: ST. LOUIS GROWS SMALL

190. **On many nights:** William Gentry Jr., "The Case of the Church Bells," *Bulletin Missouri Historical Society*, Vol. 10, No. 2 (January 1954), 183; Dacus and Buel, *A Tour of St. Louis*, 116.

190. **Neither the *Post-Dispatch*:** *St. Louis Spectator*, 12/24/1881, MHS.

190. **A few printers:** *PD*, 5/12/1881, quoted in JSR, 198–199. Eventually, after Pulitzer moved to New York, the *Post-Dispatch* permitted a closed shop.

191. **Pulitzer claimed that:** *ThJo*, 10/23/1886, quoted in JSR, 196.

192. **Pulitzer talked Daniel Houser into:** *NYT*, 6/19/1881, 5.

192. **There was one paper:** *ThJo*, 12/20/1884, 6; JN to JP, 3/10/1900.

192. **Almost as if:** WRR, 74.

193. **In September, the president:** *ChTr*, 9/10/1881, 1; *WaPo*, 9/10/1881, 1.

193. **When his turn:** *PD*, 9/10/1881, 1; George Barnes Pennock letter, *NYW*, 11/3/1911.

193. **At the beginning:** *PD*, 9/12/1881, 1. However, Pulitzer became so nervous about being alone in his negative predictions that he resorted to filing a few encouraging dispatches. Within days, though, he was back in his role as a doomsayer.

193. **On September 15:** *PD*, 9/15/1881, 1; *WaPo*, 9/16/1881, 1; *NYT*, 9/16/1881, 1.

194. **The tide of:** *NYT*, 9/17/1881, 1; *PD*, 9/17/1881, 1.

194. **On Monday morning:** *PD*, 9/19/1881, 1, quoted in WRR, 75; Ackerman, *Dark Horse*, 427.

194. **The day after:** *PD*, 9/20/1881, 4.

194. **The success of:** Circulation figures, PLFC.

195. **Pulitzer trumpeted the:** *PD*, 6/1/1882, quoted in JSR, 206.

195. **As a consequence:** *WaPo*, 1/23/82, 2.

195. **The hostility grew:** *ChTr*, 3/25/82, 5; also see JSR, 292.

196. **In March, on:** *WaPo*, 3/22/1882, 2; *PD*, 3/16/1882, 4.
197. **Perhaps inspired by:** APM, 167–177.
197. **During his years:** *ThJo*, 12/20/1884, 6.
199. **If the railroad:** *PD*, 10/14/1880, 4; *NYW*, 5/13/1883, 1.
199. **Gould became Pulitzer's:** *PD*, 3/18/1882, 4 and 7.
199. **Broadhead aroused the:** Donald F. Brod, "John A. Cockerill's St. Louis Years," *Bulletin*, Vol. 26, No. 3 (April 1970), MHS, 232.
200. **In his office:** Compiled press accounts. See, for instance, *ChTr*, 10/16/1882.
201. **News of the shooting:** *Daily Kennebec Journal*, 10/16/1882, 2.
201. **Slayback's friend Clopton:** Sarah Lane Glasgow to William Glasgow, 10/18/1882, William Carr Lane Collection, MHS.
201. **On October 18:** *Harper's Weekly*, 11/4/1882 quoted in JSR, 289; circulation figures, FP.
202. **As part of:** *ChTr*, 10/19/1882, 3; Janesville *Daily Gazette*, 10/24,1882, 2; JSR, 292, note 26.
202. **By November, Pulitzer:** *St. Louis Spectator*, 11/11/1882, MHS.
202. **One of the men:** Turner, *When Giants Ruled*, 105; *ThJo*, 1/15/87, 12.
203. **A few hours later:** Julius Chambers, quoted in APM, 231.

CHAPTER 16: THE GREAT THEATER

One of the most persistent myths about Pulitzer was that he purchased the *New York World* while in New York with Kate preparing to board a ship for Europe. In fact, Pulitzer had been stalking the paper for months. See, for example, the *Springfield Republican*, 2/19/1883, 4.

204. **On April 7:** *NYT*, 4/4/1883; Klein, *The Life and Legend of Jay Gould*, 315–319.
204. **He decided to:** *NYW*, 5/13/1883, 1. "The only changes I can suggest would cost money," one of the paper's managers had written a few months earlier—hardly glad tidings to bring to the boss (Elmer Speed to William Hurlbert, 1/15/1883, WP-CU).
204. **In January, Gould:** *WaPo*, 1/28/1878, 2; *ChTr*, 1/25/1883, 3; *PD*, 4/11/1883, quoted in JSR, 297.
204. **On the day:** R. L. Cotteret to Edwin H Argent, 3/3/1883, JP-CU. For a sample of the reporting sheet, see January–June 1883 folder, JP-CU, Box 4.
205. **On the way:** *WaPo*, 4/7/1883, 4; Smith to JP, 8/6/1887, WP-CU.
205. **This purchase, unlike:** *ThJo*, 4/19/84, 4; *ChTr*, 4/16/1883, 5.
205. **Pulitzer did not:** Renehan, *The Dark Genius of Wall Street*, 3.
206. **On April 28:** The original contract is among the JPII-LC Papers. Conkling later billed Pulitzer for the services; see JP to Conkling, 12/19/1885, WP-CU. His role as Pulitzer's lawyer in the purchase is detailed in *Atchison Daily Globe*, 11/19/1887, 1.
206. **He confessed his anxiety:** JSR, 302. Later in life, Joseph often credited Kate with giving him the resolve to go through with the deal. See RP to John C. Milburn, of Carter, Ladyard & Milburn, 1/5/1912, JP-CU. Pulitzer's friends Watterson and Melville Stone, who co-owned the *Chicago Daily News*, both later claimed that he asked them to become partners in the *World* after he bought it. That seems highly unlikely, as Pulitzer never wanted a real partner in any enterprise.
206. **Word of the:** *GlDe*, 05/06/1883, 6.
206. **On May 9:** The *New York Herald*, which printed the *Journal*, disclosed that it was running off 50,000 copies a day: *NYT*, 5/23/1883, 8; APM, 205–210.
207. **At the Fifth Avenue Hotel:** *NYH*, 5/10/1883, 8.
207. **Escorting Pulitzer around:** DCS-JP, 135–136.
208. **While Joseph made:** APM, 205–206.

209. **There may have been:** *Herald* editorial, reprinted in *NYT*, 5/23/1883, 8.

210. **A few weeks:** APM, 210.

210. **For those who had watched:** Charles Gibson to JP, 5/14/1883, JP-CU; John H. Holmes to JP, undated but certainly between May and June 1883, JP-CU, Box 5.

210. **Taking from his bag:** *NYW*, 5/12/1883, 1.

210. **Then—also as he:** Stephen Richardson, JP-LC, Box 11, Folder 8.

211. **What they found:** In Albert's unpublished memoir, he makes mention of having been the first to introduce ears. But as the *Journal* from those months no longer exists, the claim cannot be confirmed.

211. **But if the new *World*:** *NYT*, 11/5/1911, SM3.

212. **During the following days:** Walt McDougall, "Old Days on the World," *American Mercury* (January 1925) 22.

212. **As the staff:** *NYW*, 5/10/1908.

212. **Finished with the city room:** *NYS*, reprinted in *GlDe*, 5/27/1883, 10; GJ, 303.

213. **The paper abandoned:** *NYW*, 5/31/1883, 1. The *New York Times* opted for DEAD ON THE NEW BRIDGE.

213. **If the headline:** JP memo, 1899 or 1900, quoted in GJ, 48, footnote.

213. **Pulitzer had an uncanny:** *NYW*, 5/29/1883, 1.

214. **The *World*'s stories:** *NYW*, 1/25/1884, 4, quoted in GJ, 34.

215. **As was inaccuracy:** AI, 111.

215. **In his first weeks:** *NYW*, 5/29/1883, 4 and 5/30/1883, 8.

216. **The Pulitzers moved:** *ChTr*, 7/31/1883, 1.

216. **Even though work:** Among the guests were General Grant and Schurz: *NYT*, 6/8/1883, 5; WAS, 89–91, Hirsh, *William C. Whitney*, 227; *Rocky Mountain News*, 11/8/1883, 4. The club permitted entry to the Republican Roscoe Conkling.

216. **Pulitzer even found time:** The telegraphs and invitations for the boat ride may be found in JP-CU, Box 5.

216. **Pulitzer may have taunted:** *NYW*, 9/30/1883, 4.

217. **In August, Pulitzer:** *ChTr*, 8/6/1883, 2.

217. **By the end of August:** Circulation was 27,620 on August 12, 1883, according to the notarized statements that Pulitzer began publishing in the paper; see GJ, 332. Also *NYW*, 8/11/1883, 4.

218. **On August 28:** *NYT*, 8/29/1883, 2 and 8/30/1883, 8. Pulitzer knew several of his traveling companions, such as August Belmont Jr., the son of the eminent banker, and the journalists Herbert Bridgman and Noah Brooks.

218. **Pulitzer was surprised:** *NYW*, 9/9/1883, 4 and 9/10/1883, 8.

218. **During Pulitzer's absence:** *Davenport Gazette*, 09/08/1883, 2; *BrEa*, 9/30/1883, 2.

219. **The rumors were:** *NYW*, 9/26/1883, 4.

219. **As the *World*'s circulation:** NYW, 5/17/1883.

219. **When he returned:** *NYT*, 9/25/1883, 2; *Oshkosh Northwestern*, 08/26/1883, 3; *Bismarck Daily Tribune*, 9/28/83, 10.

219. **Weeks later, as:** *NYT*, 11/1/1883, 5.

220. **In November, Pulitzer:** A review of internal memos from the period confirms that the published circulation figures were quite accurate.

CHAPTER 17: KINGMAKER

221. **Despite his triumphant:** J. W. Buell to JP, 12/19/1883, WP-CU; *NYT*, 5/10/1884, 5.

221. **Characteristically, Pulitzer made:** Cunard telegram, 5/19/1884; William D. Curtis to JP, 6/18/1884, JP-CU.

222. **As the convention broke up:** *NYW*, 6/7/1884, quoted in Morris, *The Rise of Theodore Roosevelt*, 267.

222. **A Republican who:** *NYW,* 7/24/1884, 4 and 8/26/84, 4.

223. **Although Blaine had:** Pulitzer was pestered by attorneys representing disgruntled persons threatening to sue. One such case involved a college professor who felt that an article about students' wild antics had injured him and the college. See Scott to JP, 4/2 and 4/3/1884, WP-CU; WAS, 103. Pulitzer also regularly praised Conkling in his editorials. See, for instance, *NYW,* 9/5/1883, 4. That Conkling was the author of the anonymous pieces for the *World* was common knowledge, reported in the *Tribune* and other newspapers.

223. **Pulitzer could hardly:** *PD,* 11/8/1882, 4; *NYW,* 10/14/1884.

223. **With each passing day:** In March, the circulation had been 40,000: *ThJo,* 3/29/1884, 7; 4/5/1884, 5; and 5/31/1884, 3.

223. **By midsummer:** *ThJo,* 6/14/1884, 2.

224. **Nothing his competitors:** *ThJo,* 6/7/1884, 1.

224. **In July, sitting:** Quoted in JWB, 85. Pulitzer not only attended the Chicago convention but, as he had done for the *Post-Dispatch,* filed signed articles. (See *NYW,* 7/9/1884–7/12/1884.) Years later, Pulitzer unrealistically boasted, "If it had not been for the action of the *World* at this stage, he could not have been nominated." (JP to James Creelman, JC, folder 74.)

224. **On July 29:** *ChTri,* 7/30/1884, 1; *NYT,* 7/30/1884, 1.

225. **Cleveland also carried:** "There is a story in circulation concerning a record made by him 'in youth's hot blood'—*a story which* The World *will never under any circumstances print*—which may find its way into the channels of public gossip, if this lowest type of campaign tactics is to be adopted by the Blaine organization": *NYW,* 7/25/1884, 4.

225. **Pulitzer was only:** JWB, 89.

226. **The next day:** "I did not tell him that the cartoon looked like the crab's eyebrows, without proper reduction to refine its coarse lines." (McDougall, "Old Days on the World," 22.)

227. **Pulitzer had wanted:** An illustration of a man accused in the Phoenix Park murders ran in *NYW,* 5/26/1883, 8. The story of the apprehension in Montreal is told in GJ, 95–96; *ThJo,* 1/10/1885, 3.

227. **Not all the reading public:** *ThJo,* 6/7/1884, 3, quoted in GJ, 111.

227. **Pulitzer enlisted McDougall's:** GJ, 99, note.

227. **Pulitzer had no interest:** *ChTr,* 6/29/1882, 12; *NYW,* 9/29/1884, 4.

227. **The maliciousness of:** Smith to JP, 11/28/1884, WP-CU.

228. **Pulitzer interrupted his:** WRR, 206; Henry, *Editors I Have Known since the Civil War,* 273–274.

228. **As the campaign:** *NYT,* 9/30/1884, 5.

228. **As he spoke:** *NYW,* 10/30/1884, 2. The paper devoted more than an entire page to the evening rally.

229. **The crowd roared:** *ChTr,* 10/4/1884, 10.

229. **The fall campaign:** *NYT,* 10/07/1884, 2; 10/22/1884, 2. E. A. Grozier, Pulitzer's secretary in 1884, later described how reluctant Pulitzer was to accept the nomination. (Grozier to DCS, 12/10/1917, DCS-NYPL.)

229. **The nomination was:** *ThJo,* 10/11/1884, 5 and 10/18/1884, 2.

229. **On October 16:** *NYT,* October 16, 1884, 5; Hirsch, *William C. Whitney,* 238–239. For a while it seemed as if Pulitzer might have contributed $5,000 to the Republicans. What had happened was that Pulitzer had written a check to R. Hoe & Company as payment toward a new press. Hoe had given the check to the Republican Party, leading to the rumor that Pulitzer was also supporting the Republicans. See *Milwaukee Sentinel,* 4/28/1886, 3.

231. **Pulitzer was not done yet:** *NYW,* 10/30/1884, 4.

231. **The "Royal Feast":** *NYW,* 11/10/1884, 4.
231. **November 4, 1884:** Figures ibid.
232. **The *World* began:** *NYW,* 11/6/1884, 4.
232. **Pulitzer basked in:** JP to James Creelman, JC, Folder 74; *ChTr,* 1/1/1885, 3.
232. **Pulitzer capped off:** *ChTr,* 1/1/1885, 3. Remarkably, newspapers reported on the check's progress through clearing houses. So much for financial privacy.

CHAPTER 18: RAISING LIBERTY

233. **Piled on Pulitzer's desk:** Correspondence Box 7, WP-CU.
233. **It was all:** *ThJo,* 11/14/1885, 1; James Scott to JP, 3/18/1885, WP-CU; Pulitzer's friend Gibson was making inquiries for Pulitzer to determine if anyone in St. Louis would buy the *Post-Dispatch* for $500,000 or more; see Gibson to JP, 1/5/1885.
234. **The news management:** *ThJo,* 1/30/1886, 5.
234. **His election to Congress:** Correspondence in Box 5, JP-CU; Silas W. Bart to JP, 4/14/1885, JP-CU; *LAT,* 1/21/1885; *NYT,* 1/21/1885, 1.
234. **In early February:** *AtCo,* 2/4/1885, 5.
234. **Politics seemed even less:** *ChTr,* 2/6/1885, 2; *NYT,* 2/6/1885, 5; WES, 120–121.
234. **Pulitzer expected:** WRR, 199; *NYW,* 3/16/1885, 4.
235. **Cleveland didn't share:** *WaPo,* 3/9/1885, 1; *GD,* 3/14/1885; *NYT,* 3/24/1885, 1 and 4/19/1885, 3; WRR, 186–187.
236. **But Pulitzer was:** *NYW,* 8/6/1884, 4. When the dust settled after the election, Pulitzer resumed promoting the project, arguing that Cleveland's victory removed the fund-raisers' last excuse for failure. "Perhaps it has been thought hitherto that a Statue of Liberty erected in the chief harbor of a Republic virtually controlled by monopolists, corruptionists, and self-created aristocrats was both unnecessary and undesirable," Pulitzer wrote. "This is all at an end now. The people have vindicated their capacity to govern themselves and the life of the Republic has been saved." (*NYW,* 11/21/1884, 4.)
236. **The scattered editorials:** *NYW,* 3/14/1885, 4.
236. **The following Monday:** *NYW,* 3/16/1885, 1.
237. **By the next morning:** *NYW,* 3/17/1885.
237. **Rather than start:** At about the same time, other groups were raising money for the Washington Monument in the capital. But it received congressional funding and the public's donations were led not by a newspaper but rather by private organizations.
237. **The public service:** *NYW,* 6/8/1885, 4.
237. **The long hours:** The children stayed at the Thorn Mountain House resort in Jackson, NH. *BoGl,* 8/9/1885, 3.
238. **While Kate shopped:** Pulitzer traveled with letters of introduction from George Childs. Henry Moore to John Norton, 5/29/1895, JNP-MHS; *ThJo,* 6/20/1885, 2; S. P. Daniell to JP, 6/1/1885, JP-CU.
238. **Usually Pulitzer's transatlantic:** Fragment of an undated rough draft of JP letter, quoted in WRR, 134.
238. **The European sojourn:** JPII to JP, 3/21/1908, MHS; Johns, *Times of Our Lives,* 61.
239. **At home it:** WAS, 131.
239. **One friend understood:** Dillon to JP, 7/8/1885, JP-CU.
240. **On the morning of December 3:** *NYT,* 12/4/1885, 3 and 7; *ChTr,* 12/4/1885, 2; *ThJo,* 11/28/1885, 5.
240. **"All right, but":** JP to Conkling, 12/19/1885, WP-CU; Theron Crawford to JP, 12/9/1885 and 12/14/1885, WP-CU.
240. **Pulitzer and the House:** *NYT,* 12/8/1885, 4; *AtCo,* 1/8/1886, 1.

241. **To maintain this schedule:** He "took very little interest in his Congressional office, and was very irregular in his attendance in Washington" (Edwin A. Grozier to Seitz, 12/10/1917); *WaPo*, 3/4/1886, 2; Amos J. Cummings in *WaPo*, 4/18/1886, Dana's *Sun* harped on Pulitzer's poor attendance in Congress. Walt McDougall claimed that one night when he was in Washington with his boss, Pulitzer was almost arrested for drunkenness. "He was lit up to seventh magnitude by a few cocktails," he said. (Walt McDougall, "Funniest Memories of a Famous Cartoonist," *WaPo*, 8/22/1926, SM3.)

241. **Pulitzer found:** Edwin A. Grozier to Seitz, 12/10/1917, DCS-NYPL; *BoGl*, 2/16/1886, 5.

241. **Many of Pulitzer's colleagues:** *NYT*, 2/27/1886, 2; *ChTr* 2/27/1886, 1.

242. **When a committee:** *NYT*, 3/13/1886, 3; *WaPo*, 3/13/1886, 1.

242. **The gentleman in question:** JP to Crawford, 2/11/1886, WP-CU.

242. **The committee members:** An examination of the *Congressional Record* may be seen in WRR, 184; *WaPo*, 3/4/1886, 1; *WaPo*, 6/28/1886, 2.

242. **When Pulitzer was nominated for:** Gibson to JP, 10/10/1884, JP-CU. Full resignation letter appeared in *BrEa*, 4/11/1886, 1.

243. **The *World*'s Washington correspondent:** Crawford to JP, 4/13/1886, WP-CU.

243. **Pulitzer's congressional career:** JP to Board of New York Press Club, April 1886, JP-CU, Box 6; *WaPo*, 3/23/1886, 2; *Medical Record*, 3/27/1886, 366. Pulitzer also mistakenly sent his letter to the New York secretary of state instead of to the speaker of the house thereby delaying the effective date of his resignation until May. (Interview with Donald Ritchie, associate historian of the U.S. Senate Historical Office, 1/17/2008.)

243. **In late June:** The landlord, who was not consulted, was not happy. See John Hoey to JP, 9/24/1886, and 10/25/1886, JP-CU.

243. **Since Kate could not:** Thomas Davidson to William T. Harris, 10/7/1884, Harris Papers, MHS.

244. **Pulitzer was most frustrated:** WHM to JP, 7/28/1886, quoted in WRR, 121.

244. **Next Pulitzer dashed:** *NYW*, 10/28/1886, and 10/29/1886.

245. **Not being among:** *NYW*, 10/28/1886, 4.

245. **As one of:** Depew, *My Memories*, 392.

246. **"Well, gentlemen":** Depew was also willing to curry favor with Pulitzer. On the evening of the festivities honoring the Statue of Liberty, he attended a dinner the Pulitzers gave for the celebrated sculptor Bartholdi in the new residence which they had rented at 9 East Thirty-Sixth Street. During the dinner, Bartholdi's declaring an interest in seeing Niagara Falls prompted Pulitzer to ask Depew for a New York Central private railcar to convey Bartholdi and the Pulitzer family there. Depew submitted a $500 bill to Pulitzer for the ride, adding that the amount should be "strong enough to pulverize the most enlightened anti-monopolist."

246. **Hewitt was a:** JP to Davidson, 9/24/1886, TD.

246. **In the end:** Davidson to JP, 10/7/1886, JP-CU.

246. **On Election Day:** TR told Robert Underwood; Morris, *The Rise of Theodore Roosevelt,* note 70, 800.

246. **The double triumphs:** Edwin Argent to W. A. R. Robertson, 10/14/1886, WP-CU.

247. **Most vexing was:** Masy le Doll to JP, 12/11/1886, WP-CU; Walter Hammond to JP, 12/4/1886, JP-CU.

247. **Work and tension:** JP to Emile Grevillot, 11/23/1886, JP-CU; *Philadelphia Press* interview with Pulitzer, reprinted in *Bismarck Daily Tribune*, 12/07/1886; George Childs to KP, 11/27/1886, JP-CU.

CHAPTER 19: A BLIND CROESUS

248. **Joe Howard, one:** McDougall, *This Is the Life!* 110; *NYH*, 2/9/1887, 1; *ChTr*, 2/9/1887, 1; *Milwaukee Daily Journal*, 2/9/1887, 1.

249. **Howard was not:** Churchill, *Park Row*, 151.

249. **Bennett's wrath was:** *Daily Inter-Ocean*, 11/27/1887. The interview was conducted by Foster Coates, who would eventually become an editor for Pulitzer.

249. **Smith was a Kentuckian:** *ThJo*, 5/10/1884, 5.

249. **Although Smith cut:** Smith to JP, 1886, WP-CU, Box 8.

250. **With Cockerill overseeing:** Turner to JP, 2/25/1887, WP-CU.

250. **While Pulitzer waited to:** George Olney to JP, 1/27/1887, WP-CU.

250. **In the meantime:** Clippings from *Public Ledger and Daily Transcript*, 2/7 and 2/8/1887, WP-CU, Box 9. Also *ThJo*, 3/26/1887, 10; 4/7/1887, 8; and 9/10/1887, 10.

251. **For years Hearst:** Nasaw, *The Chief*, 54–55, 70–72.

253. **In late March:** *NYT*, 3/22/1887, 8; *ChTr*, 3/23/1887, 3.

253. **Lawyers who knew:** *BoGl*, 4/1/1887, 8.

253. **Pulitzer was soon:** *BoGl*, 4/1/1887, 8; Childs to JP, 4/13/1887, JP-CU; Lucille and Ralph, letters to JP and KP, 6/9/1887, JP-CU; Childs to JP, 4/13/1887, JP-CU.

254. **After a stopover:** *WaPo*, 5/2/1887 and 5/23/1887, 4; *WAS*, 156.

254. **The Pulitzers took:** *BoGl*, 6/29/1887, 8; *ThJo*, 1/9/1886, 5.

254. **An enterprising American:** *Philadelphia Times* correspondent in Paris, reprinted in several papers, including *Capital* (MD), 6/28/87, 1.

254. **Joseph and Kate:** T. C. Crawford did the investigating for Pulitzer. See Crawford to JP, 8/12/1887, WP-CU.

255. **Nothing came of:** Junius Morgan to JP, 6/4/1887, JP-NYSL.

255. **Gladstone, dressed in:** *Morning Post*, 7/11/1887, 2, 5; *Daily Telegraph*, 7/11/1887, 2; *PD*, Twenty-Fifth Anniversary Number, 12/11/1903, 4.

255. **While the ceremony:** Ford, *Forty-Odd Years in the Literary Shop*, 148.

255. **Unaware of the:** *Evening Standard*, 7/11/1887, 5; Mary Gladstone, diary entry for July 9, 1887, 46, 262, Vol. 44, December 10, 1885, to Feburary 15, 1893, BLMC.

256. **By August the Pulitzers:** Smith to JP, 8/6 and 8/25, 9/7 and 9/10/1887, WP-CU; JP to Smith, 9/1/1887, WHS-IHS.

256. **Abandoning business and:** The Pulitzers rented Windhurst, owned by General John Rathbone. Childs to JP, 8/12/1887, JP-CU; *Gleaner*, 2/16/1887; Frank K. Paddock to JP, 12/24/1887, JP-CU.

256. **The Pulitzers returned:** *BoGl*, 10/01/1887, 3; *ThJo*, 9/11/1886, 1.

257. **It was, indeed:** Strouse, *Morgan*, 225–226.

257. **While negotiating for:** Platt and Bowers to trustees of Mary Grace Hoyt, 12/22/1887, JP-CU.

257. **He invested in:** *ThJo*, 4/16/1887, 13; Blackeslee to JP, 12/2 and 12/3/1886, JP-CU; Paul S. Potter to JP, 4/10/1887, JP-CU; bill of sale for Paris paintings in JP-CU, Box 7; JP to Goupil's Picture Gallery, 1/14/1887, JP-CU; Fearing to JP, 1/16/1884, JP-CU; H. A. Spalding to JP (in Paris) 5/14/1887, JP-CU; John Hoey to JP, 10/25/1886, JP-CU. Payroll records show that the Pulitzers employed a chef, a kitchen staff, and cleaning women in addition to nannies; see JP-CU, Box 8. While waiting to move to Fifty-Fifth Street, the Pulitzers and their growing retinue of servants remained at 9 East Thirty-Sixth Street, having happily left behind the Fifth Avenue house with its allegedly bad plumbing, to the fury of the landlord. The landlord claimed that prospective renters had fled because the cleaning women the Pulitzers employed were spreading rumors that the plumbing was unhealthy.

258. **Pulitzer developed a:** JP to Metropolitan Telephone and Telegraph, 10/18/1886, WP-CU; *WaPo,* 4/17/1887, 6; *ThJo,* 11/14/1885, 1.
258. **Money bought the Pulitzers:** *NYT,* 12/30/1885, 5.
258. **The ball was held:** *NYT,* 12/30/1885, 5.
258. **The Pulitzers' rising status:** *WaPo,* 12/19/1886, 1.
259. **In particular, Joseph:** Homberger, *Mrs. Astor's New York,* 176.
259. **"J.P. always cherished":** McDougall, *This Is the Life!* 165.
259. **Pulitzer did not simply:** Newton Finney, one of the club's original founders, reluctantly sold two of his shares to Pulitzer when the project neared a critical deadline and had not obtained a sufficient number of subscribers. Kate's charm helped ease the owner's hesitancy about including Pulitzer. (McCash and McCash, *The Jekyll Island Club,* 10–11.)
260. **Despite distaste for:** Homberger, *Mrs. Astor's New York,* 143, 175.
260. **Up until now:** Burrows and Wallace, *Gotham,* 1087–1088.
260. **"To decide a bet":** Julius Esch to editor of *World,* 12/11/1885, WP-CU.
260. **"In all the multiplicity":** *ThJo,* 7/12/1884, 1.
261. **"Any man can":** *ThJo,* 7/19/1884, 2 and 6; 10/11/1884, 6.
261. **Pulitzer banned:** *LAT,* 4/28/1891, 12. Jews, according to the newspaper, possessed untold wealth and influence. "The two Pulitzers—though they are estranged—command more circulation than all the other journals combined."
261. **The rivalry between:** *ThJo,* 6/20/1885, 4; *NYT,* 4/13/1942, 15.
262. **"We have withdrawn":** *NYS,* 10/18–11/8, 1887.
263. **Dana's words hit:** McDougall, "Old Days on the World," 23.
263. **Pulitzer had reached:** Childs to JP, undated but most likely fall of 1887, JP-CU, Box 7.
264. **In 1887, optometrists:** Wells, *A Treatise on the Disease of the Eye,* 536. Which eye had failed was deduced from Dr. Hermann Pagenstecher's later comments.
264. **Pulitzer's doctors were:** JP to FC, 1/26/1909, JP-LC.
264. **"I am absolutely":** JP to Varina Davis, 11/30/1887, JP-CU.
265. **Congressman Walter Phelps:** Walter Phelps to JP, 4/19/1888, JP-CU.

CHAPTER 20: SAMSON AGONISTES

269. **On a moonlit:** *LAT,* 2/28/1888, 3 and 3/1/1888, 6.
269. **Pulitzer's doctors in New York:** Manton Marable to KP, 1/14/1888, JP-CU, quoted in WRR, 217.
269. **The journey drained:** Details regarding the Pullman car may be found in April 1888 personal ledger, JP-CU, Box 7.
270. **The Pulitzers had come:** Cashin, *First Lady of the Confederacy,* 247–250; Jefferson Davis, *Private Letters,* 553.
270. **For the next several weeks:** *Landmark,* 3/1/1888, 4.
270. **During the blizzard:** Walter Phelps to JP, 4/19/1888, JP-CU; Conkling to JP, 3/16/88, JP-CU; *WAS,* 173;
271. **Pulitzer nixed the idea:** *ThJo,* 5/12/1888, 3; Smith to JP, 5/18/1888, WP-CU.
271. **The family reached:** *NYW,* 5/10/1888, 1.
271. **Home again, Pulitzer:** *WaPo,* 6/17/1888, 1; *NYT,* 6/10/1888, 16, and 7/8/1888, 16.
271. **Once across the:** Among the doctors Pulitzer saw were Sir Andrew Clarke; Dr. Jean-Martin Charcot, one of the founders of neurology; and Dr. Charles-Edward Brown-Séquard. (See DCS-JP, 171; and *WAS,* 175.)
272. **Still smarting from:** Manuscript fragments, JP-LC, Box 11.
272. **Resigned to his exile:** *ChTr,* 9/16/1888, 12; *Mansfield Times,* 1/18/1889, 2.

273. **Infirm but not:** Number of employees was derived using the *World* directory left in the cornerstone of the building that went up that year. It may be found in WP-CU, Box 10; JWB, 133; Turner to JP, 6/7/1888, WP-CU.

273. **Aside from creating:** When a letter was read to its recipient, a report would be sent back to Pulitzer on the person's reaction. For example, in one such case, Seitz wrote to Pulitzer, "He received it in an agreeable and appreciative way." One wonders how else the recipient was to react. DCS to JP, 11/20/1900, WP-CU. Also see JP to DCS, 8/17/1900, JP-LC.

274. **For years, Pulitzer:** Chambers, *News Hunting on Three Continents*, 307.

274. **By similar means:** JP to Chambers, 2/10/1889, reprinted in Chambers, *News Hunting*, 333.

274. **While Pulitzer was in California:** *NYT,* 11/14/1886, 3; DCS-JP, 169. Pulitzer recounted his early connection to French's Hotel several times in stories published in the *World*.

274. **The architect George Brown:** Post to Barlow, 4/11/1888, WP-CU.

275. **From Paris, Pulitzer:** September/December 1888, Folder, WP-CU, Box 10.

275. **Over the winter:** JP to Turner, 4/19/1889, WP-CU.

275. **Money, of course:** JP to Turner, 3/19/1889, WP-CU.

275. **Pulitzer still considered:** JP to Turner, 3/19/1889, WP-CU.

276. **After Post's visit:** JP to John Jennings, 3/11/1889, JJJ.

276. **Pulitzer took time:** *NYT,* 4/27/1889, 4.

276. **An editor from:** *WaPo,* 5/13/1889, 4.

276. **On May 15:** Turner to Post, 5/15/1889, WP-CU.

277. **Pulitzer did his resolute best:** JP to KP, 6/11/1889, JP-CU.

277. **"Well," he added:** Ponsonby also wrote to Kate. He reported, "I am sure you will be glad to hear that he *scarcely ever* alludes to his health": Ponsonby to KP, 6/21/1889, JP-CU.

277. **In a decade:** *AtCo,* 4/21/1889, 18; *NYT,* 7/3/1889, 4; *WaPo,* 6/4/1890, 4.

278. **Pulitzer also increased:** *NYT,* 9/20/1889; Wilson, ed., *The Memorial History of the City of New York*, Vol. 5, 594–595. By 1940, 551 boys, mostly immigrant children, had gone on to become engineers, lawyers, doctors, journalists, and authors. See *Time,* 1/1/1940.

278. **In the fall:** *NYT,* 10/27/1889, 13; *WaPo,* 9/14/1889, 5. Pulitzer also donated $50,000 to try to attract the 1892 World Fair to New York City.

278. **Nothing about the project:** JP to Davis, 11/23/1889, JP-LC.

278. **On October 10:** *BoGl,* 10/11/1889, 2; *WaPo,* 10/11/1889, 4; *ChTr,* 10/20/1889, 26. Taylor used to tell Pulitzer that "he would have no appetite for breakfast if he did not see blood running down the column rules on the editorial paper of the morning *World*." (Morgan, *Charles H. Taylor*, 140.)

280. **Inside the cornerstone:** The recording, one of the earliest of a human voice, remained hidden in the box until 1955, when the building was torn down. The box fell out of a clamshell bucket and was recovered. The recording, which was transferred to a reel-to-reel format, is among the *World*'s papers at Columbia. The men were right about the New York Giants, who went on to defeat the Dodgers in the championships. They wrongly predicted, however, that New York would get the World Fair in 1892. It went to Chicago.

280. **Many of the nation's:** *NYT,* 10/11/1889, 2.

280. **Back again in Paris:** *NYT,* 10/20/1889, 12; Cashin, *First Lady of the Confederacy*, 270–271.

280. **Every day the sad group:** Winnie Davis to Jefferson Davis, *Jefferson Davis: Private Letters*, 582–583.

281. **He sent detailed:** JP to Davis, 11/23/1899, JP-LC.

282. **Just before Christmas:** JP to KP, 12/23/1889, JP-MHS.
282. **"He is certainly":** Ponsonby to KP, 12/23/1889, JP-MHS.
282. **Crossing the Arabian:** JP to KP, 1/14/1890, JP-MHS.
283. **Shortly after mailing:** Thwaites, *Velvet and Vinegar*, 53–54.

CHAPTER 21: DARKNESS

284. **That spring, the stacks:** JP to WHM, 7/23/1890, WP-CU.
284. **Earlier in the year:** Pulitzer's return to France may be dated by a canceled check signed by Pulitzer in Paris, 3/26/1889, PLFC.
284. **But over the succeeding:** JWB, 137.
285. **On October 2:** Pulitzer's ship and the *City of New York*, which left half an hour earlier, raced each other across the ocean in an intercompany competition. Passengers on each ship joined betting pools, and the two oceanliners remained within sight of each other for most of the crossing. The *Teutonic*, carrying the Pulitzer party, lost the race by an hour. The *Teutonic* completed its voyage in five days, twenty-two hours, and nineteen minutes. (*NYT*, 10/9/1890, 5.)
285. **Joseph settled into:** Stanford White to KP, 8/29/1891, JP-CU; bills, JP-CU, Box 1889–1898; *NYT*, 11/17/1890, 5; *WaPo*, 12/7/1890, 9, and 11/30/1890, 14.
286. **In such circumstances:** JP to WHM, 7/23/1890, WP-CU.
286. **The gigantic high-speed:** "The World, Its History, Its New Home," *Scientific American* (12/20/1890), 384.
287. **Kate and Hosmer:** Garrison, *An Introduction to the History of Medicine*, 578.
288. **As he struggled:** Koestler, *The Unseen Minority*, 4; Selin, *Medicine Across Cultures*, 320.
288. **News of Pulitzer's abdication:** *NYH*, 10/17/1890, 4.
289. **The final price:** *NYW*, 12/11/1890; *Fort Wayne Sentinel*, 1/17/1891, 9.
290. **For almost four months:** JWB, 143. The yacht cruised along the Spanish coast, crossed over to Africa, and then took them east to Greece and Turkey.
290. **Pulitzer defied Mitchell:** *Middletown Daily Press*, 6/27/1891, 2; *Newark Daily Advocate*, 5/21/1891; *Galveston Daily News*, 6/21/1891, 8; *AtCo*, 5/1/1890, 1. Bennett had once told Cockerill that "the life of a managing editor is only five years."
290. **Leaving Kate in Paris:** *NYT*, 6/11/1891, 8.
290. **Ballard Smith, the:** *BoGl*, 6/11/1891, 10.
291. **Pulitzer's solution to:** *WaPo*, 6/19/1891, 4; Johnson, *George Harvey*, 36.
291. **A heat wave:** *WaPo*, 6/19/1891.
291. **A few weeks:** Nasaw, *The Chief*, 88, 90–91.
292. **Pulitzer's emergency trip:** JWB, 144; *NYT*, 6/16/1891, 5; *WaPo*, 8/16/1891, 13.
293. **Pulitzer shared most:** *NYT*, 12/27/1909, 1.
294. **Unlike many of the elite:** JP memo (probably to FC), 9/19/1907, WP-CU.
294. **As 1891 closed:** JWB, 144.
294. **Again, Dr. S. Weir Mitchell:** S. Weir Mitchell to JP, 12/15/1891, JP-MHS.
295. **One of the men:** John Cockerill, Pulitzer's former editor, disclosed the proposed deal in the *Democratic Standard* (Coshocton, OH), 5/2/1892.
295. **In February, the Pulitzers:** JP to Smith, 2/28/1892, WP-CU; McCash, *The Jekyll Island Club*; *AtCo*, 3/9/1892, 4.
295. **It was Pulitzers first visit:** McCash, *The Jekyll Island Club*, 18; *WaPo*, 4/14/1892, 5, and 4/15/1892, 4; *NYT*, 4/28/1883, 1. In April Pulitzer returned to New York to catch the *Teutonic*, bound for Liverpool. In addition to the servants and secretaries, the Pulitzers' traveling party grew even larger with the addition of a companion for Kate, Mattie Thompson, traveling with her own personal French maid. Her father was the former representative Phillip "Little Phil" Thompson, of Kentucky, best-

known for having shot to death a man he accused, quite probably wrongly, of having slept with his wife. "That man took my wife to Cincinnati and debauched her," he said while still holding his smoking gun. "I swore to kill him on sight." The jury acquitted him, agreeing with Pulitzer's friend Henry Watterson's estimation, "The forfeit of the life of the wife-seducer to the vengeance of the husband is accepted as unwritten, but inexorable, law." See Kotter, *Southern Honor and American Manhood*, 45. Mattie Thompson later married Kate's brother William Davis, whom she may have met while in Kate's company.

296. **Their assumption made:** *NYW*, 2/2/1884, 4, quoted in GJ, 294.

297. **In St. Louis:** *NYW*, 3/14/1885, 4, quoted in GJ, 309.

297. **Pulitzer—who now:** *NYW*, 7/12/1892, 4.

298. **Angry about his paper's:** J. Errol, "A Visit to Professor Dr. Hermann Pagenstecher," *London Society*, Vol. 63 (January–June, 1893). Pagenstecher and Pulitzer had actually first met in their youth. Udo Brachvogel had introduced them over beers at the Schalks Salon on Broadway in New York when Pulitzer was working for the *Westliche Post*. "We sat together sipping beers and talking," said Pagenstecher, recalling the moment to his patient. "I was greatly fascinated by your original ideas and carried away an impression of my new acquaintance that I shall never forget." (Pagenstecher to JP, 12/12/1900, JP-CU.)

298. **Pagenstecher was more:** Pagenstecher to KP, 10/30/1892, JP-CU.

298. **Pulitzer rejoined his family:** Hirsch, *William C. Whitney*, 376.

298. **With the coming:** DCS-JP, 190.

CHAPTER 22: CAGED EAGLE

299. **It took the:** *NYW*, 1/13/1884, quoted in WRR, 145–146.

299. **The *Majestic*, one:** *NYT*, 5/11/1893, 12; DCS-JP, 188.

299. **Bennett admired Pulitzer:** Kluger, *The Paper*, 162–163; DCS, 182.

300. **The publishers disembarked:** DCS-JP, 192. Harvey drank and toasted a bit too much. His twenty-fifth toast was to the King irritating Pulitzer. "Oh, damn it. No Kings! No Kings!" Pulitzer said.

300. **Despite the good cheer:** JP to Harvey in Johnson, *George Harvey*, 45.

300. **Pulitzer, for his part:** Filler, *Voice of the Democracy*, 32; DCS to JP, 1/17/1901, WP-CU.

300. **Phillips received an invitation:** Marcosson, *David Graham Phillips*, 141–142.

301. **Pulitzer was so completely:** DGP to JP, reprinted ibid., 165–166.

302. **No one on the staff:** DCS-JP, 193. Seitz, who wrote the first biography of Pulitzer, began working that year at the highest levels of the paper. Much of what he describes in his book, from this point on, consists of events he witnessed himself.

302. **"It was soon":** DCS, 194; Johnson, *George Harvey*, 58.

302. **Amid the managerial confusion:** "The position of a London correspondent is extremely desirable under some circumstances but under other circumstances extremely undesirable," a frustrated Phillips wrote to Pulitzer. "It means that a man may make a reputation for himself if he can supplement energy with ability, and has the privilege of signing his name to his letters. If he has not that privilege, he is simply wasting energy, ability, and time." (DGP to JP and DGP to Jones, reprinted in Marcosson, *Phillips*, 168–169.)

303. **Pulitzer was unconvinced:** Pulitzer was stingy with bylines, which were not then a common practice. He once told another correspondent that a byline "is a privilege, but not a right." (Memorandum for James Creelman, 1896, JC.)

303. **Phillips consented to remain:** Marcosson, *Phillips*, 169.

303. **Leaving the paper:** *LAT*, 12/24/1893, 25; *ChTr*, 11/26/1893, 25. DCS-JP, 13–14.

304. **Pulitzer suffered from:** It is risky to try to identify psychological problems in historical figures. Still, "Blindness and deafness have both been recognized as causal agents in mental illness," according to Anthony Storr, *Solitude*, 51. Hyperesthesia is a real effect, not hypochondriacal, according to Edwin N. Carter, a clinical psychologist in private practice. "The peripheral nervous system," Carter says, "has an exaggerated response eliciting sympathetic nervous activity at the expense of parasympathetic activity." A common hyperesthesia can be found in children who feel that clothing is scratching no matter how soft it is, or too tight no matter how loose it is. (Carter to author, 10/24/2008.)

304. **His condition, in any case:** JP to Adam Politzer, quoted in WRR, 255–256.

304. **As if his own health:** Doctor's report of RP, 3/10/1893, JP-CU, Box 8.

304. **The older Pulitzer children:** RP to LP, 2/1/1894, JP-CU.

305. **All winter Joseph:** JP to KP, 4/27/1893, JP-CU; GWH to JP, 4/28/1894. In reporting his findings on Colorado Springs, Hosmer added, "I have not yet said any mention of this to Mrs. Pulitzer." Also JP to KP, 4/28/1894, JP-CU.

305. **In New York:** JP to Depew, 5/17/1894, CDP.

305. **Jones's ineptitude at:** *AtCo*, 12/10/1893, 18.

305. **With the problem of Jones:** *ChTr*, 6/7/1894, 2.

306. **Unlike the coterie:** ABF–2001, Box 3.

306. **Upon arriving in New York:** *BoGl*, 6/24/1894, 23.

306. **Senator David Hill:** McClellan, *The Gentleman and the Tiger*, 99–100. When he arrived for their appointment at the Normandy Hotel, McCellan found Hill talking with George Harvey, whom he met during a short stint working at the *World*, and who was now doing political work for Pulitzer's friend Whitney.

308. **On his return:** *AtCo*, 12/29/1894, 3.

308. **Jones's contract:** DCS-JP, 199. The terms of the contract described by Seitz are confirmed by a document in the Fogarty Collection.

308. **For Pulitzer, Jekyll Island's:** *AtCo*, 1/11/1895, 3.

309. **One of the few witnesses:** Correspondence of Felix Webber, 9/27/1894; 12/9/1894; 1/2/1895, JP-MHS.

310. **Kate had certainly:** JP to KP, JP-CU, Box 8. This letter was partially burned, probably in a house fire.

311. **Her separation from Joseph:** "H." to KP, Saturday, 10/10/1895 and 10/18/1895. AB-LC.

312. **In May, Pulitzer:** Moray Lodge, on Campden Hill, next to Holland Park; JP to TD, 6/30/1895, TD.

312. **That summer the remodeled:** *BoGl*, 1/10/1895, 8.

312. **The "tower of silence":** Cobb, *Exit Laughing*, 131.

312. **Roosevelt's claim that:** JLH, 108.

313. **Reading the editorial:** Morris, *The Rise of Theodore Roosevelt*, 504–505; Roosevelt, *Letters*, Vol. 1, 497.

313. **Indeed, Roosevelt's ambitions:** *ChTr*, 2/23/1896, 11.

313. **The rebuff drew:** *NYT*, 12/18, 1895, 1; *ChTr*, 12/18/1895, 1; *AtCo*, 12/18/1895, 1.

314. **Pulitzer refused to:** Quoted in DCS-JP, 203.

314. **Pulitzer had long feared:** *NYS*, 10/6/1878, 3.

314. **Pulitzer now expanded:** JLH, 119.

315. **In England, the telegrams:** *NYW*, 12/26 and 12/27, 1895, Roosevelt, *Letters*, Vol. 1, 503–505.

315. **Under such headlines:** Eggleston, *Recollections*, 328–330. Eggleston based his account on notes he wrote that evening before returning to New York.

316. **Pulitzer dismissed his men:** JLH, 137.

316. **Pulitzer won:** *NYT*, 1/8/1896, 2. A senator asked Chandler if he would read one

of the telegrams from the *World*. He said he couldn't, because the paper was now in the hands of Senator Hill of New York, arousing laughter in the chamber. The men looked over at Hill, who only months before had been currying favor with Pulitzer. "Whatever else the Senator from New York may be," Hill told his colleagues, "he is not, at this time, the defender of Mr. Pulitzer. I leave that to other gentlemen."

317. **Pulitzer mounted his:** JLH, 122.
317. **A few days later:** DCS-JP, 209.
317. **Roosevelt, in this:** *NYT*, 3/19/1896, 8.

CHAPTER 23: TROUBLE FROM THE WEST

319. **In February 1895:** APM, 322.
320. **At the beginning:** APM, 285.
320. **From its origin:** APM, 272.
320. **The *Journal*'s circulation:** Henry Kellett Chambers, "A Park Row Interlude: Memoir of Albert Pulitzer," *Journalism Quarterly* (Autumn 1963), 542. Also *NYT*, 11/24/1909, 3.
320. **But his years:** *Morning Journal*, 4/15/1895 quoted in APM, 323–324.
321. **At long last:** *AtCo*, 7/26/1896, 23.
322. **Pulitzer's men at:** DCS-JP, 211. The *Examiner*'s office was located in suite 186 in the Pulitzer Building in 1894–1895, according to Trow's City Directory.
322. **Pulitzer found out:** *AtCo*, 1/22/1896, 3; JP to James Creelman, 1/18/1896, JC.
322. **After two years:** JP to James Creelman, 2/18/1896, JC.
322. **While the party:** DCS-JP, 212–213.
323. **"The news of":** *ChTr*, 2/9/1898, 3.
323. **"The immediate effect":** DCS-JP, 213–214; Nasaw, *The Chief*, 104; Ochs to JP, quoted in Brown, *The Correspondents' War*, 28.
323. **Hearst's entry into:** DCS-JP, 217; Nasaw, *The Chief*, 105.
324. **With his newspaper's supremacy:** *AtCo*, 1/17/1897, 7.
324. **On Jekyll Island:** King, *Pulitzer's Prize Editor*, 295–304.
324. **Pulitzer found tranquillity:** *ChTr*, 7/12/1896, 14.
325. **Its pleasures were:** *WaPo*, 6/6/1896, 9; *ChTr*, 6/6/1896, 2. The entire speech is reprinted in DCS-JP, 218–224.
325. **Before returning to:** JP to Norris, 6/15/1896, JP-LC; various telegrams, JP-LC, Box 1.
326. **The strength of the silver movement:** *ChTr*, 7/12/1896, 14; Kazin, *A Godly Hero*, 61.
326. **Pulitzer summoned the *World*'s:** Eggleston, *Recollections*, 325–326.
327. **When Eggleston delivered:** "He had a wonderful judgement at prophesying and forecasting the elections," recalled Joseph Pulitzer Jr. "I can remember being impressed by that. It was uncanny the way he could do that": The Reminiscences of Joseph Pulitzer Jr., October 7, 1954, transcript, p. 67, the Oral History Collection of Columbia University.
327. **Eggleston and Pulitzer:** *NYW*, 8/11/1896.
327. **"You can, if":** JP to James Creelman, 11/4/1896, JC; Milton, *The Yellow Kids*, 107.
328. **The beauty of the setting:** AB to KP, 1/11/1897, JP-CU (misdated as 1896).
329. **Efforts to relieve:** JP to KP, 1/14/1897, JP-CU; AB to KP, 1/11/1897, JP-CU (misdated as 1896).
330. **Compounding the council's woes:** JP to DCS, 9/2/1897, JP-CU. The door consumed several letters between Bar Harbor and New York.
330. **As the day neared:** AB to DCS, 1/15/1897, JP-LC; BM to JP, 2/16/1903, WP-CU.
330. **What had been called:** See Campbell, *Yellow Journalism*, 25–49.

331. **Clubs and libraries:** *NYT,* 3/4/1897, 3.

331. **Pulitzer knew nothing:** McDougall, *This Is the Life!* 242.

331. **Pulitzer now realized:** JP to JN, 8/21/1897, JP-LC; JP to DCS, 8/28/1897, JP-LC.

331. **In a state of:** *AtCo,* 3/18/1897, 1. The paper claimed that the previous year, Morgan had bypassed Jekyll and gone to Florida when he learned that Pulitzer was on the island (*AtCo* 1/17/1897, 7).

332. **After a month's rest:** Pulitzer added a glass conservatory to the back of the house that he could use as a study and where he could tend to what he called "matters of state": DCS-JP, 232; *WP,* 3/31/1897, 7; *Eau Claire Leader,* 5/20/1897, 11.

332. **Among those who came:** JP to James Creelman, 11/4/1896, JC; JP to DCS, 4/28/1897, JP-LC; DCS-JP, 232–233.

332. **Almost as soon:** Jones to JP, March 5, 1896, PLFC.

333. **Jones grew tired:** JP to JN, 6/26/1897, JP-LC; JP to BM, 6/30/1897, JP-LC. A copy of the signed agreement is in the Fogarty Papers.

333. **With the Jones episode:** Letters and telegrams, August 1897, JP-LC.

333. **No one was exempt:** KP to AB, date unknown, 1897, JP-CU.

334. **In August 1897:** AB to KP, 3/3/1896, AB-LC.

334. **In the fall of 1897:** For a discussion of the various versions of Brisbane's departure, see Carlson, *Brisbane,* 110–111. Elizabeth Jordan, a journalist who worked with Brisbane at the *World,* told one person that she heard many rumors as to the reasons but she concluded he was asked to leave because Pulitzer was not getting his money's worth from him. Reid to Sparkes, 2/28/1938, London 1886–1897 Folder, Box 2, AB.

334. **The social season:** *ChTr,* 8/1/97, 33; *Lowell Sun,* 12/18/1897, 2.

335. **Lucille made a:** *Bangor Daily Whig and Courier,* 1/3/1898, 4; *BoGl,* 1/1/1898, 12; *NYT,* 1/2/1898, 7; and 1/5/1898, 4.

335. **In October there was:** JP to TD, 10/13/1897, 12/8/1897, and 12/14/1897.

336. **It was left to Butes:** AB to JN, 12/31/1897, JP-LC.

CHAPTER 24: YELLOW

337. **In the early morning:** *NYT,* 1/22/1899, 3. Rainsford had been picked by J. P. Morgan for the post.

337. **The moment didn't:** *WaPo,* 2/18/1898, 7; *NYT,* 10/28/1898, 1.

338. **Meanwhile, Joseph remained:** KP to JP, undated but dated by other elements to the spring of 1898, JP-CU, Box 8.

338. **The warmth between:** GWH to KP, 3/29/1898, JP-CU.

338. **Five hundred miles:** Milton, *The Yellow Kids,* 218–220.

339. **His boss already knew:** Nasaw, *The Chief,* 130–131.

339. **Within twenty-four hours:** *NYW,* 2/17/1898, 1; and 2/20/1898, 1.

340. **The staff struggled:** Ledlie to JP, 2/15/1898, JP-CU; DC to JP, 4/15/1898, JP-CU.

340. **The epic battle:** Chapin, *Charles Chapin's Story,* 179.

340. **No more stinging:** The complete story may be found in Procter, *William Randolph Hearst: The Early Years,* 124.

341. **In April, when:** *TT,* 4/7/1898, 12, quoted in Nasaw, *The Chief,* 132.

341. **From the command post:** GHL to KP, 4/8/1898, JP-CU.

341. **Trying once more:** JP to DCS, 5/23/1897, JP-LC; JP memo, April 1898, JP-LC.

342. **Pulitzer joined the chorus:** JP to DCS, 2/15/1897, and 3/27/1897, JP-LC.

342. **"If we are":** *NYW,* 4/10/1898.

343. **Upon completing his:** GHL to KP, 4/8/1898, JP-CU; *WaPo,* 4/20/1898, 8; CP to JP, 5/21/1898, JP-CU.

343. **On his return:** KP letter, 1898, JP-CU, Box 8; *NYT*, 8/28/1898, 13.

343. **The "*Journal*'s war":** Morris, *Rise of Theodore Roosevelt*, 615, 629.

343. **By the war's end:** JN to JP, 9/11/1899, WP-CU. At least the *Post-Dispatch* was making money. Its 1898 profits were better than all but two previous years.

343. **Also coming to Narragansett:** KP to CP, 1989, JP-CU. Box 8; *NYT*, 7/23/1898; *AtCo*, 7/23/1898, 1.

344. **The trip through the South:** Cashin, *First Lady*, 290.

344. **On September 21, 1898:** *NYT*, 9/22/1898, 4.

344. **The *World* was desperate:** *WaPo*, 10/10/1898, 6, and 10/14/1898, 6; John Norris, "*Journal* and *World* Revenues Compared," 11/14/1898, WP-CU.

344. **Norris, along with Seitz:** Memo, 1898, JP-CU, Box 8; DCS to JP, 11/18/1898, WP-CU.

345. **The typewriters were still:** Memo, 11/28/1898, JP-CU.

346. **Pulitzer assigned the business manager:** JP to JN, 1/31/1899, JP-CU; Noted in February 8–14, 1900 Folder, JP-CU, Box 10. A year later, Norris hinted that he thought the reason the deal to sell the *Post-Dispatch* failed was Pulitzer's inability to understand the financing arrangements. (JN to JP, 3/13/1900, JP-CU.)

346. **Kate was also:** JN to JP, 2/17/1899, WP-CU; AB to KP, 3/14/1899, JP-CU.

347. **Pulitzer told his staff:** JP to DCS, 5/4/1899, JP-LC; JP to KP, 5/31/1899, JP-CU.

347. **In Britain:** Walter Leyman to JP, 10/9/1899, JP-CU, quoted in WES, 298–299.

347. **Pulitzer headed back:** *LAT*, 5/3/1899, 5.

348. **That summer Pulitzer:** *NYT*, 5/27/1899, 2. The builder eventually sued to get his payment.

348. **His house in New York:** *NYT*, 1/10/1900, 2; personal ledger for April 1899 shows expenses and descriptions of items, JP-CU.

348. **Kate joined Joseph:** JAS to KP, 8/1/1899, JP-CU.

CHAPTER 25: THE GREAT GOD SUCCESS

349. **One icy night:** *NYT*, 2/15/1891, 5. Jacob Riis reported the story in his *Children of the Poor* but gave the children different names.

349. **Newsies, as boys:** Charles Dickens's fictional Martin Chuzzlewit encountered them when he disembarked in New York. '"Here's this morning's New York Sewer!' cried one. 'Here's this morning's New York Stabber! Here's the New York Family Spy! . . . Here's full particulars of the patriotic locofoco movement yesterday, in which the whigs was so chawed up; and the last Alabama gouging case; and the interesting Arkansas dooel with Bowie knives; and all the Political, Commercial, and Fashionable News. Here they are! Here they are! Here's the papers, here's the papers!'" (Dickens, *Martin Chuzzlewit*, 267.)

350. **Since most copies:** The headline, though it may be apocryphal, is said to have been written by Charles Chapin and appears twice in works by Irwin Cobb. See *Exit Laughing*, 140, and his novel *Alias Ben Alibi*, 126.

350. **The newsies became:** There is no existing record as to which of the two newspapers raised its wholesale price first. However, only the *World*'s managers were under orders to cut costs. Hearst was still spending money in hopes of beating the *World* and establishing his own paper. It makes sense that he would have matched the *World*'s price increase but not instigated it.

351. **The newsies demanded:** David Nasaw, "On Strike with the Newsboy Legion, 1899," *Big Town, Big Time: A New York Epic: 1898–1998* (New York: Sports Publishing, 1998), 1839; DCS, "Memo for Mr. Pulitzer on the Newsboys' Strike," July 27, 1899, WP-CU; *NYT*, 7/22/1899, 4.

351. **The strike exacted:** Pulitzer had left England on the *Majestic* on July 12, 1899, and

a special train car had brought him and the family to Bar Harbor on July 20, 1899. See *Lowell Sun,* 7/10/1899, 19, and *Daily Kennebec Journal,* 7/21/1899; DCS to JP, 7/22/1899, WP-CU; John M. Quinn, *Anaconda Standard,* 8/6/1899, 3.

351. **But enemies with:** DCS, "Memo for Mr. Pulitzer on the Newsboys' Strike." 7/22/1899, WP-CU. As Seitz left the *Journal's* office he spotted Hearst with four leaders of the newsboys. They had come from his office and had promised to call off the strike against the *Journal* if Hearst agreed to lower the price to 50 cents per 100. The meeting set off a rumor that he would give in. "I cannot believe he will be so foolish," Merrill wired to Pulitzer. "The boys cannot last many days—in spite of encouragement the other papers are giving."

351. **Advertisers abandoned the papers:** DCS, "Memorandum on the Newsboys Strike," 7/25/1899, WP-CU.

351. **Using homeless men:** DCS, "Memo for Mr. Pulitzer on the Newsboys' Strike," 7/27/1899, WP-CU.

352. **As the strike continued:** David Nasaw, "Dirty-Faced Davids and the Twin Goliaths," *American Heritage,* Vol. 36, No. 3 (1985), 46; *NYT,* 7/27/1899, 3.

352. **A clever ruse:** The compromise broke the strike but was recognized by others as a loss for the newsboys. For example, newsdealers who had supported the boys withdrew their support, declaring the strike a failure: *NYT,* 8/1/1899, 4.

352. **Facing the resolute partnership:** DCS to JP, 7/26/1899, WP-CU; DCS, "Memo for Mr. Pulitzer on the Newsboys' Strike." 7/27/1899. WP-CU Seitz also told Pulitzer he had paid no bribes: *NYT,* 7/28/1899, 4.

353. **This was no longer:** DCS to JP, 7/26/1899, WP-CU.

353. **When David Graham Phillips:** JP to GWH, 12/22/1910 reprinted in DCS-JP, xii–xiii.

353. **The pressure was:** JP to Merrill, quoted in DCS, 246.

353. **One could never:** JP to WHM, reprinted in DCS, 247.

354. **Despite the outburst:** JP to DGP, 8/17/1899, JP-LC.

354. **Pulitzer, however, was:** Maurice, *The New York of the Novelists,* 139; Marcosson, *David Graham Phillips and His Times,* 208.

354. **In Phillips's novel:** Phillips, *The Great God Success,* 11.

355. **Following the settlement:** DCS to JP, 10/5/1899, WP-CU; DCS, "Memorandum for Mr. Pulitzer on Los," 7/31/1899, WP-CU.

355. **The two managers:** DCS, "Memo for Mr. Pulitzer on Mr. Seitz' Conversation with Los," 8/14/1899, WP-CU.

355. **Proposals for a peace treaty:** Nasaw, *The Chief,* 110; JP to BM, 8/29/1898, JP-LC; DCS to JP, October 4, 1898, JP-LC; memo, 12/19/1898, JP-LC; see also Nasaw, *The Chief,* 148–149. The squabble over the wire service would not die. Hearst enraged Pulitzer when he started using wire copy from the *Journal* in his *Evening Journal.* Pulitzer sued. Faced with the threat of being personally dragged into court, Hearst vowed to terminate the negotiations and resume his attacks on Pulitzer in the paper, "making it as personal and as powerful as he can," Carvalho warned.

355. **Keenly aware of:** JP to DCS, 7/24/1899, JP-LC.

356. **Combination instead of:** JP to DGP, 8/23/1902, The Sherman act specified, "Every contract, combination in the form of trust or otherwise, or conspiracy, in restraint of trade or commerce among the several States, or with foreign nations, is declared to be illegal. Every person who shall make any contract or engage in any combination or conspiracy hereby declared to be illegal shall be deemed guilty of a felony."

356. **Remaining in Bar Harbor:** JP to DCS, 8/19/1899, JP-LC.

356. **Pulitzer placed high hopes:** JP to DCS, 8/25/1899, JP-LC.

356. **Like a nervous suitor:** JP to DCS, 9/4/1899, and 9/5/1899, JP-LC.

357. **Upon finally sitting:** DCS, "Memo for Mr. Pulitzer on Mr. Seitz' Conversation with Los," 8/14/1899, WP-CU.

357. **From the start, both:** DCS, "Memo for Mr. Pulitzer on Los and Treaty," 8/3/1899, WP-CU. "By the way," said Carvalho, "Mr. Pulitzer is taking a great deal of my time and much of our money in fighting an Associated Press suit against the *Journal*, in which he will be beaten on several important points. It seems to me that any agreement ought to be preceded by the abandonment of that suit." Seitz tried to keep the issue off the table by arguing that it would resolve itself in court. His view prevailed, and he and Carvalho decided to draft a contract to bring to Hearst and Pulitzer. "Of course," Seitz told Pulitzer, "I could see that a treaty of peace was hardly feasible while an active war went on."

357. **While the men negotiated:** JN to JP, 8/8/1899, WP-CU.

357. **Pulitzer pledged:** JP to DCS, 9/23/1899, JP-LC. The proposed contract may be found in WP-CU, Box 12, 9/1–15/1899.

358. **When Norris reviewed:** JN to JP, 9/7/1899, and BM to JP, 9/14/1899, WP-CU.

358. **Pulitzer ignored both:** JP to DCS, 9/2/1899, JP-LC; DCS, "Memo for Mr. Pulitzer on Mr. Seitz' Conversation with Los," 8/14/1899.

358. **As with crushing:** JP to DCS, 9/23/1899, JP-LC.

359. **The negotiations dragged:** DCS to JP, 11/23/1899, WP-CU.

359. **"I cannot get over":** Marcosson, *Phillips*, 98–99.

359. **With the arrival of winter:** Phillips, *The Great God Success*, 170, 274, 278–279.

CHAPTER 26: FLEEING HIS SHADOW

361. **Muffled sounds of screaming:** *NYT*, 1/10/1900, 3; *WaPo*, 1/10/1900, 3; *BrEa*, 1/9/1900, 18; *NYH*, 1/10/1900; James W. McLane to JP, 1/14/1900, JP-CU.

362. **Kate and the children:** *ChTr*, 2/21/1900, 4; NYC Fire Department Chief and Police Chief Clerk letters to DCS, 3/5/1900, JP-CU.

362. **As Pulitzer's fifty-third birthday:** *NYT*, 4/13/1900, 9; 1899 Expenditures, in January 1–7, 1900, Folder, JP-CU, Box 10.

363. **Kate had not yet:** Dr. McLane to JP, 5/7/1900, JP-CU; JAS to JP, 5/7/1900, JP-CU.

363. **At the *World*:** JP telegram, 1/5/1900, JP-LC.

363. **Since January:** JN to JP, 4/2/1900, JP-CU; Berger, *The Story of the New York Times*, 127; *ChTr*, 10/17/1902, 12.

363. **Phillips was also:** DGP to JP, 4/5/1900, JP-CU; BM to JP, 4/5/1900, WP-CU; JAS to JP, 4/14/1900, JP-CU. When Phillips returned, he got into a fight with Pulitzer over the cost of the trip.

363. **After more than a decade:** Transcript of JP talk, 1900 Folder, WP-CU, Box 14.

364. **The telegrams tested:** ABi to AB, 2/29/1901, JP-CU.

364. **People in competitive:** The only known surviving copy of the codebook once belonged to H. A. Jenks, JP-CU. Here is a sample of a coded telegram, followed by the decoded version. Coded: "Would unhesitatingly give atlas of angers aroma for arm on second art agony especially if I were anxious to get rid of management of amour." Decoded: "Would unhesitatingly give approval of Knapp's proposition for arbitration on second-class security especially if I were anxious to get rid of management of *Post-Dispatch*." JP to AB, 2/22/1899, JP-CU.

365. **This 5,000-entry book:** Sometimes Pulitzer's choice of codes must have raised an eyebrow or two. One must wonder what a telegraph operator in the 1890s made of a message that spoke of "vagina" ($27,500 in advertising for a week) or "vaginal" ($28,000). Pulitzer organized his lexicon by letter groupings. Codes for cash balances, for instance, were all words that began with H. "Ha" stood for $1,000; "hypo

crite" meant $400,000. For his private bank balance, Pulitzer used a term that many people looking at their own checkbooks could relate to: "hysterics." The complex code was rendered even more cumbersome by the addition of codes within coded messages. When Pulitzer sought to have checks sent out in his name, his requests were supposed to include one of five names from a list of cities found in the annual *World* Almanac. Without the name, no payment was authorized.

365. **To stay out of trouble:** The memo dated 2/23/1910, is bound in Jenks's codebook, JP-CU.

365. **For himself, Pulitzer:** In 2005, when the Pulitzer family announced the intention of selling the *Post-Dispatch*, a group of employees made a last-ditch effort to purchase it. They named their attempt the "Andes Project": *Guild Reporter*, 2/11/2005, 1.

366. **In late June 1900:** *NYT*, 6/26/1900, 6; RP to JP, 6/15/1900, JP-CU.

366. **Like most of:** Ralph did not want Butes to bring the matter up with his father. "I judge that the paper is worrying him considerably and I hate to talk money with him, as you know": RP to AB, 8/1899, JP-CU.

366. **Ralph's fifteen-year-old brother:** JPII to JP, 3/12/1901, JP-CU.

366. **It was not until:** Pfaff, *Joseph Pulitzer II*, 32. Seven years later, Joseph Jr. was present when his father received an appeal from a worker who had been fired after his parents refused to let him come to work on Rosh Hashanah. "I appeal to you, being that you are a Jew (otherwise, I would not appeal)," wrote Isaac Feigenbaum. Joseph Jr. told Seitz that his father said, "If this chap really has a *sincere* religious conviction, that fact should be considered. He leaves the matter with you." (Feigenbaum to JP, 9/27/1907, JP-LC.)

367. **Pulitzer supervised the children's:** JP to DCS, 10/30/1900, JP-LC.

367. **Pulitzer had even:** DWP, 33; JP to KP, 11/24–29/1901, dictation in notebook, JP-CU, Box 16, Folder 5.

367. **Pulitzer took less interest:** JP to KP, 12/4/1900, JP-CU. Pulitzer's attitude toward his daughters was typical of fathers at the time. At his death, he left his daughters each a fraction of his estate but no interest in any of the newspapers.

367. **Joseph endlessly expressed:** JP to KP, 1/14/1897, JP-CU; Adam Politzer to JP, 10/19/1900, JP-CU.

368. **As her time:** DGP to JP, 11/22/1900, WP-CU. The passage to which Phillips alludes may have been Horace, *Epistles*, Book 1, Poem 1, lines 81–93.

368. **When one of the governesses:** Ledlie to JP, 6/29/1900, JP-CU; KP to JP, no date, probably 6/29/1900, June Folder, JP-CU, Box 11; KP to JP, 7/18/1900 and 7/19/1900; JP to KP, 7/21/1900; KP to JP, 7/22/1900, KP to JP, 7/25/1900, JP-CU; JAS to JP, 8/1/1900, JP-CU.

369. **It was not a good time:** JP to KP, 10/22/1899, JP-CU.

369. **After Davidson's death:** J. Clark Murray to JP, 9/16/1900, and W. R. Warren to JP, 9/21/1900, JP-CU.

369. **In the fall of 1900:** JC to JP, no date, in 1900 folder, WP-CU, Box 14.

369. **Backing Bryan put:** Kazin, *A Godly Hero*, 105.

370. **In the early morning:** *ChTr*, 10/10/1900, 1.

370. **"In the few moments":** GHW to KP, 10/15/1900, JP-CU.

370. **The new century:** Details of the war between the large retailers and the *World* may be found in WP-CU, Box 18.

371. **An upturn in:** The modern securities laws were years away. What Pulitzer was doing was not illegal. For instance, his banker obtained confidential information about his bank's forthcoming dividends and purchased shares for Pulitzer to benefit from the higher price the stock would fetch. (DC to JP, 10/14/1904, JP-CU.)

371. **Pulitzer invested in:** In 1902 and 1904, Pulitzer asked Clarke to sell railroad and steel stocks because he was uncomfortable owning them. In one instance, Clarke

replied, "It would seem a pity to make the sacrifice simply because your sense of what is right and just is not complied with" (DC to JP, 9/2/1902, JP-CU); JP to DC, undated, JP-CU, Box 8.

371. **All the income:** DuVivier and Company to KP, 4/5/1901; Gebrüder Simon to JP, 12/5/1900; GWH to KP, 2/21/1901, JP-CU.

371. **The new mansion:** William Mead to Hughmon Hawley, 12/14/1900, MMW.

372. **Just when matters:** Stanford White to JP, 2/11/1902, MMW.

372. **In the circulation war:** DCS to JP, 9/17/1891, WP-CU. Earlier in the year, when giving instructions to his editors, Pulitzer used an example that eerily came to pass, "Not even if McKinley is assassinated."(JP comment, in Merrill summary upon return from Jekyll, 3/8–10/1901 WP-CU.)

372. **For the first:** WAS, 324; BM memo, 10/21/1901, WP-CU.

373. **On the other hand:** PB to JP, 9/10/1901, WP-CU.

373. **The combination of:** Two years later the *Wall Street Journal*, which regularly commented on the city's journalism, noted the change. "The *World* has in the past few years retained all the more desirable attributes of the 'yellow' journalism, [but] it has abandoned many of the methods of degraded demagoguery which have made the *Journal* a stench in the nostrils of people who are able to think." (*WSJ*, 5/11/1903, 1.)

373. **The calm that Pulitzer:** Figures contained in 1902 Folder, JP-CU, Box 19.

373. **In choosing art:** GHL to JP, 3/24/1902, JP-CU.

374. **Kate was willing:** JP to KP, 4/16/1902, JP-CU. In fairness, Joseph also included tender words about how much he was thinking of her. But these may well have been written to make her feel better or may have been the idea of Butes, who would have taken the dictation.

374. **Kate, however, did not:** GHL to AB, 5/23/1902, JP-CU.

374. **"I not only":** DCS-JP, 254.

375. **Joseph left Kate:** Dr. Bounus to JP, 7/3/1902, JP-CU; KP to GHL, 7/27/1902, JP-CU.

375. **Alone in Maine:** GHL to AB, 8/9/1902 and AB to GHL, 8/10/1902, JP-CU.

375. **In September, John Dillon:** *BoGl*, 10/16/1902, 4; *ChTr.* 10/17/1902, 12.

376. **For an additional:** JP to FDW, 10/16/1902. Bills, letters, and drawings, 10/29/1902; prepaid voucher, 10/29/1902, JP-CU; JP dictation to White Star, 8/28/1905, LS Folder, 1903–1905; JP to White Star, 11/17/1900, JP-CU. White Star kept the mats in storage for times when Pulitzer booked passage. See AI, 196–197.

377. **Years before, while running:** *PD*, 5/30/1879, 2. The meeting was the Thirteenth Annual Session of the Missouri Press Association, held at Columbia, MO, May 27 and 28, 1879; *Chicago Inter-Ocean*, 11/27/1887. See also *NYW*, 4/4/1887, quoted in WRR, 754.

377. **By the 1890s:** *Life*, 9/8/1898, 189. Henry Luce would later buy this magazine and turn it into the famous weekly of the twentieth century.

377. **While he was at rest:** Correspondence, 8/12/1902, JP-CU, indicates that a lawyer came to Maine to revise the will. For an example of press figures with whom Pulitzer discussed his ideas, see H. W. Steed to JP, 7/6/1904, BLMC; "Rough Memorandum," 1902, JP-CU.

378. **Although his idea:** Franklin Prentiss to JP, 11/26/1887, and "Christmas Prizes Offered by Mr. Pulitzer," 11/3/1899, JP-CU; November memo, 1899, JP-LC, Box 2.

378. **Pulitzer assigned Hosmer:** JP to KP, 5/20/1904, JP-CU.

378. **On the train:** JP to GWH, 8/11/1902, JP-CU; DCS-JP, 435; *AtCo*, 2/3/1903, 5.

379. **Ignoring Seitz's opinion:** JP to GWH, 8/11/1902, JP-CU.

379. **On Sunday, February 22:** Volo and Volo, *Family Life in Nineteenth-Century America*, 196.

379. **Pulitzer let loose:** JP telegram, 2/26/1903; WP-CU, DCS to JP, 2/27/1903; JP

memorandum, 2/27/1903; JP memo to DCS, 2/28/1903; Council notes, 3/2/1903, WP-CU.

380. **Pulitzer replied that:** Gale was awarded the Pulitzer Prize for Drama in 1921, for a play based on her novel *Miss Lulu Bett*. For more on her work at the *World*, see Morris, *The Rose Man of Sing Sing,* 155–156.

380. **When Edith arrived:** *BoGl*, 5/9/1903, 20; Edith Pulitzer to JP, 5/1903, JP-CU; *NYT*, 5/9/1903, 8.

380. **Pulitzer took great joy:** Draft of letter in July 3–6, 1903 Folder, JP-CU, as well as numerous other items in the files.

381. **In fact, not long after:** James Tuohy to JP, 7/17/1903, JP-CU. I have chosen not to use the man's name, as there is no way to ascertain his side of the story. There exists one letter in which the man is said to deny the charges.

381. **One reader in particular:** JWC to JP, February 1903, WP-CU.

382. **Writing to Joseph:** KP to JP, 6/21/1903, JP-CU.

CHAPTER 27: CAPTURED FOR THE AGES

383. **In early 1904:** JWB, 183–185.

384. **For Kate, the winter:** KP to JP, 2/19/1904; KP to JP, 2/4/1904; JP to KP, 2/22/1904; KP to JP, 2/23/1904; KP to JP, 3/1/1904, JP-CU.

385. **Remaining in New York:** JPII to JP, 4/7/1904; JP to AB, 1/29/1904, JP-CU.

385. **Harvard decided that:** JPII to JP, 2/15/1904, JP-CU.

385. **After her time:** KP to JP, 5/4/1904, KP to JP, 5/13/1904, JP-CU. J. P. Morgan was also resting in Aix-les-Bains. "If you two get together there will be an interesting time," said Pulitzer's banker Dumont Clarke (DC to JP, 5/6/1904, JP-CU).

386. **"In all my planning":** JP, "The College of Journalism," *North American Review* (May 1904), 680.

386. **However, in the year:** DCS-JP, 457.

386. **Butler consented but:** Butler to George L. Rives, 8/15/1903, quoted in Boylan, *Pulitzer's School,* 15.

387. **Realizing that the story:** *NYT*, 8/16/1903, 6; TR to Robert Underwood Johnson, 12/17/1908, Roosevelt, *Letters*, Vol. 6, 1428.

387. **None of the public praise:** DCS-JP, 460.

387. **In Aix-les-Bains:** JP to KP, 5/25/1904 (misdated as 1905), JP-CU.

387. **Joseph didn't rest:** Transcripts of Pulitzer's Pitman Shorthand Notebooks, 1903–1905, LS.

388. **When Pulitzer's mood:** JP to JPII, 5/23/1904 (misdated as 1905), JP-CU.

388. **None of Pulitzer's secretaries:** JP to KP, transcripts of Pulitzer's Pitman Shorthand Notebooks, 1903–1905, LS.

388. **His cruelty stung:** KP to JP, 9/15/1904, JP-CU.

388. **The elections of 1904:** AB to SW, 1/1/1904, WP-CU.

389. **Ralph dutifully reported:** RP to JP, 1/4/1904, and JP to RP, 1/25/1904, JP-CU. Roosevelt's interest in seeing Pulitzer is also noted in a letter from the president to Harvey on January 22, 1904. (Roosevelt, *Letters*, Vol. 3, 702.)

389. **Roosevelt extended his invitation:** TR to J. E. Smith in DCS memo to JP, 9/19/1899, WP-CU.

390. **Pulitzer sent Williams:** "Bryan Statement," 2/25/1904, JP-CU.

391. **As the Democrats settled:** *WSJ*, 6/28/1904, 3; JP to DCS, 5/6/1904, WP-CU.

391. **Pulitzer was elated:** WAS, 356. See also Stoddard, *As I Knew Them,* 56–57; Morris, *Theodore Rex,* 341. Morris believed Parker was swayed by the *New York Times*'s opposition to the silver standard. See also Kazin, *A Godly Hero,* 166–120.

391. **From Bar Harbor:** JP to WHM, 8/1904, JP-LC.

392. **Pulitzer had long sought:** JP editorial memo, September 1904, WP-CU.

392. **The ten questions:** J. W. Slaght to BM, 10/20/1904, WP-CU; Klein, *Life and Legend of E. H. Harriman*, 364.

393. **Roosevelt considered the attacks:** TR to Henry Cabot Lodge, 10/31/1904, Roosevelt, *Letters*, Vol. 4, 1006–1007; JP, draft of editorial, JP-CU, Box 31.

393. **As 1905 began:** David Francis to JP, 2/22/1905; JP to FDW, 3/18/1905; JP to Francis, 3/1/1905; Francis to JP, 3/2/1905, JP-CU.

393. **When Francis returned:** JP to Francis, 3/3/1905; JP to FDW, 3/10/1905, JP-CU.

394. **"Mr. Pulitzer is alone":** *ChTr*, 2/3/1905, 6.

394. **On April 10:** KP to JP, 4/11/1905; JP to RP, 5/25/1905, JP-CU.

394. **Newspaper management was:** GWH took down the conversation. See November 1904, JP-CU, Box 31.

395. **Kate had mailed:** JT to JP, 3/12/1902; JP to GWH, 4/15/1903, JP-CU.

395. **Finally the painter consented:** KP to JP, 4/11/1905.

396. **By mid-May:** KP to JP, 5/8/1905; notes on undated sheet, 5/15/1905, JP-CU.

396. **Her portrait complete:** MAM to JP, 5/21/1905, JP-CU.

396. **Kate wanted to leave:** JP to Edith Pulitzer, 5/12/1905; see also JP dictation, May 9–14 Folder, Box 34; JP to KP, 5/14/1905; JP dictation to KP, 5/25/1905, JP-CU.

396. **Almost in a pique:** JP to EP, 6/1/1905, and EP to JP, 6/2/1905, JP-CU.

396. **Unaware of her husband's:** KP to JP, 6/16/1905, JP-CU.

397. **Pulitzer took his turn:** James Tuohy to JP, 4/4/1905; JT to JP, 4/26/1905, JP-CU.

397. **Accompanying Pulitzer to London:** JP to Bettina Wirth, undated June Folder, 1904, JP-CU, Box 30; JP to Dr. Van Noorden, 10/1906, JP to AB, 6/18/19093, JP-CU.

397. **When Thwaites first:** Thwaites, *Velvet and Vinegar*, 51–53; Mortimer to JP, 1/19/1902, JP-CU.

398. **On this trip:** KP to JP, 5/8/1905, JP-CU; Thwaites, *Velvet and Vinegar*, 51–53.

CHAPTER 28: FOREVER UNSATISFIED

399. **The story had surfaced:** Beard, *After the Ball*, 171–178.

400. **The *World* aggressively:** DCS-JP, 275.

400. **The staff usually:** JP to FC, DCS-JP, 280.

400. **How to please:** Memo to JP, probably written by Samuel Williams, 10/1907, WP-CU.

400. **Within a month:** JP to DCS, 8/28/1905, JP-LC.

401. **Merrill was wounded:** WHM to JP, 9/14/1905, WP-CU.

401. **Worried that he might:** AB to WHM, 11/14/1905; WM to AB, 11/20/1904, WP-CU. Four years later, Pulitzer instructed Seitz to buy letters that Pulitzer had written to Townsend in the 1870s. (See JP to DCS, 4/2/1909, JP-LC.) It is unlikely that any of these letters contained anything particularly scandalous. Rather, Pulitzer probably felt that his frank comments about political figures would be embarrassing if quoted.

401. **Ralph finally screwed up his courage:** RP to JP, 7/28/1904, and Nolan and Loeb to JP, 1/9/1905, JP-CU.

402. **Money was of little concern:** RP to JP, 6/6/1905, JP-CU; KP to Sally, 9/20/1905, JP-MHS.

402. **On October 14:** *WaPo, NYT, BoGl*, 10/8/1905; KP to JP, 7/2/1905; and KP to JP, 7/12/1905, JP-CU.

402. **For a brief moment:** RP to JP, 10/14/1905, quoted in *WAS*, 374.

403. **The father expressed:** JP to RP, 10/5/1905, JP-CU.

403. **Joseph decided that:** Walker, *City Editor*, 6. See also Morris, *The Rose Man of Sing Sing*.

403. **In April, Joseph called:** Chapin, *Charles Chapin's Story*, 216.

404. **His father's continued harshness:** JPII to JP, 12/12/1906. The Reminiscences of Joseph Pulitzer Jr., October 7, 1954, transcript, p. 15, the Oral History Collection of Columbia University. For the full story of JPII's rise, see Pfaff, *Joseph Pulitzer II*.

404. **After Joe was banished:** Telegraph notes, 5/15/1906; KP to JP, 11/24/1906, JP-CU.

404. **Kate, her companion:** KP to JP, 5/16/1906, JP-CU.

405. **In London, Kate:** KP to JP, 5/7/1906, and 5/20/1906, JP-CU.

405. **After Paris, the group:** Edith Pulitzer to JP, 5/24/1906, JP-CU.

406. **Kate returned to:** KP to JP, 8/28/1906, JP-CU.

406. **After consecutive failed bids:** KP to JP, 10/28/1906, JP-CU; Nasaw, *The Chief*, 156–158.

406. **Of all of Hearst's enemies:** *WAS*, 383; JP editorial memo, 9/1904, WP-CU.

406. **Hearst, however, knew:** *ChTr*, 10/28/1906, 1.

407. **In the end:** *WaPo*, 11/18/1906, 11.

407. **Three decades after:** The Reminiscences of Joseph Pulitzer Jr., October 7, 1954, transcript, p. 39, the Oral History Collection of Columbia University.

407. **Kate was proud:** KP to JP, 11/18/1906 and 11/11/1906, JP-CU.

408. **Reaching age seventy-five:** GWH to JP, 12/25/1906, JP-CU.

408. **She stayed in New York:** KP to JP, 12/24/1906; JP to AB, 12/23/1906, JP-CU.

408. **Shortly after New Year's Day:** KP to JP, 1/12/1907, JP-CU.

409. **"You would be":** KP to JP, 2/5/1907, JP-CU.

409. **To her pleasure:** Stephen MacKenna to JP, 3/6/1907, JP-CU; *WRR*, 562.

409. **"As to the sittings":** Butler, *Rodin*, 408.

409. **Pulitzer's French:** *NYW*, 10/31/1911.

410. **The sittings with Rodin:** Doods, *Journal and Letters of Stephen MacKenna*, 32.

410. **On April 10:** *WaPo*, 4/12/1907, 4; *ChTr*, 4/11/1907, 7; *NYT*, 4/11/1907, 5.

410. **There still was no truce:** JP to JPII, 5/27/1907, JP-CU.

410. **Joseph's somber mood:** Marcosson, *Phillips*, 134–135.

411. **That Butes went:** AB to DCS, 2/27/1904.

412. **In the fall:** Undated, unsigned report, filed in December 1908 Folder, JP-CU, Box 58.

412. **The $1.5 million *Liberty*:** JP, May 1906 Folder, Box 39, JP-CU.

413. **As a result:** JP to GWH, 4/1907, JP-CU.

413. **On a Sunday morning:** The visit was on July 26, 1908. A copy boy, Alexander L. Schlosser, who later became an editor, recorded the events of Pulitzer's visit to the *World*. See JWB, 208–214.

413. **Clarke smiled but:** GWH and DCS agree on the number of visits Pulitzer had made to the building since its construction.

414. **The truth was:** JP and Clark Firestone, conversation transcript, 8/5/1908, WP-CU.

415. **Two months before:** *NYW*, 5/10/1908; *BoGl*, 5/10/1908, 13; *WaPo*, 5/2/1908, 2, AI 28.

415. **In August, Pulitzer:** FC to JP, 2/8/1908, WP-CU.

415. **In fact, Bryan's:** Ibid.

416. **Pulitzer instructed Cobb:** JP to FC, quoted in DCS-JP, 328.

416. **Pulitzer's efforts were:** Notes 7/6/1908, WP-CU.

416. **Without knowing Pulitzer's motives:** DCS-JP, 340.

CHAPTER 29: CLASH OF TITANS

417. **On the evening:** *NYT,* 10/2/1908, 3.
417. **According to rumors:** Frank Cobb, "How the Story Came into the Office," 3, EHP, Folder 21.
418. **The story had immense appeal:** Roosevelt, *Autobiography,* 553.
418. **Speer left his office:** *NYT,* 2/23/1915, 13; JP to Adolph Ochs, 3/26/1908, NYTA.
418. **After listening to:** DCS-JP, 352.
418. **Around ten o'clock:** Frank Cobb, "How the Story Came into the Office"; DCS-JP, 353.
419. **As soon as:** Whitley later claimed that he had told Van Hamm the article was untrue. But the *World* wisely kept the copy of the proof that Whitley marked up. According to Frank Cobb, "It shows that Mr. Whitley scratched out the name of Charles P. Taft and substituted Henry W. Taft. Then he erased the name of Henry W. Taft and restored the name of Charles P. Taft." (Cobb, "How the Story Came into the Office," 1–2.)
419. **"But for Mr. Cromwell":** Ibid., 4.
419. **Over the next:** JP telegram, 10/2/1909, quoted in DCS-JP, 343; *NYW,* 10/14/1908, 1, and 10/21/1908, 1.
419. **The articles, while conceding:** *Indianapolis News,* 11/2/1908.
420. **Pulitzer was sailing:** JP to FC, 11/3/1908, JP-LC; DCS-JP, 349.
420. **With the election over:** TR to William D. Foulke, 12/1/1908, reprinted in *ChTr,* 12/8/1908, 1.
420. **An astonished Pulitzer:** *WaPo,* 12/7/1908, 2; DCS-JP, 356.
421. **Roosevelt had not mentioned:** Cobb, "How the Story Came into the Office," 9.
421. **By the time the *Liberty*:** *NYW,* 12/8/1908.
422. **"I do not know":** JP conversation notes, 8/27/1908, JP-LC.
422. **"When I was":** TR to HS, 12/9/1908, HSP.
422. **Roosevelt wanted revenge:** Alfred H. Kelly, "Constitutional Liberty and the Law of Libel: A Historian's View," *American Historical Review,* Vol. 74, No. 2 (December 1968), 429–452.
422. **Stimson found the envelope:** HS to TR, 12/10/1908, HSP. To begin his research in a stealthy manner, Stimson had to obtain the Attorney General's permission to requisition $10 to buy old issues of the *World.* "No source is open to me to read the files of the *World* for that month in connection with the Panama matter without possible danger of arousing interest and publicity": HS to AB, 12/21/1908, NARA-MD.
423. **Impatient, Roosevelt looked:** Rhodes, *The McKinley and Roosevelt Administrations,* 271.
423. **"It seems to me":** TR to Knox, 12/10/1908, Roosevelt, *Letters,* Vol. 6, 1418–1419.
423. **Next, Roosevelt composed:** *WaPo,* 1/17/1909, 1.
423. **On December 15:** *ChTr,* 12/16/1908, 2.
424. **Two minutes into the message:** *NYT,* 12/16/1908, 1.
424. **While Roosevelt was seeking:** Thwaites, *Velvet and Vinegar,* 57–58.
425. **Pulitzer also summoned:** Van Hamm to JP, 1/7/1909, WP-CU.
425. **This didn't satisfy:** JP to DCS, 12/16/1908. WP-CU.
425. **There was nothing:** JP memo, phoned to Cobb, 12/15/1908, JP-LC.
425. **By nightfall, Pulitzer:** Mr. Pulitzer's statement, 12/15/1908, JP-LC.
425. **It was a half-truth:** Memo written on board *Liberty,* 6/26/1908; JP to Williams, 9/12/1908, JP-LC.

426. **Aid came from:** *ChTr,* 12/7/1908, 6. Bryan also wrote a supportive note to Cobb. Bryan to FC, 12/19/1908, WP-CU.

426. **Pulitzer believed prison:** JP note to Robert P. Porter, 12/15/1908, JP-LC; Notes, 12/16/1908, JP-LC; DCS to JP, 12/17/1908, WP-CU.

427. **The *Liberty*'s southerly course:** *WaPo,* 12/20/1908, 2; *ChTr,* 12/20/1908, 2; JP to Cobb, 12/18/1908, and Notes of Mr. Pulitzer's Conversations, 12/19–20/1908, JP-LC.

427. **Summoned, Cobb raced:** JP to DCS, 12/19/1908, and Confidential memo to Cobb, 12/23/1908, JP-LC.

428. **Legally, Pulitzer's guess:** HS to Bonaparte, 1/15/1909, CJB.

428. **Despite Stimson's hesitance:** Butt, *The Letters of Archie Butt,* 314.

428. **Later that night:** RHL to JP, 2/7/1909, WP-CU. Earl Harding reported Roosevelt's words as follows: "As to the men I'm bringing libel suit against, I will cinch them. I will cinch them in Federal Courts, if I can. If I cannot cinch them there, I will cinch them in the State Courts. But the one sure thing is we will cinch them." Harding, *The Untold Story of Panama,* 97; *WRR,* 710; *WaPo,* 1/31/1909, 1.

428. **With the clock ticking:** DCS-JP, 373; JP told DCS "get into the habit of using the cipher as much as necessity requires." (Notes dictated 2/10/1909, JP-LC); Davis to DCS, 1/18/1909, JP-LC; Notes 2/1/1909, JP-LC.

428. **Pulitzer could not restrain:** JP to FC, 1/26/1909; JP undated notes, JP-LC, Box 8.

429. **The Justice Department's attorneys:** *BoGl,* 1/17/1909, 12.

429. **Stimson was convinced:** *NYT,* 1/17/1909, 1 and 1/19/1908, 3.

429. **Ralph, who feared:** *NYT,* 1/21/1909, 1.

430. **Stimson was infuriated:** HS to Bonaparte, 1/21/1909, CJB.

430. **Cobb seized the:** "Freedom of the Press," *NYW,* 2/6/1909. Amusingly, a compositor changed "persecution" to "prosecution" in setting the editorial into type. FC to JP, 2/6/1909, WP-CU.

430. **In the legal proceedings:** *WaPo,* 2/2/1909, 1.

431. **"Thus far, we":** HS to Bonaparte, 2/8/1909, CJB; TR to HS, 1/28/1909, HSP.

431. **The following morning:** *NYT,* 1/30/1909, 3.

431. **"To put it":** Cobb, *Exit Laughing,* 156–161.

432. **"Even so," Jerome continued:** Stimson had feared this might be the case. He wrote to Bonaparte that Jerome's "personal relations with the *New York World* have naturally made him reluctant to push forward under a charge of officiousness and a desire for personal revenge." (HS to Bonaparte, 1/28/1909, CJB.)

432. **Stimson remained firmly:** Ibid. and HS to Bonaparte, 2/8/1909, and 2/10/1909, CJB.

433. **Bonaparte brought the:** Bonaparte to HS, 2/9/1909, CJB; TR to HS, 2/10/1909, HSP.

433. **Stimson did not cower:** HS to TR, 2/11/1909, HSP.

433. **On his yacht:** Reporters' notes on grand jury, WP-CU, Box 46; JP dictation, 2/10/1908, and JP notes 2/5/1909, JP-LC; *WaPo,* 2/18/1906, 1.

434. **Frank Cobb was ready:** *NYW,* 2/18/1909.

434. **Arrest warrants were:** JP to FC, 3/1909, JP-LC.

434. **McNamara consulted the attorney general:** 2/9/1909, CJB; 2/15/ 1909, 5/7/1910, NARA-MD; TR to HS, 2/13/1909, HSP; *NYT,* 2/24/1909, 2; FDW to JP, 2/26/1909, JP-CU.

435. **Meanwhile, the grand jury:** HS to George Wickersham, 3/5/1909, NARA-MD.

435. **These indictments, like:** A copy of the applicable statute can been seen in Barrows, *New Legislation Concerning Crimes, Misdemeanors, and Penalties.* The single copy sent to the federal building was not to a subscriber. Rather, it was a copy sent for inspection as required by postal laws.

435. **By the time the *Liberty* steamed:** *WaPo*, 3/6/1909, 1.
436. **His nerves agitated:** Notes, 3/8/1909, JP-LC; GWH to JP, undated but written shortly after his 4/18/1909 grand jury appearance, in April 1909 folder, JP-CU; Shakespeare, *Julius Caesar*, Act IV, Scene 1.
436. **Clearing Sandy Point:** Pulitzer's staff was always prepared for such an event. In February, money had been given to Tuohy in London for the payroll for the ship's crew should the *Liberty* suddenly be overseas. (AB to Davis, 2/9/1909, JP-CU.) JAS to JP, 4/6/1909, JP-CU; DCS-JP, 376–377.
436. **Pulitzer spent the summer:** AT to FC, 9/3/1909, JP-LC.
437. **Each side believed:** McNamara to George Wickersham, 7/27/1909, NARA-MD; Harding, *The Untold Story of Panama*, 61.
437. **Harding was among:** Harding, *Untold Story*, 67–70.
438. **Harding decided:** Guyol report, EHP.
438. **When Harding and Guyol:** The officials reported to Washington that Harding and Guyol told Colombians they were there "to right the great wrong done Colombia by the United States and restore Panama to its former state." (Huffington to Attorney General, 12/11/1909, NARA-MD.)
438. **Harding concluded:** Huffington to Attorney General, 12/11/1909, NARA-MD, Quoted in Guyol report, EHP, Folder 38. Choral hydrate is one of the oldest known sleep inducing drugs and is still used today for the purpose of date rape.
439. **Harding took matters:** Huffington to attorney general, 12/11/1909. NARA-MD. Seitz did not seem to believe the letter from the legation. "Harding was waylaid in Colombia in the belief that he carried certain documents of value—which he did not": DCS-JP, 377–378.

CHAPTER 30: A SHORT REMAINING SPAN

441. **After disagreeable stays:** NT to DCS, 10/1/1909, JP-LC.
441. **Albert had also:** JWB, 256. Fanny Barnard Pulitzer died 6/24/1909, in New York, at age fifty-three: *NYT*, 6/26/1909, 7.
442. **Over time, Albert's behavior:** *The Call*, 3/10/1909, 1. Albert's passion for the city's oysters also gave rise to a tale republished for weeks in American newspapers. A companion at luncheon recommended that Albert put horseradish on his oysters. Uncertain if his Viennese physician allowed him to eat this condiment, Albert telegraphed home. He promptly received permission. The high cost of the telegrams provided an irresistible feast of merriment for reporters, such as one who began his story with the lead, "For the privilege of eating horseradish, Albert Pulitzer paid $40." (*LAT*, 3/10/1909, 13.)
442. **While he was in San Francisco:** *Oakland Tribune*, 10/17/1909, 4; *NYT*, 4/6/1909, 1; *ChTr*, 11/6/1909, 13.
442. **By fall, his memoir:** *NYT*, 10/5/1909, 4; *ChTr*, 10/05/1909, 5. Eulogy reprinted in APM.
443. **Joseph learned of:** Thwaites, *Velvet and Vinegar*, 65–66.
443. **Several days later:** Adam Politzer to JP, 10/16/1909, JP-CU. Joseph was mentioned in Albert's will of 1881. It provided that he should receive Albert's gold Waltham watch and chain, gold cufflinks, and turquoise shirt studs and asked that he watch over Albert's son Walter. But the will in effect when Albert died made no mention of Joseph. (See JWB, 254–255.)
444. **As winter set in:** DCS-JP, 392–393.
444. **Contributing to Pulitzer's melancholy:** JAS to JP, 12/28/1909, JP-CU; JP notes for RP, 1/26/1910, JP-LC.
445. **Pulitzer's loneliness was:** JP to JPII, 5/27/1907, JP-CU.

445. **Kate did her best:** KP to JP, 9/24/1902, JP-CU.
445. **His twenty-nine-year-old son:** JPII to JP, 1/4/1910, MHS.
446. **Once again, Pulitzer revised:** JP to Edward Sheppard, 4/25/1910, JP-CU. Hughes apparently declined to be a trustee, but Pulitzer kept him in the will nonetheless: JP to KP, 5/5/1910, JP-CU. See also NT to DCS, 1/25/1910, JP-LC .
446. **"I am of":** ChTr, 10/13/1909, 8.
446. **On January 25:** NYT, 1/27/1910, 3.
447. **The law was intended:** The Roosevelt Panama Libel Case, 98; NYT, 1/26/1910, 8; WaPo, 1/26/1910, 4; The History of the United States District Court for the Southern District of New York, 12.
447. **The only party:** NYT, 2/26/1910, 8.
448. **In March, Joe:** Pfaff, Joseph Pulitzer II, 107.
448. **Even Wickham had:** JP to Elinor Wickham, 8/31/1909, quoted in Pfaff, Joseph Pulitzer II, 104.
448. **In person, Joseph:** JPII to JP, 3/18/1910, JP-MHS, quoted in Pfaff, Joseph Pulitzer II, 107–108.
448. **The children gone:** NYT, 11/14/1911, 1.
449. **Roosevelt's prosecution of:** NYT, 10/25/1910; WaPo, 10/25/1910, 11.
449. **Pulitzer's attorney once again:** Harding, Untold Story, 87.
449. **Ten weeks later:** Harding, Untold Story, 77.
450. **Pulitzer got word:** NYW, 1/4/1911; Harding, Untold Story, 82.
450. **As Phillips neared:** NYT, 1/24/1911, 1; WaPo, 1/24/1911, 1; ChTr, 1/24/1911, 1.
451. **Funeral services were held:** JP to RP, 3/10/1911; telegram, 4/11/1911; NT to RP, 3/12/1911; KP to RP, 5/28/1911, JP-LC.
451. **One of Pulitzer's many doctors:** Dr. Heinbrand to JP, June 1911, JP-CU; Wood, Pharmacology and Therapeutics for Students and Practitioners of Medicine, 103.
451. **In the summer:** JP to Emma Cunlifee-Owens, 3/4/1911, WP-CU.
452. **Pulitzer and Cobb:** Notes of conversation, 6/22/1911, in June 17–21 folder, WP-CU, Box 51. Pulitzer was an unabashed fan of Wilson's. He telegraphed Wilson after Wilson's election victory of 1910, urged Cobb to promote Wilson continually, and even proposed publishing a campaign pamphlet. (JP conversation with FC, undated 1910 Folder, JP-LC, Box 9; JP to FC, 11/21/1910, JP-LC.)
452. **Concluding his meeting:** NYT, 7/2/1911, X4, and 6/11/1911, X4.
452. **Joseph spent time:** AI, 213–214.
453. **Joseph's favorite indulgence:** Transcript of conversation written by Firestone, 8/5/1911, WP-CU.
454. **Wallace C. Sabine:** Wallace C. Sabine to McKim et al., 5/13/1902, JP-CU.
454. **The house's proximity:** JP memo for RP, 10/5/1911, WP-CU; JP to JPII, 10/9/1911, JP-CU.
455. **If his employees:** Gaynor, quoted in RHL to JP, 10/8/1911,WP-CU.
455. **Roosevelt never let up:** JP notes, 10/5/1911, JP-CU.
455. **Of the three men:** WRH to JP, 10/9/1911, WP-CU.

CHAPTER 31: SOFTLY, VERY SOFTLY

456. **On the second day:** AI, 234–236.
456. **The following day:** Syracuse Herald, 10/20/1911, 11.
457. **Pulitzer's German reader:** Christopher Hare, The Life of Louis XI: The Rebel Dauphin and the Statesmen King (New York: Scribners, 1907). The book's last words, which Pulitzer did not hear, were, "The France of Louis XII is the justification of Louis XI" taken from Stanley Leathes, Cambridge Modern History, Vol. 1, The Reformation (London, MacMillan, 1904).

457. **The following day:** *Colorado Springs Gazette,* 10/30/1911, 1.

458. **When they reached:** JP to GWH, January 7, 1911, quoted in DCS-JP, x; *New York American,* 10/30/1911.

458. **Pulitzer's death was:** Death certificate, South Carolina Room, Charleston County Main Library.

458. **So many former:** Elizabeth Jordan, "The Passing of the Chief," *New Yorker,* 12/18/1947.

461. **Kate outlived her husband:** Pfaff, *Joseph Pulitzer II,* 144.

462. **In the early morning:** Barrett, *The End of the World,* 154, 237; JWB, 438.

Bibliography

Manuscript collections are listed at the beginning of the endnotes section on page 471. Magazines, journals, and newspapers appear only in the actual notes. All other published and unpublished works cited in the endnotes are listed in full here.

BOOKS

Ackerman, Kenneth D. *Dark Horse: The Surprise Election and Political Murder of President James A. Garfield.* New York: Carroll & Graf, 2003.

Avery, Grace Gilmore, and Floyd C. Shomemaker, eds. *The Messages and Proclamations of the Governors of the State of Missouri,* Vol. 5. Columbia: State Historical Society of Missouri, 1924.

Barclay, Thomas S. *The Liberal Republican Movement in Missouri 1865–1871.* Columbia: State Historical Society of Missouri, 1926.

Barrett, James Wyman. *The End of the World: A Post-Mortem by Its Intangible Assets.* New York: Harper, 1931.

———. *Joseph Pulitzer and His World.* New York: Vanguard, 1941.

Barrows, Samuel J. *New Legislation Concerning Crimes, Misdemeanors, and Penalties.* Washington, DC: GPO, 1900.

Beach, William H. *The First New York (Lincoln) Cavalry.* New York: Lincoln Cavalry Association, 1902.

Beard, Patricia. *After the Ball.* New York: HarperCollins, 2003.

Beattie, William. *The Danube: Its History, Scenes, and Topography.* London: Virtue, 1841.

Berger, Meyer. *The Story of the New York Times: 1851–1951.* New York: Simon & Schuster, 1951.

Bowlby, John. *Attachment and Loss: Loss, Sadness, and Depression,* Vol. 3. New York: Basic Books, 1980.

Boylan, James. *Pulitzer's School: Columbia University's School of Journalism, 1903–2003.* New York: Columbia University Press, 2003.

Brown, Charles H. *The Correspondents' War: Journalism in the Spanish-American War.* New York: Scribner, 1967.

Bruns, Jette. *Hold Dear, as Always,* Adolph E. Schroeder., ed. Adolph E. Schroeder and Carla Schulz-Geisberg, trans. Columbia: University of Missouri Press, 1988.

Burrows, Edwin G., and Mike Wallace. *Gotham: A History of New York City to 1898.* New York: Oxford University Press, 1999.

Butler, Ruth. *Rodin: The Shape of Genius.* New Haven, CT: Yale University Press, 1996.

Butt, Archie. *The Letters of Archie Butt.* New York: Doubleday, Page, 1924.

Campbell, W. Joseph. *Yellow Journalism: Puncturing the Myths, Defining the Legacies.* Praeger, 2001.

Carlson, Oliver. *Brisbane: A Candid Biography.* New York: Stackpole Sons, 1937.

Cashin, Joan E. *First Lady of the Confederacy: Varina Davis's Civil War.* Cambridge, MA: Harvard University Press, 2006.

Chamberlin, Everett. *The Struggle of '72.* Chicago, IL: Union, 1872.

Chambers, Julius. *News Hunting on Three Continents.* New York: Mitchell Kennerley, 1921.

Chapin, Charles. *Charles Chapin's Story.* New York: Putnam, 1920.

Churchill, Allen. *Park Row.* New York: Rinehart, 1958.

Clayton, Charles C. *Little Mack: Joseph B. McCullagh of the St. Louis Globe-Democrat.* Carbondale: Southern Illinois University Press, 1969.

Cobb, Irvin S. *Alias Ben Alibi* . New York: George H. Doran, 1925.

———. *Exit Laughing.* New York: Bobbs-Merrill, 1941.

Collier, Peter, and David Horowitz. *The Rockefellers: An American Dynasty.* New York: Holt, Rinehart, and Winston, 1976.

Corbett, Katharine T., and Howard S. Miller. *Saint Louis in the Gilded Age.* St. Louis: Missouri Historical Society, 1993.

Corcoran, William. *A Grandfather's Legacy: Containing a Sketch of His Life and Obituary Notices of Some Members of His Family Together with Letters from His Friends.* Washington, DC: Henry Polkinhorn, Printer, 1879.

Croffut, William A. *An American Procession: A Personal Chronicle of Famous Men.* Boston, MA: Little, Brown, 1931.

Dacus, J. A., and James W. Buel. *A Tour of St. Louis.* St. Louis, MO: Western, 1878.

Davis, Jefferson. *Private Letters, 1823–1889.* New York: Harcourt, Brace, and World, 1966.

Depew, Chauncey. *My Memories of Eighty Years.* New York: Scribner, 1924.

Dickens, Charles. *Martin Chuzzlewit.* London: University Society, 1908.

Doods, E. R. *Journal and Letters of Stephen MacKenna.* New York: Read Books, 2007.

Douglas, George H. *The Golden Age of the Newspaper.* Greenwich, CT: Greenwood, 1999.

Dreiser, Theodore. *Newspaper Days.* Santa Rosa, CA: Black Sparrow, 2000.

Eberle, Jean Fahey. *Midtown: A Grand Place to Be!* St. Louis, MO: Mercantile Trust, 1980.

Eggleston, George Carey. *Recollections of a Varied Life.* New York: Henry Holt, 1910.

Emery, Edwin, and Michael Emery. *The Press and America: An Interpretive History of the Mass Media.* Englewood Cliffs, NJ: Prentice Hall, 1984.

Filler, Louis. *Voice of the Democracy: A Critical Biography of David Graham Phillips, Journalist, Novelist, Progressive.* University Park: Pennsylvania State University Press, 1978.

Foner, Eric. *Reconstruction: America's Unfinished Revolution: 1863–1877.* New York: Harper & Row, 1988.

Ford, James L. *Forty-Odd Years in the Literary Shop.* New York: Dutton, 1921.

Gallagher, Edward J. *Stilson Hutchins: 1838–1912.* Laconia, NH: Citizen, 1965.

Garrison, Fielding H. *An Introduction to the History of Medicine.* Philadelphia, PA: Saunders, 1914.

Geary, James W. *We Need Men: The Union Draft in the Civil War.* Dekalb: Northern Illinois University Press, 1991.

Gerstäcker, Friedrich. *Gerstäcker's Travels. Rio de Janeiro—Buenos Ayres—Ride through the Pampas—Winter Journey across the Cordilleras—Chili—Valparaiso—California and the Gold Fields.* London and Edinburgh: T. Nelson, 1854.

Gilman, Sander. *The Jew's Body.* New York: Routledge, 1991.

Harding, Earl. *The Untold Story of Panama.* New York: Athene Press, 1959.

Hare, Christopher. *The Life of Louis XI: The Rebel Dauphin and the Statesmen King.* New York: Scribner, 1907.

Hart, Jim Alee. *A History of the St. Louis Globe-Democrat.* Columbia: University of Missouri Press, 1961.

Heaton, John L. *The Story of a Page: Thirty Years of Public Service and Public Discussion in the Editorial Columns of the New York World.* New York: Harper, 1913.

Henry, Robert Hiram. *Editors I Have Known since the Civil War.* Jackson, MS: Kessinger Publishing, 1922.

Hirsch, Mark D. *William C. Whitney: Modern Warwick.* New York: Dodd, Mead, 1948.

The History of the United States District Court for the Southern District of New York. New York: Federal Bar Association, 1962.

Homberger, Eric. *Mrs. Astor's New York: Money and Power in a Gilded Age.* New Haven, CT: Yale University Press, 2002.

Ireland, Alleyne. *Joseph Pulitzer: Reminiscence of a Secretary.* New York: Mitchell Kennerley, 1914.

Johns, Orrick. *Time of Our Lives: The Story of My Father and Myself.* New York: Stackpole, 1937.

Johnson, Willis Fletcher. *George Harvey: A Passionate Patriot.* Boston, MA: Houghton Mifflin, 1929.

Juergens, George. *Joseph Pulitzer and the New York World.* Princeton, NJ: Princeton University Press, 1966.

Kargau, Ernst D. *The German Element in St. Louis.* Baltimore, MD: Genealogical, 2000.

Kazin, Michael. *A Godly Hero: The Life of William Jennings Bryan.* New York: Knopf, 2006.

King, Homer W. *Pulitzer's Prize Editor: A Biography of John A. Cockerill, 1845–1896.* Durham, NC: Duke University Press, 1965.

Klein, Maury. *The Life and Legend of Jay Gould.* Baltimore, MD: Johns Hopkins University Press, 1986.

———. *The Life and Legend of E. H. Harriman.* Chapel Hill: University of North Carolina Press, 2000.

Kluger, Richard. *The Paper: The Life and Death of the New York Herald Tribune.* New York: Knopf, 1986.

Knight, William, ed. *Memorials of Thomas Davidson.* Boston, MA: Gunn, 1907.

Koestler, Frances A. *The Unseen Minority: A Social History of Blindness in America.* Washington, DC: American Foundation for the Blind, 2004.

Komoróczy, Géza, ed. *Jewish Budapest: Monuments, Rites, History.* Budapest: Central European University Press, 1999.

Kósa, Judit N. *The Old Jewish Quarter of Budapest.* Budapest: Corvina, 2005.

Kotter, James C. *Southern Honor and American Manhood: Understanding the Life and Death of Richard Reid.* Baton Rouge: Louisiana State University Press, 2003.

Kremer, Gary. *Heartland History: Essays on the Cultural Heritage of the Central Missouri Region.* St. Louis, MO: G. Bradley, 2001.

Kune, Julian. *Reminiscences of an Octogenarian Hungarian Exile.* Chicago, IL: privately printed, 1911.

Lee, Alfred McClung. *The Daily Newspaper in America: The Evolution of a Social Instrument.* New York: Macmillan, 1937.

Leidecker, Kurt F. *Yankee Teacher: The Life of William Torrey Harris.* New York: Philosophical Library, 1946.

Lemann, Nicholas. *Redemption: The Last Battle of the Civil War.* New York: Farrar, Strauss, and Giroux, 2006.

Loeb, Isidor, and Floyd C. Shoemaker, eds. *Debates of the Missouri Constitutional Convention of 1875.* Columbia, MO: State Historical Society, 1930–1944.

Lupovitch, Howard N. *Jews at the Crossroads: Tradition and Accommodation during the Golden Age of the Hungarian Nobility.* Budapest: Central European University Press, 2007.

Marcosson, Isaac F. *David Graham Phillips and His Times.* New York: Dodd, Mead, 1932.

Maurice, Arthur Bartlett. *The New York of the Novelists.* New York: Dodd, Mead, 1916.

McCagg Jr., William O. *A History of Habsburg Jews.* Bloomington: Indiana University Press, 1992.

McCash, William Barton, and June Hall McCash, *The Jekyll Island Club: Southern Haven for America's Millionaires.* Athens: University of Georgia Press, 1989.

McClellan, George B. *The Gentleman and the Tiger.* Philadelphia: Lippincott, 1956.

McDougall, Walt. *This Is the Life!* New York: Knopf, 1926.

McPherson, James M. *For Cause and Comrades: Why Men Fought in the Civil War.* New York: Oxford University Press, 1997.

Milton, Joyce. *The Yellow Kids: Foreign Correspondents in the Heyday of Yellow Journalism.* New York: Harper and Row, 1989.

Mitchell, Edward P. *Memoirs of an Editor: Fifty Years of American Journalism.* New York: Scribner, 1924.

Morgan, James. *Charles H. Taylor: Builder of the Boston Globe.* Boston: Privately published, 1923.

Morris, Anneta Josephine. "The Police Department of St. Louis." Unpublished, Missouri Historical Society, 1919.

Morris, Edmund. *The Rise of Theodore Roosevelt.* New York: Ballantine, 1979.

———. *Theodore Rex.* New York: Random House, 2001.

Morris, James McGrath. *The Rose Man of Sing Sing: A True Tale of Life, Murder, and Redemption in the Age of Yellow Journalism.* New York: Fordham University Press, 2004.

Morris, Whitmore. *The First Tunstalls in Virginia and Some of Their Descendants.* San Antonio, TX, 1950.

Murdock, Eugene Converse. *One Million Men.* Madison: State Historical Society of Wisconsin, 1971.

Nagel, Charles. *A Boy's Civil War Story.* St. Louis, MO: Eden, 1935.

Nasaw, David. *The Chief: The Life of William Randolph Hearst.* New York: Houghton Mifflin, 2000.

Official Proceedings of the National Democratic Convention, St. Louis, MO, June 27, 28, 29, 1876. St. Louis: Woodward, Tiernan, and Hale, 1876.

Official Proceedings of the National Democratic Convention, 1880. Dayton, OH: Dickinson, 1882.

Paget, John. *Hungary and Transylvania.* London: John Murray, 1839.

Parsons, Miss. *The City of Magyar or Hungary and Her Institutions in 1839–1840.* London: George Virtue, 1840.

Patai, Raphael. *The Jews of Hungary: History, Culture, Psychology.* Detroit, MI: Wayne State University Press, 1996.

Perry, Charles M., ed. *The St. Louis Movement in Philosophy: Some Source Material.* Norman: University of Oklahoma Press, 1930.

Peterson, Norma L. *Freedom and Franchise: The Political Career of B. Gratz Brown.* Columbia: University of Missouri Press, 1965.

Pfaff, Daniel W. *Joseph Pulitzer II and the Post-Dispatch.* University Park: Pennsylvania State University Press, 1991.

Phillips, David Graham. *The Great God Success.* New York: Grosset and Dunlap, 1901.

Pitzman's New Atlas of the City and County of Saint Louis, Missouri, 1878. Philadelphia, PA: A. B. Holcombe, 1878.

Pivány, Eugene. *Hungarians in the American Civil War.* Cleveland, OH: 1913.

Primm, James Neal. *Lion of the Valley: St. Louis, Missouri, 1764–1980.* St. Louis: Missouri Historical Society, 1998.

Proceedings of the Liberal Republican Convention, in Cincinnati, May 1st, 2d, and 3d, 1872. New York: Baker and Godwin, 1872.

Procter, Ben. *William Randolph Hearst: The Early Years, 1863–1910.* New York: Oxford University Press, 1998.

Pulszky, Francis, and Theresa Pulszky. *"White, Red, Black": Sketches of Society in the United States during the Visit of Their Guest,* Vol. 2. London: Trubner, 1853.

Rammelkamp, Julian S. *Pulitzer's Post-Dispatch, 1878–1883.* Princeton, NJ: Princeton University Press, 1967.

Renehan, Edward. *The Dark Genius of Wall Street: The Misunderstood Life of Jay Gould.* New York: Basic Books, 2005.

Rhodes, James Ford. *The McKinley and Roosevelt Administrations, 1897–1909.* New York: Macmillan, 1922.

Riis, Jacob. *Children of the Poor.* New York: Scribner, 1892.

Robb, Graham. *Strangers: Homosexual Love in the Nineteenth Century.* New York: Norton, 2003.

Roberts, Chalmers M. *The Washington Post: The First Hundred Years.* Boston, MA: Houghton Mifflin, 1977.

The Roosevelt Panama Libel Case against the New York World and Indianapolis News. New York: New York World, 1910.

Roosevelt, Theodore. *An Autobiography.* New York: MacMillan, 1913.

———. *The Letters of Theodore Roosevelt.* Cambridge, MA: Harvard University Press, 1951.

Rosewater, Victor. *History of Cooperative News Gathering in the United States.* New York: Appleton, 1930.

Ross, Earle Dudley. *The Liberal Republican Movement.* Seattle: University of Washington Press, 1910.

Scharf, J. Thomas. *History of Saint Louis City and County,* Vols. 1 and 2. Philadelphia, PA: Louis H. Evert, 1883.

Schurz, Carl. *Intimate letters of Carl Schurz, 1841–1869.* Madison: State Historical Society of Wisconsin.

Seitz, Don C. *Joseph Pulitzer: His Life and Letters.* New York: Simon & Schuster, 1924.

Selin, Helaine, and Hugh Shapiro. *Medicine across Cultures: History and Practice of Medicine in Non-Western Cultures.* New York: Springer, 2003.

Shoemaker, Floyd C., ed. *Journal Missouri Constitutional Convention of 1875.* Jefferson City, MO: Hugh Stevens, 1920.

Silverman, Phyllis Rolfe. *Never Too Young to Know: Death in Children's Lives.* New York: Oxford University Press, 2000.

Smythe, Ted Curtis. *The Gilded Age Press: 1865–1900.* Westport, CT: Praeger, 2003.

Snider, Denton. *The St. Louis Movement in Philosophy, Literature, Education, Psychology with Chapters of Autobiography.* St. Louis, MO: Sigma, 1920.

Starr, Stephen Z. *The Union Cavalry in the Civil War,* Vol. 2. Baton Rouge: Louisiana State University Press, 1981.

Stealey, O. O. *130 Pen Pictures of Live Men.* Washington, DC: Privately published, 1910.

Stevenson, James H. *Boots and Saddles: A History of the First Volunteer Cavalry of the War.* New York: Patriot Publishing, 1879.

Stoddard, Henry L. *As I Knew Them.* New York: Harper, 1927.

Storr, Anthony. *Solitude: A Return to Self.* New York: Free Press, 1988.

Strouse, Jean. *Morgan: American Financier.* New York: Random House, 1999.

Sugar, Peter F., ed. *A History of Hungary.* Bloomington: Indiana University Press, 1990.

Swanberg, W. A. *Pulitzer.* New York: Scribner, 1967.

Taylor, J. N., and M. O. Crooks, *Sketch Book of Saint Louis.* St. Louis, MO: George Knapp, 1858.

Thwaites, Norman. *Velvet and Vinegar.* London: Grayson and Grayson, 1932.

Trefousse, Hans Louis. *Carl Schurz: A Biography.* Knoxville: University of Tennessee Press, 1982.

Turner, Hy. *When Giants Ruled: The Story of Park Row.* New York: Fordham University Press, 1999.

Twain, Mark. *Life on the Mississippi.* Boston, MA: James L. Osgood, 1883.

———. *Adventures of Tom Sawyer.* New York: Harper, 1903.

Volo, James M., and Dorothy Denneen Volo. *Family Life in Nineteenth-Century America.* Greenwich, CT: Greenwood, 2007.

Walker, Stanley. *City Editor.* New York: F. A. States, 1935.

Wass, Hannelore, and Charles A. Corr, eds. *Childhood and Death.* New York: Hemisphere, 1984.

Watterson, Henry. *Henry Marse: An Autobiography*, Vol. 1. New York: George Doran, 1919.

Wells, John Soelberg. *A Treatise on the Disease of the Eye*. Lea's Sons, 1883.

Wharton, Edith. *Old New York*. New York: Scribner, 1924.

White, Carl. *The German-Language Press in America*. Louisville: University of Kentucky Press, 1957.

Wilson, James Grant. *The Memorial History of the City of New York*, Vol. 5. New York: New York History, 1893.

Woerner, William F. *J. Gabriel Woerner: A Biographical Sketch*. St. Louis, MO: Privately published, 1912.

Wolf, Simon. *The Presidents I Have Known from 1860–1918*. Washington, DC: Press of Byron S. Adams, 1918.

Wood, Horatio C. *Pharmacology and Therapeutics for Students and Practitioners of Medicine*. Philadelphia: Lippincott, 1916.

The World, Its History, Its New Home. New York: World, c. 1890.

Yelverston, Thérèse. *Teresina in America*. London: Richard Bentley, 1875.

Young, Andrew W. *The American Statesman: A Political History*, rev. and enlarged by Geo. T. Ferris. New York: Henry S. Goodspeed, 1877.

DISSERTATIONS

Christensen, Lawrence Oland. "Black St. Louis: A Study in Race Relations 1865–1916." PhD diss., University of Missouri, 1972.

Eichhorst, Thomas. "Representative and Reporter." MA thesis, Lincoln University, 1968.

Fagan, Susan R. "Thomas Davidson: Dramatist of the Life of Learning." PhD diss., Rutgers University, 1980.

Miradli, Robert. "The Journalism of David Graham Phillips." PhD diss., New York University, 1985.

Moehle, Oden. "History of St. Louis, 1878–1882. MA thesis, Washington University, 1954.

Olson, Audrey Louis. "St. Louis Germans, 1850–1920: The Nature of an Immigrant Community and Its Relation to the Assimilation Process." PhD diss., University of Kansas, 1970.

Reynolds, William Robinson. "Joseph Pulitzer." PhD diss., Columbia University, 1950.

Saalberg, Harvey. "*The Westliche Post* of St. Louis: A Daily Newspaper for German-Americans, 1857–1938." PhD diss., University of Missouri, 1967.

Tritter, Thorin Richard. "Paper Profits in Public Service: Money Making in the New York Newspaper Industry, 1830–1930." PhD diss., Columbia University, 2000.

Tusa, Jacqueline Balk. "Power, Priorities, and Political Insurgency: The Liberal Republican Movement: 1869–1872." PhD diss., Pennsylvania State University, 1970.

Viener, John V. "A Sense of Obligation: Henry Stimson as United States Attorney, 1906–1909." Honor thesis, Yale University, 1961.

Index

GRATEFUL ACKNOWLEDGMENT IS MADE FOR
PERMISSION TO REPRINT THE IMAGES IN
THE INSERT:

Page 1: Merchant shops of Makó. (Courtesy of the Muriel Pulitzer Estate.) Pulitzer's
mother and sister. (Courtesy of the Muriel Pulitzer Estate.) **Page 2:** Albert Pulitzer
standing with books. (Courtesy of the Muriel Pulitzer Estate.) Joseph and Albert in 1873.
(Courtesy of the *St. Louis Post-Dispatch* and the Joseph Pulitzer Family.) **Page 3:** Carl
Schurz. (Courtesy of the Library of Congress.) Pulitzer Liberal Republican cartoon. (Au-
thor's collection.) **Page 4:** Pulitzer profile 1869. (Courtesy of the Muriel Pulitzer Estate.)
Cartoon of Pulitzer in fight with lobbyist that appeared in the February 5, 1870 edition of
Die Vehme. (Courtesy of the Missouri History Museum.) **Page 5:** Joseph Pulitzer and Kate
Davis. (Courtesy of the *St. Louis Post-Dispatch* and the Joseph Pulitzer Family.) Nannie
Tunstall. (Courtesy of the Virginia Military Institute Archives.) **Page 6:** Cartoon of Pulit-
zer purchasing the *Dispatch.* (Author's collection.) Illustration of John Cockerill. (Courtesy
of the Library of Congress, *New York World-Telegram & Sun* Collection.) **Page 7:** New
York *World* building owned by Jay Gould. (Courtesy of the Library of Congress, *New York
World-Telegram & Sun* Collection.) Pulitzer building (Courtesy of the Library of Congress.)
Page 8: Don Carlos Seitz. (Courtesy of the Library of Congress, *New York World-Telegram
& Sun* Collection.) Arthur Brisbane. (Courtesy of the Library of Congress.) David Graham
Phillips. (Courtesy of the Library of Congress.) **Page 9:** Charles Dana, William Randolph
Hearst, Theodore Roosevelt, and William Jennings Bryant. (Courtesy of the Library of
Congress.) **Page 10:** Opening the cornerstone. (Courtesy of the Library of Congress, *New
York World-Telegram & Sun* Collection.) Joseph and Kate Pulitzer. (Courtesy of the Rare
Book and Manuscript Library, Butler Library, Columbia University.) **Page 11:** Pulitzer
children. (Courtesy of the Rare Book and Manuscript Library, Butler Library, Columbia
University.) **Page 12:** Joseph Pulitzer walking with son Ralph, Pulitzer wearing goggles,
and Pulitzer seated outside with blanket. (Courtesy of the *St. Louis Post-Dispatch* and
the Joseph Pulitzer Family.) **Page 13:** Albert Pulitzer walking by canal. (Courtesy of the
Muriel Pulitzer Estate.) Joseph Pulitzer walking in Monte Carlo. (Courtesy of the *St. Louis
Post-Dispatch* and the Joseph Pulitzer Family.) **Page 14:** Pulitzer's East Seventy-Third
Street house and Chatwold. (Courtesy of the *St. Louis Post-Dispatch* and the Joseph Pulit-
zer Family.) **Page 15:** *Liberty.* (Courtesy of the *St. Louis-Post Dispatch* and the Joseph Pu-
litzer Family.) The Jekyll Island House. (Courtesy of the Jekyll Island Museum Archives.)
Page 16: Columbia Journalism School. (Courtesy of Columbia University Archive.) Floor
engraving. (Courtesy of the author.)